ASIA

IN THE MAKING OF EUROPE

ASIA

IN THE MAKING OF EUROPE

DONALD F. LACH

VOLUME

II

A

Century of

Wonder

BOOK ONE: THE VISUAL ARTS

THE UNIVERSITY OF CHICAGO PRESS

CHICAGO AND LONDON

THE UNIVERSITY OF CHICAGO PRESS, CHICAGO 60637
The University of Chicago Press, Ltd., London

Library of Congress Cataloging in Publication Data

Lach, Donald Frederick, 1917–
    Asia in the making of Europe.

    Includes bibliographies.
    CONTENTS: v. 1. The century of discovery. 2 v.—
v. 2. A century of wonder. Book 1. The visual arts.
Book 2. The literary arts. Book 3. The scholarly
disciplines. 3 v.
    1. Asia—Discovery and exploration. 2. Europe—
Civilization—Oriental influences. I. Title.
DS5.95.L3   901.93   64-19848
ISBN 0-226-46730-9 (v. 2. bk. 1)
ISBN 0-226-46733-3 (v. 2. bk. 2)
ISBN 0-226-46734-1 (v. 2. bk. 3)

To my mother
and
to the memory of my father

Contents

BOOK ONE

List of Illustrations   ix

Preface   xiii

Acknowledgments   xvii

Introduction   3

Chapter I: COLLECTIONS OF CURIOSITIES   7

1. Portugal and Spain   10
2. Antwerp and the Low Countries   16
3. Germany and Austria   22
4. France and England   30
5. Italy   35
   Appendix: Sample Asian Items Collected in Europe   46

Chapter II: THE INDIVIDUAL ARTS   56

1. Manueline Architecture and Sculpture   57

Contents

2. Painting   64
3. Woodcuts and Engravings   78
4. Textiles, Tapestries, and Costumes   95
5. Ceramics   104
6. Woods, Furniture, and Lacquerware   109
7. Precious Metals, Gems, and Jewelry   113

Chapter III: THE ICONOGRAPHY OF ASIAN ANIMALS   123

1. The Elephant   124
   A. Antiquity and the Middle Ages   125
   B. African Elephants of the Quattrocento   131
   C. The Elephant of Rome   135
   D. Raphael and his School   140
   E. The Vienna Elephant of 1552   144
   F. *Fin de siècle*   150
2. The Rhinoceros   158
3. The Tiger   172
4. The Simians   175
5. The Birds   178

Chapter IV: EPILOGUE: NATURALISM, SYMBOLISM, AND
               ORNAMENT   186

BIBLIOGRAPHY   200

Reference Works   200
Source Materials   204
Books   213
Articles   226
Catalogues   235

INDEX   237

Illustrations

FOLLOWING PAGE 236

1. Engraving of Catharine de' Medici
2. Engraving of Archduke Ferdinand of Tyrol
3. Archduke Ferdinand in a Triumph
4. Chinese studio painting from Ambras
5. Chinese studio painting from Ambras
6. East Asian *objets d'art* from Ambras
7. Seashells in settings from Ambras
8. Bezoar stones from Ambras
9. Rock crystal elephant
10. Woodcut of treasury of Emperor Maximilian I
11. Cabinet of curiosities at Gottorp
12. Sinhalese ivory comb with reliefs
13. Ivory chest from Ceylon
14. Bezoar cup of Emperor Rudolf II
15. Engraved portrait of Charles de L'écluse
16. Painting of the collection of Ortelius
17. Tower of Belém, Lisbon
18. Archway of the "Capelas imperfeitas," Batalha
19. Manueline window at Tomar
20. Portal of the church of Matriz Golega, Portugal
21. Portal of the Casado Capítulo, Portugal
22. Interior of the Cathedral of Guarda, Portugal
23. Stalls of Santa Cruz, Coimbra
24. Watercolor of Vishnu, Siva, Brahma

[ix]

25. Sacrifice and *pagode* in India
26. Kanarese harvesting rice
27. Nāyar marriage
28. Kanarese washing clothes
29. Two fantastic columns, drawing by Dürer
30. Adoration of the Magi by Vasco Fernandes
31. Adoration of the Magi by Gregorio Lopes
32. Adoration of the Magi, Cathedral of Evora
33. Adoration of the Magi by Francisco Henriques
34. Triumph of Asia by Pauwels Franck
35. The Japanese envoys to Europe
36. Painting of the plant *Datura stramonium*
37. Mountainous landscape, painting by Nicolas Manuel Deutsch
38. Detail from "The Return of the Herd," by Brueghel the Elder
39. Grotesque head with elephant, by Arcimboldo
40. "The Admiral (?)," after Arcimboldo
41. Composite elephant, Mughul school, *ca.* 1590
42. Composite elephants in combat
43. Composite elephant formed of female musicians and driven by Krishna
44. "People of Calicut," by Hans Burgkmair
45. Engraving of sago bread
46. Engraving of banyan tree
47. "Hunting for Wild Ducks in China"
48. "Magellan's Discovery of the Straits," by Stradanus
49. Portuguese triumphal arch at Antwerp, 1593
50. Tower of Azuchi Castle, by Philips van Winghe
51. Gate of Azuchi Castle, by Philips van Winghe
52. People of Java, by Hans Sibmacher
53. Tapestry of the India series, Tournai
54. Tapestry of the India series, Oudenarde
55. "The Camel Caravan," tapestry
56. "The Magi," tapestry *ca.* 1550
57. "Landing at Calicut," sixteenth-century tapestry
58. Gujarati bedspread, sixteenth century
59. Title page of A. de Bruyn, *Omnium pene* . . . 1581
60. Costumes of Africans, Asians, and Americans
61. Chinese matron, Vecellio
62. Indian woman of moderate quality, Vecellio
63. Indian of quality, Vecellio
64. Chinese nobleman, Vecellio
65. Lady of the Moluccas, Vecellio
66. Chinese noblewoman, Vecellio
67. Chinese of moderate quality, Vecellio
68. East Indian woman of quality, Vecellio

69. Japanese youth, Vecellio
70. Chinese export porcelain, 1557
71. Vase of Medici porcelain
72. Flask of Medici porcelain
73. Flagon of Medici porcelain
74. Ewer of Medici porcelain
75. Chinese porcelain bowl in silver mounting
76. Pitcher from "Cups and Jugs" (1548), by Cornelis Floris
77. Turtle and shell from "Cups and Jugs" (1548), by Cornelis Floris
78. Lid design on exotic chest, Milan, 1560
79. Mughul-type chest *ca.* 1580
80. Studiolo of Francesco de' Medici
81. Indian chair with ivory inlays, *ca.* 1580
82. Silver tankard, Antwerp, *ca.* 1525
83. Coconut cup of Emperor Charles V, *ca.* 1530
84. Lid ornament of Rappoltstein goblet, *ca.* 1543
85. Coconut cup in silver setting, 1590
86. "Flight from Egypt," the Book of Hours (1517) of King Manuel
87. "Elephant and People of Calicut," by Hans Burgkmair
88. Elephant title page, 1514
89. Elephant in Maximilian's Prayer Book
90. Francisco d'Ollanda's copy of Raphael's elephant
91. Hanno, after Raphael
92. Hanno in stucco, by Giovanni da Udine
93. Intarsia of Baraballo on Hanno
94. Hanno in Fanti's *Triompho di Fortuna* (1526)
95. Elephant fountain, by M. van Heemskerck
96. Elephant in "Marriage Feast of Cupid and Psyche," by Giulio Romano
97. Flemish tapestry of elephant hunt, 1535–40
98. Sinhalese ivory chest, end relief
99. Sinhalese ivory chest, end relief
100. *Flugblatt* elephant of 1552
101. Elephant medal of 1554
102. Elephant and dragon of Bomarzo
103. Elephant of Bomarzo
104. Elephant hunt, engraving by Stradanus
105. "The Triumph of Saturn," by Philippe Galle
106. Elephants in *Speculum* of Lafreri
107. "Noah's Ark," 1570, by Simone de Myle
108. "Night Festival with the Carrousel Elephant," by Antoine Caron
109. "Triumph of Sémélé," by Antoine Caron
110. "Elephant with Three Sheep," by Hans Sibmacher
111. Ape on back of elephant, by Roelant Savery
112. Elephant hunt, Tunja, Colombia

113. Detail from Ortelius' map of China, 1584
114. Woodcut of elephant, by Melchior Lorck, 1580
115. Antwerp elephant
116. Bronze elephant of Christoph Jamnitzer, *ca.* 1600
117. Caryatid of elephant and dragon
118. Sugarwork elephant
119. Dürer's drawing of rhinoceros, 1515
120. Burgkmair's drawing of rhinoceros, 1515
121. Rhinoceros of Naples
122. Rhinoceros from Maximilian's Prayer Book
123. Detail from "Triumphal Arch of Maximilian," by Dürer
124. Rhinoceros with obelisk
125. Grotto in garden of Castello
126. Combat between elephant and rhinoceros
127. Rhinoceros in Tunja, Colombia
128. Caryatid of rhinoceros and elephant
129. Rhinoceros and bear, by Hans Sibmacher
130. Bacchus and Ariadne with tiger, by Giulio Romano
131. "Triumph of Bacchus and Ariadne," by Annibale Carracci
132. Tiger, from Juan de Arphe
133. "The Story of the First Human Pair," sixteenth-century tapestry
134. "The Ape Laocoön," by Titian
135. "Young Man with a Parrot," by Niccolò dell'Abbate
136. "Madonna and Child with Parrot"
137. German woman with a parrot
138. Musk deer, by Hans Sibmacher
139. Bird of paradise, by Hans Sibmacher
140. Emu, the wonderful bird, by Hans Sibmacher
141. Crowned bird of Catigan, by Hans Sibmacher
142. Dodos, by Roelant Savery
143. "Orpheus with the Animals," by Roelant Savery
144. "Garden of Eden," by Roelant Savery
145. "Asia," in Ripa, *Iconologia* (1611)
146. Title page of J. T. and J. I. de Bry, *India orientalis* (1601)
147. Products of Asia, from De Bry
148. Temples and gods of India, from De Bry
149. Ornamental panel from the loggia of the Vatican, by Giovanni da Udine
150. Detail of elephant on panel
151. Decorative panel by the Doetechum brothers(?), after Vredeman de Vries

Preface

In the first volume of my projected series *Asia in the Making of Europe*, I discussed Europe's outward thrust toward Asia and examined the sources of information on the East as well as the channels through which it flowed into sixteenth-century Europe. The materials examined there are mainly the literary sources: state documents, travel books, missionary letters and reports, histories, memoirs, and maps. In addition to an analysis of the written records, Volume I also contains an account of spices and other Asian commodities sent to Europe. I purposely did not attempt in Volume I a systematic study of the responses within Europe to the vast new body of information about Asia, a massive and complicated undertaking in itself. That task with all its complexities was left for this volume.

The present volume, *A Century of Wonder*, refers to the most general response of sixteenth-century Europe to the revelation of the East. This particular book, *The Visual Arts*, is a study of the impact of what I have termed the "silent sources" —art objects, artifacts, flora, fauna, and crafts—upon the arts of Europe from the period of the High Renaissance to the Baroque. This book helps to fill the gap that exists between the Middle Ages and the seventeenth century in our understanding of the influences exerted by Asia upon European art. But the topics included here constitute only one aspect of Asia's total influence upon Europe. In the second book of this volume, I will discuss the impact of Asia upon the letters, ideas, and institutions of sixteenth-century Europe.

As readers will see in the details set forth in the following chapters, it is possible to assert that Asia had distinct appeal and influence despite Europe's traditional hostility to alien infiltration. Artists experimented with Asian products and design ideas quite deliberately and incorporated them into their own works. The ways in which the Europeans of the sixteenth century used Asia artistically are not always obvious at first glance, probably because we do not see with the eyes of contemporaries. What looked like a symbol of Asia to the sixteenth-century connoisseur might well look to us like a meaningless portrait or even a decadent Manneristic aberration. That we have continued to believe for a long time that Asia exercised no noteworthy influence on modern European art until the eighteenth century is attributable, in my estimation, to a lack of serious research on earlier periods and to our inability to comprehend what it was about Asia that appealed to European artists and craftsmen of the late Renaissance. It is hoped that this book will, among other things, stimulate specialists in the visual arts to examine more closely the interchanges between Europe and Asia and will encourage general students of diffusion to look for concrete evidence of influence instead of relying exclusively upon stylistic similarities or making unsubstantiated assertions about common attributes and spiritual affinities.

In undertaking the preparation of this book on the visual arts, I was well aware that I would be engaging in an enterprise that had never before been investigated thoroughly. I also knew that my own background and credentials for embarking on such a pioneering effort were hardly adequate to the task. As a consequence, I set out blithely, as amateurs incline to do, to prepare myself as best I could to undertake this study. In the process, I have received such warm and hearty support from others that I finally became pleased with my own brashness.

I have received unstinting cooperation from the art historians of the University of Chicago. On the street, at lunch, and in the corridors they have patiently answered my naive questions. They have even shared my excitement of discovery. Reverend Harrie van der Stappen, S.V.D., a specialist in East Asian art, was particularly helpful in aiding me to identify Philips van Winghe's drawings of Azuchi Castle. Edward A. Maser, who has been working for a number of years on the Habsburg art collections, lent me every possible aid, including a reading of my chapter on collections. Bertha H. Wiles, now retired, gave me the benefit of her vast knowledge in the graphic arts. Pramod Chandra kindly talked with me about Indian art, informed me about the history of *Kutūhala* (composite paintings), and obtained a copy of one of them for me from the National Museum of India in New Delhi. Herbert L. Kessler, who has one foot in Byzantium and the other in sixteenth-century Europe, read the entire manuscript and gave me hours of informal instruction in art history. Francis H. Dowley, who has unselfishly shared my enthusiasms for more years than we both like to think about, also read and improved the manuscript. As if this were not enough, I received helpful tips from Professors Phyllis Bober of New York University and Charles Mitchell of Bryn Mawr.

My education was also advanced significantly by the Rockefeller Foundation. In the academic year 1967–68 its officers presented me with an opportunity to teach at the University of Delhi. Their generosity in permitting me, in the course of performing this assignment, to travel in India from the Himalayas to Cape Comorin, to visit Ceylon, and to make a leisurely trip around the world gave me the opportunity to renew my acquaintance with both Asia and Europe and to become deeply involved for the first time in the rich and puzzling civilization of India.

When I decided to publish a section from this book as a "trial balloon," Professor Denis Sinor of the University of Indiana freely opened to me the pages of the *Journal of Asian History*, which he edits. Consequently, the section of chapter iii dealing with the elephant first appeared in the *JAH* in 1967 (Vol. I, No. 2, pp. 133–76) under the title "Asian Elephants in Renaissance Europe." Because Professor Sinor generously published sixteen plates along with my article, I have been able to omit some from the collection published in this work. By substituting others, I have had the opportunity to extend my pictorial documentation of the elephant. Nor can I forgo mentioning that Mrs. Irene Sinor shared her husband's enthusiasm for my elephants, tracked down a rhinoceros for me in Naples, and drew to my attention the charming story of Wenzel Hollar and his elephant by Johannes Urzidel.

Librarians and museum experts likewise lightened my task. Always at hand were the vast resources of the University of Chicago libraries, the Art Institute of Chicago, and the Newberry Library. Robert Rosenthal, chief of the University of Chicago's Department of Special Collections, regularly called to my attention items from his rare books. Helen Smith, as she has for many years, assiduously filled my orders for interlibrary exchange requests. Mrs Emma B. Pitcher helped me to identify birds and other fauna in my illustrations.

From research funds granted me by the Social Science Research Committee, the Committee on Far Eastern Studies, and the Committee on South Asia (all of the University of Chicago) I was able to hire graduate students in history to assist me. Amy Gordon, Kathleen Stark, Eric Stevens, and Sara Bobroff helped me during the stages of research and writing. Sister Michaela Zahner, C.S.J., labored long and hard as we saw the book through the press together.

For the past five years my wife has acted as my personal photographer. Our joint venture in scholarship began in 1965 on a three-month tour of Italy where we hunted artistic elephants and other exotica with her cameras. In India, and in all the other countries we visited on our world tour, she had more enthusiasm for shooting pictures for my project than I did myself. At home she spent countless hours taking and retaking the photographs which illustrate this book. While her photographic skills made this extensive illustration program possible, it was her verve and devotion which made the preparation of the book a delight.

Admittedly my venture into what might be called art history is a *tour de force*. For mistakes of fact and interpretation I take personal responsibility. But I do ask forbearance and compassion from those whose professional competence far exceeds my slight attainments in this complicated field.

Acknowledgments

Permissions to reproduce photographs were courteously granted to us by the following copyright holders: Kunsthistorisches Museum, Vienna (2, 3, 4, 5, 6, 7, 8, 10, 38, 135, 137); Editions Gallimard, Paris (47); André de Rache, Brussels (11, 40); Alfieri, Edizione d'arte, Venice (34, 100); Gabinetto disegni e stampe degli Uffizi, Florence (36); R. Geigy (ed.), *Acta tropica*, Basel (126); Musée du Louvre, Paris (72); Department of Prints and Drawings, The Royal Museum of Fine Arts, Copenhagen (114); A. L. van Gendt and Co., Amsterdam (15, 105); S. Schéle, Stockholm (76, 77); Victoria and Albert Museum, London (70, 85); Martinus Nijhoff, The Hague (16).

Authorizations were also obtained from The Metropolitan Museum of Art, New York (75); Jean Ehrmann, Paris (108); F. Bruckmann K. G. Bildarchiv, Munich (12, 13, 37, 81, 83, 109, 111, 142); The Albertina, Vienna (120, 123); Georges Alran, Mazamet (Tarn), France (107); Constable Publishers, London (23); Mrs. M. Fischel, Berlin, and Routledge and Kegan Paul, Ltd., London (95); Monumenti musei e gallerie pontificie, Vatican (92); Eva Bollert, Karlsruhe (78, 82, 84); Museumsabteilung der bayerischen Verwaltung der staatlichen Schlösser, Gärten und Seen, Munich (99); Academia nacional Belas Artes, Lisbon (17, 18, 19, 20, 21, 22); Kupferstichkabinett, Staatliche Museen der Stiftung preussischer Kulturbesitz, Berlin (91).

BOOK ONE

The Visual Arts

Introduction

In the century of the great overseas discoveries Europeans were struck by wonder at the extent and variety of the world that was rapidly being opened to full view. Writers of the sixteenth century described the curiosities and singularities of the outside world as beguiling, perplexing, and stupefying. Artists as well as collectors of oddities were awestruck by the alien works of nature and man that appeared to be fearfully and wonderfully made. Fear, strange as it now seems, struggled with admiration and curiosity in the perception and comprehension of marvels that were inexplicable in traditional European terms. Only the boldest spirits were prepared to admit their own perplexity and uncertainty about the meaning of the revelation of America and the East for European civilization. Others who were inclined to look to the supernatural for the explanation of baffling problems surely sighed with the Psalmist: "Thou art the God that doest wonders: thou hast declared thy strength among the people" (Psalm 77:14).

Stupefaction, bewilderment, and anxiety arrested reactions for a time. A pause was required for a more complete assessment of the revelations and for contemplation of their ultimate implications. But while wonder mixed with fear produced hesitation, it did not beget apathy or inertia. Men in all walks of life from the humble potter to eminent divines and philosophers were inspired with a desire to learn in more detail about the high civilizations of Asia and their spiritual and material works. Those aspects which could be comprehended most readily by Europeans both in Asia and Europe were naturally the surface and concrete manifestations of Asian civilization. The doctrines of Asia's great religious and philosophical systems were obviously beyond the abilities of the merchant in the field to understand. The missionaries with their strong Christian bias were initially determined to dismiss Asian beliefs and material works as heathen superstitions and vanities. In Europe the Humanists were inclined to

[3]

regard as barbarous all that was not classical and European. Some artists of the Renaissance were likewise disposed to belittle what they saw of Asian arts by categorizing them as works of talented craftsmen. But, despite the convinced ethnocentrism of Europe's artists and intellectuals, the *reality* of Asia could not forever be ignored or dismissed disparagingly. In the course of the sixteenth century, artists, writers, and scholars were required to make room in their works and thoughts for the encroaching civilizations of the East.

The accommodation of Europe to the actuality and permanence of Asia as a part of its own world came slowly and falteringly. Asia, unlike America, had had interchanges with Europe that stretched back in time before the beginnings of recorded history. In Antiquity and the Middle Ages, flora, fauna, and portable goods from Asia were brought into Europe at irregular intervals. Such imports were generally associated with a vague outer world of barbarians and enemies of civilization. Periodic invasions of the Christian West by infidel Muslims, pagan Mongols, and terrible Turks contributed to Europe's fear of and antipathy to the East. Alexandria, known in the eighth and ninth centuries as "the market of the two worlds," was the place where most of the business of Eurasia was transacted in the Middle Ages. But even here there was no firm knowledge about the exact places from which the products of Asia came, for pepper and other spices were vaguely called "grains of paradise" until the sixteenth century.

The Crusades had the effect of opening the Near East to Europeans, as, in its commercial relations with the Levant, Europe moved from a debtor to a creditor status during the twelfth century. The returning Crusaders also brought goods and stories from Asia to the hinterlands of Europe where such things had only rarely been known before. In the era of the Mongol peace (1240–1350) relations between Europe and China by the overland route were closer than they had ever been. China was brought psychologically nearer than India, which remained fabulous to Europe until the era of the great discoveries. From the middle of the fourteenth century to about 1500 the European view of Asia was again cut off by lack of intercourse, and just at a time when Europe itself was recovering its own classical past and becoming more convinced than ever before of the supreme value of Western civilization.

Europe's preoccupation with itself continued well into the sixteenth century, its energies consumed by international wars, the development of national states, and religious divisions. The discovery of America also diverted Europe's attention from Asia, for the New World had been totally unknown and its products were initially of greater novelty. In contrast to Asia, America was easily penetrated by European arms, religion, and civilization. America posed no threat, real or imaginary, as Asia did to Europe. So, at first, there was greater receptivity to and interest in America, perhaps promoted by the fact that Charles V, who ruled the Spanish conquests in the New World, was also the Holy Roman Emperor, the most powerful of Europe's kings and its protector against the Turkish incursions from the east. The "policy of secrecy" (see Vol. I, pp. 151–54) followed by Portugal about its progress in the East also had the effect until the middle of the sixteenth century of keeping solid information about Asia from circulating freely in Europe. But despite all such obstacles, knowledge of the discoveries in the East increased and the boundaries of European civilization had periodically to be stretched and adjusted to make room for Asia's products, arts, and ideas.

Not all the information about Asia was to be found in official declarations, travel accounts, or missionary letters and histories. The steady influx into sixteenth-century Europe of the spices, flora, fauna, and portable arts and crafts of Asia brought concrete examples, in quantities and varieties not known before, to the attention of Europeans in all walks of life. Even in the Middle Ages, the Chinese had been recognized as gifted craftsmen. With the opening of direct maritime access to India, its artisans and artists were likewise acknowledged ever more frequently to be skilled, versatile, and sophisticated. The Europeans who lived and worked in the East reported admiringly on the architectural and sculptural monuments of tropical Asia, esteemed its cities to be greater and wealthier than many of Europe's proudest urban centers, and relayed to the folks back home, either orally or in writing, a few of the traditions and legends they heard in the Orient. The Jesuits in the field were to conclude by the last generation of the sixteenth century that Europe had much to learn from the high civilizations of Asia.

Since the publication of Volume I of *Asia in the Making of Europe* (1965), I have been struggling with the methodological problem of how best to study and present the impact of Asia upon Europe in the sixteenth century. Some of the reviewers of Volume I rightly predicted that I would have difficulty in showing concretely how the revelation of the East moved Westerners to begin "self-consciously to question their own cultural premises ... and to initiate fundamental revisions in their own views of the world, man, and the future" (p. 835). In what follows I shall try to relate how I am attacking, for this volume, what is admittedly a complex and crucial problem.

Tracers of influence must carefully judge and determine which paths to follow to their goals. Pioneers in this kind of intellectual exploration find that certain trails are cold, that others are overly circuitous or complex, and that but few give direct and easy access. In most instances some false starts may be made before the explorer finds marks or remains which encourage him to take one path rather than the other or to follow a trail that others have assured him leads nowhere. Even after the searcher surveys a few vistas of the past which others have not seen from his peculiar angle, he must contemplate the entire perspective to determine whether his own view is a mirage, distortion, or delusion.

Once satisfied about the reality of his perception, the observer of influence must rule out other possible sources, evaluate his own perspective in relation to others, and ask himself whether a causal relationship is possible on the basis of the known facts. And, even after exercising all such precautions, he and his reader must fully realize that the vision is partial, the inferences biased, and the demonstrations hazardous. But the undertaking is justified even though it provides nothing more than a new angle from which to look upon an old scene or a new series of partial explanations of what spurred men on to do what they did.

In choosing trails I started, somewhat naively perhaps, to follow one that was most obvious and clearly marked. Of the many strange products, objects, and devices imported into Europe from Asia, I asked myself: What were they? Who received them? What questions did they provoke? How did artisans and artists in Europe see them? Were the more numerous objects of greater influence than those which were known only as samples? It was through asking myself such a series of simple questions that I decided to commence my study of the impact of Asia upon Europe with the visual arts.

Other considerations also entered into this decision. First, I suffered from a sense of guilt that, in Volume I, I had relied, as conventional historians usually do, too heavily on literary sources. From references in the literary sources I was certain that oral reports had constituted a vital source of information and inspiration. I was likewise convinced that objects imported from Asia had made a significant impression upon Europeans. These "silent sources"—art objects, artifacts, flora, fauna, and crafts—obviously needed investigation. Although they were much harder to exploit and control than the literary sources, they might provide answers to a number of vital questions not dealt with in the literary sources. It is perfectly clear that literary luminaries such as Rabelais, Montaigne, and Bodin were moved intellectually by the import and meaning of the discoveries. Natural scientists, geographers, and churchmen were likewise forced to respond, either negatively or positively, to the revelation of Eastern products, places, peoples, and religions. But what evidence, for example, was there of how the populace at large reacted to the strange new items from Asia? And what about their influence, if any, on artists and artisans? In this context, sixteenth-century European art works were clearly an unknown quantity to me and to others.

The adoption of motifs from Asia by European craftsmen has a long and revered history. Medieval architects and illuminators of manuscript books had been influenced in their designs by the exotic flora and fauna of the East. Later artists, especially in the eighteenth century, were fascinated by China and produced a vast number of chinoiseries in all facets of art. But what about the great artistic masters of the late Renaissance? Were they so imbued with the artistic prototypes of Antiquity and their own spectacular achievements that they were totally oblivious to the opening of the overseas world? I was seriously assured by many whom I talked to, or whose books I read, that this was indeed true of the artists. Rationally I found this conclusion hard to accept and so I began a few preliminary investigations. At first there were many false starts and the path was rocky and the trail unclear. But gradually as I pushed aside the tangled underbrush I began to see a clearing in the distance. Whether the clearing that I found is a mirage, distortion, or delusion will be decided by others.

CHAPTER I

Collections of Curiosities

In the long centuries before the opening of the direct passage to India, learned men certainly looked studiously and wonderingly at the isolated specimens of Asia's arts and crafts which found their way to Europe. And they were generally left to infer for themselves whatever they could about the peoples and civilizations which produced these strange items. During the sixteenth century the steady influx in quantity of exotica from Asia stimulated a more generalized and deeper curiosity about what were indiscriminately called "Indian products." No longer content merely to observe in puzzlement what came to them from afar, European intellectuals and creative artists began self-consciously and systematically to seek solid information about the East and its products.

At first the insights to be obtained through men who had been in the field were disappointingly few and generally unsatisfying to trained and inquisitive minds. Humanists, scientists, and artists often reproached the itinerant merchant or returned navigator with having failed to make the most of an opportunity to observe the strange physical and cultural features of the Asian scene. Pierre Belon (1517–64), the French naturalist, specifically complained:

Those persons who undertake a distant voyage in foreign parts for a particular purpose are usually inclined to seek out those things necessary to bring about a resolution of their own affairs, rather than to use their time making other observations for which they have no understanding: as so clearly appears in the dealings of a merchant who, no matter how often he has traveled to India and the newly found lands, has nonetheless no other object than to get his money's worth by buying goods and is not concerned to become acquainted with the countless singularities that a curious man [*un homme curieux*] would readily be able to observe.[1]

---

[1] *Les observations de plusieurs singularitez et choses mémorables, trouvées en Grèce, Asie, Indée, Egypte, Arabie et autres pays estrangés* (Paris, 1554), p. iv. For a detailed survey of the word "curiosity" in various European languages see D. Murray, *Museums: Their History and Their Use* (Glasgow, 1904), I, 187, n. 1.

Men of curiosity in all walks of life, as they became increasingly impatient with and distrustful of the superficial observations of travelers and merchants, urged the people in the field to send back specimens of the things that were to be found in Asia. Even though every fleet that returned to Lisbon carried new items to stimulate the imagination of the learned and artistic,[2] the demand for more "curiosities" intensified as the century wore on. Along with requests for rare objects there went entreaties for more acute observation of the Asian environment itself and of the way life was lived there.

To help provide the curious with reliable information, amateur artists sent back drawings or paintings of what they saw on their daily rounds of the marts of Asia.[3] Learned Jesuits wrote about and speculated on the meaning and symbolism of the religious statues and temples of Hinduism and Buddhism. Cartographers in Asia and Europe prepared routiers, artistic maps, and terrestrial globes which helped both amateurs and scholars to associate products with places, to gain a sense of the magnitude of Asia, and to acquire an elementary appreciation of the great diversity of its peoples and their achievements.[4] Cosmographers and travel writers gathered details about the jewels, textiles, flora, and fauna of the East which opened new business and intellectual vistas. And, even as the hunger of the curious was being appeased by new products and information, the appetite for collecting the wonders of the outside world constantly grew.

Royal connoisseurs, wealthy merchant princes, bourgeois businessmen, and eminent scholars competed to acquire samples of Eastern natural products, arts, and crafts. Agents were hired and friends badgered as the collectors began to acquire a taste for assembling cabinets or chambers of curiosities. The representatives of the great commercial houses sent curiosities as gifts to their employers, friends, business acquaintances, and rulers with a passion for collecting. Gerhard Mercator (1512–94) and Abraham Ortelius (1529–98), the cartographers, exchanged geographical information and books. Charles de L'écluse (1526–1609) the famous botanist, received botanical specimens from his Spanish colleague, Benito Arias Montano (1527–98). The rulers of Europe, like Oriental potentates, sent gifts of exotic animals, jewels, porcelains, and trinkets to one another. Collectors frequently complained that the Portuguese insisted upon keeping information on Asia to themselves and were sometimes deliberately misleading in what they did report.[5]

The collectors' spirit was not born in the sixteenth century, but it did receive a new stimulus and a change of emphasis as a result of the overseas discoveries.[6]

---

[2] F. de Sousa Viterbo, "O orientalismo portugues no século XVI," *Boletim da Sociedade de geographia de Lisboa*, XII (1892–93), Nos. 7–8, p. 317.

[3] See below, pp. 64–67 and pls. 24–28.

[4] On the collection and interest in globes as concrete models of the earth see F. de Dainville, "Les amateurs de globes," *Gazette des Beaux-Arts*, LXXI (1968), 51–64.

[5] For example, see the letter of Guillaume Postel to Abraham Ortelius (April 9, 1567) as reproduced in J. H. Hessels (ed.), *Abrahami Ortelii (geographi Antwerpiensis) et virorum eruditorum ad eundem et ad Jacobum Colium Ortelianum. . . . Epistulae . . . (1524–1628)* (Cambridge, 1887), pp. 43–44. Vol. I of *Ecclesiae Londino-Batavae Archivum.*

[6] For a general history of collecting and collections see Murray, *op. cit.* (n. 1); and F. H. Taylor, *The Taste of Angels: A History of Art Collecting from Rameses to Napoleon* (Boston, 1948).

King Solomon and the rulers of ancient Babylon had collected precious objects from Asia for their treasure houses. The patricians of Greece, Rome, and Byzantium prided themselves on their collections of animals and objets d'art from distant places. In medieval Europe the treasury of the cathedral and the strong room of the castle housed precious and curious objects ranging from Chinese textiles to ostrich eggs. Oddities were stored in medieval treasuries for their material and talismanic values and were not ordinarily on display.[7] The doges of Venice were among the first to exhibit in public the exotic objects which they received as gifts from the princes of the Levant or acquired by pillage or purchase in the Near East.[8] Beginning in the middle of the fifteenth century a "fever" broke out in Rome and its environs for uncovering and collecting ancient works of art, inscriptions, cameos, and coins.[9] Finally, the sixteenth century saw the appearance of the cabinet or chamber of wonders (*Wunderkammer*) in which collections of ethnographical specimens, minerals, flora, and fauna were placed on display side by side with some of the best examples of cinquecento European painting or artistic craftsmanship. What made the collections of the *Wunderkammer* distinctive was the emphasis they placed upon the systematic assembling of contemporary rather than ancient arts and crafts, of unusual specimens from the world of natural history, and of curiosities from the newly found lands.[10]

But what do we know about the availability in Europe of Asian items that were potentially of interest to artists, scientists, and collectors? Even a cursory survey of the cargoes, custom records, ambassadorial reports, company papers, diaries, and personal correspondence of those involved in overseas trade with Asia readily yields information about the many kinds of Asian imports which actually found their way through Lisbon and Venice to the other marts of Europe (see Appendix, p. 55). But not all the imports can be found listed in the extant cargo tallies or in the reports of the customhouses. It must be assumed that many items, particularly small and valuable commodities like jewels and personal curios, were brought or sent back by individual sailors as part of their own share of the cargo or were smuggled into the country. Other items were sent as gifts to the rulers of Europe by native kings in the east or by Portuguese officials in the field who were trying to keep their fences mended at home. Individuals also brought home gifts for families and friends, as well as souvenirs for themselves and the collectors of curiosa.

[7] A. Lhotsky, *Die Geschichte der Sammlungen*, Vol. II, Pts. 1 and 2 of *Festschrift zur Feier des fünfzig-jährigen Bestandes*, edited by the director of the Vienna Kunsthistorisches Museum (Vienna, 1941–45), pp. 1–4. For a survey of medieval attitudes toward the natural world and Eastern art see F. Denis, *Le monde enchanté: Cosmographie et histoire naturelle fantastiques du moyen âge* (Paris, 1843).

[8] On the relations between commerce and art in Venice see J. Alazard, *La Venise de la Renaissance* (Paris, 1956), chap. vii.

[9] For the history of private collecting in Italy see J. Burckhardt, "Die Sammler," in *Beiträge zur Kunstgeschichte von Italien* (2d ed.; Stuttgart, 1911), pp. 341–573.

[10] See J. von Schlosser, *Die Kunst- und Wunderkammern der Spätrenaissance* (Leipzig, 1908), pp. 10–18; also G. Klemm, *Zur Geschichte der Sammlungen für Wissenschaft und Kunst in Deutschland* (Zerbst, 1837), pp. 44–45.

I

PORTUGAL AND SPAIN

The city of Lisbon itself was a vast and splendid emporium where the products of Oriental industry and art were on display throughout the sixteenth century. Gifts of porcelains and textiles were brought back to King Manuel I and other highly placed persons in Lisbon by the leaders of the first expeditions.[11] The king of Melinde on Africa's east coast presented Vasco da Gama on his second voyage in 1502 with "a bedstead of Cambay [India] wrought with gold and mother of pearl."[12] Albuquerque and his aides in India had brocaded coats and a sedan chair made for the king as tokens of native craftsmanship. A sword and a crown of gold, armor, wrought arm bands and bracelets, and jewels were sent to Lisbon in 1512 as tokens of Siam's friendship and as examples of its industry. Silks, pearls, and porcelains were collected in Asia as gifts for the queen and the ladies of the court. Albuquerque sent jewels to the official chronicler, Ruy de Pina, to assure himself a favored place in the history of Portugal's endeavor in the East.[13] Diogo Lopes de Sequeira, following Albuquerque's example, sent gifts of two gold necklaces to Dom Manuel. Occasionally the king even paid for Oriental ceramics and textiles out of his own pocket.[14]

Indian elephants and a rhinoceros from Cambay were on display in Lisbon by 1513–15. The Zamorin of Calicut sent a dispatch to Lisbon in 1513 engraved on a sheet of gold. Fernão Peres d'Andrade, who was in China in 1516–17, returned to Portugal and showed King Manuel "several of their [Chinese] paintings and figures."[15] The emissaries from Ceylon in 1541 brought documents and presents to Lisbon in two ivory caskets (see pl. 13). One of the caskets contained gems and a golden statue of the prospective king of Cotta (Kotte), and a jeweled crown.[16] King John III of Portugal crowned the effigy of the prince in a symbolic investiture by which the Sinhalese tacitly acknowledged the suzerainty of Portugal. In the meantime João de Barros, according to numerous references in his *Décadas da Asia*, was collecting through the men in the East the Oriental books and manuscripts which he used in writing his history.[17]

[11] Sousa Viterbo, *loc. cit.* (n. 2), pp. 319–20.

[12] H. J. Stanley (trans. and ed.), *The Three Voyages of Vasco da Gama . . . from the Lendas da India of Gaspar Correa* (London, 1869), p. 306.

[13] According to João de Barros, as quoted in Sousa Viterbo, *loc. cit.* (n. 2), p. 319. Also see Dom Manuel's letter to Pope Leo X as excerpted in R. B. Smith, *The First Age of the Portuguese Embassies to . . . Southeast Asia* (Bethesda, Md., 1968), p. 13.

[14] See the list of bills paid in 1514 in A. Braamcamp Freire (ed.), "Cartas de quitação del Rei D Manuel," *Archivo historico portuguez*, I (1903), 202.

[15] From the translation of Osório's *De rebus* (1571) in J. Gibb (trans.), *The History of the Portuguese . . .* (London, 1752), I, 249. For discussion of Osório see my *Asia in the Making of Europe* (hereafter cited as *Asia*), I (Chicago, 1965), 196.

[16] J. de Castilho, *A ribeira de Lisboa* (2d ed.; Lisbon, 1941–48), II, 197–98.

[17] Cf. *Asia*, I, 381, 402, 410, 437, 506.

But infinitely more important at this early period for the future of Portugal were the renovation of the city of Lisbon, the commencement of the great masterpieces of Manueline architecture, the establishment of the Casa da India as the center of the spice trade, and the elevation of the city to the position of Europe's center for the distribution of Asian goods. As early as 1503, a French merchant wrote of Lisbon as the place where one can "view beautiful riches and other rarities brought . . . by Portuguese vessels plying to the East Indies." [18] Only the spices were held as a monopoly of the Portuguese crown; consequently the Rua Nova dos Mercadores, the artery on which luxury wares from abroad were sold, had become by midcentury one of the most elegant mercantile streets of Europe. [19] Under its covered galleries the prospective buyer could shop in all kinds of weather for porcelains, jewels, gold and silverware, exotic woods, and textiles from the East. [20] By 1580 six shops in this street specialized in selling fine porcelains of various types, [21] for the king had declared in 1522 that ships returning from India might carry porcelain as one-third of their total cargo. [22] Porcelain was but one of the items sold commercially on the Rua Nova. Eight hundred cases of Asiatic goods passed through the Casa da India in 1552, and these did not include the precious stones, porcelains, high quality amber, and bedspreads also imported. [23] Each year about two thousand ordinary gems and stones were imported, many of which were sold in the city. [24] The cloth merchants of the Rua Nova stocked silks, velvets, damasks, and taffetas of various kinds and prices, [25] and every week they held a fair on the Rossio of Lisbon at which they sold remnants, including Indian textiles, at bargain prices. [26]

Iberian merchants also dealt in Eastern commodities that were thought to be more useful than decorative. Aside from the spices which were often employed as medicaments and incense, the pharmacists of Lisbon kept on their shelves jars of dried rhubarb, root of China, [27] myrobalans, tamarinds, benzoin and camphor

[18] As quoted in H. Belevitch-Stankevitch, *Le goût chinois en France au temps de Louis XIV* (Paris, 1910), p. xxx.

[19] A painting of this bustling thoroughfare was made for King Manuel's Book of Hours.

[20] João Brandão (d. 1562) gives the best contemporary description in his *Estatistica de Lisboa de 1552* as reproduced in *Tratado da majestade, grandeza e abastança da cidade de Lisboa na 2.ª metade do século XVI* (Lisbon, 1923), pp. 79–80; also see Damião de Gois, *Lisboa de quinhentos* (Lisbon, 1937), p. 48. For a recent summary see A. Vieira da Silva, *As muralhas da ribeira de Lisboa* (Lisbon, 1940–41), I, 91–112.

[21] See J. A. L. Hyde and R. R. Espirito Santo Silva, *Chinese Porcelains for the European Market* . . . (Lisbon, 1956), p. 49. But when Filippo Sassetti tried in 1583 to buy porcelain for Baccio Valori in Florence, he could not find anything in Lisbon fine enough to purchase. See E. Marcucci (ed.), *Lettere . . . di Filippo Sassetti* (Florence, 1855), pp. 231, 237.

[22] Hyde and Espirito Santo Silva, *op. cit.* (n. 21), p. 48.

[23] Brandão, *op. cit.* (n. 20), p. 38.

[24] *Ibid.*, p. 42.

[25] *Ibid.*, p. 48.

[26] *Ibid.*, p. 75.

[27] *Smilax China* or Chinese Sarsaparilla. In India inferior, local roots were substituted frequently for the Chinese product. See C. Markham (trans.), *Colloquies on the Simples and Drugs of India by Garcia da Orta* (London, 1913), p. 378, n. 1. It is possibly for this reason that Nicholas Monardes, the eminent pharmacist of Seville, believes that the roots brought from America were fresher and better than those from Asia. See N. Monardes, *Joyfull News out of the Newe Founde Worlde* (New York, 1925), I, 34–35.

[11]

crystals for the treatment of common ailments. Bezoar stones, concretions found in the intestines of some Asian animals, were highly prized in India as antidotes against poison; in Portugal the bezoar was imported for both its medicinal and its amulet qualities and was sought after by many of the crowned heads of Europe. The king of Cochin sent a bezoar stone as a gift to Dom Manuel shortly after he first engaged in business with the Portuguese. Opium and bhang (Indian hemp or hashish), famed for their aphrodisiac, stimulatory, narcotic, and hallucinatory attributes, could be found in the apothecary shops of Seville.[28] Datura (thorn apple or strammony), a powerful intoxicant, entered the European pharmacopoeia in the sixteenth century and was a subject of serious interest to botanists and to illustrators of botanical books (pl. 36). Both scientists and amateur collectors competed to obtain samples of the exotic drugs for their collections of curiosities. Bezoar stones and rhinoceros horns were frequently set in silver or gold mountings by European craftsmen and were highly prized as showpieces and as antidotes against poison (pl. 8).

It was not only the royal family of Portugal that collected mementos of Lusitania's great exploits in the East. Vasco da Gama, who spent his last years in Evora, had pictures of the trees and animals of India painted on his house.[29] Afonso de Albuquerque, the son of the conqueror, bought a country house at Bacalhoa near Setubal where he built a pavilion called Casa da India that was richly decorated with Indian hangings.[30] Juan Sebastian del Cano, who brought Magellan's ship back to Spain with a large cargo of spices, petitioned Charles V to allow him to have a coat of arms of two crossed sticks of cinnamon with three nutmegs and two cloves rampant.[31] Dom João de Castro, after his tenure as viceroy of India (1545–48), built an estate near Sintra where the royal menagerie was located, which he called Pinha Verde. On the hill above his garden he planted an arboretum of rare trees and bushes brought back from India.[32] One of those he reputedly brought was the Chinese orange, the first sweet orange tree in Europe.[33] And though this is not certain, he may have had a stela in his garden with an Indian inscription carved on it.[34] In the latter half of the sixteenth century other Portuguese noblemen stocked their parks with exotic animals and plants. In Spain a most extensive menagerie was maintained by Don Hurtado de Mendoza.[35] In an inventory of a Spanish nobleman dated 1560, it is thought worthwhile to notice that his wife possessed a headdress of Indian silk with edgings of linen. The residence of Simon Ruiz, merchant of Medina del Campo,

---

[28] Monardes (*op. cit.* [n. 27], I, 89–90) tells of seeing Indian dockworkers buying opium in Seville (*ca.* 1560). Also see L. Lewin, *Phantastica: Narcotic and Stimulating Drugs, Their Use and Abuse* (New York, 1964), *passim.*

[29] A. Franco, *Evora ilustrado* (Evora, 1948), p. 116.

[30] W. C. Watson, *Portuguese Architecture* (London, 1908), pp. 26–27.

[31] F. Guerra, "Drugs from the Indies . . . ," *Analecta medico-historica*, I (1966), 40.

[32] R. S. Nichols, *Spanish and Portuguese Gardens* (New York, 1902), pp. 225–26.

[33] Gallesio, *Traité du citres* (Pisa, 1917), II, 297.

[34] Sousa Viterbo, *loc. cit.* (n. 2), p. 321.

[35] P. Delaunay, *La zoölogie au seizième siècle* (Paris, 1962), p. 146.

boasted a bed and a carved and gilded table from the Portuguese Indies.[36] Martaban jars, huge earthenware pots utilized as water and oil casks aboard Asian and Portuguese ships, were evidently brought back in sizable numbers (as they were in the following century to Holland) for use in the homes and institutions of the Iberian peninsula.[37]

The Habsburg rulers of Spain, like their German relatives, began to collect oddities at an early date. The great Charles V, even though he was not especially interested in the arts himself, possessed porcelains, golden items, and feather-works from the East.[38] Philip II was much more of a collector and connoisseur of the arts than his father. Early in his career he bought Western books on Asia for the library at the Escorial, and later a number of Chinese books sent from the Philippines were added to this collection.[39] In 1566 Queen Catharine of Portugal sent presents from India to her daughter-in-law, a Spanish princess, which included a selection of the finest porcelains. Other relatives and friends at the court of Lisbon likewise sent gifts of porcelain to Spain.[40] Many of these porcelains were so highly prized that they were kept in the jewel room and treasury of Madrid.

Portugal's vital interest in Asian trade was vividly portrayed in the triumphal arches and pedestals erected in Lisbon when Philip of Spain made his formal entry there in 1581.[41] Every major Portuguese conquest in the East was depicted as a statue presenting its products symbolically to the new king. Goa, represented as "Queen of the East," was given the central position in the display of coopera-tion erected by the merchants of Lisbon before the Ribeira Palace. The king responded positively to this overture of the merchants. He immediately ordered his servitors in the East to be on the watch in Asia for new items which might be of profit to the kingdom. The French ambassador wrote to his government on September 20, 1581, that the king himself had passed the previous day in front of a window watching with great pleasure the unloading of the ships from India.[42] Philip acquired porcelain services in Lisbon for his children and

[36] See F. L. May, *Hispanic Lace and Lace Making* (New York, 1939), p. 12; also H. Lapeyre, *Une famille de marchands: les Ruiz* (Paris, 1955), p. 77.

[37] A. C. Burnell and P. A. Tiele (eds.), *The Voyage of John Huyghen van Linschoten to the East Indies* (London, 1885), I, 101. The Museum of Leeuwarden in Holland possesses a very complete collection of Martaban jars, surpassed only by the assemblage of them at Djakarta. See M. Beurdeley, *Porcelaine de la Compagnie des Indes* (Fribourg, 1962), p. 40.

[38] See the inventory of 1560 of the treasures of Charles V in Pedro de Madrazo, "Über Kronungs-insignien und Staatsgewänder Maximilian I. und Karl V. und ihr Schicksal im Spanien," *Jahrbuch der kunsthistorischen Sammlungen des allerhöchsten Kaiserhauses*, IX (1889), 45–51. Charles V's set of porcelain plates (now at Dresden) had been decorated in China with his cipher and badge.

[39] At Antwerp in 1568 Benito Arias Montano had bought two Western books on Asia for his king. R. Beer (ed.), "Niederländische Bücherewerbungen des Benito Arias Montano für den Eskurial im Auftrage König Philip II von Spanien," *Jahrbuch der kunsthistorischen Sammlungen des allerhöchsten Kaiserhauses*, XXV (1905), vi, x. Also see *Asia*, I, 693, 779 n., on Chinese books at the Escorial.

[40] F. de Sousa Viterbo, "O theatro na corte de D. Filippe II," *Archivo historico portuguez*, I (1903), 4.

[41] See A. Guerreiro, *Relação das festas que se fizeram na entrada de el-rei D. Felipe, primeiro de Portugal*, reprint of the 1581 publication (Porto, 1950), pp. 49–80.

[42] M. Gachard (ed.), *Lettres de Philippe II à ses filles les infantes Isabella et Catherine écrites pendant son voyage en Portugal (1581–83)* (Paris, 1884), p. 121, n. 5.

certain other pieces of a type that he himself had never before seen.[43] In a letter to his family the king promised to send his young son a "desk from India" if he would persevere in learning to read and write.[44] The following month he sent his daughters some rosaries made in India.[45] When a lone ship arrived at Lagos in July, 1582, the king wrote his daughters that it had aboard an elephant which was being sent from Goa as a gift from his appointee, Viceroy Francisco de Mascarenhas, to the young prince in Madrid. But perhaps most revealing of Philip's self-conscious interest is a letter of October 25, 1582, in which he wrote to his daughters:

I am concerned to find other objects to carry back to Madrid with me; but it is difficult to find them, although they do say that they have many things on board one of their ships. I am sending you some chunks of the wax that they have brought, because they [the chunks of wax] are not of the ordinary sort, as well as some pieces of white wax, a thing that I have never before seen. Seal some of your letters to me with this wax, so that I can see how it works, although I guess that it will not be suitable.[46]

Philip's curiosity about the East was titillated again when he was visited at Madrid in November, 1584, by the young emissaries from Japan (pl. 35). Among the gifts presented to the king on this occasion were folding screens (*byōbus*), two suits of Japanese armor, a bamboo desk with drawers in it given to the Jesuit Alessandro Valignano by Oda Nobunaga, a varnished wooden basin decorated with a gold border, a fancy basket crammed with trinkets, and a small lacquered pipe.[47] In the Armería of Madrid the legates themselves were shown many jewels from Asia and three Indian desks that belonged to the king.[48] Captured weapons, as well as those acquired by other means, were also sent to the king by his men in the field to acquaint him with Asian armaments and craftsmanship.[49] The Spanish governors and missionaries in the Philippines regularly sent books, maps, and other sources of information about China for the king to see. Archbishop Vicente de Fonseca, Philip's appointee at Goa, sent his royal master a huge ivory crucifix that was so artistically carved in Ceylon that the figure of Christ "seemed to be alive."[50] The king also displayed Asian animals in Madrid and added trees and shrubs from the Orient to his arboretum at Aranjuez. As a measure of the king's interest in the Oriental trade there is the story of how in 1585 he ordered that the keel of a huge carrack, built at Goa of

[43] *Ibid.*, pp. 205–6.
[44] *Ibid.*, p. 124.
[45] *Ibid.*, p. 130.
[46] *Ibid.*, p. 186.
[47] J. A. Abranches Pinto *et al.*, *La première ambassade du Japon en Europe* (Tokyo, 1942), pp. 87–88.
[48] *Ibid.*, p. 106. These items are still in the Armería, as well as those presented by the Japanese. Also see M. Kiichi, "Armaduras japonesas en la Real Armería de Madrid," *Monumenta Nipponica*, XVI (1960–61), 175–81.
[49] Burnell and Tiele, *op. cit.* (n. 37), I, 109–10.
[50] Linschoten's words in *ibid.*, p. 81.

Indian teak twenty years before, should be transported to the Escorial once the ship was broken up at Lisbon.[51]

The inventory of Philip's collection, prepared a number of years after his death for a sale of his belongings, lists around twenty thousand articles, including his porcelain collection of over three thousand pieces.[52] It also includes paintings, musical instruments, and lacquered boxes from China. For example, one entry reads: "Three canvases painted in distemper over a very fine canvas placed upon paper, of birds native to China."[53] Daggers, cutlasses, and knives of China and India also appear in the inventory.[54] In a medal struck in Philip's honor, the reverse bears the enigmatic inscription: "Reliquum. Datura. India."[55] This is probably a reference to the offerings of India to the king and his country. Philip's personal involvement in collecting, which continued strong into the final year of his life, can be observed in a letter he wrote on May 10, 1598, to the viceroy of India, Dom Francisco da Gama. He ordered that there should be sent to himself "a good quantity of amber and chosen work [probably textiles], carpets, and a very few porcelains." And, commanded the king, "Whatever you do or send you will inform Miguel de Maura so that I may be apprised."[56]

Even though the precious metals of America and the products of the East flowed into (and through) Spain for most of the sixteenth century, the sumptuary laws imposed by the crown helped to prevent the subjects of Philip from indulging in ostentatious personal display or from spending large sums for collections of curiosa. A law of 1494, for example, prohibiting the importation and sale of textiles (except those for religious use) using gold or silver threads was reaffirmed and revised in 1534 by Charles V. While such restrictions were generally relaxed under Philip, many prohibitions remained. A decree of 1563 permitted women to wear precious stones, pearls, and gold and silver jewelry but only on the condition that they be used on the head, bust, and sleeves and never on the skirt![57] Nonetheless, by the end of the century, the jewelry shops of Spain were selling gold jewelry, porcelains, silk fabrics, fancy headdresses, and gloves for milady's hands.[58] But a decree of 1593 sternly

---

[51] C. R. Boxer, "The Carreira da India (Ships, Men, Cargoes, Voyages)," *O Centro de estudos históricos ultramarimos e as comemorações henriquinas* (Lisbon, 1961), p. 40. A royal order of 1585 ordained that carracks for the India run should be built in India rather than in Europe because those built with teak in India were esteemed to be cheaper, stronger, and more durable (*ibid.*, p. 37).

[52] Inventories prepared in 1611–13. See R. Beer (ed.), "Inventare aus dem Archivio del Palacio zu Madrid," *Jahrbuch der kunsthistorischen Sammlungen des allerhöchsten Kaiserhauses*, XIV (1893), iv–v; XIX (1898), cxxv–cxli. For appropriate extracts from these and other royal inventories see J. C. Davillier, *Les origines de la porcelaine en Europe* (Paris, 1882), pp. 125–35.

[53] Beer, *loc. cit.* (n. 52), XIX (1898), cxxix; for the musical instruments and boxes see *ibid.*, pp. cxxxiv and clxiii.

[54] *Ibid.*, XIV (1893), lxii–lxiii.

[55] A. Armand, *Les médailleurs italiens* ... (Paris, 1883), I, 239. Also see discussion of *datura* at Florence, the home of the artist Gianpaolo Toggini, who cast this medal (see below, p. 41).

[56] As quoted by Hyde and Espirito Santo Silva, *op. cit.* (n. 21), p. 50.

[57] J. C. Davillier, *Recherches sur l'orfevrerie en Espagne au moyen âge et à la Renaissance: Documents inédits tirés des archives* (Paris, 1879), pp. 120–22.

[58] *Ibid.*, pp. 113–16.

forbade silversmiths and all other persons from buying, selling, or making tables, coffers, bureaus, or buffets decorated with silver.[59] Spanish merchants, however, sold goods from America, including the costumes and headdresses of the Indians, at the metropolitan and provincial fairs in the other countries of Europe.[60] And the Spanish style in clothing was imitated by most of the other European courts (pl. 1).

Information on the Iberian collections is limited and sketchy, perhaps because so many literary and artistic sources were destroyed in the Lisbon earthquake of 1755. A better estimate of the numbers and types of imports from Asia can be obtained from studying the reports of foreigners and the lists of gifts sent by the rulers of Portugal to the prelates and crowned heads of Europe.[61] King Manuel sent to the pope many items which splendidly displayed the superb craftsmanship of Oriental artisans and artists. Gold and silver works, embroideries, brocaded clerical vestments, and rugs appear in the lists of his gifts, along with exotic animals and substantial quantities of spices and drugs.[62] Pius IV also received porcelain vessels and plates as gifts from Portugal.[63] Throughout the century, the agents of the great commercial companies and the representatives of foreign governments kept their employers informed of arrivals at Lisbon and of the prices of Oriental jewels and pearls. Johann von Schuren, a Fugger factor, bought diamonds at midcentury in Lisbon for his friends in Augsburg and for the daughters of Anton Fugger.[64] Portuguese commercial agents in France and the Low Countries, as well as students and priests in Paris and Rome, acted as informants and even agents for the collectors of curiosa in Italy and northern Europe. Through such devious routes much additional information might easily be obtained about the products of Asian provenance which arrived in Portugal, and something more could certainly be learned about the distribution of Asian curiosa among interested parties in the commercial centers outside of Iberia.

2

ANTWERP AND THE LOW COUNTRIES

From 1503 to 1553 the Portuguese and their agents in Antwerp delivered and sold almost everything that the buyer could find in Lisbon itself.[65] But after the

[59] *Ibid.*, p. 122.

[60] See E. Bonnaffé, *Causeries sur l'art et la curiosité* (Paris, 1878), pp. 94–95.

[61] See J. A. Goris, *Etude sur les colonies marchandes méridionales (portugais, espagnols, italiens) à Anvers de 1488 à 1567* (Louvain, 1925), pp. 236–39, 254–55, 269–99.

[62] Silver works, usually decorated with animals in relief, called *bastiães*, are very numerous on the list of things sent to Rome with the ill-fated embassy of 1515 which ended in shipwreck off Genoa. See Ernesto de Campos de Andrada (ed.), *Relações de Pero de Alcáçova Carneiro, conde da Idanha* (Lisbon, 1937), pp. 198–99.

[63] E. da Fonseca Brancante, *O Brasil e a louça da India* (São Paulo, 1950), p. 66. In 1554 the king presented to the papal legate in Portugal a blue-and-white porcelain bowl that is still preserved in the Museo Civico at Bologna.

[64] N. Lieb, *Die Fugger und die Künste im Zeitalter der Hohen Renaissance* (Munich, 1958), p. 136.

[65] For pertinent illustrations within this half of the century see Goris, *op. cit.* (n. 61), pp. 236–37, 254–55, 269–99. For a summary of the economic rise and decline of Antwerp see *Asia*, I, 119–31, and also the engraving of Antwerp at midcentury following p. 100.

closing of the Portuguese factory at Antwerp in 1549, the international trade of the Scheldt city began to decline seriously. Philip II's efforts to force the Hispanicization of the Netherlands from 1567 to 1580 resulted in a series of wars by which Antwerp lost whatever remained of its earlier status as the commercial heart of northwestern Europe. The emigration of the merchants to other cities brought a new order to affairs in the Netherlands by which Amsterdam and other Dutch port cities quickly replaced Antwerp in international trade. The rapid rise of the Dutch state in the last two decades of the sixteenth century culminated in the first Dutch voyages to the East and the establishment of a direct and regular trade with its marts. Antwerp's rise and decline as a commercial center and its replacement by the Dutch formed a pattern followed in many artistic, intellectual, and publishing activities as well.

Albrecht Dürer, the great German artist, was one of Antwerp's most eminent visitors in the years of its greatest glory. He traveled in the Low Countries during 1520–21; his diary contains numerous references to his activities there and imparts a genuine sense of the personal exultation he felt in being a part of Antwerp's rich and bustling life. Dürer met the Portuguese factors and became so friendly with them that he did a portrait drawing of Fernandez d'Almada and gave him as a gift the famous painting called "St. Jerome in Meditation."[66] He also sold, bartered, and gave as presents an almost incredible number of woodcuts and engravings by himself and his fellow German artists.

From his Portuguese and Flemish friends and acquaintances, Dürer, fascinated as he always was with new ideas and objects, acquired a collection of curios. His diary, used as an inventory to his collection, reveals that he acquired more than one dozen Indian coconuts, musk balls, Calicut cloths, a green jug filled with myrobalans, "two ivory saltcellars from Calicut . . . and a very pretty piece of porcelain," several pieces of sandalwood, "Calicut feathers," several green parrots, and a wooden weapon and a fish-skin shield from Calicut, and "two gloves with which the natives there fight."[67]

Almost anything of exotic interest stimulated Dürer to engage in reflection. On a visit to Brussels in the summer of 1520, he saw the royal collection of oddities from the New World which were on display for the imperial coronation. After viewing the gifts of Montezuma to Cortes, Dürer confided to his diary:

I saw the things which have been brought to the king [Charles V] from the new land of gold [Mexico], a sun all of gold a whole fathom broad, and a moon all of silver of the same size, also two rooms full of the armour of the people there, and all manner of wonderous weapons of theirs, harness and darts, very strange clothing, beds and all kinds of wonderful objects of human use much better worth seeing than prodigies. . . . all the days of my life I have seen nothing that rejoiced my heart so much as these

[66] E. Panofsky, *The Life and Art of Albrecht Dürer* (Princeton, 1955), I, 206.
[67] Compiled from W. M. Conway (trans.), *The Writings of Albrecht Dürer* (London, 1911), pp. 98, 100, 103, 104, 105, 109, 111, 113, 114, 115, 116, 123.

things, for I saw among them wonderful works of art, and I marvelled at the subtle *ingenia* of people in distant lands. Indeed, I cannot express all that I thought there.[68]

Others were likewise to marvel at the "subtle *ingenia*," but few were to leave their reactions so sharply and clearly expressed.

The feather headdresses which Dürer saw on display in Brussels were certainly products of Mexico, and consequently the featherworks known in Europe are often associated in the minds of modern students exclusively with America.[69] While feather creations were regularly imported from America, it should be recalled that even at this early date Dürer bought "Calicut feathers" in Antwerp. Hans Burgkmair in his woodcut gave feather skirts and headdresses to the "people of Calicut" (pl. 44). The feather pictures listed in the collections are also often associated with Asia,[70] and in numerous tapestries and paintings the natives of Asia are shown in feather dress. Such an association is warranted inasmuch as feathers were used in China and Japan as early as the eighth century for decorating clothes. Feathers were also appliquéd on screens in the Far East to make colorful designs, portraits, and calligraphic inscriptions. Head ornaments of feathers were as common in the islands of tropical Asia as they were in America. The sale of feathers from the kingfisher (*Halcyon chloris*) and from varicolored pheasants was a profitable export business in Cambodia, Borneo, and Japan.[71] In 1585 the Japanese legates presented featherworks to Francesco Calceolari (Calzolari), apothecary of Verona, for his collection. And it should be remembered that plumages of the bird of paradise were brought back from the Moluccas, and from the marts of Asia where they were on sale, by many of the voyagers to the East.[72] Their contemporaries in Europe, like Dürer himself, correctly associated colorful feathers, exotic plumages, featherworks, and feather headdresses with Asia as well as America.

Shortly after Dürer returned to Augsburg, the Portuguese Humanist Damião

[68] *Ibid.*, pp. 101–2. Also see Vienna, Kunsthistorisches Museum, *Sonderausstellung Karl V* (Vienna, 1958), pp. 101–2. While he was in Brussels in 1520, Dürer also did a pen drawing of the royal gardens of Brussels with its plants and beasts from different places (reproduced in Panofsky, *op. cit.* [n. 66], II, no. 1409). He also did a pen drawing of Antwerp's harbor in 1520 with its ships from far-off shores. Reproduced in *ibid.*, no. 1408.

[69] For example, see S. Schéle, *Cornelis Bos: A Study of the Origins of the Netherland Grotesque* (Stockholm, 1965), pp. 79–80.

[70] Philip Hainhofer, a professional supplier of collectors, suggested in 1610 that the feathers of Turkish chickens and Indian cocks should be purchased in Amsterdam for use as colorful decorations at weddings and parties. He also lists in 1612 a Japanese feather portrait of St. Francis. See O. Doering (ed.), *Des Augsburger Patriciers Philipp Hainhofer Beziehungen zum Herzog Philip II von Pommern Stettin: Correspondenzen aus den Jahren 1610–1619* (Vienna, 1896), pp. 53–54, 233. Also see the engraved title page of B. L. Argensola, *Conquista delas islas Malucas . . .* (Madrid, 1609), in which the woman who symbolizes the Moluccas wears a feather headdress.

[71] S. Jenyns, "Feather Jacket (*Jimbaori*) of the Momoyama Period (1573–1638). Supposed to Have Belonged to Hideyoshi (1536–1598)," *British Museum Quarterly*, XXXII (1967), 48–52.

[72] Cf. below, pp. 181–82. "Strange beasts" were also being sent from Spain to the animal park of Brussels as early as 1507. See P. Saintenoy, *Les arts et les artistes à la cour de Bruxelles* (Brussels, 1932), p. 73.

de Gois left Lisbon in 1523 for Flanders.[73] He remained in the Netherlands for the next six years as notary at the Portuguese factory. He was also a regular visitor at the court of Archduchess Margaret, daughter of Emperor Maxmilian I and ruler of Flanders from 1524 to her death in 1530. Margaret, one of the earliest royal collectors of Indian wares, probably knew the leading Portuguese merchants of Antwerp as well as Gois, as indicated by the fact that she had portraits of some of them among her possessions when she died.[74] It was probably through them and Gois that she began, within the short span of her reign, to add to Charles's collections of Americana and to begin serious collection of Asiatica in the Low Countries. While she acquired a number of oddities and textiles from Asia, Margaret was evidently partial to Chinese porcelain. According to the inventory of her possessions she assembled for the period a sizable collection of porcelain bowls, saltcellars, ewers, and plates. On her death in 1530 her collection was divided between Emperor Charles V and his brother Ferdinand.[75]

The "sinjoren," as the men of wealth and position in Antwerp were called, competed with one another and with the leaders of the foreign merchant communities in constructing, decorating, and furnishing ostentatious dwellings. The patrician interiors of their showplace homes often boasted collections of statuary, tapestries, gems, coins, and exotic curiosities. Diego Duarte, a Portuguese jewel merchant, had a town house at the Place de Meu in which he brought together a beautiful collection of paintings, tapestries, and miscellaneous objects.[76]

Scholars like Abraham Ortelius and his publisher-friend, Christopher Plantin, were part of this bourgeois society and shared its enthusiasm for collecting (pl. 16). As early as 1561 Ortelius wrote a note to remind himself to ascertain, presumably from his Portuguese correspondents, whether anything strange and new from India had come to their attention.[77] For his geographical work, Ortelius also searched far and wide in his personal travels and through his numerous correspondents in all parts of Europe for more and better books about and maps of Asia. Others wrote to Ortelius for the latest information on the East or asked his criticisms of their works on Asia.[78] Merchants who traveled

[73] M. Lemos, "Damião de Goes," *Revista de história*, IX (1920), 208.

[74] See "Inventaire des objects d'art et lingerie de luxe qui composaient le mobilier de Marguerite d'Autriche," as reproduced in *Le cabinet de l'amateur*, I (1842), 223.

[75] Cf. *ibid.*, pp. 215-23, 271-75; also H. Zimmermann (ed.), "Urkunden, Acten und Regesten aus dem K. und K. Haus-, Hof- und Staats-Archiv in Wien." *Jahrbuch der kunsthistorischen Sammlungen des allerhöchsten Kaiserhauses*, III (1885), Pt. 2, ciii-cv. Also see the catalogue entitled *Margareta van Oostenrijk en haar Hof* (Mechelen, 1958).

[76] Unfortunately only a very few written sources remain on the collections of the period before the "Spanish Fury" of 1576. See S. Speth-Hollterhoff, *Les peintres flamands de cabinets d'amateurs au XVIIe siècle* (Brussels, 1957), pp. 10, 23; also J. Denucé, *De kunstkamers van Antwerpen in de 16e en 17e eeuwen* (The Hague, 1932); on the relationships between art collecting and commerce see H. Floerke, *Studien zur niederländischen Kunst- und Kulturgeschichte* (Munich, 1905), pp. 163-73.

[77] See Hessels, *op. cit.* (n. 5), p. 24.

[78] For example, the Louvanian Jesuit Jacobus Nearchus wrote to Ortelius in 1570 asking his opinion about a Jesuit letterbook and his own work on the Tartars. See *ibid.*, p. 69; or see the letter of Gerhard Mercator from Duisburg of 1580, *ibid.*, pp. 238-40.

regularly between Lisbon and Madrid were commissioned to acquire coins for his collection.[79] From the botanists Joachim Camerarius in Germany and Benito Arias Montano in Spain, Ortelius got information about and samples of exotic plants and seeds for his own garden and for Charles de L'écluse (pl. 15), as well as drugs and books on drugs.[80] Arias Montano also sent Ortelius a bezoar stone and other gems from his own collection.[81] Ortelius, meanwhile, helped Archduke Ernest at Brussels to augment his collections of jewelry and armor from all over the world.[82]

A younger contemporary of Ortelius, Bernard ten Broecke (1550–1633) (usually called "Paludanus"), a learned physician of Enkhuizen, was simultaneously building a collection of curiosities. Enkhuizen was also the home of Jan Huygen van Linschoten, the famed traveler who worked for the Portuguese in India from 1583 to 1588, and of Dirck Gerritsz (called "China") who had spent many years in the East as a gunner with the Portuguese fleets.[83] While Paludanus had never traveled to India and points east himself, he had made a journey to Italy and the Levant, where he acquired many curios for his collection. In Italy he knew Damião de Gois and probably learned from him something of the distant East as the Portuguese knew it.[84] At any rate, by the time Linschoten returned to Enkhuizen in 1592, the fame of Paludanus as a scholarly collector had been well established.

Ortelius did not yet know his neighbor Paludanus in 1592,[85] but Duke Frederick I (ruled 1593–1608) of Württemberg, having heard of the physician's renowned *Wunderkammer*, made a special visit to Enkhuizen on September 17 of that year to see it.[86] The Duke's secretary, Jakob Rathgeb, took careful notes on the visit and eventually published an inventory of the collection in which he explained its organization and itemized its contents,[87] sometimes rather roughly. It consisted of eighty-seven numbered cabinets and chests of marked and identified exhibits of earths, clays, sands, crystals, potteries, salts, nitrates, metals, jaspers, agates and carnelians, and precious stones; exotic woods, fruits, plants, roots, seeds, flowers, cereals, gums, and resins; strange animals or parts of animals, foreign birds (including three plumages of the bird of paradise),

---

[79] *Ibid.*, pp. 320–21.

[80] *Ibid.*, pp. 374–75, 429, 498–99.

[81] *Ibid.*, pp. 429, 684–85. The agents of the Rovellascas frequently acted as intermediaries between Ortelius and his Iberian correspondents. On the Rovellascas in the spice trade see *Asia*, I, 134–36, 475.

[82] See Coremans, "L'Archiduc Ernest, sa cour et ses dépenses, 1593–95," *Bulletin de la Commission royale d'histoire* (Brussels), XIII (1847), 140.

[83] For the relations of Paludanus and Linschoten, see C. M. Parr, *Jan van Linschoten: The Dutch Marco Polo* (New York, 1964), pp. 190–98.

[84] H. de Vocht, *History of the Foundation and Rise of the Collegium Trilingue Lovaniense, 1517–1550* (Louvain, 1951–55), III, 60.

[85] He wrote to Emanuel Demetrius on August 18, 1592: "The Paludanus about whom you inquire is unknown to me" (Hessels, *op. cit.* [n. 5], p. 525).

[86] See J. Rathgeb, *Warhaffte Beschreibung zweyer Reisen . . .* (Tübingen, 1603), I, 44 n.

[87] *Index rerum omnium naturalium a B. Paludanus* in *ibid.*, following the introduction.

medicines, "things from the seas," and two chests of all sorts of manufactured objects produced in India, China, and both Indies. Among the other Eastern commodities identified by Rathgeb were clay from which porcelain is made, jaspers and rubies, carnelians from India, and various samples of clothing from both Indies.

With the return of Linschoten in 1592, Paludanus helped to prepare the *Itinerario* of his compatriot for publication. He undoubtedly also added to his own collection the souvenirs of Eastern provenance brought back for him in Linschoten's sea chest. We learn from Linschoten's own testimony that he gave the doctor a penis bell, reeds and canes, palm-leaf paper, and samples of Chinese writing and paper.[88] By 1596 Ortelius and Paludanus had come to know each other and were corresponding about the possibilities of a northern passage to China.[89] Linschoten, who was privy to this correspondence, sent the geographer a parcel of pictures, probably prepared for the *Itinerario*, and sketches of the fruits and trees that grow in India.[90] In his covering letter, Paludanus volunteered to send Ortelius curious natural items from his own cabinet.

With the death of Ortelius in 1598, Paludanus' collection stood in a class by itself as a private collection of natural curiosities. Its fame spread far and wide and in the seventeenth century an English traveler on viewing the collection composed, allegedly extempore, the following epigram:

> In the old world or new, what wondrous thing
> Did art to light or nature lately bring,
> This Paludanus house doth show a rare
> Proof of the Owners sovereign wit and care.[91]

Before his death in 1633, Paludanus gave a few objects from his collections to the museum of natural history that was then being assembled in "the Publick Theater and Anatomie Hall of the University of Leyden."[92] But the bulk of his collection remained at Enkhuizen until it was sold in 1651 to Duke Frederick III of Schleswig-Holstein-Gottorp. Frederick's agent was Adam Olearius, a celebrated Eastern traveler; in 1666 Olearius published a catalogue of the collection at Gottorp (pl. 11). In the eighteenth century most of Paludanus' collection went to Tsar Peter III, a descendant of the duke of Gottorp, and was incorporated into the Russian imperial collection at St. Petersburg. The remainder of it was acquired for the royal cabinet of curiosities in Copenhagen.[93]

---

[88] Burnell and Tiele, *op. cit.* (n. 37), I, 50, 96–97, 99–100, 142.

[89] Hessels, *op. cit.* (n. 5), pp. 677–78.

[90] *Ibid.*, p. 705. For examples of the kind of pictures Linschoten probably sent to Ortelius see portraits of the inhabitants of southeast Asia in *Asia*, I, following p. 528.

[91] As quoted and translated from Latin in [Thomas Powell], *The History of Most Curious Manual Arts and Inventions* . . . (3d ed.; London, 1675), pp. 187–88.

[92] The catalogue of the Leyden collection was prepared by its buyer, Jakob Voorn, and published in 1691. See Murray, *op. cit.* (n. 1), I, 29–30. I have not seen the English original, but I have consulted the French translation of 1704 by Gerard Blancken.

[93] *Ibid.*, I, 95–96; also see M. Boyer, *Japanese Export Lacquers* . . . *in the National Museum of Denmark* (Copenhagen, 1959), p. 45.

3

GERMANY AND AUSTRIA

The close political ties of the Habsburgs to Spain and the Low Countries and the constant commercial intercourse between Antwerp (later also Amsterdam) and the Hanseatic and south German mercantile centers brought Germany at an early date into intimate touch with the discoveries and Asian trade. Agents of the Fuggers, Welsers, Prauns, and Herwarts kept information and products flowing into Augsburg and Nuremberg, two of the great artistic and printing centers of sixteenth-century Germany. Vienna and Prague, previously oriented commercially and intellectually toward Venice and Italy, came increasingly to feel the mercantile and artistic influence of the Low Countries during the sixteenth century, sometimes directly and sometimes through the mediation of the merchants and princes. Because of the widespread ramifications of their interests, the Habsburgs, the other German princes, and the great merchants were in a position to keep abreast of the latest developments in European and overseas commerce and to make artistic and scientific collections which were far richer and more comprehensive than those of their contemporaries in other countries.[94]

The earliest German collectors, whether princes or commoners, tended, like Albrecht Dürer, to concentrate on natural curiosities from overseas and on Roman statuary, bronzes, coins, and inscriptions. Lucas Rem, a commercial agent of the Welsers assigned to Lisbon in the years between 1503 and 1506, bought "strange, new parrots, long-tailed monkeys, and other curious and delightful things."[95] Konrad Peutinger and Willibald Pirckheimer, the Augsburg Humanists, eagerly sought books and information on the East.[96] In 1507 Peutinger, who kept in close touch with the Welsers, acquired a parrot, exotic woods, a bow, seashells, and other things from India through the German merchants.[97] Pirckheimer commissioned Dürer to buy pearls and precious stones for him in Venice. He was, however, informed by the artist that prices were so high at Venice that one could do better at Frankfurt, where the goods from Antwerp were merchandised.[98] Georg Agricola (1490?–1555), who needed fossils and minerals for his scientific studies, was anxious to get specimens from Africa and Asia to strengthen his collection.[99] Albrecht Dürer, as we have

---

[94] Taylor, *op. cit.* (n. 6), pp. 127, 167–68.

[95] B. Greiff (ed.), "Tagebuch des Lucas Rem . . . ," *Jahresbericht des historischen Kreisvereins . . . von Schwaben und Neuburg* (Augsburg, 1861), p. 43.

[96] See E. König (ed.), *Konrad Peutingers Briefwechsel* (Munich, 1923), pp. 49–50, 56–58; and E. Reiche (ed.), *Willibald Pirckheimers Briefwechsel* (Jena, 1930), I, 517, 520.

[97] Itemized in Peutinger's letter to Sebastian Brant of April 7, 1507, in König, *op. cit.* (n. 96), pp. 77–78.

[98] See Reiche, *op. cit.* (n. 96), p. 520; also H. Estienne, *La foire de Franckfort* (Lisieux, 1875), p. 67.

[99] See quotation from his *De natura rerum fossilarum* as given in Klemm, *op. cit.* (n. 10), pp. 242–43.

already seen, was eager to acquire as many examples of the "subtle *ingenia*" of foreign craftsmen and artists as he could find.

The Habsburgs of the prediscovery era were more interested in collecting native historical mementos than foreign curiosa or the antiquities of Greece and Rome. Each royal establishment in the first half or the sixteenth century had its own treasury. Maximilian I, the earliest Habsburg patron of the arts, had a stronger interest than his predecessors in the collection of curiosa and contemporary art. But his collecting activities remained essentially medieval and dynastic in their aims. He kept treasuries in most of his castles, concentrated on German and family interests, and used contemporary art for political propaganda (pl. 10). Upon his death Maximilian divided his treasuries among his grandsons, Charles V and Ferdinand I. The great Charles, even with his vast imperial interests, was interested in overseas arts only as they served the Catholic faith and the dynasty.[100] So, strange as it seems in light of his interests in Iberia, Charles's collections, like those of his grandfather, contained only miscellaneous curiosities from the East: bezoar stones, roots of China, and a double coconut from the Seychelles Islands that was gilded and set in a silver mounting.[101]

Ferdinand I, who was king of Bohemia and Hungary and regent of Austria in the time of Charles V's imperial reign, was much more intellectually curious than his older brother. He had been educated in the Netherlands, was tutored by Erasmus for a time, and was fascinated by Humanism and the contemporary arts. One of the Venetian ambassadors described him as "a most searching investigator of nature, of the countries of this earth, and of animals."[102] At Vienna he collected antiquities, books, armor, and contemporary paintings. Maximilian II, the eldest son of Ferdinand, inherited his father's enthusiasm for art, science, collecting, and the patronizing of scholars and artists. He used his diplomatic emissaries, including those whom he sent to the Porte, to help in collecting oddities for his chamber of curiosities. He himself brought an Asian elephant from Iberia to Austria[103] and was instrumental in founding the animal park at Ebersdorf. When he became emperor in 1564, Maximilian II set out to make Vienna the artistic as well as the administrative capital of the empire. He sponsored artists, botanists, and astronomers and brought to central Europe a more profound concern for contemporary intellectual and artistic affairs.[104]

Collections also began to be assembled in the middle and latter half of the sixteenth century by the lesser princes and wealthy merchants of south and central Germany. The two great ministers of the Habsburgs, Nicholas Perrenot de Granvelle and his son Cardinal Antoine de Granvelle, brought together at

---

[100] Lhotsky, *op. cit.* (n. 7), pp. 72–137.

[101] For example, see above, p. 13, and in the 1527 inventory of the jewels at Pressburg in H. Zimmermann (ed.), "Regesten aus dem K. und K. Reichs-Finanz-Archiv," *Jahrbuch der kunsthistorischen Sammlungen des allerhöchsten Kaiserhauses*, III (1885), Pt. 2, lxxii.

[102] See E. Albèri (ed.), *Relazioni degli ambasciatori Veneti al Senato* (Florence, 1839–63), 1st Ser., VI, 151.

[103] See below, pp. 144–46.

[104] Lhotsky, *op. cit.* (n. 7), pp. 157–73.

their native Besançon (Franche-Comté) an artistic and ethnographic display that was one of the most sumptuous of the private collections.[105] Elector Augustus of Saxony, who ruled from 1583 to 1586, undertook the first collection for what was to become the great museum of Dresden. From the inventory of 1587 prepared by his son and successor, Elector Christian I (ruled 1586–91), it becomes clear that Augustus had a genuine predilection for Asian curiosities, a preoccupation that was certainly connected with his interest in the spice trade and with his ill-fated efforts to make Leipzig the staple of northern Europe.[106] Aside from an assortment of seashells, strange plants and animals (for example, one griffon's tongue), and Indian textiles, the list includes routiers and maps of India. Of particular interest are two pieces of "Indian" lacquered furniture presented to Elector Christian of Saxony (probably around 1586) by the grand duke of Tuscany, Francesco I (ruled 1574–87).[107] The first piece was a desk with two small drawers that was covered with leather on which golden heathen pictures were painted. The other piece was a folding "Indian" table overlaid with black leather decorated with paintings of assorted birds and animals.[108] In 1591 another grand duke of Tuscany, Ferdinand I (ruled 1587–1609), sent to the Saxon Elector John George I (ruled 1591–1656) an "Indian" strongbox decorated with gold and fabulous work, as well as a porcelain cup.[109] From these descriptions it seems clear that some of these pieces were lacquerware from China or Japan. The Saxons in their turn probably gave Oriental rarities to Christian IV (ruled 1588–1648) of Denmark for his cabinet of curiosities.[110]

While the Lutheran Saxons learned of Asia primarily through the spice traders, the Catholic Bavarians maintained ties through the Jesuits as well as the merchants. And like the Saxons, the Bavarian Dukes Albert V (ruled 1552–79) and William V (ruled 1579–97) also had numerous contacts with the grand dukes of Florence and other patrons of the arts and sciences. Albert, who was a great patron of letters as well as arts, encouraged the Jesuits to move into the university of Ingolstadt to help in halting the spread of Protestantism in his dominions. In 1559 the first Jesuits settled at Munich and soon won for themselves an

[105] Taylor, *op. cit.* (n. 6), p. 164.

[106] For the creation of the Thuringian Company and his relations with Konrad Rott see *Asia*, I, 134. On his efforts to employ Hans Ulrich Krafft, who had traveled in the Levant from 1573 to 1577, see K. D. Haszler (ed.), *Reisen und Gefangenschaft Hans Ulrich Kraffts* (Stuttgart, 1861), pp. 368–69.

[107] For the interests of Francesco in the spice trade and in India see *Asia*, I, 133, 476. It is probable that these pieces were sent to Europe by Filippo Sassetti, the Rovellasca factor at Cochin. In 1629, the Augsburg collector Philip Hainhofer visited Dresden and described the tables and desks he saw there as being of "Indianischem lakwerk." See O. Doering (ed.), *Des Augsburger Patriciers Philipp Hainhofer Reisen nach Innsbruck und Dresden* (Vienna, 1901), p. 223.

[108] Extracted from the summary of the unpublished inventory in Klemm, *op. cit.* (n. 10), pp. 168, 172, 175, 177. Also see J. L. Sponsel, *Das Grüne Gewölbe zu Dresden* (Leipzig, 1925–32), I, 3–6.

[109] O. Münsterberg, "Bayern und Asien," *Zeitschrift des Münchener Alterthumsvereins*, N.S., VI (1894), 15–16.

[110] When Prince Christian of Anhalt visited Rosenborg Palace near Copenhagen in 1623, he described its collection of Oriental rarities. He reported seeing Japanese swords, knives, paintings, and pictures in the king's chamber. He also commented on an "Indian carrier . . . built like a bed in which they carry their queen about." See G. Krause, *Tagebuch Christians des Jüngeren, Fürst zu Anhalt . . .* (Leipzig, 1858), pp. 94–96.

important place at the court. Though the Jesuits clearly stimulated an interest at Munich in their Asian missions, they were more important as purveyors of news and information than of Asian arts and products. Indeed, it is striking that in the first inventory of Albert's treasures made in 1565, only one art object, an ivory elephant with a tower on its back set with rubies, diamonds, and pearls,[111] can be clearly distinguished as of Indian provenance. In Samuel Quickeberg's description of the Bavarian art treasures in his *Inscriptiones* . . . (1565), he lists only garments of the Indians, Arabs, and Turks made of parrot feathers and strange fabrics and tissues.[112] The Jesuits, it may be assumed, were much more concerned to funnel whatever Bavarian money they could into the support of the Society and its activities than they were to help the duke squander his funds on "heathen vanities." Such a conclusion is supported by the fact that the Jesuits dedicated one of their letterbooks published at Munich in 1570 to young Duke William as part of their propaganda campaign.[113]

In the final analysis the Wittelsbach dukes had to obtain their ethnographical and artistic curiosa from the East through their commercial agents in Iberia and the agents they employed in Italy. In 1555, for example, the agents of Mark Fugger in Lisbon obtained two ivory caskets for Duke Albert, several ivory combs, and a collection of jewelry (pls. 12 and 13). The caskets and combs were of Sinhalese origin and the caskets were possibly those which the Cotta emissaries brought to Lisbon in 1541 with the golden effigy of their prince.[114] That these caskets ultimately arrived safely in Munich is attested by the fact that they are described in the manuscript inventory of the Wittelsbach treasures prepared in 1598 by J. B. Fickler (1533–1610), the scholarly curator of the Bavarian collections.[115] He also indicates that on a table in the *Kunstkammer* reposed a display of Indian ceramics, crystals, textiles, coconuts in their natural and embellished states, costumes, and weapons. Oriental coins, exotic chests (see pl. 78), seashells, and textiles also appeared within other parts of the Bavarian collection. Charles of Spain, the son of Philip II, presented Duke Albert with a rectangular table covered with mother-of-pearl inlaid with roses and foliages.[116]

The enthusiasm of the Habsburgs for collecting became a mania in the latter half of the sixteenth century. At Graz, Archduke Charles II, spurred on by his

[111] M. Zimmermann, *Die bildenden Künste am Hof Herzog Albrechts V. von Bayern* (Strassburg, 1895), p. 65.
[112] Also see Quickeberg's, *Musaeum theatrum* (Munich, 1567); and J. Stockbauer, *Die Kunstbestrebungen am bayerischen Hofe* . . . (Vienna, 1874), p. 106.
[113] The book is entitled: *Epistolae Indicae et Japonicae etc. tertia editio . . . Illustrissimo Principi. Domino D. Guilielmo Bavariae dicatae 1570.*
[114] Cf. above, p. 10. This connection was first made by V. Slomann, "Elfenbeinreliefs auf zwei singhalesischen Schreinen des 16. Jahrhunderts," *Pantheon*, XX (1937), 357–60; XXI (1938), 12–19. Also see H. Thoma and H. Brunner, *Schatzkammer der Residenz München: Katalog* (Munich, 1964), pp. 363–66.
[115] I have not actually seen this exceedingly precious work. It is discussed in Klemm, *op. cit.* (n. 10), pp. 195–96. The reference to the manuscript is "Kunstkammer-Inventar, München 1598 von Joh. Bapt. Fickler," Cod. germ. 2133, Bayerische Staatsbibliothek, Munich.
[116] For these details from the inventory see Stockbauer, *op. cit.* (n. 112), pp. 14–17; and J. Irwin, "Reflections on Indo-Portuguese Art," *Burlington Magazine*, XCVII (1955), 387.

wife Maria who took an almost childish delight in collecting costly and curious objects, began assembling a mélange of oddities in the 1570's.[117] Through Hans Christoph Khevenhüller, the Austrian diplomatic representative in Spain, the court at Graz purchased silks, embroideries, pearl necklaces, and other costly goods. According to the inventory of 1590 the archduke left no fewer than 127 tapestries as well as a collection of Tartar and Indian weapons.[118] Archduke Ernst, the contemporary regent of the Netherlands, owned exotic Asian weapons, pearls, and a cross of Oriental ebony.[119]

Emperor Maximilian's younger brother, Archduke Ferdinand (1520–95), was the most systematic of the Habsburg collectors (pls. 2 and 3).[120] While acting as regent in Prague from 1547 to 1563, he began to put together what came to be the nucleus of his great collection. It was also during his Prague days that he married Philippine Welser, of the great German commercial family. Ferdinand's commoner wife continued her family's interest in overseas activities by collecting books and other materials on the discoveries.[121] When Ferdinand was transferred to Innsbruck, he bestowed the nearby castle of Ambras upon his wife. After Philippine died in 1580, Ferdinand removed to Ambras his extensive collections of armor, portraits of great men, and ethnographic and artistic rarities. Here he organized his heterogeneous collection into logical divisions and subdivisions, and took great personal interest and pride in studying and displaying it.

Ferdinand's collection was particularly rich in examples of the arts and crafts of Asia. The Innsbruck inventory of 1596, prepared shortly after the great collector's death, is a document of first importance for the history of collecting. From it one gains a sense of the number and variety of Asian objects it was possible for an alert, wealthy, and conscientious collector to acquire in Europe before 1600. In the large *Kunstkammer* at Ambras, eighteen huge, tall cabinets housed the items most precious to Ferdinand. Cabinet no. 14 contained the porcelain and the pearl ornaments. On the first shelf stood forty-two small but deep porcelain bowls, all of one size and decorated with blue foliage; on the next shelf were sixty-six porcelain vases, a few of which were glazed with gold, all the rest being plain blue and white; on the third, thirty-eight flatter porcelain bowls; on the fourth, thirty-eight larger porcelain bowls; on the fifth, thirty-eight pieces in all, of which thirty were medium-deep bowls and eight were flat plates; on the sixth stood seven bowls of blue-and-white porcelain, one of which was decorated with strange animals; on the seventh stood six large, flat bowls,

---

[117] Lhotsky, *op. cit.* (n. 7), pp. 206–8.

[118] For inventoried items see H. Zimmermann (ed.), "Urkunden, Acten und Regesten aus dem Archiv des K. K. Ministerium des Innerns," *Jahrbuch der kunsthistorischen Sammlungen des allerhöchsten Kaiserhauses*, III (1885), Pt. 2, xxviii–xxix.

[119] Lhotsky, *op. cit.* (n. 7), p. 215.

[120] *Ibid.*, pp. 179–83.

[121] See *Asia*, I, 160, n. 40. In the portrait collection at Ambras was a portrait of Magellan and one of Tamerlane, the "Tartar terror." See F. Kenner, "Die Porträtsammlung des Erzherzogs Ferdinand von Tirol," *Jahrbuch der kunsthistorischen Sammlungen des allerhöchsten Kaiserhauses*, XIX (1898), Pt. I, 25, 143–44.

four of which were blue and white inside and outside and two blue on the inside and white on the outside; on the eighth stood six of the largest porcelain vessels, two of which were alike but without borders and decorated on the inside with heathen gods in blue, and four without decorations.[122] Here, in this collection alone, were 241 pieces of Chinese porcelain, mostly of the Ming blue-and-white type. Such a figure for the Ambras collection makes it far easier to accept the idea that Philip II contemporaneously had around 3,000 pieces in his collection. Philip, it seems, had a large number of figurines, whereas none is noted for Ambras. Naturally, it is not possible to be certain that all the porcelains listed as such were genuine porcelain or that some of them were not European imitations of originals.

Other cabinets of the *Kunstkammer* at Ambras contained porcelain-like seashells, and pearl ornaments from India stood on display alone or were set in silver or gold mountings; rock crystal elephants, horn goblets, coconuts, muscat nuts, and bezoar stone amulets and cups were likewise given European mountings (pls. 7, 8, 9).[123] Textiles, fancy work, and apparel from the East brightened other chests. Heart-shaped ceramic flasks, three plumages of the bird of paradise, native trumpets and horns, and decorated shields added to the ethnographical variety of the display.[124] But most striking of all were the three pieces in cabinet no. 17, the entries for each beginning in the inventory with the description: "an Indian fabric on which is painted . . . [*Ain Indianische tuech darauf ist gemalt . . .*]."[125] These are references to three Chinese scroll paintings on silk, two of which are still preserved in the Kunsthistorisches Museum of Vienna (pls. 4 and 5).[126] In the inventory the two extant paintings are described: the first is a picture of "a great bird, similar to a swan, along with other birds and a variety of painted plants"; the second shows "several Indian houses in which women are playing stringed instruments." The painting of which no modern record exists is described as showing "Indian houses in which the Indians are sitting down together while one of them, clad in a red coat, is writing." In the eighteenth and last of the Ambras cabinets were housed the wooden art objects so dear to the hearts of the Tirolese, and included therein were lacquerware and cloisonné, an enamel technique on metal.[127]

While the princelings of Hesse and Brandenburg aped the greater collector

[122] From Innsbruck inventory of May 30, 1596, as reproduced in W. Boeheim (ed.), "Urkunden und Regesten aus der K. K. Hofbibliothek," *Jahrbuch der kunsthistorischen Sammlungen des allerhöchsten Kaiserhauses,* VII (1888), Pt. 2, ccc. For some of the porcelains from Ambras see pl. 6.

[123] Art historians use the European mounting to date approximately the appearance in Europe of articles of foreign provenance. See W. Born, "Some Eastern Objects from the Hapsburg Collections," *Burlington Magazine,* LXIX (1936), 269. At Frederiksborg Castle in Denmark a bezoar stone as large as a human head was kept in a silk wrapper in an Indian basket (Boyer, *op. cit.* [n. 93], p. 38).

[124] For references to these items see Boeheim, *loc. cit.* (n. 122), pp. ccxxxvii, cclix–cclx, cclxxxii, ccxcii–ccxciv, ccci, cccvi.

[125] *Ibid.,* p. cccvii.

[126] According to my colleague Father Harrie Van der Stappen, these are both unsigned studio paintings of the late Ming period.

[127] See Schlosser, *op. cit.* (n. 10), p. 68 and pl. 4.

princes of Europe by assembling porcelains,[128] the wealthy private collectors of Germany usually concentrated on the antiquities and contemporary arts of Europe. The Welsers, for all their overseas interests, collected European medals and coins and possessed a comprehensive run of Dürer's prints.[129] Paul von Praun (1548–1616) collected drawings and paintings in Italy for his collection in Nuremberg, as well as coins, bronzes, engraved gems, and a "number of rare curiosities."[130] The Imhofs and the Fuggers collected paintings and gems. The Fuggers patronized Charles de L'écluse, but apparently showed little direct interest themselves in his collections of foreign plants. Konrad Gesner, Joachim Camerarius, and Gerhard Mercator likewise received the support of the patricians in their efforts to acquire information on the East. But the merchant princes of Germany seemed content to make money for themselves from the spice trade, to acquire exotic items for others, and to turn their own money into less exotic, and presumably safer, artistic investments. The Fugger newsletters are full of information and speculation on trade, islands of gold, and new discoveries of land but they contain almost nothing relating to the acquisition of Asian arts and crafts in Europe or Asia.[131]

The oldest and most varied of the private collections was that owned by Dr. Lorentz Hofmann of Halle. In 1625 a catalogue of it was published in Latin and German.[132] In terms of Asian objects, Hofmann's collection was far more varied than most of the princely cabinets. While he possessed only four large porcelains, he lists one of them as being Japanese rather than Chinese. His collection also included Indian and Chinese weapons, Chinese coins, an "Indian painting," and various "Oriental books." Like many others he refers to articles of apparel made of parrot feathers.

The most avid of the Habsburg collectors was Rudolf II, the emperor from 1576 to 1612. During the last years of the sixteenth century he virtually turned his capital city of Prague into the *Wunderkammer* of Europe.[133] In his passion for collecting, he had agents working all over Europe. Those who wanted to win the imperial favor knew that the quickest way to receive Rudolf's attentions was to send him a new oddity or work of art for his collections. The emperor's desire for accumulation knew no bounds, but the focus of his interest shifted

[128] Cf. Beurdeley, *op. cit.* (n. 37), p. 113, and L. Reidemeister, *China und Japan in der Kunstkammer der brandenburgischen Kurfürsten* (Berlin, 1932), p. 5. For the names of other princely collectors see Klemm, *op. cit.* (n. 10), pp. 201–2.

[129] Taylor, *op. cit.* (n. 6), p. 135.

[130] C. de Murr, *Description du cabinet de . . . Praun* (Nuremberg, 1797), p. viii. Stefan von Praun (1544–91), Paul's uncle, traveled widely in the Levant and the Iberian peninsula (*ibid.*, p. v).

[131] An unusual example of the interested merchant is Konstantin von Lyskirchen (d. 1581), the burgomaster of Cologne, Fugger merchant, and collector and patron of the arts. From his Portuguese contacts, he supplied the sketches and descriptions of Asian cities for G. Braun and F. Hogenberg, *Civitates orbis terrarum* (Antwerp and Cologne, 1572), I, 54, 57. For his collecting activities see O. H. Förster, *Kölner Kunstsammler vom Mittelalter bis zum Ende des bürgerlichen Zeitalters* (Berlin, 1931), pp. 21, 26. For the Fugger newsletters see *Asia*, I, 92, n. 1.

[132] Summary of the catalogue in Klemm, *op. cit.* (n. 10), pp. 214–18.

[133] O. Schürer, *Prag: Kultur, Kunst, Geschichte* (Vienna and Leipzig, 1930), pp. 132–34.

with the passage of time from one field of collecting to another. In a sense the artists and scientists who were attracted to Prague by his patronage were in themselves a collection of talent. According to recent information it appears that Rudolf had his collections of wonders divided into three large, organized sections: *naturalia, artificialia*, and *scientifica*. His was, contrary to the opinions expressed by many modern commentators, a systematic collection of the world of nature, human creation, and general knowledge—in short, a universal museum.[134] The collections were usually locked, but it was customary for visitors to be shown them on request.[135] The sackings of Prague in the course of the Thirty Years' War resulted in the dispersion of these collections.

While it is not possible to reconstruct with precision what Rudolf's collections contained, it is possible to show that they included extensive holdings of plants, animals, books, and art objects from Asia. From his correspondence and that of others, it is known that he actively sought to acquire precious stones and bezoars from Asia in the marts of Iberia and Italy.[136] His agents bought giant coconuts in the Netherlands for his jewelers to set in ornate mountings.[137] Netherlandish artists and scientists brought overseas plants and animals to Prague to enliven the imperial park on the Hradchin.[138] Khevenhüller in Madrid acquired most of Granvelle's collection of art and curiosities for Rudolf. His agents in the Levant and Russia were constantly watching for miniature paintings, an art form for which he had a special fondness.[139]

Rudolf's collection, which has been likened to an Oriental bazaar, included examples of a vast array of Asian artistic and ethnographical items. The inventories prepared in 1619 and 1621 (see Appendix), partial as they are, are replete with references to "Indian objects," no distinction being made between those of Chinese, American, or Japanese provenance. An entire section of the inventory of 1619 is given to listing the "Indianische Sachen." Analysis of both inventories reveals that Rudolf had "one case of assorted Indian paintings bound together," several other Indian paintings on paper, ten miniature paintings of which five were framed in ebony, and seven embroidered pictures some of which were featherworks. He also owned eight Indian books and "assorted printed and written [manuscript] books." The ivory collection numbered about

---

[134] See E. Neumann, "Das Inventar der rudolfinischen Kunstkammer von 1607/11," in Swedish National Museum, *Analecta reginensis* (Stockholm, 1966). The earliest and most comprehensive of the inventories of Rudolf's collection still extant, the document of 1607–11, has not yet been published. This inventory, which is more accurately a catalogue of the objects in Rudolph's collection, was compiled in all probability by Daniel Fröschl, the miniaturist, who took over supervision of the Prague collections in 1607 after the death of Ottavio da Strada. Neumann, the director of the Sammlung für Plastik und Kunstgewerbe of the Kunsthistorisches Museum in Vienna, is planning to publish in the near future his edited version of the inventory of 1607–11 discovered recently in the library of Prince Liechtenstein at Vaduz.

[135] For example, Hans Ulrich Krafft, the Levantine traveler, visited them in 1584 and was shown about by the painter Bartolomäus Spränger. See Haszler, *op. cit.* (n. 106), pp. 388–90.

[136] Lhotsky, *op. cit.* (n. 7), pp. 246–47.

[137] *Ibid.*, p. 252.

[138] K. Chytil, *Die Kunst in Prag* . . . (Prague, 1904), p. 15.

[139] *Ibid.*, p. 29.

one hundred and twenty wrought and unwrought pieces; the collection of brass and metal wares was also extensive and included representations of the gods and temples of India. The porcelains, which totaled over seven hundred pieces, were mostly kept together in cabinets following the organization of the Ambras collection. Among the other Indian oddities were chess sets and gaming boards inlaid with mother-of-pearl, dozens of lacquered boxes and chests, numerous desks, inkstands and ink, Maldive coconuts and bezoar stones in silver settings (pl. 14), musical instruments, bedsteads and chairs, costumes and silken bed covers. Among the natural objects there were cases of seashells, dried and stuffed birds and animals, large numbers of rhinoceros horns, one piece of rhinoceros hide, and five emu eggs. European paintings of Indian animals were also collected and displayed, including one of the elephant and another of the rhinoceros.[140]

In Rudolf's massive collection the *Kunst- und Wunderkammer* reached its apogee. The word "wonder" no longer meant "mystery" or "miracle" to Rudolf and his fellow collectors. Rather it had come to mean that which evoked astonishment, stimulated reflection, and provided visual aids to the investigation of the physical world.[141] In the German collections attention was focused especially on the unusual and abnormal, on the resemblances of bizarre rock formations to animals, on the similarities between malformed men and beasts. To the collectors the world included a vast array of objects which tangibly illustrated the intricate relations between nature and man, and nature and art. And, because the natural products and human creations of Asia were so strange to sixteenth-century Europe, they figured prominently in most major collections as examples of rarities which did excite wonder, provoke discussion, and inspire thought.

4

FRANCE AND ENGLAND

Political emissaries, pilgrims, travelers, and merchants periodically brought objects of Oriental provenance into medieval France. Arles, at the beginning of the ninth century, was a principal market for gold and silver items, pearls, textiles, and ivories from the East.[142] King Charles V of France (reigned 1364–80) kept in his treasury a number of Oriental jewels.[143] The dukes of Anjou and Burgundy of the fourteenth century owned a variety of Oriental rarities.

---

[140] Indian items extracted from H. Zimmermann (ed.), "Das Inventar der Prager Schatz- und Kunstkammer vom 6. Dezember, 1621," *Jahrbuch der kunsthistorischen Sammlungen des allerhöchsten Kaiserhauses*, XXV (1905), xx–xlvii; and the Czech inventory of 1619 in J. Morávek, *Nově objevený inventář rudolfinských sbírek na Hradě Pražském* (Prague, 1937), pp. 24–27. See appendix to this chapter.

[141] Lhotsky, *op. cit.* (n. 7), p. 212.

[142] J. Ebersolt, *Orient et Occident: Recherches sur les influences byzantines et orientales en France avant et pendant les croisades* (2d ed.; Paris, 1954), p. 40.

[143] E. T. Hamy, *Les origines du musée d'ethnographie: Histoire et documents* (Paris, 1890), p. 5.

A full century before the German princes became fascinated with the *Wunder-kammer*, the duke of Berry, Jean de France, had assembled an extensive cabinet of curiosities. Scattered throughout his inventory are references to coconuts (both in mounts and in their natural state), to porcelain bowls, and to strange seashells and other maritime exotica.[144] But there is no indication in these pages that Jean had any interest in systematically acquiring curiosities from overseas— no more than had the French princes of the fifteenth century who bought strange animals for their hunting preserves, gardens, and menageries.[145] It was not until the discovery of the direct overseas route to India that French collectors, scientists, and artists sought self-consciously to learn something about Asia through collecting its flora, fauna, and crafts. And then, because of the political connections of France with Turkey and because France was not in control of the spice trade, interested Frenchmen usually sought information and commodities in Constantinople as well as in Lisbon and Antwerp.

Francis I (reigned 1515–47), shortly after becoming king in his own right, began to take an interest in the East and in Portugal's activities there. In January, 1516, he took the opportunity while in Marseilles to see the rhinoceros from India that was being sent as a gift from Portugal to Pope Leo X.[146] While Francis also introduced legislation to keep the spices coming through Antwerp from flooding the French market,[147] he continually sought to add exotic beasts from overseas to his personal menagerie at Amboise.[148] He even wrote to King Manuel of Portugal asking to buy "things which arrive regularly at Lisbon in great abundance from the Province of India."[149] Jean d'Ango, sponsor of the first French voyages to the East, made a collection of overseas curiosities at Dieppe. From this accumulation he presented to the king some coconuts, rare woods, and engraved stones.[150] Florimond de Robertet, minister of Francis I, possessed, according to an inventory of 1532 prepared by his widow, some of the first porcelains "to be sent to France after the arrival of the Portuguese in China."[151]

About 1530 the king himself began to build a cabinet of foreign treasures at Fontainebleau which were gathered for him by agents in Italy, Portugal, and the Levant. In this collection were beautiful porcelain vases and bowls as well as "une infinité de petites gentillesses"[152] from the Indies, China, and Turkey.

---

[144] J. Guiffrey (ed.), *Inventaires de Jean, duc de Berry* (Paris, 1894–96). Also see M. Meiss, *French Painting in the Time of Jean de Berry* (New York, 1967), Vol. I, chap. iii.

[145] See G. Loisel, *Historie des ménageries de l'antiquité à nos jours* (Paris, 1912), I, 169.

[146] See P. de Vaissière (ed.), *Journal de Jean Barrillon, secrétaire du Chancelier Duprat, 1515–1521* (Paris, 1897), I, 193.

[147] Text of the ordinance in the *Journal d'un Bourgeois de Paris* (pp. 50–53) as cited in *ibid.*, I, 299.

[148] Loisel, *op. cit.* (n. 145), I, 263–70.

[149] As quoted in L. de Matos, "Natura intelletto e costumi dell'elefante," *Boletim internacional de bibliografia Luso-Brasileira*, I (1960), 46.

[150] For Ango's support of the French voyages see *Asia*, I, 177–78. On his collection see Hamy, *op. cit.* (n. 143), p. 8.

[151] Robertet had forty-two pieces of white porcelain decorated, according to the inventory, "with all kinds of small paintings." As cited in Belevitch-Stankevitch, *op. cit.* (n. 18), p. xxxiii.

[152] The words of Le Père Dan in *Le trésor des merveilles de . . . Fontainebleau* (Paris, 1642), p. 84.

Natural curiosities and books were bought for the king's collections in the Levant by Pierre Belon and Pierre Gilles (1490–1555). After five years in the Near East, Gilles met Guillaume Postel (1510–81) in Jerusalem during 1549, and the two collectors of Orientalia quarreled repeatedly as they competed in their book-buying enterprises—Gilles for the king and Postel for himself and the Venetian printer Bomberg.[153] The cosmographer André Thevet, who had traveled and collected in the Levant from 1549 to 1554, became guardian of the royal cabinet of curiosities at Fontainebleau in 1562[154] and evidently supervised it until his death in 1592. When he took it over, the royal collection contained numerous jewels and precious items which are described as being decorated in the "façon d'Inde."[155] Jean Mocquet succeeded Thevet in this post and under his supervision the Fontainebleau collection came to be called the *Cabinet des singularitez.*[156]

The successors to Francis I, as well as the "great names" (the Montmorency, the Guise, and others) had collections of their own in their châteaux and urban residences. King Henry II (reigned 1547–59) continued to add to the collection begun under his predecessor. His queen, Catharine de' Medici (pl. 1), who was the real ruler of France from 1559 to her death in 1589, assembled a collection of rare and precious objects including the usual coconuts and seashells, ebony and ivory chess sets, Chinese lacquered tables and boxes, Persian carpets, and porcelain, which she housed in her residence at Paris, the Hôtel de la Reine.[157] But most striking was her collection of maps showing the voyages of discovery as well as special maps of the East Indies, eastern Asia, the Moluccas, Calicut, and the Persian Gulf, all of them "figurée à la main."[158]

Jean Nicot (1530–1600), who was sent to Lisbon in 1559 to arrange a marriage between Dom Sebastian and Margaret of Valois, regularly sent news and curiosities to the court of Paris over the next two years.[159] Students and emissaries from Portugal who were studying or working in France also acted as intermediaries. The lawyer and friend of Rabelais, André Tiraqueau (1480–1558), kept in his home near Fontenay-le-Comte (Vendée) a cabinet which held Oriental costumes and other souvenirs of the East. The inventory (1599) of Gabrielle d'Estrées (1573–99), favorite of King Henry IV, lists "a canopy [pavillon] of taffetas from China on which all sorts of birds and animals are represented."[160] Bernard Palissy (1510–90), a professional potter, put together

---

[153] For evidence of their quarrels see Denis, *op. cit.* (n. 7), p. 337; also W. J. Bowsma, *Concordia Mundi: The Career and Thought of Guillaume Postel* (Cambridge, Mass., 1957), p. 16.

[154] J. Adhémar, *Frère André Thevet, grand voyageur et cosmographe des rois de France au XVI siècle* (Paris, n.d.), pp. 51–58.

[155] These are the descriptive words used repeatedly in the inventory of 1560. See *Revue universel des arts*, III (1855), 315–50; IV (1856), 445–56, 518–30.

[156] Hamy, *op. cit.* (n. 143), p. 9.

[157] E. Bonnaffé, *Inventaire des meubles de Catherine de Médicis en 1589* (Paris, 1874), pp. 76, 80, 89, 90, 93, 164.

[158] *Ibid.*, pp. 65–66.

[159] E. Falgairolle (ed.), *Nicot . . . correspondance* (Paris, 1897), pp. 35, 50–51, 147.

[160] As quoted in Belevitch-Stankevitch, *op. cit.* (n. 18), p. xxxiii.

an extensive collection of fossils, minerals, and ceramics. Pierre de l 'Estoile tells of a Parisian collector named Guitter who had a cabinet of curiosities which included porcelains of China and was famous enough to attract a visit from Queen Marie de' Medici in 1601.[161] The painter Etienne Monstier (1504–1603) maintained a collection which included rarities of the Indies, Canada, and China. Claude de Peiresc (1580–1637), the great antiquarian of Aix-en-Provence, carried on the tradition of collecting Asian products with verve and enthusiasm well into the seventeenth century. And, in 1601, two merchants of Saint-Malo outfitted two vessels to sail for the East expressly "to enrich the public with curiosities from the Orient."[162]

Leopold von Wedel, a German traveler to England in 1584–85, remarked in his diary: "Rare objects are not to be seen in England, but it is a very fertile country, producing all sorts of corn, but not wine."[163] While such a statement was not absolutely true, it serves to indicate how far away and backward England seemed to a person who had an acquaintance with the exuberant and thriving mercantile life of the Low Countries and Germany. Just a few Englishmen had acquired oddities from the East before the beginning of Queen Elizabeth's reign (1558–1603). King Henry VIII owned but one piece of porcelain, as did Archbishop Warham and Sir Thomas Trenchard.[164] But William Cecil (Lord Burghley after 1571), Elizabeth's chief adviser, watched events closely in the Low Countries as the Netherlands increased its resistance to Philip II's rule. He also urged the Portuguese on more than one occasion to set up their spice staple in London,[165] far away from the turbulence of the Low Countries. In 1579, the year of the foundation of the Dutch Republic, Burghley established a consulate in Constantinople as the English began to trade seriously with the Ottoman Empire. Burghley acquired in connection with his trading endeavors some exquisite blue-and-white porcelains which he had set in elaborate silver-gilt mounts (pl. 75)—a clear sign of how valuable they were esteemed to be.[166]

Sir Francis Drake and other marauding seamen were responsible for acquiring, either through piracy or trade, a number of curiosities for Elizabeth. On his return in 1580 from a voyage around the world, Drake brought home Javanese krises and samples of sago bread, the chief food of the Moluccans. Two pieces

---

[161] *Ibid.*, pp. xliii–xliv.

[162] As quoted in *ibid.*, p. xxxviii. But the French evidently continued to depend upon other European purveyors. In 1602 King Henry IV wrote to Secretary Cecil in London thanking him for the care that had been taken in dispatching to France some novelties from India and China destined for the king's own use. See *ibid.*, pp. xliii–xliv.

[163] G. von Bülow (trans.), "Journey through England and Scotland Made by Leopold von Wedel in the Years 1584–1585," *Transactions of the Royal Historical Society*, N.S., IX (1895), 268.

[164] Henry's is described as: "A cup of Porcelaine glasse fation with two handles garnished with silver and guilt the Cover garnished with iij Camewe heddes and thre garnettes." As quoted in II. Honour, *Chinoiserie: The Vision of Cathay* (London, 1961), p. 37. Also see Belevitch-Stankevitch, *op. cit.* (n. 18), p. xxxii.

[165] See C. Read, *Mr. Secretary Cecil and Queen Elizabeth* (New York, 1955), pp. 428–29; and the same author's *Lord Burghley and Queen Elizabeth* (New York, 1960), pp. 155–56.

[166] L. Avery, "Chinese Porcelain in English Mounts," *Metropolitan Museum of Art Bulletin*, N.S., II (1943), 266.

of sago bread and information on the sago palm were relayed in 1581 to Charles de L'écluse by Dr. Hugh Morgan, the queen's physician.[167] In a book published in the following year, L'écluse gives the story of the sago palm as it was related to him and includes in his work a print of sago bread (see pl. 45).[168] When Thomas Cavendish returned home from the East in 1588 he brought with him a map or a description of the provinces of China and remarked on his own about the "incomparable wealth" of China.[169]

But it was not until the capture in 1592 of the Portuguese carrack "Madre de Dios" that the English public was able to see for itself what wealth there was in the India trade. Dispatches to the Fuggers in Augsburg in 1592 tell how the English sailors, though forbidden to do so by royal command, stole as much as they could for themselves from the Portuguese vessel before it could be brought from the Azores to England.[170] In spite of the pillaging that took place, a rich cargo was finally disembarked at Dartmouth. Richard Hakluyt summarizes as follows the catalogue made of the prizes on September 15, 1592:

Where upon good view it was found that the principall wares after the jewels (which were no doubt of great value, though they never came to light) consisted of spices, drugges, silkes, calicos, quilts, carpets, and colours, etc. The spices were pepper, cloves, maces, nutmegs, cinamom, greene ginger; the drugs were benjamin, frankincesce, galingale [a mixture of lime and linseed oil used to make mortars], mirabolans, aloes zocatrina [Socotrine], camphire; the silks, damasks, taffatas, sarcenets, altobassos, that is, counterfeit cloth of gold, unwrought China silke, sleaved silk, white twisted silk, curled cypresse. The calicos were book-calicos, calico launes, broad white calicos, fine starched calicos, course white calicos, browne broad calicos, browne course calicos. There were also canopies, and course diaper towels, quilts of course sarcent and of calico, carpets like those of Turkey; whereunto are to be added the pearle, muske, civet and amber griece. The rest of the wares were many in number, but lesse in value; as elephants teeth, porcellan vessels of China, coco-nuts, hides, ebenwood as Blacke as jet, bedsteds of the same, cloth of the rindes of trees very strange for the matter, and artificiall [artistic] in workemanship.[171]

Some of the best items were added to the queen's collections, while others were given to the participants in the capture and to the Merchant-Adventurers. Thomas Platter of Basel, who traveled in England during 1599, records seeing in the queen's apartments at Whitehall "one Indian bed with Indian valence and an Indian table."[172] At the London residence of Mr. Walter Cope (d. 1614),

[167] Henry R. Wagner, *Sir Francis Drake's Voyage around the World: Its Aims and Achievements* (San Francisco, 1926), p. 501.

[168] *Caroli Clusii . . . Aliquot notae in Garciae aromatum historiam . . .* (Antwerp, 1582), pp. 24–25.

[169] See the reports of Cavendish as they appear in the first edition of Hakluyt's collection. D. B. Quinn and R. A. Skelton (eds.), *The Principall Navigations Voiages and Discoveries of the English Nation . . .* (facsimile of 1589 ed.; Cambridge, 1965), II, 808, 813–15. He also brought back two Japanese and a Filipino, whom Hakluyt interrogated. See E. G. R. Taylor (ed.), *The Original Writings and Correspondence of the Two Richard Hakluyts* (London, 1935), I, 48.

[170] V. von Klarwill (ed.), *The Fugger News-Letters, Second Series* (New York, 1926), pp. 240–43.

[171] Richard Hakluyt, *The Principal Navigations Voyages Traffiques and Discoveries of the English Nation* (Glasgow, 1903–5), VII, 116–17. Also see letter of Emanuel van Meteren to Ortelius in Hessels, *op. cit.* (n. 5), p. 541.

[172] C. Williams (trans. and ed.), *Thomas Platter's Travels in England, 1599* (London, 1937), p. 165.

usher to Lord Burghley and a wealthy collector, Platter, accompanied by Mathias de L'Obel (Lobelius), the Flemish botanist and physician, was led into an apartment "stuffed with queer foreign objects in every corner."[173] Among the items included in Platter's lengthy list are ornaments and costumes from China and Java, a box from China, Indian plumes and a madonna made of feathers, a palm-leaf fan, earthen pitchers and porcelains from China, a "small bone implement used in India for scratching oneself," an Indian chain of monkey's teeth, and all sorts of "heathen coins."[174] Other Londoners also collected curios, but, in Platter's estimation, Cope's was "superior to them all for strange objects, because of the Indian [?] voyage he carried out with such zeal."[175] Hakluyt in his "To the Reader" in the first edition (1589) of *The Principall Navigations* confesses that he was "ravished in beholding all the premises gathered together with no small cost, and preserved with no little diligence, in the excellent cabinets of my very worshipfull and learned friends Mr. Richard Garthe, one of the Clearkes of the pettie Bags and M. William [mistake for Walter] Cope."[176] Hakluyt did not, however, make direct use of the specimens in the Garth-Cope collections in writing up his notes. He refers to them in an effort, lame as it was, to explain to the reader why he did not feel compelled to illustrate his great work of compilation.

5

ITALY

While the relations of England and France with the East were decidedly remote and relatively recent, the story of Italy's connections is complicated by its lengthy and intimate contacts with the Levant. The seaport towns along Italy's Adriatic coast (Venice, Ravenna, and Ancona) had long maintained direct connections with the Levant and the commerce of the East. Sicily became at a somewhat later date the Mediterranean meeting place where East and West most fully merged several centuries before the opening of the Cape route to India. From Byzantium, Damascus, Jaffa, and Beirut the lanes of maritime trade and intercourse led to all the eastern ports of Italy from Venice in the north to Palermo in the south. The orientalized mosaics of Ravenna date back to the fifth century. The Church of St. Mark in Venice, a replica of the Church of the Holy Apostle in Constantinople, was consecrated in 1094. And these are, of course, only the most obvious of the artistic masterpieces that remain to document in tile and stone the depth and persistence of Italy's medieval relations with the Levant. In the twelfth and thirteenth centuries Western artists who worked in the Crusader Kingdom of Jerusalem consciously imitated Byzantine

[173] *Ibid.*, p. 171.
[174] *Ibid.*, pp. 171–73.
[175] *Ibid.*, p. 173.
[176] Quinn and Skelton, *op. cit.* (n. 169), I, xlvii.

miniature paintings and icons in the works they did there.[177] It is not at all unlikely that these European artists relayed to Italy, directly or indirectly, a host of Byzantine artistic models and ideas, some of which themselves owed a debt to Indian, Chinese, Persian, Islamic, and Steppe art.

The silk trade was especially vital to the commercial relations between Italy and Byzantium. The fine fabrics woven in the imperial workshops at Constantinople and Antioch were highly prized in Europe during the crusading era. With the political eclipse of Byzantium, the industry of silk weaving was taken over by the Norman rulers of Sicily. At Palermo captive Byzantine weavers worked side by side with Arab weavers to provide silken fabrics for Latin Europe. From Sicily the silk industry quickly moved into the Italian peninsula, the *Arte dè seta*, or guild of silk workers, being founded at Florence in 1193.[178] Lucca and Venice likewise became great centers of silk fabrication and trade as the demand for rich woven materials constantly increased. But even with the growth in Italy, and then in the rest of southern Europe, of a thriving silk industry, the demand for Chinese and Persian silks persisted. Venice, the major importer of Oriental silks, continued to be the emporium to which merchants of quattrocento Europe were required to turn for practically all commodities imported from the East.

The great commercial prosperity of Venice in the thirteenth and fourteenth centuries led to a growth of interest there in collecting exotica from the East. The city's patricians invested in precious stones, carpets, and Oriental antiquities. In many Venetian paintings of the fifteenth century Oriental rugs appear as part of the background or among the decorative furnishings.[179] Ceramics, metal works, and jewelry from the workshops of the Levant were sold and collected in Venice in constantly increasing quantities. The treasury of St. Mark still has on display a Chinese porcelain vase reputedly brought back to Venice in 1295 by Marco Polo.[180] Wild beasts and exotic plants were imported from Constantinople via Venice for the menageries which came into vogue in Italy beginning in the thirteenth century.[181]

During the quattrocento the craze for collecting began in earnest in Italy. Although the remains of Roman antiquity were most highly cherished, certain individuals began quite self-consciously to collect foreign arts and crafts. Pope Nicholas V (ruled 1447–55) sent Cyriac of Ancona (1391–1452) to the Levant and Egypt for the purpose of making collections in those lands. The Malatesta rulers of Rimini were interested in foreign beasts, as is demonstrated by the numerous uses to which they put their elephant insignia.[182] But it is worth

---

[177] See H. Buchthal, *Miniature Painting in the Latin Kingdom of Jerusalem* (Oxford, 1957); and Kurt Weitzmann, "Icon Painting in the Crusader Kindgom," *Dumbarton Oaks Papers*, No. XX (1966), pp. 51–83.
[178] G. R. B. Richards, *Florentine Merchants in the Age of the Medicis* (Cambridge, 1932), p. 44.
[179] G. Bandmann, "Das Exotische in der europäischen Kunst," in *Der Mensch und die Künste: Festschrift Heinrich Lützeler* (Düsseldorf, 1962), p. 340.
[180] See reproduction in Taylor, *op. cit.* (n. 6), facing p. 64.
[181] Loisel, *op. cit.* (n. 145), I, 148.
[182] See below p. 132.

noting that very few ivories were collected in Italy.[183] Most of the extant inventories of Italian families show that in the fifteenth century they were great amateur collectors of porcelain, especially the Este and the Medici. In 1487, the sultan of Egypt presented to Lorenzo the Magnificent some celadon vases from China.[184] Wild beasts, especially lions, were sent to Florence as gifts from the rulers of the Levant as the menagerie came to be a necessary part of the entourage of the Renaissance prince. "It belongs to the position of the great," asserted Federico Matarazzo, "to keep horses, dogs, mules, falcons and other birds, court jesters, singers, and foreign animals."[185] Nor is this combination of human and animal curiosities a mere slip of the pen. It is well known that early in the sixteenth century the famous Cardinal Ippolito de' Medici kept a human menagerie at his strange court, including Tartar bowmen and Indian divers.[186]

Most fascinating as an example of the growing interest in the East among Italian artists is the story of Leonardo da Vinci (1452–1519) as revealed in his *Notebooks*. From letters that he wrote it appears that Leonardo might have traveled in the Levant, possibly in 1498–99, or just at the time when Vasco da Gama made his voyage to India.[187] Leonardo in these letters describes the topography of the Levant eastward to the boundaries of India, possibly from his own experiences in part and certainly with the aid of the nomenclature of Ptolemy.[188] He also owned the books of Pliny, Strabo, and Sir John Mandeville, and was sufficiently impressed by the Asian customs he read about in these works to take notes on them.[189] From Mandeville he learned that people in certain parts of India (meaning China) cut up their wooden idols and ground the pieces into a fine powder that they sprinkled on their food and ate.[190] Long fingernails, he noted, are venerated among the "Indians" (Chinese) as a sign of gentility, especially if they are perfumed and painted.[191] He collected maps of the world and even had a look at "a map of Elephanta in India, which belongs to Antonello the merchant."[192] On the basis of either a literary description or the object

---

[183] See Burckhardt, *loc. cit.* (n. 9), p. 393.

[184] Beurdeley, *op. cit.* (n. 37), p. 118.

[185] As quoted in J. Burckhardt, *The Civilization of the Renaissance in Italy* (London, 1898), II, 290.

[186] *Ibid.*, pp. 291–92.

[187] E. McCurdy (trans. and ed.), *The Notebooks of Leonardo da Vinci* (New York, 1958), I, 18; II, 1133–36. The artist left Milan in 1498 and went to Venice, where he gave advice on how to fortify the city against the Turks. It may have been in connection with this assignment that he went to Armenia. For the history of this debated question see E. McCurdy, *The Mind of Leonardo da Vinci* (New York, 1939), pp. 230–55.

[188] McCurdy, *Notebooks*, I, 359–60.

[189] For the complete list of his personal books see *ibid.*, II, 1164–68. Andrea Corsali in a letter sent from India to Giuliano de' Medici compares Leonardo's vegetarian habits to those of the Gujaratis. See McCurdy, *The Mind*, p. 78.

[190] McCurdy, *Notebooks*, I, 85; for a reference to the feast of idols at the Grand Khan's court see M. Letts (ed.), *Mandeville's Travels: Text and Translations* (London, 1953), I, 161.

[191] McCurdy, *Notebooks*, II, 1185; on the fingernails of the Grand Khan see Letts, *op. cit.* (n. 190), I, 219–20.

[192] McCurdy, *Notebooks*, I, 365. Elephanta is the island in the harbor of modern Bombay famous for its cave temple carved out of solid rock. Leonardo was interested in rock caves and this may account for his knowledge of Elephanta.

itself, Leonardo drew and commented in his *Notebooks* upon an air tube that was used by pearl divers in the Indian Ocean.[193] Finally, in his *Prophecies*, Leonardo gloomily predicted: "Shadows will come from the East which will tinge with much darkness the sky that covers Italy." And then he goes on to assert that "all men will take refuge in Africa." [194] His forebodings were probably based on the fear that was quite general in the early sixteenth century that the Turks were about to mount a new and devastating offensive in the eastern Mediterranean region.

The Venetians, because of their self-interest in Oriental trade through the Levant, tried hardest of the Italian states to keep informed about the commodities being brought by sea into Lisbon and Antwerp after 1500. While the reports of their agents deal primarily with the quantities and prices of the spices and drugs being imported, they also indicate, but in no great detail, that dyes, hides, wax, and woods were also important in the early cargoes and that their prices in Lisbon were far lower than those obtaining in Venice. Notes on the imports in quantity of pearls, precious stones, and textiles also appear with greater frequency in the Venetian reports beginning in 1506.[195] Speculation about whether or not the Portuguese king would be financially able to continue sending out annual fleets was almost constant. The panic of the Venetians was not unwarranted, for in the decade from 1505 to 1515 over four times the quantity of pepper imported by Venice entered Lisbon.[196] Andrea Navagero, the Venetian Humanist, nervously sent a dispatch from Seville to Venice in March, 1526, reporting that two Portuguese ships had but recently arrived from India richly laden with gold, spices, and precious stones.[197] Even after Venice had regained a substantial share of the spice trade in the latter half of the sixteenth century, its emissaries continued to report in detail on the size and wealth of Lisbon and even on the numbers of merchants, Jews, and slaves living within its confines.[198] Still, the Venetians led the way among the Italian collectors in assembling exotic specimens from Asia. Early in the sixteenth century, Andrea Odoni had a collection of natural rarities and porcelains which was among the first assembled in Italy.[199]

While the Venetians were legally and effectively excluded from the Portuguese spice monopoly, the Florentines were especially welcomed as investors and as participants in the voyages from the beginning of the direct trade with India.[200]

---

[193] *Ibid.*, II, 791.

[194] *Ibid.*, p. 1118.

[195] See for example, G. Scopoli (ed.), "Relazione di Leonardo da Ca'Masser . . . ,"*Archivio storico italiano*, Ser. L, Appendix 2 (1845), p. 23.

[196] Cf. *Asia*, I, 119.

[197] As quoted in E. A. Cicogna, *Della vita et delle opere di Andrea Navagero* . . . (Venice, 1855), p. 187.

[198] For example, see the report of 1572 by Matteo Zane as reproduced in V. Marchesi, "Le relazioni tra la repubblica Veneta e il Portogallo dall' anno 1522 al 1797," *Archivio veneto*, XXXIII (1887), 25.

[199] Burckhardt, *loc. cit.* (n. 9), p. 551. For Odoni's porcelains see listing in M. Michiel, *Notizia d'opere di disegno*. . . (Bologna 1884), p. 159.

[200] Cf. *Asia*, I, 103–4.

The Florentines, unlike the Germans in Lisbon, had continually good relations with the Portuguese, and their business and banking houses profited from this harmony and cooperation. Interest in, and information about, Portugal's progress in the East was consequently more genuine and current in Florence than in any other part of Italy. The Florentine merchants were also more influential at Antwerp than any other Italian group. Through its closer ties with Portugal and the Atlantic trading community, Florence began to challenge Venice as a purveyor of information and goods from the East.

The Medici rulers of Florence, long-time patrons of the arts, and several of the leading patricians of Tuscany became collectors of Asian arts and crafts in the sixteenth century. In Tuscany the collecting impulse was not new; in a certain sense it was merely the Renaissance form of the medieval spirit of encyclopedism and curiosity. In Florence and elsewhere the emphasis switched gradually, however, from the collection of European antiquities to the acquisition of examples of contemporary art and activity. At the same time, a new vitality was infused into collecting by the growth of a spirit of scientific curiosity which sought to find cosmic relationships between the marvels of art and nature. The "virtuosity" of the prince and the man of learning included disinterested curiosity in every aspect of culture, even in the bizarre and the fantastic as Saba Castiglione indicates in his *Ricordi* (1554). And here, as in most other aspects of Renaissance activity, the Tuscans led the way.[201]

Typical of the virtuosity of the sixteenth-century Tuscan was the collection of natural and artistic curiosities assembled by Bernardo Vecchietti in his villa named Il Riposo near Florence. Raffaello Borghini in his famous book called *Il Riposo* (1584) reported that Vecchietti's *scrittojo* (chest for valuables)[202] located in the top room of his villa contained "vessels of porcelain and of mountain crystal, seashells of many types, stone pyramids of great value, jewels, medals, masks, fruits and animals . . . and all the new and rare things that come from India and from Turkey which cause stupefaction to anyone who observes them."[203] In another chest were more porcelains, oriental daggers, and objects of ivory, ebony, and mother-of-pearl.[204] Ridolfo Sirigatto, another Florentine collector, assembled in the second of his five storage rooms rarities from the world of nature, such as seashells, animal horns, and hides.[205] Cosimo I (duke of Florence, 1537–69, and grand duke of Tuscany, 1569–74), according to an inventory of his collection dated 1553, possessed 373 pieces of porcelain which he housed in the Palazzo Vecchio. The duke also received a book on the route from Lisbon to the Moluccas from Portugal and one on the West Indies from

---

[201] S. Castiglione, *Ricordi, overo anmaestramenti* . . . (Venice, 1554), p. 14. For discussion see L. Salerno, "Arte, scienza e collezioni nel manierismo," in *Scritti di storia dell'arte in onore di Mario Salmi* (Rome, 1963), pp. 194–97.

[202] For discussion of this translation and for other Italian terms used in relation to collections see Burckhardt, *loc. cit.* (n. 9), pp. 537–44.

[203] R. Borghini, *Il Riposo* (reprint, 3 vols. in one; Milan, 1607), I, 15.

[204] *Ibid.*, p. 16.

[205] Cf. Burckhardt, *loc. cit.* (n. 9), pp. 548–51.

Spain. On the basis of these routiers Ignatio Danti (1536–86) drew a map of the world in 1563 for Cosimo that was four yards in diameter.[206] The agents of Niccolò Gaddi (1537–91) ransacked the markets of Italy and the Low Countries to find curiosities for his collection.[207] The Florentine botanist Matteo Caccini cultivated rare plants from all over the world in his garden, including what was then called the "orange of China."[208] Notable also was the botanical collection of Pier Andrea Mattioli (1501–77) of Siena.

It was Grand Duke Francesco I (ruled 1574–87) of Florence who most enthusiastically brought Asia within the field of vision of Italian Humanism.[209] Several years before assuming his post as ruler of Tuscany, Francesco had ordered work begun on a studiolo (pl. 80), designed by Bernardo Buontalenti to be "a cabinet of things rare and precious, in terms of both costliness and art, such as jewels, medals, engraved gems, cut crystals, vases, ingenious devices, and similar objects that are not too large."[210] The studiolo was lined with ebony and decorated with precious stones and paintings. According to its program similar objects were to be displayed within it from both nature and art and their relationship symbolized in the decoration by a god from antiquity; Pluto, god of the nether regions, was to be shown with precious metals in their natural state and with metal works of art such as clocks, enamels, and medals.[211] Battista Naldini, Francesco Morandini (1544–97) called Poppi, and Jan van der Straet (1523–1605) called Stradanus, the "masters of the studiolo," worked on the decorations and Alessandro Allori (1535–1607) painted his famous "Pearl Fishery" for the room in which it was housed. Ebony, pearls, and precious stones were, as we shall see, ordinarily associated in the cultivated mind of the sixteenth century with a resplendent East.[212]

Francesco I, as is indicated by the program of the studiolo, was an amateur of natural science. In the Boboli gardens he experimented with mulberries;[213] elsewhere in Tuscany he encouraged the cultivation of rice and bamboo.[214] He

---

[206] For the list of porcelains in Cosimo's cabinets see R. W. Lightbown, "Oriental Art and the Orient in Late Renaissance and Baroque Italy," *Journal of the Warburg and Courtauld Institutes*, XXXII (1969), 232–33. On the *mappemonde* of Cosimo see letter of Danti to Ortelius in Hessels, *op. cit.* (n. 5), p. 242. Also see George Kish, "The Japan on the 'Mural Atlas' of the Palazzo Vecchio, Florence," *Imago mundi*, VIII (1951), 52–54.

[207] See A. E. Popham, "On a Letter of Joris Hoefnagel," *Oud-Holland*, LIII (1936), 146.

[208] P. G. Conti (ed.), *Lettere inedite di Charles de L'Escluse . . . à Matteo Caccini . . .* (Florence, 1939), pp. 120–23. This orange was probably the *citrus aurantium cortice eduli* of Linnaeus. See A. Targioni-Tozzetti, *Cenni storici sulla introduzione di varie piante nell'agricoltura ed orticoltura* (Florence, 1896), pp. 162–63.

[209] For his relations to the Indian trade and Filippo Sassetti, see *Asia*, I, 475–77.

[210] As quoted from V. Borghini in Salerno, *loc. cit.* (n. 201), p. 199.

[211] See *ibid.*, pp. 199–200. The studiolo was restored in the Palazzo Vecchio in 1910 by G. Poggi.

[212] On the ebony furnishings of the studiolo see D. Heikamp, "Zur Geschichte der Uffizien-Tribuna und der Kunstschränke in Florenz und Deutschland," *Zeitschrift für Kunstgeschichte*, XXVI (1963), 193–94.

[213] G. Masson, *Italian Gardens* (New York, 1961), p. 81.

[214] L. G. T. Malespini, *Oratione de le lodi di Francesco I de' Medici* (Florence, 1587), p. 27.

collected specimens of plants, seeds, and fruits from the overseas world, corresponded with Ulisse Aldrovandi, (1522–1605), the great naturalist of Bologna, and assigned to Jacopo Ligozzi (1547–1626) the task of drawing and painting naturalistic representations of the strange plants and animals in his own and Aldrovandi's collections (see pl. 36).[215] In the meantime he was given various examples of Japanese craftsmanship by the legates from Japan who visited Florence in March, 1585: ricepaper, cocoons, and stone razors.[216] But it is in his interest in porcelain that we can best see the meeting of art and science in the virtuosity of the grand duke. He was determined to learn the secret of porcelain manufacture and to produce ceramics in Florence to rival the Chinese products in design, color, and quality.[217]

It was in the time of Giovanni de' Medici, Pope Leo X (1513–21), that Rome first became acutely aware of the discoveries being made by the Portuguese in Asia. The mission of obedience sent to Rome by Dom Manuel in the spring of 1514 brought with it a cornucopia of exotic gifts: spices, porcelains, ecclesiastical vestments garnished with precious stones, a Chinese book, parrots, a Persian horse, and an Indian elephant.[218] The pope, it is reported, eagerly showed off the Chinese book to his friends.[219] The poets and artists at Leo's court were likewise attracted by the curiosa of Asia, and in their creations they immortalized the elephant especially.[220] A hospital for "Indians" was founded at Rome in 1525 along with a number of other special "national" hospitals.[221] But these first contacts were not long followed up in the Eternal City. The sack of Rome in 1527 forced the emigration of the artists and literati and brought a temporary halt to the development of the papal court as an international center of culture.

The popes of the Counter-Reformation were not prone to collect "heathen vanities." The following story illustrates how far behind the other princes of Europe the successors of Leo were in their appreciation of Oriental goods. In 1562, Pope Pius IV (reigned 1559–65) invited to dinner the Archbishop of Braga and the Portuguese ambassador to the Council of Trent, Bartolomeu dos Martires (1514–90). The Portuguese prelate was astounded to see the lavish display of silver tableware on which the dinner was served and expressed his indignation that the Church should squander its wealth on massive silver plate when it was surrounded on all sides by the poverty of the faithful. He informed the pope of his indignation and told him that "we have in Portugal . . . a type

[215] See O. H. Giglioli, "Jacopo Ligozzi disegnatore e pittore di piante e di animali," *Dedalo*, IV (1923–24), 556.

[216] Cf. *Asia*, I, 694.

[217] See below, pp. 107–8.

[218] See below, pp. 136–38.

[219] According to Guido Panciroli (1522–99) in his *De rebus inventio et peditis* . . . (Amberge, 1607). I have used only the English version, *The History of Many Memorable Things Lost, Which were in Use among the Ancients* (London, 1715), p. 342.

[220] See below, pp. 138–39.

[221] "Indians," in this case, probably refers to all Asians, Africans, and Americans. See J. Delumeau, *Vie économique et sociale de Rome* . . . (Paris, 1957), p. 409.

of baked earthenware which is far superior to silver in elegance and neatness." The archbishop went on to explain that this earthenware was called porcelain and was made in China of clay so fine that it surpassed in luster both crystal and alabaster, and that its relatively low price compensated for its fragility. In response to these remarks, the pope agreed that he would certainly prefer porcelain to silver and requested the archbishop on his return to Portugal to have a porcelain service sent to the Vatican.[222]

While the Council of Trent made permanent the secession of the Protestants, the new possibilities and horizons opened to the Church by overseas expansion began to have their effects upon Rome even before the Council concluded its deliberations in 1563. The organization and growth of the Society of Jesus with its direct responsibility to the pope quickly brought to the Vatican the realization that as the capital of Catholicism its future was linked to the world beyond as well as to Europe itself. In the period after Trent all the roads in Catholic Europe again led to Rome. The overland route from Madrid to Lyons to Rome was the busiest in Europe, and Portugal was added to it after Philip II became king in 1581. Pilgrims, couriers, and carters cluttered the highways to Rome. Embassies from all parts of the Catholic world, including the Congo, Japan, Persia, and Muscovy, came to Rome as the various congregations of the Latin church realigned or aligned themselves for the first time with Rome. In 1585 the Japanese legates presented to Pope Gregory XIII two folding screens (*byōbus*) and an ebony desk, which he added to the Vatican collections. The city itself grew rapidly in size and impressiveness as the Vatican building program was resumed and as the Jesuits commenced building their mother church, the Gesù. The mural in the room of the Vatican Library named for Sixtus V shows the Japanese legates in one of the Coronation processions of 1585.

Cosmographers, literati, artists, and printers again began to gravitate toward Rome as they had in the time of Leo X and Raphael. People meanwhile crowded into the city from all over the Lazio to work in the revivified metropolis. Domestic servants and slaves of all colors, conditions, and backgrounds were imported from the countries of the Mediterranean basin.[223] While the last session of the Council of Trent was being held in 1563, the Loggia della Cosmographia was being completed in the Vatican.[224] In 1571 *avvisi* (newsletters) on the overseas world printed in Portugal were sold on the streets of Rome.[225] In 1600 the Galleria delle Carte geografiche, completed in the pontificate of Gregory XIII (1572–85), a staunch supporter of the Jesuits, had on display a special depiction of the city of Quinsay, or Hangchow, in China.[226] Michele

---

[222] L. de Souza, *Vida de Dom Fr. Bartolomeu dos Martires* (Viana, 1619), pp. 60–62. Evidently the porcelains thereafter sent to the Vatican are no longer extant. See Beurdeley, *op. cit.* (n. 37), p. 119.
[223] P. Pecchiai, *Roma nel cinquecento* (Bologna, 1948), pp. 371–72.
[224] *Ibid.*, p. 485.
[225] Delumeau, *op. cit.* (n. 221), p. 29.
[226] See A. Merens (ed.), "De reis van Jan Martensz. Merens . . . anno 1600," *Mededeeling van het Nederlandsch Historisch Instituut te Rome*, 2d ser. VII (1937), 139.

Mercati (1541–93), physician to Pope Gregory, organized a natural history collection that was housed in the Vatican.[227] As the first Jesuits returned from the East in the 1580's, Rome came to be a center of information that rivaled Lisbon and Venice. Ortelius, for example, began to receive cartographical data on the East from his correspondents in Rome.[228] But, despite all this activity, the extant records of the Vatican collections, the treasury of the Gesù, and the inventories of individual Roman collectors do not indicate that systematic efforts were made in Rome to assemble natural or artistic curiosities from the East.[229]

Venice and Florence were the greatest Italian centers of collection, but there were notable collections in many other Italian cities. Mattioli at Siena, Girolamo Cardano (1501–76) at Milan, Aldrovandi at Bologna, and Francesco Calceolari (1521–ca. 1600) at Verona had extensive collections of natural history in which were included botanical and geological specimens from the East as well as a miscellany of other curiosities.[230] At Naples the museum of Ferrante Imperato (1550–1631) was well stocked with rarities of nature,[231] and at Padua the botanical gardens of the university contained growing specimens of Eastern trees and plants. The collections of the naturalists had a scientific objective, but they are important as well for the history of art. For, in the preparation of their books on natural science, the botanists worked with painters and engravers who prepared the illustrations for their massive works. And, as we shall see, other artists of the time copied these illustrations of plants, animals, and oddities and used them for their own purposes in other works of art.

Asia had different meanings for the various types of collectors. The patrician families in the major commercial cities of Lisbon, Venice, and Antwerp collected precious textiles, gems, and porcelains to satisfy a taste for splendid furnishings. Francesco Sansovino (1521–86) in his *Venetia, città nobilissima e singolare* (1581) describes the opulence of Venetian life:

There are innumerable houses the ceilings of whose apartments are worked in gold and all other colors and carved with paintings and excellent decoration. Nearly all of their interiors are covered with the very best tapestries, coverings of silk, gilded leathers and other materials according to the different seasons. And the chambers are for the most part adorned with bedspreads and chests decorated in gold, and paintings with frames also in gold. The silver services and other wares of porcelain, pewter, and inlaid copper and bronze are without end.[232]

[227] Delaunay, *op. cit.* (n. 35), p. 155.

[228] Hessels, *op. cit.* (n. 5), pp. 444, 522, 754.

[229] Cardinal Gaddi was the only private Roman collector who assembled natural rarities. See Burckhardt, *loc. cit.* (n. 9), p. 558.

[230] Aldrovandi, for example, in his *Musaeum mettalicum* (Bologna, 1648), shows (pp. 156–58) beautifully hafted examples of stone knives and axes used in India and a bowl of Ming porcelain (p. 231).

[231] An engraving which shows his collection is included in his *Historia naturale* (Naples, 1599).

[232] As quoted in Taylor, *op. cit.* (n. 6), p. 611.

The princely collectors were not generally so hedonistic in their interests; they often collected Eastern products to increase the prosperity of their realms or to display their personal erudition, virtuosity, or glory.[233] The learned collectors—geographers, naturalists, and artists—sought to acquaint themselves, in Dürer's words, "with the subtle *ingenia* of people in distant lands"[234] and to acquire what they could from study of them.

The Renaissance *virtuoso*, as the heir of the Middle Ages, possessed a tradition of individualism in taste and an undifferentiated concern for nature, science, and art. No wonder then that the cabinets of curiosities contained a mélange of oddities and that the menageries sometimes included exotic human beings as well as animals. But with the sixteenth century a subtle change began to take place in the manner, meaning, and objectives of collecting. Oddities were no longer collected exclusively as curiosities. The collection of antique remains was consciously supplemented by the addition of products from other civilizations. In a certain sense the remains of Antiquity themselves became exotic curiosities when displayed in company with rarities from overseas.[235] The *homme curieux*, as Pierre Belon said,[236] was eager to become acquainted with "countless singularities" from distant places, to compare them with those that he knew, and to integrate them into his own world view. His cabinet of curiosities was not a haphazard collection of odd objects but a systematic display which tried to transmit concretely the relations that were thought to obtain between the worlds of nature and art.

Natural curiosities of all times and places were considered to be works of art from the hands of the Creator and were objects of wonder to both the artist and the scientist. The artist, who had but recently become socially superior to an artisan, remained a close student of nature and the crafts. The exotic creations of foreign craftsmen were equally fascinating to artists and scientists; the interest in porcelain and its manufacture provides an example of their common concern. Cartography, which invokes art, science, and discovery, was of abiding interest, and maps and globes figured prominently in many of the major collections. Geography had lost its traditional connection with astronomy (which had best been exhibited in the works of Ptolemy) and had become much more concerned with mapping and describing the new parts of the world that were being revealed at a bewildering rate. To geographers like Ortelius and Mercator, the collection of curiosities was a valuable visual aid to studies and a treasure-trove of illustrative material. And it was not coincidental that André Thevet, the cosmographer, was selected to be guardian and organizer of the royal collection of France, or that Hakluyt tells his readers to investigate the collections of curiosities to see illustrations of the things mentioned in his collection of travels.

[233] See G. Händler, *Fürstliche Mäzene und Sammler in Deutschland von 1500–1620* (Strassburg, 1933), pp. 1–8.
[234] Cf. above, p. 18.
[235] See J. Seznec, "Erudits et graveurs au XVIᵉ siècle," *Mélanges d'histoire et d'archéologie*, XLVII (1930), 136–37.
[236] Cf. above, p. 7.

The artist, likewise, whether or not he worked at illustrating the new books of cosmography or natural history, also had accessible for study the products of strange and sophisticated arts and crafts by men of his own time. While the artist often found these foreign *ingenia* uncongenial to his taste, they added to his growing uneasiness about the presuppositions and conventions of European classical art. His sense of being on the brink of momentous change was succinctly expressed in 1575 by the Humanist physician Cardano in his autobiography: "The conviction grows that as a result of the [overseas] discoveries, the fine arts will be neglected and but lightly esteemed, and certainties will be exchanged for uncertainties."[237] Virtuosity in the sixteenth century thus involved looking for a new certainty based on discovering the invisible ties which were assumed to link science with art, antiquity with modernity, and Europe with the rest of the world. The collection of curiosities was conceived of as such a synthesis in miniature, a tangible cosmography, a universal mirror which reflected, even though vaguely, the relationships between discovery, whether of the past or present, and the transformation and expansion of the contemporary arts and sciences.

[237] As translated from the Latin by Jean Stoner in *The Book of My Life* (*De vita propria liber*) (New York, 1929), p. 189.

Sample Asian Items Collected in Europe

Excerpts from two inventories follow which were compiled in 1619 (No. 1) and 1621 (No. 2) respectively, as catalogues of the Prague Collections of Emperor Rudolf II. Notice that the "Indianische Sachen" listed may be of any provenance outside of Europe. Only occasionally do any of the European inventories distinguish individual objects more definitely, that is, as being from Asia, Africa, or America. They are relatively consistent, however, in identifying objects from Turkey, and occasionally even refer to some of them as coming from China or Japan. In most instances, however, the modern reader must determine or guess for himself the place of origin. For example, "Nine 'Indian' painted works rolled together" (p. 50) leads me to believe that this is a reference to nine Chinese scroll paintings. Other items are unfortunately not so readily identifiable. It is for this reason that I have compiled and added a list (No. 3) to this appendix of items imported into Europe from Asia that is derived from a host of sources; cargo lists, travel books, and the inventories of other collections.

I

Inventory of 1619 (Prague Collection of Rudolf II)*

INDIANISCHE SACHEN UNGESCHECZT

Ain indianisch gemaltes trühel, darinnen vierzehn kleine schwarze schalichen.

Ain indianisch geflochtenes trühel mit zwei fachen, darin ein klein kästl, mit 4 geflocht-enen pecherle, 3 duppelte schalen und 5 schüsslichen.

* From J. Morávek, *Nově objevený inventář rudolfinských sbírek na Hradě Pražském* (Prague, 1937), pp. 24–7.

[46]

Ain indianisch trühel gemalt, darinnen drei kleine kästl, in dem ainem ein schön viere-
kicht porczulan, in den andern zweien nichts, dabei aber 10 viereckichte schalichen.

Ain indianisch gemaltes trühel, darinnen zwei runde skatlichen und zwei trinckschalichen.

Ain indianisch gemaltes trühel, darinnen zwei in einander schwarze skatln und drei gelbe
geflochtene schalichen.

Ain indianisches gemaltes trühel, darinnen ein lenglichtes skatlichen und 2 runde duppelte
und 1 einfaches skatlichen.

Ain indianisch gemaltes trühel, darinnen zwei schöne geschirl, mit gar klenien perln
und coralen geziert, und dann zwei klaine schalichen.

Ain klaines indianisch gemaltes trühl, darinnen ein ander klaines trühl.

Ain kleines indianisch gemaltes trühl, darinnen zwei andere klainere trühel.

Ain indianisch gemaltes viereckichtes grosses castl, darinnen zwölf klaine und 1 mittel-
messige schalen.

Ain dergleichen grosses viereckichtes indianisch gemaltes trühel, darinnen 2 par indianische schuh, ain heubl von schilf, 12 schalichen.

Ain lange indianisch gemalte skatl, darinnen 2 cästl, in einem etliche indianische schlechte
halsgeheng, das ander ist verschlossen, dass man nicht aufmachen können, ain schalen,
darinnen 6 schalichen.

Ain viereckichte indianische skatl, darinnen vier geflochtene schalichen.

Ain indianisch viereckichte niedrige skatl, darinnen nichts verhanden.

Ain viereckichte etwas hohe rote indianische skatl, darinnen 5 schöne runde schalichen,
in aim cästl, und dann absonderlich zwei schalichen.

Ain viereckicht indianisch gemalte skatl, darin nichts verhanden.

Ain runde indianische skatl, darinnen 7 indianisch kupferne gemalte schüsseln und dann
vier kleinere geflochtene schüsseln.

Ain indianisches hohes etwas durchbrochenes trühl, darinnen drei schwarze skatlichen
und 3 kleine schalichen.

Aine achteckichte indianisch geflochtene skatl, darinnen eine runde skatl, mit 5 kupfernen
und einer geflochtenen schüssel.

Ain klaines viereckichtes indianisch skatlichen, darinnen 5 indianische gauckelmännel.

Ain indianische messinge lenglichte achteckichte schalen, darinnen 11 schalichen, 6 weisse
skatlichen, die deckl gemalt, 3 klaine neppel und ein klein rund skatlichen mit aim deckl.

Ain indianische achteckichte vierfache skatl, darinnen eine runde durchbrochene skatl, in
der wiederumb ein duppelte geflochtene, darinnen drei kleine schalichen, und über denselben vier schwarze schüsslichen.

Ain indianisch gemalte skatl, darinnen eine duppelte skatl mit 9 gelben schüsseln und
über denselben drei schwarze schüsslichen.

Ain indianische geflochtene skatl, darinnen ein gemaltes schwarzes und wieder darin ein
schön rot mit gold gemalt skatlichen.

Ain runde indianische skatl, darinnen zwei dergleichen geflochtene duppelte skatlichen.

Ain runde schwarze indianische skatl, darin zwei duppelte geflochtene skatln.

Ain lenglichte indianische geflochtene skatl, darinnen ein indianischer kampfl, mit silber
eingefast, und drei schälichen.

Ain lenglichte indianische geflochtene skatl, darinnen 3 schälichen, zwei mit deckeln.

Ain klein viereckicht indianisches skatlichen.

Ain messings indianisch trühel mit 2 fachen, im obern 16 schälichen und 4 skatlichen, im untern 5 geflochtene schälichen, 4 runde und zwei viereckichte und gar ein kleines, 4 messinge, und 7 gar kleine messinge gemalte schälichen, zwei plechene indianische mans- und weibesbild oder göczen, ain indianisch schloss.

Ain indianische runde grosse skatl, darinnen etliche messinge gemalte schüsseln.

Ain lange viereckichte indianisch geflochtene skatl, darinnen nichts zu finden.

Ain lange viereckichte indianisch gemalte skatl, darinnen indianisch vöglichen, so mehrerntheils verdorben.

Ain lang viereckichte indianisch skatl, darinnen nichts zu finden.

Ain lang viereckichte indianische skatl ohne deckl.

Aine viereckichte indianisch gemalte skatl, darinnen 4 kleine schälichen.

Ain viereckicht indianisch skatl, darinnen 5 schälichen.

Ain lenglichtes viereckichtes trühel mit aim schloss, darinnen ein par indianische schuh.

Ain schwarz lenglicht zugespiczte indianische skatl, darinnen ein schwarz skatlichen, in welchem 2 klingende kugeln, neun schalichen und ein püchsel als ein pulverflasch.

Sechs grosse geflochtene achteckichte schüsseln.

Aine grosse achteckichte geflochtene skatl, mit zweien fachen, im obern 3 schüsseln, im untern eine schwarze mit gold gezierte runde schüssel.

Ain indianisch achteckichte geflochtene skatl, darinnen 3 runde messinge und drei geflochtene schalen.

Aine achteckichte indiansch geflochtene skatl, darinnen 9 geflochtene schälichen und 2 schwarze schüsslichen.

Ain runde geflochtene skatl, darinnen nichts zu finden.

Ain dreifacher korb mit einer handhab, darinnen ein viereckicht skatlichen, aine schwarze kugel, so man nicht wissen können was es sei, ain meercompass, ain schwarz rundes skatlichen und zwei runde geflochtene schälichen.

Ain indianisch achteckicht hohe messinge skatl, darinnen aine runde geflochtene skatl mit 15 schälichen.

Ain runde indianisch skatl, darinnen nichts zu finden.

Ain indianische flaschen von messing, mit aim langen hals gemalt.

Ain grosse runde indianische skatl, darin 2 kleine schälichen.

Ain grosse runde indianische skatl, darinnen nichts zu finden.

Ain lenglichte indianische skatl, darinnen nichts zu finden.

Ain indianische orgel mit hülzernen pfeifen.

Drei indianische sonnenschirmen von fischhaut, die man zusammen legen kan.

Ain gross gebund mit indianischem rot und weissen papier.

In etlichen skatln unterschieden allerlei indianisches samenwerk.

Ain werck von alocs, schön geschnitten, wie paum oder laubwerck, darinnen etliche figuren.

Ain indianisch geflochtener lenglichter korb, darinnen eine flasche von gelben horn in
silber gefasst und mit silbern ketteln in aim futteral, item zwo in einander runde hohe
schwarze skatln mit gold gemalt.

Ain indianischer geflochtener lenglichter korb, darinnen zwei indianisch kästl von horn,
mit silber beschlagen, in dem grossen seind zwei grosse und 3 kleinere schalen von horn,
item ein pulverflaschen von perlnmutter, in silber vergult eingefast, item ein indianischer schurcz von geferbten federn, item ein fucher von helfenbain schön durch-
brochen, item ein pürstel, item sechs instrument von ebenholcz, mit silbern plech
beschlagen.

Ain indianisch geflochten lenglichter korb, darinnen zwei indianische göczen, dabei ein
messingschalen und ain messigfläschl mit farben.

Zwo runde ubereinander indianische schalen, in silber vergult eingefasst.

Ain indianische flasch von gelben horn mit silber beschlagen in aim futteral.

Ain achteckichte schwarze mit gold gezierte skatl, darin nichts zu finden.

Ain lenglichte viereckichte skatl, darinnen 8 schlechte schälichen.

Ain achteckichte runde indianische skatl, darin ein ander viereckichte, schön mit gold
geziert.

Ain achteckichte runde indianische skatl, darinnen nichts zu finden.

Ain grosse runde indianische achteckichte skatl, darinnen nichts zu finden.

Ain gross indianisch mit gold gemaltes kästl, darinnen ein ander schön cästl, welches
ganz über mit kleinen perln und corallen gestickt, in welchem 12 kleine schalichen.

Mehr ein indianisch cästl mit gold geziert, darinnen ein ander cästl ganz über mit kleinen
perln und corallen gestickt, in welchem 12 indianische schälichen.

Mehr ein indianisch cästl mit gold geziert, darinnen ein ander cästl ganz über mit kleinen
perln und corallen gestickt, darinnen 10 schälichen.

Ain lenglicht viereckicht niedriges schön gemaltes indianisch cästl, darinnen ein schön
indianisch, auf weissen taffet gemaltes küsszichen, item zwo indianische bünden und 12
schalichen.

Ain dergleichen viereckichtes lenglichtes cästl, darinnen 12 schalichen.

Ain viereckicht mit gold gemalte indianisch skatl, darinnen ein ander dergleichen
achteckichte skatl.

Ain indianisch gemalte kupferne flaschen in aim schön geflochtenen körbel.

Zwei grosse indianisch mit gold gezierte handbecken in aim rot ledernen futteral.

Ain indianisch braiter hut von geschipten gefarbtem horn.

Ain indianisch balbierbecken mit einer scharten.

Ain viereckicht schreibzeug mit weiss- und schwarzem helfenbain eingelegt.

Ain par indianisch gemalte pantofeln.

Allerlei zusammen gebundene stuck holzart, so in des Indiis wechst.

Ain indianisch von stroh geflochtene klaine decken.

Ain grosse tabackpfeifen.

Ain klein indianisch keulichtes geschirl.

Ain indianischer cranz von gefarbten gelben und roten federn.

Ain indianische schwarze rüstung mit gold geziert, in aim casten.

Ain andern indianische schöne rüstung in einem kasten.

Ain indianisch zimblich grosses trühel mit perlnmutter eingelegt, darinnen gemaltes plumwerck, in einem schlecht mit eisen beschlagenen futteral.

In aim futteral ein schön cästl über und über mit perlnmutter eingelegt, welches der könig in Persia durch seinen oratorem kaiser Rudolfo präsentieren lassen, dabei ein verzeichnis zu befinden, was darinnen gewesen; es hat sich aber im aufmachen nur zwei kleine porczulanichen, ain gefarbter orientalischer dupasi, ain stuck weiss dupasi, ain schwarz halbrunde kugl von dupasi, ain stuck weisslich amathist, ain klaines fläschl von weissem stain wie ein schnecken und ein ledernes fläschl mit eim gulden mund-stuck befunden.

Ain indianisch kleines schreibtischl mit vergulten fachen.

Ain schön persianisch schachtbrett, über und über mit perlnmutter eingelegt.

Ain indianisch pretspiel mit inliegenden stainen von helfenbain und ebenholcz.

Ain mit eisen beschlagenes schlechtes trühl mit rotem leder überzogen.

Gar ein kleines trühel mit indianischen sachen, daraus man dinten soll machen können.

Neun stuck zusammengerultes indianisch malwerck.

Ain lange viereckichte niedrige schwarze mit gold gemalte skatl, darinnen 15 viereckichte schalichen, und 1 viereckichtes trühel, darinnen zwei indianische stahlerne spigl.

Ain dergleichen lenglicht viereckicht niedrige schwarze mit gold gezierte skatl, darinnen nichts zu finden.

Ain viereckichte schöne indianische niedrige skatl, mit perlnmutter eingelegt und mit gold gemalt.

Ain viereckicht dergleichen indianische niedrige skatl, darin 5 runde geflochtene schä-lichen.

Ain dergleichen viereckicht lenglicht indianische skatl, darinnen 8 viereckicht schalichen.

Ain indianisch viereckichte schüssel oder schalen.

Drei zusamben gebundene achteckichte indianische schalen mit handgriffeln.

Ain indianisch geflochtener korb mit aim deckl und handhab, darinnen 4 stuck zur indianischen dinten, item acht viereckichte schalichen, aine grosse und darin sieben geflochtene runde schalichen, und drei kleine runde hülczerne schalichen.

Ain dergleichen indianischer geflochtener korb mit aim deckl und handhab, darinnen 5 etwas hohe achteckichte und 3 runde geflochtene schalen.

Ain rundes indianisches mit gold geziertes skatlichen.

Viel schnäbel von indianischen vogeln.

Neun indianische lange schwarze gerade und krumpe gewundene hörner, zusammen gebunden, dabei zwei par klainere.

Zwei indianisch thierle, armadillo gennant.

Ain grosser langer schnabel von einem indianischen vogl, in aim blausammeten futteral.

Ain gross indianische fledermaus.

Vier indianische heydexen.

Ain schwarz horn von einer indianischen ziegen.

Mehr fünf indianische jagerhörner von weissem bain.

Ain schwarzes gewundenes horn von einem indianischen thier.

Fünf indianische gürtl, daran klingendes schellwerck, in eim kästl.

Ain indianische helfenbeine büxen.

Allerlei indianisch gartengewechssamen.

Ain zweig von eim indianischen baum, daran noch die frucht henget.

Ain indiansch keulicht geschir wie ein tiefe schalen.

Ain indianische grosse flaschen.

Ain stuck indianische materia wie ein salben.

Vier indianische schildkröten.

Ain indianische armband von weissen bain, schön geschnitten.

Ain gedreheter pecher mit eim deckl, von indianischem holz.

Ain ander gedreheter pecher von indianischem holz.

Ain indianisch pecherle von schildkrot.

Ain runde skatl mit indianischen fliegen.

Zwei kästl, darinnen indianische merkrebs.

Elf grosse indianische nuss.

Ain indianische schildkrot.

DRECHSELWERK VON HELFENBAIN

Ain hundert und achtzehn kästl, darinnen allerlei schönes gross und klein kunstreiches drechselwerk von helfenbain.

SCHÖNE STUCK VON MARMELSTAIN

Fünf grosse köpf von marmelstain.

Vier kleine köpf von marmelstain.

Sechzehn kleine bilder von marmelstain.

Ain hundl von marmelstain.

PORCZELLANEN

In zweien almarn, alle fach voll, übereinander geseczte, gross und klaine porczellanengefäss, darunter etliche in silber eingefast, ungeschäczt.

Absonderlich siebenzehen grosse und kleine porczellanenkrüeg auf einer almar in der vordern kunstcammer stehend, ungeschäczt.

ZWENE SCHÖNE GROSSE KRÜGE VON *majolica*, ungeschäczt.

ALLERLEI GLÄSERNE TRINKGESCHIR, ungeschäczt.

SCHÖN ERDENGESCHIR

In einer doppelten almar mit dreien fachen, florentinisch schön gemaltes erdengeschir, als gross und klaine kruge, flaschen, schalen, handbecken, schüsseln und leichter, ungeschäczt.

FRANCZÖSISCH GESCHIR

In einer mit eisern banden beschlagene truhen, schön franczösisch geschir von schüsseln, tellern und andern, so von kupfer mit glas überlaufen und schön gemalt, ungeschäczt.

GESCHIR VON TERRA SIGILLATA

Allerlei geschir von terra sigillata, darunter ain schöne gisskandel in aim rotsammeten futteral.

Etliche kästl mit terra sigillata.

GROSS UND KLEIN ERDENGESCHIRL, SO IN DER ERDEN GEFUNDEN WORDEN.

NACKENDE BILDER

Fünf grosse nackende bilder von weisser materia, deren eines in einer almar auf rot duppeltaffetern polstern und vorhengen ligt.

ZWEI GROSSE WILDE SCHWEIN von materia als gibs.

AIN SCHWEINSKOPF, welchem ein bauer den hirnschädel eingeschlagen, und hat doch das schwein noch etlich jahr gelebet, in einem grünen kästl.

DIE UNTERN KIENBACKEN VON EINEM WILDEN SCHWEIN, mit einem sehr selczamen wunderbahren krummen zahn, in einer skatl.

AIN OBER UND UNTER KIENBACKEN VON ain wilden schwein mit ungewöhnlichen krummen zähnen, in einer skatl.

VIEL STUCK ALLERLEI SELCZAMES MERGEWECHS, welches etlichs zu stain worden. In einer skatl absonderlich allerlei wunder mergewechs.

MERMUSCHELN ODER MERSCHNECKEN

In vielen unterschiedenen almarn und skatlichen sehr viel allerlei mermuscheln und schnecken klain und gross.

ETLICHE MERFISCHL

Ain wunder merfisch stella arborescens genannt.

Zwo lange zungen von merfischen.

Vier schwertfischschnabel.

Ain fischhaut so man zappen nennet.

FÜNF STRAUSSENAYER
FÜNF AYER VON VOGEL EME [emu].

Allerlei merwunder und thierlein, in einer lenglichten skatl.

Ain merkraben, in aim kästl.

Ain grosser merkrebs in einem langen trühel.

Noch ein grosser merkrebs.

Etwas kleiner merkrebs, beisammen in drei trüheln.

DREI MERSCHLANGEN
NATERZUNGEN VON MALTA, DABEI AIN KROTENSTEIN, in einen runden skatlichen.
ZWEI GROSSE NATTERBELGE.

ARMADILIA

Zwei armadilia in einem trühel.

Ain armadilia, dabei zwei solcher häut in einem lenglichten trühel.

Ein grosse haut.

2

Inventory of 1621 (Prague Collection of Rudolf II)*

Inventarium aller derjenigen sachen, so nach der victori in ihrer majestät schaz- und kunstcamer zue Praag seind gefunden und auf ihrer mayestät und ihrer fürstlich gnaden von Lichtenstein bevelch seind den 6. decembris anno 1621 inventirt worden, wie volgt:

NO. I. IN EINER ALMAR, IN OBERN THEIL:

1. Ein oberteil eines weibesbild von fleischfarben gips, auf einen fleischfarben und rothen daffenten polster liegend.

   In bemelter almar, im untern theil:

2. Etliche schachteln von allerlei indianischen geferbten federn und schlechten sachen.

NO. 2. EIN ALMAR MIT 3 FACHEN:

Im obern fach:

3. Schöne gemachte indianische schalen und unterschiedliche geschirr, dreissig stuck.

   Im andern fach:

4. Eine schachtel mit allerlei türkischen servetlen.
5. Zwo boratschen mit silbern knöpfen ⎫
6. Item 9 flaschen   ⎬   indianisch.
7. Mehr 4 baukhen ⎭
8. Mehr eine runde schachtel mit etlichen krüglen von terra sigillata.
9. 5 indianische schreibzeug, darunter einer mit perlemutter.
10. Mehr ein schachtel mit einem schachtspiel und roth geferbtem helfenbein.
11. 5 indianisch trinkgeschirr.
12. 7 indianische täschlein und 2 sammacken.
13. 1 messinge runde schaal mit indianischer schrift.
14. 3 andere schlechte indianische stuck.

    Im dritten fach:

15. 18 stuck gross und klein erdene egyptische antiquen.
16. 1 khessel mit zwo messingen decken und ein indianische schellen sambt den pfeifen.

NO. 3. IN DER ALMAR MIT NO. 3, HAT 3 FACH:

Im obern fach seind:

17. 28 stuck von stroh und holz indianische gemahlte geschirr, alle mit kleinen stücklein mit dergleichen sorten gefüllt.

    Im andern oder mittlern fach:

18. Ein truhlen und 2 andere indianische stuck von geferbtem metall, darinnen viel kleine stücklein von indianischen stroh und holz sambt einem kleinen krüglein.

---

* From H. Zimmermann, "Das Inventar der Prager Schatz- und Kunstkammer vom 6. Dezember 1621," *Jahrbuch der kunsthistorischen Sammlungen des allerhöchsten Kaiserhauses*, XXV (1905), Pt. 2, p. xx.

19. Mehr 22 stuck allerlei sorten an indianischen geschirr, darunter etliche leer und etliche mit kleinen stücklein gefüllt.
Im dritten fach:
20. Eine indianische orgell und unterschiedliche indianische saamen sambt dergleichen gar geringen sachen.

NO. 4. IN DER ALMAR MIT NO. 4, HAT 2 FACH:

Im obern fach:
21. 3 truhlen von indianischem stroh, darinnen allerlei kleine sachen.
22. 12 stuck von indianischen holz, darunter 1 mit 2 indianischen truhlen und eins von perln.
23. Ein hölzerner berg geschnizt.
24. Zwei gross indianische becken.
25. 1 bar indianische pantoffel.
26. 1 doppelt indianisch trinkgeschirr von einer schildkrotten, mit silber und vergult eingefast.
27. 1 indianische flaschen von gelben agtstein im futteral.
28. 1 indianisch krüegl in einem strohenem körbel.
29. 8 indianische bücher.
30. 2 stuck indianische tinten.
31. 1 indianisch dacken.
Im untern fach:
32. 1 indianische truhlen in einem futteral.
33. 1 schachtspiel, mit perlemutter eingelegt.
34. 2 pretspiel, mit helfenbein eingelegt.
35. 2 hölzerne truhlen, darinnen indianische rüstungen.
36. 1 hölzern schreibzeugtruhlen.
37. 2 leere futteral.

NO. 5. IN DER ALMAR MIT NO. 5, HAT 3 FACH:

Im obern fach:
38. 1 buschen zusambengebunden allerlei indianische gemähl.
39. 21 schnäbel von allerlei indianischen vögeln.
Im mittlern fach:
40. 6 schachtele gemalte, in 4 allerlei vogeleier, in der einen meergewechs und in der andern beinwerch.
41. 2 indianische körb, gefüllt mit kleinen stücklein.

European Imports from Asia

(Excluding Spices)*

Peoples of Asia
Indians, Chinese
Malays, Japanese,
  Filipinos
sailors
navigators
prisoners
slaves

Fauna
parrots and lorys
birds of paradise
  (plumages)
elephants
rhinoceroses
emu
monkeys and apes
dodos

Flora: Dried and Fresh
coconuts
seeds
myrobalans
oranges
trees, plants, shrubs
double coconuts
durians

Dyes
myrobalans
vermilion
indigo
lac
Indian saffron
alum

Incense and Perfume
pepper
musk
civet

Ceramics
porcelain
Martaban jars
seashells

Precious Metals
gold (from Sumatra)

silver (from Japan)
golden items; chests,
  goblets, necklaces
coins

*Precious and Semiprecious
Stones*
diamonds
rubies
sapphires
emeralds
spinels
carnelians
bezoar stones
rocks (sometimes with
  inscriptions on them)
amber
cat's eyes

Ivory
wrought and unwrought

Woods
ebony
sandalwood
aloeswood
teak
camphor of China,
  Borneo, and Sumatra
bamboo
cocopalm

Furniture
lacquered bowls and
  boxes
desks
sedan chairs
tables
bedsteads
chairs

Textiles
silk, raw and processed
cotton cloths, primarily
  from India
bedspreads and quilts
embroidery and needle-
  work

rugs, primarily from
  Ormuz
native costumes
hangings

Drugs
datura (thorn apple or
  strammony)
rhubarb
myrobalans (used also for
  dye)
tamarins
root of China
opium
bhang (Indian hemp or
  hashish)
benzoin
camphor (wood, oil, and
  crystals)
rhinoceros horn

Miscellaneous
musical instruments
buffalo horn
wax
resin
hides
pearls and mother-of-
  pearl
feathers and featherworks
palm products
caulking
chess sets
folding screens (*byōbus*)
armor and swords
maps and charts
manuscripts, books
native costumes and
  slippers
paintings, Chinese and
  Indian
sexual appliances
reeds (*Calumus rotang*)
ambergris
varnish (tung oil)
parasols

* For the spice trade see *Asia*, Vol. I, chap. iii.

CHAPTER II

The Individual Arts

The European artist, then as now, was likely to be more curious about the works produced by his opposite numbers in Asia than by exotic flora, fauna, and miscellaneous oddities. But the Asian artistic creations available, even in the greatest of the collections, were not numerous. Access to the collections was not always easy for the artists to obtain, and very few artists had collections of their own. It was fairly simple for any interested artist to see and study Chinese porcelains or lacquerware, for they were widely diffused and readily available in most of the artistic centers of western Europe. Elaborately worked textiles and rugs were likewise widely dispersed as can be seen from the frequency of their appearance in European paintings. Oriental ceramics, lacquerware, and textiles were not new to the European scene in the sixteenth century, even though they were on hand in greater numbers and variety than ever before. They had long exercised their influence upon the minor arts of Europe, but even when available in larger quantities were not of primary interest to practitioners in the major arts.

The impact of Asia, and the speculations of modern students about it, will be examined in what follows in each of the individual arts where influences are discernible. In the major arts the effects of the discoveries and the revelations of the East were not profound and were limited to the introduction of decorative and symbolic elements, or to naturalistic subject matter derived from the collections and from the specimens of Asian exotica sold in the marketplace. The influence of Asia in the graphic arts was probably most apparent in the prints prepared as illustrations for books. In the related decorative arts of ceramics, woodworking, jewelry, and tapestry making, efforts were made to use Asian materials or to find adequate substitutes for them as artists and craftsmen in these fields tried to create products competitive with those being imported.

Although no European art form underwent basic transformation in response to the challenge of Asia's arts and crafts, new dimensions were added to most of them in subject matter, ornament, and symbolism. And although no identifiable movement in the arts owed its inspiration directly to the overseas discoveries, the Mannerist artists were inclined to experiment with motifs derived from exotica. The very presence, in quantity, for the first time in history, of foreign arts and crafts of high quality helped to speed the unsettling of Renaissance preconceptions about the nature and possibilities of the arts.

I

MANUELINE ARCHITECTURE AND SCULPTURE

The exuberance felt by King Manuel and his subjects over the successes of the Portuguese in India was given tangible expression at Lisbon and elsewhere in Portugal by the building and rehabilitation of national shrines. Between 1510 and 1514 the nave and a chapter room were added to the Convent of Christ at Tomar in recognition of the prominent role played by the Order of Christ in the discoveries. Additions were also undertaken at the famous monastery of Batalha, the symbol of Portugal's deliverance from the yoke of Castile begun in the late fourteenth century. The Tower of Belém, originally conceived of as a fortress on the Tagus to guard the port of Lisbon, was built on Manuel's orders between 1514 and 1519 as a monument to the discoverers (pl. 17). Close by the tower on the river, the construction of the great monastery of the Jerónimos (Order of St. Jerome) went on from 1499 to the middle of the sixteenth century, partially financed by a royal grant of one-twentieth of the proceeds from overseas trade assigned to the support of the Jerónimos.[1] The new wealth of Portugal likewise went into the construction of numerous other less impressive public works and edifices. King Manuel before his death in 1521 paid for sixtytwo building projects. But many of those erected in Lisbon and its environs were destroyed or damaged beyond restoration by the earthquake of 1755.

The architectural masterpieces undertaken in the time of Manuel (1495–1521) set the pattern for a national style called Manueline, though its influence long outlived the king himself and extended into the other arts as well. Historians of architecture have generally agreed that the Manueline style is a peculiar Portuguese form of flamboyant Gothic which acquired its individuality through lavish use of decorative motifs derived from various European and foreign prototypes.[2] A great debate has ensued, however, for more than a century now, with reference to the sources of the multiple foreign influences behind this florid, polyglot style. Some authorities have argued that it is not a "true style"

---

[1] J. de Sigüenza, *Historia de la Orden de San Gerónimo* (Madrid, 1907), II, 73.
[2] Authoritative and judicious assessments may be found in G. Kubler and M. Soria, *Art and Architecture in Spain and Portugal* (Baltimore, 1958), pp. 101–3; and J. Barreira *et al.*, *Arte portugesa* (Lisbon, 1948), IV, 77–78, 167–68.

at all, since it is not an architecture of new forms but an undigested assortment of decorative motifs from a host of local and international sources.[3] At the other extreme stand those who see it as an absolutely unique Portuguese style that is free from all foreign influences.[4] But most interesting in the context of this work are those historians who see the Manueline as a style of European architecture which draws heavily, both in form and decoration, from Indian edifices.

Even among those who agree that they discern Indian influence, wide divergences of opinion exist on how far it extends. Among the earliest to propose a relationship between Indian and Gothic architecture was the Romantic German philosopher, Friedrich W. J. von Schelling.[5] Albrecht Haupt, while discounting Spanish or Italian influence, was the first to propound the theory that the peculiar features of the Manueline additions to Tomar and Batalha (pls. 18 and 19) could be accounted for as efforts to imitate details from the Jain temple of Ahmadābād.[6] The parallels drawn by Haupt between Portuguese and Indian details were soon challenged by W. C. Watson[7] and others. Haupt's critics have generally averred that resemblances to the Manueline can be found in Gothic decorations and, if one must look to a distance, even in Mexican temples. But Haupt was not without his followers, too. Ernst Diez in his essay "Oriental Gothic" claims that the pointed arch, along with the gesture of folding the hands in prayer, was borrowed from India.[8]

Raul da Costa-Tôrres went much further than any other student of the subject in his efforts to discern Asian influence in Portuguese architecture. For the architecture of the epoch of the discoveries he distinguished three periods: the Pre-Manueline, or the Gothic-Morgebrino (North African), 1415–95; the Manueline, or the Gothic-Hindu Baroque, 1495–1540; and the Joannine-Jesuit, or the Classic Chinese, 1540–80.[9] On the basis of such associations, Costa-Tôrres, and more recently Eugenio d'Ors, have sought the origins of the Baroque in the Manueline style and, by extension, in the influence of Asia.[10] Lees-Milne, on the other hand, sees the Manueline and Baroque styles as "a sort of prolongation of the Romanesque," and he discerns a relationship in spirit between the naturalistic fantasy of the Manueline and the playfulness of the Rococo.[11]

The architects responsible for creating the Manueline masterpieces were

[3] For the most recent statement of this view see J. Lees-Milne, *Baroque in Spain and Portugal* . . . (London [1960]), pp. 145–46.

[4] R. dos Santos, *O estilo manuelino* (Lisbon, 1952).

[5] Cf. quotations and discussion in P. Frankl, *The Gothic: Literary Sources and Interpretations through Eight Centuries* (Princeton, 1960), p. 458.

[6] *Die Baukunst der Renaissance in Portugal* (Frankfurt am Main, 1890).

[7] *Portuguese Architecture* (London, 1908).

[8] As cited in Frankl, *op. cit.* (n. 5), p. 748.

[9] *A arquitectura dos descobrimentos* (Braga, 1943).

[10] For commentary of Ors's view of the Tomar window as the synthesis of the "Barocchus Manuelinus," see P. Dony, "Der Manuelstil in Portugal (1495–1521)," *Das Münster*, XIX (1966), 229.

[11] *Op. cit.* (n. 3), pp. 142, 152.

Diogo Boytac (active 1490–1525 ?), João de Castilho (active 1515–52), Diogo de Arruda (active 1508–31), Francisco de Arruda (active 1510–47), and Mateus Fernandes (active 1514–28). Practically all Manueline buildings are identifiable because they display the armillary sphere of the king, which symbolized the cosmos, or the cross of the Knights of Christ, which decorated the sails of the Portuguese ships. Early Manueline creations tend to be moribund Gothic with admixtures of Moorish or North African elements; the postdiscovery works tend to combine late Gothic with naturalistic, maritime elements and a flamboyant iconography, possibly inspired by Muslim and Indian art; in the declining phase Renaissance elements from Italy overlay the basically Gothic character of the Manueline constructions.[12] The greatest of the Manueline edifices belong to the middle period, and the features characteristic of this period have sometimes been designated as the attributes of the "true Manueline" style. Particularly distinctive features are the rounded (almost never pointed) arches of door and window, the frequent appearance of arches made up of three or more convex curves,[13] and the generally undulatory rhythm of both the simplest and most elaborate archways. Also remarkable is the widespread use of nave piers (pl. 22) which look like twisted strands of rope, palm-tree columns, eight-sided capitals ornamented with molded leaves or branches, and rounded moldings twined together to give a spiral effect. But perhaps most impressive and distinctive are the ornate portals which appear as a central motif in practically all the great Manueline churches and monasteries (pls. 20 and 21).

While many of the distinctive features of Manueline architecture can be shown to have medieval or Gothic antecedents,[14] there can be no doubt that the style, seen as a totality, is utterly unique. Even when dismissed as eccentric, or as little more than maritime decorative incrustations superimposed upon basically Gothic structures, the Manueline style has for the viewer a distinctly exotic character that is un-European and Oriental.[15] The predominance of the decorative over the architectonic elements gives the Manueline structures the appearance of gigantic sculptures. And in the best examples, such as the great portal to the Unfinished Chapels ("Capelas imperfeitas") at Batalha (pl. 18), the architects show respect for form and appear to be trying for a kind of planned asymmetry in which sculpture and architecture find unity. The stylized lines and ornamentation of Gothic architecture are consciously replaced by sinuous and oscillating lines, eccentric planes, and bizarre ornaments of naturalistic

[12] Here I have obviously departed radically from the periodization and characterization of Costa-Tôrres as cited above (p. 58).

[13] Costa-Tôrres (*op. cit.* [n. 9], pp. 182–83), argues that the rounded arch is of Oriental origin, that it was introduced to the Occident by the Manuelists, and that it is as much an identifying mark of the Manueline style as the armillary sphere or the cross of Christ. Watson (*op. cit.* [n. 7], p. 143) concedes that the arches which are made up of a series of convex curves "probably derived from Moorish sources."

[14] Twisted columns can be found, for example, in the thirteenth-century cloister of St. John Lateran in Rome. See Lees-Milne, *op. cit.* (n. 3), p. 146.

[15] For a similar opinion see J. Evans, *Pattern* (Oxford, 1931), II, 59.

inspiration. A list of the naturalistic ornaments includes, among other things, a wide variety of exotic fruits, plants, and animals as well as maritime and nautical motifs.[16] The architectural sculptor seems in some instances, as in the famous window of Tomar (pl. 19), to be arranging these into an abstract geometrical composition designed to catch in stone the exuberant and expansive spirit of Manuel's Portugal.

Speculation about the sources for Manueline decoration is so prevalent and diverse because the history of the architects and their monuments is notable for its sparsity of documentation. Particularly conspicuous by their absence are concrete data to show that the architects had anything more than the vaguest impressions of Indian architecture derived from the amateurish drawings (pl. 148) and literary descriptions of men in the field. The first stone was laid for the church of the Jerónimos in 1502 and it was virtually completed by Manuel's death in 1521. But almost nothing is known about Diogo Boytac, its first architect, about his successors, or about the details of its construction. And no literary evidence is available to show that its Orientalized features owe a direct debt to Indian or to any other Asian civilization.

Traces of Indian influence have frequently been assigned to the Manueline additions to Tomar and Batalha and to the Tower of Belém. Diogo de Arruda, a military architect who had spent some time in North Africa, constructed the additions to Tomar and invented for them a nautical iconography to celebrate the maritime exploits of the Portuguese. Carvings in stone of billowing sails, coral growths, and seaweed decorate the chapter room and the church. The famous capitular window (pl. 19) is set in a maze of coiled, snarled rope with cork floats threaded upon a cable.[17] While Tomar's decorations clearly reflect the maritime interests of Portugal, no pictorial or literary evidence exists to support the view that Arruda's naturalistic carvings owe a direct debt to specific Indian prototypes or even generally to the "aesthetic principles of Hindu art."[18]

Mateus Fernandes, the creator of the magnificent portal to the Unfinished Chapels at Batalha, has left no records for posterity to consult other than his architectural triumphs. Scholars have sought repeatedly to link him to Tomas Fernandes, the military architect in India, whom Albuquerque praised so lavishly in his letters, or to Diogo Fernandes of Beja, who went to Gujarat as a member of an embassy in 1513.[19] No definite connection has yet been established, however, and so the commentators on Batalha must also refer vaguely to the similarity in design, technique, or spirit between its portals and those of Indian temples. Others who prefer to bring their conjecturing closer to home point out the resemblances between the portal of Batalha and the fourteenth-century doorway to the north porch of St. Mary Redcliffe at Bristol.[20] Such remote

[16] Costa-Tôrres (*op. cit.* [n. 9], p. 198) gives such a list.

[17] Kubler and Soria (*op. cit.* [n. 2], p. 103) compare Diogo de Arruda's creations to the modern works in Barcelona of Antonio Gaudi.

[18] Phraseology of Costa-Tôrres, *op. cit.* (n. 9), p. 177.

[19] See Watson, *op. cit.* (n. 7), p. 159, and Barreira *et al.*, *op. cit.* (n. 2), IV, pp. 177–78.

[20] Lees-Milne, *op. cit.* (n. 3), pp. 147–48.

resemblances, whether in Europe or India, are not enough by themselves to support arguments for artistic influence.

The third of the great Manueline monuments, the Tower of Belém (pl. 17), was the work of Francisco de Arruda, brother of Diogo, a military architect, and one of the least-known artists of the sixteenth century. It has been conjectured that the tower, probably built between 1514 and 1519, was modeled on coastal fortresses of North Africa or India. Resemblances have been noted between its balconies and ribbed cupolas and those of the palace of Udaipur in Rajasthan, or those of the temple of Politana in Gujarat. But such attributions to Indian influence have been roundly denied by Reynaldo dos Santos, the closest student of the Tower of Belém.[21] He stresses, particularly with reference to the cupolas and balconies, the greater importance of Islamic and North African prototypes and argues that the resemblances between the tower and the Indian structures merely show their common debt to Islam—the Mughul influence in India and the Moorish in Portugal. But such arguments, cogent as they may be, have not silenced the proponents of Indian influence. Costa-Tôrres argues that it is not in details or in the technique of decoration that the resemblances lie, but in the organic harmony of the perfectly finished structure in which, as in Indian monumental art, the interior is subordinate to the exterior and the parts to the whole.[22]

Hundreds of art monuments in Portugal have been identified as having Manueline features.[23] But in no single instance is it possible to establish a clear link between them and Indian counterparts. Even the wooden stalls in the upper choir of the church of Santa Cruz in Coimbra (pl. 23), on which are carved scenes supposedly illustrating the voyages of Vasco da Gama and of Pedro Alvares Cabral, show that the carvers had no clear idea of the appearance of Indian towns or of the luxuriance of tropical vegetation.[24] Although drawings of life in India may have been available to the artists at home, they were probably all by Indians or by European amateurs. An extant painting (pl. 25), done in India by an amateur watercolorist before 1540, shows an Indian temple that looks more like a poor attempt at a European church than anything Indian. Filippo Sassetti wrote in 1585 to Lorenzo Canigiani in Florence describing the dwellings of Cochin and comparing certain of them in their external projections to the *sporti* of Santa Croce in Florence.[25] Father Manuel Pinheiro, writing from Ahmadābād in 1595 about the beautiful tombs of Sirkej, concludes that they are "a work of barbarians which is not at all barbarous."[26] While a number

[21] *A Torre de Belém, 1514–20* (Coimbra, 1922).

[22] *Op. cit.* (n. 9), pp. 211–12.

[23] *Ibid.*, pp. 215–16.

[24] Lees-Milne (*op. cit.* [n. 3], pp. 146–47) asserts that they are "purely and simply late Gothic in style [and] repeat the familiar traceral patterns to be found at this time all over Europe."

[25] E. Marcucci (ed.), *Lettre . . . di Filippo Sassetti* (Florence, 1855), pp. 295–96.

[26] See my *Asia in the Making of Europe* (hereafter cited as *Asia*), I (Chicago, 1965), p. 461. For additional suggestive detail see W. Varde-Valivlakar, "An Account of the Expedition to the Temples of Southern India Undertaken by Martin Alfonso de Souza, the 12th Governor [1542–45] of Portuguese India," *Indian Antiquary*, XLI (1912), 238–48.

of capable artists went to India in the second half of the sixteenth century, little is known of what they sent back home. And, irrespective of what they might have sent back, the decline of the Manueline style and the beginning of Italian influence in Portugal had taken place before they even left Europe.

The carriers of Portuguese culture to the rest of Europe—the exiled Jews, merchants, seamen, students, and Jesuits—apparently did not spread abroad a taste for the Manueline style. In Spain the Plateresque ("silversmith-like") style seems to have grown parallel to but independent of the Manueline. Both of these Iberian national styles owe far more to their common Moorish backgrounds than to each other, especially in their indebtedness to *mudéjar*, the folk art of wall ornament. Similarities between the architecture of the French Renaissance and the Manueline likewise seem to be coincidental, or at least to have nothing more in common than their Gothic backgrounds. And, by mid-century, intrusions from Italy and the Low Countries brought an abrupt end to these national styles of architecture, as a common European style began to emerge which was to develop into the Baroque.

Claims have been made, particularly by Costa-Tôrres, for the importance of overseas influence in the development of the Baroque. Costa-Tôrres, who contends that unique particularities are not so important in assessing influence as are common aesthetic or spiritual principles, avers that Far Eastern art, which is fundamentally Chinese rather than Indian, has structural and organic affinities with Italian neoclassicism.[27] Portuguese architects learned, he assumes, either from direct observation or from study of Chinese structures depicted on porcelains, lacquerware, textiles, paintings, and books something of the style, line, and architectonic character of Chinese art. On the basis of these observations they constructed pavilions, kiosks, balconies, and porches which showed distinctive Chinese features and were incorporated into the type of habitation commonly called *antiga portuguesa*. The pavilions and kiosks have disappeared from the gardens and squares which they once graced, but the houses have preserved the slanting roofs, extended eaves, and decorative features borrowed from China. The art style called "Jesuit," sometimes used as a synonym for Baroque, departed, Costa-Tôrres argues, from the heavy lines of medieval architecture, borrowed decorative features from Hindu art, and adopted lighter architectonic qualities from Chinese art. The concave arch, the sinuous lines, and the pillared façade pierced with a window of Oriental architecture became features of the new Jesuit churches built in Portugal even before the Gesù was begun in Rome.[28] Edifices constructed in Flanders and Germany in the later sixteenth century likewise are said to owe a debt to Portuguese architecture and to the East.[29]

The theory of Costa-Tôrres on the Portuguese-Oriental origin of the Jesuit-Baroque style has a certain elementary logic to support it, and little else. On the

[27] Costa-Tôrres, *op cit.* (n. 9), pp. 257–60.
[28] *Ibid.*, pp. 264–68.
[29] *Ibid.*, pp. 270–71.

surface it seems reasonable to assume that the Jesuits with their great interest in Portugal and the East would have borrowed elements from the Manueline, and from the Far East directly, to add a missionary aspect to their architectural creations. This seems particularly likely when it is recalled that the Jesuit letter-writers remarked in astonishment on the grandiose edifices of Asia and even described a number of them in detail.[30] Unfortunately for this theory, not a scrap of concrete evidence exists, and Costa-Tôrres does not provide any, to show that Giacomo da Vignola or Giacomo della Porta, the planners of the Gesù in Rome, knew anything about either Portuguese or Asian architecture. The Jesuits, in fact, had almost nothing to say about the construction of the Gesù. Their patron, Cardinal Alessandro Farnese, employed the architect Vignola and his own painters (in 1568) without consulting the Society or trying to ascertain its wishes in the matter. When Farnese died in 1589, the work on the Gesù stopped and the Jesuits, limited by their lack of funds, were forced to abandon the work of decorating the interior of the central church for generations and to confine their activities to the side chapels.[31] The building itself does not evoke reminiscences of the Orient or of the Society's activities there. Indeed, it is remarkable to see in Macao and in Goa how European the remains of the Jesuit structures look in a totally Asian environment.

Nothing would give me greater satisfaction than to be able to document Costa-Tôrres' rationale for the Asian origins of the Baroque. Certainly other theories of its origin have been equally unsatisfactory in terms of evidence and have likewise relied heavily on hypothetical resemblances. But study of the history of the Gesù shows, if anything, that its planners were not aware of either Asian or Portuguese architecture. The only bits of evidence of Asian influence which I have turned up tend to prove that Asia was still too remote to be seriously considered in any search for architectonic models. In 1599, for example, a portal made of wood from the Portuguese Indies was hung at one of the entrances to the Gesù,[32] but that is all that is known. Even the Jerónimos with their several congregations in Italy were national in their orientation and little interested in transmitting knowledge of Asia to Rome. And the international Jesuits, with their several houses in Portugal, seemed not to derive inspiration from the Jerónomite monastery at Belém with its maritime, Manueline features.[33] The Jesuit churches, other than the Gesù, likewise reveal in the sixteenth century no direct debt either to the forms or the decorative motifs ordinarily associated with the East.[34] Until further artistic and literary evidence can be produced to reinforce the case for an Oriental contribution to the

[30] See *Asia*, I, esp. pp. 280, 684–65.

[31] F. Haskell, *Patrons and Painters: A Study in the Relations between Italian Art and Society in the Age of the Baroque* (New York, 1963), pp. 65–66.

[32] J. Delumeau, *Vie économique et sociale de Rome* . . . (Paris, 1957), pp. 120–21.

[33] E. Mâle, *L'art religieux après le Concile de Trente* (Paris, 1932), pp. 500–501.

[34] For notice of a few relics from the East preserved in the Gesù see P. Pecchiai, *Il Gesù di Roma* (Rome, 1952), pp. 331, 345.

Baroque, the more traditional explanations must remain in the forefront. It might be wise, however, for serious students to consider the possibility of a Manueline contribution to the origins and development of the enigmatic Baroque, especially in its decorative aspects.

2

PAINTING

The painting of the early Renaissance was certainly subject to Oriental influence.[35] From the thirteenth century onward, the opening of the land route to China, the presence of European artists in the Crusader Kingdom of Jerusalem, the increase in the number of Oriental slaves in Europe, and the dissemination of descriptions in travel accounts helped to make the peoples and products of Asia known to Europeans. Nor was the availability of Chinese art to European artists so limited as it had previously been. Traders brought Chinese paintings as well as illustrated books, porcelains, textiles, and lacquerware into Constantinople in the fifteenth century, and these presumably could have been seen and studied in the Italian merchant colonies by Western artists as they were by Turkish miniaturists of the time.[36] Study of the Renaissance paintings themselves shows frequent use of Oriental persons and products and the introduction of lesser typological and stylistic elements which are comprehensible only in terms of borrowings from Chinese art.[37] Oriental subjects and decorative detail thus enriched European painting and helped to accelerate its break with medieval forms even before the discoveries began.

The opening of maritime relations with southern Asia in the sixteenth century brought Europeans into direct touch with a new and fantastic world that could have been best interpreted to Europe through the medium of sketches, drawings, and paintings. Oriental paintings were certainly brought to Europe at an early date, for Fernão Peres d'Andrade reportedly showed some Chinese paintings to King Manuel in 1520.[38] But European painters, like architects, seem not to have accompanied the early fleets sent out from Lisbon, though by the end of the century Hakluyt lists a "paynter" among those specialists required for the voyage to India.[39]

The earliest extant collection of paintings of Eastern life and peoples, probably

[35] See *Asia*, I, 72–74; also see R. A. Jairazbhoy, *Oriental Influences in Western Art* (Bombay, 1965).

[36] M. Loehr, "The Chinese Elements in the Istanbul Miniatures," *Ars orientalis*, I (1954), 89.

[37] H. Goetz, "Oriental Types and Scenes in Renaissance and Baroque Painting," *Burlington Magazine*, LXXIII (1938), 55–56; Y. Yashiro, "The 'Oriental' Character in Italian Pre- and Quattrocento Paintings," *East and West*, III (1952), 81–87.

[38] See above, p. 10. Bernardino de Escalante in his book on China (see *Asia*, pp. 742–43) wrote in 1577 that he had seen Chinese paintings of armored horsemen (chap. xvi in John Frampton's translation). Mendoza (see *Asia*, pp. 770–71) used Chinese paintings and porcelains as sources for his discussion of Chinese sailing chariots.

[39] E. G. R. Taylor (ed.), *The Original Writings and Correspondence of the Two Richard Hakluyts* (London, 1935), II, 482.

[64]

by a European, is the series of 141 colored drawings housed today in the Biblio-teca Casanatense in Rome.[40] The unknown painter was obviously an amateur artist of Portuguese or Luso-Indian origin[41] who made his sketches from life in India, probably in Goa and Cambay. From internal evidence it may be deduced that the watercolors were executed between 1533 and 1546.[42] It is possible that they were intended as illustrations for a book or routier, for they are arranged in a geographical order similar to those followed in the great travel accounts and histories of the era. They depict peoples, costumes, and customs of each land known to the Portuguese from the Cape of Good Hope to China.

The majority of the watercolors show scenes of India and its various peoples, but there are also pictures of the natives of Africa, Arabia, Persia, Indonesia, Indochina, Malacca, the Moluccas, and China. At the great marts of western India the artist probably saw and sketched the foreign Asian merchants, usually in their native costumes. The Indian scenes are rich in ethnographical detail and show people engaged in their common occupations: plowing, sowing, harvesting, driving oxen caravans, selling water, bathing, washing clothes, and hunting birds. Others of the paintings are of social and religious significance: sacrifices before the gods, marriages, pilgrimages, ritual suicide, and portraits of the *trimurti* (Shiva, Vishnu, and Brahma); others illustrate Indian military customs: Pathan warriors on horseback, war elephants, Nāyar warriors on foot, naval engagements, and duels. In his portraits of people of various castes and of foreign origin the artist tries, within the limits of his capabilities, to depict faithfully their peculiarities of feature, hairdress, and costume. While the artist does not see his subjects with the keen eye of the skilled painter, his renditions are simple, literal, and free from the artistic con-ventions that a more sophisticated artist might have brought to them.

That these are faithful depictions of Asia and Asians of the early sixteenth century there can be no question, particularly when the watercolors are checked against the literary sources of the period or compared to Asian paintings. It is not clear, however, when and how the watercolors got to Europe, or if they were ever used as models by European artists. In the register of the Biblioteca Casanatense they are designated simply as "Album di disegni indiani" (MS. 1889). It seems that the colored drawings were given to the Jesuits of the College of Goa and were then sent to Portugal and eventually to Rome.[43] It has been suggested that Fernão Mendes Pinto might have acquired and given them to the Jesuits. To support this contention we know that Pinto was a wealthy merchant in the East at midcentury, that he was for a period a member of the Society of

---

[40] For a description see G. Schurhammer, "Desenhos orientais do tempo de S. Francisco Xavier," in *Garcia da Orta*, Special Number (Lisbon, 1956), pp. 247–56. For reproductions of a number of these, see the plates in *Asia*, I, following p. 356, and, in this volume, plates 24–28.

[41] The captions and explanations on the paintings are all in Portuguese.

[42] Schurhammer, *loc. cit.* (n. 40), pp. 252–53.

[43] At the Casanatense, the former library of the Dominican fathers in Rome, the librarians told me in February, 1965, that they had no special information on the history of the collection. Also see *ibid.*, pp. 247–48.

Jesus, and that he describes Indian rituals in his *Peregrinations* in a way reminiscent of their depiction in the drawings.⁴⁴ Whatever Pinto's relations to the paintings may be, I have so far not seen any trace of their influence in sixteenth-century European art.

In the middle and latter half of the sixteenth century, other artists, both professional and amateur, European and native, drew, sketched, and painted scenes of life in the East and of the Portuguese activities there. Gaspar Corrêa, the author of the famous *Lendas de India,* "understood how to draw"⁴⁵ and so was ordered in 1547 by the governor D. João de Castro to paint the portraits of all the governors of India. He and a native artist of great skill painted on planks the portraits of the early governors on the basis of Corrêa's memory of them. They also directed their joint efforts to painting the Portuguese fortresses and armadas, and Corrêa certainly copied some of the portraits into the *Lendas.*⁴⁶ That the practice was continued throughout the sixteenth century of painting and hanging the portraits of the viceroys in the Great Hall of the Palace of Goa is attested to by Linschoten, who also reports that pictures of the ships that arrived in India were hung in an anteroom of the palace.⁴⁷ The gallery of the armadas no longer exists, but the portraits of the viceroys may still be seen in Goa at the Archaeological Museum.⁴⁸ Those on display today are copies or have been extensively retouched by later artists.⁴⁹

Other Indian artists painted portraits of the viceroys and ships of Portugal for the *Livro de Lizuarte de Abreu, 1558–64,* and for the *Livro das Armadas* both preserved in the Academy of Sciences at Lisbon.⁵⁰ In 1586 Sassetti wrote from Cochin to Grand Duke Francesco I of Tuscany that he knew of a local painter who could draw and color plants so well that he could depict clearly and in detail all the peculiarities of the many novel plants found in India.⁵¹ Linschoten brought sketches back from India which he published as engravings in 1596 in his *Itinerario,* and some of which he sent to Ortelius. These sketches are reminiscent of the Casanatense watercolors, particularly in their depiction of individuals, costumes, and decorative detail. It is distinctly possible that Linschoten's collection of sketches was produced by collaborative efforts between European amateurs and Indian professionals, even as were the portraits of the early viceroys.

⁴⁴ *Ibid.,* pp. 254–55.
⁴⁵ As quoted in A. Cortesão and A. Teixeira da Mota, *Portugaliae monumenta cartographica* (Lisbon, 1960–62), I, 168.
⁴⁶ *Ibid.,* p. 132.
⁴⁷ A. C. Burnell and P. A. Tiele (eds.), *The Voyage of John Huyghen van Linschoten to the East Indies* (London, 1885), I, 219.
⁴⁸ The Archaeological Museum established by the government of India is located in a modest building adjoining the cathedral in Old Goa. I viewed the 200 portraits on December 18, 1967, and found them to be in good condition.
⁴⁹ Most of the portraits were sent to Lisbon in 1956–57 for retouching and cleaning. See Cortesão and Teixeira da Mota, *op. cit.* (n. 45), I, 168.
⁵⁰ *Ibid.,* p. 170; also see J. A. Frazão de Vasconcellos, *As pinturas das armadas da India . . .* (Lisbon, 1941), pp. 27–30.
⁵¹ Marcucci, *op. cit.* (n. 25), p. 374; cf. below, p. 83.

The Jesuits, for all their avowed interest in art and in the architectural monuments of the East, did little to encourage the visual depiction of Asian life. Father Emmanuel Alvares (1526–1606), a painter, was sent to India in 1560, but he evidently spent most of his time either painting or teaching natives to paint Christian religious subjects.[52] The churches of Goa and its environs were designed, built, and decorated by Brother Aranha, a Portuguese Jesuit, and by John Storey, the English painter who arrived at Goa in 1583 with Ralph Fitch.[53] In 1583 Father Giovanni Nicolao, a Neapolitan painter, arrived in Japan and set to work teaching the young converts of the Jesuits to paint religious subjects.[54] That the Jesuits were eager to convert native artists is clear from their letters to Europe. But the missionaries appeared to be fearful of the religious side effects that might be expected if pagan subjects or art forms should be adopted or tolerated. Generally they insisted that the native artists should follow Christian designs as closely as possible, particularly when painting Christian subjects, constructing chapels and churches, or preparing sculptures of Christ and the saints.[55] Still it is fascinating to see, as in the Cathedral of Goa itself, how "idols" like Rama and Sita finally managed to invade the sacrosanct precincts of Christian iconography and sculpture.

In Portugal the century of empire building coincided with, and perhaps stimulated, a period of independent development in painting that has not been rivaled there since.[56] Close artistic relations with Flanders in the fifteenth century had helped to develop Portuguese artists of European significance, such as Nuno Gonçalves (fl. 1450–71), and a tradition which would come to flower in the first half of the sixteenth century at Lisbon, Evora, Coimbra, and Viseu. Painting in Portugal was placed under strict supervision by King Manuel, possibly as a part of his policy of royal control over information.[57] In 1508,

---

[52] Alvares also did a drawing in 1561 of a shipwreck off the coast of Sumatra, and it is preserved in the Jesuit Archives at Rome. As recently as 1941, the Armenian painter Sarkis Katchadourian bought a painting in Bombay which shows Vasco da Gama's fleet rounding the Cape of Good Hope and which seems to have been painted in India around the end of the sixteenth century by a European artist (see W. Born, "An Indo-Portuguese Painting of the Late Sixteenth Century," *Gazette des Beaux-Arts*, XXX [1946], 165–78). Might the unidentified painter be Father Alvares or one of his pupils?

[53] On Fitch's travels see *Asia*, I, 478–79; for other details see P. Brown, *Indian Painting under the Mughals, A.D. 1550 to A.D. 1750* (Oxford, 1924), p. 169.

[54] G. Schurhammer, "Die Jesuitenmissionäre des 16. und 17. Jahrhunderts und ihr Einfluss auf die japanische Malerei," *Jubiläumsband 1933 der deutschen Gesellschaft für Natur- und Völkerkunde Ostasiens*, I, 118. For further details see Kenji Toda, "The Effect of the First Great Impact of Western Culture in Japan . . .," *Journal of World History*, II (1954), 435–36.

[55] J. Irwin, "Reflections on Indo-Portuguese Art," *Burlington Magazine*, XCVII (1955), 387. The Jesuits often sent religious portraits painted by their converts in Asia as gifts to their patrons in Europe. For example, D. Leonor Mascarenhas in Portugal received in 1584 an "Ecce Homo" painted in Miyako by a Japanese convert. See J. A. Abranches Pinto et al., *La première ambassade du Japon en Europe* (Tokyo, 1942), p. 94.

[56] On the history of Portuguese painting see Barreira et al., *op. cit.* (n. 2), III, 229–75; R. dos Santos, *Oito seculos de arte portuguesa: Historia e espirito* (Lisbon, 1967), pp. 41–148; Kubler and Soria, *op. cit.* (n. 2), pp. 328–41; *L'art portugais de l'époque des grandes découvertes au XX siècle* (Paris, n.d.); G. Martin-Méry, *L'Europe et la découverte du monde* (Bordeaux, 1960).

[57] Cf. *Asia*, I, 151–54.

three years after the creation of the royal spice monopoly, the king named Jorge Afonso (d. 1551) as supervisor of painting. In 1529, Afonso was reconfirmed in this office by King John III. In his will, prepared in 1540, Jorge Afonso bequeathed to posterity the details which have enabled scholars to reconstruct the system of royal supervision over painting which he was responsible for creating and administering until his death in 1551 or 1552. It is possible that this strict supervision over information had the effect of discouraging the Portuguese artists from choosing subjects too closely related to the discoveries.

Jorge Afonso had a large atelier at Lisbon in which he trained a number of the leading masters of the Manueline era. Associated with him were other great Manueline painters: Gregório Lopes, Cristóvão de Figueiredo, Garcia Fernandes, and Gaspar Vaz. Since most of the masters eventually set up their own workshops, attributions to individual artists are often difficult to make with certainty even when the painters possessed personal styles of distinction. Outside the workshops, cooperative works were commonly undertaken by two or more painters. This system of cooperation under general supervision helped to produce a national style of painting, comparable to Manueline architecture, which displayed a high degree of iconographic and stylistic unity and permitted only a token amount of individuality to develop.

The pupil and son-in-law of Jorge Afonso, Gregório Lopes, had a career that spanned forty years (*ca.* 1510–50). Royal painter to the two kings who ruled during his lifetime, Lopes rubbed elbows with the royal servitors who had been to the East. His paintings, when compared to those of his contemporaries, show a preoccupation with the sea and the Orient not common in the western Europe of his day. His paintings, like those of many Venetian artists, are colorfully decorated with Oriental rugs and beturbaned persons clothed in rich brocades. His Adoration of the Magi (*ca.* 1520–30), like those of many of his contemporaries, shows a tawny Indian king wearing a rose-colored turban, pearl ear ornament, and a jacket and bodice fringed with pearls, who carries before him a large golden chalice as his gift to the Christ Child (pl. 31).[58] A member of Lopes' atelier seems also to have painted the portrait of Vasco da Gama around 1524, shortly before the admiral's departure for his last voyage to India. In the years just before 1539 Lopes himself executed the paintings which were destined to decorate the Manueline rotunda of the Templar church at Tomar.

The early paintings of Vasco Fernandes, a contemporary of Lopes and leader of the school of Viseu, are likewise reminiscent of Manueline architectural decoration in the serpentine undulations and rhythmic lines given to draperies and costumes. In Fernandes' Adoration of the Magi (post 1530) one of the kings

---

[58] Francisco Henriques (d. 1518), the Flemish painter who worked in Portugal, had painted a picture of the Magi for the Cathedral of Evora in which the dark king, negroid in his looks, wears an elaborate headdress with streamers and a heavy brocaded gown that makes him look much more affluent than the other two kings. In his hand he carries what could be a coconut in an elaborate silver mounting. See below, p. 75.

is a barefoot, spear-bearing Oriental with a circular feather headdress and neck piece, ear jewels, pearl necklace, and wrist and ankle bracelets. Feather costumes of this type seem to be associated in various other displays, as we have seen, with the natives of the insular regions of Asia. In his left hand the king is carrying as his gift what appear to be three lacquered bowls (pl. 30).

Garcia Fernandes, a pupil of Jorge Afonso and an associate of Lopes, likewise introduced Oriental elements into his paintings. He was considered by contemporaries to be the continuator of Francisco Henriques, the Flemish painter, whose daughter he married. In 1540 Fernandes stated that he had painted works for India, probably his "St. Catherine," which later hung in the Cathedral of Goa. His painting of the Annunciation now in the museum of Oporto includes a depiction of a Ming porcelain jar. In most of his later works, and in those of his followers, a tendency toward Manneristic experimentalism, a concern with complexity for its own sake, and a taste for the bizarre are displayed in the elongation of figures, in the treatment of space, and in the attention to still life.

The individual most responsible for bringing to Portugal the artistic viewpoint of the Italian Renaissance was Francisco D'Ollanda (1517–84), architect, miniaturist, and art theorist. With the aid of a grant from King John III, D'Ollanda spent the years 1537–41 in Italy studying art and sketching the antiquities of Rome. While there he claims to have had the good fortune to meet and discourse with Michelangelo and his circle. The record of his alleged conversations with the great Italian master are preserved in his book *Da pintura antiqua*, completed in 1548. Though this and his other writings were not published until modern times, they were circulated in manuscript and certain portions of them translated into Spanish. His sketchbook, preserved in the Escorial, is one of the best sources extant on the antiquities of Rome, as his drawings were made before the rehabilitation of the city and the new constructions undertaken at the Vatican in the latter half of the sixteenth century.[59]

D'Ollanda, who while in Rome became much enamored of the great empires of the past, was disdainful of European painting outside Italy. Time after time in his writings he sighs for the day when Rome will be rebuilt and the true art of Antiquity universally revived.[60] It is from Antiquity, he asserts, that one best understands the relations of man to nature. Antiquity is not to be confused with the old or aged. The old are the decrepit and valueless paintings done in Spain and Portugal. Antiquity does not include only the classical age of Greece and Rome; it also includes the Renaissance of the Italians. Antiquity is worthy of emulation because it chose man, the most perfect being on earth, as its subject and combined his most perfect parts and forms into ideal pictures. Its canon of beauty therefore necessarily sets the standard for all peoples at all times. The plastic and architectonic remains of Antiquity, not only of Athens

[59] For a reproduction see E. Tormo y Monzó, *Os desenhos das antigualhas que vio Francisco d'Ollanda, pintor português* (Madrid, 1940).

[60] See J. de Vasconcellos (ed.), *Francisco de Hollanda: Vier Gespräche über die Malerei geführt zu Rom 1538* (Vienna, 1899).

and Rome but also of France, Catalonia, Spain, Portugal, and North Africa, were designed according to the same basic principles. Indeed, "All of Asia reeks and smells of Antiquity."[61] Thus from D'Ollanda we learn that European artists of the mid-sixteenth century were concerned enough with the aesthetic implications of Asian art to try to find a place for it in the Antiquity idealized by Humanistic and artistic thought.

An intellectual-artistic readjustment was likewise taking place contemporaneously among the Europeans in Asia. The Jesuit Humanists in the East, from Xavier to Valignano, admired the temples of India and Japan and sent back word pictures of some of them to Europe. Certain observers even attributed the magnificent ruins they saw in the East to Alexander the Great or the Romans.[62] To the century that had witnessed the rediscovery of the Laocoön and the Golden House of Nero, the artistic deeds of the Greeks and Romans certainly seemed beyond comparison. So to associate Asiatic art with the revered treasures of western Antiquity was to accord it the greatest possible deference. The state of knowledge in Europe about the civilizations of Asia, and the state of knowledge prevailing with respect to Europe's relative position in the world, would not allow the art theorist of the sixteenth century to think in terms of independent artistic traditions which might rival in sophistication the greatest artistic achievements of the West. But, separated as they were by great physical and intellectual distances from Asia, thoughtful art theorists of the sixteenth century nonetheless clearly tried, though hesitantly, to explain as well as they could where Asia might be fitted into prevailing Humanistic and artistic canons.

In Part II of *Da pintura antiqua*, D'Ollanda gives his rendition of the conversations which he says he had with Michelangelo in Rome in 1538. Like many another convert to a new dispensation, D'Ollanda shows himself to be more literal and conventional than the great master in his view of Antiquity. He is especially troubled by the tendency of the Italian painters of his day—unquestionably the early Mannerists—to include grotesqueries, specters, and strange beasts and men in their works. He seems not to have had any feeling for what the unearthing of the "grotte" or the ruins of the Golden House of Nero had done to revolutionize mural and miniature painting from the time of Raphael onward.[63] When queried by D'Ollanda about the fantasizing of his contemporaries, Michelangelo replied that such freedom of expression, unnatural and strange as it might seem, is both excusable and commendable if it liberates the mind and pleases the eye of the viewer.[64]

Liberation of art, mind, and spirit from traditional restraints was one of the major revolutionary drives behind the Italian Mannerist movement (1520–1600)

---

[61] *Ibid.*, pp. lxxx–lxxxi.

[62] *Asia*, I, 280, 562 n., 684.

[63] For an excellent discussion of the influence of the Golden House on decoration and grotesqueries see A. von Salis, *Antike und Renaissance* (Zurich, 1947), pp. 39–43.

[64] Vasconcellos, *op. cit.* (n. 60), pp. 101–2.

in painting.[65] It began in Rome, Florence, and Venice and soon spread to the lesser Italian cities and to the artistic centers of France and northern Europe. In the artistic experiments of the early Mannerists the emphasis was upon creativity and originality as the artists, in the words of Benedetto Varchi, strove to produce in their works "an artificial imitation of nature."[66] Michelangelo, like Leonardo and Raphael, was attracted by the bizarre, the grotesque, and the exotic as he sought to find the meaning behind the reality.[67] But most of the Mannerist painters of Italy, like the Renaissance masters, remained sublimely unaware of the many ways in which they might have used the "subtle *ingenia*" of artists from another culture for their own creative purposes.

This is not to say that Italian painting completely escaped the impact of the discoveries. From the time of Giovanni da Udine, one of Raphael's pupils, to the end of the century, Asian designs and motifs appeared in arabesque and grotesque decorations (pls. 149, 150). But of course the acanthus, the palm leaves, and fantastic birds and animals had long been an accepted part of the European decorative vocabulary and but few new items were added to the painter's repertoire in the sixteenth century. The most favored plant decoration of the Mannerist was the moresque or arabesque, which was described by contemporaries as "heathen work" patterned after models of Levantine or Indian origin.[68] Later Mannerist painters, such as Jacopo Ligozzi (1547–1627) at Florence, were commissioned to paint pictures of the specimens of exotic plants which were acquired by Grand Duke Francesco I and by his scientific correspondent, Aldrovandi (pl. 36).[69] But Ligozzi's realistic paintings of exotica had no particular influence upon Mannerist ornament, or upon the prints portraying European findings in the East.

Nothing was more moving to the Jesuits and their artists in Europe than the conquests of Xavier in Asia and the story of his tragic death off the coast of China. This Christian Alexander, who fought the good fight without an army, died alone, almost like Christ himself, within sight of his ultimate goal. Episodes from the life and martyrdom of Xavier were painted on the walls of Jesuit chapels, houses, and colleges as reminders to the faithful of the efficacy of sacrifice in realizing the church triumphant. Erasmus Quellin (1607–78), for example, painted in the seventeenth century a continuous frieze in the Jesuit church of Malines which depicted Xavier preaching to the Asians, performing

[65] For general discussion see F. Baumgart, *Renaissance und Kunst des Manierismus* (Cologne, 1963); C. H. Smyth, *Mannerism and Maniera* (Locust Valley, N.Y., 1963); F. Würtenberger, *Der Manierismus* (Vienna, 1962); G. Briganti, *Italian Mannerism* (London, 1962); J. Bousquet, *La peinture manieriste* (Neuchâtel, 1964).

[66] As quoted in J. Shearman, *Mannerism* (London, 1967), p. 18.

[67] See M. Praz, *Bellezza e bizzurria* (Milan, 1960), p. 256.

[68] Based on a quotation from a sixteenth-century work on moresques in the Royal Library of Stockholm as given in E. Forssmann, *Säule und Ornament: Studien zum Problem des Manierismus in den nordischen Säulenbüchern und Vorlageblätter des 16. und 17. Jahrhunderts* (Stockholm, 1956), p. 127.

[69] O. H. Giglioli, "Jacopo Ligozzi disegnatore e pittore di piante e di animali," *Dedalo*, IV (1923–24), 556; also see Galleria degli Uffizi, *Mostra di disegni del Ligozzi (1547–1626)* (Florence, 1924), pp. 13–22.

miracles, and making conversions.[70] In the recreation room of the novices at Saint-André-en-Quirinal in Rome the future apostles to the Indies had frescoes before them of the martyrdoms suffered by the Jesuits at Salsette in India in 1583 and at Nagasaki in Japan in 1597.[71] But, even though these depictions all took place in Asia, the only traces of local color in the paintings are the feather and turban headdresses given to a number of the natives.

The painters in Italy showed relatively little interest in the strange physical features of the Japanese emissaries who visited there from February to August, 1585.[72] Although contemporaries remarked on their costumes, the artists seem not to have been interested in painting the envoys in native garb. The only commemorative portraits extant show the Japanese in the European garments given to them by Pope Gregory XIII (pl. 35).[73] The great Tintoretto (1518–94) was ordered by the Venetian senate to paint the portraits of the envoys. He evidently finished one of Mancio Itō, but not of the others, and it hung for a period in the great hall of the senate. But no modern record exists of the portrait itself and the earlier writers make no more than a mere mention of it.[74] It is possible that the Tintoretto portrait was taken back to Japan by the emissaries as an example of European painting, but nothing exists aside from circumstantial evidence to support this conclusion.[75] From the evidence that does remain to us in other extant portraits, it is striking to see that the artists paint the legates almost as if they were Europeans (pl. 35).

The Flemish painters, in their initial responses to the discoveries, restricted their experiments with overseas oddities to book and border ornaments. Pieter Coecke van Alost, Cornelis Bos, Cornelis Floris, and Colijn de Nole produced title pages and colophons which lent a great impulse to the growth of a Netherlandish ornament that was strikingly grotesque and exotic.[76] Flowers, fruits, animals, and plants from the Orient appear more frequently and more realistically in Netherlandish ornament than they do in painting elsewhere.[77] Miniature paintings of insects and other small creatures reached a high level of realistic perfection in the latter half of the century in the work of Georg Hoefnagel (1542–1600). He collected drawings of oddities for Ortelius' cabinet of curiosities[78] and painted rare flowers and animals for his patron, Emperor

[70] Mâle, *op. cit.* (n. 33), p. 438.

[71] *Ibid.*, pp. 117–20.

[72] Cf. *Asia*, I, 692–701.

[73] See *ibid.*, plates following p. 656; also see Abranches Pinto *et al.*, *op. cit.* (n. 55), pp. xxii, 162.

[74] See especially C. Ridolfi, *Vita di Giacopo Robusti detto il Tintoretto* . . . (Venice, 1642), p. 89. See the print of the Japanese youth in Western costume in C. Vecellio, *Habiti antichi et moderni di tutte il mondo* (2d ed.; Venice, 1598), facing p. 477. Is it possible that Vecellio has reproduced the Tintoretto portrait in this engraving?

[75] Cf. C. R. Boxer, "Portuguese Influence in Japanese Screens from 1590 to 1614," *Connoisseur*, XCVIII (1936), 80–81.

[76] See G. Marlier, *La renaissance flamande, Pierre Coeck d'Alost* (Brussels, 1966), p. 385.

[77] See M. L. Hairs, *Les peintres flamands de fleurs au XVIIᵉ siècle* (Brussels, 1955), pp. 7–8. Cf. especially the still life by Frans Snyders (fl. 1579) which shows a lobster on a Chinese porcelain plate along with a monkey and a parrot (National Museum, Stockholm, No. 637).

[78] A. E. Popham, "On a Letter of Joris Hoefnagel," *Oud-Holland*, LIII (1936), 147–49.

Rudolf II. The drawing and painting of exotic objects for the collectors helped to stimulate the growth of still life in the sixteenth century. Some of the still lifes produced then are themselves pictorial collections of rarities.[79]

As still-life and flower paintings became genres in themselves, the depiction of flowers, fruits, and plants was done with such accuracy and care that most species can be readily identified. The painters, especially the watercolorists, evidently did not work from engravings of plants in scientific books; the flowers in their bouquets are all drawn from actual specimens.[80] The porcelains in their still lifes and the seashells which decorate their flower paintings are likewise readily identifiable. The vases and ewers are almost always Chinese porcelains. The seashells so far studied by conchologists are never local varieties; they all come from distant places, especially Asia and America.[81] The textiles in early "breakfast pieces" are so clearly drawn that in a number of cases their places of origin can be determined by studying the pattern of the weave.

Landscape painting, like still lifes, became an end in itself in the sixteenth century, especially in the works of Pieter Brueghel the Elder (*ca.* 1525–69). In the Gothic landscape the enclosed garden (called "Paradise" in Persian) had been a piece of protected perfection outside of which there lay nothing but twisted, tortured rocks, forbiddingly dark forests, and brooding mountains.[82] In the painting of the fifteenth century the backgrounds were often spectacular, realistic landscapes. Bosch, Patinir, and Jean de Cock produced rocky and tortuous landscapes as grounds for the exotic plants, animals, and people with which they crowded their paintings of a fantastic world.[83] In 1551, when Brueghel went to Italy, the Mannerists there were already painting fantastic panoramas from an elevated viewpoint with distant prospects of craggy mountains, serpentine rivers, and jagged coast lines. Niccolò dell'Abbate (1505–71) in his mythological landscapes helped to turn the attention of Italian painters away from their preoccupation with the human figure to the portrayal of nature in which man is but a part rather than the center of the universe.[84] Brueghel, during his travels to Italy, painted atmospherically the sharp and lofty peaks and the deep ravines of the Alps.[85]

A number of art historians—Oskar Münsterberg, Charles Sterling, Jorge Baltrušaitis, Jacques Bousquet—have recently pointed out the analogies in composition and spirit between these early Western panoramas and Chinese

[79] I. Bergström, *Dutch Still-Life Painting in the Seventeenth Century* (London, 1956), p. 41.

[80] Hairs, *op. cit.* (n. 77), pp. 14–15.

[81] Bergström, *op. cit.* (n. 79), pp. 64–65; also see W. S. S. van Benthem-Jutting, "A Brief History of the Conchological Collections at the Zoölogical Museum of Amsterdam, with Some Reflections on 18th Century Shell Cabinets and Their Proprieters . . . ," *Bijdragen tot de Dierkunde*, XXVII (1939), 167–246.

[82] K. Clark, *Landscape Painting* (New York, 1950), pp. 4–10, 26–27.

[83] For further discussion see P. Fierens, *Le fantastique dans l'art flamand* (Brussels, 1947), p. 58. As examples see pls. 37 and 38.

[84] Bousquet, *op. cit.* (n. 65), pp. 270–75.

[85] F. Grossmann, *Bruegel: The Paintings* (rev. ed.; London, 1966), p. 17.

landscape paintings.[86] At Paris in 1960 an exposition was held at the Louvre on landscape painting in the Orient and the Occident from Antiquity to the present century.[87] The commentator on the exposition, Charles Sterling, sees the sixteenth-century European landscape as an idealization of nature. It stands as a symbol for the planet as the perfect courtier symbolizes the ideal man. Nature, which realizes its ideal beauty only when comprehended in its complete fullness, is presented by the landscape painters in both its savage and its civilized detail. Everywhere, as in the Chinese landscapes, the eye is on a level with each detail. The multiple perspective of the painting enables the eye to travel down every valley, to the top of every peak, and to the edge of each precipice. And often the landscape is in monochrome, a synthetic, artistic device which enables the Western panoramas to present something of the poetic unity demanded by the landscape ideal evolved in Sung China. But, while a similarity seems to exist between the Chinese and Western conceptions of nature, the fundamental difference in viewpoint—palpable naturalism in the West and an abridged realism impregnated with spirit in the East—precluded any concrete similarities in painting except for sporadic borrowing of motifs.

But from where might the motifs be borrowed? Most obviously they could have been copied from the pictorial motifs on the ceramics, lacquerware, and textiles that were available from the fourteenth century onward.[88] They might also have been borrowed from illustrations in Chinese books or from the paintings on Japanese screens that became increasingly numerous in sixteenth-century Europe.[89] The rugged rocky outgrowths and rolling banks of clouds, the dragons and phoenixes that appear in Renaissance paintings, look as if they might have been derived from such sources.[90] A Florentine *cassone* of 1448, now at Berlin, is studded with Oriental motifs, the clouds in it forming an easily discernible Chinese dragon. In the painting called "Sodom in Flames" attributed to Lucas van Leyden (1494–1533) a Chinese phoenix, similar to those commonly found on lacquerware, descends from heaven. The buildings in the

[86] O. Münsterberg, "Leonardo da Vinci und die chinesische Landschaftsmalerei," *Orientalisches Archiv*, XII (1910), 92–100; C. Sterling, "Le paysage dans l'art européen...," *L'Amour de l'art*, 1931, pp. 9–21, 101–12; J. Baltrušaitis, *Le moyen-âge fantastique* (Paris, 1955), p. 211; Bousquet, *op. cit.* (n. 65), p. 275.

[87] Catalogue published under the direction of Germaine Cart is entitled *Le paysage en Orient et en Occident* (Paris, 1960). This exposition followed one held two years previously at the Musée Cernuschi.

[88] *Ibid.*, pp. 13–14.

[89] For mention of some of the Chinese books in Europe see *Asia*, I, 738, 745, 747, 750n., 756n., 778–80, 803, 805n. Many of these books were illustrated. For example, see the pages reproduced from a sixteenth-century collection of Chinese plays and lyrics that is now in the library of the Escorial and that was probably brought to Spain before 1585. See J. J. Y. Liu, "The Fêng-yüeh Chin-nang: A Ming Collection of Yüan and Ming Plays and Lyrics Preserved in the Royal Library of San Lorenzo, Escorial, Spain," *Journal of Oriental Studies* (Hongkong), IV (1957–58), pls. I–XI. But, since these illustrations show personages mainly, this particular work would certainly have little meaning for landscape painting. It is introduced at this point merely to show that illustrated Chinese books were available and that some of them might well have contained depictions of landscapes as well as portraits of individuals.

[90] For an illustration of how the Chinese cloud motif might have become a European tear motif see V. Slomann, *Bizarre Designs in Silks* (Copenhagen, 1953), p. 142.

paintings of Hieronymus Bosch (*ca.* 1460–1516), the master who most directly inspired Brueghel, seem likewise to owe a debt to Chinese and Indian motifs. Dürer, in his drawings of fantastic pillars, apparently used Ming porcelain vases as models for some of his eccentric designs (pl. 29).[91] And, finally, we know that Chinese paintings on silk were collected in Europe, because two of those collected at Ambras are still preserved in Vienna.[92] Georg Hoefnagel, who was employed at Ambras from 1582 to 1590, painted more than one hundred pictures of its natural history collections,[93] and could certainly have studied the Chinese studio paintings there—especially the one that is full of flowers (pl. 4).

Several biblical and classical themes painted regularly in the sixteenth century have the Orient as their locale. In the literary traditions of the early Church the Magi were generally thought of as coming from Persia, and in the most ancient depictions of them it is clear that they were understood to be servants of Mithra, the ancient cultic god of Persia and India.[94] In the Middle Ages the Magi were fixed at three in number and were elevated in rank from Wise Men to Kings. They were also given the names of Melchior (Persia), Caspar (India-Ethiopia), and Balthazar (Arabia), and were declared in the thirteenth-century *Golden Legend* of Jacobus de Voragine to represent the three different generations of humanity: European, Asian, and African. Caspar, the youngest of the Three Kings, begins to be depicted by the beginning of the fifteenth century as a black king from Africa, while Balthazar shows up with increasing regularity as an Oriental of indeterminate origin. In the sixteenth century the gifts that both bear appear more frequently to be portraits of Oriental products available to the artists of Europe, and the youngest of the kings turns up occasionally as an Afro-Asian primitive with feather headdress, spear, and arm bracelets (pl. 30). The black kings in the triptychs of the Magi executed by the Netherlandish painters often carry a gift of rhinoceros horn set in and decorated with silver.[95] Hieronymus Bosch, Jan Gossaert Mabuse, and Roger van der Weyden include swarthy kings in rich Oriental robes in their paintings of the Magi.

The Flemish painters throughout the sixteenth century treat the Magi with a secularized extravagance and vigor which contrasts markedly with the quiet piety shown in the paintings of the kings by the masters of the fifteenth century.[96] To Brueghel the Elder is attributed an Adoration of the Magi, now located in Brussels, in the background of which there stand numbers of Orientals as well as camels and elephants. In his Adoration of 1563, now in Vienna, the dark

[91] For discussion see R. Schmidt, "China bei Dürer," *Zeitschrift des deutschen Vereins für Kunstwissenschaft*, VI (1939), 103–6.

[92] Cf. above, p. 27.

[93] G. Händler, *Fürstliche Mäzene und Sammler in Deutschland von 1500–1620* (Strassburg, 1933), pp. 49–50.

[94] H. Kehrer, *Die "Heiligen Drei Könige" in der Legende und in der deutschen bildenden Kunst bis Albrecht Dürer* (Strassburg, 1904), *passim;* and H. Baudet, *Paradise on Earth: Some Thoughts on European Images of Non-European Man* (New Haven, Conn., 1965), pp. 17–18. Also see above, p. 68.

[95] See the numerous reproductions of Netherlandish triptychs in Marlier, *op. cit.* (n. 76), pp. 117–63. Also cf. above, p. 7.

[96] See Fierens, *op. cit.* (n. 83), p. 60.

king holds as his gift a silver sailing vessel that bears a beautiful nautilus shell and in the background stands a camel.[97] Certain commentators, such as Jean Macer, seek to prove all three kings came from afar to the Holy Land, not merely from the surrounding Levantine peoples. The three Magi should thus be shown, he contends, as coming from east of the Holy Land, specifically from "Therse," Turkestan, and Cathay.[98] When Caesar Baronius (1538–1607) in his *Annales ecclesiastici* . . . discusses the Magi, he does not concern himself with questioning their names, ages, or colors, but is far more interested to know what parts of Asia they really came from.[99]

Italian painters from Raphael to Annibale Carracci (1560–1609) portray the mythological triumph of Bacchus in India. In his magnificent composition for the center of the ceiling of the Farnese Gallery in Rome, Carracci brings India into the upper left-hand corner of his painting by showing an elephant with rider and a beturbaned Oriental carrying a pitcher on his head (pl. 131). The Asian atmosphere is heightened by having Bacchus' chariot pulled by two tigers.[100] The problem of how to depict Asia and its people had also to be resolved in the allegorical paintings of the "four parts of the world." Until the discovery of America, the pictorial maps showed only Asia, Africa, and Europe. In the late sixteenth century the designers and painters began to produce paintings showing the triumph of Europe over the rest of the world. Hans Fugger in 1580 ordered a "Triumph of the Four Quarters of the World" for his new castle at Kirchheim to show allegorically the wealth and extent of the Fugger interests. The triumph of Asia painted for this series by Pauwels Franck (1540–96), a Flemish artist, is considered to be the best of the four portrayals (pl. 34).[101] But it shows no advance in realism over the Venetian triumphs of the fifteenth century or over the beturbaned Orientals of Martin Schongauer (*ca.* 1430–91).

The painters who worked at Prague in the court of Rudolf II climax the sixteenth-century interest in the bizarre and exotic. Georg Hoefnagel and Roelant Savery (*ca.* 1577–1639) brought to the imperial court the Flemish interest in the painting of exotic animals and flowers. The four volumes of animals painted by Hoefnagel at Prague were evidently intended for use in wall decorations.[102] The exotic animals and plants in Savery's many paintings form a kind of artistic biological garden in themselves.[103] Savery brings the birds and animals from all parts of the world into his naturalistic paintings. Orpheus is shown with

[97] A. L. Romdahl, "Pieter Brueghel der Ältere und sein Kunstschaffen," *Jahrbuch der kunsthistorischen Sammlungen des allerhöchsten Kaiserhauses*, XXV (1905), 100 and pl. XIV.

[98] J. Macer, *Les trois livres de l'histoire des Indes* (Paris, 1555), pp. 47–49.

[99] As discussed in Mâle, *op. cit.* (n. 33), p. 249.

[100] For complete reproduction see J. R. Martin, *The Farnese Gallery* (Princeton, N.J., 1965), pl. 69.

[101] See S. M. Rinaldi, "Appunti per Paolo Fiammingo," *Arte veneta*, XIX (1965), 99. Also see below, p. 192.

[102] E. Kris, "Georg Hoefnagel und die wissenschaftliche Naturalismus," *Festschrift für Julius Schlösser* (Zurich, 1927), pp. 243–53.

[103] For a general survey of his exotic works see J. Bialostocki, "Les bêtes et les humaines de Roelant Savery," *Musées royaux des Beaux-Arts Bulletin* (Brussels), No. 1 (March, 1958), pp. 69–97.

animals from Asia that he could not possibly have known, a clear indication of Savery's determination to depict the chronological and geographical unity of the world of nature (pls. 111, 143).

Giuseppe Arcimboldo (1527–93), artist at the Habsburg court from 1560 to 1587, produced a large number of paintings now referred to as *têtes composées*. He arranged animals, fish, flowers, fruits, and vegetables into fantastic portraits of human heads and faces; he also arranged human figures into animal portraits (pls. 39, 40). Art historians have sought antecedents for these grotesque compositions in the sketches and remarks of Leonardo,[104] in the bizarre paintings of Bosch, in the ornamental grotesques of Giovanni da Udine,[105] in the experiments of the Mannerists with masks, in the reflected human image in ancient depictions of Bacchus where the wine god is made of grapes and the vine, in the satirical medals and caricatures of the Reformation where the pope is given the head of a donkey, and even in the murals designed for covered markets and inns to provide atmospheric backgrounds.[106] But the works which most closely resemble in idea and execution the composite heads of Arcimboldo are the Mughul miniature paintings of fantastic animals[107] which are mosaics of intertwined animal and human forms (pls. 41, 42, 43).[108] In the Hindu tradition such paintings possibly represent the belief in the internal unity of all beings and illustrate the doctrine of the transmigration of souls through successive reincarnations. It is possible, though precise documentation does not exist, that Arcimboldo was stimulated to experiment with composite figures after seeing Indian miniature paintings on ivories or in books that belonged to the imperial collection of curiosities.[109] In Arcimboldo's works also, and in the calligraphic Indian portraits of animals, as well as in the interesting and provocative displays of the *Wunderkammer*, an effort was obviously made to stress the mystical and ambiguous relationship of man to the natural world. It is even possible that Arcimboldo, like the Indian painters, was trying to express a belief in metempsychosis, a popular doctrine of his day and one that almost certainly had appeal for his enigmatic imperial master.

---

[104] In his *Notebooks* Leonardo tells how to make an imaginary animal appear real by making each part of it from a known beast (E. McCurdy [trans. and ed.], *The Notebooks of Leonardo da Vinci* [New York, 1958], I, 15); for some experiments along the line of Leonardo's suggestion see B. Geiger, *I dipinti ghiribizzosi di Giuseppe Arcimboldi* . . . (Florence, 1954), pp. 36–40, 46–47.

[105] P. Wescher, "The 'Idea' in Giuseppe Arcimboldo's Art," *Magazine of Art*, XLIII (1950), 3.

[106] For details see F. C. Legrand and F. Sluys, *Arcimboldo et les arcimboldesques* (Brussels, 1955), pp. 71–75.

[107] The artistic analogue between the "marvelous" miniatures of India and the composite heads of Arcimboldo was first pointed out in J. Strzygowski *et al.*, *Asiatische Miniaturenmalerei* (Klagenfurth, 1933), p. 223.

[108] See also "The Combat of Elephants" reproduced in K. M. Ball, *Decorative Motives of Oriental Art* (London, 1927), pp. 74–75.

[109] Legrand and Sluys, *op. cit.* (n. 106), pp. 72–73; a specific denial of Asian influence on Arcimboldo's art is made by R. Caillois, *Au coeur du fantastique* (Paris, 1965), p. 25. Such denials are based on the assertion that Arcimboldo painted composite heads in Milan before he even went to Prague. Ordinarily it is asserted that Rembrandt was the first of the European artists to be inspired by the Indian miniatures. See Brown, *op. cit.* (n. 53), pp. 24–25.

3

WOODCUTS AND ENGRAVINGS

In China the art of printing with wood blocks on textiles and paper developed as early as the eighth century A.D., and pictures printed from wood blocks began to appear shortly thereafter. In Europe textile printing was common throughout the Middle Ages, but the European technique seems not to have been influenced at this period by the Chinese method of textile printing. Woodcuts imprinted on paper and vellum were not produced in Europe until the late fourteenth century. The appearance of block books in Europe during the early fifteenth century preceded by a number of years the invention of typography. Chinese printed textiles, playing cards, and image prints which circulated in late medieval Europe certainly influenced the development of block printing there. To what extent the European technique of printing with movable type was indebted to the Chinese and Korean examples is a complicated problem that is still being debated by specialists.[110]

In the early blockbooks produced in fifteenth-century Europe the text and the illustrations were cut upon the same block of wood. The blockbooks reached the height of their popularity in the Low Countries around the middle of the fifteenth century.[111] But with the invention of movable type about 1450, book illustrations had to be cut into separate blocks. In the sixteenth century many books appeared in which the illustrations were accorded far more space and prominence than the texts. The hieroglyphic books, for example, are today far more important for their woodcuts than for their texts. Woodcuts continued also to be issued independently and singly throughout the fifteenth and sixteenth centuries.

Line engraving upon metal, an art closely related to the techniques of the gold- and silversmiths, was first experimented with in northern Europe in the mid-fifteenth century.[112] It proved, however, to be far less convenient for book illustration than the woodcut and was consequently not developed further for this purpose until the sixteenth century. As time went on, the need for a finer technique, particularly for the reproduction of maps,[113] stimulated

[110] For the transmission of block printing westward see T. F. Carter and L. C. Goodrich, *The Invention of Printing in China and Its Spread Westward* (2d ed.; New York, 1955), pp. 201–8, 241–43; for a sixteenth-century acknowledgment of Europe's debt to China see G. Panciroli, *The History of Many Memorable Things Lost . . .* (London, 1715), Pt. II, p. 338; for the European history of woodcuts see C. Dodgson, *Catalogue of Early German and Flemish Woodcuts* (London, 1903), I, v–vi; and A. M. Hind, *An Introduction to a History of Woodcut . . .* (Boston and New York, 1935), I, 64–96.

[111] A. Stevenson, "The Quincentennial of Netherlandish Blockbooks," *British Museum Quarterly*, XXXI (1967), 83–84.

[112] S. Colvin, *Early Engraving and Engravers in England* (London, 1905), p. 26.

[113] See A. M. Hind, *A History of Engraving and Etching . . .* (London, 1927), pp. 19–22, 105–10. On the revival and final triumph of copperplate engraving in cartography see R. A. Skelton, *Decorative Printed Maps of the 15th to 18th Centuries* (London, 1952), pp. 42–50.

Plantin, Mercator, Ortelius, and others to use engraved illustrations. Etching, or the art of engraving with acid on metal plates and the making of prints therefrom, likewise developed in the sixteenth century and was widely used in book illustration. By the last generation of the sixteenth century prints derived from plates began to replace the woodcut in a wide variety of scientific and technical books that required sharp and accurate illustrating. Maps, plants, animals, human portraits, and religious themes were among the subjects most commonly engraved or etched in Germany, the Netherlands, and Italy.

The cities of south Germany, shortly to be followed by those of the Low Countries, led the way in the development of printing and in the related arts of woodcuts and metal engraving. German, Flemish, and Dutch artists were called upon in the early sixteenth century to supply illustrations for the expanding industry of book production. The preparation of single sheet prints and woodcut illustrations for books took up a large share of the creative industry of Albrecht Dürer at Nuremberg, Hans Burgkmair at Augsburg, Lucas Cranach at Wittenberg, Hans Baldung at Strassburg, Lucas van Leyden at Leyden, and of a great many others at Antwerp and Amsterdam. These cities, besides being centers of book production, were intimately involved in international commerce and in the financing of the discoveries. The book illustrations and the separate prints produced in the shops of these cities helped from the beginning of the sixteenth century to diffuse knowledge of the overseas world. The superb quality of their woodcuts made the German books on the discoveries much more popular for general reading than the unillustrated or crudely illustrated books which were at first produced in southern Europe.

Emperor Maximilian I (ruled 1493–1519) lent his moral and financial support to the development of the print in Germany. Ever eager to glorify his own achievements, the emperor corralled the finest literary and artistic talents among his subjects to prepare a series of allegorical "Triumphs" that would tell his story in verse and woodcut for the benefit of posterity. To this end he employed the vast talents of Dürer, Burgkmair, Hans Schäufelein (1480–1538), and a bevy of lesser artists. His famous "Triumphal Arch," first printed in 1517, was composed and executed by Dürer and his circle. In this symbolic and fanciful arch the memories of Maximilian's reign that were dearest to his heart and best for his public image are preserved in woodcuts of the emperor's ancestors, battles, and key successes. To highlight the emperor's claim to universal dominion, Dürer included three small woodcuts under the title "The Isles of India and the Ocean" (pl. 123) which symbolically depict Maximilian's control over Africa (the elephant), over Asia (the rhinoceros), and over America (a seascape dotted with rocky islets). The "Triumph of Maximilian," a sequence of 137 woodcuts depicting a procession of persons and events connected with the emperor's reign, was uncompleted when Maximilian died in 1519. So great a series of woodcuts could not, however, be left unpublished. The first edition of the "Triumph," as it appeared in 1526, included the famous three sheets (nos. 129–31) executed by Burgkmair, possibly aided by Albrecht Altdorfer (1488–1578), and entitled "People of Calicut" (pls. 44 and 87).[114] Among the verses attached to those woodcuts is one which boasts:

> The Emperor in his warlike pride,
> Conquering nations far and wide,
> Has brought beneath our Empire's yoke
> The far-off Calicuttish folk.
> Therefore we pledge him, with our oath
> Lasting obedience and troth.[115]

Dürer, like Burgkmair and Altdorfer, also drew pictures of Oriental people. Most of Dürer's Oriental subjects are from before 1500 and seem to be adaptations of the Turks and the Circassian slave girls drawn by Gentile Bellini.[116] Both Dürer and Burgkmair did droll drawings of Orientals and Asian scenes as marginal illustrations for the Prayer Book of Maximilian I. And Dürer did drawings of two emblematic columns (pl. 29) which include fantastic vases that have been identified as Chinese porcelains. In 1515 Dürer possibly had a part in designing the terrestrial map of the Eastern Hemisphere which was published under the auspices of Johannes Stabius.[117] Dürer also made singularly fine drawings of Asian animals, including the rhinoceros, parrots, and monkeys.

Burgkmair, who was closely associated with the Welsers of Augsburg, prepared in 1508 a series of five great woodcuts called the "King of Cochin" series. These were designed as illustrations for the book published in 1509 recounting Balthasar Springer's experiences in India during 1505–6.[118] The inscriptions on the woodcuts link them directly to the book and the subjects discussed in the text, such as the ceremonial processions of the king of Cochin, are depicted in the illustrations. Students of Burgkmair have advanced various theories about his sources for these woodcuts. Most commonly they have linked the woodcuts to Springer's narrative descriptions and to the changes that came in Burgkmair's work with his return from Venice in 1508.[119] It has also been argued, however, that he based his drawings upon watercolors made by an artist who had actually been on the voyage. This argument is advanced to

[114] On Altdorfer's role see F. Winzinger, "Albrecht Altdorfer und die Miniaturen des Triumphzuges Kaiser Maximilian I," *Jahrbuch der kunsthistorischen Sammlungen in Wien*, N.S., LXII (1966), 165–66 and pl. 18*b*.

[115] The inclusion of the "People of Calicut" was probably the emperor's own idea when he dictated in 1512 the plan for the triumph. The English translation is from Stanley Appelbaum (ed.), *The Triumph of Maximilian I* (New York, 1964), p. 19.

[116] E. Panofsky, *The Life and Art of Albrecht Dürer* (Princeton, 1955), II, nos. 1249–58, includes a list of his drawings in which the subjects are Orientals.

[117] *Ibid.*, no. 405.

[118] Entitled *Die Merfart . . .*, the contents of this small book are summarized in *Asia*, I, ·163. For reproductions of two of the woodcuts see *Asia*, I, plates after p. 164 and p. 356. For descriptions of the originals in the Welser archives see Dodgson, *op. cit.* (n. 110), II, 71.

[119] On the critical importance to his work of Burgkmair's Venetian interlude see E. von Huber, "Die Malerfamilie Burgkmair von Augsburg," *Zeitschrift des historischen Vereins für Schwaben und Neuburg*, I (1874), 313–14.

explain why the physiognomy of the Orientals is more realistic on Burgkmair's woodcuts than on those of Theodor de Bry of almost a century later.[120] Others have pointed out that Burgkmair's elephant in the "People of Calicut" series is more realistic than the conventional elephants in Andrea Mantegna's "Triumph of Caesar."[121] It has also been observed that the parasol or *chattra* held over the king of Cochin's head as a symbol of his exalted position is of a type that is clearly recognizable as of south Indian origin.[122] For my own part I prefer the watercolor theory because of the close resemblances of the Oriental figures, costumes, and weapons in Burgkmair's series to those in the watercolors preserved in the Biblioteca Casanatense of Rome.[123] In both instances the shields of the individual Indian warriors are circular, the breechcloth is similarly knotted about the middle, the right arm which holds the sword is held at about the same angle, the hair is gathered into a topknot, and the elaborate ear ornaments are circular. On the basis of these comparisons I think that the theory of derivation from watercolors is tenable and a more likely explanation than one that relies exclusively on the literary text as the source.

While Dürer, Burgkmair, and Altdorfer executed their drawings of the Indian rhinoceros in 1515,[124] other south German artists worked on illustrations for travel and geographical books. Burgkmair's engravings in the "King of Cochin" series appear to have been pirated by Jan van Doesborch, the Flemish publisher of early travel accounts.[125] The forty-four woodcuts of Jorg Breu (1480–1537),[126] a native of Antwerp who worked at Augsburg from 1508 to 1534, were used in the German version of the *Itinerario* of Ludovico di Varthema (*ca.* 1470–1517) published at Augsburg in 1515 and again in 1518.[127] Michael Ostendorfer (*ca.* 1490–1559) of Ratisbon drew a heart-shaped projection of Apian's world map (1530) on which the busts of Ptolemy and Vespucci appear in fantastic Oriental costume.[128] Other artists prepared woodcuts of Asiatic plants, such as rhubarb, for publication in the printed newsletters of the day.[129]

The Germans also took the lead in the illustration of botanical and zoological books. The German *Herbarius* (also called the *Ortus sanitatis*) published in 1485 set a standard for botanical illustration that went unchallenged for the next fifty years.[130] In the beginning years of the sixteenth century the only herbals with illustrations approaching in realism those of the *Ortus sanitatis* were the

---

[120] W. F. Oakeshott, *Some Woodcuts by Hans Burgkmair* (Oxford, 1960), pp. 8–9.

[121] Appelbaum, *op. cit.* (n. 115), pp. 18–19, n. 71. But also see below, pp. 133–34.

[122] H. Goetz, "An Indian Element in 17th Century Dutch Art," *Oud-Holland*, LIV (1937), 224–25.

[123] See above, pp. 64–66, for discussion of the Casanatense watercolors.

[124] See below, pp. 163–65, for discussion.

[125] See Oakeshott, *op. cit.* (n. 120), pp. 12–13.

[126] For commentary and one selected reproduction see F. W. H. Hollstein, *German Engravings, Etchings, and Woodcuts* (Amsterdam, 1954), IV, 177.

[127] Entitled *Die Ritterlich und lobwirdig raisz des gestregen und uber all ander weyt erfarnen ritters un landt-farers, herrn Ludowico Vartomans von Bolonia.* A copy is in the British Museum.

[128] Dodgson, *op. cit.* (n. 110), II, 249–50.

[129] *Ibid.*, p. 140.

[130] W. Blunt, *The Art of Botanical Illustration* (London, 1950), p. 33.

botanical books then being produced at Venice. A new epoch in the history of botanical illustration was ushered in with the publication in 1530 of the first volume of Otto Brunfels' *Herbarum vivae icones* (Living Portraits of Plants). Brunfels (d. 1534) was an unoriginal and doctrinaire botanist; the excellent reception accorded his work he owed to the great draftsmanship of Hans Weiditz (*ca.* 1500–*ca.* 1536), whose portraits of domestic plants were so distinguished that they were once thought to be the work of Dürer.[131] The *De historia stirpium* (History of Plants) of Leonhard Fuchs (1501–66), published in 1542, is most valuable for its original and lifelike illustrations of European plants. P. A. Mattioli, personal physician to Emperor Maximilian II, brought a new popularity to the book of Dioscorides by introducing into his 1554 edition of it illustrations by Giorgio Liberale and Wolfgang Meyerpeck.[132] Indeed, an opinion has been expressed that the naturalism of the illustrations in the old herbals and natural histories possibly slowed down the development of the art of literary description in botany.[133] The generally low level of understanding of the early botanists about the geographical distribution of plants certainly had the effect of keeping botany parochial and its leaders unaware of the scientific implications of the new plants that were being imported from overseas. It was even uncommon before midcentury for the botanist to press and dry exotic specimens that could be used by the artist as models.[134]

Floriculture developed in Europe on an extensive scale only in the latter half of the sixteenth century. The garden founded at the University of Padua in 1543 became the model for the scientific garden and the botanical counterpart and outdoor adjunct of the *Kunstkammer*. Here the scientist could grow exotic plants from the seeds and bulbs brought from distant places; here the artist could sketch the plants from life. Most of the Oriental plants imported came into Europe through Venice from the Levant. But, in the latter half of the century, the Portuguese and the Jesuits also began to describe more frequently the plants they had seen and to send back dried samples of plants, seeds, and bulbs.

A revolution in the European view of Asian plant life was sparked by the publication in India of the *Coloquios* (1563) of Garcia da Orta, a Portuguese physician.[135] The original work and the Latin epitome of it published by Charles de L'écluse (Clusius) at Antwerp in 1567 were not illustrated. It was left to the Spanish botanist, Cristobal de Acosta (d. 1580), to publish in his extended version of Orta's work the first illustrations of Asian plants. In his *Tractado* (1578) Acosta provided moderately well-drawn woodcuts of forty-six plants, including the roots.[136] L'écluse, who also epitomized Acosta's work in

[131] *Ibid.*, p. 45.
[132] For discussion see J. Stannard, "Dioscorides and Renaissance Materia Medica," *Analecta medico-historica*, I (1966), 9–10.
[133] A. Arber, *Herbals: Their Origin and Evolution* (Cambridge, 1938), p. 150.
[134] *Ibid.*, pp. 138–39.
[135] For details on Orta and the publication history of his book see *Asia*, I, 192–95. A recent evaluation of the importance of the *Coloquios* to the history of botany is C. das Neves Tavares, "A botânica nos *Colóquios* de Garcia da Orta," in *Garcia da Orta*, XI, No. 4 (1963), 667–93.
[136] For reproductions of several of his plant portraits, see *Asia*, I, following p. 100.

Latin translation, considered his illustrations poor and unlifelike. To remedy this deficiency L'écluse soon began to work with Christopher Plantin, the publisher of Antwerp, to have drawings and engravings made of exotic plants. Pieter van der Borcht (1545–1608), Plantin's principal designer, drew and painted for the Flemish botanists an almost incredible number of plants.[137] Most of the drawings of plants from India and America were made from living specimens, some of them grown in the botanical garden of Leyden supervised by L'écluse. Borcht's plant and flower portraits are so detailed that they appear to have been done with the aid of a magnifying glass.[138]

L'écluse was the only one of the renowned European botanists to accumulate information systematically on new plants from people in the field. His connections with Plantin also enabled L'écluse to have accurate drawings, paintings, woodcuts, and engravings made of rare plants that came under his eye.[139] While many other European naturalists had similar interests, they were not as well placed as L'écluse to collect plants directly from Asia or to have illustrations of their exotic specimens published.[140] Most of the other botanists had to rely upon intermediaries, usually friends, patrons, agents, or other botanists for the dried plants, seeds, and bulbs from distant lands. L'écluse himself received many of his finest specimens from the Levant, but he was never completely dependent on this route. It was possibly through his contacts with Portuguese merchants and sailors that L'écluse was led to recognize that the *rhaponticum* (rhubarb) of commerce was of Chinese origin.[141] The Italians seem to have received exotic plants from the maritime purveyors only during the last generation of the sixteenth century, and then but irregularly and in small numbers.

The botanical artists of northern Italy generally used dried plants as their models. The systematic pressing and drying of plants was probably initiated by Luca Ghini (*ca* 1490–1556), a professor of botany at Bologna. His pupil Aldrovandi was the first to attempt making collections of dried plants from all over the world. Mattioli, and other great naturalists, even though they had botanical gardens themselves, continued throughout the sixteenth century to collect and catalogue dried plants, probably for comparative purposes. To restore the natural appearance of the dried plants for the artist, they were soaked in water.[142] The illustrations in the Italian books are consequently not so naturalistic as those produced from living models in northern Europe. But both the illustrations and the texts of their works stress, as their *herbaria* do, the similarities

[137] For example, 1,856 paintings of plants by Borcht are preserved in the State Library at Berlin. See Blunt, *op. cit.* (n. 130), pp. 65–66.

[138] G. Bazin, *A Gallery of Flowers* (London, 1960), p. 14.

[139] See especially his *Rariorum plantarum historia* (Antwerp, 1601).

[140] For example, a book of 2,191 engravings that had been executed for the works of Dodoens, de l'Obel, and L'écluse was published at Antwerp by Plantin in 1581 under the title *Plantarum seu stirpium icones*. For relations between Plantin and the botanists see Colin Clair, *Christopher Plantin* (London, 1960), pp. 115–16, 147–48.

[141] See Stannard, *loc. cit.* (n. 132), p. 14.

[142] Arber, *op. cit.* (n. 133), p. 140.

and differences rather than the individual characteristics of the plants themselves. In the long run, the Italian drawings probably contributed more to the development of comparative plant morphology than the more detailed and exquisite illustrations of the German and Flemish works.

The Swiss and German naturalists from Konrad Gesner (1516–65) onward were more encyclopedic than analytical in their interests. Gesner collected drawings and woodcuts on all subjects and from every conceivable source as illustrations for his books on natural history. The fifteen hundred drawings of plants which he assembled passed after his death into the hands of Joachim Camerarius the Younger (1534–98). After being trained as a physician at Bologna, Camerarius settled in Nuremberg, his birthplace. Like Paludanus and other physicians of the period, he collected oddities and cultivated rare plants in his garden. The merchants of Nuremberg and his fellow botanists kept him supplied with rarities.[143] Camerarius, however, was more than a collector and physician. He was also a speculative thinker. His chief work reveals in its title, *Hortus medicus et philosophicus* (Medical and Philosophical Garden) (1588) the range and depth of his diverse interests. In his desire to probe behind the mysteries of nature, Camerarius helped to bring the exotic natural world of the East more sharply within the focus of European speculative thought.

Camerarius stands at the end of a long line of sixteenth-century thinkers and scholars who sought to express abstract thought in visual form by inventing emblems. It was Marsilio Ficino (1433–99) and the Neoplatonists of the quattrocento, who first popularized the notion that Hermes Trismegistus, an ancient Egyptian sage, had attained through his use of hieroglyphs as emblems a penetration of the universe comparable to that divinely revealed to the Evangelists. The hieroglyphs of Egypt were thought to be a unique form of symbolic writing which expressed highly abstract conceptions through the portrayal of material objects. In this sacred system of writing each individual subject and phenomenon was thought to be an idea made objective, or God made animate. Only the initiated could comprehend the true meaning of the hieroglyphs. Enlightenment came to these favored ones through pious contemplation, philosophical speculation, or artistic creation.[144]

In the Renaissance the principal source of information on the symbolic significance of Egyptian writing was the *Hieroglyphica* of Horapollo. A manuscript copy of this work was found in 1419 by a Florentine traveler to Greece. From 1422 on, manuscript copies were circulated in Florence, and Horapollo's misleading ideas about the symbolic nature of the hieroglyphs came to be accepted as doctrine. His work was first printed in 1505 and over the next century no fewer than thirty editions of it were published.[145] The writers of

[143] He was the first to make extensive use of the botanical observations in the Near East of Leonhard Rauwolf of Augsburg. See K. H. Dannenfeldt, *Leonhard Rauwolf* (Cambridge, Mass., 1968), p. 227.
[144] For a thorough study of the hieroglyphic tradition of the late Renaissance see E. Iversen, *The Myth of Egypt and Its Hieroglyphs . . .* (Copenhagen, 1961), pp. 60–65.
[145] G. Boas, *The Hieroglyphics of Horapollo* (New York, 1950), p. 29.

the emblem books of the sixteenth century used it as a model, and their readers employed it as a key to the emblems.

The pious object of the composers of the emblem books was to speak "hieroglyphically" or to depict through symbols the true nature of things divine and human. In 1522 Andrea Alciati compiled the first great collection of emblems. He drew his raw materials from Horapollo and other hieroglyphic writers as he sought through his Latin stanzas, allegorical pictures, and proverbs to create an indissoluble artistic unity of iconography and poetry. A volume of emblems based upon Alciati's collection was published at Augsburg in 1531; it contained the first set of excellent emblematic woodcuts, probably the work of Hans Schäufelein.[146]

From the beginning the elements of wonder and rarity were conspicuously employed by the composers of emblem books as media for stimulating insight and speculation.[147] In their quest for wonderful fables and pictures the emblem-ists ransacked the classical authors, the medieval bestiaries and lapidaries, and the cosmographies, natural histories, and travel books. To be acceptable as the main subject of a device the fable had to be founded on truth and had to stress a noble or didactic theme.[148] New themes which could meet these specifications were not always easy to find. Consequently, from Alciati onward the emblem collectors copied unblushingly from their predecessors and from other works. They were particularly prone to reuse the prints, sometimes with the same but more often with a new text. Such revisions were possible because consistency in symbolic meaning was not an essential of device-making. Indeed, the switch from a conventional to a novel symbolism made the emblem more cryptic and its meaning more delightfully ambiguous. In Alciati's collection, for example, the emblem of the elephant is used to illustrate both peace and military glory, perhaps because they were thought to be two sides of the same coin!

The association of emblems with hieroglyphs was maintained throughout the sixteenth century, even though Renaissance artists had no possibility of decipher-ing the original Egyptian pictographs.[149] The successor to Horapollo as the final authority on hieroglyphics was Giovanni Pietro Valeriano (1477–1588?). After a lifetime of compiling information on the symbolic meaning of Egyptian writing, he published his *Hieroglyphica* at Basel in 1556. Through the publication of these fifty-eight books, Valeriano hoped to reconstruct and revivify the Egyptian "mute and symbolical language of ideas"[150] and to provide the basis for expressing allegorically through hieroglyphs the fundamental philosophical conceptions of his day. He devoted whole books to discussion of the allegorical significance of individual animals, such as the elephant and the rhinoceros.

[146] See H. Green (ed.), *Andreae Alceate Emblematum* (Manchester, 1870), pp. 14–16. This edition was dedicated to Konrad Peutinger.

[147] See M. Praz, *Studies in Seventeenth-Century Imagery* (2d ed.; Rome, 1964), pp. 62–63.

[148] *Ibid.*, pp. 68–70.

[149] Iversen, *op. cit.* (n. 144), p. 66.

[150] *Ibid.*, p. 72.

Monsters, strange birds and fish, exotic plants and stones, and foreign costumes likewise figured prominently in his choice of concrete subjects with enough symbolic power to transmit abstract moral, religious, and metaphysical concepts to the enlightened viewer. The popularity of Valeriano's erudite work with scholars and artists caused it to be reprinted and discoursed upon throughout Europe.[151] Along with Horapollo's, Valeriano's work also became a major source for artists who wanted to incorporate hieroglyphs into their decorative and ornamental designs.[152]

To the Neoplatonists any work of art was in itself a piece of sacred allegorical writing, a manifest expression of the mystical relationship binding matter to idea and man to God. Both the artist and the interpreter of the emblem were thought to act under divine inspiration: the artist is given insight into the ideal nature of matter when he creates, and the gifted interpreter when he correctly reads the metaphysical message of the emblem. The work of art, whether emblem or not, thus necessarily becomes a bit of divine revelation. But not all the inventors of emblems could maintain such a lofty conception of the hieroglyphs and allegories. The popularity of the emblem books with all levels of literate society gradually led to their vulgarization. Once the floodgates had opened to popular fantasy, especially in France, the emblems were debased and the simplest puns, pranks, and conundrums were called hieroglyphic.

Joachim Camerarius in his *Symbolorum ac emblematum* ... (Nuremberg, 1590–1604)[153] stands somewhere between the philosophical emblematists and the unabashed vulgarizers. The emblems in the four lengthy *centuriae* of his work are more clearly inspired by the natural histories, cosmographies, and travel books than are those of any other author.[154] The very fact that his works lack the terse and enigmatic quality of the more sophisticated emblems adds to the impression that he is beginning to break with the classical hieroglyphic tradition. The novelty of his representations also required more textual explanation and documentation than was conventional. For example, he brings the tulip, which had but recently been imported into Europe from Turkey, into emblematic iconography for the first time (Centur. I, chap. lxxxviii). Four-footed beasts from India also receive their fair share of attention: the rhinoceros,

---

[151] For the remarks of Torquato Tasso on the *imprese* see E. Raimondi (ed.), *Torquato Tasso Dialoghi: Edizione Critica* (Florence, 1958), II, Pt. II, 1029–1134.

[152] Some painters before Valeriano's time had used hieroglyphs as sources of inspiration for their motifs, especially Pinturicchio, Leonardo, Mantegna, Giovanni Bellini, Dürer, and Giorgio Vasari. See Praz, *op. cit.* (n. 147), pp. 24–25.

[153] Title of the complete edition of 1697 used in this study is *Joachimi Camerarii symbolorum ac emblematum ethico-politicorum centuriae quatuor: prima, arborum et planetarum; secunda, animal quadrupedium; tertia, avium et volatilium; quarta, piscium et reptilium.* German translations were issued in 1671 and 1672.

[154] Similar naturalistic emblems, but many fewer, may be found in A. Freitag, *Mythologia ethica* ... (Antwerp, 1579), and in a derivative work entitled *Viridarium moralis philosophiae per Fabulas Animalibus brutus attributas traditae, iconibus artificiosissime in aes insculptis exornatum* (Cologne, 1594). The animals depicted here are fabulous in large part; the texts in these two works are identical; most of the etchings in both books seem to be by Marc Gheeraerts. For further detail on these delightful etchings see Clair, *op. cit.* (n. 140), pp. 195–96.

elephant, tiger, the Indian "dog," and the musk deer.[155] In the division on birds he shows the Indian parrot, the bird of paradise, and what he calls the crowned birds of Catigan Island, in the South Seas.[156] The explanatory material added to each of these prints in derived from both classical and contemporary sources. The four hundred etchings themselves were executed at Nuremberg by Hans Sibmacher (d. 1611).[157] Camerarius' literary sources on Asia included Maximilian of Transylvania on Magellan's expedition, Sebastian Münster's *Cosmographia*, Juan González de Mendoza on China, Fernão Lopes de Castanheda on the Portuguese empire, and Orta and Monardes on plants and drugs. Camerarius' emblems were extremely popular and his work was republished repeatedly in the seventeenth and eighteenth centuries.

Emblematists and cosmographers of the late sixteenth century also brought Asia to the attention of their readers through the creation of emblems based upon maps. This practice evidently began with the geographical and cosmographical woodcuts printed by John Day in William Cunningham, *The Cosmographical Glasse* (London, 1559).[158] But most of the map emblems seem to have originated with the engravers of Antwerp, especially Philippe Galle (1537–1612). A typical example of the map emblem supported by a Latin motto can be seen in the *Emblemata* of Joannes Sambucus (1531–84).[159] Or for variety see the collection of emblematic poems by Hugo Favolius (1523–85) illustrated with small engraved maps by Galle.[160] The engraved maps of Asia, Tartary, and India are here supported by lengthy Latin poetic mottoes from the pen of Favolius.[161] The book on the most famous islands of the world by Thommaso Porcacchi (*ca.* 1530–85) likewise takes on the form of an emblem book.[162] Small prints of Giacomo Gastaldi's maps of Taprobane and the Moluccas are followed by motto-like captions based upon information taken from the ancients, Conti, Varthema, and Ramusio. The map engravers in preparing their elaborately detailed and sharp delineations of the new maps and routiers added through their conventional signs—ships, monsters, and allegorical figures—iconographical elements which helped to enlarge the vocabulary of contemporary decoration and ornamentation (see pl. 113).[163] Franz Hogenberg (fl. 1558–90), from his workshop at Cologne, inaugurated the golden age of

---

[155] Centur. II, chaps. i–v, vii, xxxv, lviii, lxiv. Also see pls. 129 and 138.

[156] Centur. III, chaps. xliii, vliv, and xlvi. Catigan is possibly a reference to Canigao island southwest of Leyte in the Philippines, which Magellan passed by. Also see pls. 139 and 141.

[157] Praz, *op. cit.* (n. 147), p. 295, calls them engravings on copper. But see A. Andresen, *Der deutsche peintre-graveur, oder die deutsche Maler als Kupferstecher* . . . (Leipzig, 1872–78), II, 280–409, for discussion of Sibmacher's etchings.

[158] See esp. fols. 7 and 8.

[159] (Antwerp, 1564), p. 113.

[160] *Theatri orbis terrarum enchiridon* . . . (Antwerp, 1585).

[161] *Ibid.*, pp. 5–7, and 135–37.

[162] *L'isole piu famoso del mondo* (Venice, 1576), pp. 185–88, 189–92.

[163] Also see the animal decorations for playing cards of Virgil Solis (1514–62) in F. Rumpf, "Beiträge zur Geschichte der frühen Spielkarten," *Festschrift Adolph Goldschmidt* (Berlin, 1935) p. 85.

decorative cartography by the profusely illustrated maps he produced for Ortelius' *Atlas* published in 1570.[164]

The cosmographies, which were often illustrated with decorative maps, also included engravings of Asian flora, fauna, peoples, and cities that were based on woodcuts and sketches assembled by the compilers and their artists. Sebastian Münster (1489–1552), the German geographer, was among the first to bring illustrations of the contemporary East into his work. The woodcuts in the first edition of his *Cosmographia universalis* (1544) were executed by Hans Holbein the Younger and Konrad Schmitt. For his definitive German edition of 1550, Münster's main art collaborator was Hans Rudolph Manuel Deutsch (1525–71). The profusion of illustrations in this edition indicates that Deutsch must have ransacked the printing houses of central and western Europe for drawings and woodcuts. In the section of the work on Asia, woodcuts of the mythological dog-headed Indians and pygmies are balanced with illustrations which purport to show the cities of "Narsinga" (Vijayanagar), Tenasserim, and Pegu along with crude engravings of the pepper plant, clove tree, parrots, and the musk deer of Cathay.[165] An improvement in accuracy occurs in Ramusio's *Navigationi* (Vol. I; 1554) where the engraver, probably working from a dried sample, shows the obverse and reverse sides of the betel leaf in detail.[166]

André Thevet, in the course of his voyage to the Levant from 1549 to 1552, collected or made drawings which, upon his return to France, he had cut in wood by Jean Cousin and his workshop, and in copper at Antwerp by Leonard Gaultier (*ca.* 1561–1641).[167] In addition, he acquired drawings from others, some made in Asia and others in Europe. From a pilot in Spain he received a drawing of "Mandelaph," king of the island of Taprobane, and from the natural histories he took his illustration of peeling cinnamon bark, the pepper vine, and of pearl fishing at Ormuz; from an imaginative European artist he derived his illustrations of Indian temples and religious processions and even of the combat between Magellan and the natives of the island of Mactan.[168] Georg Braun and Franz Hogenberg received sketches of the Indian cities of Diu, Goa, Calicut, Cannanore, and Ormuz through Konstantin von Lyskirchen (d. 1581) of Cologne. Lyskirchen had evidently obtained the sketches through his Fugger contacts who had, in turn, received them from their Portuguese representatives. The sketches were engraved, probably by Hogenberg, and

[164] Skelton, *op. cit.* (n. 113), pp. 17–18. For a study of how ship decorations passed from one engraver to the other see J. von Beylen, "Schepen op kaarten ten tijde van Gerard Mercator," *Duisburger Forschungen*, VI (1962), 131–33.

[165] Summary based on the revised German edition of 1550 produced in Basel under Münster's personal direction. For further discussion see K. H. Burmeister, *Sebastian Münster* (Basel, 1963), pp. 120–21.

[166] See *Asia*, I, 204–8; Giulio della Torre, a Veronese artist, struck a medal honoring Ramusio, the reverse side of which is decorated with a map. A. Armand, *Les médailleurs italiens...* (Paris, 1883), I, 134.

[167] J. Adhémar, *Inventaire du fonds français: Graveurs du XVIᵉ siècle* (Paris, 1939), II, 108.

[168] A. Thevet, *La cosmographie universelle...* (Paris, 1575), I, 330r, 383r, 425v, 436v; "Mandelaph" may be Manzor, sultan of Tidore. See *Asia*, I, 595–96.

included as illustrations in the first volume of the *Civitates orbis terrarum* (Antwerp and Cologne, 1572).[169] François de Belleforest in his *Cosmographie universelle* (Paris, 1575) likewise included views of several Indian cities.

A number of European artists made contact with Eastern art through their own travels in Europe. Of more than usual interest are two sketches by Philips van Winghe (1560–92), an itinerant artist of Louvain.[170] Sometime after 1585 and before his death in 1592, van Winghe visited the collections of the Vatican in Rome. Here he evidently saw and was attracted by the two Japanese folding screens (*byōbus*) which had been brought to Europe as a gift for Pope Gregory XIII.[171] On these screens, as we know from the Jesuit sources, were painted scenes of Azuchi, the capital of Oda Nobunaga on the northeastern shore of Lake Biwa in Japan. The screens evidently featured Azuchi Castle, a magnificent edifice constructed high on a rocky cliff between 1576 and 1580 which was the original prototype of the Japanese castle. The sketches of Van Winghe (pls. 50 and 51) which show respectively the tower and the gate of Azuchi Castle are the only pictorial representations extant,[172] as far as can be determined, of the castle which was completely destroyed in 1582. No record can be found of the whereabouts of the screens themselves.

Other itinerant artists journeyed as far east as the Levant. Pieter Coecke van Alost was sent to Constantinople in 1533, possibly by the Brussels tapestry weaver Van der Moyen, to arrange for the sale of tapestries to the sultan or to establish a weaving plant there.[173] Certain of the drawings which he did during his year in Turkey were published by his widow in 1553 in a book of woodcuts on the customs of the Turks.[174] Melchior Lorck (*ca.* 1527–1583), a Danish

---

[169] On the Portuguese emigration from Antwerp to Cologne see H. Kellenbenz, *Unternehmer-kräfte im Hamburger Portugal- und Spanienhandel* (Hamburg, 1954), p. 201. The views obtained from the Portuguese are similar to those of the fortresses and towns shown in the *Lendas da India* of Gaspar Corrêa and in the *Livro de Lizuarte de Abreu*, both completed before 1564. See the facsimile edition with introduction by R. A. Skelton of G. Braun and F. Hogenberg, *Civitates orbis terrarum: The Towns of the World*, 1572–1618 (Cleveland, 1966), I, xviii, 54, 57. Also see for the iconographic history of Goa, L. Silveira, *Ensaio de iconografia das cidades portuguesas do ultramar* (Lisbon, 1957), III, 361.

[170] For his artistic biography see G. J. Hoogewerff, "Philips van Winghe," *Mededeelingen van het Nederlandsch Historisch Instituut te Rome*, VII (1927), 59–82.

[171] These screens were especially prepared in 1581 as a gift for Father Valignano, and were probably painted by an artist of the Kano school. See Abranches Pinto *et al.*, *op. cit.* (n. 55), pp. 1, n. 7, 185, n. 659.

[172] Prints of Van Winghe's sketches first appeared in V. Cartari, *Le vere e nove imagini de gli dei della antichi* (Padua, 1615). They are included in the appendix relating to the gods of the East and West Indies added to Cartari's work by Lorenzo Pignoria, possibly to honor the Japanese embassy of 1615. In the caption beneath the engraving of the gate Pignoria incorrectly calls it (or perhaps both these engravings) a portrayal of a temple which houses the Japanese gods. To anyone who has ever seen a Japanese temple or castle, such an identification is clearly impossible. For further discussion of the Japanese gods see R. W. Lightbown, "Oriental Art and the Orient in Late Renaissance and Baroque Italy," *Journal of the Warburg and Courtauld Institutes*, XXXII (1969), 242–47.

[173] A. J. J. Delen, "Bücherillustrationen des Pieter Coecke van Alost," *Gutenberg Jahrbuch* (1930), p. 191; and Marlier, *op. cit.* (n. 76), p. 57.

[174] Entitled *Les moeurs et fachons de faire des Turcs*, it was reproduced in facsimile by W. S. Maxwell in London in 1873.

engraver, went to Constantinople in 1555, possibly as a member of Augier Ghiselin de Busbecq's mission.[175] His artistic objective was to find and examine the true sources of classical Antiquity.[176] After more than four years in the Levant, Lorck returned to Vienna in 1560 with sketches of Turkish antiquities, costumes, flora, and fauna (pl. 114). In 1574 he was employed by Christopher Plantin, the Antwerp publisher. While in the city on the Scheldt, he worked as an engraver with Galle and became friendly with Ortelius. Lorck, if we may judge by his engravings, was primarily interested in depicting Turkish costumes, an interest which was shared by many other artists and engravers of his day. It may have been Lorck who did the woodcuts that illustrate N. de Nicolay, *De Schipvaert ende Reysen gedlaen int Landt van Turckeyen* (Antwerp, 1576).

The engravers of the latter half of the sixteenth century became especially fascinated by the differences in national costumes. Separate drawings and paintings of individuals in unusual dress preceded the collections which were published in costume books. But from 1562 to 1600 no fewer than twelve costume books were published in Europe, primarily in Venice, Paris, and Antwerp.[177] In the small collections that were first published the emphasis in the prints was on the national and European costumes of the day. But the collection of 1562 published in Paris included engravings by François Desprez, of an Indian man and woman, a Tartar, and "a woman of Asia,"[178] as costume interests became more universal. The Parisians, then as now, seem to have had a particular interest in dress, for the workshop of Guillaume le Bé (1539–98) turned out two series of woodcuts around 1585 showing in costume the natives of "Magellan" (the Philippines), China, and Goa as well as the Grand Khan of Tartary and the Emperor of China in their imperial trappings.[179] The earliest costume books prepared in Venice do not include Asians, but they were quick to appear in the works issued under French influence at Antwerp. Abraham de Bruyn (*ca.* 1538–90), the Antwerp engraver, in 1572 reissued the figures from the first edition of the *Recueil*, though in a somewhat different order.[180] The Asians in these depictions show no Oriental physical features and their costumes probably were inspired by the Turkish costumes of Coecke van Alost and Lorck. The

[175] For Lorck's life and works see H. Harbeck, *Melchior Lorichs* (Hamburg, 1911); the catalogue by E. Fischer, *Melchior Lorck: Drawings from the Evelyn Collection . . . and from the Department of Prints and Drawings, the Royal Museum of Fine Arts, Copenhagen* (Copenhagen, 1962); and P. Ward-Jackson, "Some Rare Drawings by Melchior Lorichs," *Connoisseur*, CXXXV (1955), 88–89; also see J. Sthyr, *Dansk Grafik, 1500–1800* (Copenhagen, 1943), I, 34.

[176] See O. Benesch, "The Orient as a Source of Inspiration of the Graphic Arts of the Renaissance," in *Festschrift Friedrich Winkler* (Berlin, 1959), p. 251.

[177] F. Bertelli, *Trachtenbuch: Venedig, 1563* (Zwickau, 1913), p. 1; and H. Doege, "Die Trachten-bücher des 16. Jahrhunderts," *Beiträge zur Bücherkunde und Philologie: August Wilmanns zum 25 März 1903 gewidmet* (Leipzig, 1903), pp. 429–44.

[178] *Receuil de la diversité des habits qui sont de present en usaige tant es pays d'Europe, Asie, Afrique et isles sauvages* (Paris, 1562), plates 94, 103, 120. This book was published by Richard Breton.

[179] Based on description of the woodcuts in the Département des Estampes of the Bibliothèque nationale as given in Adhémar, *op. cit.* (n. 167), II, 356–57.

[180] Issued by Abraham de Bruyn under the title *Omnium pene Europae, Asiae, Aphricae atque Americae gentium habitua.* For a reproduction of the exotic figures in costume, see pls. 59 and 60.

improvement in De Bruyn's presentation is that he shows the Asians next to Americans, Africans, and Moors and thereby depicts concretely how Europeans conceived of these people and their differences in dress. Jean Jacques Boissard (1528–1602), poet and author, published a collection of costume prints in 1581 which is especially good in its sharp and clear depiction of Oriental costume.[181] Though the artist is not named, it would seem from the fidelity of his work that he actually worked from authentic models.

The most comprehensive of the sixteenth-century costume books was that published by Cesare Vecellio (1521–1601) at Venice in 1590 under the title *Habiti antichi et moderni di tutte il mondo.*[182] The first edition contained 420 woodcuts; the second edition of 1598 was enlarged to include 522. Most of the additions to the second edition were of Oriental and American costumes. None of the Vecellio prints of Asians is a duplicate of the *Recueil* or De Bruyn plates, but they seem to be dependent upon the Boissard illustrations for certain of the Oriental costumes.[183] Vecellio's whole conception of Asian life is implicitly more sophisticated than that of his predecessors. He clearly distinguishes one Asian from the other and tries to depict Indians and Chinese of different social levels. The features and costumes of most of his figures continue to be European, but the Chinese take on a new realism in both aspects. His Japanese youth is outfitted with a copy of one of the costumes presented to the doge in 1585 by the Japanese legates and housed in the hall of arms of the Council of Ten.[184] The truer depiction of Chinese physiognomy, costume, and class distinctions derives from the fact that the artist, according to Vecellio's own statement (Bk. II), used figures from Chinese paintings as his models.[185]

The leading engravers of Antwerp, on the contrary, seem not to have used "porcelain Chinese," paintings on silk, or other Asian sources, in their works on Oriental subjects. Jan van der Straet (1523–1605), commonly known as Stradanus,[186] collaborated with others on a fair number of engravings which purport to be depictions of life in overseas places, especially Asia and America. For their sources these Antwerp artists relied on literary materials to which they gave their own artistic interpretations. One in a series of engravings prepared around 1590 to glorify the overseas discoveries of about a century before symbolizes the achievements of Ferdinand Magellan.[187] Like all the others the

---

[181] Entitled *Habitus variarum orbis gentium* (Paris, 1581).

[182] For commentary see C. Lozzi, "Cesare Vecellio e i suoi disegni e intagli per libri di costumi e di merletti," *La bibliofilia,* I (1900), 3–11; and M. von Boehn, *Modes and Manners* (London, 1932), II, 108–9.

[183] Doege, *loc. cit.* (n. 177), pp. 441–42.

[184] But in the engravings showing the Japanese legates being received by Pope Gregory XIII they are shown in European costume, probably the garments which were gifts from the pope himself. For two of these commemorative engravings see Abranches Pinto *et al., op. cit.* (n. 55), facing p. 163.

[185] For reproductions see pls. 61–69.

[186] For discussion of his interest in maps and geography while in Florence see J. A. F. Orbaan, *Stradanus te Florence, 1553–1605* (Rotterdam, 1903), p. 89.

[187] For further discussion see R. Wittkower, "Miraculous Birds," *Journal of the Warburg Institute,* I (1937–38), 255–56.

Magellan engraving (pl. 48) shows an idealized portrait of the hero surrounded by animals, plants, and figures which are designed to illustrate his accomplishments through the realistic, emblematical, and mythological ideas that they represent. For example, the figure of Apollo, the sun god, is included, according to the inscription, to remind the viewer that Magellan by his voyage around the earth was the first of the discoverers to emulate the sun. More puzzling is an unexplained and fantastic picture in the upper left-hand corner of the engraving which shows a huge bird carrying an elephant. The source for this strange design is clearly the story which Pigafetta tells in his account of Magellan's voyage about the marvelous birds[188] which are native to the South China Sea and are "so large that they can lift any large animal into the air."[189] The Antwerp artists probably read this statement in the first volume of Ramusio's popular collection, which included an epitomized version of Pigafetta's story. In the second volume of his *Navigationi*, Ramusio also included Marco Polo's description of the world. Here a variant of the same fable, probably of Arabian origin, is recounted in connection with Marco's description of Madagascar. The "ruch," as the gigantic bird is named in this narrative, "is able to carry an elephant in its claws."[190] It is certainly reasonable to suppose that Stradanus was inspired by this fable to introduce the "ruch" into his design as a symbol of the marvels that Magellan experienced in sailing across the Pacific Ocean. The pictorial design itself was probably the invention of Stradanus, for the elephant shown here is one of the type that commonly appears in northern woodcuts and engravings. In the 1599 edition of his *Ornithologiae* (Book X, p. 610), the Italian naturalist Aldrovandi reproduces the Stradanus engraving as an illustration of one of the birds he categorizes as fabulous.[191]

Another example of the joint efforts of the Antwerp artists is to be seen in the engraving completed around 1570 called "Hunting for Wild Ducks in China" (pl. 47). The theme of this picture is certainly derived from a literary source. In the comprehensive history of China prepared in the eighteenth century on the basis of earlier sources by Father Jean-Baptiste Du Halde (1741 ed.; II, 237–38), it is asserted:

Besides the Domestick Birds, they have on the Rivers and Lakes great Plenty of Water-Fowl, and principally Wild-Ducks: The Manner in which they are taken deserves

[188] Probably a reference to the Indian solar bird called *garuda* which carries off the *naga* ("snake" or possibly "elephant" in Sanskrit) in the two great Sanskrit epics, the *Mahabharata* and the *Ramayana*. In the definitive Pigafetta text the name *garuda* is actually assigned to this bird. See C. E. Nowell (ed.), *Magellan's Voyage around the World: Three Contemporary Accounts* (Evanston, Ill., 1962), p. 248. For the history of the *garuda* in Indian lore see A. de Gubernatis, *Zoölogical Mythology, or The Legends of Animals* (London, 1872), II, 94–95.

[189] G. B. Ramusio, *Delle navigationi . . .* (Venice, 1550–59), I, 407r.

[190] *Ibid.*, II, 58r. On the "ruch" see H. Yule and H. Cordier (eds.), *The Book of Ser Marco Polo* (New York, 1933), II, 415–24.

[191] My analysis runs counter to that advanced by Wittkower (*loc. cit.* [n. 187], pp. 256–57), who concludes that the bird has no part in the idea of the engraving and surmises that Stradanus based his picture on an original Persian representation that he might have seen while in Florence. On the woodcut elephants see below, p. 157.

to be mention'd; they put on their Heads the Shells of large Calibashes or Gourds, wherein they make Holes to see and breathe through, then they go naked into the Water, or swim deep with their Bodies that nothing may appear above the Water but the Calibash; the Ducks, being accustomed to see Calibashes floating approach them without Fear, at which time the Duck-hunter, taking them by the Feet, pulls them into the Water to prevent their Noise, wrings their Neck, and ties them to his Girdle, and pursues his Exercise till he has got a great number.

Neither the hunters nor the features of the landscape have anything Chinese about them. Similarly, a Stradanus-Galle collaborative engraving of Justinian shows the emperor receiving the silkworm in a bamboo cane from the hands of an Oriental who has nothing Oriental about him, except possibly his costume.[192] Their engraving of an elephant hunt likewise seems to be based upon literary descriptions (pl. 104).[193]

The prints of the triumphs and processions which took place in Antwerp usually show the East in connection with the depictions of the arches and displays erected by the Portuguese merchant community as its contribution to the celebrations.[194] The Portuguese nation at Antwerp played only a token part in the *joyeuse entrée* of Prince Philip of Spain in 1549, probably because its members were discomfited and uncertain about their future under his regime.[195] But after Philip became king of Portugal in 1580 his Lusitanian subjects at Antwerp took a prominent part in the *entrées*. For the celebrations connected with the *entrée* of July 18, 1593, of Archduke Ernest of Austria, the Portuguese nation erected a huge arch on which its overseas possessions are depicted in terms of animals and riders (pl. 49). Ethiopia is symbolized by the elephant and Asia by the rhinoceros. A huge print of the procession designed by Pieter van der Borcht shows at the bottom right a delegation of dark, occasionally beturbaned, people who are leading camels and asses and carrying a man on a litter who looks like a native king.[196] This portion of the procession is reminiscent of Burgkmair's "People of Calicut" in the "Triumph of Maximilian." The royal triumphs held in France often followed exotic themes also, and frequently included dancers and other persons clothed in picturesque costumes that were

---

[192] Plate 8 in the fascinating collection called *Nova reperta* (Antwerp, 1592). The first picture in this book shows Columbus landing on American shores in commemoration of the centennial of that momentous event. The native woman in this picture looks for all the world like a Renaissance depiction of a Greek goddess!

[193] Discussed in E. Tietze-Conrat, "Die Erfindung im Relief," *Jahrbuch der kunsthistorischen Sammlungen in Wien*, XXXV (1920), 131.

[194] Compare the use made of American Indians and symbols in the triumphs of Charles V. See M. Bataillon, "La cour découvre le nouveau monde," in J. Jacquot (ed.), *Fêtes et cérémonies au temps de Charles Quint* (Paris, 1960), pp. 13-27.

[195] The Portuguese did not contribute a triumphal arch, and but twenty of them and their aides walked in the procession. See C. Grapheus, *Le triomphe d'Anvers faict en la susection du Prince Philip, Prince d'Espaigne* (Antwerp, 1550); includes twenty-nine woodcuts of triumphal arches by Pieter Coecke van Alost. For the role of the Portuguese in this and in other Antwerp triumphs see J. M. Lopes, *Les Portugais à Anvers au XVIe siècle* (Antwerp, 1895), pp. 12-16.

[196] J. Boch, *Descriptio publicae gratulationis, spectaculorum et ludorum, in adventu . . . Ernesti archiducis Austriae, an. MDXCIII, XVIII kal. iulias, aliisque diebus Antwerpiae editorum . . .* (Antwerp, 1595), pp. 140-41.

designed along lines that were supposed to be "Oriental." Whenever possible, as in the royal *entrée* at Rouen in 1550, natives from the overseas world were invited, as they may have been at Antwerp in 1593, to take part in the celebration to lend it color and authenticity.[197]

The inauguration of direct Dutch relations with Asia brought to the public a new series of travel accounts and a fresh set of engravings and maps. The *Itinerario* (1596) of Linschoten included a number of maps based on Portuguese and Dutch originals that were engraved for the publisher Cornelis Claesz by Arnoldus F. à Langrens.[198] The illustrations of people, flora, and fauna of Asia were engraved by Joannes and Baptista à Doetechum from sketches brought back by Linschoten, from the objects themselves available in the collection of Paludanus, and from the rich store of woodcuts and engravings already on hand in the Low Countries.[199] The engravings themselves help to reveal the artists' sources. Seminaturalistic coconut palms stand everywhere in the backgrounds to give the scenes a tropical ambiance. The individual plants, fruits, jewels and ornaments, fans, parasols, palanquins, and Martaban jars are realistic and were probably done from examples on hand. The fauna, however, seem to be taken from older woodcuts, paintings, and tapestries. All the faces, except for a few Chinese with thin and sparse goatees, are Western and are usually reminiscent of Greek statues. The beturbaned merchants and long-gowned women of aristocratic status look like copies of Schongauer's and Bellini's people. The buildings, while basically Western, are sometimes elongated and given curved eaves as the artist tries to Orientalize them (pl. 148). While these illustrations are still essentially Western in the total impression they convey, closer study reveals that the artists used all the means at their disposal to transmit as much as they could, particularly in details, of Asian landscape, life, and customs.

That the Linschoten maps and illustrations constitute a watershed in Europe's pictorial impression of Asia is best indicated by their constant reappearance in the works of others. John Wolfe, who published an English translation of Linschoten's *Itinerario* in 1598, had engravings of Langrens' maps cut in London which are inferior both in accuracy and artistry to the originals. He does not include any other illustrations.[200] Theodor de Bry,[201] on the other hand, in his series of picture books entitled *India orientalis* which began to appear at Frankfurt in 1598, is often heavily indebted to the Linschoten engravings and

[197] See J. Chartrou, *Les entrées solennelles et triomphales à la Renaissance (1484–1551)* (Paris, 1928), pp. 111–17; also N. Ivanov, "Fêtes à la cour des derniers Valois," *Revue du XVIe siècle*, XIX (1932), 96–122.

[198] For his map of eastern Asia see *Asia*, I, following p. 164.

[199] See reproductions in *Asia*, I, following pp. 356, 528, and 752.

[200] Wolfe's book is entitled *John Huighen van Linschoten, his Discours of Voyages into ye Easte and West Indies. . . .* It should also be recalled that Hakluyt did not include either maps or illustrations in the first edition of his work published in 1589. Perhaps this deficit is to be accounted for by the state of English engraving.

[201] For general discussion of his career see *Asia*, I, 216.

other earlier Netherlandish and German sources. In the main, the De Bry engravings (see pls. 146, 147, 148) are found on comparison to be inferior to the originals in artistic fidelity and vigor.[202] But the De Bry collection, aside from being a convenient compendium, has preserved many works of earlier artists that would otherwise have disappeared completely.

Levinus Hulsius (d. 1606),[203] a native of Ghent, began issuing his series of German travel books in 1598 at Nuremberg. The first volume published was the account of the Dutch voyage to the East Indies of 1595 to 1597.[204] Thirteen of the engravings in this book were executed by Hans Sibmacher of Nuremberg, the artist who etched the emblems for Camerarius' collection.[205] A number of oddities brought back from the first Dutch voyage, including Chinese coins and a Javanese kris, were available to Sibmacher when he did his sketches and engravings. He was so impressed with the "devil" cut into the hilt of the kris that he reproduced an enlarged copy of it in connection with his depiction of the people of Java (pl. 52).[206] Into his engraving of Chinese persons he inserted realistic depictions of two Chinese copper coins (cash) and did a remarkably good copy of the Chinese characters on them. And he apparently had available a sketch of the emu, a bird which the captain of the "Amsterdam" received as a gift from the ruler of Sidayu in Java and took back to Europe with him. His portrayal of the emu is lifelike and the subject is clearly recognizable as the *Struthio casuarius* of Linnaeus (pl. 140).[207] Thus in Sibmacher's engravings, as in those of the Doetechums (pl. 151), the artist's endeavor is to introduce as many realistic features of Asian life as he can to give his studies an authentic tone. In Sibmacher's case he makes the kris and the Chinese coins the main features in his prints of Asian peoples who continue themselves to look for all the world like Greek statues. From the evidence of Sibmacher's engravings, it can be asserted that he was certainly aware of the limits of his knowledge and was doing his best to compensate for his deficiency.

4

TEXTILES, TAPESTRIES, AND COSTUMES

References in Western literature to Oriental textiles as prized possessions begin to appear in Greek times. Chinese silk yarns and raw silk were worked at

[202] A similar opinion is expressed in A. G. Camus, *Mémoire sur la collection des grands et petits voyages* (Paris, 1802), p. 195.

[203] For general discussion of his career see *Asia*, I, 216–17.

[204] Entitled *Erste Schiffart an die orientalischen Indien, so die Hollandisch Schiff, im Martio 1585 aussgefahren, und im Augusto 1597 wiederkommen, verzicht* . . . (5th ed.; Frankfurt am Main, 1625).

[205] See above, p. 87. Also Andresen, *op. cit.* (n. 157), pp. 366–69.

[206] Compare ornaments on European daggers and sheaths in S. Schéle, *Cornelis Bos: A Study of the Origins of the Netherlands Grotesque* (Stockholm, 1965), pls. 45–46.

[207] A native of Seram island, this bird is today usually called the Seram cassowary. The name "eme" given to the bird in the Hulsius book (p. 43) was said to be the name in use in Java. L'écluse also described this bird.

Palmyra beginning in the second century A.D., and within the next two centuries silk weaving spread to Asia Minor, Egypt, and Greece. Chinese silks were so common in Rome that Pliny complained about the drain of gold to pay for them. Charlemagne received silken garments from Harun al-Rashid, the caliph of Baghdad, which he proudly displayed at the Abbey of St. Denis. The Muslim rulers of the Levant made it a practice to give costly gifts of robes to favored officials and foreign potentates. But from the fourth to the eleventh century silk export was a monopoly of the Byzantine state. Byzantine, Egyptian, and Islamic silks were used for ecclesiastical vestments in Rome as early as the ninth century. Wall hangings and carpets from Persia were kept among the sacred relics in church treasuries even before the period of the Crusades. It was, however, the returning Crusaders who brought back vast numbers of easily portable textiles as souvenirs of their experiences in the East. In the period between the Fourth Crusade (1198) and the Latin conquest of Constantinople (1204), the independent Italian silk industry began to produce silks competitive with those of Byzantium. The Muslims of Spain also acted as intermediaries in the textile trade and were responsible for supplying many of the brocades used as coronation and burial robes for Christian ecclesiastics and the secular rulers of the West.[208] The technique of drawn work and lacemaking was adopted in Venice during the fifteenth century, in imitation of the Asian laces imported there.[209]

From the tenth to the twelfth centuries the designs in the textiles imported from the Orient had a profound effect upon the development of Romanesque ornament.[210] Patterns of Indian and Chinese origin were borrowed by the Sassanid weavers of Persia (third to seventh centuries A.D.), who transmitted them in the form of textile decorations to Byzantium and western Europe. The naturalistic figures and animals of Asian origin in Romanesque designs seem to have been copied from non-Muslim textiles, for Islam forbade the representation of living things in art.[211] Dragons, fabulous birds, and floral motifs from Chinese textiles, or from Levantine imitations and stylizations, helped to enrich European iconography and to give a rhythmical quality to Romanesque ornament. In the thirteenth century the free play previously enjoyed by Oriental motifs in European art was checked abruptly, but never completely, by the pervasive influence that Gothic art came to have upon all styles of decoration.

The weaving of silk textiles was introduced into Europe through weavers brought from Byzantium and the Islamic world. The cities of Islamic Spain

[208] Based on the discussion of the Western awakening to the Orient in Jairazbhoy, *op. cit.* (n. 35), pp. 30–37.

[209] M. Schuette, "History of Lace," *Ciba Review*, No. 73 (1949), p. 2685.

[210] Evans, *op. cit.* (n. 15), I, 161; for more specific illustrations see M. B. Rogers, "A Study of the Makara and Kirttimukha with Some Parallels in Romanesque Architectural Ornament of France and Spain," Ph.D. diss., Department of Art, University of Chicago, 1965, *passim*.

[211] A. Leix, "Early Islamic Textiles," *Ciba Review*, No. 43 (1942), pp. 1573–74; also F. M. Heichelheim, "Byzantine Silks," *Ciba Review*, No. 75 (1949), pp. 2761–62.

were producing imitations of Egyptian textiles as early as the tenth century. On the island of Cyprus ateliers of silk weavers meanwhile made materials in imitation of Chinese silk damasks. Roger II of Sicily brought silk weavers from Byzantium to Palermo in the twelfth century. By 1300 the craft of silk weaving had passed from Sicily to the mainland of Italy. In the fourteenth century Lucca became the most important center of the Italian textile industry, and the resplendent, heavy silks produced there considerably modified the Oriental decorative motifs preserved in the Sicilian textiles. The rounded frames of the Islamic type disappeared and the animals of the older tradition were incorporated into heraldic forms. On the Luccan silks the designs were less symmetrical, lighter, and much more directly indebted to the motifs of Chinese textiles. Flying birds, the lotus flower, waterfalls, rocks, stylized cloud forms, and often entire landscapes were borrowed from Chinese textiles (perhaps at times through the agency of Persian imitations) and treated with the naturalism so esteemed by Gothic artists.[212] In other Italian silks, many of which were done in imitation of Luccan silks, the Asian motifs exhibit a vigor and freedom of movement which was likewise borrowed directly from Chinese art and which contributed significantly to the growth of asymmetry and Gothic naturalism in European decoration of the fourteenth century.[213] That the feeling of proximity to China was possibly greater in the fourteenth century as a result of the pilgrimages being made across the land route to the distant East is reflected in the term "Tartar cloths," a generic name applied to Oriental or Orientalized textiles.[214]

Venice took the leadership in silk weaving from Lucca in the fifteenth century. With this shift the designs, including those borrowed from Oriental textiles, were Europeanized. The delicate leaf work of the Chinese design was transformed or replaced by stolid depictions of European plants. Dragons and tortoises gave way to deer, lions, and other beasts commonly recognized as European. A few traces of Chinese influence remained in the depiction of seascapes in which the diagonal movement of the waves continued to be clearly shown. But, in general, the Venetian weavers eschewed the fantastic and asymmetrical patterns of the Luccan silks and only rarely retained the Chinese freedom of movement that had been so strikingly captured by the Luccan weavers. The development of the technique of collective weaving in fifteenth-century Italy also contributed to the popularity of symmetrical and static patterns, particularly simple floral designs that could be easily copied by the less skilled technicians of the weaving groups.[215] In 1490 Venice, to protect its textile industry, forbade the importation of Oriental textiles. In the late fifteenth century even the Venetian painters reduced the number of textiles

---

[212] F. E. de Roover, "Lucchese Silks," *Ciba Review*, No. 80 (1950), p. 2925.

[213] O. von Falke, "Chinesische Seidenstoffe des 14. Jahrhunderts und ihre Bedeutung für die Seidenkunst Italiens," *Jahrbuch der preussischen Kunstsammlungen*, XXXIII (1912), 176–92. Also see Evans, *op. cit.* (n. 15), pp. 162–64.

[214] See P. Toynbee, "Tartar Cloths," *Romania*, XXIX (1900), 559–64.

[215] O. von Falke, *Kunstgeschichte der Seidenweberei* (Berlin, 1921), pp. 38–40. On the role of flora in Indian design see Slomann, *op. cit.* (n. 90), pp. 42–43.

they brought into their works, for the heavy and florid designs of the weavers had nothing like the interest for the painter that the Oriental textiles had.[216]

With the opening of the direct sea route to the East the European writers of travel accounts commented regularly on the costumes of the natives, from the silk robes of the rich Chinese merchants to the palm-leaf skirts and bark-cloth breech garments worn by the South Sea islanders.[217] They also were quick to indicate that Bengal, St. Thomas (Madras), and Cambay in India were the main Eastern centers of cotton textile production. Both Varthema and Barbosa remark on the *sinabafos* of Bengal, the fine muslins made at Dacca which were generally used in Asia for turbans and skirts.[218] Linschoten esteems the cotton cloth of Cambay to surpass in fineness "any Holland cloth." He observes, however, that the carpets woven in Cambay are not as good as the Persian rugs sold in Ormuz. Gujarati colchas, or quilts, he describes as "very fair and pleasant, stitched with silks, and also of cotton of all colors and stichings."[219] All the commentators indicate that silken materials (damasks, satins, and brocades) are made in China, and a number of them assert that the heavy Chinese silken materials were rewoven into diaphanous fabrics at Chaul in India and at other Asian centers.[220] Linschoten guesses that the patterned textiles and painted calicoes of the Madras area were more highly prized in India than silk "because of the fineness and cunning workmanship."[221]

It was the exquisitely worked textiles of Asia which most attracted upper-class Europeans and which were increasingly imported throughout the sixteenth century. In 1511 Albuquerque sent from the region of Malacca a number of women skilled in needlework, but they were unfortunately lost at sea before arriving in Portugal.[222] The embroideries themselves arrived in Europe where they were used as counterpanes and canopies in the bedchambers of the upper classes. Most of the embroidered pieces brought into Europe during this period were executed in Bengal, Sind, and Gujarat. In Bengal the embroidered designs were worked in heavy tussore silk, in Sind on leather, and in Gujarat in bright silks on a cotton or satin ground.[223] In all three places the craftsmen quickly began to produce "export embroideries" designed especially to appeal to

---

[216] The great Venetian painters of fabrics were Carlo Crivelli, Gentile Bellini, Vittore Carpaccio, and Paolo Veronese; see G. de Francesco, "Silk Fabrics in Venetian Paintings," *Ciba Review*, No. 29 (1940), p. 1047.

[217] See W. Naumann, "Bark Cloth in the Reports of the First Explorers of the South Seas," *Ciba Review*, No. 33 (1940), pp. 1175–79. Also see Hakluyt's inventory as quoted above, p. 34.

[218] R. C. Temple (ed.), *The Itinerary of Ludovico di Varthema of Bologna from 1502–1508* (London, 1928), p. 79; and M. L. Dames (ed.), *The Book of Duarte Barbosa* (London, 1921), I, 93. On the Persian derivation of the word "Sinabafos" see H. Yule and A. C. Burnell, *Hobson-Jobson: A Glossary of Colloquial Anglo-Indian Words and Phrases . . .* (New Delhi, 1968), p. 623.

[219] Burnell and Tiele, *op. cit.* (n. 47), I, 60–61.

[220] *Ibid.*, p. 64.

[221] *Ibid.*, p. 91.

[222] See J. Irwin, "The Commercial Embroidery of Gujarat in the Seventeenth Century," *Journal of the Indian Society of Oriental Art*, XVII (1949), 51–52. He was sending the needleworkers to Queen Maria.

[223] See plate 58, for an embroidered Gujarati bedspread of the sixteenth century.

European tastes. European elements supplied by the Portuguese and their agents were worked into the Indian designs to produce what have since been labeled works in the "Indo-Portuguese style." The so-called Goan embroideries preserved in our museums are pictorial works of Bengal made by an organized industry that produced for export beginning in the late sixteenth century.[224]

Silk-embroidered quilts from India reached the peak of their popularity in Europe during the latter years of the sixteenth century. The art of quilting likewise began to develop in Europe at this same period, as the European textile workers sought to acquire part of this profitable market.[225] The chain stitch, the principal technique of Chinese embroideries throughout history, became increasingly popular in Europe with the importation of Asian embroideries. While the technique was not unknown to European needleworkers of the prediscovery era, the popularity of the chain-stitched Asian embroideries helped to maintain and spread the use of chain stitching in Europe.[226] The lace industry of Spain and Portugal actually adopted the technique only in the mid-sixteenth century.[227] By the end of the century the sumptuary edicts of Philip II and the Inquisition brought an abrupt drop in the production and importation of rich silks and brocades in the Iberian states. The center of the European industry moved thereafter to Italy and France.[228]

The French connoisseurs, while buying textiles from their neighbors, began independently to develop the industry of carpet and tapestry weaving. Imitations of Saracenic carpets were produced in the fourteenth century by the weavers of Paris. In the fifteenth century the tapestry makers of Arras, possibly inspired by Islamic and Persian miniature paintings, began to incorporate Oriental motifs into their designs.[229] The early verdure tapestries of Flanders possibly owe a direct debt to the floral textile prints of India.[230] That floral and animal carpets were being imported into Europe in large numbers, and that they were imitated by European weavers, is clearly illustrated in the numerous Renaissance paintings in which they are shown draped over balconies, lining gondolas, hanging on walls, and covering tables and altars.[231] In 1580 Ancona, which made a specialty of importing Oriental rugs from the Levant, sought to persuade Cardinal Montalto (elected Pope Sixtus V in 1585) to act as the city's protector in Rome by presenting the prelate with two bundles of Oriental

---

[224] J. Irwin, "Indo-Portuguese Embroideries of Bengal," *Arts and Letters: Journal of the Royal India, Pakistan, and Ceylon Society*, XXVI (1952), 65–70.

[225] M. Schuette and S. Müller-Christensen, *The Art of Embroidery* (London, 1964), p. xxiii.

[226] *Ibid.*, p. ix.

[227] F. L. May, *Hispanic Lace and Lace Making* (New York, 1939), p. 271; see also M. A. Moeller, "An Indo-Portuguese Embroidery from Goa," *Gazette des Beaux-Arts*, XXXIV (1948), 118–19.

[228] D. Réal, *Tissus espagnoles et portugais* (Paris, 1925), introduction.

[229] Jairazbhoy, *op. cit.* (n. 35), pp. 47–48.

[230] W. Born, "Textile Ornaments of the Post-Classical East and of Medieval Europe," *Ciba Review*, No. 37 (1941), p. 1344.

[231] K. Erdmann, "Orientalische Tierteppiche auf Bildern des 14. und 15. Jahrhunderts," *Jahrbuch der preussischen Kunstsammlungen*, I, (1929), 263–94; and G. Soulier, "Les influences persanes dans la peinture florentine du XVe siècle," *L'Italia e l'arte straniera* (Rome, 1922), pp. 194–98.

carpets.[232] Persian rugs were meanwhile being imported into western Europe from India by way of Portugal for 40 per cent less than the cost of bringing them from the Levant into Venice.[233]

Antwerp, whose tapestry weavers had been granted the legal right to organize themselves as a separate guild in 1415,[234] came to be a leading center of tapestry manufacture in the fifteenth century. At the same time the city on the Scheldt became the emporium for the tapestries of Brussels, Oudenaarde, and Enghien. As early as 1504 Jehan Grenier of Tournai was paid by Archduke Philip the Fair to design a series of rich tapestries made "à la manière de Portugal et de l'Indye."[235] The series, including therein various tapestries, celebrated the Portuguese conquest of the East (pls. 53, 54). In the three panels which survive, fantastic animals and strange peoples, presumably of India, dominate the scene and remind the viewer of the nearly contemporary woodcuts by Burgkmair labeled "People of Calicut."[236] In one of the panels the words "Indiae novae" are inscribed above a door opening onto a city before which strange animals are being put aboard ship for dispatch to Europe. In 1510 Emperor Maximilian purchased a tapestry from Arnold Poissonnier of Tournai called "History of Wild Beasts and People" designed by Gilles le Castro "in the manner of Calicut," apparently as a variation on the tapestries of 1504.[237] Between 1513 and 1516 the same weaver provided King Henry VIII of England with another exotic production in five pieces which is called in contemporary records "Voyage de Caluce" and which was given as a present to Robert Wyftel, a royal councillor. When Poissonnier died in 1522, nine hangings from the India series were left in his workshop.[238] From the extant literary and tapestry fragments, it is possible to see that the tapestry artists of the early sixteenth century were certainly influenced in their choice of themes by the Portuguese successes in the East.

The tapestry artists responsible for the India series, and the variations on it, were obviously striving for exotic effects by jamming strange animals into triumphal marches and onto crowded ships (pls. 55 and 57). Naked children carrying banners and trumpets tumble about on the backs of zebras. The clothing of the adult figures can be best labeled "half Burgundian and half Oriental."[239]

---

[232] Delumeau, *op. cit.* (n. 32), pp. 99–100.

[233] Assertion of Filippo Sassetti in Marcucci, *op. cit.* (n. 25), pp. 147–48.

[234] J. Denucé, *Antwerp Art-Tapestry and Trade* (The Hague, 1936), p. x.

[235] H. Göbel, *Die Wandteppiche* (Leipzig, 1928), Pt. I, Vol. I, p. 253; W. G. Thomson, *A History of Tapestry* (London, 1930), p. 209; P. Ackerman, *Three Early Sixteenth-Century Tapestries . . .: The Rockefeller-McCormick Tapestries* (New York, 1932), pp. 8–9.

[236] Cf. above, p. 81.

[237] From literary records in the Torre do Tombo at Lisbon, it appears likely that King Manuel also ordered tapestries from this series. See the preface by Reynaldo dos Santos in Martin-Méry, *op. cit.* (n. 56), p. xviii. Simone de Ricci, a Florentine weaver of tapestry who was at Lisbon in 1512, received an order from the king for commemorative tapestries that were to be paid for in pepper. See P. Peregallo, *Cenni intorna alla colònia italiana in Portogallo* (Genoa, 1907), pp. 146–47.

[238] E. Soil, *Les tapisseries de Tournai* (Tournai, 1892), pp. 41–42, 282. One tapestry from this series hangs in the National Museum (NM 17/1918) at Stockholm.

[239] Göbel, *op. cit.* (n. 235), Pt. I, Vol. I, p. 277.

The verdure and hunting scenes woven at Tournai seem to be related to the India tapestries, especially in their use of mythological flora and fauna. The hunting tapestries in particular show Asian and African beasts when they depict exotic chases. The artists possibly got their models by sketching the live beasts that were imported into the Low Countries for the menageries of the Burgundian lords.[240]

Pieter Coecke van Alost, a master painter of tapestries at Brussels, was selected in 1515 by Pope Leo X to translate Raphael's cartoons of the renowned "Acts of the Apostles" into tapestry. The revolution effected by this great production was to make the tapestry into a woven fresco with open spaces rather than crowded and elaborate patterns. Around 1522, Coecke van Alost completed, possibly for his Fugger patrons, a series of six tapestries in his new style that was entitled "Histoire indienne a oliffans et jeraffes."[241] Other merchant princes likewise began to purchase tapestry frescoes, and they came increasingly to demand woven masterpieces that would celebrate the worldly achievements, such as commerce and the discoveries, in which the patrons had a part.[242] By midcentury, tapestries, previously limited in sale to princes and nobles, were being exported in numbers from Antwerp to Portugal, Spain, and the German states. Especially favored at this time were marine, hunting, and garden scenes, mythological and biblical episodes, the heroic exploits of legendary and national heroes, and decorative maps.

Specifically with regard to the overseas deeds of the Portuguese, records exist of four series of Netherlandish tapestries of the latter half of the sixteenth century which celebrate the feats of the Da Gamas, the conquest of Tunis, the exploits of Nuno Alvares, and the triumphs of João de Castro.[243] Originally a part of the Habsburg collections, the tapestries celebrating the deeds of Castro in India from 1538 to 1547 are Austrian state property and are today preserved in the Kunsthistorisches Museum of Vienna.[244] On those panels which remain are recorded by the weavers of Brussels their artistic impressions of Castro's siege of Diu (1538), one of his campaigns against the *hidalcão* (the sultan of Bijapur), his naval descent upon Dabhul, and his triumphal entry into Goa (1547). While the persons and the landscapes of these scenes look European, the tapestry artists strive for a few Asian effects by the turbans that they put on the native prisoners, soldiers, and dancers; by the elephants that are shown drawing the war machines; and by the camels that appear in the backgrounds. Were it not, however, that inscriptions on some of the tapestries indicate what

[240] *Ibid.*, p. 169.
[241] *Ibid.*, pp. 306–8.
[242] Denucé, *op. cit.* (n. 234), pp. xiii–xiv.
[243] L. Keil, *As tapeçarias de D. João de Castro* (Lisbon, 1928), pp. 5–7. A. Faria de Morais ("Les tapisseries de D. João de Castro," *Bulletin des études portugaises et de l'Institut français au Portugal*, N.S., XIX ([1955–56], 64–138) claims that the ten panels in the Castro series were produced early in the seventeenth century by the atelier of Henri de Nève.
[244] First described in 1883 by Ernst von Birk in his inventory of the Habsburg collections. For more recent discussion see L. Baldass, *Die Wiener Gobelins-Sammlung* (Vienna, 1921).

they are meant to depict, it would be hard to determine by the representations alone where the scenes of Castro's triumphs were laid.

In tapestries, paintings, and engravings depicting Asians the costumes are among the earliest features to be Orientalized. The costume books of the last generation of the sixteenth century, as we have seen, make a heroic effort to show examples of Oriental costumes.[245] In terms of the history of European costume the interest in Oriental dress may possibly be related to the prevalence of Spanish fashion in Europe at large and to the gradual disappearance among the upper classes of distinctive national apparel.[246] Silken gowns became ever more popular in the course of the century,[247] and France and Saxony sought to keep money at home by establishing royal silk-weaving industries at Lyons and Dresden.[248]

A distinction developed near the end of the sixteenth century between fabrics woven for clothing and for other uses. The designs on the textiles woven for clothes tended to be naturalistic and to include tulips, sunflowers, palm fronds, and other exotic touches.[249] The native dress of the Japanese legates of 1584 to 1586 was universally described, judged as either ludicrous or delightful, and possibly imitated in Portugal by courtiers.[250] In Venice, where Oriental rather than Spanish dress was imitated, the robe of the Japanese included in Vecellio's book on costume (pl. 69) is called a *zimarra*, the name of a Venetian robe of black that probably evolved in imitation of the long caftan of Turkey or Persia.[251] In Paris, costumers kept on hand all sorts of Orientalized vestments that could be purchased or rented for the divertissements of the court, marriage celebrations, and masquerades.[252] While some of these fanciful costumes were possibly inspired by the prints in costume and cosmographical books, it should be recalled that authentic Asian costumes were available in the collections of connoisseurs and that the artist of Boissard's costume collection seems to have copied Oriental costumes in his drawings. When Thomas Platter was received by Queen Elizabeth at Nonsuch Castle in 1599, she wore "a gown of pure white satin, gold-embroidered, with a whole bird of Paradise for panache, set forward on her head studded with costly jewels."[253] The Virgin Queen, who was

---

[245] See above, pp. 90–91.

[246] Boehn, *op. cit.* (n. 182), II, 111–15.

[247] For an example of how many silks and brocades a woman of means possessed see the list of bequests to Monte Cassino made in her testament of 1545 by Isabella Castreata; reproduced in A. Caravita, *I codici e le arti a Monte Cassino* (Montecassino, 1871), III, 129–34.

[248] *Ibid.*, p. 164.

[249] Falke, *op. cit.* (n. 215), p. 44.

[250] On their visit to Dona Catherina at Villa-Viçosa in Portugal and her interest in imitating their dress see *Asia*, I, 692; also see for descriptions the following contemporary writers: G. Gualtieri, *Relationi della venuta de gli ambasciatori giaponesi a Roma . . .* (Venice, 1586), p. 54; M. A. Ciappa, *Compendio delle herioche et gloriose attioni, et sante vita di Papa Greg. XIII* (Rome, 1591), p. 63; and A. de Herrara, *Historia general del mundo* (Madrid, 1601), II, 450.

[251] Vecellio, *op. cit.* (n. 74), p. 477, and Boehn, *op. cit.* (n. 182), II, 160.

[252] G. Wildenstein, "Un fournisseur d'habits de théâtre et de mascarades à Paris sous Henri III," *Bibliothèque d'Humanisme et Renaissance*, XXIII (1961), 100–102.

[253] C. Williams (trans. and ed.), *Thomas Platter's Travels in England, 1599* (London, 1937), p. 192.

something of a collector of Asian curiosities, thus showed her continental visitor that she, like any ruler of the distant Moluccas, knew how to wear a plumage headdress of the rare bird of paradise found only in the East.

Milady's headdresses and accessories shown in European paintings and preserved in museums also possibly owe a debt to the East. Parallels have been shown to exist, such as the conical hats worn by ladies both in China and in Europe in the Middle Ages.[254] The arc-shaped diadems attached to the fantastic caps of the Dutch ladies shown in the paintings of a number of sixteenth-century Netherlandish artists have been traced to Indian prototypes.[255] The parasol and the folding fan, two of the major weapons in the arsenal of feminine coquetry, appear in the hands of the French women represented in the *Diversarium nationum ornatus* (1593) of Alexandre di Fabri.[256] Parasols or umbrellas, the *chattra* of India, appear in art both as symbols of power and as protection against the elements. Catharine de' Medici, the Italian queen of Henry II of France, is generally credited with having introduced the Chinese (or Japanese) folding fan as part of the costume of courtly ladies (pl. 1).[257] And it has even been suggested that the exposure of the female breast among court ladies may have been inspired by the transparent smocks (*bajus*) that were worn in Goa by the wives and mistresses of the Portuguese.[258]

The rich influx of cotton cloths into Europe from India may also have affected the dyeing and handling as well as the style of ordinary dress. Indigo, which had been costly and used sparingly in Europe before 1500, gradually replaced the native woad as a blue dye during the sixteenth century. The resist dyeing technique commonly used in the East for producing textile patterns was reportedly used in Europe for the first time by Pieter Clock, a Dutch painter.[259] The washing, pleating, and starching of robes was a custom of long standing in India and Ceylon. The stiffening of clothes by the use of starch made from rice or pulse was not common in Europe until the last generation of the sixteenth century. The popular enthusiasm for large collars and starched ruffs among the burghers of the Netherlands and England was probably related to the greater varieties of cotton and linen textiles available, and to the devotion of the upper classes in these countries to personal cleanliness and outward neatness. In Italy women of gentility wore drawers of silk or linen, and the custom was reputedly introduced into France by Catharine de' Medici. The plenitude of inexpensive cotton cloth from India, it has been suggested, probably brought underwear within the financial range of persons of very moderate means. It may even be

[254] Baltrušaitas, *op. cit.* (n. 86), p. 177. Also see G. Schlegel, "Hennins or Conical Lady's Hats in Asia, China and Europe," *T'oung pao*, III (1892), 422–29.

[255] Goetz, *loc. cit.* (n. 122), pp. 228–30.

[256] S. Blondel, *Histoire des éventails chez tous les peuples et à toutes les époques* (Paris, 1875), p. 65.

[257] A. Varron, "From the History of the Umbrella and the Sunshade," *Ciba Review*, No. 42 (1942), p. 1520. On the umbrella of Diane of Poitiers, mistress to King Henry II of France, see *ibid.*, p. 1544.

[258] Slomann, *op. cit.* (n. 90), p. 98 n. For discussion of the *baju* in Portuguese literature see *Asia*, I, 354.

[259] W. A. Vetterli, "The History of Indigo," *Ciba Review*, No. 85 (1951), pp. 3066–68. On the resist technique see Carter and Goodrich, *op. cit.* (n. 110), p. 248.

that the ritual bathing of the Indians, which the Europeans thought of as a good means for mitigating the worst effects of a tropical climate, had something to do with the upsurge of interest in bathing and personal hygiene in sixteenth-century Europe.[260]

5

CERAMICS

In medieval Europe the potter usually spent his time making simple vessels for the everyday use of the common people. His wheel shaped crude earthenware, terracotta, and stoneware utensils that were ordinarily unpainted, drab, and starkly utilitarian. The dazzlingly white, gayly ornamented, and thrillingly thin and resonant porcelains of China that occasionally found their way into medieval Europe must have looked to these simple potters like creations of another world. Celadons from Sung China were used as tableware in Egypt and the Levant as early as the eighth century.[261] Collections of Ming blue-and-white porcelains were later assembled at locations along the land routes, particularly at Ardebil in Iran and at Constantinople by the sultans of Turkey.[262]

In Spain, where the Moors had long been manufacturing exquisite vases and colorful tiles, efforts were made beginning in the fifteenth century to develop the art of pottery painting, especially in Valencia. In Italy, too, it was not long before the potters began to experiment with decorative painting as they sought to compete with the finer wares that the nobility was buying from the Levant and Spain. A vitreous coating that was either transparent (glaze) or opaque (enamel) was applied to colored, porous terracottas to give them the ground required for painting. This polychromed type of faience called majolica was not a successful imitation of porcelain; nonetheless it helped to satisfy the demand for native ceramic vessels of beauty. Once his product had become appealing to the upper classes, the Italian potter was patronized by the Renaissance princes and was elevated in status from simple craftsman to sponsored artist.[263]

Even though the chemical composition of porcelain remained a mystery,

[260] On this intimate subject see Slomann, *op. cit.* (n. 90), pp. 94–100; also C. W. Willett and P. Cunningham, *The History of Underclothes* (London, 1951), pp. 37, 47, 52.

[261] Compare the account of the discoveries recently unearthed at Fustat near Cairo (*New York Times*, January 12, 1969).

[262] For detailed studies of these two Near Eastern collections see J. A. Pope, *Fourteenth-Century Blue-and-White: A Group of Chinese Porcelains in the Topkapu Sarayi Müzesi, Istanbul* (Washington, 1952); and the same author's *Chinese Porcelains from the Ardebil Shrine* (Washington, 1956). Also see Soames Jenyns "The Chinese Porcelains in the Topkapu Saray, Instanbul," *Transactions of the Oriental Ceramic Society* (*London*), XXXVI (1964–66), 43–72.

[263] The best general studies are: W. B. Honey, *European Ceramic Art from the End of the Middle Ages to about 1815* (London, 1949); G. Liverani, *Five Centuries of Italian Majolica* (New York, 1960); A. Lane, *Italian Porcelain* (London, n.d.); J. C. Davillier, *Les origines de la porcelaine en Europe* (Paris, 1882).

the potters of Renaissance Italy could successfully imitate the shapes and decorations of the Oriental wares. The drug pot, or *alberèllo*, was probably made in terracotta by the potter in imitation of the bamboo containers that were used to transport spices over the land routes to Europe. Bulbous Valencian vases of the fifteenth century seem to be directly copied from Chinese and Levantine originals.[264] In imitation of porcelain the sides of majolica dishes and pots became thinner. The Persian palmettes which appeared on fifteenth-century majolica were possibly in imitation of the designs commonly seen on textiles. Border designs, central figures, and softer shadings were copied from the Ming porcelains available in Europe. Continuous trailing sprays and wavy lines in monochrome blue interrupted by a lotus-like flower, called the "porcelain flower" by botanists, were copied from Chinese porcelains. Birds, ducks, silkworms, rosettes, and reeds set in a stylized landscape were incorporated into majolica design at an early date. Arabesques and strictly European ornamentation were often painted in monochrome blue *alla porcellana* by the decorators of majolica in Tuscany, Faenza, and Venice.[265]

Speculation about the composition of true porcelain occurred repeatedly in the travel books and technical works of the sixteenth century. Part of the confusion was produced in Europe by the fact that the word "porcelain," whose ultimate etymology is still unknown, was used so broadly that it included agates, precious stones, mother-of-pearl, and seashells within its meaning. In the inventory of 1611–13 of Philip II's porcelains and other ceramics, listings may be found for "porcelains" of crystal, of agate, and of stone.[266] The Portuguese factor Duarte Barbosa was evidently responsible for lending his authority as a direct observer of life in the East to older European stories about the manufacture of porcelain from seashells and about maturing it underground for a century.[267] Guido Panciroli (1522–99) enshrined for posterity in his book on inventions the common belief that porcelain was compounded of broken shells, beaten eggs, and gypsum (plaster of paris).[268] Damião de Gois, the Portuguese Humanist, wrote in 1541 that porcelain made of seashells was so expensive that a single piece of it cost as much as several slaves.[269] Pierre Belon, who witnessed many porcelains being sold in Cairo, was uncertain how they were made and was inclined to doubt that such fragile items had been safely brought to Egypt from the distant East.[270] Two renowned Humanists, Cardano and J. C. Scaliger (1484–1558), debated learnedly at midcentury about the nature of porcelain and

[264] Liverani, *op. cit.* (n. 263), p. 17; also see discussion of Catalan inventories in A. W. Frothingham, *Lustreware of Spain* (New York, 1951), p. 170.

[265] For a summary of the motifs on Ming porcelains see Pope, *Fourteenth-Century Blue-and-White...* (n. 262), pp. 34–48.

[266] R. Beer (ed.), "Inventare aus dem Archivo del Palacio zu Madrid," *Jahrbuch der kunsthistorischen Sammlungen des allerhöchsten Kaiserhauses*, XIX (1898), Pt. 2, cxxxv–cxli, *passim*.

[267] Dames, *op. cit.* (n. 218), II, 214.

[268] Panciroli, *op. cit.* (n. 110), pp. 281–82. Probably derived from Barbosa through Ramusio.

[269] *Opúsculos históricos* (Porto, 1945), letter to Nanio, 1541.

[270] *Les observations de plusieurs singularitez et choses mémorables, trouvées en Grèce, Asie, Judée, Egypte...* (Paris, 1554), pp. 236v–37v.

its relation to the myrrhine vases of the ancients. Loys Guyon (d. 1630), who wrote on porcelain near the end of the sixteenth century, averred that many of the collectors and connoisseurs of his day were still ignorant of what it was made of and where it came from.[271] But Filippo Sassetti informed his correspondents in Florence in 1580 that Chinese porcelain was produced from a white, malleable clay.[272] The author of the Jesuit treatise of 1590 on China, first published by Hakluyt in 1599, clearly described Chinese porcelain as "the best earthen matter in all the world," and extolled it for "the clearnesse, the beauty, and the strength thereof."[273]

In Portugal, where a flood of porcelains followed in the wake of the discoveries, the makers of ceramic vessels and tiles were as ignorant as those of Italy about the composition of porcelain.[274] The Portuguese were quick, however, to have porcelain made in China to Western specifications and following European models. European mugs, porringers, and goblets of pewter or tinware were copied down to the last detail by the Chinese ceramicists, sometimes along with the royal insignia or with inscriptions in Portuguese (pl. 70).[275] The arms of the European monarchs were possibly copied from the European coins which circulated in China.[276] On the porcelains destined for export the Chinese and Japanese painters sometimes depicted Western scenes or persons copied from the European engravings that were available in the East at the end of the sixteenth century.[277] The earliest of the export porcelains still preserved is a flagon decorated with the armillary sphere of King Manuel which is dated from about the time of his death in 1521. Because such wares were initially obtained through intermediaries, the Portuguese referred to the porcelains of China as "louças da India." The regular appearance in Lisbon of Chinese ceramics designed especially for the European market further stimulated the European potters to produce wares that would compete with those of Chinese manufacture.

Like the Italian makers of majolica, the Portuguese and Spanish potters were unable to produce true porcelain and were limited to imitating the shapes and decorative motifs of the Chinese wares. Even though majolica imitations of Chinese porcelains were known in Portugal before the discoveries, they were

[271] See chapter iii of his *Les diverses leçons* (Lyons, 1625).

[272] Marcucci, *op. cit.* (n. 25), pp. 147–48.

[273] R. Hakluyt (ed.), *The Principal Navigations* . . . (London, 1599), II, Pt. II, 90. Da Cruz, Mendoza, and Linschoten likewise take issue with the tradition that porcelain is made from seashells and affirm that it is a clay product. Paludanus, the Humanist physician, cannot refrain from inserting an annotation to the effect that he believes Linschoten's assertion even though so great a scholar as J. C. Scaliger accepted the older story in the account of how to make porcelain given in his book *Subtleties*. See Burnell and Tiele, *op. cit.* (n. 47), I, 130.

[274] Barreira *et al.*, *op. cit.* (n. 2), I, 159–60.

[275] M. Beurdeley, *Porcelaine de la Compagnie des Indes* (Fribourg, 1962), pp. 78–79; also J. G. Phillips, *China–Trade Porcelain* (Cambridge, Mass., 1956), pp. 18–19. In 1956 at London there were pieces on display with inscriptions and emblems dated 1520, 1541, 1552, and *ca.* 1577. See R. dos Santos, "A exposição de arte portuguesa em Londres," *Belas Artes* (Lisbon), 2d ser., No. 9 (1956), p. 7.

[276] Beurdeley, *op. cit.* (n. 275), p. 90.

[277] See the preface by Reynaldo dos Santos in Martin-Méry, *op. cit.* (n. 56), pp. xv–xvi.

too rare to have profoundly influenced Iberian pottery design and decoration.[278] It was probably the overwhelming presence of Chinese porcelains, including export wares, which inspired the potters of Talavera in Spain to make their "perfect imitations of Oriental china."[279] Other literary references also testify to the imitative efforts that were being made throughout the sixteenth century in the Iberian countries, though samples of the actual vessels produced are exceedingly rare.[280] Porcelain jars and dishes shown in Portuguese paintings of the period seem to be the only other visual remains,[281] except for a few of the tiles (*azulejos*) that are still to be seen in the old gardens and edifices of Portugal. Some of these tiles were possibly produced in Goa or in other parts of Portuguese Asia for sale in Europe, as were the textiles and items of furniture now commonly called Indo-Portuguese.[282] And, when Philip III (Philip II in Portugal) visited Lisbon in 1619, the potters erected an arch in his honor on which an inscribed verse boasts that the faience workers of Lusitania now produce what previously had to be brought from China at exorbitant prices.[283]

Carrying on the majolica tradition of earlier times, Italian ceramicists of the early sixteenth century continued to decorate their wares with Orientalized borders. But the more enterprising potters were not satisfied with faience decorated in imitation of porcelain. They unflaggingly tried to determine the composition of true porcelain in order to produce it at home. The Venetians and their neighbors seemed to believe that the translucent Ming porcelains were a combination of glass and pottery. Early in the sixteenth century "counterfeit porcelain" made of opaque white glass painted with enamel was for sale in the city of canals. In 1519 Duke Alfonso I of Ferrara sought to hire a Venetian who boasted that he could "make porcelain of every kind."[284] In 1561–62 Duke Alfonso II of Ferrara hired Camillo da Urbino, a maker of majolica, to fabricate porcelain. The product he turned out was little more than another form of majolica. While the Italians experimented with glass and clay, there is no record to show that serious potters actually tried to make porcelain from crushed seashells.

Europeans of the sixteenth century made their best attempt to produce true porcelain as a result of experiments carried on under the prodding of

---

[278] Barreira *et al.*, *op. cit.* (n. 2), I, 160–61. For a somewhat less positive view see R. dos Santos, *Faiança portuguesa, séculos XVI e XVII* (Lisbon, 1960), p. 21.

[279] From the manuscript history of Talavera as quoted in J. F. Riano, *The Industrial Arts in Spain* (London, 1879), p. 171; for the history of Talavera and its products see J. Ainaud de Lasarte, *Cerámica y vidrio*, Vol. X of *Ars hispaniae* (Madrid, 1952), pp. 251–59.

[280] For a reproduction of a faience plate of the late sixteenth or early seventeenth century decorated with "Chinoiseries" see Santos, *op. cit.* (n. 278), p. 34, fig. 11.

[281] Barreira *et al.*, *op. cit.* (n. 2), I, 161.

[282] *Ibid.*, II, 70–71. The Goanese trade in ceramics from China was so enormous that an industry developed there of making decorative plates from the fragments of broken Chinese dishes. These reconstituted wares were mounted in rings of lacquer. See Evans, *op. cit.* (n. 15), II, 60.

[283] Arch and inscription shown in an engraving in J. B. de Lavanha, *Viage de la catholica real magestad del rei D. Felipe III, N.S., al reino de Portugal* (Madrid, 1622).

[284] Lane, *op. cit.* (n. 263), p. 2.

Duke Francesco I of Tuscany. Andrea Gussoni, Venetian legate to Florence, wrote in 1575 that Francesco and his workers had rediscovered the secret of making "Indian porcelain" after years of experimenting.[285] Still, the Florentine ruler continually sought information thereafter on the composition of Chinese porcelain from Filippo Sassetti in Lisbon. In his enterprise for making porcelain Francesco was singularly aided by a Levantine (or possibly he was a Greek) who had taken a journey to the Indies. The "Medici porcelain" of Francesco was a translucent soft-paste product reminiscent of similar wares that had long been turned out in Turkey. Although the imitation porcelain manufactured in Francesco's factory was finer than majolica, it was not translucent or resonant enough to be mistaken for the superb hard-paste porcelain of China.

Production of the Medici porcelains ended with Francesco's death in 1587. The records show that at least fifty-nine pieces were turned out within a span of twelve years; it is probable that others were produced for which no listing exists.[286] Forty-five of the recorded pieces have been located and are extant (for examples see pls. 71–74).[287] According to a contemporary recipe the Medici porcelain was a mixture of twelve parts of glassy material (sand, glass, and powdered rock crystals) with five parts of white clay from Vicenza. The surviving pieces betray through technical defects their experimental character. Almost all of them are decorated in blue on a white ground that is covered with a cloudy glaze bespecked with minute bubbles. The shapes are quite conventional and seem not to be modeled on Oriental prototypes. The painted designs, by contrast, are almost all of Oriental derivation and quite distinct from the older Orientalized motifs used by the painters on majolica.[288]

The Chinese porcelains available in Florence in the Medici collections were probably used as models by the experimenters, for the ornamentation and painted designs of the Medici porcelains are obviously borrowed from Chinese vessels made in the reigns of the Chia-ch'ing (1522–66) and Wan-li (1573–1619) emperors. A Western-shaped vase has attached to it a dragon spout and a handle shaped as a fantastic animal. Painted designs which include pine trees, deer, and birds are frank imitations of common Ming porcelains. A dish exhibits a broad frieze surrounding a center in which rocks, bamboo, water plants, and "clouds" are displayed in the Chinese manner. Some of the Medici bowls are signed on the bottom with a mark that is probably supposed to be a Chinese character.[289] From these indications it can clearly be seen that the Medici porcelains were imitations, as far as it was within the technical competence of Europeans to carry it out, of Ming blue-and-white porcelains.

The Medici porcelains, like the true porcelains of China, possessed a magical quality for the sixteenth century. The secret of their composition, the mystery

---

[285] The best account of this enterprise is in *ibid.*, pp. 3–4.
[286] G. Liverani, *Catalogo delle porcellane dei Medici* (Faenza, 1936). Also see above, p. 5, for Medici porcelains collected by Emperor Rudolf II.
[287] Lane, *op. cit.* (n. 263), p. 4.
[288] *Ibid.*, pp. 4–5.
[289] *Ibid.*, pp. 5–6.

surrounding their manufacture and firing, the fragile transparency of their bodies, and the strangeness of their decoration, helped to give the porcelains a recondite and enigmatical character. The popular belief in their relationship to weird seashells and the mystical egg, or seat of life, made them curiosities of more than ordinary value and spiritual power. "Their admirable Nature," asserts Panciroli, "is conspicuous in this, that they immediately break upon the Reception of Poyson." [290] And in the paintings and collections of curiosities the porcelain vessel is prized quite as often for its mysterious and cosmic qualities [291] as for its delicate, shell-like beauty. For, like the shell, it appears to be the work of the Creator and beyond the ability of ordinary mortals to manufacture or fully comprehend. The shell carries mysteriously the roar of the sea; the porcelain dazzles the eye and confounds reason.

6

WOODS, FURNITURE, AND LACQUERWARE

The exotic woods of tropical Asia—sandal, teak, camphor, ebony, and aloes—were known to Europe in classical Antiquity. The aromatic woods, particularly aloes and sandal, were burned as incense, and in the medieval kitchen red sandal was added to dishes as a flavoring. Camphor and aloes and their by-products were especially valued as medicaments and dyes. Ebony and teak were imported into the Roman Empire to help meet the need for durable construction wood. But ebony was also made into cups, from Antiquity to the sixteenth century, because of its alleged antagonism to poison. The hardness and deep black color of ebony possibly gave rise to the tradition repeated by Pausanias (fl. A.D. 174), the Greek traveler and geographer, that the ebony tree produced neither leaves nor fruit, was never exposed to the sun, and lived in the shade of other trees. Bamboo, employed in Asia for all sorts of mundane purposes from book-making to bridge-building, was known in medieval Europe only as the famous cane that reputedly carried the silkworm in its hollow interior into the Byzantine Empire. New information about the woods of Asia and their uses had to await the establishment of direct contacts between maritime Europe and Asia.

Sixteenth-century writers of travel accounts comment on the aromatic woods of Asia in connection with their discussions of the spice trade. Garcia da Orta devotes several of his colloquies to the place of origin, description, and uses of, and the commerce in, aloes, sandal, and camphor wood. In the process he challenges and corrects many of the impressions and beliefs of the ancients and

[290] *Op. cit.* (n. 110), p. 282; also cf. G. Bandmann, "Das Exotische in der europäischen Kunst," in *Der Mensch und die Künste: Festschrift Heinrich Lützeler* (Düsseldorf, 1962), p. 343, n. 30.

[291] In the breviary of Mayer van den Bergh a Chinese blue-and-white vase filled with flowers is included, but in different positions, in the scenes illustrating the months of January and October. See C. Gaspar (ed.), *Le bréviaire du musée Mayer van den Bergh à Anvers* (Brussels, 1932), fols. 406 and 558. Also see A. I. Spriggs, "Oriental Porcelain in Western Paintings, 1450–1750," *Transactions of the Oriental Ceramic Society* (London), XXXVI (1964–66), 73–76.

of his contemporaries in Europe about the medicinal qualities of the woods and their by-products. The coconut palm and its numerous products he also discusses at length, and he concludes that its many attributes "make it good merchandise for Portugal."[292] Linschoten, who likewise remarks on the woods, goes a step further than most of his predecessors by commenting on the furniture made in India that he judges to be finely "wrought and inlaid very workman-like."[293]

Aside from the woods themselves, Europe received in the sixteenth century a selection of furniture made by the craftsmen of the East. Tables, beds, cabinets, chairs, chests, boxes, and chessboards made in India and China of exotic woods and often inlaid with mother-of-pearl, bone, or ivory were brought back to Europe by the Portuguese.[294] The market for Asian furniture, once it opened in Europe, was widened by the production in India of "export furniture."[295] Furniture in Portugal itself began to be more commonly finished in ebony and teak and with inlays added. Decorated bedsteads from the East, sometimes painted or covered with embroidered silk, inspired the legislation in Portugal setting the standards to be followed in making the monumental beds that came into vogue there.[296] The ornamentation on the bedsteads manufactured in Portugal usually followed Oriental models closely.

Outside of Portugal the rulers of Europe collected "Indian" desks, tables, and lacquered boxes for their own chambers of curiosities or as gifts for other notables. A chair and a chest with ivory inlays were evidently made in India especially for Catharina Steinbeck, the last consort of King Gustavus I Vasa of Sweden (pls. 79, 81).[297] Japanese lacquer, or Urushi ware, was given to King Philip II of Spain in 1584 by the legates.[298] A Chinese chair, presumed to have been used by Philip II of Spain during his last years in the Escorial, might have been "export furniture" made in Manila or Mexico after a Chinese model.[299] In Spain cabinets inlaid with ivory and fitted with drawers covered with silk embroideries in different colors were manufactured in the late sixteenth century in imitation of Indian furniture.[300] The lid design on a chest made in Milan around 1570 for Duke Albert V of Bavaria follows patterns common on inlaid chests of Indian manufacture (pl. 78). A huge tent bed dated 1596 was

[292] G. da Orta, *Colloquies on the Simples and Drugs of India*, ed. C. Markham (London, 1913), p. 141.
[293] Burnell and Tiele, *op. cit.* (n. 47), I, 61.
[294] On Chinese chairs and bedsteads see Gaspar da Cruz's discussion as translated in C. R. Boxer (ed.), *South China in the Sixteenth Century* (London, 1953), p. 125. Escalante (see *Asia* pp. 742–43) bought a chest in Lisbon that was so admirably made that "none [in Europe] could take upon them to make the lyke. . . ." See Frampton's translation, chap. ix.
[295] Barreira, *et al.*, *op. cit.* (n. 2), I, 378–79; and J. F. da Silva Nascimento and A. Cardoso Pinto, *Cadeiras portuguesas* (Lisbon, 1952), p. 48.
[296] Varreira *et al.*, *op. cit.* (n. 2), I, 373–74. Even ivory bedsteads were sent to Lisbon.
[297] V. Slomann, "The Indian Period of European Furniture," *Burlington Magazine*, LXV (1934), p. 120.
[298] Abranches Pinto *et al.*, *op. cit.* (n. 55), p. 88.
[299] Slomann, *loc. cit.* (n. 297), p. 204.
[300] Riano, *op. cit.* (n. 279), p. 121.

made of ebony and decorated with elaborate figures for the Nuremberg patrician and silk merchant Paulus Schewl.[301]

It is in the widespread use of ebony for furniture and interior decoration that the greatest change took place in wood turning and joinery during the sixteenth century. In Italy, where the Venetians had brought ebony into vogue even before the opening of the sea route to India, the princes furnished their special chambers with ebony chairs and cabinets, many of them the work of German craftsmen. The studiolo (pl. 80) or curiosity cabinet, of Francesco de' Medici was decorated with ebony set with a variety of precious stones. For this work and others, cabinetmakers journeyed to Florence from Munich, Prague, and elsewhere to help establish workshops.[302] For, along with his efforts in porcelains and the lapidarial arts, Francesco had a profound desire to establish Florence as the center of cabinetwork in ebony and other exotic woods.[303] This was, of course, part of his effort to concentrate the luxury trades in Florence and to make the city into the artistic center that it has been ever since.

While Florence specialized in producing costly studiolo pieces in ebony, Augsburg became the center for beautiful cabinetwork in all kinds of wood.[304] German chests and art cabinets were sold to most of the princely collectors in Europe during the last years of the sixteenth century. The ornamentations on these artistic pieces of woodwork continued to follow the Oriental designs that had been derived from Asian furniture and from Orientalized Venetian patterns. The ebony writing tables designed in 1617 for Duke Philip II of Pomerania-Stettin had the four parts of the world and the four elements as inlaid decorations on the doors enclosing its drawers.[305] Exotic flora and fauna of the East are depicted in such pieces in their natural colors and in a style reminiscent of the inlays in Mughul furniture.

The attraction of ebony as the wood most appropriate to the studiolo may not be entirely attributable to its durability, beauty, and rarity. Like the other objects in the chamber of curiosities, the ebony itself had a metaphysical quality for the men of the time. It was grown only in distant lands, was harder and blacker than European woods, and could be given a glossy sheen. Where ebony was combined with other woods, the drawers and various interior parts were normally made of exotic woods of extraordinary color. The precious stones used to decorate the ebony cabinets were themselves believed to possess various mystical qualities, thus continuing the theme of making the studiolo into a kind of *Wunderkammer* in miniature. In it the valuable and mysterious

[301] A. Feulner, *Kunstgeschichte des Möbels seit dem Altertum* (Berlin, 1927), fig. 180 and p. 186.

[302] D. Heikamp, "Zur Geschichte der Uffizien-Tribuna und der Kunstschränke in Florenz und Deutschland," *Zeitschrift für Kunstgeschichte*, XXVI (1963), 195–96.

[303] It may have been coincidental that in 1585 the Japanese legates presented Francesco with gifts of wood. See *Asia*, I, 694. Thevet (*op. cit.* [n. 168], I, 409) comments at length on the "good ebony" of India, as compared to that of Brazil.

[304] T. Hausmann, "Der Pommersche Kunstschrank," *Zeitschrift für Kunstgeschichte*, XXII (1959), 337.

[305] O. Doering (ed.), *Des Augsburger Patriciers Philipp Hainhofer Beziehungen zum Herzog Philip II von Pommern-Stettin: Correspondenzen aus den Jahren 1610–1619* (Vienna, 1896), p. 317.

objects of foreign provenance were combined aesthetically and allegorically to produce a concrete and beautiful sample of the harmony existing between nature and art, between man and the universe.[306]

Along with valuable woods from the East, the ancients imported lac,[307] a resinous incrustation produced on certain trees by the puncture of the lac insect. In India, lac was used as sealing wax, dye, and varnish, while in Europe it was prized mainly for its dark red coloring matter. But lacquerware, so-called because it was commonly thought to be finished with lac varnish, was not brought into Europe in any quantity until the sixteenth century (pl. 6).[308] Then the type of lacquer called "Coromandel" was imported into Europe, principally by Venice.[309] This lacquerware, which was manufactured in East Asia, is actually not finished with lac varnish or Indian shellac; in China, Japan, and Korea the lacquer is obtained from the sap of a tree botanically related to the American poison oak. Lacquered furniture was made in the East, especially for the use of the Jesuit missionaries there, which was German in form and Asian in decoration.[310] In Europe the recipe for making lacquer, by either of the two Asian methods, was as unknown in the sixteenth century as the formula for making porcelain.

Europeans tried, as in the case of porcelain, to produce lacquered objects that could compete with Oriental wares. In the sixteenth century Venetian artisans began to make boxes, cabinets, frames, and caskets that were varnished with Indian shellac in red, black, or dark green in imitation of Eastern lacquerware.[311] Albrecht Dürer, a close student of Near Eastern lacquerware, wrote to a friend in 1509 seeking the recipe for a special varnish that nobody in his circle could produce.[312] In 1515 Leonardo, as a reminder to himself, wrote this note: "Learn how to melt gum into lacquer-varnish." [313] Decorative motifs were also borrowed by the Europeans from Near Eastern, Indian, and East Asian wares. In the earliest imitations the European lacquers were decorated with figures in Chinese costumes, ladies holding parasols and fans, exotic plants and

---

[306] Cf. Heikamp, *loc. cit.* (n. 302), pp. 193–94; 235–36.

[307] Sanskrit, *lākshā;* Hindi, *lākh;* Persian, *lak;* Latin, *lacca.* The Western word "lacquer" is derived from this term. See Yule and Burnell, *op. cit.*, pp. 499–500.

[308] F. W. Gibbs, "Historical Survey of the Japanning Trade," *Annals of Science*, VII (1951), 401. The few pieces which reached Europe as early as the fourteenth century were kept in the treasuries of the churches and the vaults of the princes. See Hans Huth, *Europäische Lackarbeiten, 1600–1850* (Darmstadt, n.d.), p. 5.

[309] It appears that ships from Burma (Pegu), Martaban, and Malacca brought both lac and lacquerware to the ports of the Coromandel Coast, where the Arab and Western merchants then purchased them. Hence the name "Coromandel" was applied to the lacquerware imported from the East in the sixteenth century. The lac itself was often called "lac of Sumatra," presumably because Sumatra was another of the principal markets in which it was purchased. On this trade see Linschoten's account in Burnell and Tiele, *op. cit.* (n. 47), II, 88. Some of the "Coromandel" pieces were lacquered screens.

[310] J. Irwin, "A Jacobean Vogue for Oriental Lacquer-Ware," *Burlington Magazine*, XCV (1953), 194.

[311] The best survey of the history of European lacquer is W. Holzhausen, *Lackkunst in Europa* (Brunswick, 1959); also see the forthcoming book by Hans Huth, *Lacquer of the West* (Chicago, 1970).

[312] Holzhausen, *op. cit.* (n. 311), p. 32.

[313] McCurdy, *op. cit.* (n. 104), II, 1124.

animals, and even Oriental buildings and gardens.[314] Elsewhere in Italy, as well as in Portugal, France, England, and Holland, efforts were likewise made to produce a local product to compete with the brilliant lacquers of the East. But because they had no concrete notion of Eastern lacquer techniques, the Europeans could not match the perfection of the Oriental lacquers. It was not until the late seventeenth century that the secret of the "art of Japanning" became known to Europe.[315]

7

PRECIOUS METALS, GEMS, AND JEWELRY

Asia was a deficit area in gold and silver throughout the sixteenth century. Between the Cape of Good Hope and the Pacific just two regions supplied the bulk of the gold circulated in the Orient. Most of the gold mined in Ethiopia and southeast Asia was attracted to the marts of coastal and continental India.[316] Gold was constantly in short supply in eastern Asia, and the price of it mounted sharply in the last third of the sixteenth century. Silver, mined primarily in Japan and China, was more readily available than gold in the Far East. Asian supplies of precious metals were augmented in the sixteenth century by European silver and American gold and silver brought into the region by the Portuguese and Spaniards. Despite the fact that the Europeans knew full well that gold and silver were more highly prized in Asia than any other commodities, they persistently believed, as Mandeville had, that they would find a "land of gold" in Asia comparable to what they had found in America.[317] Eventually, it could be said, they found it in Australia.

The persistence in Europe of the belief in an Asian "land of gold" may be shrugged off by attributing it simply to the naive hope that man has always had about finding gold at the end of the rainbow. Or it may be ascribed to the simple fact that European sailors sought out, cherished, and perpetuated the local Asian stories of an Eldorado in some unidentified place located always farther to the east. But dreams of mineral wealth were also given substance by the lavish use that the Indians, especially, made of precious metals and stones in their arts and crafts. The gems, pearls, and fine pieces of jewelry and metalwork of India which were carried back to Europe conveyed explicitly the idea that Asia was a region of incalculable wealth which was becoming even wealthier through its importation of European and American precious metals.

---

[314] See the article on "lacquer" by Giovanni Mariacher in the *Encyclopedia of World Art*. Also see the high praise expressed for Chinese lacquer by Gaspar da Cruz (in Boxer, *op. cit.* [n. 294], p. 125) and by Linschoten (in Burnell and Tiele, *op. cit.* [n. 47], I, 61, 64, 97; II, 90).

[315] Interestingly enough, John Evelyn and Robert Boyle, the pioneers in the discovery of "English Japanning," turned for information on lacquering techniques to the sixteenth-century account by Linschoten. See Gibbs, *loc. cit.* (n. 308), pp. 403–4.

[316] V. Magalhães-Godinho, *Os descobrimentos e a economia mundial* (Lisbon, 1963), I, 243, 398–99.

[317] For example, see Belon, *op. cit.* (n. 270), pp. 86v–87v.

The European conception of Asia as a land overflowing with gold and precious stones can be traced back to Herodotus and Ctesias.[318] But it was not until Alexander's time (early fourth century B.C.) that the polished stones of India were actually imported into Europe. The Indians seem never to have cut designs into the gems; the art of engraving gems, an invention of the seal-cutters of Nineveh in the eighth century B.C., passed through the Phoenicians to the Asiatic Greeks and the Etruscans. The heads of the gods and the rulers of Hellenic Greece were engraved upon the stone of the signet as they were upon the coins of the time. At first the engravers worked with the softer stones, especially the lapis lazuli and the common amethyst. The Romans, who took the Etruscans for their masters in the glyptic art, produced deeply cut figures in harder stones and gems. The collecting of engraved gems and cameos became a vogue in the Roman Republic with its taste for the extravagant. In the imperial era of Augustus, when gem engraving reached its zenith in Rome, imitation intagli of paste and glass were produced for the common people. The declining economic prosperity of the empire in the third century A.D. brought with it a sharp drop in the importation of precious stones and in the cutting of real gems. Long after it had disappeared in Rome, the technique of counterfeiting precious stones was practiced at Constantinople. By the end of the Middle Ages the craft of making glass jewels passed from Byzantium to Venice, the European center of Eastern trade.

In Europe at large the art of gem engraving became all but totally extinct during the Middle Ages. Jewel merchants like the Polos were possibly more interested in the medicinal and magical properties of jewels than in their ornamental use. Marco described the jade workings of Turkestan and identified the various qualities of jade in terms of their affinities with stones commonly known in Europe.[319] The legends of the stones and their catalogue of secret properties collected in the lapidarial writings of the Middle Ages were derived from the comments of Pliny, the Book of Revelation, and the famous *Book of Stones* falsely attributed to Aristotle.[320] The *De lapidibus* (written 1067–81) of Marbodius was a popular Christian treatise written in Latin hexameters that had an influence on mineralogy comparable to that exerted on zoology by the *Physiologus*. In the twelfth century antique stones were used to decorate the reliquaries made in northern Europe and soon ceremonial vessels were likewise encrusted with them.[321] The theological mineralogy of the medieval lapidaries, like those of the Orient, ordained that jewels should be worn as prophylactics and talismen rather than as mere ornaments. The amethyst, which neutralizes the intoxicating

[318] For the general history of precious stones and engraved gems see G. F. Kunz, *The Curious Lore of Precious Stones* (New York, 1938); C. W. King, *The Handbook of Engraved Gems* (London, 1866) and *Antique Gems and Rings* (London, 1872); and E. W. Streeter, *Precious Stones and Gems: Their History, Sources, and Characteristics* (6th ed.; London, 1898).

[319] L. Olschki, *Marco Polo's Asia* (Berkeley, 1960), pp. 162–63. Odoric of Pordenone described in vivid detail the great jade jar belonging to the khan. See J. Goette, *Jade Lore* (New York, 1937), p. 45.

[320] See J. Ruska, *Das Steinbuch des Aristoteles* (Heidelberg, 1912).

[321] Baltrušaitis, *op. cit.* (n. 86), pp. 24–26.

effects of alcohol, was made into cups. The topaz kept the soul pure and chaste, its name being related to *tapas* in Sanskrit, or to the word which is applied to the process by which the Indian ascetic frees himself from sensual desires. Bracelets, rings, and metallic charms were inscribed with magical words to protect their wearers from enemies, both natural and supernatural.[322]

The lapidarial writings of the early Renaissance were not affected significantly by the revival of classical learning because the medieval writings preserved most of the ancient traditions. In their lapidarial books on precious stones and engraved gems, the Renaissance investigators sought to provide philosophical and scientific explanations for the virtues conventionally attributed to the jewels.[323] With regard to the jewels themselves the Renaissance craftsmen, beginning around 1400, revitalized the art of gem engraving. Stones of brilliance and color were sought, as the jewelers began once again to make pins, brooches, buckles, necklaces, and rings for personal ornament.[324] Still, a belief persisted in the medicinal, antidotal, and talismanic virtues of precious stones, and of the other rare items used in jewels such as the rhinoceros horn and the bezoar stone.

The Renaissance desire for ornament and antidote were both satisfied and stimulated by the gems, oddities, and lapidarial fables imported from the East. The cornucopia of pearls and cut and uncut gems also held a host of fabulous and ancient Asian traditions about the virtues of the stones which flowed into Europe. The writings of the medieval and Renaissance travelers contained detailed information on the sources, prices, and availability of the much esteemed pearls and precious stones of Asia. Mandeville, in particular, related many stories about gold and precious stones, and about the uses of jewels as charms in the East. Along with these accounts, and by other means as well, the writers relayed to Europe some of the Asian traditions about the medicinal, antidotal, and magical virtues of jewels, drugs, and a miscellany of exotic objects. For example, Duarte Barbosa wrote early in the sixteenth century:

And here they find [in Cambay] a great abundance of . . . [chalcedony], which are stones with grey and white veins in them which they fashion round, and after they are bored the Moors wear them on their arms in such a manner that they touch the skin, saying that they are good to preserve chastity; as these stones are plentiful they are not worth much.[325]

The cosmographies and the travel collections likewise give a fair share of attention in their discussions of the Orient to details of the trade in precious

---

[322] For a detailed history of the lapidarial writings and for the legends enshrined in them see J. Evans, *Magical Jewels of the Middle Ages and the Renaissance, Particularly in England* (Oxford, 1922), esp. pp. 35–37, 121–25.

[323] For a list of precious metals and stones and their Christian symbolism see L. Réau, *Iconographie de l'art chrétien* (Paris, 1956), I, 135–36.

[324] At the end of the fifteenth century engraved jewels were widely diffused in Italy according to Camillo di Leonardo in his *Speculum lapidum* . . . (1502).

[325] Dames, *op. cit.* (n. 218), I, 144–45.

stones.[326] Hans Ulrich Krafft, a merchant of Augsburg who traveled in the Levant from 1573 to 1577, observes with respect to jewelry that "many of the objects produced by these barbarian peoples are so subtly and decoratively worked that they surpass those of the Germans and other Christian nations."[327] Garcia da Orta devotes two of his colloquies on the drugs and simples of India to the lore current in Asia about diamonds and precious stones. References to the sources, prices, and virtues of pearls and the available jewels appear as well in other of his colloquies. Later European writers on precious stones, such as Anselm Boetius de Boodt, court physician to Rudolf II, derived much of their information on the diamonds and rubies of India and Burma from Orta and Linschoten.[328]

Once they established relations with Vijayanagar and Ceylon in 1505, the Portuguese sought to gain direct access to and information on the sources of the precious stones. A Portuguese factory was set up at Bhatkal in 1510, an important town on the route to the city of Vijayanagar and a market for the pearls from the Fishery Coast. Domingo Pacs, who visited Vijayanagar from 1520 to 1522, gathered information on diamond mining.[329] Georg Pock, the factor of the German firm of Hirschvogel, reported to Nuremberg from Vijayanagar in 1521 that the collection of jewels of Krishna Dēva Rāyya was far greater than anything possessed by a European monarch.[330] A manuscript report by two lapidaries that is dated around 1548 identifies five diggings in Vijayanagar and states that others exist in Orissa.[331]

The diamonds of India were judged by contemporaries to be smaller in size but heavier in weight, finer in clarity, and higher in virtue than the diamonds of Arabia, Scythia, Macedonia, Ethiopia, and Cyprus.[332] In Lisbon diamonds of all sizes, cut and uncut, were for sale, but diamonds from India became hard to get in the 1560's when war and famine, attendant upon the fall of Vijayanagar, prevented the mining and transport of the precious stones.[333] The lapidaries

[326] Sebastian Münster in the 1550 edition of his *Cosmographia* (pp. 168–71) devotes a large share of his attention to diamonds; Richard Eden in the 1577 edition of *The History of Travayle* (pp. 423r–426v) gives all the data available to him on the traffic in precious stones.

[327] K. D. Haszler (ed.), *Reisen und Gefangenschaft Hans Ulrich Kraffts* (Stuttgart, 1861), p. 125.

[328] A. Boetius de Boodt, *Gemmarum et lapidum historia* . . . (Leyden, 1636), pp. 33–37, 120–21. For the influence of Orta see *Asia*, I, 192–95. Also see discussion in C. F. Torre de Assunção, "A mineralogia nos Colóquios," *Garcia da Orta*, Special Commemorative Volume (1963), pp. 712–21.

[329] Cf. *Asia*, I, 374, 471.

[330] Pock was also a correspondent of the Herwart merchant group, the German family most interested in the jewel trade between India and Europe. See H. Kömmerling-Fitzler, "Der Nürnberger Georg Pock (d. 1528–1529) in Portugiesisch-Indien und im Edelsteinland Vijayanagara," *Mitteilungen des Vereins für Geschichte der Stadt Nürnberg*, LV (1967–68), 168–69.

[331] A. de A. Calado, "Livro que trata das cousas da India e do Japão," *Boletim da biblioteca da universidade de Coimbra*, XXIV (1960), 69–71.

[332] G. M. Bonardi, *La minera del mondo* (Venice, 1589), p. 23v. On the sale of Indian gems at Baghdad in 1574 see the account of Leonhard Rauwolf as summarized in Dannenfeldt, *op. cit.* (n. 143), p. 121.

[333] See letter of the Viceroy Antão de Noronha of December 30, 1564, to Queen Catharine of Portugal in J. Wicki (ed.), "Dokumente und Briefe aus der Zeit des indischen Vizekönigs D. Antão de Noronha (1563–1568)," in H. Flasche (ed.), *Aufsätze zur portugiesischen Kulturgeschichte* (Münster, 1960), I, 239.

working in Lisbon in the sixteenth century were among the finest diamond cutters the world has ever known.[334] Johann von Schuren, the Fugger agent, reports buying at Lisbon a solitaire of 67.5 carats as well as many smaller diamonds to be set in rings and other kinds of jewelry.[335] At Antwerp the Affaitadi merchants imported diamonds and pearls "en gros" from Lisbon, maintained a lapidary, and furnished quantities of uncut stones to the tapestry makers for use as decorations on their more elaborate creations. Diamonds from India were also marketed in Venice by the Affaitadi.[336]

The pearls from the Persian Gulf and the Straits of Manaar were more highly prized than the pearls found in European and American waters. All pearls were judged in terms of the "perfect pearls of the Orient" which brought the highest price on the Antwerp market.[337] Leonardo prepared a recipe for melting small pearls in order to make "pearls as large as you wish."[338] Dresses stitched all over with pearls were in vogue before 1550, and in the latter half of the century pearls were lavishly used as trimmings and in embroidery. Many of the leading collectors had so many pearls that they noted them in their inventories by weight rather than by number.[339] Mother-of-pearl was used in making medallions, game boards, and inlays in furniture.[340] Infusions of pulverized pearls were administered as a physic after all less drastic measures had failed.

Precious stones available in the Indian coastal towns likewise arrived in Europe in quantity. Linschoten noted that Cambay sold amethysts, garnets, crystals, agates (cat's eyes), fine amber, and carnelians. Ceylon marketed all the precious stones except diamonds, and Arakan and Pegu in Burma furnished rubies, sapphires, emeralds, and spinels.[341] Jades and nephrites from China competed in Europe with the kidney-shaped nephrites of America. Until the end of the sixteenth century the English language used one transliteration or the other from the Chinese word *yü* (stone) as its word for jade.[342] Common belief had it that a piece of jade placed over the kidney would cure ailments connected with that organ.

The ready availability in Europe of precious stones and metals from the overseas world combined to promote the art of the jeweler and the other

[334] Streeter, *op. cit.* (n. 318), p. 23.

[335] N. Lieb, *Die Fugger und die Künste im Zeitalter der hohen Renaissance* (Munich, 1958), p. 136. Also see the list of jewels, including rubies, sapphires, and diamonds, which Lucas Rem, the Welser merchant, gave to his bride in 1518. See B. Greiff (ed.), "Tagebuch des Lucas Rem . . .," *Jahresbericht des historischen Kreisvereins . . . von Schwaben und Neuburg* (Augsburg, 1861), p. 53.

[336] J. Denucé, *Inventaire des Affaitadi, banquiers italiens à Anvers de l'année 1568* (Antwerp, 1934), p. 63.

[337] J. A. Goris, *Etude sur des colonies marchandes méridionales . . . à Anvers de 1488 à 1567* (Louvain, 1925), pp. 260–61. For a comparison of European and Oriental pearls see the letter to Ortelius by Daniel Engelhardus (March 23, 1598) in J. H. Hessels (ed.), *Abrahami Orteliis . . . Epistulae* (Cambridge, 1887), p. 746.

[338] McCurdy, *op. cit.* (n. 104), I, 191.

[339] Boehn, *op. cit.* (n. 182), II, 184.

[340] E. Bonnaffé, *Inventaire des meubles de Catherine de Médicis en 1589* (Paris, 1874), p. 90.

[341] Burnell and Tiele, *op. cit.* (n. 47), I, 61, 80, 97.

[342] Goette, *op. cit.* (n. 319), p. 24.

workers in metal. The European workers also had available, whether or not they were influenced by them, a variety of bracelets, rings, and signets made in the East. Like other artists, the jewelers came to be patronized by royal and papal connoisseurs. Both Charles V and Pope Clement VII employed Valario Brilli il Vicentino to set jewels for them. Matteo del Nazzaro, master of the mint to Francis I, founded an atelier in which he taught pupils to work in precious metals. Jacopo da Trazzo, the first European to engrave a diamond, became wealthy in the service of Philip II of Spain. As time went on, the techniques of engraving on gems were greatly refined, particularly through the use of the magnifying glass.[343] In England and Venice jewels in the form of ships were highly favored. Queen Elizabeth was presented with a ship jewel whose hull was made of ebony set with a table diamond and whose masts and rigging were fashioned from enameled gold set with pearls.[344]

One-fourth of the jewelers and silversmiths plying their craft in Lisbon in 1513 were foreigners, mostly Spanish Jews.[345] Raulu Xatim, a goldsmith of Goa, worked in Lisbon for the king from 1518 to 1521.[346] This concentration of skilled workers in gold and silver forced Dom Manuel to issue his decree of April 19, 1514, ordaining that the workers in precious stones and gold should keep shop on the Rua Nova, and the silverworkers on the Rua Dourivesaria.[347] Diogo Roiz was silversmith to the consort of Manuel and one of the greatest artists working in Lisbon. It was probably Roiz who was responsible for establishing separate guilds of gold- and silversmiths, each with its own recognized masters and rules. That such an organization was necessary, and possibly effective, is demonstrated by the fact that by 1550 the city counted an impressive total of 430 workers in precious metals.[348]

The most celebrated of the early Portuguese creations of the goldsmith's art is the famous custodial of Belém. It was made in 1506 by Gil Vicente from gold that Vasco da Gama brought to Lisbon in 1503 from his second voyage to India. Dedicated to Dom Manuel, the custodial of the Jerónimos resembles in its form and decoration the south portal of the Belém monastery.[349] Like so many other Manueline creations, the heavy golden custodial is richly decorated with reliefs of exotic flowers, fruits, and birds. Many of the silver and gold works produced in Lisbon for sale to the general public were equally massive, profusely decorated with exotic and maritime objects, and artistically analogous to the Manueline ornamentation on the monasteries of Belém and Tomar.[350] One of the treasures most cherished by Diogo de Sousa, the Manueline bishop

[343] King, *Engraved Gems* (n. 318), p. 170.
[344] J. Evans, *A History of Jewellery, 1100–1870* (London, 1953), pp. 127–28.
[345] J. Couto and A. M. Gonçalves, *A ourivesaria em Portugal* (Lisbon, 1962), p. 102.
[346] R. dos Santos, "A India Portuguesa e as artes decorativas," *Belas Artes* (Lisbon), 2d ser., No. 7 (1954), p. 9. The Goa worker had made a dagger and other items for the king before he came to Lisbon.
[347] Couto and Gonçalves, *op. cit.* (n. 345), p. 17.
[348] *Ibid.*, pp. 120–21.
[349] For pictorial reproductions of both see *ibid.*, p. 104.
[350] Barreira *et al.*, *op. cit.* (n. 2), I, 44.

of Braga, was the episcopal throne that he had made in the form of a splendid galleon whose high prow was studded with jewels and precious stones. It seemed to lie at anchor under the Gothic reticula of the cathedral's arched roof as if it were tied up in the shade of a palm tree.[351] A wider variety of religious and secular objects in precious metals and stones were also made by Indo-Portuguese goldsmiths and jewelers for sale in Europe.

The tendency toward a profuse, exotic decoration was replaced in Portugal during the latter half of the century by the adoption of classical and Renaissance motifs. In Spain, with its long and distinguished tradition in silverware, the exotic trend in decoration began to appear only in the creations of the last generation of the sixteenth century. Goblets, ewers, and basins of the sort that had previously been decorated with Greek goddesses or Roman triumphs now became grounds on which fantastic animals, fish, and birds disported.[352] Juan de Arphe (1532–1602) in his instructional manual for silversmiths devotes a whole book to drawings of and discussion about the proportions and shapes that should be followed in animal designs (pl. 132).[353]

In the Low Countries and Germany, the silversmiths, like the woodcut artists, reacted sensitively to the discoveries. Their designs, like those of the Manueline artists in Portugal, often have few open spaces and are crowded with exotic flora and fauna. The body of a silver tankard made in Antwerp around 1525 is profusely decorated with "natives" in the foreground and palm trees and camels in the background. On the cover of the tankard, sailing vessels ply their way toward palm-lined shores (pl. 82).[354] A knob on the lid of a Rappoltsteiner goblet created around 1543 by the Strassburg master, Georg Kobenhaupt, is global in shape with a world map cut into it that is decorated with astrological animals and exotic maritime life (pl. 73).[355] Erasmus Hornick of Nuremberg in 1562 issued a book of jewel designs many of which were explicitly calculated to use the pearls that were so fashionable in pendants shaped as dragons and sea horses.[356] Grotesques consisting of foliage twining about satyrs and fantastic human and animal figures are also frequently seen on silverworks of the Renaissance.[357]

The widespread interest of the north in the collection and display of oddities led to the mounting of porcelains and natural curiosities in gold and silver settings. Coconut, nautilus, and bezoar stone cups in elaborate and bejeweled settings were made for the wealthier collectors (pls. 83, 85). Around 1570 Georg Berger in Germany began mounting Chinese porcelains in silver.[358]

[351] *Ibid.*, IV, 235.

[352] J. C. Davillier, *Recherches sur l'orfèvrerie en Espagne au moyen âge et à la Renaissance* (Paris, 1879), pp. 89–90.

[353] See Book III of his *Varia commensuracion para la escultura* (Madrid, 1598).

[354] For a detailed description see H. Thoma, *Kronen und Kleinödien* (Munich, 1955), p. 22.

[355] *Ibid.*, p. 23.

[356] Evans, *op. cit.* (n. 344), pp. 119–20.

[357] M. H. Gans and T. M. Duyvené de Wit-Klinkhamer, *Dutch Silver* (London, 1961), p. 11.

[358] For an illustration of his work see *Reallexikon zur deutschen Kunstgeschichte*, ed. O. Schmitt (Stuttgart, 1937), III, 442.

Around 1585 a London silversmith set at least five pieces of excellent blue-and-white porcelain in silver mounts (pl. 75) for William Cecil, Lord Burghley, who evidently presented one or more of them to Queen Elizabeth for her collection.[359] In a document found in the city library of Nuremberg, there is a description of a silver mounted cup made of a coconut so huge that it was esteemed a "marvelous work of nature." A member of the family of Wenzel Jamnitzer, a most highly esteemed goldsmith of Nuremberg, cut a scene from the "Feast of Bacchus" into the nut itself and inscribed the costly cover "worthy of an emperor's attention" with the date 1593. The Jamnitzer coconut was added to the curiosity cabinet of a substantial family of Nuremberg who displayed it between 1593 and 1606 to more than one thousand visitors of distinction.[360]

Commonplace oddities of this kind were valued as much for their presumed occult powers as for their beauty. The nautilus shell was accorded particular attention because of its mother-of-pearl interior and the mysterious regularity of its spiral form. Precious stones, like other curiosities, were regarded as works of art by the Creator. On their mystical qualities, Anselm Boetius de Boodt declared in his *Gemmarum et lapidum historia* (Hanau, 1609):

What God can do by Himself, He could do also by means of ministers, good and bad angels, who, by special grace of God are enabled to enter precious stones and to guard men from dangers or procure some special grace for them.[361]

In India, likewise, the precious stones were prized for their power to work good or evil upon man. The Hindus even classified diamonds and rubies according to the four castes. That such Asian ideas about the precious stones had an effect upon European thought is exemplified by Cardano's reference to the onyx as a talisman for cooling the ardors of passion, a belief that he contends is held in India, where people everywhere wear it on the neck for this purpose.[362]

The West, for the first time in history, was faced in the sixteenth century with direct competition from the high civilizations of the East which possessed independent artistic traditions of great antiquity, towering accomplishments, and enduring vitality. The artistic histories of Islam and Byzantium were, by contrast, less ancient, less impressive, and too closely related to Europe's own traditions to produce either ready acceptance or shocked aversion. But despite the enormity and strangeness of the competition, Europe's artistic reactions to the establishment of direct maritime contacts with the East were slow in coming

[359] For a description of both the mountings and the porcelains, now in the Metropolitan Museum of Art, see L. Avery, "Chinese Porcelain in English Mounts," *Metropolitan Museum of Art Bulletin*, N.S., II (1943), 266–72.

[360] See for the full description M. Frankenburger, *Beiträge zur Geschichte Wenzel Jamnitzer und seiner Familie* (Strassburg, 1901). Also see the pitcher fashioned from a double-coconut and set in a silver and gilt mounting by Anton Schoenberger in Prague (National Museum at Stockholm, No. 6872).

[361] As quoted in Kunz, *op. cit.* (n. 318), pp. 5–6.

[362] G. Cardano, *Les livres . . . intitulez De la Subtilité et subtiles inventions . . .* (Paris, 1584), Bk. VII, p. 454. Also see J. Lucas-Dubreton, *Le monde enchanté de la Renaissance: Jérôme Cardan l'halluciné* (Paris, 1954), pp. 151, 156.

and initially limited to superficialities. Europe's hesitant response is usually accounted for by reference to the fact that direct relations began at a time in Europe's own history when the visual arts had attained a level of qualitative excellence not equaled before or since. Or to the fact that many of the best of Asia's portable arts were well known in Europe and had already exercised their influence upon design and ornament long before the sixteenth century began. Or, it is sometimes argued, that Europe's imagination was initially fired more by the voyages themselves than by the lands and peoples revealed, and so European artists were more inclined to celebrate maritime exploits than to emulate Asia's arts.

Close scrutiny of the individual arts and artists shows, however, that Europeans were at no time oblivious to the challenge of Asia's arts. Albrecht Dürer was fascinated by the "subtle *ingenia*" of foreign works; the Medicis were determined to produce porcelains that would compete with the wares of China; and Cardano was distressed by the "uncertainties" that the revelation of the East was producing in the arts of Europe. In all of the art forms examined, the practitioners gradually made adjustments to bring Asian elements into their works for variety, novelty, and exotic effect. And what becomes entirely clear is the simple fact that the artists of the Renaissance, whatever the degree or direction of their cultural bias, felt free to bring exotica into their works and to experiment with and copy techniques that were then unknown in Europe.

Earlier efforts to imitate Asian porcelains, textiles, and lacquerware were intensified as the result of closer and more regular contacts. The makers of the Medici porcelains imitated the composition, shapes, ornaments, and colors of Ming blue-and-white ware in what was the most successful effort to produce porcelain in Europe before the eighteenth century. The technique of lacemaking was introduced to Europe around 1500, and pattern books were later prepared in Venice and Germany to show lace workers how to create Oriental designs. The chain stitch was more widely used as Europeans from Italy to Spain sought to imitate the Asian textiles in texture as well as in design and ornament. Artisans engaged in quilting, dyeing, marquetry, and jewel engraving and design were stimulated to adopt new techniques to meet the competition of products from the East. Lisbon and Antwerp became major markets for the superior jewels, pearls, embroideries, and works in precious metals of the East. Jewelry for personal adornment, perhaps in imitation of Indian customs, became increasingly common, and sumptuary laws were issued in some countries against its manufacture and use. Books on jewel design and manuals for silversmiths, embroiderers, and lacemakers were prepared to help European craftsmen to create competitive works. And enterprising merchants and craftsmen of both Europe and Asia cooperated to produce "export products" in Asia of porcelain, furniture, featherworks, and textiles that were designed to appeal to European tastes.

In architecture and sculpture the influences of the discoveries were limited to the maritime ornamentation employed by Manueline artists. In European painting, Asian rugs, textiles, porcelain, flora, and fauna were regularly used for their decorative qualities and their exotic appeal. The presence in the Netherlands of strange flowers, oddities, and seashells from the East helped to stimulate innovations which contributed to the development of the related arts of flower painting and still life. Tapestries and woodcuts in their adoption of new themes reflected the widespread interest in the discoveries evinced in northern Europe. Costume was among the first features to be Orientalized in paintings, tapestries, and prints. The depictions of Chinese in the prints became quite realistic by the end of the sixteenth century. And, at all periods, it was common for the graphic artists quickly to create representations of the novel products, animals, and oddities of Asia. It was probably because of their close association with book publication and cartography that the woodcut artists and engravers of northern Europe were more responsive than any other group to the arrival of curiosities of the East.

Practitioners in the major arts were more limited in the Asian sources they had at hand and were consequently not so well informed or fundamentally concerned with what their Asian counterparts had done or were doing. The architects of Europe were unable to view the great monuments of Asia and could learn about them only by report or by portraits in other media. The sculptors could see only the inferior works of Asian craftsmen or lesser artists, for the great sculptures were too large or too highly prized to be taken off to Europe. Asian paintings in small numbers were available in Europe, but no concrete evidence exists to show that European painters were moved to study, imitate, or experiment with the foreign techniques they represented. While it is possible to see resemblances between European and Chinese landscape paintings, the problem needs much more study before anything definite about influence can be said. The same conclusion must also be reached in the case of the possible debt of Arcimboldo to Indian miniatures for the idea behind his *têtes composées*. But while such cases are still conjectural, it does appear plain that Asian sources were at hand and that the artists might have used them. The likelihood that painters were inspired by such examples is reinforced by the fact that the graphic artists unhesitatingly used the collections of curiosities as sources for their prints.

Obviously there was no unbreachable cultural bias against using Asian arts as models, or against copying foreign techniques. Indeed, some artists were *positively* attracted by the "subtle *ingenia*" of Asian art objects. And it certainly is clear that they used them in painting for their exotic and symbolic qualities. In the graphic arts generally, the "heathen objects" had appeal as examples of the new and fantastic, and these qualities were especially appreciated by the innovating Mannerists. But the full impact of Asia on European art is not limited to such obvious responses. To see more clearly how the exotica from Asia relentlessly worked their way into European art, we will in the following chapter trace selected examples through the various European arts and examine the ways in which they were adapted by individual artists to their own artistic ends.

CHAPTER III

The Iconography of Asian Animals

To appreciate the effects of the importations from Asia upon artistic conceptions and symbolism it is necessary to trace in detail the movement of selected, dramatic examples of exotica through the arts of Europe. The new plants, for example, had attraction for and influence upon the engravers of botanical books and the flower painters, and their trail could be followed through numerous related arts. Or decorative elements and designs from textiles and porcelains could be tracked through the arts of tapestry weaving, engraving, and costume. But it is far simpler, and certainly more striking, to show how the arts and artists of Europe responded to the strange and wonderful animals imported from Asia.

Beasts were brought into Portugal as oddities in some of the first fleets to return from India.[1] The largest of the living animals imported by sea were the elephant and rhinoceros of India. The Bengal tiger was the only one of the larger beasts that came from the animal markets of the Levant. Smaller animals were also brought regularly from the East as pets of the sailors, especially monkeys and parrots. Along with the animals, the adventurers also brought plumages of the bird of paradise and various living birds to Europe that had never before been known there, such as the emu and the dodo. Along with the animals themselves there entered a host of Asian traditions and stories about the animals' origins, characteristics, and functions that were to influence the depiction and figurative meanings assigned to them by European artists.

---

[1] I. de Vilhena Barbosa, *Apontamentos para a história das collecções e dos estudos de zoologia em Pórtugal* (Lisbon, 1885), pp. iv–vii.

I

THE ELEPHANT[2]

Maritime transport of pachyderms must have posed stupendous problems. Adult elephants, aside from any overcrowding or security problems they might cause, are voracious eaters. A single elephant, were it to be kept in reasonably good health, would certainly eat and drink the rations of many men.[3] The elephants brought back to Europe, consequently, seem to have been young beasts which had not yet attained their full size, weight, or strength, but which were manageable and old enough to be trained. They were usually accompanied, at least at first, by their mahouts or Indian trainers. It was possibly because they were tractable that Asian elephants, once they became available, were brought into Renaissance Europe in preference to their less docile African cousins.

Thirteen Asian elephants, at least, were imported into Europe via Portugal during the sixteenth century. No elephants entered, so far as is known, from Egypt or the Levant. Of the elephants brought in through Lisbon, one reached Rome, two got to Vienna by different routes, one arrived at Madrid, and one lodged for a period at Dieppe before being taken across the channel to England. On its peregrinations from Lisbon to other European cities, the Asian elephant was viewed for the first time by throngs of Frenchmen, Englishmen, Spaniards, Italians, Flemings, Walloons, and Germans, as brief stopovers were made in urban centers such as Alicante, Civitavecchia, Genoa, Milan, Brussels, Antwerp, Cologne, and in many smaller towns and villages.

Everywhere they went the elephants of Asia stimulated the curiosity of artist, scientist, Humanist, and the man in the street. Learned Latin poets and vulgar versifiers celebrated the beast and its presumed virtues. Humanists and naturalists debated learnedly, and without noticeable humor, the differences between the beast before their eyes and the ones described by their revered authorities of Antiquity. Amateur artists and painters as great as Raphael depicted the elephant from the living model. Reigning monarchs, in an effort to keep abreast or forge ahead of their fellows, sent requests to Portugal for elephants, and more than one ruling potentate hoped to begin raising these majestic beasts in his own menagerie.

The initial curiosity stirred by the elephant quickly evaporated as it became better known. The effusions of rhymesmiths and Humanists were quickly forgotten. The natural scientist, inclined at this time to be subservient to the authorities of Antiquity, vainly sought to reconcile the elephant of fact with the elephant of tradition. It was mainly in the field of art that the Asian elephant

[2] In its essentials this section has been published as D. F. Lach, "Asian Elephants in Renaissance Europe," *Journal of Asian History*, I (1967), 133–76. A number of the plates published there are not reproduced in this book but are cited in the following notes.

[3] "... no less than 600 pounds of fodder is the proper daily allowance for an elephant" (S. W. Baker, *Wild Beasts and Their Ways* [London, 1890], I, 22).

left a lasting impression upon Renaissance culture. Not only did the living model invest the depiction of the elephant with a new naturalism, it also helped to bring profound changes into symbolism. But to comprehend the changes which were introduced by the living Asian elephants into Renaissance art and thought, it is first necessary to examine the traditions and lore about elephants which the men of the sixteenth century inherited from their European past.

A. ANTIQUITY AND THE MIDDLE AGES

Within historical times the range of the elephant, the largest living land mammal, has been narrowed greatly by the encroachments of civilization. Originally native to most of Africa and the Eurasiatic continent, the elephant is found today only in sub-Saharan Africa, India, Ceylon, and southeast Asia. By Roman times the elephant had been reduced to two genera, the African and the Indian. The major differences between the two types, especially useful for studying them in art, are the greater height of the African, its concave back which slopes sharply to the rump, its longer tusks, and its larger ears. Since most depictions show the elephant in profile, the line of the back, concave in the African and convex in the Asian, is especially useful as a distinguishing mark.

Knowledge of the elephant spread gradually westward in Antiquity.[4] Exotic animals were sent as tribute to the kings of Assyria, the renowned obelisk of Salmanassar II (ruled 1019–1007 B.C.) showing a procession of animals led by an Indian elephant.[5] Ctesias of Cnidus, physician to the Persian king Artaxerxes Mnemon (436–358 B.C.), introduced the elephant, though in a highly fanciful description, into Greek literature. The Persians, long before the time of Ctesias, had recruited Indian auxiliary corps with elephant mounts into their armies. Europeans had their first experience on record with elephants on the occasion of Alexander the Great's final defeat of Darius III (336–330 B.C.) at Arbela in 331 B.C. The Macedonian conqueror evidently captured fifteen elephants from his desperate Persian foe, and it may have been one of these animals which Aristotle observed and eventually described so accurately in his *History of the Animals*.

From his campaign in India (326–324 B.C.), which ended with a victory over Porus, Alexander brought back to Babylon a number of Indian war elephants. Tradition has it that the conqueror entered the city in a chariot drawn by elephants, and Diodorus Siculus reports that the funeral chariot of Alexander was decorated with a representation of his triumphal return from India. Alexander

---

[4] Compare the history of the elephant and its depiction in the East as summarized in K. M. Ball, *Decorative Motives of Oriental Art* (London, 1927), chaps. x and xi.

[5] For a reproduction see O. Keller, *Die antike Tierwelt* (Leipzig, 1909), I, 374, fig. 130. It is possible that the "Indian elephant" was actually native at this period to the swamps of the upper Euphrates. Assyrian kings went on elephant hunts in this region, for the animal appears to have lived there until about 800 B.C. See F. S. Bodenheimer, *Animal and Man in Bible Lands* (Leyden, 1960), p. 103. On the prehistoric animals see Emiliano Aguirre, "Evolutionary History of the Elephant," *Science*, CLXIV (June 20, 1969), 1366–75.

himself ordered that a coin should be cast to commemorate his victory over the Indian ruler: on its reverse side it shows Alexander on horseback fighting against Porus, who is riding an elephant. Like the god Dionysius, Alexander celebrated his victories in India with a triumphal procession that ultimately became the archetype for the *trionfi* of the Renaissance.[6] The successors of Alexander in the Levant, the Seleucids, continued long after the conqueror's death to use elephants as shock forces in their armies.[7] A dramatic confrontation occurred at the Battle of Raphia (217 B.C.) between the Indian elephants of the Seleucids and the African of the Ptolemies. The decisive defeat handed to the African elephants on this occasion served to enhance the reputation of the Indian elephants and their mahouts.[8]

Both the Seleucids and the Ptolemies kept elephants for spectacular displays as well as war. Alexandria boasted the largest and most complete zoological collection known to the Hellenistic world. Elephants were paraded in Egypt on festival occasions, for example in the great processions honoring Dionysius held in the early years of Ptolemy II's reign (283–246 B.C.). Twenty-four chariots, each drawn by four elephants, followed immediately behind a huge representation of Dionysius returning from India. "Quadrigas," following this model, were to become conventional in the triumphal processions of Roman times and in the later artistic representations of them.[9] Especially valuable as models for the Renaissance artists were the Roman sarcophagi showing the triumph of Dionysius (or Bacchus) in India.[10]

The Greek city-states were not wealthy or powerful enough to collect expensive animals for war or spectacles. The Greeks themselves had no taste for circuses or gladiatorial combats involving beasts. They collected small exotic animals as pets and curiosities, but large animals like elephants are almost never depicted on Greek vases, coins, reliefs, mosaics, or wall paintings.[11] The word ἐλέφας is obviously preserved in "elephant," but we possess little undisputed information on its pre-Greek etymology.[12] Aristotle includes a variety of references to the elephants in his biological writings, and seems especially fascinated

---

[6] See W. S. Heckscher, "Bernini's Elephant and Obelisk," *Art Bulletin*, XXIX (1947), 159, fig. 7.

[7] The victory monument erected *ca.* 275 B.C. by Antiochus I shows a representation of an elephant crushing a soldier in its trunk, a motif that appears repeatedly in both Asian and European depictions of the elephant. See Keller, *op. cit.* (n. 5), I, 377–78, fig. 132.

[8] See G. Jennison, *Animals for Show and Pleasure in Ancient Rome* (Manchester, 1937), p. 38.

[9] A fine example of this motif in Roman art is the ivory carving of the early fourth century A.D. commonly called "Apotheosis of Romulus." For reproductions see O. M. Dalton, *Catalogue of the Ivories of the Christian Era* (London, 1909), pl. I. In 1912 a wall painting of a "quadriga" was unearthed at Pompeii. See A. Maiuri, *Pompei-Ercolana: I nuovi scavi* (Naples, 1927). A Roman medal of Maxentius depicts the emperor standing in a chariot drawn by four elephants, as does a coin on which Nero and his mother are represented. See G. F. Kunz, *Ivory and the Elephant in Art, in Archaeology, and in Science* (New York, 1916), pp. 174, 179.

[10] See especially the plates in K. Lehmann-Hartleben and E. C. Olsen, *Dionysiac Sarcophagi in Baltimore* (Baltimore, 1942).

[11] Keller, *op. cit.* (n. 5), I, 381. On some later coins the head of Socrates is combined with the head and trunk of the elephant. See Kunz, *op. cit.* (n. 9), p. 183.

[12] For a review of its etymology see H. Yule and A. C. Burnell, *Hobson-Jobson: Glossary of Anglo-Indian Colloquial Words and Phrases* . . . (2d ed.; New Delhi, 1968), pp. 337–41. For a summary of its development and usage in the idioms and symbols of the Romance and Germanic languages see R. Riegler, *Das Tier im Spiegel der Sprache: Ein Beitrag zur vergleichenden Bedeutungslehre* (Leipzig, 1909), pp. 81–91.

by the multiple functions of its stupendous and pliable nose or trunk. The great philosopher is the first writer to record, while denying its veracity, the common belief current in his day that the elephant has no joints in its legs—a misconception which in Europe retained broad acceptance until the mid-seventeenth century.[13] Megasthenes in his *Indica* (302 B.C.) makes frequent references to the elephant and is possibly responsible for India's being known in Europe as "the land of the elephant."

The Romans first became acquainted with elephants when Pyrrhus II, king of Epirus, invaded Italy early in the third century B.C. Thanks to the surprise and shock created among the Romans by the elephants, Pyrrhus won quick victories in 280 and 279 B.C. Four years later, however, the Romans under Curius Dentatus defeated him at Beneventum near Naples. Four elephants were among the captives taken by the victorious consul, and they were brought to Rome to march in his triumphal procession.[14] Twenty-four years later, the consul Lucius Caecilius Metellus defeated the Carthaginians at Palermo (251 B.C.) and returned to Rome with over one hundred African elephants.[15] The mahouts of the captured elephants, probably Indians or persons trained by Indians, were integrated into the Roman service, but the Romans seem never to have used elephants, these or others, for military purposes. The Roman term "African beasts" was thereafter indiscriminately applied to a broad range of foreign animals brought to the capital for processions and games (*ludi*).[16] From this time on, the elephant frequently appears as a device on the coins of the Metelli.

Animal shows and combats became a standard feature of Roman life beginning in the first century B.C. Elephants were pitted in the arena against bulls, gladiators, and each other. Most of those so mistreated were evidently African elephants captured by the Romans in their wars against the Carthaginians and Numidians. At Pompey's celebration in 55 B.C. over twenty elephants and an Indian rhinoceros were on display.[17] Torchlight parades featuring elephants celebrated the glories of the empire under Julius Caesar. Since the elephants bore torches in their trunks, it seems likely that they were trained Indian elephants rather than captive war elephants of the African variety. This conclusion is reinforced by the fact that in the Augustan Age and thereafter the elephant trained to perform

[13] See Aristotle, *Parts of Animals*, trans. A. L. Peck (London, 1955), 2. 16. 659*2*, for discussion of the trunk; also see *ibid.* ("Progression of Animals"), 9. 709*2* and 712*2*, for discussion of how the elephant walks and bends its legs. An analogue of the popular belief in the jointless elephant is a similar Chinese story which makes the rhinoceros jointless (cf. Kunz, *op. cit.* [n. 9], pp. 144–45); among the Muslim writers this feature of jointless legs is associated sometimes with the elephant and at others with the rhinoceros (cf. R. Ettinghausen, *The Unicorn* [Washington, 1950], p. 15); in Europe, from Aelian throughout the Middle Ages, the rhinoceros was also believed to be jointless. In the Hindu tradition, the best elephants, those fit for a prince, have "invisible joints" in both their fore and hind legs. See Franklin Edgerton, *The Elephant-Lore of the Hindus* (New Haven, Conn., 1931), p. 55.

[14] On this first Roman triumph and on later ones as well see Ferdinand Noack, "Triumph und Triumphbogen," *Vorträge der Bibliothek Warburg, 1925–1926* (Leipzig-Berlin, 1928), pp. 185–90.

[15] See Pliny, *Natural History*, trans. H. Rackham (Cambridge, Mass., 1949), 8. 6. 13–15.

[16] Jennison, *op. cit.* (n. 8), pp. 3, 44.

[17] *Ibid.*, pp. 52, 54.

circus tricks entertained in the arena ever more frequently.[18] A herd of state elephants was kept permanently under the two Caesars in Latium between Rome and the sea. Since these beasts were not used in war service, one must conclude that the state bore the expense of their keep to have them on hand for ceremonial processions, animal displays, and circuses.

Pliny the Elder (A.D. 23–79) summarizes in his *Natural History* (8. 1–13) much of what the Roman world knew or believed about the elephants. The great compiler rates the elephant as the beast which most nearly approaches man in intelligence: it comprehends the vernacular language and understands and remembers orders and duties. Moral virtues attributed to the elephant are honesty, wisdom, justice, modesty, affection, and gentleness. It is said to show "respect for the stars and reverence for the sun and moon." [19] In India, wild elephants are hunted and captured by mahouts riding domesticated elephants; in Africa elephants are caught by means of pitfalls and hunted with spears and javelins for their ivory and flesh. Indian elephants, Pliny incorrectly asserts, are larger in size than their African cousins.[20]

Pliny is also guilty of lending his authority to the popular misconceptions about the great longevity[21] of the elephant and its fear of mice. He describes a fight between a rhinoceros and an elephant and implies that the rhinoceros wins the encounter by stabbing the elephant in the belly with its horn.[22] From the evidence of Roman coins, medals, and sculptures there can be little doubt that Pliny and other ancient authors were probably much more familiar with African than with Asian elephants.[23] Indeed, the elephant head on many of Caesar's coins and in extant marble and bronze sculptures seems for the Romans to symbolize "Africa" and their empire there.[24]

As an allegorical symbol, the elephant achieved the peak of its prestige during

[18] Cf. *ibid.*, pp. 58, 65–66. Tradition has it, but the evidence is not substantial, that a white elephant from Asia was on display in Rome during the reign of Augustus. See P. Armandi, *Histoire militaire des éléphants, depuis les temps les plus reculés jusqu'à l'introduction des armes à feu* (Paris, 1843), pp. 380–81.

[19] Compare the stories in the *Panchatantra* of the elephant's devotion to the moon as discussed in V. S. Naravane, *The Elephant and the Lotus* (Bombay, 1965), p. 54.

[20] A mistaken belief that was current in Antiquity, possibly because the African elephants used at the battle of Raphia were smaller and younger than the Indian elephants pitted against them. Cf. Jennison, *op. cit.* (n. 8), pp. 39–40.

[21] Pliny asserts that they live from 200 to 300 years. Indian estimates range from 80 to 120 years. See Edgerton, *op. cit.* (n. 13), p. 23. Modern scholars tend to feel that elephants not in captivity live for about the same span of years as humans.

[22] It is probably true that the elephant fears the rhinoceros as well as many other wild beasts. See Baker, *op. cit.* (n. 3), p. 292.

[23] Jennison, *op. cit.* (n. 8), pp. 196–98; for a discussion of the elephant as an allegorical portrait of Julius Caesar on a Roman coin see D. and E. Panofsky, "Iconography of the Galerie François Iᵉʳ," *Gazette des Beaux-Arts*, 6th ser., LII (1958), 123. For an Indian elephant see the Roman medal struck for the consul Curius Dentatus and reproduced in Keller, *op. cit.* (n. 5), I, 357, fig. 131. The best survey of the elephant on coins and medals is G. Cupertus, *De elephantis in nummis obviis* (The Hague, 1719). A copy of this work with its 126 splendid cuts of coins and medals may be found in the collection of the American Numismatic Society in New York. Also see H. A. Grueber, *Coins of the Roman Republic in the British Museum* (London, 1910), II, 5; and S. L. Cesano, "Le monete di Cesare," *Atti della pontifica Accademia Romana di Archeologia*, 3d ser., *Rendiconti*, XXIII–XXIV (1947–49), 107.

[24] Cf. V. Waille, "Note sur l'éléphant, symbole de l'Afrique à propos d'un bronze récemment découvert à Berrouaghia (Algérie)," *Revue archéologique*, XVII (1891), 380; Keller, *op. cit.* (n. 5), I, 381–82. Also the article on elephants in P. Lavedan, *Dictionnaire illustré de la mythologie et des antiquités grecques et romaines* (Paris, 1931).

the Middle Ages. Christian teachers and writers, beginning in the second century A.D., regularly applied myths and legends about animals to their allegorical interpretations of the Holy Scriptures and the doctrines of the Church.[25] Because of its high moral standing in classical writings, the elephant soon became a standard emblem for a number of ethical and religious precepts. Traditions regarding the elephant, as well as some fifty other "Christianized" animals, were collected in Alexandria, possibly in the fifth century, in the book of allegories called *Physiologus*, or *The Naturalist*.[26] While the collection itself has been preserved only in later manuscripts, it is clear that most of the bestiaries of the Middle Ages and many of the animals described or depicted in the manuscripts of the Alexander Romance are derived from the stories enshrined in the *Physiologus*. Modifications and additions to the *Physiologus* conception of the elephant start to appear in medieval writing and art only in the twelfth century and are based mainly on the writings of Isidore of Seville and the *De Universo* (842–48) of Rabanus.[27]

The medieval writers of the bestiaries clearly knew that elephants are native to India and Africa; at that point fact ceases and fantasy takes over. For them the elephant always symbolizes virtue, is beloved of God, and may even be an emblem of the Church. The dragon is equated with the serpent in the Garden of Eden and is the mortal enemy of the elephant. When they mate, which they do only for the purpose of procreation, the elephants retire to the earthly paradise in the East. Elephants give birth in the water, a symbol to medieval writers and artists of regeneration through baptism. Elephants never lie down to sleep, because being jointless they could not rise again. When sleeping, the elephant leans against a tree that it has specially selected as its favorite resting place. To catch an elephant, the hunter need only discover and cut down the tree while the elephant is sleeping against it. A fallen elephant may be raised by a small elephant and a group of twelve large elephants—a symbolic reference to Christ and the twelve disciples. Elephants will tolerate everything except evil, and they crush the symbols of evil in their trunks or under their feet.[28]

Fantasy reigned supreme to the thirteenth century even though live elephants were known in medieval Europe. Harun al-Rashid, the caliph of Baghdad, sent an elephant accompanied by two of his courtiers to Charlemagne as a gift.

[25] The elephant, as such, is not mentioned in the Bible, except in the apocryphal books. Hinduism and Buddhism, like Christianity, have their share of elephant legends.

[26] For an English rendition of the "sermon" on the elephant see W. Rose, *The Epic of the Beast* (London, n.d.), pp. 201–3.

[27] See G. C. Druce, "The Elephant in Medieval Legend and Art," *Archaeological Journal*, LXXVI (1919), 5.

[28] Examples of this bestiary tradition may be readily seen by consulting the discussions of the elephant in M. Goldstaub and R. Wendriner, *Ein Tosco-Venezianischer Bestiarius* (Halle, 1892); and T. H. White, *The Book of Beasts* (London, 1954). For pictorial examples of the medieval elephant see L. M. C. Randall, *Images in the Margins of Gothic Manuscripts* (Berkeley and Los Angeles, 1966), figs. 167–70. For the continuation of the bestiary tradition into the Renaissance see Leonardo's description of the elephant in E. McCurdy (trans. and ed.), *The Notebooks of Leonardo da Vinci* (New York, 1958), II, 1084–86.

"Abulabaz," as the elephant was called, disembarked at Pisa in 801, traveled overland to Aix-la-Chapelle, and was on display at Charlemagne's court for the next four years. An ivory chess set was possibly among the other gifts sent to Charlemagne, one piece of which is carved into an elephant holding a man in its trunk.[29] "Abulabaz" seems not to have been represented in Carolingian art, but later medieval elephants were. Emperor Frederick II returned from the Holy Land with an elephant and actually used it in his successful siege of Cremona in 1229.[30] This or another live elephant was at Cremona in 1241 when Earl Richard of Cornwall, the crusading earl, visited there.[31] St. Louis, on his return to France in 1254 from the Holy Land, brought an elephant with him. In the following year he sent the beast as a gift to Henry III of England.

St. Louis' elephant may have inspired the realistically sculptured elephant which stands among the *chimères* of Notre Dame de Paris; it was certainly the model for the convincing likeness in the manuscript (Parker 16) by Matthew Paris at Cambridge. From this depiction, it may be safely concluded that St. Louis had returned with an African elephant.[32] But such realistic portraits were rare and apparently had little influence on the configurations of the elephant portrayed in bestiaries, embroidered on sacerdotal vestments, drawn in manuscripts of the Alexander Romance, or depicted in ecclesiastical carving, decoration, and heraldry.[33] Many of them seem to be copied from Oriental ivories and textiles. The elephant with the castle on its back figures prominently in medieval religious and civil processionals and in illustrations, even though the elephant is only rarely depicted in the bestiaries as being warlike.[34] This form

---

[29] This chess piece, probably of Persian craftsmanship, is in the Cabinet des Medailles in Paris. The tradition that it was sent by Harun al-Rashid is based on a seventeenth-century account and so its veracity may be open to question. See H. and S. Wichmann, *Schach: Ursprung und Wandlung der Spielfigur in zwölf Jahrhunderten* (Munich, 1960), pp. 16–17, pl. 1–3. For another elephant chess piece see W. Born, "Some Eastern Objects from the Hapsburg Collections," *Burlington Magazine*, LXIX (1936), 875 and pl. IID. For the history of the elephant as a chessman in Europe see H. J. R. Murray, *A History of Chess* (London, 1913), pp. 791–92.

[30] It is perfectly possible that Frederick II possessed more than one elephant. He had a passion for animals that was almost Oriental, and at Palermo he kept a menagerie that was unique in the Europe of his day. When traveling in Italy, he was usually accompanied by an entourage of exotic animals. See E. Kantorowicz, *Kaiser Friedrich der Zweite* (Berlin, 1931), p. 137; and G. Loisel, *Histoire des ménageries de l'antiquité à nos jours* (Paris, 1912), I, 145–46.

[31] Matthew Paris shows the elephant conventionally with a castle on its back and a huge bell around its neck. See A. E. Popham, "Elephantographia," *Index to Life and Letters*, V (1930), 179–80. Also see Heckscher, *loc. cit.* (n. 6), p. 163.

[32] Druce, *loc. cit.* (n. 27), p. 1; also Heckscher, *loc. cit.* (n. 6), p. 164. For a reproduction of the elephant of Matthew Paris see Lach, *loc. cit.* (n. 2), pl. I.

[33] In the thirteenth-century Cathedral of Ripon (England) a realistically carved elephant with a castle was turned into a poppy head, and it now graces a pew at the right end of the choir stall. It probably originated outside the bestiary tradition, but such exceptions are few. See Druce, *loc. cit.* (n. 27), p. 65 and pl. XV, no. 2.

[34] Heckscher (*loc. cit.* [n. 6], p. 16) asserts that in medieval convention we find "tower-carrying elephants where the text does not call for the tower at all." For examples see the elephant in a Latin treatise of the thirteenth century on beasts (Harley MS. 3244, fol. 39 [Brit. Mus.]), or the page from the "Evangiles de Lothaire" (B.N., MSS. Lat. 266, fol. 73v) as reproduced in J. Ebersolt, *Orient et Occident: Recherches sur les influences byzantines et orientales en France avant et pendant les croisades* (2d ed.; Paris, 1954), pl. 22. For a bestiary elephant with a howdah occupied by four men see M. R. James, *The Bestiary, Being a Reproduction in Full of the Manuscript II.4.26 in the University Library, Cambridge* . . . (Oxford, 1928), p. 37 and fol. 46b.

harks back to classical prototypes or even to the frequent references in Roman and apocryphal writers to battles involving elephants.[35]

Medieval illustrators sometimes show the elephant with the body of a wild boar, depict its trunk to look like an elongated duck's bill or trumpet, or make its rear legs look like the hind legs of a horse. In French sculptures of the eleventh and twelfth centuries, fantastic elephants based on designs evidently borrowed from manuscripts, textiles, and ivories appear at least twenty times on a variety of Romanesque monuments.[36] On *mappae mundi* of the Middle Ages, such as the Hereford map of the thirteenth century, elephants are placed as landmarks within the confines of India. Elephants introduce a light element into Luccan silk designs of the fourteenth century as they are shown dancing and pulling wagons guided by monkeys.[37] Elephant heads and demi-elephants appear as watermarks on paper manufactured in the Kingdom of Aragon beginning in 1375.[38] The watermark elephants, like practically all the others of the period, show distinctive medieval characteristics.[39] With almost nothing but such caricatures available, European artists clearly had to await the reappearance of live elephants in Europe before they could again create more realistic illustrations.

B. AFRICAN ELEPHANTS OF THE QUATTROCENTO

Wild beasts came to Europe through Constantinople, Alexandria, and Venice long before the Portuguese became active in Africa. That elephants were well known in Constantinople is readily adduced from the evidence of Byzantine art.[40] Silk textiles of the tenth century, for example, employ elephant motifs as central figures in their designs.[41] But the Byzantine elephants are only slightly more realistic than the bestiary elephants of the West,[42] perhaps because the Byzantine artists derived their conceptions of elephants from Persian designs.

[35] For references to the elephant of war in the Apocrypha see 1 Maccabees 3:33; 6:34-37; 7:8-9. To this day the elephant and castle appear as chess pieces, in heraldic emblems, and on tavern signs. See G. R. Kernodle, *From Art to Theatre: Form and Convention in the Renaissance* (Chicago, 1944), p. 15.

[36] See M. Thibaut, "L'éléphant dans la sculpture romane française," *Bulletin monumental*, CV (1947), 183-95.

[37] See F. E. de Roover, "Lucchese Silks," *Ciba Review*, No. 80 (1950), p. 2928.

[38] F. de Bofarull y Sans, *Animals in Watermarks* (Hilversum [Holland], 1959), p. 26.

[39] "A French Book of Hours of the Late Fifteenth Century" (Newberry Library, Ayer Collection, MS. 43) shows a trumpet elephant of the medieval type in the bottom border of the "Annunciation to Shepherds."

[40] Compare the triumphal arch of Arcadius with its elephant statue and mahout as described in P. Gyllius, *Antiquities of Constantinople*, trans. J. Ball (London, 1729), p. 289. Further commentary in Kunz, *op. cit.* (n. 9), p. 172, and Loisel, *op. cit.* (n. 30), I, 190. Also see the mosaic of the elephant in combat with the lion still on display in Istanbul at the palace museum.

[41] For a reproduction of the elephant within a circular design as it appears in the famous purple silk preserved in the treasury of the cathedral at Aix-la-Chapelle see A. Grabar, "Le succès des arts orientaux à la cour Byzantine sous les Macédoniens, "*Münchner Jahrbuch der bildenden Kunst*, 3d ser., II (1951), 35, fig. 3.

[42] See the two cameo elephants in H. Wentzel, "Abseitige Trouvaillen aus Goldschmiedearbeiten," in F. Dettweiler *et al.* (eds.), *Studien zur Buchmalerei und Goldschmiedekunst des Mittelalters* (Marburg, 1967), pp. 72-73.

A sketch of a live African elephant was made in Egypt by Cyriac of Ancona (1391–1452) on one of his numerous trips to the Levant.[43] Possibly this sketch was used by the artists employed by the Malatesta of Rimini as the model for that family's badge.[44]

In the Malatesta medals, emblems, carvings, sculptures, and friezes dating from the time of Sigismund I in the mid-fifteenth century, the elephant figures prominently, possibly as a symbol of the family's fortitude and strength.[45] The famous Malatesta "temple" included numerous heraldic elephants: two guarded the main portal, others supported the pilasters in the two western chapels, and others formed the seat for a statue of Sigismund or held on their backs the sepulcher of Isotta, his mistress and wife. The Malatesta elephant had its secular uses as well; it stood above the door of the Biblioteca Malatestiana at Cesena, and the little bronze elephants with upturned trunks which are extant were apparently intended as decorative sculptures symbolizing "good fortune."[46] While the Malatesta elephant looks African and retains medieval features, most puzzling is the Latin inscription which appears on the elephant used as a device on the Biblioteca Malatestiana: "Elephas indus culices non timet" ("The Indian elephant does not fear insects [gnats]").[47]

Enamored of classical pageantry, the princes and lords of the quattrocento revived the Roman triumph to celebrate victories and other noteworthy events. The elephants of Antiquity, probably copied from the representations on Roman sarcophagi or coins,[48] often figured in the *trionfi* as automatons. At the banquet held on February 17, 1453, in Lille to honor Philip of Burgundy, an elephant-automaton in life size was the center of attraction.[49] Twenty-five years later, according to tradition, King Christian I of Denmark founded the Order of the Elephant, a very select religious organization that has as its decoration a chain

[43] Text of letter and reproduction in C. Mitchell, "Ex libris Kiriaci Anconitani," *Italia medioevale e umanistica*, V (1962), 285, pl. XXII.

[44] Cyriac's elephant is much cruder than the ones created by the artists of Rimini. Therefore, other possible sources must be sought. The manuscript book, *Regalis Ystoria*, of anonymous thirteenth-century authorship, shows an elephant with a crown on its head in its illuminated border. This item, preserved in the Biblioteca Gambalunga at Rimini, would seem to indicate an earlier relationship between the elephant and the rulers of Rimini. See Corrado Ricci, *Il tempio malatestiano in Rimini* (Milan and Rome, n.d.), p. 313, pl. 374, p. 316, pl. 379. The Malatesta elephant might also have been modeled upon Roman prototypes, or might even combine, judging from its appearance, both Roman and medieval characteristics. Also see *ibid.*, pp. 323–24.

[45] Cf. G. de Tervarent, *Attributs et symboles dans l'art profane, 1450–1600* (Geneva, 1958), I, 154.
[46] See *ibid.*, pls. 391 and 392.
[47] For a reproduction of this piece see C. Yriarte, *Un condottiere au XVᵉ siècle* (Paris, 1882), p. 305, fig. 162. Probably refers to Pliny's remarks (Pliny, *op. cit.* [n. 15], p. 25) to the effect that elephants crush insects on their skin simply by wrinkling up the creases. For further comment on the Renaissance use of the elephant and fly motif see Heckscher, *loc. cit.* (n. 6), pp. 172–73.

[48] Available by the mid-sixteenth century were Roman coins depicting numerous elephant quadrigas and the elephant stepping on the dragon with the inscription CAESAR. See E. Vico, *Omnium Caesarum verissimae imagines ex antiquis numismatis desumptae* (Venice, 1554), *passim*.

[49] Oliver de la Marche, chief of the Burgundian school of rhetoric, acted as master of ceremonies and sat on the back of the artificial elephant disguised as a nun. See Heckscher, *loc. cit.* (n. 6), p. 167. Other authors seem to believe that Philip's elephant was a live beast. See R. Schwoebel, *The Shadow of the Crescent: The Renaissance Image of the Turk (1453–1517)* (Nieuwkoop, 1967), p. 87.

of interlinked elephants supporting a pendant elephant that has an Oriental driver on its back (see pl. 114). In this context the elephant is not the symbol of pomp, triumph, and power, but of docility, sobriety, and piety.[50]

Not all the references to elephants in fifteenth-century Europe were based on traditional drawings, imitations, or symbols. In the report of his African experiences Luis de Cadamosto (1432–88), a Venetian navigator in the service of Portugal, describes the live elephants and tells of hunting them.[51] About 1477 King Alfonso V of Portugal apparently sent a live African elephant and other exotic beasts as a gift to René the Good, duke of Anjou and count of Provence. At the Frankfurt fair of 1480 an African elephant was exhibited in a garden in the Gallus-Gasse, and a picture of it in life size was painted on the gardener's house.[52] It is possible that this same elephant was on display at Cologne in 1482.[53] Probably it was this elephant which was the model used by the German artists of the time; for most of the realistic elephants shown in the prints, paintings, and sculptures of the later fifteenth and early sixteenth centuries generally exhibit features typical of the African elephant.

The earliest printed books include numerous woodcut illustrations which show the African elephant. In the *Meditations* of Cardinal Turrecremata, first printed at Rome in 1467, the woodcuts depict murals in the Church of Santa Maria sopra Minerva. Among them there is a woodcut of the Creation in which a lifelike African elephant grazes with a variety of other wild beasts.[54] A woodcut of an elephant in the German *Herbarius*, or *Ortus sanitatis* (1485), is possibly a portrait of the beast exhibited at Frankfurt in the 1480's.[55] Some later artist took the elephant from the *Herbarius*, perched it on a mound of ivory, and published this grotesque representation in the Latin *Ortus sanitatis* printed at Mainz in 1491. About the same time, Martin Schongauer produced a distinctly comical woodcut of an African elephant with a highly imaginary tower on its back that was to be used repeatedly as a serious depiction of the elephant in natural histories of the sixteenth century.

Between 1485 and 1492 Andrea Mantegna (1431–1506) painted his famous tempera pictures which depict the "Triumph of Caesar" and revive Antiquity

---

[50] Kunz, *op. cit.* (n. 9), p. 187. Cf. the royal canopy made in Denmark in 1586 on the order of King Frederick II by Hans Knieper on which elephants with castles decorate the borders (National Museum at Stockholm).

[51] Cadamosto's account was first published in 1507 in the *Paesi novamente ritrovati* of Montalboddo. It was republished in Vol. I (p. 112r) of G. B. Ramusio's *Delle navigationi et viaggi* (Venice, 1554), and was thereafter cited repeatedly by natural historians in their descriptions of the elephant.

[52] J. W. Thompson (ed.), *The Frankfurt Book Fair: The Francofordiense Emporium of Henri Estienne* (Chicago, 1911), p. 62. In a letter, recently found, the city officials of Frankfurt were asked permission to bring an "Helffandt" into the city (*Washington Post*, December, 6 1967).

[53] A. Kaufmann, "Über Thierliebhaberei im Mittelalter," *Historisches Jahrbuch der Görresgesellschaft*, V (1884), 409.

[54] For a reproduction from the edition of 1473 see W. M. Ivins, "A Neglected Aspect of Early Print-Making," *Metropolitan Museum of Art Bulletin*, VII (1948), 53.

[55] See J. F. Payne, "On the 'Herbarius' and 'Hortus Sanitatis,'" *Transactions of the Bibliographical Society*, VI (1900–1901), 98. The artist was evidently a contemporary of Erhard Rewick, the sketcher who accompanied Bernard von Breydenbach on his travels in the Levant.

by showing a quadriga of African elephants carrying candelabra on their backs —the artist's version of a Roman torchlight procession.[56] In Hieronymus Bosch's paintings the elephant, especially the one in the "Garden of Delights," is distinctly African and lifelike and in startling contrast to the fantastic creatures and things which surround it.[57] The elephants shown in the woodcuts of Hans Burgkmair seem to follow the quattrocento tradition, even the so-called Indian elephant which appears in the "King of Cochin" series of 1508 (pl. 87).[58] The India series of tapestries, prepared after 1504 by the workshop of Jehan Grenier of Tournai, likewise depict an elephant that is African and medieval.[59] "The Triumph of Fame," a tapestry of the early sixteenth century now in the Austrian state collection, likewise retains the medieval African elephant (pl. 55). The sculptured elephant on the Palazzo Fantuzzi of Bologna (built between 1517 and 1521) depicts the elephant and tower in a manner reminiscent of Schongauer and the Malatesta elephants.[60]

But perhaps most striking of all in this transitional period is the allegorical treatment accorded the elephant, particularly in the woodcuts illustrating the *Hypnerotomachia Poliphili* (1499) of Francesco Colonna. The artist who did the sketches for these woodcuts must be classified as the person who best synthesizes the quattrocento view of the elephant. He uses elephants, reminiscent of the Malatesta beast, in a lavish scene of triumph in which he marches them along two by two. More allegorical is his hieroglyphic emblem of elephants and ants which is designed to illustrate the Sallustian maxim that concord makes small things great and discord great things small. Implicit in this emblem is the welding of the classical, Egyptian, and Christian traditions, a synthetic idea which Colonna shared with the Neoplatonists of his day. This theme reaches a crescendo in the elephant with an obelisk on its back, the obelisk being inscribed with mysterious hieroglyphs which recall Horapollo. To the Neoplatonist the elephant probably symbolized zeal, industry, and divinity objectivized, while the obelisk that pierces the body of the elephant possibly symbolized the intellectual insight to be obtained through using the hieroglyphs as intermediaries between the human intellect and the divine idea.[61] In terms of art history the

---

[56] Cf. above, p. 127. And see the drawing of the triumph by Bernado Parentino (1437–1531) as reproduced in M. Muraro, *Catalogue of the Exhibition of Venetian Drawings from the Collection Janos Scholz* (Venice, 1957), p. 17 and fig. 5.

[57] Popham, *loc. cit.* (n. 31), pp. 182–83.

[58] W. F. Oakeshott (*Some Woodcuts by Hans Burgkmair* [Oxford, 1960], pp. 10–12) conjectures that Burgkmair depended for his figures in this series on watercolors made in India by a German who accompanied the Portuguese fleet of 1505. To strengthen his contention that this is possible, I suggest looking at the watercolor of the elephant painted in India by a Portuguese amateur artist and reproduced in my *Asia in the Making of Europe* (hereafter cited as *Asia*), I (Chicago, 1965), following p. 356. Also see the border drawing of the hindquarters of an elephant which Burgkmair includes in a tropical scene in the Prayer Book of Emperor Maximilian (pl. 89).

[59] See H. Göbel, *Die Wandteppiche* (Leipzig, 1928), I, 253.

[60] Reproduced in C. Ricci, *L'architecture italienne au XVIᵉ siècle* (Paris, n.d.), pl. 232.

[61] E. Iversen, *The Myth of Egypt and Its Hieroglyphs in European Tradition* (Copenhagen, 1961), pp. 64–68. The text accompanying the woodcut of the elephant tells only about Poliphilo's dream of the elephant's appearance and seems not to be closely correlated with the woodcut itself.

elephant with the obelisk is important as a partial prototype for Bernini's famous elephant statue (erected in 1667) which stands in the Piazza Minerva in Rome.[62] No elephant prior to the woodcut in Colonna's book bears the obelisk on its back;[63] no elephant between it and Bernini's seems to carry on this theme even though interest in the hieroglyphs continued unabated during the sixteenth century.[64]

C. THE ELEPHANT OF ROME

While the elephant retained its allegorical symbolism and many of its medieval attributes, a new and realistic dimension was quickly added to Europe's knowledge of it as a consequence of the discoveries. In the *Itinerario* of Ludovico di Varthema,[65] published at Rome in 1510, the gentleman from Bologna describes the Indian elephant in detail in his account of the Hindu kingdom of Vijayanagar.[66] He tells of riding an elephant, estimates it as being larger than three oxen, with the tallest elephant standing thirteen or fourteen palms (about 9 to 9.5 feet) high. He itemizes the elephant's uses in war and in the occupations of peacetime. The female, though smaller, he declares to be stronger than the male. The elephant procreates in secret places, fears fire, and on its foot has five nails, each "as large as the shell of an oyster." He claims to have seen "some elephants which have more understanding, and more discretion and intelligence than any kind of people I have met with." In commenting on Cambay (Gujarat) he records that fifty elephants regularly do reverence before its king.[67]

Shortly after Varthema's book appeared in Rome, King Manuel I of Portugal began to behave like an Indian potentate himself. With his empire in the East prospering, the Portuguese ruler began to collect "elephants of state" and soon erected a stable for them near the Paço d' Estãos, his residence in the Rossio of Lisbon.[68] It is possible that certain of these beasts had been captured at Malacca

---

[62] Heckscher, *loc. cit.* (n. 6), p. 155, and *passim.*

[63] A possible earlier prototype is that on a wall at the side entrance to the thirteenth-century Church of San Corona in Vicenza. On examination I felt that this seemed to be a simple pyramid rather than an obelisk. It is also possible that the fifteenth-century artist was imitating the Catania monument, but since the original no longer exists it is impossible to determine whether the eighteenth-century Catania elephant now standing in the Piazza del Duomo follows the antique elephant which previously stood there or whether it follows the elephant of Colonna and Bernini. Cf. *ibid.*, p. 176, n. 115.

[64] The only monuments of the sixteenth century directly inspired by Colonna's elephant were the rhinoceros with obelisk erected in 1549 to celebrate Henry II's entrance into Paris (see Iversen, *op. cit.* [n. 61], p. 812), and the Antwerp elephant which is shown in an engraving of 1595 with a pillar on its back (pl. 115).

[65] On Varthema see *Asia*, I, 164–66.

[66] R. C. Temple (ed.), *The Itinerary of Ludovico di Varthema of Bologna, from 1502 to 1508* (London, 1928), pp. 51–54.

[67] *Ibid.*, p. 45.

[68] G. de Brito, "Os pachidermes do estado d'El Rei D. Manuel," *Revista de educação e ensino,* IX (1894), 81.

in 1511, when seven elephants fell into the hands of the Portuguese conquerors. On ceremonial occasions, as when he paraded from his palace to the cathedral, Manuel tried to have no fewer than five elephants in the procession. Led by gaily clad drivers, they would perform tricks and feats for the amusement of the admiring throng.[69] An elephant also appeared as a decorative figure on the Tower of Belém, completed during Manuel's reign. In the king's Book of Hours (pl. 86) a realistic elephant with a driver on its back is shown at the bottom of a depiction called "The Flight from Egypt" (1517).[70] To complete his simulation of an Oriental potentate, Manuel sent rare beasts as gifts to his fellow rulers in Europe, and in Asia the Portuguese kings later demanded elephants as tribute from their princely vassals.[71]

In Europe it was tradition that reigning monarchs should dispatch to Rome a mission of obedience to each new pope.[72] But the mission sent by Manuel in 1514 to Pope Leo X was no ordinary embassy of obedience. Led by Tristão da Cunha, commander of the Portuguese fleet to India in 1506, it was designed to dazzle the Holy See with Portugal's great conquests in Asia. Among the exotic gifts sent to Rome was an Indian elephant accompanied by the royal equerry, Nicolau de Faria, and a Hindu driver. It was later rumored in Rome that the elephant at first refused to board the ship at Lisbon because the Hindu trainer, who had fallen in love with a Portuguese girl, had painted the sea voyage and life in Italy to the elephant in the blackest colors. When Manuel learned of the driver's perfidy, he ordered him on pain of death to reassure the elephant and to see to its embarkation.[73]

The embassy of Tristão da Cunha left Lisbon by sea early in 1514.[74] Eight days later it called at Alicante, where the elephant created a sensation. The elephant and the other foreign beasts were evidently put on display for a short time

---

[69] *Ibid.*, p. 79. It is even possible that after 1510 Manuel rode on a litter which had been sent to Lisbon from India. See F. de Sousa Viterbo, "O orientalismo portugues no século XVI," *Boletim da Sociedade de geografia de Lisboa*, XII (1892–93), Nos. 7–8, p. 319.

[70] See F. de Sousa Viterbo, *Diccionario historico e documental* . . . (Lisbon, 1899), I, vii; and R. dos Santos, *Oito séculos de arte portuguesa* (Lisbon, 1967), fasc. 32, pl. 376.

[71] P. S. S. Pissurlencar (ed.), *Regimentos das fortalezas da India* (Bastorà [Goa], 1951), pp.359–60; also P. E. Pieris, *Ceylon and Portugal* (Leipzig, 1927), p. 56.

[72] L. Matos, "Natura intelletto e costumi dell'elefante," *Boletim internacional de bibliografia Luso-Brasileira*, I (1960), 44. Also see S. de Ciutius, *Une ambassade portugaise à Rome au XVIᵉ siècle* (Naples, 1899), pp. 4–8.

[73] This story is told by Piero Valeriano in his *Hierolyphica sive de sacris Aegyptiorum* . . . *literis commentarii* (Basel, 1556), fol. 21v. The Paduan Francesco Chalderia, who lived for two years in Lisbon, describes the embarkation of the elephant in his tract *Rerum et regionum Indicarum per Serenissimum Emanuelem Portugalliae regem partaram narratio verissima*. See citation to Chalderia in Matos, *loc. cit.* (n. 72), p. 46. Also see the version of this story as it was used to prove the ability of the elephant to understand human languages and emotions in S. de Priezac. *L'histoire des éléphants* (Paris, 1650), pp. 63–64.

[74] The travels of the elephant and its reception in Rome were minutely recorded by João de Faria, second legate, and Nicolau de Faria, in letters to King Manuel of March, 1514. See L. A. Rebello da Silva (ed.), *Corpo diplomático portuguez* . . . (Lisbon, 1862), I, 234–38, 238–42. For excellent summaries of these and additions from other sources see Matos, *loc. cit.* (n. 72), pp. 45–47, and M. Winner, "Raffael malt einen Elefanten," *Mitteilungen des kunsthistorischen Institutes in Florenz*, XI (1964), 83–86.

on the islands of Iviza and Majorca when the ships touched there. The embassy finally landed at Port' Ercole in Italy, a harbor under the jurisdiction of Siena located about seventy miles north of Rome. A bark had to be borrowed at the port to make a bridge for the elephant between the ship and the shore.[75] From Port' Ercole the elephant proceeded overland along roadways lined with curious observers. It was accompanied from Montalto onward by a papal escort of one hundred mounted men. In Corneto, when the elephant entered the inn, the building shook so hard that the tiles fell off the roof and such confusion reigned that the elephant had to spend the night in the middle of the public square. When the procession finally arrived in Civitavecchia, two days of rest were ordained while nobles from all over Romagna came to see the elephant. Wet weather kept the procession waiting for several more days outside the walls of Rome before the embassy could make its formal entrance.

Around 2:00 P.M. on Saturday, March 12, 1514, the grand entry began, in streaming sunshine, to wind its way through the Porta del Popolo. All eyes were riveted upon the exotic gifts, especially the elephant. Prelates and dignitaries were a common sight in the Eternal City, but no living elephant had been seen in Rome since Antiquity. Guided by the Hindu trainer, the elephant carried on its back a richly clad Moor, a splendid covering worked with the arms of Portugal, and a silver castle which contained costly gifts for the Holy See. The people thronged the narrow streets, sat in the windows, and perched on the roofs and crossbars; the assemblage was so great that the bailiffs had difficulty opening a passage for the elephant legate.[76] It is possible that Leonardo da Vinci was one of the startled spectators.[77]

Finally reaching the Castel San Angelo, the diplomatic procession stopped before the pope and the cardinals, who were seated in the apertures of the fortress. The elephant, in response to a command, bowed three times before His Holiness. To the delight of the populace, it then sucked water into its trunk from a bucket and sprayed the high prelates; then the elephant turned to the throng and favored it with the same treatment. Leo X was delighted with the whole display and laughed like a child at the elephant's antics. To the roar of the cannons and the fanfare of trumpets, the procession then moved across the Ponte San Angelo to the other side of the Tiber and to an inn and a stable in

[75] A Roman polychrome mosaic, unearthed several generations ago on the site of the ancient Etruscan city of Veii, depicts how elephants were similarly embarked and disembarked in Antiquity and how they were chained to the mast and secured to the deck. See R. Cagnat, "La première représentation connue du mode d'embarquement de l'éléphant," *L'ami des monuments et des arts* (Paris), XIV (1900), 67–70.

[76] Interest was so profound and enduring in the "diplomatic elephant" that its entrance to Rome was chronicled three years later by a French observer. See L. Madelin (ed.), "Le journal d'un habitant français de Rome au XVIe siècle (1509–40)," *Mélanges d'archéologie et d'histoire*, XXII (1902), 277. An engraving of Tristão da Cunha (in P. Jovius, *Elegia virorum . . . illustrium* [Basel, 1575]) has an elephant looking over the diplomat's shoulder.

[77] The great artist was in Rome when the elephant arrived there. He was also acquainted with Giovanni Battista Branconio dell'Aquila, the papal chamberlain and keeper of the elephant. See McCurdy, *op. cit.* (n. 28), II, 1177.

the Campo dei Fiori. A few days later the elephant was taken to the Belvedere Gardens, its permanent home.

The Romans soon named the elephant "Hanno,"[78] and he was known under this name to his keepers at the Vatican and in the contemporary accounts. Hanno, unlike the panthers and other wild animals brought to Rome, was treated with great care and even assigned an overseer. His personal attendant was the papal chamberlain and friend of Raphael, Giovanni Battista Branconio dell' Aquila, who was aided by a stablehand called Alfonso.[79] Pope Leo even refused, out of concern for the elephant's health, to lend Hanno to Lorenzo de' Medici for the Triumph of the Camillus held in Florence in June, 1514. Hanno was permitted, however, to take part in Roman festivals and was ordinarily the center of attraction on these occasions. A street and an inn were renamed after the elephant.[80]

One of Hanno's most notable public appearances took place on September 27, 1514, when he appeared in the ludicrous proceedings put on for the festival of Saints Cosmas and Damian, the protectors of the House of Medici.[81] The butt of the pope's humor on this day was a vain grayhaired poet named Baraballo of Gaeta, who was listed in the account books of the Vatican at a somewhat lower level than Alfonso, the elephant keeper. A mere rhymster with an inane desire to be recognized as the "new Petrarch," Baraballo himself suggested that he should be crowned poet laureate at the Capitol. When the pope agreed and proclaimed that he should ride to the Capitol on Hanno's back, the delighted courtiers prepared satirical poems and comedies to magnify the occasion.[82] The "archpoet," as Filippo Beroaldo called him, dressed in a Roman toga, mounted the "arch-elephant" to the sound of trumpets. On its back the elephant wore a covering inscribed "Poeta Barabal." The mock ceremony ended when Hanno,

[78] Winner (*loc. cit.* [n. 74], p. 81, n. 22) and most others are inclined, quite understandably, to look to classical sources in accounting for this name. They take it to be a reference to one of the numerous "Hannos" of Carthaginian history, or to a lion tamer mentioned in Pliny. I would suggest the possibility that when the Romans asked the Hindu trainer (probably a native of Malabar) what the elephant was called, he replied "Ana," the Malayālam word for "elephant." See T. Burrow and M. B. Emeneau, *Dravidian Etymological Dictionary* (Oxford, 1961), entry no. 4235. Garcia da Orta in his *Coloquios* (1563) notes that "Ani" is the Malayālam word in use in India during the sixteenth century. For Orta see below, p. 154. In the Italian version of Cristobal de Acosta's *Trattato* (Venice, 1585), p. 322, it is reported that the Malabar name is "Anne." Other Italians of the time wrote the name of Leo's elephant as "Annone."

[79] According to later accounts, Alfonso allegedly died under mysterious circumstances on the same day as Hanno. See Winner, *loc. cit.* (n. 74), p. 86.

[80] E. Rodocanachi, *La première Renaissance: Rome au temps de Jules II, et de Léon X* (Paris, 1912), p. 319, n. 2.

[81] See, for details, the account in D. Gnoli, "La Roma di Leon X," in *Quadri e studi originali annotati e publicati a cura di Aldo Gnoli* (Milan, 1938), pp. 114–17; also Rodocanachi, *op. cit.* (n. 80), pp. 121–23.

[82] For a summary of the comedy prepared by Filippo Beroaldo the Younger, see Winner, *loc. cit.* (n. 74), p. 87; see also in the *Carminum* (Rome, 1530) of Beroaldo, the "Prologus in comoediam habitam in coronatione Barabelli." Also see Gnoli, *loc. cit.* (n. 81), p. 115. Also see the Latin poem by Ia. Manius Philoenus as reproduced in W. Roscoe, *The Life and Pontifical of Leo X* (London, 1805), II, 104–5.

made skittish by the noise and music, refused to cross the bridge of San Angelo and Baraballo was forced to dismount. News of this great farce ran throughout Italy. Machiavelli in his poem *Asino d'Oro* (chap. vi) takes note of the poet's downfall.[83] And, a few years later, Giovanni Barili portrayed the mock crowning of Baraballo in an intarsia which may still be seen in the Vatican on the upper right-hand corner of one of the portals to the Stanza della Segnatura (pl. 93).

Hanno appeared in several other Roman festivals, and was a source of constant delight to the populace.[84] Marino Sanuto, the Venetian diarist, comically describes him as being "as large as three oxen, as understanding the Portuguese and Indian languages, and as trumpeting like a woman."[85] But, despite all the care lavished upon him by his keepers, Hanno's health gradually failed. Ulrich von Hutten, hardly a sympathetic observer, has Magister Wilhelm in the *Letters of Obscure Men* describe the pope's great anguish at the elephant's illness, his frantic appeals to the doctors for aid, and his sorrow when Hanno died on June 16, 1516.[86] Others baited the pope about his childlike devotion to the elephant and Pietro Aretino wrote, possibly in 1516, a polemical tract called *The Last Will and Testament of the Elephant* in which he satirizes Leo and the entire curia. Hanno, in Aretino's burlesque, willed his tusks to Cardinal San Giorgio on condition that the prelate's "thirst, like that of Tantalus, for the papacy may be moderated"; his knees to Cardinal Santa Croce "to enable him to imitate my genuflections" on the condition that "he tells no more lies in council"; and his jaws to Cardinal Santi Quattro "so that he can devour more readily all of Christ's revenues."[87] Martin Luther, writing four years after Hanno's death in his tract *On the Papacy of Rome*, indirectly criticizes the pope for his frivolity in playing with elephants.[88]

[83] For a delightful pasquinade on this episode see G. A. Cesareo, *Pasquino e pasquinate nella Roma di Leone X* (Rome, 1938), pp. 193–94. Animals, including the elephant, figured prominently in the pasquinades on Leo (lion). See Gnoli, *loc. cit.* (n. 81), p. 301, and *Opere di Niccolò Machiavelli, cittadino segretario fiorentino* (n.p., 1813), V, 407.

[84] See, for example, the part Hanno played in the reception held in March, 1515 (Rodocanachi, *op. cit.* [n. 80], p. 97).

[85] *I Diarii* (Venice, 1887), Vol. XVIII, col. 59.

[86] U. von Hutten, *Opera quae extant omnia* (Munich, 1807), VII, 246. Also see Giovanni Capito's Latin elegy to the elephant as reproduced in Roscoe, *op. cit.* (n. 82), II, app. C, 103–4. A little book of verse on the elephant from this period is in the British Museum (P.B. 11426. d. 54). Entitled *Natura intellecto et costumi delle Elephante . . .* , it reviews the writings of Aristotle, Pliny, and Solinus on the elephant. For a reproduction see Matos, *loc. cit.* (n. 72), pp. 47–55, who contends that it was probably printed in Rome around 1514. The woodcut of the elephant on the title page is of the quattrocento type.

[87] From the manuscript in the Museo Correr (Codex Cicogna 2673, fol. 240v–241r) of Venice as published in Vittorio Rossi, *Dal Rinascimento al Risorgimento* (Florence, 1930), pp. 232–38. It was Rossi who first attributed this manuscript to Aretino. For a partial English translation see T. C. Chubb, *Aretino, Scourge of Princes* (New York, 1940), pp. 50–51.

[88] G. Scheil, *Die Tierwelt in Luther's Bildersprache in seinen reformatorisch-historischen und polemischen deutschen Schriften* (Bernburg, 1897), p. 19. Luther asserts that the pope catches flies while he lets elephants cavort, a possible paraphrase of the biblical text: "Ye blind guides, which strain at a gnat, and swallow a camel" (Matt. 23:24).

D. RAPHAEL AND HIS SCHOOL

Tradition avers, based on the remarks of Paulus Jovius in his *History of My Own Times* and other works,[89] that Raphael was commissioned by the pope to paint Hanno's picture. But no painting or drawing from Raphael's hand has actually survived, though Jovius seems to have been acquainted with a Raphael representation of some kind. Jovius also relates that after Hanno's death an epitaph to the elephant was painted on the wall near the tower at the Vatican's door. It is likely that the epitaph appeared on an outside wall of the Vatican with Raphael's depiction of Hanno standing over it, for Jovius reports that Leo fulfilled the people's wish for a picture of their "incomparable townsman."[90] This work was probably destroyed in the renovation of the Vatican undertaken in the time of Pope Paul IV (1555–59),[91] the Carafa pope who was so hostile to the worldliness of his predecessors.

The epitaph itself was written by Branconio, the elephant's keeper, and to it was appended an epigram by Filippo Beroaldo the Younger. The only source which depicts the elephant fresco with the epitaph and the epigram below it is from the pen of Francisco d'Ollanda and is preserved today in the Escorial (pl. 90).[92] D'Ollanda, a Portuguese architect, was in Rome in 1539–40 to study and sketch in the ancient capital. He probably sketched the memorial to Hanno out of a sense of duty to country and king, for his tour was being sponsored by King John III of Portugal, the son of King Manuel. The sketch is poor and the rendition of the epitaph faulty, but both the fresco and the inscription are clear enough to lead us back to Raphael.

The entire epitaph is dedicated to D(eus) M(aximus)[93] and reads:

Beneath this enormous mound I lie buried, the huge elephant, which King Manuel, after he had conquered the East, sent as a prisoner to the tenth Leo. I, the elephant, was much admired by the Roman people—since such a beast had not been on view for centuries—and in the body of a beast they discerned human intelligence. Fate envied me my home in happy Latium and would not permit me to serve my lord for as much as three years. Therefore, O Gods, add those years which destiny has filched from me to the life of the great Leo.

[89] See *Pauli Iovii novocomensis episcope Nucerini Elogia virorum bellica virtute illustrim veris imaginibus supposita, quae apud Musaeum spectantur . . .* (Florence, 1551), p. 205.

[90] Winner, *loc. cit.* (n. 74), pp. 89–90.

[91] Roscoe, *op. cit.* (n. 87), II, 338–39.

[92] For discussion see E. Tormo y Monzó, *Os desenhos das antigualhas que vio Francisco D'Ollanda, pintor português* (Madrid, 1940), p. 142.

[93] In this I agree with Tormo (*ibid.*) rather than Winner (*loc. cit.* [n. 74], p. 91), who interprets the "D" and "M" as being abbreviations for "gods" and "manes." It seems likely that a dedication on the wall of the Vatican, even in Leo X's time, would be headed by an invocation to the Christian God rather than to pagan deities and shades.

He lived to seven years of age, died of angina, and was twelve palms [8 ft. 10 in.][94] tall. This memorial was placed here by Giovanni Battista of Aquila, papal chamberlain and the elephant's headkeeper, on June [?], 1516, in the fourth year of the pontificate of Leo X.
What nature took away, Raphael of Urbino has with art restored.[95]

But did the great Raphael actually execute a portrait of Hanno from life? On the basis of the excellent work of Matthias Winner,[96] it now seems most likely that he did. Winner has been able to depict with superb detail the close relationships between D'Ollanda's elephant and a pen drawing now preserved in the *Kupferstichkabinett* of Berlin, which is a close copy of the missing sketch by Raphael (pl. 91). He also shows with great clarity the similarities between the Berlin elephant and the intarsia of Barili (pl. 93), and between the Berlin elephant and another pen drawing in the Fogg Museum at Cambridge, Massachusetts. While each depiction has its distinctive characteristics, Winner convincingly stresses the following identities: the gait and positioning of the elephant, the strikingly short tusks, the little bell hanging around the neck, the ribbed muscular structure in the ear, the curvature of the trunk, and the placement of the driver's left hand on the trunk. The misrepresentation of the elephant's proportions in the sketch book of D'Ollanda he attributes to the copyist's lack of talent. Hanno's gait, proportions, and leg placement and the representation of the driver seated on the elephant's neck in the Berlin drawing correspond perfectly to the depiction in the intarsia; the D'Ollanda and the Cambridge elephants are faulty in having all four feet placed on the same level, and they do not correspond in other ways to the intarsia. He therefore concludes that the Berlin drawing is closer to the Raphael original than any of the other extant copies. But all the depictions, faulty or not, seem to have a portrait by Raphael as their common source.

Raphael certainly drew the elephant before its death in 1516, for the scientific naturalism of his depiction must have come from a living model. Such an assumption is reinforced by the fact that Raphael promised to paint Leo's elephant for Isabella d'Este. The lady from Ferrara visited Rome in 1514–15, and on March 3, 1516, her agent, Carlo Asnelli, wrote saying that Raphael had agreed to do a painting of the elephant.[97] This being the case it is likely that Raphael, careful workman that he was, had sketched not just one but several preliminary studies of the living model before agreeing to undertake the commission. Possibly some of the studies were sent off to Ferrara for approval. That such drawings were available in Ferrara seems to be confirmed by the woodcut (pl. 94) which

[94] Derived from the figures given by Winner, *loc. cit.* (n. 74), p. 96. Elephants do not grow nearly so slowly as they are commonly supposed to and may reach maturity when twelve to fifteen years of age. See O. P. Breland, *Animal Life and Lore* (New York, 1963), p. 78. Hanno, though tall for his seven years, seems not to have been extraordinary even though the epitaph calls him "huge." "Jumbo," the famous African elephant bought by P. T. Barnum from the London zoo, was 11 feet 10 inches tall at 23 years of age and weighed 11,000 pounds. See Kunz, *op. cit.* (n. 9), p. 188.
[95] On Beroaldo's authorship of this epigram see Winner, *loc. cit.* (n. 74), p. 90.
[96] *Ibid.*, esp. pp. 92–96.
[97] *Ibid.*, pp. 98–99.

appears in the *Triompho di Fortuna* (1526) of the Ferrara mathematician, Sigismondo Fanti. Here Hanno appears in a reverse woodcut looking almost exactly as he does in the Berlin drawing. He is used here as the center of an astrological wheel of fortune with which Fanti casts the future of Leo's family, the House of Medici. Several years later, after 1517, Raphael negotiated with Alfonso d'Este to paint a "Triumph of Bacchus in India." Raphael evidently sent a drawing of his "Bacchus" with Hanno in it to Ferrara for approval but then decided that he would rather do another subject. Alfonso persisted in his wish for a "Bacchus," and eventually handed the commission over to Titian. While Raphael's drawing is no longer extant, it may be preserved in an eighteenth-century aquatint for which Sir Joshua Reynolds made the drawing, possibly on the basis of Raphael's original.[98]

The drawings of Hanno made from life seem to cast their influence over the depiction of the elephant in European art throughout the sixteenth century. One of the best tracers by which to follow Hanno's career in art is the moon-shaped hook (*ankus*) which the elephant's driver holds in the Berlin drawing. This prod was certainly imported from India along with the elephant and its driver, for identical goads appear in Indian sculptures[99] and miniatures.[100] Other characteristics to watch for are the ribbed muscular structure of the ear, the short tusks, and the curvature of the trunk. It is important to watch closely for these features of the Berlin elephant because there is a tendency, which begins with the pupils of Raphael after his death in 1520, to fantasize Hanno by giving him physical attributes which seem to be derived from ancient, medieval, and quattrocento depictions of the elephant.

It appears quite likely, on the basis of later paintings and sketches, that Giulio Romano and Giovanni da Udine also made drawings of the elephant, either from life or on the basis of Raphael's drawings. In the garden of the Villa Madama, which was erected after Raphael's plans on the slope of Monte Marino outside of Rome, Giulio Romano and Giovanni da Udine constructed an elephant head in plaster using the trunk as a fountain. Copies of this delightful piece were sketched by D'Ollanda and Martin van Heemskerck (pl. 95), and in their renditions something of the joyful spirit of Hanno seems to live on.[101] Traces of Hanno's portrait and memories of the fountain at the Villa Madama extend to Mantua. Giulio Romano's sketch for a decorative stucco elephant

---

[98] On this attribution see *ibid.*, pp. 100–101. For Raphael's relations with Alfonso see G. Gruyer, *L'art ferrarais à l'époque des princes d'Este* (Paris, 1897), I, 151.

[99] Winner, *loc. cit.* (n. 74), p. 101, n. 97.

[100] See, for example, the seventeenth-century miniature in the Vienna National Library (Min. 64, fol. 28), reproduced in J. Strzygowski *et al.*, *Asiatische Miniaturenmalerei* (Klagenfurth, 1933), pl. 9, no. 29. The "noble sages" of India recognized just four elephant hooks, those resembling respectively "a thunderbolt, half-moon, nail, and *keteka* thorn." See Edgerton, *op. cit.* (n. 13), p. 109. For a photographic reproduction of the ankus see J. L. Kipling, *Beast and Man in India* (London, 1904), p. 227.

[101] On the garden's history see O. Fischel, *Raphael* (London, 1948), I, 164–65. Obviously the giant plaster head is not derived from Raphael's drawing (Winner, *loc. cit.* [n. 74], p. 104); it seems likely, however, that it was modeled on some other unknown sketch, possibly made from life or the artist's memory of Hanno.

with putti scrambling on its back reproduces exactly the small ear muscle of Hanno: it also wears a bell though other of its features are quite different from the Raphael elephant.[102] The roistering elephant (pl. 96) shown in the "Marriage Feast of Cupid and Psyche" (completed *ca.* 1528 in the Sala di Psiche of the Palazzo del Te) is highly reminiscent of the fountain elephant of the Villa Madama, but only in spirit.[103] In Rome, meanwhile, the Raphael students working there continued to follow the master's drawing in every particular. Especially faithful to the original are a stucco relief (pl. 92) and an elephant ornament (pls. 149,150) preserved in the loggia of the Vatican by Giovanni da Udine and a drawing for a table ornament, probably by Polidore da Caravaggio, in which Hanno wears a saddle decorated with the Medici arms.[104]

It was the fantasized elephants of Giulio Romano which first spread from Italy to the rest of Europe, perhaps because others had not seen Hanno or Raphael's portrait of him. At Mantua, the stucco panels and medallions of the Sala delle Aquile and the filigrees and cartouches in the Camerino degli Ucelli of the Ducal Palace show decorative elephants frolicking with other exotic beasts. King Francis I of France, who was certainly interested in collecting live elephants for his menagerie at Amboise,[105] seems to have been entranced by fantastic pachyderms as well. Rosso Fiorentino, who had worked earlier both in Rome and Mantua, painted, sometime shortly after 1531, a fresco in the gallery of Fontainebleau which includes a gigantic, elongated elephant. Iconographically, it and the fantasized copy of it by Antonio Fantuzzi show no resemblance to Raphael's and Giulio Romano's naturalistic elephants.[106] Symbolically, the Fontainebleau elephant, and perhaps its artistic prototype as well, hark back to the elephants of the Roman triumphs. It is possible that the Fontainebleau elephant, decorated with the fleur-de-lis of France, is intended to be an allegorical portrait of Francis I as a wise and virtuous ruler, a "new Alexander" who had won both military and cultural victories.[107]

While the Fontainebleau fresco was being completed, a series of tapestries representing the triumph of Scipio Africanus was being prepared in Brussels

---

[102] Winner, *loc. cit.* (n. 74), p. 101. This sketch, prepared for the Sala delle Aquile in the Palazzo del Te, is reproduced in F. Hartt, *Giulio Romano* (New Haven, 1958), II, 296, fig. 220.

[103] Cf. Hartt, *op. cit.* (n. 102), I, 128, quoting E. Gombrich on this subject.

[104] See Winner, *loc. cit.* (n. 74), pp. 102–4. Compare the decorative stucco of the classical quadriga, probably from the 1520's in "L'Odeo" of the Villa Cornaro in Padua. It was possibly worked on also by Giovanni da Udine, but it shows no debt to Hanno. See G. Mazzotti, *Ville Venete* (Rome, 1963), p. 107.

[105] Francis I, shortly after Hanno's death, wrote a letter to the king of Portugal and sent his agent, Antoine de Conflans, to Lisbon to try to buy a male and female elephant for his menagerie (Matos, *loc. cit.* [n. 72], p. 46). The king also sent emissaries to Constantinople to purchase exotic animals, and around 1545 his ambassador to the Porte arranged to have an elephant sent from Persia to France. Cf. below, p. 147.

[106] For commentary, see P. Barocchi, *Il Rosso fiorentino* (Rome, 1951), pp. 110, 134–36, 157–58. The elephants in the "Triumph of Bacchus in India" painted in 1530 by Perino del Vaga as a fresco decoration in the Palazzo Doria of Genoa likewise owe no debt to Hanno. See P. Askew, "Perino del Vaga's Decorations for the Palazzo Doria, Genoa," *Burlington Magazine*, XCVIII (1956), 50, fig. 28.

[107] Based on discussions in Panofsky, *loc. cit.* (n. 23), pp. 132–33.

for Francis I. The drawings for these tapestries by Giulio Romano and Gianfrancesco Penni were published for the first time in 1907. All but two of the themes represented in the drawings are derived from Appian's *Punic Wars* (8. 9. 66). Two elephants, along with oxen and camels, are depicted as trophies of war in one of the sketches (no. 260). The lead elephant is shown with a rider holding a goad in a manner reminiscent of Hanno's driver; only the head of the other elephant appears, and it seems to be vaguely similar to Giulio Romano's marriage-feast elephant.[108] Cornelius Cort, while in Rome in 1567, redid his earlier engraving, "The Battle of Scipio against Hannibal," after a drawing by Giulio Romano which he saw in the collection of Thomas Cavallerius, a Roman gentleman.[109] The four elephant figures depicted in Cort's engraving (two heads one facing and one moving away from the viewer) are realistic-fantastic and seem to owe nothing directly to Raphael's Hanno.[110] They appear to be much more closely related to the fountain of the Villa Madama and to the elephants of Giulio Romano. When compared to the older type of elephants still being used at the time,[111] the elephants deriving from Giulio Romano constitute a new type—naturalistic elephants fantasized by the artists. Hanno, in company with the fantasized elephants, can be clearly seen in one engraving from the collection published by Antonio Lafreri in his *Speculum Romanae magnificentiae* (pl. 106).[112] Two of the naturalistic elephant portraits from Lafreri show up prominently in the painting "Noah's Ark" (1570) by Simone de Myle (pl. 107).

E. THE VIENNA ELEPHANT OF 1552

In 1551 King John III of Portugal bestowed an Indian elephant as a gift upon Archduke Maximilian II of Austria, the eldest son of Emperor Ferdinand I and the elected king of Bohemia who had been stationed in Spain for many years. When Maximilian was recalled to Vienna, he left Spain with the elephant in his entourage. The royal party and the elephant landed at Genoa and went overland

---

[108] For a reproduction see Hartt, *op. cit.* (n. 102), fig. 475.

[109] See J. C. J. Bierens de Haan, *L'oeuvre gravé de Cornelis Cort . . . 1533–1578* (The Hague, 1948), pp. 178–80 and pl. 50. The drawings of elephants in the Ashmolean collection at Oxford, attributed usually to the "school of Raphael," seem to be copied from Cort's engraving. See Winner, *loc. cit.* (n. 74), pp. 92–93.

[110] Cf. Winner, *loc. cit.*, pp. 102–3.

[111] See, for example,.the quadriga of elephants in the "Triumph of Pompey" shown in the edition of Plutarch by Giovanni Zonara published in Latin in 1557; and the "Triumph of Saturn," a woodcut after P. Brueghel by Philip Galle in 1574 as reproduced in plate 105; or the Flemish tapestry called "Elephant Hunt," by a Brussels master of *ca.* 1535–40 as reproduced in plate 97. In all these cases, as well as in many others not here cited, the elephants shown hark back to the pre-Hanno depictions.

[112] In the large collection at the University of Chicago, two engravings show Hanno. One depicts him with the Asian elephants of Giulio Romano and the other (possibly by Giovanni Battista Franco), shows him with fantasized African elephants. Also see the engravings of Roman triumphs for other sorts of elephants, possibly copied from ancient sarcophagi.

to Milan. About thirteen years old at the time, the elephant bowed and trumpeted before the archbishop of Milan and was subjected to the scrutiny of the mathematician Girolamo Cardano.[113] From Italy the royal party evidently approached the Alps by way of the Tyrol. The oldest inn at Brixen (Bressanone) in the heart of the Tyrol has a life-sized elephant painted on it with an inscription dated 1551, a probable indication that Maximilian and his party halted there.[114] From this center they evidently took the Brenner Pass to the Inn Valley and then proceeded to work their way northward. A *Flugblatt* portraying the elephant (pl. 100) announced its imminent appearance at the Habsburg court with an inscription which indicated that it had arrived at Wasserburg in Upper Bavaria on January 24, 1552.[115] The procession, which must necessarily have moved at a slow pace, evidently followed the Inn River to Passau and the valley of the Danube. The last several stages of its journey were made by river barge.

The official entry of Maximilian took place in Vienna on May 7, 1552. The sophisticated Viennese who watched the procession were unimpressed by the gilded coach and eight which carried the royal couple, by the lavish costumes of the Spanish courtiers, and even by the sight of the Indian parrots which were carried out in the open for all to see. But they were overwhelmed by suddenly seeing before their eyes a colossal four-footed beast which walked along between armed guards swinging its trunk gracefully from side to side. Near the Kärntner Gate the crowd almost panicked at the sight of the elephant and quieted down only after Wolfgang Laz, the imperial physician, had explained that the beast was not a vicious monster and that it performed useful service in its homeland.[116]

Once a few of the courtiers approached the beast, the people bravely surged around to admire and touch it. Then the procession moved slowly toward the Michaelsplatz and to a large shed where the elephant was to be put on display. Tradition has it that the elephant won the hearts of the public by picking up in its trunk a little girl who had fallen down in the press. Whatever may be the truth of this story, no doubt exists that the elephant moved the Viennese. A house numbered 619 on the corner of the Graben and the Stephansplatz was known until its demolition in 1866 as the "Elephant House."[117] On its wall a relief of the elephant was executed in 1552 which showed a driver on the elephant's back carrying a goad in his right hand and a yellow rein in his left hand which was tied to the two long tusks. Beneath the sandstone relief appeared Latin and German inscriptions. The German verse read, in part, as follows:

[113] G. Cardano, *De subtilitate* (Basel, 1554), Bk. X, chap. 204.

[114] See Kaufmann, *loc. cit.* (n. 53), p. 409, n. 3.

[115] The *Flugblatt* initialed M. M. shows a realistic Indian elephant with a driver on its back who holds a hook in his left hand.

[116] See M. Bermann, *Alt-und-Neu Wien* (Vienna, 1880), II, 702–6; and W. Kisch, *Die alten Strassen und Plätze Wiens* (Vienna, 1883), pp. 117–18, 128.

[117] See the engraving by J. E. Fischer von Erlach and J. A. Delsenbach of the vegetable market of the Graben (dated around 1713), which shows the head of this elephant with its rider perched on the neck. A. May, *Wien in alten Ansichten* (Salzburg, 1965), pl. 18.

Dieses Thier heisst ein Elephant,
Welches ist weit und breit bekannt,
Seine ganze Gröss, also Gestalt,
Ist hier ganz fleissig abgemalt.[118]

Several other houses and inns affected doorplates inscribed "Zum Elephanten," and No. 47 Kärntnerstrasse retained its commemorative inscription and elephant portrait to 1880. After a time the elephant itself was taken to the menagerie at the pleasure palace and hunting lodge of Ebersdorf in the outskirts of Vienna.

The elephant died at Ebersdorf on December 18, 1553, just a little more than one and a half years after its arrival in Vienna. To commemorate the elephant's short residence in Austria, a leaden medal was struck in 1554 by Michael Fuchs (pl. 101). Rather than bury the elephant, the Viennese apparently decided to commemorate its visit in its own bones. Sebastian Huetstocker, mayor of Vienna, had an armchair made of its bones with his family arms inscribed on the two front legs. The armchair, which is housed today in the Baroque collection of the Stiftsbibliothek of Kremsmünster,[119] also had an inscription carved into the seat. An incised elephant led and followed by Orientalized drivers encircles the inscription. The support beneath the seat has carved into it an elephant quite evidently copied from the *Flugblatt* portrait of 1552, or from some source common to them both. The Latin inscription on the seat reads in translation:

When his Serene Highness Prince Maximilian, King of Bohemia, Archduke of Austria, etc., came (along with his royal wife Maria, daughter of the Roman Emperor Charles V., and their two children)[120] from Spain to Vienna on May 7, 1552, he brought with him an Indian elephant—which elephant died in the following year [1553] on December 18 at the residence of the governor [*rectoris*] in a suburb of Vienna. The weight of the deceased amounted to 42 Centner, 73 Pfund [i.e., 5,200 pounds]. From its remains, and on the order of the king, there was given to me, Sebastian Huetstocker, then mayor [*consuli*] of the city of Vienna, by Francisco Delasso, the supreme equerry, a gift of the right front shoulder from which part this armchair was made.[121]

A limestone relief (*ca.* 1560) by Severin Brachmann of Maximilian II and Maria shows an elephant based on the *Flugblatt* portrait standing behind the emperor while a dromedary stands behind his wife.[122]

[118] Bermann, *op. cit.* (n. 116), II, 704. The original elephant portrait was so weathered and unclear that it was replaced in 1727 by a large fresco which showed the elephant being led by its driver. In 1789 this picture was plastered over and the elephant was not restored. The name, however, continued to be used until the house itself was demolished in 1866.

[119] The armchair was purchased by Kremsmünster when the *Kunstkammer* of Schloss Windhaag bei Prag (Mühlviertel, Oberösterreich) was broken up—probably in 1869. Today it is housed in the newly rehabilitated *Kunst- und Raritätenkammer* of the Stiftsbibliothek of Kremsmünster (letter of April 2, 1966, from the Stiftsbibliothek). For further information see K. Werner, *Die Sammlungen Kremsmünster* (Berlin, 1936), pp. 22–23.

[120] Parentheses added.

[121] For Latin text see reproductions in Lach, *loc. cit.* (n. 2), pl. VII.

[122] Reproduced in A. Lhotsky, *Die Geschichte der Sammlungen* (Vienna, 1941–45), Vol. II, Pt. II, pl. 23.

The number of artistic representations of elephants from living models increases considerably after the demise of the Vienna elephant, even though distorted African and Asian types continue to appear both separately and in conjunction with more naturalistic elephants.[123] It is next to impossible to connect, even indirectly, all of the realistic elephants with their living or artistic models. Part of the problem stems from the fact that masses of material in zoological institutes remain unexplored or unknown and also that too little work has so far been done in determining the part played by artists in the illustrations of zoological works.[124] Examination of a number of natural histories of the mid-sixteenth century reveals that the illustrators commonly adhere to the quattrocento depiction of the elephant.[125] P. A. Mattioli, the Sienese physician and naturalist, in the section on ivory in his *Commentaries* (1544) on Dioscorides introduces a note of realism into his text and illustrations. He describes the elephant's hide on the basis of what he learned from Hanno's attendants and quotes much more from Cadamosto than from Pliny. His two woodcuts of African elephants are more naturalistic than many of those included in the natural histories before and after his time.[126] In 1548 from Aleppo in northern Syria Pierre Gilles wrote a detailed description of the elephant based on dissection. The beast he describes was one that had been purchased as a gift for King Henry II by the French ambassador to the Porte from a brother to the shah of Persia. This elephant died near Aleppo, and Gilles' careful description of it was not published until 1562.[127] Konrad Gesner, in his section on the elephant in *Historiae animalium* (Zurich, 1551–58), still uses Schongauer's highly fantastic depiction. Ambroise Paré's *Oeuvres* (Paris, 1585) contains several woodcuts in which the elephants show very little improvement in realism over some of those found in medieval bestiaries. From these and other examples it seems clear that many of the early scientists had little knowledge of the available naturalistic descriptions and illustrations. Indeed the author of "Second Voyage to Guinea," who studied

---

[123] For example, the elephant in the background of Brueghel's "Adoration of Kings," painted around 1556, is of the quattrocento type, possibly because of Brueghel's indebtedness to Bosch. See F. Grossmann, *Brueghel: The Paintings* (rev. ed.; London, 1966), p. 190 and pl. 4.

[124] For elaboration of this point see E. K. J. Reznicek, *Die Zeichnungen von Hendrick Goltzius* (Utrecht, 1961), I, 207–8. Also note that the Sinhalese carvings of the elephant were available as models for European artists. See above, p. 25. So far as I can ascertain, European artists of the time seem not to have modeled their representations on these Sinhalese carvings.

[125] Most fascinating is the woodcut of a small elephant pulling a plow in the 1548 version of P. de Crescentio, *De omnibus agriculturae partibus et de plantarium animalium natural et utilitate libri XII* (Basel). For earlier versions of the woodcut used in the Crescentio book see A. Tchemerzine, *Bibliographie d'éditions originales et rares d'auteurs français . . .* (Paris, 1927–33), III, 70. In India, the small, spindly "deer elephants" were used for plowing.

[126] Based on the edition of 1572 published at Lyons of his *Commentaires . . . sur les six livres de Ped. Dioscoride . . .*, pp. 229–31. Interesting for its naturalistic descriptions of the circus tricks performed by an elephant in Constantinople is the "Turkish letter" dated 1555 in E. S. Forster (ed. and trans.), *The Turkish Letters of Ogier Ghiselin de Busbecq, Imperial Ambassador at Constantinople, 1554–62* (Oxford, 1927), pp. 38–39.

[127] P. Gilles, *Aeliani de historia animalium libri XVII* (Lyons, 1562), pp. 497–525. Also see E. T. Hamy, "Le père de la zoölogie française: Pierre Gilles d'Albi," *Revue des Pyrénées*, XII (1900), 582–85.

African elephants closely, wrote in 1555 that "Painters and Arras workers are deceived" in their depictions of the tusks.[128] He might also have pointed out that many of them also were wrong in their drawings of the legs, trunk, and ears (pls. 104, 105).

The sculptured elephants of this epoch are likewise very little dependent upon living models, or even naturalistic drawings. The fountain elephant of the Villa Madama, for example, is far more naturalistic than the crude elephant head done at midcentury which now occupies a niche at the base of the fountain in the Piazza Pretoria of Palermo.[129] Equally unrealistic is the elephant head that is carved, along with other animals, in the interior of the grotto of the Medici villa at Castello.[130] Of the sculptures the most natural in appearance are the marble elephants which guard the sepulchers of King Sebastian and the Cardinal-King (Prince Henry) in the monastery of the Jerónimos at Belém in Portugal.[131] The most puzzling of the sculptured elephants is the huge stone creature which dominates the garden of Bomarzo in central Italy.

Sometime before 1564, Vincino Orsini had constructed in the "Sacred Wood" at the base of the hill on which the village of Bomarzo stands a fantastic garden "which resembles itself and nothing else."[132] Orsini, running directly counter to prevailing ideas of classical symmetry and proportion, had this section of his garden designed around the irregular outcroppings of stone along the hillside.[133] In the "Sacred Wood" gigantic human, animal, and mythical figures are cut from the stone. In the center of this fantastic mélange stands a mammoth elephant (pl. 103) with an ornate girdle and square castle on its back, a driver on its neck, and a soldier in its trunk. The tusks have apparently disappeared, the ears are large and open, and the legs are four-square, heavy, and straight.

While the head and ears are reminiscent of D'Ollanda's elephant and the position of the rider similar to Barili's driver in the intarsia of the Vatican, it is certainly not possible to assert that the sculptor of Bomarzo is portraying Hanno in stone. The motif of the elephant holding the soldier in its trunk is seen frequently in the temple elephants of India,[134] but prototypes employing the same

[128] As published in R. Hakluyt, *The Principal Navigations Voyages Traffiques and Discoveries of the English Nation* (Glasgow, 1904), VI, 164.

[129] Possibly completed in Florence *ca.* 1555, it was the work of Francisco Camillo and Michelangelo Nascherino. It was acquired by Palermo in 1573 and assembled by 1585; see L. Russo, *La fontana di Piazza Pretoria in Palermo* (Palermo, 1961), p. 55 and pl. X.

[130] See below, p. 166.

[131] For discussion see J. de Sigüenza, *Historia de la Orden de San Gerónimo* (Madrid, 1907), II, 72; for an early description of the tombs and their elephant guardians see J. B. de Lavanha, *Viage de la catholica real magestad del rei D. Felipe III, N.S., al reino de Portugal* (Madrid, 1622), p. 7.

[132] Quotation from the Italian inscription still visible in the park. The fullest account of the garden is in G. Zander *et al.*, "Gli elementi documentari sul Sacro Bosco," *Quaderni dell'istituto di storia dell'architettura* (Rome), April, 1955, pp. 19–32. Also see M. Praz, *Belleza e bizzarria* (Milan, 1960) pp. 248–49.

[133] See G. Masson, *Italian Gardens* (New York, 1961), pp. 144–45.

[134] For an example see R. Piper, *Das Tier in der Kunst* (Munich, 1922), pl. 28. For a listing of elephants in stone in India see Navarane, *op. cit.* (n. 19), p. 55.

device could have been available to the artist in Europe.[135] It is also possible that the sculptor or Orsini, or both, had seen the live elephant at Milan in 1551 and that it was the inspiration for the Bomarzo mammoth. Whatever the case may be, the elephant, as well as the entire garden, seems to owe a considerable debt, either directly or indirectly, to medieval themes. The elephant, for example, looks as if it is being attacked by a dragon (pl. 102), a theme that constantly recurs in the bestiaries. But what makes Bomarzo unique is the fact that both the dragon and the elephant seem to hark back to Oriental prototypes as well. It is this strange blend of Oriental and medieval in Bomarzo that helps to create a mysterious atmosphere for the viewer and an all but insoluble iconographic problem for the art historian.[136]

At Bomarzo and elsewhere, the elephant continued throughout the mid-sixteenth century to retain its earlier symbolic and emblematic significance. In the lavish *entrées* of the kings of France, as earlier in the triumphal arch of Emperor Maximilian I, the elephants of medieval and quattrocento art occupy an important place as symbols of power and virtue. In the engravings celebrating the *entrée* of Henry II into Rouen in 1550, a quadriga of elephants carrying torches and castles recalls the painting of Mantegna and the literary fancy of the *Hypnerotomachia*.[137] In the *Hieroglyphia* (Basel, 1556) of Piero Valeriano an entire book is devoted to the allegorical significance of the elephant throughout history.[138] Elephants of the Schongauer type appear repeatedly in the various editions of the *Emblemata* of Andrea Alciati as emblems of justice and peace, and as a symbol of the continuity in spirit between Rome and the Renaissance.[139] Woodcuts of two fabulous elephants looking at snakes wound around a pole illustrate the idea that "little things are effaced through concord."[140] The elephant fighting a wild boar is given as a Medici emblem.[141] The emblematical

[135] The elephant chess piece sent to Charlemagne has a warrior in its trunk (Wichmann, *op. cit.* [n. 29], pl. II); a poppy head in Ripon Cathedral (thirteenth century) is carved in the shape of an elephant with a castle on its back and a warrior in its trunk (Druce, *loc. cit.* [n. 27], p. 65 and pl. XV); also see the engraving after H. Bosch by H. Cock (*ca.* 1562) in F. W. H. Hollstein, *Dutch and Flemish Etchings, Engravings, and Woodcuts, ca. 1450–1700* (Amsterdam, n.d.), III, 147.

[136] For various speculations about the Oriental origins of the Bomarzo mammoths and about their influence on other gardens, and on paintings, see Zander *et al., loc. cit.* (n. 132), pp. 27–29. Masson (*op. cit.* [n. 133], p. 145) stresses the relationship in sculptural and architectural detail between Bomarzo and the gardens of nearby villas; René Hocke (*Die Welt als Labyrinth* [Hamburg, 1957], *passim*) relates the stupendous creatures of Bomarzo to the giants of the Palazzo del Te and alleges that both have their spiritual *Urheimat* in the Africa and India celebrated in the travel books. Praz (*op. cit.* [n. 132], p. 246) asserts that Italians have no eye for the bizarre, except when inventing new forms of macaroni, and so he is inclined to place the inspiration for Bomarzo in the East. Whatever else may be said: "Il problema storica resta ancora aperto" (L. Benevolo, "Saggio d'interpretazione storica del Sacro Bosco," in Zander *et al., loc. cit.* [n. 132], p. 61).

[137] See J. Chartrou, *Les entrées solennelles et triomphales à la Renaissance (1484–1551),* (Paris, 1928), p. 86. These were actually horses in disguise.

[138] Cf. Iversen, *op. cit.* (n. 61), pp. 71–72; also see G. Boas, *The Hieroglyphics of Horapollo* (New York, 1950), pp. 104–5; also G. C. Capaccio, *Delle imprese ... in tre libri divisio* (Naples, 1952), Bk. II, chap. viii, pp. 17v–21v; and C. Ripa, *Iconologia...* (Padua, 1611), pp. 232–33, 325, 427, 456, 509.

[139] See H. Green (ed.), *Andreae Alceate Emblematum* (Manchester, 1870), *passim*.

[140] G. Gueroult, *Le premier livre des emblèmes* (Lyons, 1550), p. 36.

[141] H. Junius, ... *Medici emblemata ...* (Antwerp, 1565), p. 8.

personal badges of Astorre Baglione of Perugia and of Emanuel Filiberto, duke of Savoy, also feature the elephant prominently.[142] To illustrate a victory of the Romans over the Huns, Virgil Solis and Jost Amann chose to symbolize the Romans as elephants in a woodcut for the *Thurnierbuch* of S. Feyerabend.[143] On the copperplate portraits of the Habsburgs of Austria the elephant appears in the rich ornamental decorations as a symbol of strength and diligence.[144] The first illustrated edition (1571) of Cartari's *Imagini* includes an engraving by Bolognino Zaltieri, a Venetian artist, which shows Bacchus riding on the back of an elephant. Crude woodcuts of elephants fighting dragons and wild boars, grazing peacefully with sheep (pl. 110), or piously worshipping the moon, continue to be used as emblems down to the end of the century.[145] Most spectacular is the use of the elephant as caryatid in the *New Termis Buch* of Joseph Boillot published in 1592 (pl. 117). The information in the explanatory captions which accompany the elephant caryatids derives from both the authorities of Antiquity and from the reports on Hanno's activities in Rome. Torquato Tasso, the great Italian poet, likewise recalls Hanno's visit to Rome in his dialogues dealing with *imprese* that were written late in the sixteenth century.[146] From these examples it is clear that the elephant continued to be an emblem of piety, virtue, and peace. But artistically, the elephants depicted in these books are uniformly fantastic and owe almost nothing to the realistic paintings, engravings, and woodcuts that were contemporaneously being produced.

F. FIN DE SIÈCLE

A new opportunity to increase the realism of elephant portraiture came in 1563.[147] In September of that year another Indian elephant was sent from Portugal to Maximilian, now the king of Bohemia. It was transported by sea to

[142] G. Ruscelli, *Le imprese . . .* (Venice, 1566). The capital letter "E" as the initial letter of the word "Essendo" is decorated with an elephant and driver in this and other books printed in Venice at this time. For example, see also G. Benzoni, *La historia del mondo nuovo* (Venice, 1565), p. 1.

[143] (Frankfurt am Main, 1566), p. vii. Also see the Feyerabend elephants in N. Reusner, *Emblemata . . .* (Frankfurt, 1581), Bk. II, fig. 13; and in Georg Schaller, *Eigentliche und auch gründliche Beschreibung allerley vier und zweyfüssigen Thieren* (Frankfurt am Main, 1592).

[144] See F. Terzo (Tertius), *Austriacae gentis imaginum . . .* (Innsbruck, 1569–73), *passim*.

[145] For example see P. Fabrici, *Delle allusioni, imprese et emblemi . . .* (Rome, 1588), pp. 174, 228; Capaccio, *op. cit.* (n. 138), Bk. III, p. 22r; J. Mercier, *Emblemata* (Bourges, 1592), pp. 47v–48v; J. Camerarius, *Symbolorum et emblematum . . .* (Mainz, 1590), Bk. II, pp. 2, 4, 6. For additional examples see A. Henkel and A. Schöne, *Emblemata: Handbuch zur Sinnbildkunst des XVI. und XVII. Jahrhunderts* (Stuttgart, 1967), cols. 408–20.

[146] E. Raimondi (ed.), *Torquato Tasso Dialoghi: Edizione critica* (Florence, 1958), II, Pt. II, 1075.

[147] Two years earlier Pope Pius IV had requested that King Sebastian of Portugal send a pair of elephants, a male and a female, to Rome for the papal menagerie. See letter of the Portuguese ambassador of October 28, 1561, as quoted in Sousa Viterbo, *loc. cit.* (n. 69), p. 318. The ambassador apparently believed that elephants, as well as other Asian animals, were readily available in Lisbon; the king in his reply promised to find a pair of elephants for the pope as soon as possible. But no record exists of the receipt in Rome of the elephants requested.

Zeeland and was driven overland to Antwerp. There, the eight-year-old beast immediately became the center of attention. Ludovico Guicciardini, who was at that time preparing his *Description* of the Low Countries, reports that though this was not the first elephant seen in the Netherlands people came from far and wide to view it.[148] Flemish scholars, scientists, and artists, as well as common curiosity-seekers, eagerly commented upon the young elephant. Justus Lipsius, himself a brash sixteen-year-old Humanist at the time, scathingly attacked the elephant as being insignificant and juvenile.[149] And Guicciardini caustically observed:

... we did not find the great attributes and rare qualities in this animal which the ancient authors give it in their writings; being as crude in intelligence as it is in body and proportions, exhibiting in its behavior the unconstraint of a pig; taking its nourishment by eating and drinking everything it encounters; one time it drank so much wine that for twenty hours it was thought to be dead before it finally revived: and [it awakened] much greedier than ever and with a greater appetite.[150]

Other commentators do not share this contemptuous evaluation. An anonymous broadside published at Antwerp for the occasion is enthusiastic in its praise of the beast. Charles de L'écluse comments on the elephant's docility and speaks of its intelligence as being almost human.[151]

Representations of the elephant of 1563 in the Low Countries are numerous and of lasting influence. The woodcut of the commemorative broadside shows the elephant standing in the streets of Antwerp in the midst of a curious throng. Dr. Paludanus (Bernard ten Broecke) had an etching done of the elephant which shows it in eight different positions.[152] A drawing of 1563 attributed to Master B., a Netherlandish artist, and now in the Cabinet des Dessins of the Louvre, depicts an elephant from front and back. Even though the Louvre drawing looks like the picture of a child's stuffed animal, the mere fact of its being dated 1563 possibly indicates that it was inspired by the presence of the live elephant in the Low Countries.[153] By contrast, the chalk drawing of Lambert van Noort dated Antwerp, October 1, displays all the earmarks of a scientific, naturalistic

---

[148] L. Guicciardini, *Description générale de touts les Pays-Bas* (Amsterdam, 1613), p. 35. This is a fascinating assertion, because no other record exists of elephants in the Low Countries before 1563. There is, however, a black chalk drawing of an elephant in the Sloane Collection in the British Museum with a Flemish inscription dated 1550 (see Popham, *loc. cit.* [n. 31], p. 187). Also a faience plaque on a house in the Longue-Rue-Neuve of Antwerp had painted on it the picture of a white elephant grazing in a meadow. Beneath the picture is the inscription: "Oit is inde olifant." See catalogue of the exposition held at the Bibliothèque Nationale of Paris and entitled *Anvers, ville de Plantin et de Rubens* (Paris, 1954), pl. X.

[149] See Lipsius' derisive tract in satirical praise of the elephant in his *Dissertationum ludicrorum et amoenitatum, scriptores vanii* (Leyden, 1638), pp. 419–43. Also see the woodcut of a Roman elephant stable in J. Lipsius, *Admiranda, sive de magnitudine Romana* (Antwerp, 1605), Bk. III, p. 157.

[150] Guicciardini, *op. cit.* (n. 148), p. 35.

[151] Popham, *loc. cit.* (n. 31), p. 188.

[152] *Ibid.*, p. 188.

[153] For a reproduction see Lach, *loc. cit.* (n. 2), pl. XV. The anonymous artist, "Master B," was a Flemish disciple of Franz Floris. See Reznicek, *op. cit.* (n. 124), I, 208.

study in which the artist even notes the weight of the elephant.[154] A new version of Hieronymus Bosch's "Siege of the Elephant," engraved either for or by Hieronymus Cock, appeared in Antwerp about the same time.[155] The hybrid animal created by the engraver is possibly derived from the Bosch original with revisions inspired by the presence in Antwerp of the living elephant or a replica of it.

The people of Antwerp expressed their admiration by having a life-sized wooden image of the elephant constructed to accompany the Antwerp Giant, the city's symbol, in the processions held for gala and official celebrations (pl. 115).[156] The Antwerp elephant on its wheeled platform figured prominently in the triumphal entry staged on February 19, 1582, to welcome François d'Alençon, duke of Anjou, brother of King Henry III of France, and successor to Philip II as sovereign in the Low Countries.[157] Since François' ascendancy was a victory for France, his triumphal entry into Antwerp was obviously watched closely by the court at Paris. The elephant, as a symbol of triumph and ceremony, was picked up about this time by the French court painter, Antoine Caron, for his joyous "Night Festival with the Carrousel Elephant" and for his somber "Triumph of Sémélé" (pls. 108, 109); the elephants depicted here are derived from the Giulio Romano elephants in Cort's engraving "The Battle of Scipio against Hannibal."[158] The elephant in the Valois tapestry called "Siege of the Elephant," probably executed by Lucas de Heere around 1582, much more nearly recalls the Antwerp elephant and Cock's "Siege of the Elephant" than the prancing beast in Caron's "Night Festival."[159]

The progress of the elephant of 1563 from Antwerp to Vienna is not clearly known, nor is the date of its arrival in the imperial capital.[160] At one time or

---

[154] Reznicek, *op. cit.*, and for a reproduction, see the exhibition catalogue of the Stockholm Museum, *Dutch and Flemish Drawings* (Stockholm, 1953), No. 25. Also cf. "L'éléphant armé" of Alart du Hamel as reproduced in P. Fierens, *Le fantastique dans l'art flamand* (Brussels, 1947), pl. XXV.

[155] For comment see Hollstein, *op. cit.* (n. 135), III, 147.

[156] Popham, *loc. cit.* (n. 31), p. 189. There is a superficial resemblance in the ears, tusks, and curvature of the trunk between the elephant of the Cock engraving and the wooden model of Antwerp.

[157] Described and portrayed in *La joyeuse et magnifique Entrée . . .* , published by Plantin in 1582; for an English translation of the text see John Nichols (ed.), *Progresses of Queen Elizabeth* (London, 1788–1805), II, 354–85. Also see F. A. Yates, *The Valois Tapestries* (London, 1959), p. 34 and pl. 19. That the Antwerp elephant was still in use a century later is shown in the etching of Gaspar Bouttats which depicts a cortège of 1684. See *Anvers, ville de Plantin* (n. 148), p. 30.

[158] Notice, by contrast, the elephants which follow Mantegna's "Caesar" on either side of the bier in "Le Triomphe de Sémélé."

[159] J. Ehrmann ("Drawings by Antoine Caron for the Valois Tapestries," *Art Quarterly*, XXI [1958], 60–61) believes that the Valois tapestry in the Uffizi is based upon Caron's carrousel elephant; Yates (*op. cit.* [n. 157], p. 98) takes a more qualified view of the relationship between the Caron elephant and the tapestry depiction. Comparison of the Caron elephant with Cort's and of the tapestry elephant with the Antwerp elephant and Cock's engraving leads me to reject Ehrmann's conclusion regarding the relationship between the Caron and the tapestry elephants. Much more reasonable is the suggestion of Jean Adhémar (*Revue des arts*, IV [1954], 64) to the effect that Caron apparently used the Lafreri engraving (pl. 106), one of which includes Hanno and the elephants from Cort's "The Battle of Scipio against Hannibal."

[160] Popham, *loc. cit.* (n. 31), p. 189; the major source is J. Lipsius, *Epistolae* (Antwerp, 1592), cent. I. ep. 50.

another in 1563 it visited Brussels, where it ate a cauldron of rice and drank a good quantity of wine before being promenaded about the town. To commemorate the occasion a chronogram was composed that read: "Brabantini vidervut Elephantem."[161] On October 10, 1563, it halted in Cologne and was paraded through the city's streets with a young driver clad in yellow and armed with a goad, riding astride its neck.[162] L'écluse relates that he saw it on several occasions at the court of the animal-loving Maximilian II;[163] Henry III of France, on his return from Poland in 1574, was shown an elephant at the menagerie of Ebersdorf.[164] Possibly to commemorate the elephant's popularity, or perhaps because he disliked the painting itself, Maximilian ordered that in Pieter Baltin's "Preaching of St. John the Baptist" the saint should be removed and replaced by a portrait of the elephant. Automatically the enraptured congregation listening to the preacher was thus transformed into a gaping throng staring at an elephant. Since this portrait has unfortunately disappeared, no depiction of the elephant of 1563 from its Viennese days seems to have been preserved.[165]

In Germany the elephant nonetheless continued to appeal to collectors and to makers of oddities. Archduke Albrecht of Bavaria (d. 1579) was said to own a stuffed elephant.[166] On the death of Cardinal Elector Albert of Mainz, a number of valuable elephant-shaped trinkets were found among his possessions.[167] The Ambras collection included an elephant and castle topped with a ship, the entire piece being carved from ivory.[168] The inventory of the collection of Octavius Fugger dated 1600–1601 includes mention of an old French sword with an elephant engraved on the blade.[169] Gems engraved with elephants were included in the collection of Abraham Gorlé (1549–1609) of Antwerp.[170] The collections at Innsbruck and Dresden each boasted a clock made in the form of an elephant with a tower on its back.[171] At the wedding of the duke of Jülich-Cleve-Berg in 1585 a feature of the festivities was a table loaded with exotic animals, trees, and buildings in sugarwork, the entire scene being dominated by a large elephant with a tower on its back (pl. 118). And even today one can see on display at the Charlottenburg in Berlin the magnificent elephant and castle in gilt bronze

---

[161] P. Saintenoy, *Les arts et les artistes à la cour de Bruxelles* (Brussels, 1932), pp. 75–76.

[162] From a note in the journal of the Cologne official, Hermann Weisberg, as quoted in Kaufmann, *loc. cit.* (n. 53), p. 410.

[163] *Ibid.*

[164] Loisel, *op. cit.* (n. 30), I, 234.

[165] Popham, *loc. cit.* (n. 31), p. 190; also see C. van Mander, *Dutch and Flemish Painters: Translations from the Schilderboeck* (New York, 1963), p. 256. It is possible that the realistic Indian elephant used as an illustration by Joannes Sambucus is a representation of the elephant seen in Antwerp in 1563; see his *Emblemata cum aliquot nummis antiqui operis* . . . . (Antwerp, 1564), p. 184. Or perhaps its portrait was in the collection of Emperor Rudolf II, see above, p. 30.

[166] F. H. Taylor, *The Taste of Angels* (Boston, 1948), p. 49.

[167] M. von Boehn, *Modes and Manners* (London, 1932), II, 183.

[168] G. Klemm, *Zur Geschichte der Sammlugen für Wissenschaft und Kunst in Deutschland* (Zerbst, 1837), p. 194.

[169] N. Lieb, *Die Fugger und die Kunst* . . . (Munich, 1958), p. 41.

[170] A. Gorlé, *Dactyliothecae* . . . (Leyden, 1707), Pt. II, pl. 26.

[171] O. Doering (ed.), *Des Augsburger Patriciers Philipp Hainhofer Reisen nach Innsbruck und Dresden* (Vienna, 1901), pp. 42, 173.

created by Christian Jamnitzer of Nuremberg at the close of the sixteenth century (pl. 116).

Scientific materials on the elephant and its habits began to become more authoritative after the publication in India of Garcia da Orta's *Coloquios dos simplos, e drogas . . . da India* (1563).[172] One entire colloquy is devoted to the elephant by the Portuguese physician who had lived in Goa for a full generation before publishing his book. In 1567 Charles de L'écluse published at Antwerp an abbreviated Latin version of Orta's text. Cristobal de Acosta, on the basis of Orta's book and his own observations in the field, published at Burgos in 1578 his *Tractado de las drogas . . .*, to which he added illustrations, including one of a realistic Indian elephant leaning against the trunk of a coconut palm, and another of a war elephant with a castle on its back. Acosta implies that he sketched these elephants from life,[173] but such is obviously not the case. The entire body of the elephant leaning against the palm and the body and head armor of the war elephant seem to be taken directly from Cort's engraving "The Battle of Scipio against Hannibal," or from another depiction that was likewise based on the elephant drawings of Giulio Romano.[174] The important point is that Acosta, who had traveled in the East, denominates these as naturalistic representations. The text, like the woodcuts, is based upon observations in the field and includes a studied effort to test Pliny's assertions about the elephant against experience.[175]

Gifts of living elephants continued to be made in Europe even after Portugal lost its independence. In 1581 on the occasion of becoming king of Portugal, Philip II of Spain received a gift from Lisbon of an elephant and a rhinoceros. Both were put on display in Madrid.[176] Juan de Arphe y Villafañe, who is often called the "Spanish Cellini," prepared a book, *Varia commensuracion para la escultura* (Book III), in which he presented for artists and architects a scientific discussion of the proportions and shapes of the animals and birds then commonly being used in decorations. His elephant, which resembles one of those shown by Mattioli, is a fairly realistic beast. A scale stands to the left of the elephant to guide the artist in getting its height and proportions right.[177] An example of Arphe's elephant design appears as the central figure on a silver

---

[172] See *Asia*, I, 192–94, for discussion of Orta.

[173] See his list of the drawings of plants according to nature at the front of the book (Italian ed. of 1585). Included in this list are the two elephant portraits. In the written text accompanying the portraits he is evasive about their origin and leads the reader to think that they are his own. Certainly the tower and body of the war elephant, as well as the coconut palm, are probably his work. But he cannot take credit for the rest. See Lach, *loc. cit.* (n. 2), pl. XIV.

[174] See above, p. 144; compare the group of three elephants in the Lafreri engraving (pl. 106) likewise extracted from Giulio Romano. The elephants on either end are those used by Acosta.

[175] For a study of the Acosta texts see *Asia*, I, 194–95.

[176] An elephant is also shown as a symbol for humility in one of the emblems of Philip II. See J. de Boria, *Empresas morales a la S.C.R.M. del Rey Don Phelipe nuestro Señor* (Madrid, 1581); also see the woodcut in F. Felice Milensio, *Dell' impressa dell' Elefanta . . .* (Naples, 1595).

[177] Based on the representation reproduced in the sixth printing (Madrid, 1773), p. 196. The printer claims, in the prologue addressed to the reader, to have reproduced the original text faithfully, even while purging it of errors, and to have reproduced the original illustrations, but only the most curious. See Lach, *loc. cit.* (n. 2), pl. XV for a reproduction of Arphe's elephant.

ewer created by Felipe Roz in 1597 as part of his examination to qualify as a master silversmith.[178]

Philip II, a decade after receiving his own elephant of congratulation, sent an identical gift to the new Bourbon king of France, Henry IV; possibly Philip had it in the back of his mind that the pious elephant of Catholic tradition might give the heretic king a nudge on the road to conversion! The elephant arrived at Dieppe in July, 1591, and Henry shortly wrote from his camp before Noyon to his receiver-general of finance that he should pay for its keep "because we desire that the elephant which has been sent to us from the Indies should be maintained and cared for as a rare thing the like of which has never before been seen in this Our Realm."[179] Evidently Henry did not know that two of his greatest predecessors, Charlemagne and St. Louis, had elephants of their own. For Henry himself the novelty of the elephant quickly wore off as the expenses for its maintenance mounted. So, on September 4, 1592, the king sent an order from his camp at Provins to the governor of Dieppe that he should arrange for the safe dispatch of the elephant as a gift to Queen Elizabeth of England. Evidently the elephant made the channel crossing successfully, for references to it may be found in contemporary English writings.[180] Unfortunately, however, no clear-cut representation of the elephant of 1591 has yet been found.

What pictorial records remain in painting from the last two decades of the sixteenth century are varied, semi-fantastic, and probably have little to do with living models. Jacopo Ligozzi, a late Mannerist painter, produced a sketch in 1591 that was designed to appear as a colossal fresco in the Palazzo Vecchio in Florence. It represents the reception of the Florentine ambassadors by Pope Boniface VIII. In the background over the portal of the reception chamber there hangs a large painting which shows an Indian with a feather headdress holding a club in his hand. He is seated beside another native who holds palm branches in his hand and wears a crown of palm and dangling earrings. Behind these semi-nude savages, who possibly represent America and Asia, the head of an elephant peers out of the picture.[181] Annibale Carracci's elephant in his "Triumph of Bacchus and Ariadne" painted about 1600 and now in the Farnese Gallery, was almost certainly copied from a Dionysiac sarcophagus (pl. 131). Whatever its origins, the head and ears of the elephant are realistic but the eyes seem to be too prominent and slanted. The hook that the rider carries is almost photographic in its accuracy and is far superior to any other I have seen.[182]

[178] J. C. Davillier, *Recherches sur l'orfèvrerie en Espagne au moyen âge et à la Renaissance: Documents inédits tirés des archives* (Paris, 1879), pp. 89–90, 223–27, pl. 17.

[179] L. Delisle, "L'Eléphant de Henri IV," *Bibliothèque de l'Ecole de Chartes*, LIV (1893), 358–59.

[180] Popham, *loc. cit.* (n. 31), p. 190. For a listing of references to the elephant in late sixteenth-century English literature see W. M. Carroll, *Animal Conventions in English Renaissance Non-Religious Prose (1550–1600)* (New York, 1954), p. 102.

[181] See H. Voss, *Die Malerei der Spätrenaissance in Rom und Florenz* (Berlin, 1920), II, 415; also O. H. Giglioli, "Jacopo Ligozzi disegnatore e pittore di piante e di animali," *Dedalo*, IV (1923–24), 554–55. For a reproduction see Lach, *loc. cit.* (n. 2), pl. XVI.

[182] For a reproduction of this section of Carracci's ceiling see J. R. Martin, *The Farnese Gallery* (Princeton, N.J., 1965), pl. 70. In his commentary (p. 119), Martin unqualifiedly asserts that the elephant and mahout with hook were copied from the sarcophagi. For confirmation of this see the triumph of Dionysius in India on a sarcophagus of the third century A.D. as reproduced in Lehmann-Hartleben and Olsen, *op. cit.* (n. 10), pp. 12–13, fig. 7.

Striking in its effort to bring fauna of the overseas world into European art and imagery is the painting of the Garden of Eden (pl. 144) executed around 1600 by Roelant Savery which shows the elephant, the rhinoceros, the tiger, and the bird of paradise, all identifiable as animals from Asia, cavorting with all of the other animals, real and imaginary, in the artist's repertoire.[183] Savery's contemporary, Arcimboldo, used an elephant as the central figure in one of his grotesque human heads composed entirely of animals (pl. 39). In commenting on this elephant portrait in 1591, Don Gregorio Comanini remarked: "All these beasts Arcimboldo has painted from life. . . . Imagine his cleverness; there is something stupefying about it."[184] And Rudolf II's collection of paintings included an elephant which is being looked at by many people "from the brush of the younger Pieter Brueghel (1564–1637)."[185]

The literary descriptions from the last years of the sixteenth century are both fanciful and factual. In 1580 Filippo Sassetti wrote from Cochin to his friends in Florence about the useful work performed by elephants in India.[186] The *Viaggio* (1587), in which the Venetian, Cesare Fedrici, describes his travels in India and southeastern Asia, contains a detailed description of the "white elephant" revered in Pegu (Burma).[187] In Georg Schaller's animal book, published in 1592, woodcuts show the elephant in four different poses (both sides, front, and rear) and each is described in a verse based upon ancient authors and legends.[188] Cesare Ripa in his *Iconologia* (Rome, 1593) still describes the elephant as the most religious of all animals.[189] In his romance of *Vitei*, the great king of China, Ludovico Arrivabene discusses the elephant of Asia both in traditional Western terms and as a living animal that works in its homeland.[190] In his *Itinerary* Fynes Moryson tells about seeing a live elephant while in Constantinople in 1597.[191] And, in the meantime the De Bry brothers in their Latin travel collection were bringing together whatever they could find out about the elephant from literary and artistic sources in Europe. The result, as might be expected, was to produce

[183] Also see pl. 111. Such depictions were quite numerous in the last generation of the sixteenth century. For example, see C. Murer's *Animaux au paradis* (1580), and the animal drawings of Georg Hoefnagel. For further discussion see J. Bialostocki, "Les bêtes et les humains de Roelant Savery," *Musées royaux des Beaux-Arts Bulletin*, No. 1 (March, 1958), pp. 69–97.

[184] *Il Figino, overo del fine della pittura* (Mantua, 1591), p. 44. In Arcimboldo's painting the elephant's ear is the man's ear; the man's head, it should be noticed, supports a crown of horns!

[185] H. Zimmermann (ed.), "Das Inventar der Prager Schatz und Kunstkammer vom 6. Dezember, 1621," *Jahrbuch der kunsthistorischen Sammlungen des allerhöchsten Kaiserhauses*, XXV (1905), Pt. 2, p. xlvi. Cf. Pieter Baltins, "Preaching of St. John the Baptist" discussed above, p. 153.

[186] E. Marcucci (ed.), *Lettere . . . di Filippo Sassetti* (Florence, 1855), pp. 252–53, 273.

[187] Details on Fedrici and the history of his book in *Asia*, I, 469–73. A white elephant was possibly in Rome in the time of Emperor Augustus. Many travelers to Asia, before Fedrici, mention the white elephant. The white elephant was not seen in modern times in Europe until one was brought to Holland in 1633 (Armandi, *op. cit.* [n. 18], p. 381, citing the *Gazette de France*, July 30, 1633).

[188] These elephant woodcuts are semirealistic and could possibly hark back to depictions of the elephant of 1563, though I can make no certain identification. See the section entitled "Von Elephanten Geschichten" in Schaller, *op. cit.* (n. 143).

[189] Cf. L. Réau, *Iconographie de l'art chrétien* (Paris, 1956), I, 103–4.

[190] *Il magno Vitei* (Verona, 1597), pp. 445–50.

[191] *An Itinerary . . . Written by Fynes Moryson* (Glasgow, 1907), II, 96.

written descriptions of the elephant and other fauna of Asia which were far more factual than the woodcut illustrations.[192] Indeed, some of the woodcuts used by De Bry are simple reproductions of the elephant as it was known to Burgkmair and other European engravers who had never had a chance to see the live Asian animal or a naturalistic representation of it.[193]

Definite records exist to show that besides Hanno at least five Asian elephants were subjects of general attention in sixteenth-century Europe. Once naturalists, artists, and scholars had the opportunity to observe and inspect these living animals, the elephant of tradition underwent a gradual transformation. The semi-divine creature of medieval tradition was secularized by Pope Leo X himself. Hanno started off his career in the Eternal City by performing circus tricks. While he delighted his audience, he also helped immeasurably to reduce the elephant to the status of a mundane creature. Nor was secularization the only change that took place. Many Humanists were clearly unimpressed by the elephant of flesh and blood, and disappointed that it did not measure up in majesty or virtue to the descriptions of Pliny and the *Physiologus*. Although not all observers were repelled by the living beast, everyone had become convinced that the elephant could be ludicrous as well as majestic, frivolous as well as wise, earthly as well as otherworldly.

Through his painting of Hanno, Raphael naturalized the elephant in European art and set a new standard of realism for its depiction. Giulio Romano, Raphael's direct heir, introduced the naturalized, secularized elephant into society as he made it take part in a riotous marriage feast, gambol with putti, and disport in friezes with other exotic creatures. In the hands of Rosso and Fantuzzi the elephant of Fontainebleau was treated in a deliberately antinaturalistic manner. They elongated its legs and trunk, and distorted its proportions as they reconstructed the elephant for their own subjective, artistic ends. Their fantasized elephant (or the "Manneristic" elephant) made its way from painting into tapestry and seems to have died there. But Hanno and the elephants attributed to Giulio Romano continued to reappear, though sometimes not very sharply or clearly, in numerous paintings, engravings, woodcuts, and tapestries.

The medieval and quattrocento elephants also reappear repeatedly in the course of the sixteenth century, especially in the engravings and woodcuts produced in the Low Countries and Germany. In their book illustrations, the northern woodcut artists tend to portray the elephant as a symbol of secular or religious virtue. It rarely appears in their woodcuts as a jovial, pagan beast. In architecture and sculpture the elephant likewise continues to be staid and traditional in both appearance and symbolism.

[192] But Hakluyt, in supplementing a mariner's log reporting on a voyage to the Guinea coast, writes a detailed account of the elephant almost exclusively from Pliny. See P. A. Robin, *Animal Lore in English Literature* (London, 1936), p. 72.

[193] For a reproduction from the *India orientalis* (1601) of the "Animals of India" see *Asia*, I, facing p. 101. Also see De Bry's engravings in J. J. Boissard, *Theatrum vitae humanae* (n.p., 1596), pp. 23, 29.

The naturalists, somewhat like the artists, seem to be baffled by the problem of reconciling the living creature with the prevailing traditions. Gesner presents a mélange of tradition, myth, and contemporary observations of the elephant which makes strange reading indeed. He quotes Aelian and Varthema on the same page, and evidently gives equal weight to their testimony. The later editions of Gesner fail completely to note the report of Pierre Gilles, who dissected the elephant at Aleppo in 1545 and published his semianatomical description in 1562. The essentially factual material in Orta's *Coloquios*, as relayed to Europe through L'écluse and Acosta, seems not to have entered the mainstream of natural history until the seventeenth century.[194] Throughout the sixteenth century writers about animals continued to treat seriously the stories and traditions surrounding all monstrous creatures. But then, who is to blame the naturalists for their hesitation in identifying the dragon and the unicorn as mythical creatures when, within a single century, living exemplars of the behemoth of the past (not to mention the absurd giraffe and the ridiculous rhinoceros) had presented themselves for all to see and to wonder about?

2

THE RHINOCEROS

The Indian rhinoceros, like the Indian elephant, was brought to Europe early in the sixteenth century by the Portuguese. The *ganda*,[195] or rhinoceros of Cambay, was originally sent as a gift to King Manuel by the sultan of Gujarat. And then, like Hanno, the rhinoceros was sent off as a gift to Rome. The *ganda* quickly began to compete with the elephant for the attention of royalty, aristocracy, Humanists, and artists. And, while Hanno found his Raphael, the *ganda* contemporaneously found his artist in a sketch and a woodcut by Albrecht Dürer. The print of the *ganda* completed by Dürer in 1515, was to set the

---

[194] Elephants, both in reality and art, become more numerous in the seventeenth century. King Christian IV of Denmark in 1620 tried, though unsuccessfully, to buy two big elephants with tusks and two elephants for work (see M. Boyer, *Japanese Export Lacquers . . . in the National Museum of Denmark* [Copenhagen, 1959], p. 30). Wenzel Hollar sketched and engraved from life an elephant that was on display at Frankfurt and Nuremberg in 1629. For a fascinating fictional account of Hollar's life and his interest in "Trompette," the female elephant, see the delightful story by the modern writer Johannes Urzidil, entitled "Das Elefantenblatt." A white elephant imported into Amsterdam in 1633 was drawn by Rembrandt four years later (see the pencil drawings in the Albertina [Vienna], H26). An African elephant sent to Louis XIV in 1668 is preserved in an etching by Pieter Borel (see Popham, *loc. cit.* [n. 31], p. 191). At Rome, in 1691, Marcello Malpighi observed a living elephant and wrote an exact scientific description of it. See H. B. Adelmann, *Marcello Malpighi and the Evolution of Embryology* (Ithaca, N.Y., 1966), p. 623. For a complete dissection of the elephant see P. Blair. "Osteographia elephantina . . . ," *Philosophical Transactions* (London), XXVII (1710–12), 53–168.

[195] Sanskrit for rhinoceros; Hindi, *gainda*; Marathi, *genda*; cf. Denis Sinor, "Sur les noms altaïques de la licorne," *Wiener Zeitschrift für die Kunde des Morgenlandes*, LVI (1960), 173–74.

standard for the artistic depiction of the rhinoceros up to the eighteenth century (see pl. 119).[196]

The one-horned rhinoceros of India was much more alien than the elephant to European writers and artists of the prediscovery era. Possibly the earliest literary description of the Indian rhinoceros is the story in the *Indica* (dated *ca.* 400 B.C.) of Ctesias about the "wild asses of India." These are one-horned beasts, presumably rhinoceroses, to whom the fanciful Ctesias adds features derived from the traditions associated with the unicorn and other real and fabulous animals.[197] Ctesias tells of the medicinal virtues of the horn, a belief of commoners and kings in sixteenth-century Europe which has lived on into the twentieth century in Asia.[198] Aristotle in his *History of the Animals* vaguely refers to the one-horned "Indian ass," and he mistakenly asserts in his discussion of parts of the body that its hoof is not cloven. Biblical references to the unicorn are too vague to tell whether or not the authors are alluding to the rhinoceros. The probability is that they were repeating stories about the unicorn that were current everywhere in the ancient world.[199]

Strabo (*ca.* 63 B.C.–A.D. 21), the author of six geohistorical books on Asia in Greek, gives the first literary description of the Indian rhinoceros based on personal observation. He is likewise the first to use the word "rhinoceros" (Greek, ῥινόκερως, meaning nose horn; German, *Nashorn*) and to mention the *plicae*, or folds, of the skin. Strabo, on the basis of stories he heard, mentions the combat between the rhinoceros and the elephant, a powerful tradition that was to be tested practically at Lisbon in 1515.[200]

Pliny the Elder is the earliest of the Roman writers to comment on the rhinoceros. He records that it first appeared at Rome in 61 (?) B.C., the occasion being the games organized to celebrate the return to Italy of Pompey the Great. The

[196] The best studies of the *ganda* are A. Fontura da Costa, *Les d'esambulations du Rhinocéros de Modofar, roi de Cambaye, de 1514–1516* (Lisbon, 1937); C. Dodgson, "The Story of Dürer's Ganda," in A. Fowler (ed.), *The Romance of Fine Prints* (Kansas City, 1938), pp. 45–54; C. Coste, "Anciennes figurations du rhinoceros," *Acta tropica*, III (1946), 116–29; F. J. Cole, "The History of Albrecht Dürer's Rhinoceros in Zoölogical Literature," *Science, Medicine, and History: Essays on the Evolution of Scientific Thought and Medical Practice, Written in Honour of Charles Singer*, collected and edited by E. Ashworth Underwood (London, 1953), I, 337–56; and L. de Matos, "Forma e natura e costumi del rinoceronte," *Boletim internacional de bibliografia Luso-Brasileira*, I (1960), 387–98.

[197] For critical commentary see C. Gould, *Mythical Monsters* (London, 1886), chap. X; and O. Shepard, *The Lore of the Unicorn* (New York, 1930), pp. 26–32.

[198] In sixteenth-century Europe even the prehistoric cave sites were searched for the rare rhinoceros horn. By 1600 dozens of prized alicorns (mounted horns and tusks) were on display in Europe (Shepard, *op. cit.* [n. 197], p. 105). S. H. Prater, curator of the Bombay Historical Society, in *The Book of Indian Animals* (2d ed.; Bombay, 1965), pp. 229–30, warns that the rhinoceros of Asia is today in danger of extinction, largely owing to the exaggerated value and the mythical beliefs still attached to the virtues of its horn, blood, and urine.

[199] For a succinct summary see Shepard, *op. cit.* (n. 197), pp. 41–45.

[200] There is no reference, as far as I know, to a fight between the elephant and the rhinoceros in classical Indian literature or art. In a fresco of the third century B.C. found at Marissa in Palestine a rhinoceros is shown with an elephant, but it is not clear whether or not they are in combat. It should be noted also that this story of mortal enmity which seems to have originated in the Roman world was kept alive and embellished by Muslim authors. See Ettinghausen, *op. cit.* (n. 13), pp. 29–30, 78–90.

Indian rhinoceros was seen again repeatedly in ancient Rome down to the time of Vespasian, even though it came from a vast distance. The two-horned African rhinoceros was also displayed in Rome, but not so frequently. The one-horned Indian rhinoceros is very hardy, thrives in small quarters, and has a life expectancy in captivity double that of the two-horned African rhinoceros.[201] Hence it is not surprising that it appeared more frequently in Rome than its African cousin from much closer by.

Pliny, Aelian, Diodorus Siculus, and Julius Solinus were stimulated by the presence of living animals to learn all they could from others about the origins and habits of the rhinoceros. From their investigations they concluded that it was the original of the unicorn and so attached to the rhinoceros (both Asiatic and African) many of the beliefs about the unicorn current in the markets of the Levant and Egypt. The mosaic artists of Palestrina and Perugia depicted in early Roman times the two-horned rhinoceros as did the minters of two coins in the first century A.D.[202] On a medal struck for Emperor Caracalla (ruled A.D. 211–17) there is a device of a wrecked ship with a number of animals engraved below it, including a clear portrait of the one-horned rhinoceros.[203]

From the fall of the Roman Empire to 1515 there is no literary or artistic record which would confirm the presence in Christian Europe of the living rhinoceros.[204] And, among Muslim authors of the Middle Ages, the only one to give a fairly accurate description of the rhinoceros was al-Biruni in his book on India.[205] So, the rhinoceros, like most other exotic animals, was invested by the writers of the bestiaries with all the traditional attributes of the unicorn and with Christian symbolism as well. The writer of a Tuscan-Venetian bestiary summarizes the medieval view as follows:

The rhinoceros, one of the most fierce of animals, has between its eyes a terribly sharp horn which no armor in the world can withstand. Because of its ferocity this animal can be captured by humans only through a ruse; a pure virgin approaches it, and drawn by her smell of virginity, it lies down at her feet where it falls asleep and is killed by the hunter.

The rhinoceros symbolizes fierce and savage people whom no human can withstand, but who may be overcome through the power of the divinity and reformed. As this power proved itself with Saul, so it effects the same [reform] upon many others.[206]

The rhinoceros as the symbol of Saul-become-Paul also appears in a Latin hymn to St. Paul written by Abelard early in the twelfth century.[207] In his

---

[201] Jennison, *op. cit.* (n. 8), pp. 34–35.

[202] Cole, *loc. cit.* (n. 196), pp. 337–38.

[203] For a reproduction see Jennison, *op. cit.* (n. 8), p. 82.

[204] There is a curious mosaic in the pavement of St. Mark's in Venice, close by the Door of the Madonna, which displays clearly the head of the rhinoceros. Traditionally this is dated in the thirteenth century and is associated vaguely with Marco Polo. It has been conjectured that the unknown mosaicist was trying to depict the unicorn. See Shepard, *op. cit.* (n. 197), p. 216.

[205] See Ettinghausen, *op. cit.* (n. 13), p. 12.

[206] Translated from Goldstaub and Wendriner, *op. cit.* (n. 28), pp. 310–14. The story of capture by a virgin is likewise associated with the unicorn. See Shepard, *op. cit.* (n. 197), pp. 47–51.

[207] As cited by Cole, *loc. cit.* (n. 196), pp. 338–39.

poem "De laudibus divinae sapientae" Alexander Neckam mentions that the dragon and rhinoceros, respectively the symbols of sin and ferocity, are in league against the elephant, symbol of good, and that the rhinoceros with its sharp horn tears open the belly of the elephant.[208] In a Latin manuscript of the early thirteenth century and in the work of Bartholomew Glanvil the identity of the rhinoceros with the unicorn is forthrightly asserted. But Marco Polo and Jordan of Severac in their eye-witness accounts of the rhinoceros are firm in saying that the beasts they saw could not be captured by maidens. Jordan therefore concludes that the rhinoceros is different from the "real unicorns." Such testimony from the field had the effect for a time at least of reinstating the legendary unicorn as an independent beast.[209]

Throughout the Middle Ages the depiction of the rhinoceros was confined to the miniatures in the bestiaries. And in most of these imaginary pictures it looks more like a unicorn than a genuine rhinoceros. In the *Physiologus* of Cosmas Indicopleustes it is shown as a horse with two horns on its nose.[210] The artists of the Italian Renaissance, with all of their interest in exotic animals, did not try to depict the true rhinoceros in painting, sculpture, or textiles. It was left to Dürer to produce the first modern depiction of the Indian rhinoceros on the basis of a sketch which was forwarded to Nuremberg from Lisbon in 1515 (pl. 119).

The inspiration for Dürer's rhinoceros was the living exemplar sent as a gift from India to King Manuel of Portugal. In 1514, Albuquerque dispatched a mission from Goa to Cambay to request permission of Sultan Modafar II to build a fortress on the island of Diu. In September of that year the embassy returned to Goa with the *ganda*. This animal, judging from Dürer's depiction of it, was of the variety now called the Great Indian one-horned rhinoceros (*Rhinoceros unicornis*). It was sent to Portugal in the fleet that left Cochin at the beginning of January, 1515, and arrived in Lisbon on May 20, 1515. Because the *ganda* was the first rhinoceros to be seen in Europe since Roman times, it caused an immediate sensation.

The king and his circle were anxious to "test by experience," as Gois remarks,[211] the assertions of Roman writers about the natural enmity of the rhinoceros and the elephant. It was therefore arranged that the meeting of the two beasts should be made into a public spectacle. On June 3, 1515, they confronted each other in a courtyard enclosed by high walls between the Paço da Ribeira and the Casa da India.

The native Oçem [its Indian keeper] had led the rhinoceros by its chain to a place behind the tapestries covering the passageway, where it remained well hidden. Then the elephant,

[208] See Druce, *loc. cit.* (n. 27), p. 41.
[209] Robin, *op. cit.* (n. 192), frontispiece and pp. 75–76. Also see distinction that is made by Nicolò de' Conti in the fifteenth century in R. H. Major (ed.), *India in the Fifteenth Century* (London, 1857) p. 13.
[210] J. Strzygowski, *Der Bilderkreis des griechischen Physiologus des Kosmas Indicopleustes . . .* (Leipzig, 1899), p. 62.
[211] D. de Gois, *Chronica do felicissimo rei Dom Emanuel* (Lisbon, 1566), Pt. II, chap. xlii.

a young one with short tusks, was brought into the arena. When the tapestries were pulled aside revealing the rhinoceros, the elephant took flight and sought refuge in the shelter where it was usually kept.[212]

The rhinoceros, proclaimed victor by default, was heralded as the vindicator of the ancient writers,[213] and it became immediately one of King Manuel's most prized possessions. In his Book of Hours (1517) a realistic rhinoceros appears in the right margin of the illustration "Flight from Egypt" (pl. 86).

The *ganda* was dispatched by ship in December, 1515, to Pope Leo X. It was sent by Manuel to Rome, along with other gifts, in appreciation of the "Golden Rose" he had been awarded by the papacy in July, 1515. It may have been Manuel's intention, as Jovius suggests, to give the spectacle-loving pope the opportunity to match the *ganda* against Hanno, his own elephant. Among the other gifts taken aboard were lavish silverworks of animals (*bastiães*), silks, large quantities of pepper and other spices, and a green velvet harness for the rhinoceros decorated with gilded roses and carnations and edged with fringe.[214] The ship commanded by João de Pina arrived at the roads of Marseilles in January, 1516, and the rhinoceros was put ashore for rest and refreshment on one of the islands in the bay. King Francis I, who had been on a campaign in Provence, was in Marseilles at this time and he went out to the island to see the "wonderful beast called Reynoceron."[215] After departing from Marseilles, Pina's vessel was struck by a storm off Genoa, in February, and sank with all on board. The corpse of the rhinoceros was washed ashore near Villefranche.[216] After being stuffed it was sent to the pope and arrived in Rome in February, 1516,[217] about eight months after Hanno's death.

In the meantime a Latin poet, possibly in anticipation of the rhinoceros' arrival in Rome, wrote a stanza of twelve lines celebrating the beast.[218] And the Florentine physician Giovanni Giacomo Penni published in Rome, during July, 1515, a poem entitled "Forma e natura e costumi de lo Rinocerothe stato con-

---

[212] From the letter of Valentim Fernandes to a friend in Nuremberg, of June, 1515. Italian translation of the text in A. de Gubernatis, *Storia dei viaggiatori italiani nelle Indie Orientali* (Leghorn, 1875), pp. 389–92.

[213] As an indication of how important this event was to the scholars of the sixteenth century, see the letter of Gerardus Suberinus Corcquires of April 27, 1595, to Ortelius (in J. H. Hessels [ed.], *Abrahami Ortelii . . . Epistulae . . . [1524–1628]* [Cambridge, 1887], p. 637). Corcquires sent the geographer in this letter a collection of anagrams for the foremost events of particular years. The victory of the rhinoceros he used for 1515, Charles V's birth for 1500, and Luther's attack on the pope for 1517.

[214] For the complete list with quantities see E. de Campos de Andrada (ed.), *Relações de Pero de Alcaçova Carneiro, conde da Idanha* (Lisbon, 1937), pp. 198–99.

[215] See P. de Vaissière (ed.), *Journal de Jean Barrillon, secrétaire du Chancelier Duprat, 1515–1521* (Paris, 1897), I, 193.

[216] Paulus Jovius wrote in 1555: ". . . for it was not possible that such a beast could save itself being chained, albeit it swam miraculously among the sharp rocks which are along this coste . . . (*The Worthy Tract . . . Contaynng a Discourse of Rare Inventions, both Militarie and Amorous called Impresse*, trans. of the Italian version of 1555, London, [1585], p. D ii verso).

[217] Matos, *loc. cit.* (n. 196), p. 390.

[218] Published in *Pauli Iovii novocomensis Episcopi Nucerini Elogia virorum bellica virute illustrium veris imaginibus supposita . . .* (Florence, 1551), p. 206.

dutto im Portogallo dal capitanio de larmata del Re. . . ."[219] Penni, from the evidence of his poem, was well informed about the activities of the *ganda* in Lisbon. The probability is that he had learned of the "battle" with the elephant from the letter of Valentim Fernandes of May, 1515, which was circulated in Florence and today exists only in its Italian translation.[220] The artist who prepared the crude woodcut which graces the title page of Penni's poem was evidently not in possession of a sketch done from life, for his woodcut shows but slight improvement over the rhinoceros of the bestiaries.

Dürer himself had probably never seen a rhinoceros, living or dead, before he received the sketch from Lisbon in 1515. It is possible that he had seen a depiction of the rhinoceros on the Roman coins and medals that his German contemporaries were avidly collecting. But there is no evidence, in either literature or art, to indicate that Dürer had a source other than the Lisbon sketch.[221] While the sketch itself is not extant, the drawing by Dürer (pl. 119) labeled "Rhinoceron 1515" seems to be an elaborated rendition of it, and the caption beneath is evidently a German translation from Portuguese of the textual material that accompanied the Lisbon sketch.[222] In English translation the caption reads:

It was in the year 15[1]3,[223] on May 1, they brought our King of Portugal at Lisbon such a beast alive from India, which they call a Rhinoceros. For the wonder's sake, I have had to send you a likeness of it. It has a colour like a tortoise and is covered nearly all over with thick scales, and in size is like the elephant, but lower, and is the elephant's mortal enemy. It has in front on its nose a strong sharp horn, and when the beast comes at the elephant to fight him, it has always first whetted its horn sharp against the stone and runs at the elephant with its head between his forelegs, and rips him up where the skin is thinnest, and so kills him. The elephant is very badly afraid of the rhinoceros, for it kills the elephant whenever it comes at him, being well armed and very lively and active, This beast is called rhinoceros in Greek and Latin, but in the Indian language, "Ganda."[224]

The text of the caption placed above the woodcut of Dürer's rhinoceros, also dated 1515,[225] is essentially the same as the text on the sketch. The only omission is the reference to its being known in India as a "Ganda." While the sketch

[219] The only extant copy of this little book is today in the Biblioteca Colombina of Seville. It was brought to Rome in November, 1515, by Fernando Colombo. It is reproduced photographically in Matos, *loc. cit.* (n. 196), pp. 395–98.

[220] Gubernatis, *op. cit.* (n. 212), p. 389.

[221] Hermann Dembeck (*Animals and Men* [Garden City, N.Y., 1965], p. 279), asserts that Dürer depended upon a description by the Welser agent, Lucas Rem. Examination of Rem's *Tagebuch* fails to disclose such a description. Rem, according to the diary, was in Antwerp, but not in Lisbon, between 1513 and 1516.

[222] While Fontura da Costa (*op. cit.* [n. 196], pp. 23–25) argues that this drawing is by a Portuguese, the Dürer experts agree in attributing it to the master. See Dodgson, *loc. cit.* (n. 196), p. 46. Original of Dürer's drawing is in the British Museum.

[223] This seems to be an error for 1515; the date May 1 should also be May 20.

[224] Translation by Campbell Dodgson as printed in *loc. cit.* (n. 196), p. 46. This account of the fight between the elephant and rhinoceros is based on ancient authors rather than on the confrontation of June 3, 1515, at Lisbon. Hence, it may be conjectured that this letter was written before June 3, since it makes no mention of the actual meeting at which the elephant was not killed but ran in terror.

[225] See plate in *Asia*, I, following p. 356.

exists only in a single exemplar today, the woodcut went through many editions and is still commonly reproduced as an example of Dürer's treatment of animals. The first edition of the woodcut published in 1515 was followed by two editions published between 1540 and 1550. As many as five editions of the woodcut may have been in circulation by 1600. Throughout history the woodcut has had around ten editions, as nearly as can be reckoned from the extant versions.[226]

While Dürer prepared his sketch and woodcut, his contemporary and associate, Hans Burgkmair, prepared an excellent large woodcut (pl. 120) called "Rhinoceros M.D.X.V." Today but one copy of Burgkmair's rhinoceros exists, in the Albertina of Vienna. By 1515 Burgkmair, even more than Dürer, was acquainted with the activities of the Portuguese traders and their associates, the south German commercial agents. In the woodcuts prepared for his India series of 1508–9 which he printed as illustrations to Balthasar Springer's account of his journey to the East, he reproduced sheep, elephants, cattle, and camels. Since Burgkmair possibly based his animal woodcuts upon watercolors made by an artist who had been in the East,[227] it may not be too farfetched to suggest that his rendition of the rhinoceros may likewise have been based upon a watercolor which remained in his possession and which he had not seen fit to use in the preparation of the earlier series. Certainly, both he and Dürer produced realistic woodcuts of the rhinoceros and probably from different artistic sources.[228] But it is also possible that both worked from the same drawing.[229]

Dürer's rhinoceros differs strikingly from Burgkmair's by the imposing coat of armor made of scales, laminae, and shells with which he embellished the *plicae* of the skin. Particularly striking and completely fictitious is the dorsal spiral horn which Dürer added to the cervical vertebrae. Perhaps he decided to introduce this quaint element because he was uncertain of the accuracy in detail of the sketch sent from Lisbon. Or he certainly might have seen a two-horned rhinoceros depicted on Roman coins.[230] Or it may be that he related it to the defense tusk of the narwhal which was valued in Europe as a substitute for ivory and rhinoceros horn.[231] Whatever the reason for its introduction the spiral protuberance gives the art historian interested in tracing the influence of Dürer's rhinoceros an identification mark that is easy to follow.

A third rhinoceros (pl. 122) dated *ca.* 1515 is usually attributed to Albrecht Altdorfer (1488–1578).[232] It is to be found in that portion of Emperor Maximilian's Prayer Book preserved at Besançon and is a red ink drawing at the bottom of

---

[226] Dodgson, *loc. cit.* (n. 196), pp. 51–52.

[227] See above, pp. 80–81.

[228] For a general discussion of the resemblances and differences between the Dürer and Burgkmair rhinoceroses see Dodgson, *loc. cit.* (n. 196), pp. 55–56.

[229] E. Ehlers, "Bemerkungen zu den Tierdarstellungen im Gebetbuch des Kaisers Maximilian I," *Jahrbuch der königlichen preussischen Kunstsammlungen*, XXXVIII (1917), 168.

[230] Cole, *loc. cit.* (n. 196), p. 340, considers it possible that he might have been trying to depict a two-horned animal but fails to observe that Dürer might have seen the two-horned rhinoceros on Roman coins.

[231] Suggested by Coste, *loc. cit.* (n. 196), p. 119.

[232] For the debate over the attribution to Altdorfer see Dodgson, *loc. cit.* (n. 196), p. 55.

one of the marginal illustrations which make the Prayer Book an art treasure. While the authorship of the drawing is in dispute, the Prayer Book rhinoceros carries the dorsal spiral and armor plate of Dürer's animal. But the steeper slope of the neck, the rope around the forefeet, and the tail whose end straggles off into a disarray of hairs make it equally reminiscent of Burgkmair's portraiture. The artist of the Prayer Book rhinoceros appears to have used Burgkmair's animal as the base for his drawing and to have added to it embellishments copied from Dürer as well as a cross-hatched pattern across the center part of the back which is of his own devising.[233]

The Burgkmair and Altdorfer rhinoceroses fall from view after 1515. This was perhaps due to the greater fame of Dürer and to the repeated publication of the woodcut of his bizarre rhinoceros. Dürer himself incorporated a tiny reduction of his rhinoceros into the "Triumphal Arch of Maximilian I" first printed in 1517 (pl. 123). It has also been alleged that Dürer's rhinoceros figures in one of the sculptures in the Tower of Belém at Lisbon, which was probably built between 1514 and 1519.[234] But it would seem more likely, if we can depend upon the dating of Belém's construction, that the sculptor in Lisbon worked from a drawing similar to the one that was used in King Manuel's Book of Hours.[235] Indeed, it might even be possible that both the Portuguese and the German portraits of the rhinoceros derive from the same original drawing of the *ganda* made in Lisbon.

The second and third editions of Dürer's woodcut appeared between 1540 and 1550 and evidently stimulated much more general artistic interest than the first edition. Rabelais tells of examing one of Dürer's prints shown to him at Lyons by the German merchant Hans Kleberger. To celebrate the entry into Paris of Henry II and Catharine de' Medici in 1549, Jean Goujon erected a monument on which a rhinoceros stood bearing an obelisk topped by a sphere on which a warrior stands who symbolizes France. According to the *Ordre de l'entrée* the rhinoceros monument was intended to symbolize "Force and Vigilance." It may also have been meant to symbolize union with the Medici, who used the rhinoceros as one of their emblems. While this creation probably owed a certain amount to the inspiration of the elephant and obelisk in the *Hypnerotomachia Poliphili* (1499) of Francesco Colonna, the rhinoceros itself is copied directly from Dürer's woodcut (pl. 124).[236] A drawing for a tapestry attributed to Pieter Coecke van Alost and dated 1550 shows Dürer's rhinoceros at the center of a depiction which features wild animals, including an elephant.[237]

---

[233] S. Killermann (*Dürers Tier- und Pflanzenzeichnungen und ihre Bedeutung für die Naturgeschichte* [Strassburg, 1910], p. 86) suggests that the Prayer Book animal might be a portrait based on the stuffed rhinoceros sent to Rome. This seems highly dubious since it so closely resembles the portraits by Dürer and Burgkmair.

[234] Matos, *loc. cit.* (n. 196), p. 389.

[235] See above, p. 162.

[236] For commentary see Chartrou, *op. cit.* (n. 137), pp. 111–17.

[237] For a reproduction see G. Marlier, *La renaissance flamande, Pierre Cock d'Alost* (Brussels, 1966), p. 352.

A catalogue of 1556 giving the marbles held in the collection of Metello Varro Porcari of Rome lists a rhinoceros "without its head."²³⁸ Today the National Museum at Naples possesses a marble relief of a rhinoceros to which the head has obviously been added and which prominently displays the dorsal spiral of Dürer's beast (pl. 121). While it was at one time believed that this Naples rhinoceros came from the ruins of Pompeii, it now seems much more likely that it is of the sixteenth century and that it was once in the possession of M. V. Porcari.²³⁹

That Italian sculptors knew Dürer's rhinoceros and used it as a model is best illustrated by its presence as one of the animals in the grotto of the Medici villa at Castello (pl. 125). Niccolo Pericoli, often known as Tribolo, planned the gardens at Castello at the request of Archduke Cosimo I de' Medici.²⁴⁰ Tribolo's grotto, completed before 1568, was divided into three enclosed niches in each of which sculptured animals stand against the rear walls and behind large basins. The theme of the grotto is based on the story of the unicorn at the water with the animals that appears in the Greek *Physiologus*. Along with common beasts the elephant, lion, giraffe, camel, monkey, and rhinoceros are represented. The rhinoceros stands behind the monkey and giraffe in the left-hand niche. Its dorsal horn is so elongated as to make it roughly the same size as the nose horn, and its other features are likewise based upon Dürer's beast. But what is most striking is the acceptance by Tribolo and his followers of the exotic rhinoceros as one of the realistic beasts and as being quite different from the mythical unicorn whose symbolism provided the artistic inspiration for the grotto. And, since the rhinoceros was the device of Duke Alessandro de' Medici (ruled 1532–37),²⁴¹ the predecessor of Cosimo, the conviction is strengthened that the allegorical intent of the grotto was to glorify the achievements of the Medici.²⁴².

The first author to use Dürer's woodcut as a book illustration was Sebastian Münster in his *Cosmographei* . . . (1550).²⁴³ In the accompanying text he recounts the story of its meeting with the elephant in Lisbon. His woodcut is a fairly faithful copy of Dürer's original except that the hairs around the mouth are more profuse. Konrad Gesner in his *Historiae animalium* (1551–58) likewise reproduces in reduced size a faithful copy of the original, acknowledges Dürer as its creator, and comments admiringly on the merits and popularity of the

---

²³⁸ See L. Mauro, *Le antichità de le città di Roma* (Venice, 1556), p. 246. For this reference I am indebted to Professor Phyllis P. Bober of New York University.

²³⁹ Before going to the Museo Borgiano, the marble relief was the property of Count Borgia, an inveterate collector of oddities. Otto Keller (*op. cit.* [n. 5]) was responsible for assigning it to Pompeii. The great student of Pompeian antiquities, V. Spinazzola ("Di un rinoceronte marmoreo del Museo Nazionale di Napoli," *Bollettino d'arte*, VII [1913], 143–46), was the first modern to see that it was not from Pompeii but was based on Dürer's rhinoceros.

²⁴⁰ For the history and program of the grotto see L. Châtelet-Lange, "The Grotto of the Unicorn and the Garden of the Villa di Castello," *Art Bulletin*, L (1968), 51–58.

²⁴¹ See below, p. 167.

²⁴² Cf. Châtelet-Lange, *loc. cit.* (n. 240), p. 57, who stresses the profane and political implications of the grotto's program. She fails, however, to point out the profane symbolism of the individual animals.

²⁴³ Woodcut on p. 1171.

woodcut.[244] Valeriano in his *Hieroglyphica* (1556) includes Dürer's rhinoceros in two emblematic woodcuts.[245] In the first he shows it with a bear, a reference to Martial's observation to the effect that the rhinoceros can toss a bear with its horn (or horns?).[246] The second emblem shows the rhinoceros puncturing the soft underbelly of the elephant.

Paulus Jovius, the solon of collecting and making emblems, evidently had a copy of Dürer's rhinoceros on display in his museum.[247] And when the great Humanist and bishop was asked to design a device for Duke Alessandro de' Medici of Florence, Jovius turned to the rhinoceros as a symbol of invincibility. In telling of this episode, Jovius relates the story of the *ganda* of Lisbon and how its meeting with the elephant confirmed the reports of Pliny.[248] In response to Jovius' suggestion that he adopt the rhinoceros as his emblem, the duke first had it embroidered on the covers for the Barbary horses which he raced in Rome. "This devise pleased him [Alessandro]," reports Jovius, "so that he caused it to be engraven in his breast plate."[249] The rhinoceros that was actually engraved on the armor was a copy of Dürer's woodcut with the dorsal spiral somewhat elongated. Above it was engraved the motto coined by Jovius: "Non bueluo sin vincer" ("I warre not but I win").[250] The rhinoceros as a symbol of unconquerable might continued to appeal to the Medici successors of Alessandro as is illustrated by the Castello rhinoceros and by engravings on armor of later times.[251] The contemporary of Alessandro in Ferrara, Duke Ercole II d'Este (ruled 1534–59), had a medal struck, possibly by Alfonso Ruspagiari, with his own portrait on the front and a rhinoceros on the reverse with the inscription "urget maiora" ("He presses harder").[252]

André Thevet in *La cosmographie universelle* (Paris, 1575) is the first of the sixteenth-century authors and collectors of prints who attempts to depart from the Dürer depiction.[253] In his description of the rhinoceros he writes, perhaps unjustifiably, with the authority of an eyewitness but continues to describe a beast which resembles nothing so much as Dürer's rhinoceros. Its head is like that of a pig, its tail like that of a cow, its skin armored naturally like that of a

[244] I, 953. For further commentary see Cole, *loc. cit.* (n. 196), pp. 340–41.

[245] Bk. II, p. 21 recto and verso.

[246] For discussion of whether Martial referred to a one- or two-horned rhinoceros see Cole, *loc. cit.* (n. 196), p. 338.

[247] P. Giovio (Jovius), *Elogios o vidas breves de los cavalleros antiguos y modernos, q estan al bivo pintados en el museo de Paulo Iovico*, trans. from Latin to Spanish by Gaspar de Baeca (Granada, 1568), fols. 127–28.

[248] See *The Worthy Tract* (n. 216), p. Ciii recto.

[249] *Ibid.*

[250] For a woodcut of this device see J. Nestor, *Histoire des hommes illustrés de la Maison de Medici . . .* (Paris, 1564), p. 174. Also see Tasso's comment on this device in Raimondi, *op. cit.* (n. 146), pp. 1076–77.

[251] See the engraving of the armor preserved at Ambras which shows Giovanni Medici holding a shield on which the rhinoceros badge is clearly discernible at the bottom. Published in J. Schrenck von Nozing, *Augustissimorum imperatorum . . .* (Innsbruck, 1601).

[252] A. Armand, *Les médailleurs italiens des quinzième et seizième siècles* (Paris, 1883), I, 219.

[253] Cf. I, 403r–404v; also see the elephant and rhinoceros symbols on his map of Sumatra (*ibid.*, p. 419r). Here the natives allegedly call the elephant "Celbarech" and the rhinoceros "Ganda."

crocodile, and its proportions roughly the same as those of the elephant. His rhinoceros has a horn on the nose and a second one on the back between the shoulders which is not as large as the nose horn but is equally tough and sharp. He claims to have obtained a dorsal horn while in Cairo in 1554 from a "merchant of Bengal named Maldard" which can be seen in his collection of oddities in Paris. He then goes on to attack Girolamo Cardano[254] for saying that the rhinoceros has shorter legs than the elephant; he claims personally to have seen them both and he knows they are of equal height.

The absurdity of Thevet's written claims is matched only by the woodcuts of the rhinoceros fighting the elephant which illustrate his account. The dorsal horn is larger than in Dürer's depiction, the external armor plate has lost all relation to the *plicae* of the skin, and the three toes on the foot are changed into an uncloven hoof. Thus, the depiction of Dürer is rendered even less realistic by making it conform to the fabrications of Thevet.[255] The elephant and rhinoceros are likewise shown to be of the same height in a pictorial refutation of Cardano.

Ambroise Paré, councillor and first surgeon to Henry II and Henry III of France, inserted a woodcut of the *ganda* into his *Deux livres de chirurgie* (Paris, 1573).[256] A caricature of Dürer's woodcut, this shapeless rhinoceros appeared repeatedly in the various editions of Paré's works. In the edition of 1579 he added to his work Thevet's woodcut (pl. 126) showing the combat between the rhinoceros and the elephant.[257] The indomitable rhinoceros is also celebrated by G. de Saluste du Bartas (1544–90) in the sixth "day" of his long poem called *Hiérosme de Marnaf* which was published in 1585, the year when Paré's *Oeuvres* appeared.

In the meantime a second live rhinoceros, referred to in Europe as the *bada*,[258]

---

[254] Cardano (*De subtilitate* [Basel, 1554], p. 626) describes the rhinoceros mainly on the basis of Varthema's account, the only eyewitness description generally available in his day. Varthema, first published in 1510, describes two live "unicorns" which had been presented as gifts to the sultan of Mecca by the king of Ethiopia. See R. C. Temple (ed.), *The Itinerary of Ludovico di Varthema of Bologna from 1502 to 1508* . . . (London, 1928), p. 22. Ramusio (*op. cit.* [n. 51], p. 165r) published Varthema's description of the unicorn in 1550. Ramusio also published a brief mention of the rhinoceros and its hostility for the elephant in his epitomized version of Niccolo Conti's fifteenth-century travels to India as written down by Poggio Bracciolini (see *ibid.*, p. 376v). In 1575, Leonhard Rauwolf saw a young rhinoceros at Aleppo that was on its way to the animal market in Constantinople. See K. H. Dannenfeldt, *Leonhard Rauwolf* (Cambridge, Mass., 1968), p. 143.

[255] It is possible that Thevet based himself upon what correspondents from India told of its height. For example, a letter from Cochin (January 16, 1563) written by Andreas Fernandes to his fellow Jesuit, Pedro da Fonseca, in Portugal, asserts that the rhinoceros is "not much shorter than the elephant." See J. Wicki (ed.), *Documenta Indica* (Rome, 1948–62), V, 731.

[256] For a commentary and reproductions of Paré's woodcuts see Coste, *loc. cit.* (n. 196), pp. 122–23, and Cole, *loc. cit.* (n. 196), pp. 342–43.

[257] Also see the Dürer rhinoceros in A. Lonitzer, *Kreuterbuch* . . . (Frankfurt am Main, 1598).

[258] Gaspar da Cruz in his *Tractado* . . . published at Lisbon in 1569 describes the rhinoceros on the basis of his experiences in Cambodia. He says that they are called *badas* (*abada*), an old Portuguese word for rhinoceros derived from the Malay *badoh* which is pronounced *bada* in certain dialects of Malay. For Cruz see C. R. Boxer (ed.), *South China in the Sixteenth Century* (London, 1953), pp. 77–78. In 1592, James Lancaster, while trading in the Straits of Malacca, exchanged "ambergris for the horns of 'Abath.' " See Hakluyt, *op. cit.* (n. 128), VI, 399. In modern Portuguese the word *abada* means the female rhinoceros. For further discussion see Yule and Burnell, *op. cit.* (n. 12), pp. 1–2.

had been brought to Portugal. Filippo Sassetti wrote in 1579 to his correspondents in Florence that the *bada* is "the marvel of Lisbon."[259] And he applies to it Petrarch's line: "Che sol se stessa e null'ultra simiglia."[260] Dom Jean Sarrazim (1539–98), the abbé of St.-Vaart and first councillor to Philip II in Artois, visited Portugal with an embassy in 1582. In his correspondence he reported on the rhinoceros of Lisbon in the time of King Manuel and on the *bada* that he saw there. From his own experience he found the rhinoceros to be "as admirable among the works of nature as the monastery of Belém is among the works of art."[261] It was evidently after 1582 that this rhinoceros was sent to Madrid as a gift to King Philip II.[262] On public display in Madrid by November, 1584, it was shown, along with an elephant, to the Japanese legates.[263] Juan González de Mendoza in his book *China* (first published in 1585) also tells of its being there and comments on the reactions of the spectators.[264] The rhinoceros, which long remained on display in Madrid, had its horn sawn off and was blinded to keep it from harming persons.[265]

At Seville, meanwhile, Juan de Arphe y Villafañe published in 1585 his manual on decorations in which he presents both a written description and a print of the rhinoceros.[266] His rhinoceros resembles Dürer's woodcut in its general proportions, but differs markedly from it in that the dorsal spiral is missing. A copy of Arphe's rhinoceros in mural size (pl. 127) in a ceiling decoration of a late sixteenth-century house at Tunja in the highlands of Colombia differs similarly from Dürer's rendition, showing the nose horn as longer and the feet uncloven.[267] It is perhaps possible that the departures from Dürer's beast were introduced into these Spanish studies as a result of information conveyed to the artists by sketches of the Madrid animal.

Such a conclusion is reinforced by reference to the text in Joachim Camerarius' *Symbolorum*. . . .[268] Here the author acknowledges that his source of information about the rhinoceros is an accurate drawing received from Spain. Hans Sibmacher, the graphic artist who illustrated this work, must certainly have been acquainted with Dürer's woodcut, since they were both natives of the same city. But, as even a cursory examination of Sibmacher's rhinoceros will show, he eschewed the great master's rendition and followed the depiction done from nature (pl. 129). In the text Camerarius describes Dürer's dorsal horn as a mere

[259] For his comment see his letter to Francisco Bonciani in Marucci, *op. cit.* (n. 186), pp. 134–35.
[260] As quoted in R. Jorge, *Amato Lusitano* (Lisbon, 1962), p. 263, n. 1.
[261] From P. de Caverel (ed.), *Ambassade en Espagne et en Portugal (en 1582) de R. P. en Dieu, Dom Jean Sarrazim* . . . (Arras, 1860), as extracted in *Boletim de bibliografia portugueza*, I (1879), 162.
[262] J. Castilho, *A ribeira de Lisboa* (2d ed.; Lisbon, 1941–48), II, 173.
[263] J. A. Abranches Pinto *et al.*, *La première ambassade du Japon en Europe* (Tokyo, 1942), p. 106, n. 399.
[264] G. T. Staunton (ed.), *The History of the Great and Mighty Kingdom of China* . . . (London, 1854), II, 311–12.
[265] S. de Cobarruvias, *Tesoro de la lengua Castellana o Española* (Madrid, 1611), *s.v.* "Bada."
[266] *Op. cit.* (n. 177), p. 206.
[267] Cf. E. W. Palm, "Dürer's Ganda and a XVI Century Apotheosis of Hercules at Tunja," *Gazette des Beaux-Arts*, 6th ser., XLVIII (1956), 46–71.
[268] (Nuremberg, 1590–1604), Bk. II, No. V, p. 10. Also see Cole, *loc. cit.* (n. 196), pp. 344–45.

tuberosity on the back and not a true horn. And he goes on to criticize Martial for referring misleadingly to a two-horned rhinoceros. Camerarius, it is evident, was unaware of the fact that the two-horned rhinoceros from Africa (or perhaps even from Asia) was known to the Romans even though he himself had never heard of it.

While Camerarius and Sibmacher strove for a more realistic depiction of the rhinoceros, other artists of the latter half of the sixteenth century continued to base their renditions upon Dürer's woodcuts. One of the famous Brussels tapestries dated 1565 and attributed to Guillaume Tons l'Ancien shows Dürer's rhinoceros in combat with an elephant.[269] A Viennese silver tankard with lid is decorated with a Düreresque rhinoceros.[270] The west portal of the cathedral at Pisa, left side at the base, completed around 1595, shows Dürer's rhinoceros by itself and in a confrontation with an elephant.[271] On a map of Africa, prepared by Arnoldus F. à Langren for the frontispiece to Linschoten's *Itinerario*, Dürer's rhinoceros is shown as a symbol for the region of Angola. The triumphal arch of the Portuguese erected in Antwerp to celebrate the solemn *entrée* of July 18, 1593, shows Dürer's rhinoceros as a symbol of India (pl. 49). Astride the rhinoceros sits an Indian woman with a child on her back and a coconut in her left hand. And Joseph Boillot's *New Termis Buch*, which contains designs for fifty-five animal caryatids, includes one which shows Dürer's rhinoceros twisted triumphantly around an elephant (pl. 128). The dorsal spiral is shown almost as prominently as the nose horn and the cloven hoofs and the legs are bedecked with armor. In the accompanying text Boillot relates the story of the *ganda* of 1515 in Lisbon and discusses its victory over the elephant. He explains that in his drawing of the caryatid he has interlocked the two animals on the pillar with the weight resting on the elephant and with the rhinoceros triumphantly supporting the entablature.[272]

The rhinoceros as it was depicted on ancient coins and in medieval bestiaries was completely replaced after 1515 by Dürer's depiction. The more realistic rhinoceros of Burgkmair was never any competition for Dürer's armor-plated beast. The early edition of Dürer's woodcut seems to have been known mainly in Germany; the two editions of the 1540's inspired artists in France, Italy, Switzerland, Germany, and the Low Countries. After the mid-sixteenth century the artists who employed Dürer's woodcut as a model began to fantasize it by elongating the dorsal spiral and by redesigning the armor. As they increasingly used the rhinoceros in conjunction with other animals or people, they sometimes felt required to modify Dürer's animal simply for the sake of artistic design.

[269] M. Roethlisberger, "La tenture de la licorne dans la Collection Borromée," *Oud-Holland*, LXXXII (1967), 92, pl. 5.

[270] For a photograph see H. Thoma and H. Brunner, *Schatzkammer der Residenz München: Katalog* (Munich, 1964), p. 221, no. 535.

[271] See H. M. von Erffa, "Das Programm der Westportale des Pisaner Domes," *Mitteilungen des kunsthistorischen Institutes in Florenz*, XII (1965), pl. 2 and 27, and p. 93 n.

[272] See the suggestive discussion of fused and interlocked fauna in R. A. Jairazbhoy, *Oriental Influences in Western Art* (Bombay, 1965), chap. xv.

But that there was genuine dissatisfaction with Dürer's portrayal becomes evident as artists of the last decade of the century, even in Dürer's home city, began to look to contemporary drawings of the Madrid rhinoceros for inspiration.

But Dürer's *ganda*, despite its bizarre appearance, was not replaced in the sixteenth century and traces of its influence on the "scientific" depiction of the rhinoceros can be discerned as late as the eighteenth century.[273] In the sixteenth century the Dürer woodcut was used as a model by other graphic artists, by workers in metal, by ecclesiastical and secular sculptors, by tapestry makers and embroiderers, and by designers of emblems, maps, monuments, and caryatids. Unlike Hanno, the *ganda* seems not to have appealed to European painters, the only sixteenth-century painting of which I have seen a copy being the mural in the Spanish colony of Tunja, Colombia.[274] On medals, monuments, and armor plate the rhinoceros continued to represent patient invincibility, force, and ferocity. And it was used increasingly as a symbol for Asia, an honor that it often shared with the elephant.[275]

What is most remarkable is the fact that the Indian rhinoceros, unlike the elephant, has occupied a much less significant place in Indian and Far Eastern than in Western art. This is particularly hard to understand when it is recalled that the rhinoceros was revered in ancient India as a sacred animal and is today worshipped by the Nepalese.[276] The rhinoceros, it is true, appears on seals found at the archaeological sites of the Indus Valley and clay figurines of the animal made by children seem to indicate that it was well known to the Mohenjo-daro civilization.[277] Somewhat later it is used on Indian coins. In Hindu and Buddhist lore the rhinoceros symbolizes the pious recluse,[278] a meaning that it seems never to have acquired in the Christian West. But it is rarely, if ever, shown in the famous animal sculptures which appear around and on the Hindu temples. Carpets and a few miniatures of the Mughul period show the rhinoceros and rhinoceros-like animals, but these are probably derived from Persian art. The rhinoceros is conspicuously ignored by the Indian designers of the decorative motifs which have long been and are still used commonly on textiles, metalwork, and jewelry.[279]

[273] Coste, *loc. cit.* (n. 196), pp. 124–26.

[274] A painting of a rhinoceros is mentioned in the 1621 inventory of Rudolf II's collection. See R. Beer (ed.), "Inventare aus dem Archivio del Palacio zu Madrid," *Jahrbuch der kunsthistorischen Sammlungen des allerhöchsten Kaiserhauses*, XIX (1898), Pt. 2, xlviii.

[275] For example see the engraving on the title page of Theodor de Bry, *India orientalis* (Frankfurt am Main, 1601), reproduced in pl. 146.

[276] G. W. Briggs, "The Indian Rhinoceros as a Sacred Animal," *Journal of the American Oriental Society*, LI (1931), 281. It should also be observed that the rhinoceros is the official emblem of modern Nepal.

[277] Ettinghausen, *op. cit.* (n. 13), p. 95.

[278] See the famous refrain in the Buddhist canonical book of the third century B.C. called *Sutta Nipāta*: "Let him wander alone like a rhinoceros."

[279] Examination of five thousand traditional Indian designs turned up just one in which the rhinoceros figures, a crude design based on a Harappa seal. The elephant by contrast appears regularly in these designs. For the rhinoceros see Indian Institute of Art in Industry, *5000 Indian Designs and Motifs* (Calcutta, 1965), p. 1.

Whatever the reason for the greater appeal of the rhinoceros to Western artists, there can be no doubt that it was Dürer's woodcut which gave it an initial popularity. And that Dürer's woodcut made the rhinoceros familiar to Europeans is attested to textually by Fray Luís de Urreta in his book on Ethiopia published in 1610.[280] The *ganda* itself helped to sustain the interest of Humanists and artists by defeating the elephant to vindicate the authorities of Antiquity. And, like Hanno, it symbolized for the Western artists the remote and fascinating overseas world, an exotic appeal that neither animal could possibly have had in its homeland.

3

THE TIGER

Ctesias, the Greek physician who was the source of much fabulous lore about Indian animals, is often credited with reporting on the tiger for the first time. Through informants in Persia he learned about a marvelous Indian beast called "Martichoras" (from Old Persian *martijaqâra* meaning literally "man-slayer").[281] According to his description this beast resembles a lion, possesses a human face, carries a stinger in its tail, and shoots spines like arrows from its tail. The likelihood is that Ctesias is here repeating Persian lore about the Bengal tiger. His stories were then picked up and embellished by Pliny and Aelian.[282]

Specimens of tigers and reports based on actual observations reached the Greek world as a result of Alexander's invasion of India. Seleucus, the successor to Alexander, sent a tiger as a present to the people of Athens late in the fourth century. Although tigers were native at this period to the southern reaches of the Caspian Sea, it is possible that Seleucus had a tiger sent from India as a symbol of his efforts in the subcontinent to take up where Alexander had left off.[283] Aristotle, it appears, did not have an opportunity to observe the living tiger.[284]

Tigers were not brought into the Roman Empire until the time of Augustus. Dio reports that the Indian embassy received at Samos by the Romans in 20–19 B.C. brought tigers as gifts. About a decade later a caged tiger was exhibited in Rome at the festivities attending the dedication of the temple of Marcellus. On this same occasion as many as six hundred panthers and similar animals from Africa were killed. In the time of Claudius (*ca.* A.D. 50) four tigers were shown to the Roman public. To celebrate the return to Rome of Emperor Domitian, a number of tigers were exhibited in A.D. 93. And, at the marriage of Emperor

---

[280] As cited in Shepard, *op. cit.* (n. 197), p. 67.
[281] This word is possibly of Indian origin.
[282] Robin, *op. cit.* (n. 192), p. 4.
[283] Cf. Jennison, *op. cit.* (n. 8), p. 24.
[284] Keller, *op. cit.* (n. 5), I, 62.

Heliogabalus (*ca.* A.D. 218) it is reported that fifty-one tigers were killed in the arena.[285]

Since the tiger was not native to the Roman world, romantic stories were legion about its characteristics and habits. Pliny and other Roman writers describe it as the swiftest, most fearsome, and wildest of beasts. To take a tigress the hunter has to resort to trickery as he tries to capture her cubs. Since the tigress is reputedly fascinated by her own image, the wily hunter is supposed to put a mirror in her path and then steal her cubs while she admires herself. The swift tigress, as she pursues the mounted hunter, can best be delayed by dropping a cub every so often. Ultimate escape from her pursuit can be found only by boarding a ship and putting out to sea. But, according to Plutarch, tigers may be frightened by drums, bells, and other noisemakers—a story that was probably founded on fact.

Because of its wildness, the tiger is often associated by Roman poets and artists with the gods of wine and love.[286] A triumph of Bacchus in a mosaic of the third century A.D. shows the roistering god being drawn in his chariot by a quadriga of realistic tigers.[287] In a diptych of Constantine the Great, a tiger is shown with an elephant to symbolize the fearlessness and wisdom of the emperor.[288] The tigress as predator is clearly shown in a fourth-century *opus sectile* of marble which depicts its attack upon a bull.[289] In these, and other artistic representations, the tiger can easily be differentiated from panthers, leopards, and other cats by the close attention given by the artists to its stripes.

In the Middle Ages there was so much uncertainty about the nature of the tiger that it was classified in certain bestiaries as a serpent and in others as a bird. The bestiary writers merely repeat the stories of Antiquity about its swiftness, agility, and cruelty.[290] They also recount the story of the mirror but seem not, strangely, to attach any symbolic significance to this story. And, since living specimens of the tiger seem not to have been known in medieval Europe, miniatures of it in bestiaries are highly fanciful and virtually unrecognizable.

Living specimens of the tiger began to reappear in Europe during the last generation of the fifteenth century. They were probably brought to southern Europe from the animal market of Constantinople, for no record exists of any being brought into Europe by ship after the discovery of the sea route to India. Certain Greeks exhibited a tiger at the "Château" of Turin in 1475.[291] At the end of the fifteenth century another tiger was acquired by the court of Ferrara

---

[285] Jennison, *op. cit.* (n. 8), pp. 67, 70, 76, 91.

[286] Keller, *op. cit.* (n. 5), I, 62.

[287] A villa mosaic preserved in the Musée de Sousse. See G. C. Picard, "La mosaique romaine en Afrique du Nord," *Gazette des Beaux-Arts*, 6th ser., LII (1958), 200, fig. 10.

[288] Jennison, *op. cit.* (n. 8), p. 76. In China the tiger was also a symbol of courage. See Ball, *op. cit.* (n. 4), chap. iii.

[289] For a reproduction see Jairazbhoy, *op. cit.* (n. 272), pl. 42.

[290] For example, see Goldstaub and Wendriner, *op. cit.* (n. 28), pp. 307-10; and Randall, *op. cit.* (n. 28), fig. 662.

[291] See Loisel, *op. cit.* (n. 30), I, 246.

for its animal collection. In sixteenth-century Spain the nobility reportedly kept tigers to pit against bulls in the arena.[292] Caspar Schwenkfeld (1563–1609), the Silesian physician, reported that a tiger was on exhibition at Emperor Rudolf's menagerie in Prague.[293] In the last years of the sixteenth century the collection of Tuscany also included a tiger.[294] Literary documentation of this sort is understandably sparse and is suspect, because European writers used the word "tiger" indiscriminately to designate a number of catlike beasts.[295]

It is only when the artists begin to depict the tiger in their works that one moves to firmer ground. As early as 1528, Giulio Romano included an excellent naturalistic depiction of a tiger in his "Bacchus and Ariadne," a fresco in the Sala di Psiche of the Palazzo del Te at Mantua (pl. 130). In the Camera degli Uccelli of the Ducal Palace in Mantua, Giulio shows tigers among the animals which frolic through the scrollery.[296] Annibale Carracci has two realistic tigers pulling the chariot of Bacchus in his painting on the Farnese ceiling completed around 1600 (pl. 131). Two sculptures of the tiger in metal dated from about 1576 and attributed to Paglio Banchelli are listed in the inventory of the Medici collections made between 1567 and 1588.[297] Juan de Arphe in Book III of his *Varia commensuracion* shows a tiger in a springing position (pl. 132). And in Roelant Savery's painting of the Garden of Eden, two excellent tigers, one lying down and the other standing on four feet, are at the center (pl. 144).

The tiger, like other strange animals, appealed to the emblem-makers. Valeriano in his *Hieroglyphica* clearly distinguishes the leopard from the tiger. His first woodcut, following the tradition of Antiquity, shows two tigers pulling Bacchus in a chariot under the epigram "Fero emolita"; the second shows a tiger eating a horse under the word "Ultio"; the third depicts a man standing beside a seated tiger under the epigram "Musicae hostis."[298] An emblem of a tiger attacking a horse and another showing it looking at itself in a mirror are depicted in the emblems of Camerarius. The first illustrates the idea that revenge lessens pain; the second, that looking into a mirror leads to self-deception. These emblems are accompanied by a lengthy commentary on the propensities of the tiger drawn from the authors of Antiquity.[299] In his *New Termis Buch*, Boillot shows the tiger as a caryatid surrounded by drums, horns, and bells by which it may be frightened.[300] From these depictions, and from

[292] *Ibid.*, pp. 201, 212.

[293] P. Delaunay, *La zoölogie au seizième siècle* (Paris, 1962), p. 149.

[294] J. Rathgeb, *Wahrhaffte Beschreibung zweyer Raisen . . .* (Tübingen, 1603), II, 57r.

[295] Cf. Robin, *op. cit.* (n. 192), p. 21. Charles V, for example, in 1524 sent his brother a cloak trimmed with "tiger skin" that came from America. Lhotsky, *op. cit.* (n. 122), p. 127. Gesner (*Historiae animalium* [Zurich, 1551–87], I, 1060–65) is likewise not clear whether or not the tiger comes from America.

[296] Hartt, *op. cit.* (n. 102), I, 169.

[297] M. Müntz, "Les collections d'antiquités des Médicis," *Mémoires de l'Académie des Inscriptions,* XXXV, Pt. 2, 148–49.

[298] Valeriano, *op. cit.* (n. 73), pp. 84v–84r.

[299] Camerarius, *op. cit.* (n. 145), Bk. II, No. xxxv, p. 70.

[300] *New Termis Buch . . .* (n.p., 1604), p. B iiii verso.

Capaccio's discussion,[301] it becomes clear that the tiger retained throughout the sixteenth century the symbolism which it had acquired in Antiquity: the personification of untamable wildness, indomitable courage, remorseless cruelty, and unrelenting vengeance.

4

THE SIMIANS

Ctesias reported to the Greek world that monkeys in astonishing numbers live in the mountains of India. Megasthenes asserted that the Indians in compliance with royal orders feed cooked rice to the monkeys of the forests.[302] These are references to macaques and langurs, tailed monkeys, which are still commonly seen in India from the Himalayas to Cape Comorin. In the Athens of Aristotle, the tailless Barbary ape of North Africa was a common household pet. No records, literary or artistic, testify to the presence of living specimens of Indian monkeys in either Greece or Rome.[303]

In art, it is generally impossible to distinguish tailed Indian monkeys from tailed African monkeys, respectively the guenons and guerezas.[304] Therefore it is necessary to limit discussions to those depictions in which the general design makes it clear that the artist is seeking to portray the monkey of India. For example, in Assyrian reliefs dating back to the ninth century B.C. the monkey is shown along with other Indian animals sent as tribute from the East.[305] On a silver dish from Lampsacus of the first or second century A.D., India is represented as a woman who sits on a chair supported by elephant tusks. On each side of her chair a tame monkey stands on all fours with a collar around its neck. Despite the poor representation of the faces, it is clear from the general design that the artist is here seeking to depict the long-tailed Indian monkey, the Hanuman langur.[306]

Aristotle and Galen described the anatomy and physiology of the primates but seem not to have concerned themselves consciously with the similarities and differences between ape and man.[307] Aelian, conscious of the striking physical and behavioral resemblances among primates, asserted that the red apes of India chase human women to cohabitate with them. Such statements seem to be derived from an awareness among certain of the ancients of the anthropoid apes of Africa, the gorilla and chimpanzee. Or they may go back to the stories of

---

[301] *Op. cit.* (n. 138), Bk. II, chap. xxxvi, pp. 83v–84r.

[302] Keller, *op. cit.* (n. 5), I, 9.

[303] Cf. Jennison, *op. cit.* (n. 8), p. 128. An orangutan of India might be represented on a Greek vase of the fourth century B.C. (*ibid.*, p. 21).

[304] W. C. McDermott, *The Ape in Antiquity* (Baltimore, 1938), p. 241.

[305] Keller, *op. cit.* (n. 5), I, 9.

[306] McDermott, *op. cit.* (n. 304), p. 241. The silver dish is today preserved in the Museum of Antiquities in Istanbul.

[307] H. W. Janson, *Apes and Ape Lore* (London, 1952), p. 73.

Ctesias about the "wild men" of India with furry bodies and animal-like habits.[308] Whatever its origin, the belief was current in the Roman world by the time of Pliny that apes and monkeys were degenerate forms of humanity.

In the *Physiologus* tradition, as perpetuated by the medieval bestiaries, the ape is portrayed as a fallen angel and as the symbol of the sinner incarnate. Apes were sent to Charlemagne along with the elephant, and subsequently in Gothic art the ape is sometimes shown riding on the back of the elephant. The medieval artists possibly derived their inspiration for this symbolic combination of sin upon the back of virtue from the Indian tradition, exemplified by the reliefs in the stupa of Barhut, of apes riding on elephants.[309] Oriental tales about the ape that became known in Europe through Alexander Neckam also contributed their share to the symbolic depiction of the ape as sinner, or as the devil in animal form.[310] As with other animals not native to medieval Europe, the ape was given moral—or immoral—attributes which would serve the evangelizing objectives of medieval writers and artists.

A new naturalism appears in literary and visual references to the ape beginning in the twelfth century. In this crusading era the expansion of Mediterranean commerce brought Europe into closer touch with the products of Africa and the Levant. As a consequence the townsmen of Europe had the opportunity to see for the first time since Antiquity the live Barbary ape. The depictions of performing apes along with their trainers, dressed in Orientalized costumes, which appear in Romanesque sculpture were certainly based upon such living models.[311] Other apelike figures, especially in Spanish ecclesiastical sculpture,[312] were possibly inspired by African slaves who were sometimes identified with the "wild men" and fabulous races of the overseas world.[313] Marco Polo comments on the orangutans of southern India who have the appearance of men. The ape with the Negro is also shown repeatedly in medieval religious painting and sculpture.[314] But practically all the naturalistic apes of medieval art are of the tailless Barbary type. The few examples of tailed apes depicted before 1400 show little more than indirect knowledge of the living animals.[315]

After 1400 the tailed guenons of Africa began to appear in Europe in numbers large enough to be identified by artists as a new simian variety. Basing their work upon depictions shown in the standard sketchbooks, German engravers quite quickly began to juxtapose the tailed and tailless apes in their woodcuts. Martin Schongauer, who designed a fantastic elephant, treated the ape with sharp realism in his drawing of a sitting ape.[316] The apelike creature in Breydenbach's

[308] See R. Bernheimer, *Wild Men in the Middle Ages* (Cambridge, Mass., 1952), pp. 84–93.

[309] Janson, *op. cit.* (n. 307), p. 67, n. 105; p. 353, n. 74.

[310] *Ibid.*, p. 35. For an example of the ape as devil see the verse in R. Reinsch (ed.), *Le Bestiaire: Das Thierbuch des normannischen Dichters Guillaume le Clerc* (Leipzig, 1892), pp. 307–8.

[311] Janson, *op. cit.* (n. 307), pp. 30, 49.

[312] *Ibid.*, pp. 44–45.

[313] Bernheimer, *op. cit.* (n. 308), pp. 92–93.

[314] Janson, *op. cit.* (n. 307), p. 65, n. 97.

[315] *Ibid.*, p. 129.

[316] See reproduction in F. Winzinger, *Die Zeichnungen Martin Schongauers* (Berlin, 1962), pl. 50.

Journey (1486) became the model for several later simian depictions.[317] Along with the more naturalistic depiction of the apes, both in the late Middle Ages and the Renaissance, its symbolism underwent a change. The ape, like other Asian animals, was gradually secularized, and instead of symbolizing the sinner it came to stand for the fool. And since folly, unlike sin, is a common and inescapable quality of human nature, in the Renaissance the ape's antics were increasingly regarded with less horror and a more bemused tolerance.[318] The rediscovery of the "phallic ape" of Antiquity also had the effect of making the identification with man and his follies an even closer one.

In the age of exploration it was not long before the great apes of Africa and Asia were discovered and remarked upon. The orangutan and gibbon of south and southeastern Asia were known by report to most of the zoological encyclopedists of the sixteenth century. But it was not until the seventeenth century that a living orangutan was brought to Europe.[319] Reports of these manlike creatures, however, did not stimulate speculation among either scientists or philosophers about the nature of man and his relation to the other primates.[320] The great apes were generally accepted as belonging to the lower animals, all of whom were in one sense or another related to man.

It was left to the physiologist to point out the structural differences[321] and to the artist to suggest the behavioral parallels between simians and man. Albrecht Dürer, who collected monkeys while in Antwerp, seems to have studied both their physiognomy and habits. In his "Affentanz" (1523) he has apes disporting themselves like humans.[322] Long-tailed monkeys were acquired in Lisbon by Lucas Rem, who sent several of them to the Welsers in Augsburg.[323] Two realistic monkeys stand in front of a fireplace in the fresco of St. Michael in the Castel San Angelo in Rome. They represent sin and paganism, the enemies of Christianity, which were overcome by the sword of the saint. Cranach shows a long-tailed monkey holding a family conclave in his drawing for Maximilian's Prayer Book.[324] In a Brussels tapestry of the mid-sixteenth century a long-tailed monkey follows the first human pair as they are driven out of Paradise (pl. 133). Titian, in his woodcut called "The Ape Laocoön," is evidently caricaturing the Galenist enemies of Vesalius for whom he was preparing illustrations (pl. 134).[325] The anthropoid ape in the center is realistic enough to suggest that Titian probably observed and sketched a living beast.

Annibale Carracci, one of the late Manneristic painters of Italy, shows apes

[317] Janson, *op. cit.* (n. 307), p. 332.

[318] *Ibid.*, p. 199.

[319] *Ibid.*, p. 270.

[320] *Ibid.*, p. 327.

[321] *Ibid.*, p. 335; Leonardo in his writing on comparative anatomy considers the baboon and ape to be "almost of the same species" as man. McCurdy, *op. cit.* (n. 28), I, 191.

[322] These have been identified as green apes and nun apes from Africa. See Killermann, *op. cit.* (n. 233), pp. 45–46.

[323] See above, p. 22.

[324] Monkeys from India were almost certainly his models. Ehlers, *loc. cit.* (n. 229), pp. 166–67.

[325] For a lengthy discussion of the meaning of this woodcut see Janson, *op. cit.* (n. 307), pp. 355–64.

in the company of a dwarf, a dog, and a parrot in a work portraying the oddities of nature, a taste that had much in common with the interests of the northern painters. At the end of the sixteenth century Pieter van der Borcht produced an etching which shows a schoolroom of monkeys learning their lessons.[326] An ape on the back of an elephant, in a black-pencil drawing by Roelant Savery (pl. 111), places a medieval theme in an Asian landscape. Whether the ape continues to symbolize sin for Savery is not of concern here.[327] It is certain from study of his drawing that he associated the ape with the overseas world (seashells), the tropics (palms), and with the Asian elephant.[328] The ape, like other exotic animals, was used by Boillot as the basis for one of his fantastic caryatids. In the accompanying caption Boillot writes:

The ape is a cunning, joyful, subtle, and quick animal, with the intelligence, face . . . and other parts which makes it resemble a human more than an ass does a turnstile. . . . Throughout Asia in general one finds varieties called guenons, baboons, etc. . . . and this is enough talk about apes; if you want to know more about them, go look in your mirror.[329]

The physical and behavioral resemblances between man and ape were clearly mirrored in the arts of the sixteenth century. It is also possible to see that in depictions by artists simians were increasingly associated with Asia rather than Africa. Medieval traditions about the ape and its symbolism continue to haunt the artists of the Renaissance. But, as with the elephant, monkeys are no longer assigned exclusively a religious or moral symbolism. They have become, like men, both the victims and the makers of folly. The ape is driven from Paradise, suffers the torments of Laocoön, and engages in hapless frivolity.

5

THE BIRDS

The green parrots of India were among the birds most commonly brought back to Europe by travelers and sailors. It was possible to buy caged birds, then as now, in most Oriental bazaars. Parrots were universally popular because of their amusing ability to perform tricks and to repeat a few words in any language whatsoever.[330] Ctesias in his *Indica* (chap. 3) described a bird ("*Bittacus*") with a human tongue and voice that could speak an "Indian" language naturally a full

---

[326] Painting by Carracci now in the National Museum, Naples; for the etching of the monkeys at school see A. J. J. Delen, *Histoire de la gravure dans les anciens Pays-Bas* . . . , Pt. II (Paris, 1935), pl. XLIV.

[327] Compare the ape on the back of a dog in "Christ and the Centurion" by the Mestre de Charola de Tomar; reproduced in J. Barreira *et al.*, *Arte portuguesa* (Lisbon, 1948–54), III, 238.

[328] Compare the monkey in association with other exotic animals on the title page of A. Freitag, *Mythologia ethica* . . . (Antwerp, 1579).

[329] See the final page of Boillot's *New Termis Buch* (n. 300).

[330] For a modern description of the green Indian parrots or parakeets see S. Ali, *The Book of Indian Birds* (7th ed.; Bombay, 1964), pp. 32–33.

century before Aristotle mentioned the "psittace" in his animal history.[331] Nearchus, one of Alexander's officers, brought live parrots to the West and others were displayed at Alexandria in the great processions sponsored by Ptolemy II. By the time of Augustus the increase in trading relations between India and the countries of the eastern Mediterranean brought to Italy all sorts of exotic beasts and birds which had probably been bought in the animal market of Alexandria.

The ring-necked parakeet became a household pet in the Roman Empire and was commonly exhibited at public spectacles. Pliny in his *Natural History* (10. 117) records that "India sends us this bird." He also describes it as having a green body with a red band around its neck, and it can, he declares, "say 'Hail Caesar,' learn words repeated to it, and is particularly merry *in vino*." The winged mimic which Ovid's mistress kept was given poppy seeds to stop it from chattering and to put it to sleep. The gray African parrot, which was probably not so well known to the Romans as the green Indian variety, is today esteemed to be the better mimic. Both the African and Indian varieties were kept by the Romans in cages of ivory and silver and were fed upon nuts and seeds bought for their owners' tables.[332] There are extant very few artistic representations of the Indian parrot dating from Roman times. One of the best depictions is a mosaic from Pompeii which shows two green parrots and a dove sitting around a bird bath.[333]

In the bestiaries of the Middle Ages the parrot is explicitly identified with India alone, or with that part of the Orient "where it never rains."[334] It is also given Christian attributes like the other animals from the East:

The parrot is a symbol [*typus*] for Christ which has had and will not have an equal in purity, a consequence of its Immaculate Conception, of its stainless birth as well as its sinless thoughts, words, and actions: so it alone remains pure and faultless in this world of sin.[335]

In the late Middle Ages and early Renaissance the gray parrots of Africa were imported into Europe in greater numbers. They were cherished for their mimicry, and Chaucer says satirically that they could "cry 'Wat!' as well as can the Pope."[336] A Roman cardinal, it is said, in the year 1500 bought a gray parrot for one hundred pieces of gold because it could repeat clearly and without hesitation the entire Apostles' Creed.[337] The south German merchant princes bought parrots at Antwerp, and in 1505 agents of the Nuremberg merchants were robbed on their way home from Antwerp of a basket load of parrots they

[331] Keller, *op. cit.* (n. 5), II, 45.

[332] See Jennison, *op. cit.* (n. 8), pp. 17–18, 120; also D. M. Stuart, *A Book of Birds and Beasts* (London, 1957), pp. 10. 32–33.

[333] Mosaic No. 9992 in the National Museum, Naples. For a reproduction see Keller, *op. cit* (n. 5), II, pl. 19.

[334] See White, *op. cit.* (n. 28), p. 112.

[335] Goldstaub and Wendriner, *op. cit.* (n. 28), p. 420.

[336] As quoted in Stuart, *op. cit.* (n. 332), p. 30.

[337] E. Phipson, *Animal Lore of Shakespeare's Time* (London, 1883), p. 214.

were carrying.[338] Six years later the Fuggers sent gray parrots as a gift to Bishop Johann Thurzo of Breslau for services he had rendered them.[339] Regent Margaret of Austria carried a parrot on her arm while walking in her garden at Malînes.[340] Dürer, in his early drawings of parrots, portrays the gray African variety, with its red tail, now called *Psittacus erithacus*.[341] But, when he collected parrots at Antwerp in 1520–21, he acquired green parrots along with other Asian exotica.

Whether the parrots were gray or green, the artists of the sixteenth century seem always to have associated them with the East and with the sinless bird of the bestiary tradition.[342] In a study by an Antwerp painter who was active between 1520 and 1530, the parrot is shown in association with the Madonna and the Christ child (pl. 136).[343] A painting on wood of about the same time, possibly by Bartholomäus Bruyn, depicts a German woman with a green parrot seated on her right arm (pl. 137). Filippo Sassetti in a letter of 1580 to Florence disclaims all knowledge of a "white parrot" that he had been asked about and indicates that many green parrots were being brought into Europe from the Moluccas.[344] The green parrot, it seems, once it became commoner in Europe, was favored by painters over the gray variety for its gayer coloring.

In the natural histories and emblem books of the latter half of the sixteenth century the parrot is associated with India, America, and Africa. Sebastian Münster discusses the animals and birds of Calicut and reproduces two woodcuts of Indian parrots.[345] Valeriano places the parrot in Africa and appropriately includes a woodcut of a parrot as the symbol for eloquence.[346] Matthias Holtzwart (*ca.* 1543–89) shows the parrot in a cage, poetically relates to the viewer that it is well known in India, and attaches to it the motto: "As the shepherd is, so is his flock."[347] The *Symbolorum et emblematum* of Camerarius includes an etching of an American parrot that sleeps all winter in a tree.[348] Capaccio in his *Delle imprese* calls the parrot a symbol of liberty and eloquence.[349]

Notices of the purple-capped lory, a close relative of the parrot and a native of southeast Asia, began to appear in Europe during the last generation of the sixteenth century. G. M. Bonardi observes that there are certain birds of Sumatra

[338] Letter of the *Nürnberger Rat* to Anton Tetzel and Pirckheimer (July 10, 1505) in E. Reiche (ed.), *Willibald Pirckheimers Briefwechsel* (Jena, 1930), I, 258.

[339] G. F. Pölnitz, *Jakob Fugger* . . . (Tübingen, 1949–51), II, 179.

[340] Delaunay, *op. cit.* (n. 293), p. 150.

[341] Killermann, *op. cit.* (n. 233), pp. 56–57.

[342] For general commentary see H. Friedman, *The Symbolic Goldfinch* (New York, 1946), pp. 54–55.

[343] See M. J. Freidländer, "Der Meister mit dem Papagei," *Phoebus*, II (1949), 49–52.

[344] Marcucci, *op. cit.* (n. 186), pp. 146–47.

[345] *Cosmographia* (1550), p. 1175; also see K. Gesner, *Historiae animalium* (Zurich, 1551–87), II, 689–94.

[346] *Hieroglyphica* (1556), 166 recto and verso; cf. also Ripa, *op. cit.* (n. 138), p. 139.

[347] *Emblematum* . . . (Strassburg, 1581), fig. 19.

[348] *Op. cit.* (n. 145), Bk. III, pp. 92–93.

[349] *Op. cit.* (n. 138), Bk. II, p. 108.

called "nuri" (Malay for lory) which are of the size of a parrot but more colorful.[350] Linschoten asserts that they are native to the Moluccas and that "both in color and beauty of feathers they surpasse all birds and Parrots [whatsoever]."[351] He also reports that efforts were made to bring living lorys to Portugal as a present for the king, but that the birds were too delicate to stand the voyage and always died on the way. But perhaps Linschoten was not fully informed. The painting of Niccolo dell'Abbate called "Young Man with a Parrot" (pl. 135) seems to depict a Malayan lory rather than an Indian parrot.[352]

The parrot was sometimes called a "bird of paradise," even after the word "parrot" had come into common usage during the sixteenth century.[353] As described originally by Vincent of Beauvais in his natural history of the thirteenth century, the "bird of paradise" had nothing in common with the exquisite birds (*Paradiseidae*) of the East Indies to which the name was eventually applied in the sixteenth century.[354] The islanders, who made a business of selling the plumages of these birds, removed both the wings and legs of those they put on the market to give more prominence to the valuable tuft of plumes. Since the Europeans regularly brought these costly plumages back home, the idea gained currency, based upon examination of the plumages and upon stories told to their purchasers, that these birds never alight, live only from the dews of heaven, and fly only with the wind and always into the sun.[355] The German word commonly used in the sixteenth century to describe them was *Lufftvogel*. In Europe the plumages were given as gifts to monarchs, nobles, and prelates for their collections of curiosities.[356]

Brueghel and Frans Francken the Elder in their "Paradise" landscapes were among the first to use these birds of the Moluccas and New Guinea in their paintings.[357] Two studies in water color and gouache of a plumage are preserved

[350] *La minera del mondo* (Venice, 1589), p. 106v.

[351] A. C. Burnell and P. A. Tiele (eds.), *The Voyage of John Hughen van Linschoten to the East Indies* (London, 1885), I, 307.

[352] For a colored painting of a later date see the "Collared Parrot" in J. Barraband's *Exotic Birds* (New York, 1963).

[353] For example, see the poem by John Skelton (1460?–1529) which begins: "My name is parrot, a bird of Paradise." The word "parrot" is of unknown origin, but it may be related to the French *Pierrot*, a diminutive of *Pierre*.

[354] Robin, *op. cit.* (n. 192), p. 155. On the Latinized forms of the Malay names that were first used in Europe see *Asia*, I, 598. The term "Mamuco Diata" (*Manuk dewato* in Malay) was first used by Maximilian of Transylvania, and it continued to be used by many other writers of the sixteenth century.

[355] Compare Camoëns' lines as translated by Sir Richard Burton: "Here dwell the golden fowls whose home is air and never earthward save in death may fare." Also see the poetic description of them in the *Divine Weekes* of Du Bartas. For lore based on Cardano's account see Delaunay, *op. cit.* (n. 293), p. 154. The European commentators often confuse the "bird of paradise" with the mythical phoenix.

[356] For example, the doge of Venice in 1461 sent a beautiful and costly plumage to King Matthias Corvinus of Hungary (see Killermann, *op. cit.* [n. 233], p. 57). Queen Elizabeth of England kept a plumage of the bird of paradise at Windsor Castle (C. Williams [trans. and ed.], *Thomas Platter's Travels in England* [London, 1937], p. 215). Ambroise Paré and J. C. Scaliger also had plumages in their collections (Delaunay, *op. cit.* [n. 293], p. 154).

[357] Killermann, *op. cit.* (n. 233), p. 57.

in the university library at Erlangen. Probably works of the early sixteenth century, they are careful depictions of both sides of a single plumage. For a time the Erlangen studies were attributed to Dürer, but it is now thought to be highly improbable that he painted them.[358] In the Uffizi at Florence there is a painting by Jacopo Ligozzi which shows two birds of paradise standing on a fig branch, a posture that runs counter to the tradition that they have no feet. In his "Garden of Eden" (pl. 144), Roelant Savery shows two birds of paradise streaking across the sky, typically without their wings and feet.

The woodcut artists likewise depict the bird of paradise in accord with the prevailing traditions. Konrad Gesner, who evidently received a plumage through Peutinger, includes a woodcut of it in his *Historiae animalium*.[359] Juan de Boria, in the moral emblems he designed for Philip II, shows it as a symbol for no middle ground, since it must be either completely in repose or constantly in flight.[360] In an emblematic chapter entitled "It cannot know Intercourse with Land" Camerarius includes an etching (pl. 139) by Sibmacher showing the bird of paradise flying high above mountains, lakes, and castles as a symbol of ethereal elevation above earthly affairs. In the text which accompanies the etching he repeats most of what Maximilian of Transylvania reported early in the century and notes that other writers tell of a bird of Mexico, similar to the bird of paradise, whose feathers are used by the Chinese to make colorful feather pictures.[361]

Various other exotic birds from the East were added to the repertory of European artists during the sixteenth century. The peacock, which had been admired in India by the soldiers of Alexander, was eventually raised in northern Europe and used as a model by painters and weavers. When served at the banquet table, roast peacock was usually "eaten with gynger."[362] Early in the sixteenth century a watercolor was produced in Europe of the cormorant,[363] a European bird that was trained in England and Scandinavia, as it was in Persia and China, to catch fish. Aldrovandi and Jacob Bontius, the great naturalists, describe the horned corbeau of the East Indies and call it the rhinoceros bird.[364] Bontius includes an engraving of it in his *Historiae naturalis . . . Indiae orientalis* (1658).[365] Two birds from Japan, a male and a female, were dispatched to Pope Pius V (reigned 1566–72), but the male died and the female soon languished to death. It may be this bird whose portrait (pl. 141) is shown in Camerarius' *Symbolorum*. It is pictured as having a high ruff and crown, and in the caption it, or one like it, is said to be native to the island of Catigan (Canigao?) in the Philippines.[366] On December 4, 1596, Dutch voyagers to Java were given a gift of an emu by

---

[358] See E. Bock (comp.), *Die Zeichnungen in der Universitätsbibliothek Erlangen* (Frankfurt, 1929), I, 53, n. 164; II, pl. 164. Also see Panofsky, *op. cit.* (n. 23), II, nos. 1341–42.

[359] *Op. cit.* (n. 244), II, 612.

[360] Boria, *op. cit.* (n. 176), p. 50; also see Capaccio, *op. cit.* (n. 138), Bk. II, p. 21.

[361] Camerarius, *op. cit.* (n. 145), Bk. III, pp. 86–87. Also see above, p. 18.

[362] As quoted in Phipson, *op. cit.* (n. 337), pp. 220–21.

[363] For a reproduction see Panofsky, *op. cit.* (n. 23), II, no. 1309.

[364] *Dictionnaire raisonné et universel des animaux* (Paris, 1759), III, 703.

[365] Pp. 63–64.

[366] Camerarius, *op. cit.* (n. 145), Bk. III, pp. 88–89.

the prince of Sidayu in whose port they lay at anchor. In the account of this episode the author reports that the emu, or *eme* in the "Indian languages," is a native of the island of Banda. The emu, which returned to Holland in 1597 aboard the "Amsterdam," was studied by L'écluse, and engraved by Hans Sibmacher (pl. 140).[367] Eventually the emu was purchased by the Elector of Cologne as a gift for Emperor Rudolf's menagerie, and its eggs were added to the emperor's collection of natural rarities.[368] It was sketched at Prague by Georg Hoefnagel, and Roelant Savery includes it at the center of his "Orpheus with the Animals" (pl. 143).[369] The emperor's collection of animals also included two dodo birds from Mauritius, which Savery sketched in pencil and chalk (pl. 142).

All the foregoing Asian animals, except the tiger, came to Europe over the sea route and were consequently associated with the discoveries and with south Asia. Rarity, rather than large numbers, was the keynote to the popularity and impressiveness of these foreign beasts. Thirteen monstrous elephants and three unbelievable rhinoceroses made a far greater impact upon art than the more numerous and more commonly known monkeys and parrots. The rarer beasts, including the first and only emu, were sketched from life immediately after their appearance in Europe. In the case of the elephants and the rhinoceroses, a rash of depictions followed the arrival of each newcomer at Europe's artistic centers. Because exotic animals were often sent as presents from one ruler to another, they were seen by a wide public as living exemplars of Europe's great adventure in Asia. The most eminent artists, possibly because of official or public pressure as well as genuine interest, undertook their portrayal. The elephant had his Raphael, the tiger his Giulio Romano, and the rhinoceros his Dürer.

The animals drawn from life, such as Raphael's elephant or Giulio's tiger, were delineated naturalistically for the first time since Antiquity. And these naturalistic portraits became the artistic authorities for the true depiction of the Asian beasts throughout the sixteenth century. But the fantasizing of such naturalistic portraits began almost at once, and it could be argued that the greater the popularity of the beast the more varied became its depictions. Often the beasts were fantasized by reviving physical attributes from ancient or medieval prototypes and by adding them to or substituting them for features in the naturalistic portraits. Where there was no earlier artistic tradition of consequence, as in the case of the rhinoceros, the physical attributes of the naturalistic beast were sometimes suppressed, elongated, or redesigned. Dürer's rhinoceros itself, as contrasted to Burgkmair's more naturalistic animal, might be thought of as a fantasy based on the naturalistic sketch sent to him from Lisbon.[370] The persistence of the prenaturalistic tradition appears to be particularly strong among the

[367] For this story see L. Hulsius, *Erste Schiffart an die orientalische Indien* . . . (Frankfurt am Main, 1625), pp. 42–43.
[368] See above, p. 52.
[369] J. Fechner, "Die Bilder von Roelant Savery in der Eremitage," *Jahrbuch des kunsthistorischen Institutes der Universität Graz* (Graz, 1966–67), II, 97.
[370] For discussion of this point in relation to the importance of artistic prototypes as contrasted to the living or real model, see E. H. Gombrich, *Art and Illusion* (New York, 1965), p. 82.

woodcut artists, some of whom claim to have seen the living animal but none-theless depict it from earlier artistic prototypes. The Asian beasts, perhaps because they were not completely conventionalized, were also widely employed experimentally by sculptors, metalworkers, and decorative artists.

All the Asian animals, except the rhinoceros, figured prominently in sixteenth-century painting and had special appeal for the Mannerists. The elephant and the rhinoceros, possibly because of their greater plastic possibilities, were the only Asian beasts sculptured in stone. Among metalworkers the elephant, with medieval attributes added, was particularly popular. All the animals appeared in tapestries and woodcuts, where they were usually shown in fantasized depictions harking back to prenaturalistic prototypes. The bird of paradise, known only through its plumage and through literary descriptions, was depicted naturalisti-cally in numerous prints and paintings to the degree that information on it was available. Increasingly, over the course of the sixteenth century, the animals of Asia appeared in decorative designs, in the borders of tapestries, on ceramics, and as caryatids.

The symbolism connected with all the Asian animals, except the tiger, under-went profound change. The tiger, probably because it did not come to Europe via the sea route and was not therefore associated with the discoveries, is the only one of the animals to retain its symbolic meaning intact from the past. The rhinoceros, confused with the unicorn throughout history, was for the first time thought of as a separate beast. Since it was unknown to the Middle Ages, the rhinoceros was never Christianized. Its symbolism from Antiquity thus became the basis for its meaning to the sixteenth century, perhaps because of all the animals it most nearly lived up to the reputation given it by ancient writers. In the sixteenth century the animals that had been Christianized received secular attributes as well, perhaps in recognition of their heathen origin. The elephant became a symbol for the wise and virtuous ruler (Maximilian I, Francis I, and the Medicis), a hallmark of the overseas interests of the city of Antwerp, and a representation of the frivolous social creature. The monkey, more than the elephant, lost its medieval attributes. It exchanged the taint of the sinner for the symbolism of the clown, as it became less closely identified with barbarians and more with civilized man. The parrot forfeited its medieval virtue and increasingly became, as it had been to the ancients, an amusing mimic. The bird of paradise, which had no symbolic meaning for Europe before the sixteenth century, was simply assigned attributes by the writers of emblem books on the basis of what they knew, or thought they knew, about its characteristics.

The changing depiction and symbolism of the Asian animals show in micro-cosm something of Europe's response to the opening of direct and regular connec-tions with the East. The simple, overwhelming fact was that beasts which had been either completely or partially mythological were to be seen in Europe in the flesh and in accurate, naturalistic portraits. Artists, as might be expected, were quick to incorporate the overseas creatures into traditional European themes and designs. They did not hesitate to use Asian elephants in the depictions of Roman wars, or to show Orpheus surrounded by animals from a world unknown to him. Bosch and Savery, it might be argued, brought realistic foreign beasts into their paintings simply because Asian animals still continued to be fanciful and exotic in their appeal. But it is also true that the rhinoceros, which had previously been completely unknown, became a substantial and identifiable reality in life, literature, science, and art. Its mere existence provided confirmation both for the veracity of the writers of Antiquity and for the startling accounts of contemporary travelers to Asia. European artists, even while using the Asian animals for their own artistic purposes, had likewise to reckon with the fact, as the users of Dürer's woodcut did, that their creations could now be compared to the living models. The presence of the Asian beasts on European soil and in European art, coupled with the knowledge that they came from specific locales, helped substantially to produce a growing sense in Europe of the *reality* of Asia in all its aspects.

CHAPTER IV

Epilogue
Naturalism, Symbolism, and Ornament

The revelation of Asia did not fundamentally transform any of the European art forms. It did help to accelerate and perpetuate trends that were already in progress in naturalism, symbolism, and ornament. In the first half of the sixteenth century European painters and print-makers portrayed Asian products and animals naturalistically. Throughout the century the vocabulary of ornament was enriched and enlarged by the incorporation of maritime and Asian objects and motifs. Exotic and fantastic appeal was added to several art forms, especially monumental art and landscape architecture, by the employment of motifs and symbols which evoked the Orient. Asia and its exports furnished the makers of emblems with new challenges and suggestions. And, as time passed, many of Europe's traditional symbols lost their old meaning or acquired new ones as the *reality* of Asia increasingly became intellectually worrisome. The problem of integrating Asia into Europe's conceptions of civilization and art finally contributed to the unsettling of some traditional beliefs and revered conventions.

A host of analogues and resemblances between European and Asian arts have long titillated students of "migration art." It has often been pointed out that monsters, demons, and animals were similarly depicted in both artistic traditions as stock features from the earliest times onward. The transparent globes of Bosch, as well as those of other Flemish and a number of Venetian artists, have been compared to the cosmic glass globes of Eastern painters which purport to show that the real world is as fragile and as readily destructible as glass. The animation of unlikely objects such as rocks has been related to a sensitivity felt in both East and West to the mysterious agitations of the material world.[1]

[1] J. Baltrušaitis, *Le moyen-âge fantastique* (Paris, 1955), pp. 207–20. For a more detailed statement and illustrations see my *Asia in the Making of Europe*, I (Chicago, 1965), 71–74, and following p. 52. Also L. Olschki, "Asiatic Exoticism and the Italian Art of the Early Renaissance," *Art Bulletin*, XXVI (1944), 95–108.

Vague references to the spiritual relationships between Manueline and Indian architecture likewise reflect the feeling that the interactions between the arts of Europe and Asia have never been fully explored or comprehended.

The opening of the sea route to India brought about more intimate artistic contact but only slightly affected the speculations of certain art historians about affinities.[2] Students of Indo-Portuguese arts have been able to show definitively that export textiles, furniture, featherworks, and porcelains were made in Asia to appeal to the tastes of Europeans. In most instances Indo-Portuguese products were European in design or shape and Oriental in ornament. The correspondences in subject matter and artistic treatment between European and Sung and Ming landscape paintings have repeatedly been debated by scholars. But so far no definite evidence has been adduced to establish Europe's debt to the landscape art of China. The resemblances in idea and technique between the composite pictures of the Indian miniaturists and Arcimboldo have suggested to some that the Italian master was inspired by composite Indian paintings that were possibly available to him. Still others have proposed that the heads of death on Jesuit sarcophagi have intellectual and spiritual affinities with Bushidō and with Oriental depictions of the cycles of death.[3] The serpentine line has been identified as a link between Oriental and Western ornament, and in the West between the decorative techniques employed in the Gothic, Manneristic, and Rococo styles.[4] Mere multiplication of such analogues does not add substantially to the case for influence. It does heighten the desire, particularly when taken in conjunction with what Asian artistic prototypes have been found in the collections, for more serious investigation of the possible Asian influences upon the arts and artists of sixteenth-century Europe and upon the origins of the Baroque style.

Examples of most of the portable arts of Asia arrived in Europe over the course of the sixteenth century. Porcelains, jewels, pearls, and textiles were brought into European markets and collections in greater quantities than ever before. Porcelain table services at some periods in the sixteenth century were reckoned to be far cheaper than those of massive silver. Chinese paintings, at least ten of them, were acquired by European collectors and two are still preserved in Vienna. Japanese folding screens (*byōbus*) were given as gifts to Philip

[2] J. Strzygowski (*Asiatische Miniaturenmalerei* [Klagenfurth, 1933], p. 222) contends that the artists of sixteenth-century Europe, who were subject to the academic conventions of Renaissance art, must have greeted the appearance of art objects which did not follow these rules as a shower is welcomed after a long drought. He also contends that European art at this period had no influence upon the arts of Asia because of its sterile, academic approach. Benjamin Rowland, Jr., a recent commentator, in his *Art in East and West* (Cambridge, Mass., 1954) frankly eschews all efforts to study the influence of one culture upon the other and contents himself with comparing how the artists of Asia and the West treat the same subjects. Also see T. Bowie *et al.*, *East-West in Art* (Bloomington, Ind., 1966).

[3] E. Mâle, *L'art religieux après le Concile de Trente* (Paris, 1932), pp. 207–8.

[4] L. Salerno, "Arte, scienza e collezioni nel manierismo," in *Scritti . . . in onore di Mario Salmi* (Rome, 1963), III, 210. It should also be observed that Jahangir was much impressed by the European engravings brought to the Mughul court by the Jesuits, that he had some of them copied by native artists and had others framed in ornamental borders reminiscent of Netherlandish ornament of the latter half of the sixteenth-century. See E. Kuhnel and H. Goetz, *Indische Buchmalereien . . .* (Berlin, 1924), pp. 50–51.

II and the Vatican. Indian miniature paintings on ivory and in books are listed in the Prague collections of Rudolf II. Lacquered furniture, boxes, chests, and musical instruments from the East appear repeatedly in the inventories of all the great collections. Chinese books, some with illustrations, were available in Lisbon, Rome, the Escorial, Madrid, Paris, and Prague. Asian featherworks, as distinguished from those of Mexico and Peru, evoked constant interest.

European amateur artists in Asia, sometimes in collaboration with natives, prepared drawings and watercolors of daily life in those Eastern centers held by the Portuguese. Other Europeans sent or brought specimens of Asian flora and fauna to Europe. Oddities of every conceivable kind—back scratchers, peculiarly shaped rocks, and fans—were collected by the voyagers to titillate the curious. Indigo replaced woad in the dyeing vats of Europe as blue coloring. Princely and scholarly collectors sought to learn more clearly about the geographical dimensions of Asia by collecting maps. A few Asians, natives of India, China, Japan, and the Philippines, could be found in Europe at various times throughout the century.

Collections of art and "wonders" were assembled by many of the leading rulers, prelates, merchants, and scholars of Europe. Only a few artists and artisans had collections of their own. But over the course of the century most of the major collections were opened to an increasingly larger public. Artists in Florence, Rome, Vienna, Antwerp, and Prague used the collections as sources for their works. Craftsmen, like the makers of the Medici porcelains and the Venetian workers in wood, sought to imitate the Chinese porcelains and lacquers that were on display in those cities. "Indian products," a generic term which never disappears from the inventories (see Appendix to chapter i, p. 46), are supplemented in the listings of some of the collections by specific references to Chinese, Japanese, and East Indian products. A consciousness grew, without doubt, that Asian arts were products of several rather than a single civilization. The collections of wonders of the worlds of nature and art provoked astonishment, stimulated discussion, and inspired reflection about the arts and the civilizations from which they came.

But how did European artists themselves respond to the presence of these "subtle *ingenia*" of people in distant lands? Dürer, stirred by their "wonderful works of art," was moved to collect Eastern oddities in Antwerp. Raphael painted the Asian elephant naturalistically and Giulio Romano brought it and the Bengal tiger into his works. Woodcut artists, flower painters, and book illustrators studiously copied those samples of Asian flora which they knew. Philips van Winghe of Louvain sketched the tower and gate of Azuchi Castle from the Japanese folding screens in Rome (see pls. 50 and 51). Persian carpets, Chinese porcelains and lacquerware, and Asian animals were incorporated into European paintings. Exotic effects were achieved in various art forms by bringing lifelike palm trees, monkeys, and seashells into the depictions. The illustrators of the costume books of the late sixteenth century modeled their designs on the Oriental costumes themselves, or copied their depictions from the costumes shown on porcelains and paintings. From this evidence it is clear that no implacable cultural, philosophical, or religious hostility to the distant East prevented artists from bringing Asian objects into their creations and depicting them realistically and naturalistically.

Naturalism, or the effort of Renaissance artists to copy nature faithfully, certainly received a stimulus from the introduction into Europe of strange new plants, animals, and objects from Asia. In drawing and painting particularly, the artists copied animate and inanimate models with sincere fidelity.[5] Depicting exotic beasts from live models lent a naturalism far surpassing in realism any of the medieval artistic prototypes which were on hand. Artists were careful to give correct proportions to their beasts and to show them in their proper relationships to one another. And the sixteenth-century artist asked questions, explicit or implicit, which would not have occurred to earlier artists. Should the elephant be depicted as taller than the rhinoceros? Was the elephant really as crude in its bodily proportions as it was often portrayed? How much did an elephant weigh, and how much food and drink could it consume? Possibly in response to these questions, some of the artists showed the elephant in different poses, in scale, and with other beasts, especially the rhinoceros and monkey, as well as with humans. Many questions of the same type were also raised about the naturalistic treatment of exotic plants, fruits, trees, and flowers.

As each new elephant appeared in Europe, it was first portrayed naturalistically. A clear tradition developed in the painting of elephants which led back to Raphael's beast as the prototype for naturalistic depiction. But Raphael's successors almost at once began to fantasize his elephant, perhaps because it was better known to them. Those who fantasized elephants usually did so deliberately for their own artistic purposes. The art objects of Asia, on the other hand, were not fantasized by the Mannerist painters, perhaps because they were less adaptable to such treatment than elephants and other beasts.

Beturbaned Orientals, as well as naturalistic Asian beasts and flowers, are common in sixteenth-century paintings. Although Oriental costumes were one of the first features to be depicted realistically, European artists were slow to copy the distinctive features of Asian persons. The Japanese legates, drawn from life, were made to look only slightly Oriental, perhaps because they were sketched in their European clothes (pl. 35). But by the end of the century woodcut illustrations showed persons more clearly identifiable as Chinese (pl. 64). Paintings of carpets, textiles, and porcelains were sometimes accurate enough to reflect the provenance and period of the originals.

The print-makers tended generally to be less consistent than the painters in their response to the products and curiosities of Asia. Perhaps this was related

---

[5] Naturalism in the minor arts of the sixteenth century exhibited a strange form called "le style rustique." Bronze and plaster snakes, shells, and insects were made from molds cast around the creatures themselves. Bernard Palissy created (1570–89) a grotto in this style for the gardens of the Tuileries which inspired many imitations. See E. Kris, "Der Stil 'Rustique,'" *Jahrbuch der kunsthistorischen Sammlungen in Wien*, N.S., I (1926), 137–208.

to the fact that the earliest reports reached northern Europe, and thus the major print-makers, through intermediaries. But it does not follow that the print-makers were less responsive than the painters to external stimuli. Three major artists of the woodcut—Dürer, Burgkmair, and Altdorfer—produced individualistic sketches of the rhinoceros in the year 1515. It is very likely that they all used as sources the sketches of the rhinoceros drawn by unknown artists from the living model. The depictions by Burgkmair and Altdorfer were unfamiliar to or ignored by later artists, while Dürer's woodcut, for all its peculiarities, became the prototype of the rhinoceros in art. Certain later artists sought to give their own individualistic touches to Dürer's rhinoceros by elongating, distorting, or suppressing its distinctive attributes. And the appearance of a second rhinoceros in Spain in 1581 brought about a brief and unsuccessful effort to throw off the dominance of Dürer's woodcut. Nonetheless Dürer's partly fanciful beast, even more so than Raphael's very naturalistic elephant, managed to retain its predominance long after more realistic depictions were known in Europe.

But while remaining subservient to Dürer's rhinoceros, the print-makers brought more Asian-related subjects into their depictions than the painters. In all probability this tendency was stimulated by their closer association with book illustration and map production. They ransacked the collections of curiosities, borrowed from earlier depictions, and created from their own imaginations the illustrations of oddities described in the travel, natural science, and cosmographical books. There is also good evidence to show that they based certain of their works upon literary descriptions alone, a facet of their activity which finds no parallel among the painters.[6] Like the painters and tapestry weavers, the graphic artists were inclined to use the palm tree and Asian animals to achieve exotic effects. Unlike the painters, they did not ordinarily incorporate colorful objects into their representations. A few of the graphic artists (especially Hans Sibmacher) depicted the latest oddities as they arrived to give examples of what the discoverers were finding in the East. Others followed sketches made in the field, the main example being the De Bry family (pls. 147 and 148).

The print-makers and tapestry weavers were more experimental and topical than the painters in their choice of themes. Victories won by the Portuguese in the East were celebrated in woodcuts and tapestries shortly after they became known in Europe. The painters ordinarily restricted themselves to traditional themes: Bacchus in India, Noah's ark, adoration of the Magi, the flight from Egypt, four parts of the world, the exile from the Garden of Eden, Orpheus and the animals. While the figures, landscapes, and varieties of animals in these paintings became more Eastern, the themes themselves underwent no fundamental change. It was left to Jean Macer, a commentator rather than an artist, to suggest that all three of the Magi should be depicted as kings of countries to the east of the Holy Land.

[6] A notable exception is the painting "The Discovery of America" by Jan Mostart (d. 1556). For a reproduction see A. F. Mirande and G. S. Overdiep (eds.), *Het Schilder-Boek van Carel van Mander* (Amsterdam, 1936), facing p. 233.

The painters, it appears, were more firmly bound by artistic conventions than the print-makers, perhaps because of the domination wielded over their art by the Italian masters. They also were more firmly committed to Humanism and the revival of Antiquity and less involved than the graphic artists in matters that brought them into touch with commerce, cartography, and current affairs. Humanists and artists were openly fearful that European art might suffer from contact with Asia. From the mid-thirteenth century onward, Tartars and Mongols had been depicted in European art and literature as legions of the Anti-Christ, demons of hell, and heralds of the world's end.[7] Leonardo confided fears of this sort to his *Notebooks*. Michelangelo, according to D'Ollanda, sought to reckon with Asia by including it within his conception of Antiquity. A woodcut artist, Melchior Lorck, went to the Near East for the express purpose of seeking the true roots of Antiquity. Many of the Jesuit commentators in Asia associated its art monuments with the remains of Antiquity and even expressed the belief that some of them were built by Alexander the Great and his successors. The conviction grew, as Cardano expressed it, that the discoveries had unsettled Europe's certitude about the objectives and possibilities of the arts.

While Asia evoked sentiments of fear and uncertainty, it came to have other meanings as well for Europe. Perhaps most overwhelming was the impression of limitless wealth as Europeans viewed Asia's seemingly inexhaustible outpouring of precious stones, woods, and spices. Asia also had strong associations with the mysterious and exotic. Not only was Asia remote and distant from the concerns of Europe, but it was also the habitat of prodigious beasts, its soil produced aromatic woods and hallucinatory drugs, and its peoples created recondite porcelains and lacquerware that could not be duplicated in Europe. In the collections of curiosities, where seeds, earths, and stones from Asia were ranged alongside its gems and featherworks, the observer was able to view in miniature the mystical and cosmic relationship between art and nature. The works of nature from Asia were obviously thought to be as subtle and foreign as its works of art. Asia's rarities produced stupefaction, in the words of R. Borghini, and caused comparisons to be made between the admirable qualities of the rhinoceros (nature) and the monastery of Belém (art).

It is these varied meanings which Asia had for sixteenth-century Europe that helped to produce new symbolic attributes for the Asian animals, jewels, and woods that Europeans had long known. The animals were secularized in their symbolism as it became clear that they came from heathen lands of great wealth and high civilization. Eastern traditions were mingled even more intimately with European beliefs in the new attributes ascribed to rare woods and precious stones. Landscape gardens like those at Lisbon, Bomarzo, and Castello were given a mysterious and bizarre appearance by the mythical and Asian beasts sculptured in stone that decorated them. The makers of hieroglyphic emblems increasingly favored symbols of Asia in constructing those of their allegorical

7 Baltrušaitis, *op. cit.* (n. 1), pp. 183–88.

pictures and proverbs which stressed rarity and wonder. Creators of medals and coats-of-arms increasingly used the rhinoceros and the elephant as emblems, for the symbolism of these beasts had come to have an accepted secular significance.

Throughout the sixteenth century an effort was made in the triumphs to produce a permanent, symbolic representation of Asia with universal appeal. In the "Triumph of Maximilian" (1526) the people of Calicut and the elephant (pl. 87) represented Asia. King Henry II's entry into Paris in 1549 was symbolized by Dürer's rhinoceros as an emblem of courage, and possibly as a symbol of his marriage to Catharine de' Medici, whose family also used the rhinoceros as one of its emblems (pls. 124, 125). When the French royal couple visited Rouen in 1550, the triumphal procession was led by horses dressed as elephants carrying towers and trophies. Triumphal arches and pedestals were erected in Lisbon in 1581 to celebrate the formal entry of Philip II in which every major Portuguese conquest in the East was depicted as a woman presenting her gifts to the king. The engraving by Pieter van der Borcht (see above, p. 93) of the entry of Archduke Ernst of Austria into Antwerp in 1593 shows beturbaned people leading Asian animals, a return in spirit to the "people of Calicut." The elephant, in particular, was the living manifestation of Asia throughout most of the sixteenth century, and a replica of it in wood eventually became one of the symbols of the city of Antwerp (pl. 115). To the triumphal processions themselves, the symbols of Asia lent a new note of exoticism which evoked Europe's connections with the overseas world.

In the last generation of the sixteenth century, artists again took up the classical theme of representing each continent by an allegorical figure. Ideally these personifications of the "four parts of the world" were conceived of as pictorial epitomes of each continent's essential characteristics. But the allegorical figures which represent Asia have for the modern eye few discernible attributes which set them apart. The personification of Asia prepared by Tommaso Laureati for the Vatican in the time of Pope Gregory XIII (reigned 1572–85),[8] or that of Pauwels Franck painted in the 1580's for the Fugger castle at Kirchheim, show few characteristics themselves which evoke the Asia of reality. In Franck's triumphal procession the lady who represents Asia carries a sign to tell the viewer what she personifies (pl. 34). Her attendants wear turbans and carry exotic gifts; her cart is decorated with bejeweled hangings and drawn by a pair of camels. Similar to these depictions was that in the Caprarola Palace (built after 1555) of the Farnese near Viterbo.[9]

It is conceivable, however, that the modern viewer of these depictions does not react sensitively to the elements that were considered exotic and emblematic by sixteenth-century artists and connoisseurs. The title page of Ortelius' *Theatrum orbis terrarum* (1570), a copper engraving by Frans Hogenberg and his

---

[8] Mâle, *op. cit.* (n. 3), pp. 399–401.

[9] For a contemporary description of the Farnese painting see J. A. F. Orbaan (ed.), *Documenti sul Barocco in Roma* (Rome, 1920), p. 381. A world map, displayed as early as 1578, was in the same room, decorated with portraits of Columbus, Vespucci, Magellan, Cortez, and Marco Polo.

assistants, features symbolic figures of the "five continents" ("Magellanica" is the continent added). Verses in the frontispiece (p. A3) by Adolf van Meetkerke, a philologist and alderman of Bruges, identify and explain the portraits of the continents. According to Meetkerke, "Asia," at the left of the title page, is a richly clad and bejeweled Oriental princess who holds a thurible in her left hand in which Eastern gums burn to give off incense.[10] Cesare Ripa in his *Iconologia* (first published at Rome in 1593),[11] a handbook on allegories and their meanings, proposes a similar symbol for Asia. In his view Asia is a lady crowned with a beautiful garland of flowers and fruits and clad in a lavish costume completely embroidered with gold thread, pearls, and precious stones. "Asia" carries in her left hand a bough decorated with the leaves and fruits of cassia, pepper, and cloves; in her right hand she holds a censer from which arises an aromatic cloud of smoke. Behind the lady a camel sits on its knees in a resting position (pl. 145). Ripa explains that the garland signifies Asia's temperate climate. The lavish gown symbolizes "the great plenty which exists in this happiest part of the world" and illustrates the costume of its people. Ripa suggests that models for the fruits and leaves of spices can be seen by artists in Mattioli's commentary on Dioscorides. The smoking censer, like the bough, reminds the viewer that Asia is the land which exports aromatic spices, woods, resins, and gums. From the modern viewpoint such interpretations, particularly of the burning censer, seem vague and dubious. But it is precisely this difference in understanding that makes it difficult for the modern student to sense clearly what Asia meant or what had exotic appeal for Renaissance thought and art.

The most explicit of the representations of Asia is the engraving executed by the De Bry brothers that graces the title page of their *Pars quarta Indiae orientalis* (Frankfurt, 1601). The frame which surrounds the title and the publication data epitomizes on one engraved page what products of Asia attracted the attention of artists (pl. 146). Constructed like the proscenium of a theater or a triumphal arch, the frame is supported by a semirealistic elephant on the left and a replica of Dürer's rhinoceros on the right. Through an archway which supports the stage is a maritime scene in which naked and breech-clothed fishermen are trying to land a whale, a depiction which harks back to Dürer's famous print of the whale and stands as a possible reference to the ambergris that was imported from the East. On each side of the stage are vases of exotic flowers, those on the right being easily identifiable as irises (here called *Crocus Indicus*) and those on the left as yuccas. On the top level of the framework emus stand on either side, facing each other. Under the tail of each emu a censer burns, its gums and resins giving off aromatic smoke. The apex of the proscenium is crowned with a bowl of exotic fruits and flowers in which pineapples and tulips can readily be recognized. On either side of the bowl stands a parrot, each of which faces one of the

[10] Further discussion in C. Koeman, *The History of Abraham Ortelius and His "Theatrum orbis terrarum"* (Lausanne, 1964), pp. 33–34.
[11] I have here paraphrased the edition of 1611 (Padua), pp. 356–58. The first edition of Ripa had no illustrations and was intended primarily for the use of literary artists. Woodcut illustrations were first added to this work in the edition of 1611.

emus. The construction of the frame and its scrollery are strictly Western and classical, but all the overt decoration is Oriental, contemporary, and naturalistic.

Ornament and decoration were the artistic means most commonly employed to evoke the exotic Orient. From Romanesque times onward, the decorative motifs, devices, and patterns of Eastern art were periodically added to the vocabulary of European ornament. The interlaced arabesques of Muslim metal works were imitated by European goldsmiths and ironworkers and were adapted to the decorative plans of ceramicists and woodworkers. Chinese designs appeared mainly in European textiles, but the ornamentation on the gates of St. Mark's Cathedral in Venice consists likewise of Chinese scrolls, lozenges, and bats.[12] Designers of book covers used dragon motifs from China that they copied from Persian or other Near Eastern arts.[13] The great voyages of discovery began as early as the fifteenth century to inspire decorative motifs in the arts of the maritime countries which symbolized the great achievements being made on the high seas.[14] The rediscovery in Rome of the Golden House of Nero with its subterranean rooms decorated with "monstrous" paintings helped to stimulate a lively interest during the sixteenth century in experimenting with new, exotic ornamental motifs. About 1520 Giovanni da Udine brought the Asian elephant into his ornamental paintings in the loggia of the Vatican (pls. 149, 150). And the steady arrival in Europe of products of Asia and creations of Asian art with their novel forms and decorative designs continued to enrich the repository of motifs available to European designers of ornament.

The following quotation from the autobiography of Benvenuto Cellini (1500–1571) reveals how one sixteenth-century artist reacted to the ornament on products of foreign art:

About this time [1530] there fell into my hands some little Turkish poniards; the handle as well as the blade of these daggers was made of iron and so too was the sheath. They were engraved by means of iron implements with foliage in the most exquisite Turkish style, very neatly filled in with gold. *The sight of them stirred in me a great desire to try my own skill in that branch, so different from the others which I practiced; and finding that I succeeded to my satisfaction, I executed several pieces. Mine were far more beautiful and more durable than the Turkish, and this for diverse reasons.* One was that I cut my grooves much deeper and with wider trenches in the steel; for this is not usual in Turkish work. Another was that the Turkish arabesques are only composed of arum leaves with a few small sunflowers; and though these have a certain grace, they do not yield so lasting a pleasure as the patterns which we use. It is true that in Italy we have several different ways of designing foliage; the Lombards, for example, construct very beautiful patterns by copying the leaves of briony and ivy in exquisite curves which are extremely agreeable to the eye; the Tuscans and the Romans make a better choice, because they imitate the leaves of the acanthus,

12 L. Einstein, "A Chinese Design in St. Mark's at Venice," *Revue archéologique*, 5th ser., XXIV (1926), 28.
13 R. Ettinghausen, "Near Eastern Book Covers and Their Influence on European Bindings," *Ars orientalis*, III (1959), 113–31.
14 J. Evans, *Style in Ornament* (London, 1950), p. 39.

commonly called bear's-foot, with its stalks and flowers, curling in divers wavy lines; and into these arabesques one may excellently well insert the figures of little birds and different animals by which the good taste of the artist is displayed. Some hints for creatures of this sort can be observed in nature among the wild flowers, as, for instance, in snapdragons and some few other plants, which must be combined, and developed with the help of fanciful imaginings by clever draughtsmen. Such arabesques are called grotesques by the ignorant. ... Well, then, I designed patterns of this kind, and filled them in with gold, as I have mentioned; and they were far more pleasing to the eye than the Turkish.[15]

Like Cellini, Albrecht Dürer was fascinated by the new decorative possibilities he saw in foreign arts. As we know from his own testimony, he acquired "a very pretty piece of porcelain" while he was in Antwerp in 1520–21.[16] Several years earlier (*ca.* 1515) he seems to have been attracted by Chinese porcelains and lacquers as sources for new design ideas. In his drawings of fantastic pillars (pl. 29) he copied vases of the late Sung or early Ming periods and incorporated them into his drawings to provide new shapes and lines for his ornamental composition. The lotus-leaf frieze shown on the vase with a broad middle and the thin dragon-like handles on the taller vase help to link these Dürer ornamental drawings definitively to the inspiration of Chinese porcelains.[17] Possibly under Dürer's influence the "Antwerp Mannerists," who flourished between 1505 and 1530, sought to bring a new and restless spirit to traditional subjects by elongating and slenderizing the human body, by clothing it in overly elegant finery, and by adding Oriental decorative elements to traditional European objects.[18]

In the Netherlands the midcentury experiments of Cornelis Floris with grotesques also provide an excellent example of how overseas and Asian objects were incorporated into ornament. While continuing in their designs to employ elements from the ornamental grotesques of Rome and Fontainebleau, Floris and his followers introduced specific traits into their compositions which were derived from extra-European sources. The most singular of the new traits were the circular feather headdresses which Floris placed on his human figures.[19] Significantly, he first introduced this element into the series of ornamental designs called "Cups and Jugs" (1548) (pls. 76, 77). Examination of the cups and jugs themselves shows that Floris, like Dürer, was attracted by the shapes

---

[15] J. A. Symonds (trans.), *The Autobiography of Benevenuto Cellini* (New York, 1910), pp. 62–63. Italics mine.

[16] See above, p. 17.

[17] R. Schmidt, "China bei Dürer," *Zeitschrift des deutschen Vereins für Kunstwissenschaft*, VI (1939), 103–6.

[18] G. Marlier, *La renaissance flamande, Pierre Coeck d'Alost* (Brussels, 1966), pp. 110–12.

[19] See S. Schéle, *Cornelis Bos: A Study of the Origins of the Netherland Grotesque* (Stockholm, 1965), pp. 79–80. Schéle associates the featherdress idea with ancient Mexican art, and mentions the display of headdresses shown at the Royal Palace of Brussels in 1520. But, it should be noted that Burgkmair in his woodcut "People of Calicut" shows the natives of the Malabar Coast wearing circular feather headdresses. As stated earlier (see above, p. 18), I am convinced that European artists throughout the entire sixteenth century correctly associated the feather headdresses with both tropical Asia and America. For a description of Asian head ornaments see article by Carl A. Schmitz in *Encyclopedia of World Art*, Vol. V, col. 382.

and designs of Chinese porcelains.[20] The presence of seashells in Floris' ornamental designs makes even clearer the association of their idea with the overseas world. The exotic tendencies of Floris were further elaborated in the ornamental designs of Hans Vredeman de Vries (1527–1604), architect and painter of Antwerp. The cartouche (pl. 151) prepared for his *Grottesco in diversche Manieren* (Antwerp, 1555) brings together mythical and Asian birds and beasts into a design that anticipates the kinds of patterns which are generally associated with the chinoiserie of the eighteenth century. And, when it is noted that Floris' and Vredeman de Vries' grotesques were repeatedly used by other Netherlandish designers in ornamental frames and borders, it can be asserted that Asia made its contribution to the evolution of a Netherlandish ornament that became less graphic and more pictorial in the latter half of the sixteenth century.[21] The effects of this naturalistic, exotic Netherlandish ornament were felt as far away as Prague and Lisbon, where it had important influence during the sixteenth and seventeenth centuries on decoration in architecture, sculpture, and engraving.[22]

Joseph Boillot, who was employed by Henry IV of France as engineer and engraver, prepared a book of suggestions for caryatids that brought in the whole range of Asian animals as both functional elements and embellishments in his pillars.[23] He prepared sixty-four plates for his *Nouveaux pourtraits et figures de termes pour user en l'architecture* (Langres, 1592), and in a number of these he used the elephant, rhinoceros, tiger, and simians of the East as bases for the capital. In one instance he used the elephant as *termis*, and in another he attached it to the rhinoceros caryatid as an embellishment and as a symbol of the rhinoceros' traditional superiority in valor over the elephant (pls. 117, 128). Boillot's Asian animals, like other Asian objects in the works of European designers of ornament, are essentially naturalistic.

In addition to the contributions that Asia's exports made to the ornamental and design ideas of identifiable art modes and artists, the decorations on textiles, porcelains, and lacquerware continued to stimulate ornamental experiments in all branches of the visual arts. Ceramicists copied textile designs; architectural ornament inspired metalwork designs; painters imitated porcelain and lacquer decorations. Hieroglyphic designs from emblem books and iconographical elements—ships and sea monsters—from maps were incorporated into the patterned borders of tapestries. The naturalistic and flamboyant fantasies of the architectural ornament on Manueline edifices had their counterparts on gold and silverware. The Asian animals from Bosch's paintings turned up in engravings and on painted pottery. On the early tapestries and silver works the designs were

[20] Schéle (*op. cit.* [n. 19], pp. 79–80), does not associate the "Cups and Jugs" with Chinese porcelains.
[21] P. Fierens, *Le fantastique dans l'art flamand* (Brussels, 1947), p. 61; also A. J. J. Delen, *Histoire de la gravure dans les anciens Pays-Bas . . .* (Paris, 1935), II, 139–47.
[22] K. Chytil, *Die Kunst in Prag zur Zeit Rudolf II* (Prague, 1904), p. 5; M. S. Soria, "Francisco de Campos (?) and Mannerist Ornamental Design in Evora, 1555–1580," *Belas Artes* (Lisbon), 2d ser., No. 10 (1957), p. 37.
[23] Compare the caryatids of Turks shown in Pieter Coecke van Alost's *Moeurs et Fachons des Turces* (Antwerp, 1553). Also see discussion of them in Marlier, *op. cit.* (n. 18), pp. 60–61.

crowded with strange flora, fauna, people, and maritime motifs. Even some of the later silver settings for natural curiosities exhibited a profusion of exotic detail. Arcimboldo, like many Indian painters, arranged plants and animals in his paintings to portray human faces and figures in a clearly recognizable decorative plan. His flower mosaics were similar in spirit and intent to the feather mosaics of Asia and America, to Indian paintings of animals made up of people and gods, and reminiscent of the display techniques sometimes used by the collectors of curiosities.

The European preoccupation with adding exotica to the vocabulary of ornament was part of an effort to accommodate the strange and to bring it within the framework of traditional art. In the late Middle Ages church ornament in Spain and Gothic art in northern Europe had incorporated monstrous beasts and floral motifs without changing the subjective European character of the decorations. The objective inclusion of strange objects and motifs in European ornament continued into the sixteenth century, but with a subtle change taking place in its meaning for the artist and the viewer. During the Middle Ages exotic motifs streamed into Europe from various unidentified sources and seemingly without any relationship to the artistic tradition of a foreign culture of high achievement. In the sixteenth century the sources of the motifs became more localized for the European artist as he became aware of the relationship of the object before him to a civilization that was esteemed by many observers to be as cultivated as his own. Ornaments naturally continued to be borrowed and modified unconsciously in the decorative arts. A striking example is the case of the centipede-like creatures which figure prominently in the quilt designs made in Portuguese Asia. They are nothing but Indian efforts to reproduce the dragon-headed scrolls conventionally employed in ornament of the Italian Renaissance.[24] Nonetheless, with the awakening of consciousness about provenance, respect increased, and passive receptivity of eclectic features was gradually replaced by an active search for tighter artistic ties. Perhaps most striking of all was the tendency among most designers of ornament to depict the objects of Asia as naturalistically as they could, possibly because they were strange and exotic even so. But this was about as far as the influence went, for no evidence can be adduced to show that European artists of this period were even vaguely aware of the fundamental differences—for example, in perspective—between European and Chinese art.[25]

But it does not follow that the impact of Asia upon European ornament was negligible. In the new dispensation inaugurated by Raphael and his school a playful mood prevailed as ornament and design made room for more exuberant and colorful patterns that incorporated a variety of things—fantastic candelabra,

[24] See J. Irwin, "Reflections on Indo-Portuguese Art," *Burlington Magazine*, XCVII (1955), 388.

[25] For further discussion see R. dos Santos, "A India Portuguesa e as artes decorativas," *Belas Artes* (Lisbon), 2d ser., No. 7 (1954), pp. 5–16; also G. Bandmann, "Das Exotische in der europäischen Kunst," in *Der Mensch und die Künste: Festschrift Heinrich Lützeler* (Düsseldorf, 1962), pp. 341–44.

miniatures of the elephant Hanno (pl. 149), strands of pearls twining sinuously among bouquets of bright flowers.[26] The great voyages of discovery were reflected in the galleries painted with decorative maps which became popular, in tapestries ornamented with tawny goddesses, in bejeweled pendants shaped like ships, and in the real and mythical sea life carved in marble or chased in silver. In the maritime countries marine foliage, coral forms, nereids, and tritons were added to the repertory of ornament by architects, silverworkers, and tapestry weavers.[27]

In the northern countries a new orientation in design began with the masters of the minor arts as they looked for a new relationship between ground and ornament and for space in which to experiment with the grotesques of Antiquity and with the "heathen works" of Asia. These new designs, sometimes called "moresques," are distinctively ground ornaments without plastic attributes or possibilities. The effects of the "moresques" are entirely dependent upon the play of line and the use of two-toned contrast as they are painted, engraved, or etched on the ground. For example, an Elizabethan virginal or spinet preserved in the Victoria and Albert Museum is decorated with acanthus "moresques" and strewn flowers which recall the embellishments commonly used on the Nishiji lacquerware of Japan.[28] When so combined with more traditional motifs, the "moresques" contributed to the creation of an ornament that was, like the chamber of curiosities itself, an emblem of the cosmos. The "moresques" were therefore the ornaments most favored by late Manneristic artists in their search for mystical, universal symbols.[29]

The revelation of the East had its most profound effects upon the design of ornament and upon the new decorative features added to many art forms. In most cases the inclination was to bring naturalistic Asian objects into traditional European depictions in order to evoke exotic or unusual effects. Traditional biblical and classical themes remained dominant in painting, but the Magi were Orientalized and the strange animals in Noah's ark naturalized. A few new Asian themes, particularly relating to the overseas conquests, were added to the European repertory, but they were usually treated by artists along conventional lines. Although efforts were made to create a permanent and universal artistic symbolism for Asia, it was mainly the introduction of realistic Asian objects as decorative features that won acceptance. Like the displays of the *Wunderkammer*, the ornaments composed of realistic Asian objects, persons, or animals were strange enough to produce wonderment, to encourage experiment, and to invite contemplation.

---

[26] See A. von Salis, *Antike und Renaissance* (Zurich, 1947), pp. 37–43.

[27] J. Evans, *Pattern* (Oxford, 1931), I, 178.

[28] W. Holzhausen, *Lackkunst in Europa* (Brunswick, 1959), pp. 33–34.

[29] E. Forssmann, *Säule und Ornament: Studien zum Problem des Mannerismus in den nordischen Säulenbüchern und Vorlageblättern des 16. und 17. Jahrhunderts* (Stockholm, 1956), pp. 127–28; and G. Bandmann, "Ikonologie des Ornamentes und der Dekoration," *Jahrbuch für Asthetik und allgemeine Kunstwissenschaft*, IV (1958–59), 243–49.

While the artists made room for Asia's objects in their decorations and embellishments, the cultivated minds of Europe were likewise forced to accommodate their ideas to the *reality* of Asia and its civilization. Humanists, who had been inclined to regard everything as barbaric and contemptible which did not follow the ideals of European Antiquity, felt required to enlarge their definition of the scope of Antiquity to include Asia within it. The temples of India were compared to the great monuments of the Romans and were acknowledged to be the works of barbarians about which there was nothing barbarous.[30] Duarte Nunes de Lião in his *Descripção do reino de Portugal* (1610) wrote of Chinese porcelains: "the vases are the most beautiful things that man has invented."[31] Admiration for the wealth and creativity of Asia was accompanied by fears and uncertainty about its implications for the traditional arts and civilization of Europe. Generalized fears were given substance by the mystery which the East evoked through its strange products and unmatchable artistic creations. A sense prevailed among intellectuals that change was inevitably coming, and probably from the East. But, up to 1600, the menace of Asia was still very distant from the concerns of most Europeans. They were much more aware of Asia as another field in which the civilization of Europe had a new opportunity to display its flexibility, adaptability, and superiority.

In Europe both thought and art were being liberated from tradition as revolutionary changes were being faced in religion, politics, and the arts. To a society experiencing such profound internal changes, Asia was a peripheral problem that could best be handled by accommodation. The integrity of European civilization could readily remain unassailable by extending its benign rule to the rest of the world. For the artists of Mannerism, like the poets of the Pléiade, the arts and curiosities of the East were illustrations to support a neo-Pythagorean belief in the essential harmony of a universe that had the West as its nexus. The God of the Europeans, they believed, still ruled heaven and earth even though his domain was larger and more variegated than previously supposed. The God of the Christians inspired creation and provided enlightenment even for the heathen makers of "subtle *ingenia*" living and working in the remotest parts of the world. The clear stream of Western, Christian civilization still flowed strongly, but occasional streaks in its waters gave evidence that erosion of its banks was beginning.

[30] On this change of attitude toward the barbarians and their works see F. Chabod, *Machiavelli and the Renaissance* (New York, 1965), p. 199; also see R. W. Lightbown, "Oriental Art and the Orient in Late Renaissance and Baroque Italy," *Journal of the Warburg and Courtauld Institutes*, XXXII (1969), 243.

[31] As cited in J. A. L. Hyde and R. R. Espirito Santo Silva, *Chinese Porcelain for the European Market* (Lisbon, 1956), p. 48.

Bibliography

REFERENCE WORKS

Adam, Melchior. *Vitae germanorum philosophorum.* Heidelberg, 1615.

Adhémar, Jean. *Inventaire du fonds français: Graveurs du XVIe siècle.* 2 vols. Paris, 1939.

Ainaud de Lasarte, Juan. *Cerámica y vidrio.* Vol. X of *Ars Hispaniae: Historia universal del arte hispánico.* Madrid, 1952.

Ali, Salim. *The Book of Indian Birds.* 7th rev. ed. Bombay, 1964.

Anand, M. R., *et al.* "Indian Lacquerware," entire issue of *Marg: A Magazine of the Arts* (Bombay), XIX, No. 3 (June, 1966).

Archer, Mildred. *Natural History Drawings in the India Office Library.* London, 1962.

Armand, Alfred. *Les médailleurs italiens des quinzième et seizième siècles.* 2 vols. Paris, 1883.

Asher, A. *Bibliographical Essay on the Collection of Voyages and Travels, Edited and Published by Levinus Hulsius and His Successors at Nuremberg and Francfort from anno 1598 to 1660.* London, 1839.

Baglione, G. *Le vite de' pittori, scultori, architetti dal pontificato di Gregorio XIII.* Rome, 1640.

Ball, Katherine M. *Decorative Motives of Oriental Art.* London, 1927.

Bernt, W. *Die niederländischen Zeichnungen des 17. Jahrhunderts.* 2 vols. Munich, 1958.

Bhusan, J. B. *The Costumes and Textiles of India.* Bombay, 1958.

⸻. *Indian Jewellery, Ornaments, and Decorative Designs.* 2d ed. Bombay, 1964.

⸻. *Indian Metalware.* Bombay, 1961.

Bibliotheca exotica. . . . 2 vols. Frankfurt am Main, 1610–11.

Bock, Elfried, (comp.). *Die Zeichnungen in der Universitätsbibliothek Erlangen.* Frankfurt am Main, 1929.

Bode, Wilhelm. *Die italienischen Bronzestatuetten der Renaissance.* Berlin, 1922.

Bofarull y Sans, Francisco de Asís de. *Animals in Watermarks.* Hilversum, Holland, 1959.

Borroni, F. *Il cicognara bibliografia dell' archeologia e dell' arte italiana.* Florence, 1957.

Bourjot St.-Hilaire, Alexandre. *Histoire naturelle des perroquets.* 3 vols. Paris, 1837–38.

Bretschneider, Emil. *History of European Botanical Discoveries in China.* 2 vols. London, 1898.

Brito Aranha, Pedro Wenceslau de. *Bibliographie des ouvrages portugais pour servir à l'étude des villes, des villages, des monuments, des institutions, des mores et coutumes etc. de Portugal . . . et possessions doutremer.* Lisbon, 1900.

Brown, P. *Indian Architecture.* 5th ed. Bombay, 1965.

Bucher, Bruno. *Geschichte der technischen Künste.* 3 vols. Stuttgart, 1875.

Burrow, T., and Emeneau, M. B. *Dravidian Etymological Dictionary.* Oxford, 1961.

Calvi, Emilio. *Bibliografia di Roma nel'Cinquecento.* Rome, 1910.

Camus, A. G. *Mémoire sur la collection des grands et petits voyages.* Paris, 1802.

Cirlot, J. E. *A Dictionary of Symbols.* New York, 1962.

Cobarruvias, Don Sebastian de. *Tesoro de la lengua Castellana o Española.* Madrid, 1611.

Colmeiro, M. *La botanica y los botanicos en la peninsula hispanolusitana.* Madrid, 1858.

Costa, Luiz Xavier da. *Bibliografia artistica portuguesa.* Lisbon, 1944.

Croft-Murray, Edward, and Hulton, Paul. *Catalogue of British Drawings.* Vol. I: *XVI and XVII Centuries.* London, 1960.

Cunha Rivara, J. H. da. *Inscripçoes lapidares da India portugueza.* Lisbon, 1894.

Dalton, O. M. *Catalogue of the Ivory Carvings of the Christian Era.* London, 1909.

Debes, D. *Das Ornament, Wesen und Geschichte.* Leipzig, 1956.

Delen, A. J. J. *Histoire de la gravure dans les anciens Pays-Bas . . . des origines jusqu'à la fin du XVIIIᵉ siècle.* 3 vols. in two parts. Paris, 1924–35.

Dictionnaire raisonné et universel des animaux. Paris, 1759.

Dodgson, Campbell. *Catalogue of Early German and Flemish Woodcuts.* 2 vols. London, 1903, 1911.

———; Hind, A. M.; and Popham, A. E. *Catalogue of Drawings by Dutch and Flemish Artists . . . in the British Museum.* 5 vols. London, 1915–32.

Droulers, Eugène. *Dictionnaire des attributs, allégories, emblèmes et symboles.* Turnhout, Belgium, 1948.

Dubler, César de, (ed.). *La 'Materia Medica' de Dioscórides traducida y comentada por D. Andrés de Laguna.* 5 vols. Barcelona, 1955.

Dymock, William; Warden, C. J. H.; and Hooper, David. *Pharmacopoea Indica: A History of the Principal Drugs of Vegetable Origin Met with in British India.* London, 1889.

Encyclopedia of World Art. London, 1965.

Flemming, Ernst. *An Encyclopedia of Textiles.* New York, 1927.

Freeman, Rose. *English Emblem Books.* London, 1948.

Frimmel, Theodor von. *Geschichte der Wiener Gemäldesammlungen.* 3 vols. Leipzig, 1898–1901.

Gallardo, Bartolomé José. *Ensayo de una biblioteca española de libros raros y curiosos.* 4 vols. Madrid, 1863–89.

George, Wilma. *Animals and Maps.* Berkeley and Los Angeles, 1969.

Göbel, Heinrich. *Die Wandteppiche.* 2 vols. Leipzig, 1928.

Graesse, J. G. T. *Orbis latinus*. . . . Dresden, 1861.

Grueber, H. A. *Coins of the Roman Republic in the British Museum*. 2 vols. London, 1910.

Gruner, Ludwig. *Specimens of Ornamental Art*. London, 1850.

Haebler, Konrad. *Spanische und portugiesische Bücherzeichen des XV. and XVI. Jahrhunderts*. Strassburg, 1898.

Henkel, Arthur, and Schöne, Albrecht. *Emblemata: Handbuch zur Sinnbildkunst des XVI. und XVII. Jahrhunderts*. Stuttgart, 1967.

Hiler, Hilaire, and Hiler, Meyer. *Bibliography of Costume*. New York, 1939.

Hind, Arthur M. *Early Italian Engravings*. 7 vols. New York, 1938–48.

―――. *A History of Engraving and Etching from the Fifteenth Century to the Year 1914*. London, 1927.

―――. *An Introduction to a History of Woodcut with a Detailed Survey of Work Done in the Fifteenth Century*. 2 vols. Boston and New York, 1935.

Hirth, Georg. *Kulturgeschichtliches Bilderbuch aus drei Jahrhunderten*. 6 vols. Leipzig and Munich, 1881–90.

Hollstein, F. W. H. *Dutch and Flemish Etchings, Engravings, and Woodcuts, ca. 1450–1700*. 15 vols. Amsterdam, n.d.

―――. *German Engravings, Etchings, and Woodcuts, 1400–1700*. 7 vols. Amsterdam, 1945–54.

Hubert, Robert. *Catalogue of Many Natural Rarities*. London, 1665.

Indian Institute of Art in Industry. *5000 Indian Designs and Motifs*. Calcutta, 1965.

Jessen, Peter. *Meister des Ornamentstiches*. 4 vols. Berlin, 1922–24.

Kendrick, A. F. *Victoria and Albert Museum. Catalogue of Tapestries*. London, 1914.

Kern, H. *Manual of Indian Buddhism*. Delhi, 1968.

King, C. W. *Antique Gems and Rings*. London, 1872.

―――. *The Handbook of Engraved Gems*. London, 1866.

Kuypert, Giesbert, (Cupertus, Gisbertus). *De elephantis in nummis obviis*. The Hague, 1719.

Lafreri, Antonio. *Speculum Romanae magnificentiae*. Rome, 1575(?).

Landwehr, J. *Dutch Emblem Books: A Bibliography*. Utrecht, 1962.

Laurie, Arthur P. *The Pigments and Mediums of the Old Masters*. London, 1914.

Lavedan, Pierre. *Dictionnaire illustré de la mythologie et des antiquités grecques et romaines*. Paris, 1931.

Leggett, William F. *The Story of Silk*. New York, 1949.

Levaillant, François. *Histoire naturelle des perroquets*. 4 vols. Paris, 1801–5, 1837–38, 1857–58.

Maças, Delmira. *Os animais na linguagem portuguesa*. Lisbon, 1950–51.

MacMillan, H. F. *Tropical Planting and Gardening*. 5th ed. London, 1962.

Mehta, R. J. *The Handicrafts and Industrial Arts of India*. Bombay, 1960.

Melvin, Arthur G. *Gems of World Oceans: A Guide to World Sea Shell Collecting*. Healdsburg, Calif., 1964.

Merrill, E. D., and Walker, E. H. *A Bibliography of Eastern Asiatic Botany*. New York, 1938.

Pariset, E. *Histoire de la soie*. 2 vols. Paris, 1862–65.

Reference Works

Parker, John. *Books to Build an Empire: A Bibliographical History of English Overseas Interests to 1620*. Amsterdam, 1965.

Pavière, S. H. *A Dictionary of Flower, Fruit, and Still Life Painters*. 3 vols. Amsterdam, 1962.

Pereira, Gabriel. *A collecção de desenhos e pinturas da Bibliotheca d'Evora em 1884*. Lisbon, 1903.

Prater, S. H. *The Book of Indian Animals*. 2d ed. Bombay, 1965.

Praz, Mario. *Studies in Seventeenth-Century Imagery*. 2d ed. Rome, 1964.

Raczynski, Atanazy. *Dictionnaire historio-artistique du Portugal*. Paris, 1847.

Reallexikon zur deutschen Kunstgeschichte. Edited by Otto Schmitt. 4 vols. to date. Stuttgart, 1937——.

Réau, Louis. *Iconographie de l'art chrétien*. 3 vols. in 6 parts. Paris, 1956.

Schlosser, Julius von. *Die Kunstliteratur*. Vienna, 1924.

Schmitt, Otto. See *Reallexikon*. . . .

Schönbrunner, Josef von (ed.). *Handzeichnungen alter Meister aus der Albertina und anderen Sammlungen*. 12 vols. Vienna, 1896–1908.

Seba, A. *Locupletissimi rerum naturalium thesauri accurata descriptio et iconibus artificiosissimis expressio per universam physices historiam*. . . . 3 vols. Amsterdam, 1758.

Sepp, Herman. *Bibliographie der bayerischen Kunstgeschichte bis Ende 1905*. Munich, 1906.

Sigüenza, José de. *Historia de la Orden de San Gerónimo*. 2 vols. Madrid, 1907.

Singer, Charles, *et al. A History of Technology*. 5 vols. Oxford, 1954–58.

Sousa Viterbo, Francesco Marques de. *Diccionario historico e documental dos architectos, engenheiros e constructores portuguezes ou a serviço de Portugal, coordenados por Sousa Viterbo e publicado por indicação da Comissão dos Monumentos*. 3 vols. Lisbon, 1899.

———. *Noticia de alguns pintores portuguezes e de outros que, sendo estrangeiros exerceram a sue arte em Portugal*. 3 vols. in 1. Lisbon, 1903–11.

Streeter, Edwin W. *Precious Stones and Gems: Their History, Sources and Characteristics*. 6th ed. London, 1898.

Suida, W. *Österreichische Kunstschätzte*. Vienna, 1911.

Tchemerzine, Avenir. *Bibliographie d'éditions originales et rares d'auteurs français des XVe, XVIe, XVIIe et XVIIIe siècles contenant environ 6,000 facsimiles de titres et de gravures*. 10 vols. Paris, 1927–33.

———. *Bibliographie d'ouvrages sur les sciences et les arts édites aux XVe et XVIe siècles*. Courbevoie (Seine), 1933.

Thiele, J. M. *Handbog i den kongelige Kobberstiksamling*. Copenhagen, 1863.

Thieme, Ulrich, and Becker, Felix. *Künstlerlexicon*. 37 vols. Leipzig, 1907–50. Continued by new publication under same title after 1950.

Vasari, Giorgio. *Le vite de piu eccellenti pittori, scultori ed architetti*. G. Milanesi edition. Florence, 1878–85. English edition. 10 vols. London, 1912–14.

Venturi, Adolfo. *Storia dell'arte italiana*. 11 vols. Milan, 1901–33.

Volbach, W. F. *I tessuti del Museo Sacro Vaticano*. Vatican City, 1942.

Watt, Sir George. *The Commercial Products of India*. London, 1909.

Wild, Angenitus Martinus de. *The Scientific Examination of Pictures: An Investigation of the Pigments Used by the Dutch and Flemish Masters*. London, 1929.

[203]

Willetts, Wilham. *Foundations of Chinese Art from Neolithic Pottery to Modern Architecture.* London, 1956.

Yule, Henry, and Burnell, A. C. *Hobson-Jobson: A Glossary of Colloquial Anglo-Indian Words and Phrases.* . . . New ed. by William Crooke. 2d ed. New Delhi, 1968.

SOURCE MATERIALS

Acosta, Cristobal de. *Trattato di Christoforo Acosta Africano* . . . *della historia, natura et virtu delle droghe medicinali, et altre semplici rarissimi, che vengono portati dalle Indie Orientali in Europa.* Venice, 1585. First edition in Spanish. Burgos, 1578.

Aelian. *On the Characteristics of Animals.* English translation by A. F. Scholfield. 3 vols. Cambridge, Mass., 1958–59.

Albèri, E. *Relazioni degli ambasciatori Veneti al Senato.* 1st ser., Vols. I–VI; 2d ser., Vols. I–V; 3d ser., Vols. I–III. Florence, 1839–63.

Albuquerque, Afonso de. *Cartas de Afonso de Albuquerque.* 7 vols. Lisbon, 1884–1935.

Alcaçova Carneiro, Pero de. *Relaçoes de Pero de Alcaçova Carneiro, conde da Idanha, do tempo que êle e seu pai, Antonio Carneiro, serviram de secretários (1515 a 1568).* Lisbon, 1937.

Aldrovandi, Ulyssis. *Ornithologiae, hoc est de avibus historiae.* 3 vols. Bologna, 1599–1603.

———. *Musaeum metallicum.* Bologna, 1648.

Amann, Joost. *The Theatre of Women.* London, 1872. Reprint of London edition of 1572.

Amzalak, Moses B., (ed.). *Duarte Gomez Solis, fl. 1600: Discoursos sobre los comercios de las dos Indias.* Lisbon, 1943.

Anania, Giovanni Lorenzo d'. *L'universale fabrica del mondo, overo Cosmographia* . . . *diviso in 4. trattati.* Venice, 1576.

Antoni, Niccola de, (publisher). *Ornati delle Loggie del Vaticano.* Rome, s.d.

Apianus, Petrus, and Frisius, Gemma. *Cosmographia sive descriptio universi orbis.* Antwerp, 1584.

Argensola, B. L. *Conquista de las islas Malucas.* Madrid, 1608. Reprinted by the "Biblioteca de escritores aragoneses." Saragossa, 1891.

Aristotle. *Parts of Animals.* Translated by A. L. Peck. London, 1955.

Arphe y Villafañe, Juan de. *Varia commensuracion para la escultura.* Madrid, 1598. 6th ed. 1773.

Arrivabene, Lodovico. *Istoria della China di Lodovico Arrivabene,* . . . *nella quale si tratta di molti cose marovigliosi di quell'amplissimo regno.* . . . Verona, 1599.

———. *Il magno Vitei.* Verona, 1597.

Augustín, Antonio, (Augustinus). *Dialogos de medallas.* Tarragona, 1587.

Barbosa, Duarte. *The Book of Duarte Barbosa* . . . *Completed about the Year 1518* A.D. Translated from the Portuguese by Manuel Longworth Dames. "Hakluyt Society Publications," 2d ser., nos. XLIV, XLIX. 2 vols. London, 1918–21.

Beer, Rudolf, (ed.). "Inventare aus dem Archivio del Palacio zu Madrid," *Jahrbuch der kunsthistorischen Sammlungen des allerhöchsten Kaiserhauses*, Vol. XIV (1893), Pt. 2, pp. ix–lvv; Vol. XIX (1898), Pt. 2, pp. cxvii–clxxvii.

——— (ed.). "Niederländische Büchererwerbungen des Benito Arias Montano für den Eskurial im Auftrage König Philip II von Spanien," *Jahrbuch der kunsthistorischen Sammlungen des allerhöchsten Kaiserhauses*, Vol. XXV (1905), Pt. 2, pp. i–xi.

Belleforest, François de, (ed. and trans.). *La cosmographie universelle* [*of Sebastian Münster*] *de tout le monde.* . . . 2 vols. in 3. Paris, 1575.

Belon, Pierre, *Les observations de plusieurs singularitez et choses mémorables, trouvées en Grèce, Asie, Judée, Egypte, Arabie et autres pays estranges.* Paris, 1554.

Benacci, Alessandro. *Breve raguaglio dell'isola del Giappone et di questi Signori, che di la son venuti à dar obedientia alla Santità di N.S. Papa Gregorio XIII.* Bologna, 1585.

Benzoni, Girolamo. *La historia del mondo nuovo.* Venice, 1565. Edition of 1572 reprinted in Graz, Austria, 1962.

Beroaldo, Filippo. *Carminum.* Rome, 1530.

Bertelli, Ferdinando. *Omnium fere gentium nostrae aetatis habitus unquam ante hac editi.* Venice, 1563. Reprinted, with many plates added, in 1589, 1591, and 1594. Modern reprint. Zwickau, 1913.

Boch, Jean. *Descriptio publicae gratulationis, spectaculorum et ludorum, in adventu . . . Ernesti archiducis Austriae, an. MDXCIII., XVIII kal. iulias, aliisque diebus Antwerpiae editorum.* . . . Antwerp, 1595.

Boeheim, Wendelin, (ed.). "Urkunden und Regesten aus der K. K. Hofbibliothek," *Jahrbuch der kunsthistorischen Sammlungen des allerhöchsten Kaiserhauses,* Vol. VII (1888), Pt. 2, pp. xci–cccxiii.

Boillot, Joseph. *New Termis Buch, von allerley grossen vierfüssigen Thieren zugerichtet, mit beygefügter Thieren contrafieteten.* N.p., 1604. Reproduced and translated from first French edition. Langres, 1592.

Boissard, Jean Jacques. *Habitus variarum orbis gentium.* Paris, 1581.

——. *Theatrum vitae humanae—A.I.I. Boissardo Vesuntino conscriptum, et à Theodoro Bryio artificiosissimis historiis illustratum.* N.p., 1596.

Bonardi, Giovan Maria. *La minera del mondo.* Venice, 1589.

Bontius, Jacob, (Jakob de Bondt). *Historia naturalis et medicae Indiae oreintalis libri sex,* appended to *Gulielmi Pisonis . . . de Indiae utriusque re naturale et medica libri quatuordecim.* . . . Amsterdam, 1658.

Borghini, Raffaello. *Il Riposo.* Florence, 1584. Reprinted, 3 vols. in 1. Milan, 1807.

Boria, Juan de. *Empresas morales a la S.C.R.M. del Rey Don Phelipe nuestro Señor.* Madrid, 1581.

Boxer, C. R., (ed.). *South China in the Sixteenth Century.* "Hakluyt Society Publications," 2d ser., No. CVI. London, 1953.

Brandão, João. *Tratado da majestade, grandeza e abastança da cidade de Lisboa, na 2.ª metade do século XVI.* Lisbon, 1923.

Brásio, António. "Uma carta inédita de Valentim Fernandes," *Boletim da biblioteca da universidade de Coimbra,* XXIV (1940), 338–58.

Braun, Georg, and Hogenberg, Franz. *Civitates orbis terrarum.* Antwerp, 1572. English translation: *The Towns of the World, 1512–1618.* Introduction by R. A. Skelton. 6 vols. in 3. Cleveland, 1966.

Bruyn, Abraham de. *Omnium pene Europae, Asiae: Imagines gentium peculiaris vestitus.* Antwerp, 1581.

Bülow, Gottfried von, (trans.). "Journey through England and Scotland Made by Leopold von Wedel in the Years 1584–1585," *Transactions of the Royal Historical Society,* N.S., IX (1895), 268–78.

Bibliography

Burnell, A. C., and Tiele, P. A., (eds.). *The Voyage of John Huyghen van Linschoten to the East Indies.* "Hakluyt Society Publications," O.S., Vols. LXX, LXXI. London, 1885.

Calado, Adelino de Almeida. "Livro que trata das cousas da India e do Japão," *Boletim da biblioteca da universidade de Coimbra,* XXIV (1960), 1–138.

Ca'Masser, Leonardo da. "Relazione . . . alla Serenissima Republica di Venezia sopra il commercio dei Portoghesi nell'India . . . 1497–1506," edited by G. Scopoli, *Archivio storico italiano,* 1st ser., Appendix 2 (1845), pp. 9–51.

Camerarius, Joachim. *Hortus medicus et philosophicus.* . . . Nuremberg, 1588.

──────. *Symbolorum ac emblematum ethico-politicorum centuriae quatuor: prima, arborum et planetarum; secunda, animal quadrupedium; tertia, sevium et volatiluum; quarta, piscium et reptilium.* Nuremberg, 1697. First published between 1590 and 1604 in four sections.

Campos de Andrada, Ernesto de, (ed.). *Relações de Pero de Alcaçova Carneiro, conde da Idanha, do tempo que êle e seu pai, Antonio Carneiro, serviram de secretários (1515 a 1568).* Lisbon, 1937.

Cap, Paul Antoine, (ed.). *Bernard Palissy. Oeuvres completes.* Paris, 1944.

Capaccio, Giulio Cesare. *Delle imprese . . . in tre libri divisio.* Naples, 1592.

Cardano, Girolamo. *De subtilitate.* . . . Basel, 1554.

──────. *Les livres . . . intitulez De la Subtilité, et subtiles inventions.* . . . Paris, 1584.

──────. *The Book of My Life (De vita propria liber).* Translated from the Latin by Jean Stoner. New York, 1929.

Carlill, James, (ed. and trans.). *Epic of the Beast.* London, [1924].

Cartari, Vicenzo. *Imagini delli dei de gl'antichi.* Facsimile of the Venice edition of 1647, edited by W. Koschatsky. Graz, 1963.

Castiglione, Saba. *Ricordi, overo anmaestramenti . . . ne quali con prudenti, e christiani discorsi si ragiona di tutte le materie honorate.* . . . Venice, 1554.

Catelanus, L. *Von der Natur . . . des Einhorns.* Frankfurt am Main, 1624.

Celius, Caspar. *Caspari Celii Zeitung auss Jappon was in derselben nechst verschienen 1582. von den jesuitern, so wohin bekehrung der Heyden, als in erzehlung der neuwen Christenheit gehandelt worden.* Dillingen, 1586.

Centeno, Amaro. *Historia de cosas del Oriente primera y segunda parte. Contiene una descripcion general de los Reynos de Assia con las cosas mas notables dellos.* Cordova, 1595.

Ciappa Antonio. *Compendio delle heroiche et gloriose attioni et Santa vita di Papa Greg. XIII . . . nuovamête corretto et i molte parti accresciuto.* . . . Rome, 1596.

Comanini, Don Gregorio. *Il Figino, overo del fine della pittura.* Mantua, 1591.

Conti, P. G., (ed.). *Lettere inedite di Charles de L'Escluse . . . a Matteo Caccini.* . . . Florence, 1939.

Conway, W. M., (comp. and trans.). *The Writings of Albrecht Dürer.* London, 1911.

Coremans. "L'Archiduc Ernest, sa cour et ses dépenses, 1593–95," *Bulletin de la Commission royale d'histoire* (Brussels), XIII (1847), 85–147.

Corrêa, Gaspar. See Stanley, H. J., (trans.).

Crescentio, Pietro de. *De omnibus agriculturae partibus et de plantarum animalium natural et utilitate lib. XII.* Basel, 1548.

Cunningham, William. *The Cosmographical Glasse, Conteinying the Pleasant Principles of Cosmographie, Geographie, Hydrographie, or Navigation.* London, 1559.

Cupertus, Gisbertus, (Giesbert Kuypert). *De elephantis in nummis obviis.* The Hague, 1719.

Dames, Manuel Longworth, (trans.). See Barbosa, Duarte.

Dan, Le Père. *Le trésor des merveilles de . . . Fontainebleau.* Paris, 1642.

De Bry, Johann Theodor. *Alphabeta et characteres jam inde a creato mundo ad nostra usque tempora apud omnes nationes usurpati in aere efficti.* Frankfurt, 1596.

———. *Pars [dua et] quarta Indiae orientalis. . . .* Frankfurt, 1599–1601.

Dene, Edewaerd de. *De warachtighe Fabulen der Dieren.* Bruges, 1567.

[Du Bois], Balthazar Sylvius. *A Little Book of Geometrical Designs, Commonly Termed 'Moorish' . . . Very Useful to Painters, Goldsmiths, Weavers, Damasceners . . . and also to Needle-Workers.* [London], 1554.

Du Halde, Jean-Baptiste. *The General History of China. Containing a Geographical, Historical, Chronological, Political and Physical Description of the Empire of China, Chinese-Tartary, Corea and Thibet. Including an Exact and Particular Account of their Customs, Manners, Ceremonies, Religion, Arts and Sciences. The whole adorn'd with curious maps, and Variety of Copper Plates. Done from the French of P. Du Halde by R. Brookes.* 3d ed. London, 1741.

Eden, Richard, (ed.). *The History of Travayle in the West and East . . . done into Englyshe. . . .* London, 1577.

Fabri, Alessandro di. *Diversarum nationum ornatus.* Padua, 1593.

Fabrici, Principio. *Delle allusioni, imprese, et emblemi del Sig. Principio Fabricii da Ieramo sopra la vita, opere, et attioni di Gregorio XIII. . . .* Rome, 1588.

Falgairolle, Edmond, (ed.). *Jean Nicot, ambassadeur de France en Portugal au XVIᵉ siècle, sa correspondance diplomatique inédite.* Paris, 1897.

Fanti, Sigismondo. *Triompho di Fortuna.* Venice, 1526.

Favolius, Hugo. *Theatri orbis terrarum enchiridion, minoribus tabulis per Philippum Gallaeum exaratum: et carmine heroico, ex variis Geographis et Poëtis collecto, per Hugonem Favolium illustratum.* Antwerp, 1585.

Feyerabend, Sigmund. *Thurnierbuch von Anfang, Ursachen, Ursprung und Herkommen, der Thurnier im heyligen Römischen Reich.* Frankfurt am Main, 1566.

Forster, E. S., (ed. and trans.). *The Turkish Letters of Ogier Ghiselin de Busbecq, Imperial Ambassador at Constantinople, 1554–62.* Oxford, 1927.

Foster, William, (ed.). See Roe, Thomas.

Franck, Sebastian. *Weltbuch: spiegel un bildtniss des erdbodens. . . .* Basel, 1534.

Freitag, Arnold. *Mythologia ethica, hoc est Moralis philosophiae per fabulas brutis attributas, traditae, amoenissimum viridarium. . . .* Antwerp, 1579; also Cologne, 1594.

Gachard, M., (ed.). *Lettres de Philippe II à ses filles les infantes Isabelle et Catherine écrites pendant son voyage en Portugal (1581–83).* Paris, 1884.

Gazzoni, Tommaso. *La piazza universale de tutte le professioni del mondo.* Venice, 1585.

Gesner, Konrad. *. . . Historiae animalium.* 5 vols. in 3. Zurich, 1551–87.

———. *De rerum fossilum, lapidum et gemmarum maxime, figuris et similitudinibus liber. . . .* Zurich, 1565.

Gibb, James, (trans.). *The History of the Portuguese during the Reign of Manuel [of Osório].* 2 vols., London, 1752.

Giehlow, Karl. *Kaiser Maximilians I Gebetbuch.* Vienna, 1907.

Gilles, Pierre. *Aeliani de historia animalium libri XVII.* Lyons, 1562.

Giovio, Paolo, (Paulus Jovius). *Dialogo dell'imprese militari et amorose.* Rome, 1555.

———. *Elogia virorum . . . illustrium.* Florence, 1551; Basel, 1575.

———. *Elogios o vidas breves de los cavalleros antiguos y modernos, q estan al bivo pintados en el museo de Paulo Iovico.* Translated from Latin into Spanish by Gaspar de Baeca. Granada, 1568.

———. *Opera. . . .* 4 vols. Rome, 1556–64.

———. *The Worthy Tract of Paulus Iovius, Contayning a Discourse of Rare Inventions, both Militarie and Amorous Called Impresse, by Samuell Daniell.* London, 1585.

Gois, Damião de. *Chronica do felicissimo rei Dom Emanuel.* Lisbon, 1566.

———. *Lisboa de quinhentos.* Lisbon, 1937.

———. *Opúsculos históricos.* Porto, 1945.

———. *De rebus aethiopicis, indicis, lusitanicis, et hispanicis, opuscula. . . .* Cologne, 1574.

Goldstaub, M., and Wendriner, R., (eds.). *Ein Tosco-Venezianisches Bestiarius.* Halle, 1892.

Gomara, Francisco López de. *Primera y segunda parte de la historia general de las Indias con todo el descubrimiento y cosas notables que han acaecido dende que se ganaron āta el año de 1551.* Saragossa, 1553.

González de Mendoza, Juan. *The History of the Great and Mighty Kingdom of China. . . .* Reprinted from the translation of R. Parke. Edited by Sir George T. Staunton. "Hakluyt Society Publications," O.S., Vols. XIV, XV. 2 vols. London, 1853–54.

Gorlé (Gorlaeus), Abraham. *Dactyliothecae seu annulorum sigillarium quorum apud priscos tam Graecos quam Romanos usus, ex ferro, aere, argento, et auro.* Leyden, 1707.

Grapheus, Corneille. *Le triomphe d'Anvers faict en la susection du Prince Philip, Prince d'Espaigne.* Antwerp, 1550.

Green, Henry, (ed.). *Andreae Alceate Emblematum.* "Publications for the Holbein Society." Manchester, 1870.

Greiff, B., (ed.). See Rem, Lucas.

Gualandi, Michelangelo. *Memorie originali italiane risguardanti le belle arti.* Bologna, 1845.

Gualtieri, Guido. *Relationi della venuta de gli ambasciatori giaponesi a Roma, sino alla partita di Lisbona. . . .* Venice, 1586.

Gueroult, Guillaume. *Le premier livre des emblèmes.* Lyons, 1550.

Guerreiro, Afonso. *Relação das festas que se fizeram na cidade de Lisboa, na entrada de el-rei D. Felipe, primeiro de Portugal.* 1581. Reprint. Porto, 1950.

Guicciardini, Ludovico. *Description générale de touts les Pays-Bas.* Amsterdam, 1613.

Guiffrey, Jules, (ed.). *Inventaires de Jean, duc de Berry.* 2 vols. Paris, 1894–96.

Guyon, Loys. *Les diverses leçons.* Lyons, 1625.

Hakluyt, Richard. *The Principal Navigations Voyages Traffiques and Discoveries of the English Nation.* 12 vols. Glasgow, 1903–5.

Haszler, K. D., (ed.). *Reisen und Gefangenschaft Hans Ulrich Kraffts. . . .* "Bibliothek des literarischen Vereins in Stuttgart," Vol. LXI. Stuttgart, 1861.

Herrera, Alonso de. *Historia general del mundo.* 2 vols. Madrid, 1601.

———. *Libro de agricultura.* Madrid, 1598.

Hessels, Joannes Henricus, (ed.). *Abrahami Ortelii (geographi Antwerpiensis) et virorum eruditorum ad eundem et ad Jacobum Colium Ortelianum. . . . Epistulae . . . (1524–1628).* Cambridge, 1887. "Ecclesiae Londino-Batavae Archivum," Vol. I.

Heyns, Pierre. *Esbatement moral des animaux.* Antwerp, 1587.

Hoefnagel, Georg. *Archetypa studiaque patris Georgii Hoefnagellii.* Frankfurt am Main, 1592.

Hofmann, Lorenz. *Thesaurus variarum rerum antiquarum et exoticarum tam naturalium. . . .* Halle, 1625.

Holtzwart, Matthias. *Emblematum. . . .* Strassburg, 1581.

Hulsius, Levinus. *Erste Schiffart an die orientalische Indien, so die Holländisch Schiff, im Martio 1585 aussgefahren, und im Augusto 1597 wiederkommen, verzicht. . . .* 5th ed. Frankfurt am Main, 1625. 1st ed. Nuremberg, 1598.

Hutten, Ulrich von. *Opera quae extant omnia.* Munich, 1807.

Imperato, Ferrante. *Dell' historia naturale.* Naples, 1599.

James, M. R. *The Bestiary, Being a Reproduction in Full of the Manuscript Il.4.26 in the University Library, Cambridge. . . .* Oxford, 1928.

Jovius, Paulus. See Giovio, Paolo.

Junius, Hadrianus. . . . *Medici emblemata, ad D. Arnoldum Cobelium, eiusdem aenigmatum libellus, ad D. Arnoldum Rosenbergum.* Antwerp, 1565.

Klarwill, Viktor von, (ed.). *The Fugger News-Letters, Second Series.* Translated by L. S. R. Byrne. New York, 1926.

König, E., (ed.). *Konrad Peutingers Briefwechsel.* Munich, 1923.

Krafft, Hans U. *Ein deutscher Kaufmann des sechzehnten Jahrhunderts: Hans Ulrich Krafft's Denkwürdigkeiten.* Göttingen, 1862.

Krause, G., (ed.). *Tagebuch Christians des Jüngern, Fürst zu Anhalt. . . .* Leipzig, 1858.

Landucci, Luca. *A Florentine Diary from 1450 to 1516. . . .* London, 1927.

La Perrière, Guillaume de. *Le théâtre des bons engins, auquel sont contenus cent emblèmes. . . .* Paris, 1539.

Lavanha, João B. de. *Viage de la catholica real magestad del rei D. Felipe III, N.S., al reino de Portugal.* Madrid, 1622.

L'écluse, Charles de. *Caroli Clusii . . . Aliquot notae in Garciae aromatum historiam. Eiusdem descriptiones nonnullarum stirpium . . . que à . . . Francisco Drake . . . observatae sunt.* Antwerp, 1582.

———. *Rariorum plantarum historia.* Antwerp, 1610.

Leonardo, Camillo di. *Speculum lapidum. . . .* Venice, 1502.

Leonardo da Vinci. *The Notebooks.* Edited and translated by Edward McCurdy. 2 vols. in 1. New York, 1958.

Letts, Malcolm, (ed.). See Mandeville, Sir John.

Levi, C. A. *Le Collezioni Veneziane d'arte e d'antichità.* 2 vols. Venice, 1900.

Linschoten, Jan van. *Itinerario, Voyage ofte Schipvaert, van Jan huygen van Linschoten naer Oost ofte portugaels Indien. . . .* Amsterdam, 1596. English translation by John Wolfe. London, 1598.

Lipsius, Justus. *Admiranda, sive de magnitudine Romana.* Antwerp, 1605.

———. *Dissertationum ludicrorum et amoenitatum, scriptores varii.* Leyden, 1638.

Lipsius, Justus. *Epistolae.* . . . Antwerp, 1592.

———. *Epistolarum selectarum centuria prima [tertia] ad Belgas.* 3 vols. in 1. Antwerp, 1602–5.

Lobel, Matthias de. *Plantarum, seu stirpium historia.* Antwerp, 1576.

Lonitzer, Adam. *Kreuterbuch.* . . . Frankfurt am Main, 1598.

Luzio, Alessandro. *Isabelle d'Este ne' primordi del papato di Leone X e il suo viaggio a Roma nel 1514–15.* Milan, 1907.

———. *Il trionfo di Cesare di Andrea Mantegna.* Rome, 1940.

McCurdy, Edward, (trans. and ed.). See Leonardo da Vinci.

Macer, Jean. *Les trois livres de l'histoire des Indes.* Paris, 1555.

Machiavelli, Niccolò. *Opere.* 7 vols. N.p., 1813.

Madelin, Louis, (ed.). "Le journal d'un habitant français de Rome au XVIᵉ siècle (1509–1540)," *Mélanges d'archéologie et d'histoire,* XXII (1902), 251–300.

Major, R. J., (ed.). *India in the Fifteenth Century.* "Hakluyt Society Publications," O.S., Vol. XXII. London, 1857.

Malespini, L. G. T. *Oratione de le lodi di Francesco I de' Medici.* Florence, 1587.

Mander, Carel van. *Dutch and Flemish Painters: Translations from the Schilderboeck.* New York, 1963.

———. *Het Schilder-Boek.* Edited by A. F. Mirande and G. S. Overdiep. Amsterdam, 1936.

Mandeville, Sir John. *Mandeville's Travels: Texts and Translations.* Edited by Malcolm Letts. "Hakluyt Society Publications," 2d ser., Nos. 101 and 102. 2 vols. London, 1953.

Marcucci, E., (ed.). See Sassetti, Filippo.

Margaret of Austria. "Inventaire des objects d'art et lingerie de luxe qui composaient le mobilier de Marguerite d'Autriche," *Le cabinet de l'amateur,* I (1842), 222–23.

Markham, Clements (trans.). See Orta, Garcia da.

Mattioli, P. A. *Commentaires . . . sur les six livres de Ped. Dioscoride.* . . . Lyons, 1572. 1st ed. 1544.

Mauro, Lucio. *Le antichità de la città di Roma.* Venice, 1556.

Mercier, Jean. *Io. Mercerii I.C. Emblemata.* Bourges, 1592.

Merens, A., (ed.). "De reis van Jan Martensz Merens door Frankrijk, Italië en Duitschland, anno 1600," *Mededeelingen van het Nederlandsch Historisch Instituut te Rome,* 2d ser., VII (1937), 49–157.

Milensio, F. Felice. *Dell' Impressa dell' Elefante dell' Illustrissimo e reverendiss. Signore il sig. Cardinal Mont' Elarpo Dialogi [sic] Tre, di F. Felice Milensio Agostiniano.* Naples, 1595.

Mirande, A. F., and Overdiep, G. S., (eds.). See Mander, Carel van.

Monardes, Nicholas. *Joyfull News out of the Newe Founde World.* Reprint in 2 vols. New York, 1925.

Morávek, Jan, (ed.). *Nově objevený inventář rudolfinských sbírek na Hradě Pražském.* Prague, 1937.

Moryson, Fynes. *An Itinerary.* . . . Glasgow, 1907.

Münster, Sebastian. *Cosmographei oder Beschreibung aller Länder etc.* Basel, 1550.

Murr, Christophe T. de. *Description du cabinet de M. Paul de Praun à Nuremberg.* Paris, 1797.

Navagero, Andrea. *Opera omnia.* Venice, 1754.

Nestor, Jean. *Histoire des hommes illustrés de la Maison de Medici.* . . . Paris, 1564.

Nichols, John, (ed.). *Progresses of Queen Elizabeth.* 3 vols. London, 1788–1805.

Nowell, Charles E., (ed.). *Magellan's Voyage around the World: Three Contemporary Accounts.* Evanston, Ill., 1962.

Olearius, Adam. *Gottorffische Kunst-Kammer.* Schleswig, 1664.

Orbaan, J. A. F., (ed.). *Documenti sul Barocco in Roma.* Rome, 1920.

Orta, Garcia da. *Colloquies on the Simples and Drugs of India.* Translated by Sir Clements Markham. London, 1913.

Osório, Jeronymo, Bishop of Silves. See Gibb, James, (trans.).

Othmayr, Caspar. *Symbola illustrissimorum principum.* Nuremberg, 1547.

Panciroli, Guido. *The History of Many Memorable Things Lost, Which Were in Use among the Ancients.* 2 vols. in 1. London, 1715.

Paré, Ambroise. *Oeuvres.* Paris, 1585.

Pieris, Paul E. *Ceylon and Portugal from Original Documents at Lisbon.* Leipzig, 1927.

Pissurlencar, P. S. S. *Regimentos das fortalezas da India.* Bastorà (Goa), 1951.

Plantin, Christophe, (publisher). *La joyeuse et magnifique Entrée.* . . . Antwerp, 1582.

Pliny. *Natural History.* Translated by H. Rackham. Cambridge, Mass., 1949.

Porcacchi, Thommaso. *L'isole piu famoso del mondo.* . . . Venice, 1576.

Quickeberg, Samuel. *Inscriptiones.* . . . Munich, 1565.

———. *Musaeum theatrum.* Munich, 1567.

Quinn, D. B., and Skelton, R. A., (eds.). *The Principall Navigations Voiages and Discoveries of the English Nation.* . . . Facsimile of 1589 edition of Hakluyt. Cambridge, 1965.

Raimondi, Ezio, (ed.). *Torquato Tasso Dialoghi: Edizione critica.* 2 vols. Florence, 1958.

Ramusio, G. B. *Delle navigationi et viaggi.* 3 vols. Venice, 1550–59.

Rathgeb, Jakob. *Warhaffte Beschreibung zweyer Raisen.* . . . 2 vols. Tübingen, 1603.

Rebello da Silva, Luiz Augusto, (ed.). *Corpo diplomático portuguez contendo os actos e relações politicas e diplomaticas de Portugal com as diversas potencias do mundo desde o seculo XVI até os nossos dias.* Lisbon, 1862.

Reiche, E., (ed.). *Willibald Pirckheimers Briefwechsel.* 2 vols. Jena, 1930.

Reinsch, Robert, (ed.). *Le Bestiaire: Das Thierbuch des normannischen Dichters Guillaume le Clerc.* "Altfranzösische Bibliothek," Vol. XIV. Leipzig, 1892.

Rem, Lucas. *Tagebuch des Lucas Rem aus den Jahren 1494–1541.* Edited by R. Greiff. In *Jahresbericht des historischen Kreisvereins . . . von Schwaben und Neuburg,* Vol. XXVI. Augsburg, 1861.

Reusner, Nicolas. *Emblemata.* . . . Frankfurt, 1581.

Ripa, Cesare. *Iconologia, overo descrittione d'imagini delle virtu, vitij, affetti, passioni humane, corpi celesti, mondo e sue parti.* Padua, 1611. 1st ed. Rome, 1593.

Roe, Thomas. *The Embassy of Sir Thomas Roe to the Court of the Great Mogul, 1615–1619, as Narrated in His Journal and Correspondence.* Edited by William Foster. "Hakluyt Society Publications," 2d ser., Nos. 1, 2. 2 vols. London, 1899.

Roersch, A., (ed.). *Correspondance de N. Clenard.* 3 vols. Brussels, 1940–41.

Ruscelli, Girolamo. *Le imprese illustri con espositioni et discorsi del Sg. Jeronimo Ruscelli.* Venice, 1566.

Sambucus, Joannes. *Emblemata cum aliquot numm is antiqui operis.* . . . Antwerp, 15 64.

Sanuto, Marino. *I Diarii . . . MCCCCXCVI–MDXXXIII.* . . . Edited by Rinaldo Fulin and others. 58 vols. in 35. Venice, 1879–1903.

Sassetti, Filippo. *Lettere edite e inedite di Filippo Sassetti.* Edited by Ettore Marcucci. Florence, 1855.

Scaliger, J. J. *Autobiography.* Cambridge, Mass., 1927.

Schaller, Georg. *Eigentliche und auch gründliche Beschreibung allerley vier und zweyfüssigen Thieren.* Frankfurt am Main, 1592.

Schrenck von Nozing, Jacob. *Augustissimorum imperatorum.* . . . Innsbruck, 1601.

Scopoli, G., (ed.). See Ca'Masser, Leonardo da.

Simeoni, Gabriele, *Le imprese heroiche et morali.* . . . Lyons, 1559.

Soderini, Giovanni Vittore. *Opere.* 4 vols. "Collezione di opere inedite o rare dei primi tre secoli della lingua," Vols. 86, 87, 88, 95. Edited by Alberto Bacchi della Lega. Bologna, 1902–7.

Stanley, Henry J., (trans. and ed.). *The Three Voyages of Vasco da Gama . . . from the Lendas da India of Gaspar Correa.* "Hakluyt Society Publications," O.S., Vol. XLII. London, 1869.

Staunton, G. T., (ed.). See González de Mendoza, Juan.

Straet, Jan van der, (Stradanus). *Venationes.* Antwerp, 1578.

——— and Galle, P. *Nova reperta.* Antwerp, 1592.

Symonds, J. A., (trans.). *The Autobiography of Benevenuto Cellini.* New York, 1910.

Taylor, E. G. R., (ed.). *The Original Writings and Correspondence of the Two Richard Hakluyts.* "Hakluyt Society Publications," 2d ser., Nos. 76–77. 2 vols. London, 1935.

Temple, R. C., (Sir Richard Carnac) (ed.). *The Itinerary of Ludovico di Varthema of Bologna, from 1502 to 1508.* Translated by J. W. Jones. London, 1928.

Terzo (Tertius), Francesco. *Austriacae gentis imaginum, pars prima-[quinta].* Innsbruck, 1569–[73].

Thevet, André. *La cosmographie universelle . . . illustrée de diverses figures des choses plus remarquables vivës par l'Auteur et incogneuës de noz Ancients et Modernes.* 2 vols. Paris, 1575.

Tomasini, Jacopo Filippo. *V. C. Laurentii Pignorii . . . bibliotheca et museum.* . . . Venice, 1632.

Vaissière, Pierre de, (ed.). *Journal de Jean Barrillon, secrétaire du Chancelier Duprat, 1515–1521.* Paris, 1897.

Valeriano, Giovanni Pietro. *Hieroglyphica sive de sacris Aegyptiorum aliarumque gentium literis commentarii.* Basel, 1556.

Vasconcellos, Joaquim Antonio da Foneseca e. *Francisco de Hollanda, 1517–84: Vier Gespräche über die Malerei geführt zu Rom 1538.* Vienna, 1899.

Vecellio, Cesare. *Habiti antichi et moderni di tutte il mondo.* 2d ed. Venice, 1598.

Vico, E. *Omnium Caesarum verissimae imagines ex antiquis numismatis desumptae.* Venice, 1554.

Vigenére, Blaise de. *Traicte des chiffres, ou secretes manieres d'escrire.* Paris, 1586.

Books

Vredeman de Vries. *Grottesco in diversche Manieren.* . . . Antwerp, 1555.

Whitney, Geoffrey. *A Choice of Emblemes, and Other Devises.* . . . Leyden, 1586. Facsimile ed. by H. Green. London, 1866.

Wicki, J. (ed.). *Documenta Indica.* 7 vols. Rome, 1948–62.

———— (ed.). "Dokumente und Briefe aus der Zeit des indischen Vizekönigs D. Antão de Noronha (1563–1568)." In H. Flasche (ed.), *Aufsätze zur portugiesischen Kulturgeschichte* (Münster, 1960), I, 225–315.

Williams, C., (trans. and ed.). *Thomas Platter's Travels in England, 1599.* London, 1937.

Yule, Henry, and Cordier, Henri., (eds.). *The Book of Ser Marco Polo.* 4th ed. 2 vols. New York, 1933.

Zimmerman, Heinrich, (ed.). "Das Inventar der Prager Schatz- und Kunstkammer vom 6. Dezember 1621," *Jahrbuch der kunsthistorischen Sammlungen des allerhöchsten Kaiserhauses,* Vol. XXV (1905), Pt. 2, pp. xiii–lxxv.

————. "Regesten aus dem K. und K. Reichs-Finanz-Archiv," *ibid.,* Vol. III (1885), Pt. 2, pp. iii–cii.

————. "Urkunden, Acten und Regesten aus dem Archiv des K. K. Ministerium des Innerns, 1497–1586," *ibid.,* Vol. III (1885), Pt. 2, pp. cxx–clxxvi; Vol. VII (1888), Pt. 2, pp. xv–lxxxiv.

————. "Urkunden, Acten und Regesten aus dem K. und K. Haus-, Hof- und Staats-Archiv in Wien," *ibid.,* Vol. III (1885), Pt. 2, pp. ciii–cv.

BOOKS

Abranches Pinto, J. A.; Okamoto, Yoshitomo; and Bernard, Henri. *La première ambassade du Japon en Europe, 1582–1592.* Tokyo, 1942.

Ackerman, Phyllis. *Three Early Sixteenth-Century Tapestries with a Discussion of the History of the Tree of Life: The Rockefeller-McCormick Tapestries.* New York, 1932.

Adelmann, H. B. *Marcello Malpighi and the Evolution of Embryology.* Ithaca, N.Y., 1966.

Adhémar, Jean. *Frère André Thevet, grand voyageur et cosmographe des rois de France au XVIe siècle.* Paris, n.d.

Alazard, Jean. *L'art italien au XVIe siècle.* Paris, 1955.

————. *La Venise de la Renaissance.* Paris, 1956.

Allemagne, Henri d'. *Les accessoires du costume et du mobilier.* 3 vols. Paris, 1928.

Almeida Paile, Miguel d'. *Santo António dos Portugueses em Roma.* 2 vols. Lisbon, 1951–52.

Andresen, Andreas. *Der deutsche peintre-graveur, oder die deutschen Maler als Kupferstecher.* . . . 5 vols. Leipzig, 1872–78.

Antal, F. *Florentine Painting and Its Social Background.* London, 1947.

Appelbaum, Stanley, (ed.). *The Triumph of Maximilian I: 137 Woodcuts by Hans Burgkmair and Others.* New York, 1964.

Arber, Agnes. *Herbals: Their Origin and Evolution.* Cambridge, 1938.

Armandi, P. *Histoire militaire des éléphants, depuis les temps les plus reculés jusqu'à l'introduction des armes à feu.* Paris, 1843.

Avalon, Jean. *Le bestiaire des Triomphes de Pétrarque.* Paris, 1943.

Averdunk, Heinrich, and Mueller-Reinhard, J. *Gerhard Mercator und die Geographen unter seinen Nachkommen.* Gotha, 1914.

Bachmann, F. *Die alten Städtebilder.* Leipzig, 1939.

Baker, George P. *Calico Painting and Printing in the East Indies in the XVII and XVIII Centuries.* London, 1921.

Baker, Samuel White. *Wild Beasts and Their Ways: Reminiscences of Europe, Asia, Africa and America.* 2 vols. London, 1890.

Baldass, Ludwig. *Der Künstlerkreis Maximilians.* Vienna, 1923.

————. *Die Wiener Gobelins-Sammlung.* Vienna, 1921.

Baltrušaitis, Jurgis. *Anamorphoses.* Paris, 1955.

————. *Le moyen-âge fantastique.* Paris, 1955.

————. *Réveils et prodiges.* Paris, 1960.

Barocchi, Paola. *Il Rosso fiorentino.* Rome, 1951.

Barraband, Jacques. *Exotic Birds.* New York, 1963.

Barreira, João, *et al. Arte portuguesa.* 4 vols. Lisbon, 1948–54.

Battisti, E. *L'Antirinascimento.* Milan, 1962.

————. *Rinascimento e Barocco.* N.p., 1960.

Baudet, Henri. *Paradise on Earth: Some Thoughts on European Images of Non-European Man.* New Haven, Conn., 1965.

Baumgart, Fritz. *Renaissance und Kunst des Manierismus.* Cologne, 1963.

Bazin, G. *A Gallery of Flowers.* London, 1960.

Beard, Miriam. *A History of the Business Man.* New York, 1938.

Beau, Albin Eduard. *As relações germânicas do humanismo de Damião de Góis.* Coimbra, 1941.

Bebiano, José Bacelar. *O porto de Lisboa, estudo de história económica, seguido de um catálogo bibliográfico e iconográfico.* Lisbon, 1960.

Béguin, Sylvie. *L'Ecole de Fontainebleau: Le manierisme à la cour de France.* Paris, 1960.

Behling, L. *Die Pflanze in der mittelalterlichen Tafelmalerei.* Weimar, 1957.

Belevitch-Stankevitch, H. *Le goût chinois en France au temps de Louis XIV.* Paris, 1910.

Benesch, Otto. *The Art of the Renaissance in Northern Europe.* Cambridge, Mass., 1945.

Bergström, Ingvar. *Dutch Still-Life Painting in the Seventeenth Century.* London, 1956.

Bermann, Moritz. *Alt-und-Neu Wien.* 2 vols. Vienna, 1880.

Bernheimer, R. *Wild Men in the Middle Ages.* Cambridge, Mass., 1952.

Bertaux, Emile. *La Renaissance en Espagne et en Portugal.* Paris, 1916.

Beurdeley, Michel. *Porcelaine de la Compagnie des Indes.* Fribourg (Switzerland), 1962.

Bierens de Hann, J. C. J. *L'oeuvre gravé de Cornelis Cort, graveur hollandais, 1533–1578.* The Hague, 1948.

Bigard, Louis. *Le trafic maritime avec les Indes sous François I.* Paris, 1939.

Blondel, S. *Histoire des éventails chez tous les peuples et à toutes les époques.* Paris, 1875.

Blunt, Anthony. *Artistic Theory in Italy, 1450–1600.* Oxford, 1959.

Blunt, Wilfred. *The Art of Botanical Illustration.* London, 1950.

Boas, George. *The Hieroglyphics of Horapollo.* New York, 1950.

Bodenheimer, F. S. *Animal and Man in Bible Lands.* Leyden, 1960.

Boehn, Max von. *Modes and Manners.* 4 vols. London, 1932.

Books

Boetius de Boodt, A. *Gemmarum et lapidum historia.* . . . Leyden, 1636.

Boncompagni, Francesco L. *Le prime due ambasciate dei Giapponesi a Roma (1585–1615). Con nuovi documenti.* Rome, 1903.

Bonaffé, Edmond. *Causeries sur l'art et la curiosité.* Paris, 1878.

———. *Inventaire des meubles de Catherine de Médicis en 1589.* Paris, 1874.

———. *Le meuble en France au XVIe siècle.* Paris, 1887.

Bosch, F. D. K. *De gouden kiem.* Amsterdam, 1948.

Bousquet, Jacques. *La peinture manieriste.* Neuchâtel, 1964.

Bowie, Theodore, *et al. East-West in Art: Patterns of Cultural and Aesthetic Relationships.* Bloomington, Ind., 1966.

Bowsma, William J. *Concordia Mundi: The Career and Thought of Guillaume Postel.* Cambridge, Mass., 1957.

Boyer, Martha. *Japanese Export Lacquers from the Seventeenth Century in the National Museum of Denmark.* Copenhagen, 1959.

Braun, J. *Die belgischen Jesuiten-Kirchen.* Fribourg, 1907.

Breland, O. P. *Animal Life and Lore.* New York, 1963.

Brésard, Marc. *Les foires de Lyon aux XVe et XVIe siècles.* Paris, 1914.

Briganti, G. *Italian Mannerism.* London, 1962.

Brown, Percy. *Indian Painting under the Mughals, A.D. 1550 to A.D. 1750.* Oxford, 1924.

Buchthal, H. *Miniature Painting in the Latin Kingdom of Jerusalem.* Oxford, 1957.

Burckhardt, Jakob. *The Civilization of the Renaissance in Italy.* London, 1898.

Burmeister, Karl Heinz. *Sebastian Münster: Versuch eines biographischen Gesamtbildes.* Basel, 1963.

Cagigal e Silva, Maria Madalena de. *A arte Indo-Portuguesa.* Lisbon, [1966].

Caillois, Roger. *Au coeur du fantastique.* Paris, 1965.

Calmette, Joseph L. A. *Les grandes heures de Vézelay.* Paris, 1951.

Caravita, Andrea. *I codici e le arti a Monte Cassino.* 3 vols. Montecassino, 1871.

Cardoso, Nuno C. *Arte portuguesa.* Lisbon, 1935–37.

Carmody, Francis J., (ed.). *Versio Y of the Physiologus.* "University of California Publications in Classical Philosophy," Vol. XII, No. 7. Berkeley, 1941.

Carrington, Richard. *Elephants.* London, 1958.

Carroll, W. M. *Animal Conventions in English Renaissance Non-Religious Prose (1550–1600).* New York, 1954.

Carter, T. F., and Goodrich, L. C. *The Invention of Printing in China and Its Spread Westward.* New York, 1955.

Castilho, Julio. *A ribeira de Lisboa.* 2d ed. 5 vols. Lisbon, 1941–48.

———. *Lisboa antiga.* 2d ed. 5 vols. Lisbon, 1902–4.

Castro, José de. *Portugal em Roma.* 2 vols. Lisbon, 1939.

———. *Portugal no concilio de Trento.* 6 vols. Lisbon, 1946.

Caverel, Philippe de. *Ambassade en Espagne et en Portugal (en 1582) de R. P. en Dieu, Dom Jean Sarrazin, abbé de St. Vaast du conseil d'estat de Sa Majesté Catholique, son premier conseiller en Artois.* . . . Arras, 1860.

Bibliography

Cesareo, G. A. *Pasquino e pasquinate nella Roma di Leone X.* Rome, 1938.

Chabod, Federico. *Machiavelli and the Renaissance.* New York, 1965.

Chartrou, Josèphe. *Les entrées solennelles et triomphales à la Renaissance (1484–1551).* Paris, 1928.

Chinard, Gilbert. *L'exotisme américain dans la littérature française au XVIᵉ siècle.* Paris, 1911.

Chubb, Thomas C. *Aretino, Scourge of Princes.* New York, 1940.

Chytil, Karl. *Die Kunst in Prag zur Zeit Rudolf II.* Prague, 1904.

Cicogna, E. A. *Delle vita et delle opere di Andrea Navagero.* . . . Venice, 1855.

Ciutius, Salvatore de. *Une ambassade portugaise à Rome au XVIᵉ siècle.* Naples, 1899.

Clark, Kenneth. *Landscape Painting.* New York, 1950.

Coelho Gasco, Antonio. *Primeira parte das antiguidades da muy nobre de Lisboa, imporio do mundo, e princeza do mar occeano.* Coimbra, 1924.

Cohen, Carl. *Zur literarischen Geschichte des Einhorns.* Berlin, 1896.

Colvin, Sidney. *Early Engraving and Engravers in England.* London, 1905.

Correia, Vergilio. *As obras de Santa Maria de Belem de 1514 a 1519.* Lisbon, 1922.

———. *Azulejos datados.* Lisbon, 1916.

———. *Etnografia artistica portuguesa.* Barcelos, 1937.

Cortesão, A., and Teixeira da Mota, A. *Portugaliae monumenta cartographica.* 5 vols. Lisbon, 1960–62.

Costa-Tôrres, Raul da. *A arquitectura dos descobrimentos.* Braga, 1943.

Couto, Gustave do. *Historia da antiga Casa da India.* Lisbon, 1932.

Couto, João, and Gonçalves, António M. *A ourivesaria em Portugal.* Lisbon, 1962.

Cox, Raymond. *Les soieries d'art depuis les origines.* Paris, 1914.

Croft-Murray, E. *Decorative Painting in England, 1537–1837.* London, 1962.

Dam, Peter. *Fabulous Beasts.* London, 1952.

Dannenfeldt, Karl H. *Leonhard Rauwolf, Sixteenth-Century Physician, Botanist, and Traveler.* Cambridge, Mass., 1968.

Davillier, Jean Charles. *Les arts décoratifs en Espagne au moyen-âge et à la Renaissance.* Paris, 1879.

———. *Les origines de la porcelaine en Europe.* Paris, 1882.

———. *Recherches sur l'orfèvrerie en Espagne au moyen âge et à la Renaissance: Documents inédits tirés des archives.* Paris, 1879.

Delaunay, Paul. *La zoölogie au seizième siècle.* Paris, 1962.

Delen, A. J. J. *Christophe Plantin, imprimeur de l'humanisme.* . . . Brussels, 1944.

———. *Iconographie van Antwerpen.* Brussels, 1930.

Delisle, Leopold. *Fabri de Peiresc.* Toulouse, 1889.

Delumeau, Jean. *Vie économique et sociale de Rome dans la seconde moitié du XVIᵉ siècle.* Paris, 1957.

Dembeck, Hermann. *Animals and Men.* Translated from German by R. and C. Winston. Garden City, N.Y., 1965.

Denis, Ferdinand. *Le monde enchanté: Cosmographie et histoire naturelle fantastiques du moyen âge.* Paris, 1843.

Denucé, J. *Antwerp Art-Tapestry and Trade.* Vol. IV in *Historical Sources for the Study of Flemish Art.* The Hague, 1936.

————. *De konstkamers van Antwerpen in de 16ᵉ en 17ᵉ eeuwen.* The Hague, 1932.

————. *Inventaire des Affaitadi, banquiers italiens à Anvers de l'année 1568.* Antwerp, 1934.

Der Nersessian, Sirarpie. *L'illustration du roman de Barlaam et Joasaph.* Paris, 1937.

Didot, Ambroise Firmin. *Essai typographique et bibliographique sur l'histoire de la gravure sur bois . . . pour faire suite aux costumes anciens et modernes de César Vecellio.* Paris, 1863.

Doering, Oscar, (ed.). *Des Augsburger Patriciers Philipp Hainhofer Beziehungen zum Herzog Philip II von Pommern-Stettin: Correspondenzen aus den Jahren 1610-1619.* In R. Eitelberger von Edelberg and Albert Ilg (eds.), *Quellenschriften für Kunstgeschichte und Kunsttechnik des Mittelalters und der Neuzeit,* N.S., Vol. VI. Vienna, 1896.

————. *Des Augsburger Patriciers Philipp Hainhofer Reisen nach Innsbruck und Dresden.* In *ibid.,* Vol. X. Vienna, 1901.

Ebersolt, Jean. *Orient et Occident: Recherches sur les influences byzantines et orientales en France avant et pendant les croisades.* 2d ed., Paris, 1954.

Eça de Quieroz, José. *Ceramica portuguesa.* Lisbon, 1907. 2d ed. 2 vols. Lisbon, 1948.

Edgerton, Franklin. *The Elephant-Lore of the Hindus.* New Haven, Conn., 1931.

Ehrmann, Jean. *Antoine Caron, peintre à la Cour des Valois, 1521-99.* Geneva, 1955.

Entwisle, E. A. *A Literary History of Wallpaper.* London, 1960.

Estienne, H. *La foire de Francfort.* Lisieux, 1875.

Ettinghausen, Richard. *The Unicorn.* Freer Gallery of Art, "Occasional Papers," Vol. I, No. 3. Washington, D.C., 1950.

Evans, E. P. *Animal Symbolism in Ecclesiastical Architecture.* New York, 1896.

Evans, Joan. *A History of Jewellery, 1100-1870.* London, 1953.

————. *Magical Jewels of the Middle Ages and the Renaissance, Particularly in England.* Oxford, 1922.

————. *Pattern.* 2 vols. Oxford, 1931.

————. *Style in Ornament.* London, 1950.

Falke, Otto von. *Kunstgeschichte der Seidenweberei.* Berlin, 1921.

Ferrara, Orestes. *Le XVIᵉ siècle, vu par les ambassadeurs vénitiens.* Paris, 1954.

Feulner, Adolf. *Kunstgeschichte des Möbels seit dem Altertum.* Berlin, 1927.

Fierens, Paul. *Le fantastique dans l'art flamand.* Brussels, 1947.

Fischel, Oskar. *Raphael.* Translated from the German by Bernard Rackham. 2 vols. London, 1948.

Floerke, Hanns. *Studien zur niederländischen Kunst- und Kulturgeschichte.* Munich, 1905.

Förster, Otto H. *Kölner Kunstsammler vom Mittelalter bis zum Ende des bürgerlichen Zeitalters.* Berlin, 1931.

Fonseca, Quirino da. *A representação artistica das armadas da India.* Lisbon, 1933.

Fonseca Brancante, Eldino da. *O Brasil e a louça da India.* São Paulo, 1950.

Fontura da Costa, A. *Les d'esambulations du Rhinocéros de Modofar, roi de Cambaye, de 1514-1516.* Lisbon, 1937.

Forssmann, Erik. *Säule und Ornament: Studien zum Problem des Manierismus in den nordischen Säulenbüchern und Vorlageblättern des 16. und 17. Jahrhunderts.* Stockholm, 1956.

Bibliography

Franco, Antonio. *Evora ilustrado.* 1st ed. Evora, 1728. New version, 1948.

Frankenburger, Max. *Beiträge zur Geschichte Wenzel Jamnitzer und seiner Familie.* Strassburg, 1901.

Frankl, Paul. *The Gothic: Literary Sources and Interpretations through Eight Centuries.* Princeton, 1960.

Frazão de Vasconcellos, J. A. do A. *As pinturas das armadas da India e outras representacões artisticas de navios portugueses do século XVI: Subsídios históricos e bibliográficos.* Lisbon, 1941.

Frey, K. *Der literarische Nachlass G. Vasaris.* Munich, 1923.

Friedländer, Max. *Die altniederländische Malerei.* 14 vols. Berlin, 1924–37.

Friedländer, W. *Mannerism and Anti-Mannerism in Italian Painting.* New York, 1957.

Friedman, H. *The Symbolic Goldfinch.* New York, 1946.

Frimmel, Theodor von. *Geschichte der Wiener Gemäldesammlungen.* 3 vols. Leipzig, 1898.

Frothingham, Alice. *Hispanic Glass.* New York, 1941.

———. *Lustreware of Spain.* New York, 1951.

Gabriels, Juliane. *Het Nederlandse Ornament in de Renaissance.* Louvain, 1958.

Gallesio. *Traité du citres.* 3 vols. Pisa, 1917.

Gans, M. H., and Duyvené de Wit-Klinkhamer, T. M. *Dutch Silver.* Translated by Oliver Van Oss. London, 1961.

Gaspar, Camille, (comp. and ed.). *Le bréviaire du musée Mayer van den Bergh à Anvers.* Brussels, 1932.

Geiger, Bruno. *I dipinti ghiribizzosi di Giuseppe Arcimboldi, pittore illusionista del cinquecento (1527–1593).* Florence, 1954.

Gerard, P. *Anvers à travers les ages.* 2 vols. Brussels, 1888.

Gimma, Giacinto. *Della storia naturale delle gemme, delle pietre, e di tutti i minerali.* . . . 2 vols. Naples, 1730.

Gnoli, Domenico. *La Roma di Leon X: Quadri e studi originali annotati e publicati.* Milan, 1938.

Goette, John. *Jade Lore.* New York, 1937.

Gombrich, E. H. *Art and Illusion: A Study in the Psychology of Pictorial Representation.* New York, 1965.

———. *The Story of Art.* New York, 1951.

Gomes de Brito, José Joaquim. *Ruas de Lisboa.* 3 vols. Lisbon, 1935.

Goris, Jan Albert. *Etude sur les colonies marchandes méridionales (portugais, espagnols, italiens) à Anvers de 1488 à 1567.* Louvain, 1925.

Gould, Charles. *Mythical Monsters.* London, 1886.

Graça Barreto, J. A. da. *A descoberta da India ordenada em tapeçaria por mandado de El-Rei D. Manuel: Documento inedito do século XVI.* . . . Coimbra, 1880.

Graul, Richard. *Ostasiatische Kunst und ihr Einfluss auf Europa.* Leipzig, 1906.

Grossmann, F. *Bruegel: The Paintings.* Rev. ed. London, 1966.

Gruyer, Gustave. *L'art ferrarais à l'époque des princes d'Este.* 2 vols. Paris, 1897.

Gubernatis, Angelo de. *Storia dei viaggiatori italiani nella Indie Orientali.* Leghorn, 1875.

———. *Zoölogical Mythology, or the Legends of Animals.* London, 1872.

Guimarães, Alfredo. *Mobiliário do Paláçio Ducal de Vila Viçosa*. Lisbon, 1949.

Gyllius, Petrus, (Gilles, Pierre). *Antiquities of Constantinople*. Translated by J. Ball. London, 1729.

Händler, Gerhard. *Fürstliche Mäzene und Sammler in Deutschland von 1500 bis 1620*. Strassburg, 1933.

Hairs, M. L. *Les peintres flamands de fleurs au XVIIe siècle*. Brussels, 1955.

Hamy, Alfred. *Essai sur l'iconographie de la Compagnie de Jésus*. Paris, 1875.

Hamy, E. T. *Les origines du musée d'ethnographie: Histoire et documents*. Paris, 1890.

Harbeck, Hans. *Melchior Lorichs*. Hamburg, 1911.

Hartlaub, G. F. *Zauber des Spiegels: Geschichte und Bedeutung des Spiegels in der Kunst*. Munich, 1951.

Hartt, F. *Giulio Romano*. 2 vols. New Haven, Conn., 1958.

Haskell, Francis. *Patrons and Painters: A Study in the Relations between Italian Art and Society in the Age of the Baroque*. New York, 1963.

Haupt, Albrecht. *Die Baukunst der Renaissance in Portugal*. Frankfurt am Main, 1890.

Haydn, Hiram. *The Counter-Renaissance*. New York, 1950.

Hedicke, Robert. *Cornelis Floris und die Florisdekoration*. Berlin, 1913.

Hempel, Eberhard. *Baroque Art and Architecture in Central Europe*. Baltimore, 1965.

Herculano de Moura, J. *Inscripções indianas em Cintra: Notulas de archeologia historica e bibliographia acerca dos templos Hindus de Somnáth-Patane e Elephante*. Nova Goa, 1906.

Hocke, René. *Die Welt als Labyrinth (Manier und Manie in der europäischen Kunst)*. Hamburg 1957.

Hodgen, Margaret T. *Early Anthropology in the Sixteenth and Seventeenth Centuries*. Philadelphia, 1964.

Holzhausen, W. *Lackkunst in Europa*. Brunswick, 1959.

Honey, W. B. *European Ceramic Art from the End of the Middle Ages to about 1815*. London, 1949.

Honour, Hugh. *Chinoiserie: The Vision of Cathay*. London, 1961.

Howe, William Norton. *Animal Life in Italian Painting*. London, 1912.

Huth, Hans. *Europäische Lackarbeiten, 1600–1850*. Darmstadt, n.d.

———. *Lacquer of the West: The History of a Craft and an Industry, 1550–1950*. Chicago, 1970.

Hyde, J. A. Lloyd, and Espirito Santo Silva, Ricardo R. *Chinese Porcelains for the European Market, Water Colors and Descriptions by Eduardo Malta*. Lisbon, 1956.

Ilg, Albert, and Boeheim, W. *Das K. K. Schloss Ambras in Tirol*. Vienna, 1882.

Iñiguez, Almech F. *Casas reales y jardines de Felipe II*. Madrid, 1952.

Iversen, Erik. *The Myth of Egypt and Its Hieroglyphs in European Tradition*. Copenhagen, 1961.

Jacquot, Jean, (ed.). *Fêtes et cérémonies au temps de Charles Quint*. Paris, 1960.

Jairazbhoy, R. A. *Oriental Influences in Western Art*. Bombay, 1965.

Janson, H. W. *Apes and Ape Lore*. London, 1952.

Jennison, G. *Animals for Show and Pleasure in Ancient Rome*. Manchester, 1937.

Jenyns, Soames, and Watson, W. *Chinese Art: The Minor Arts.* Fribourg, 1965.

Jorge, Ricardo. *Amato Lusitano.* Lisbon, 1962.

Kantorowicz, Ernst. *Kaiser Friedrich der Zweite.* Berlin, 1931.

Kayser, Wolfgang. *Das Groteske: Seine Gestaltung in Malerei und Dichtung.* Hamburg, 1957.

Kehrer, Hugo. *Die "Heiligen Drei Könige" in der Legende und in der deutschen bildenden Kunst bis Albrecht Dürer.* Strassburg, 1904.

Keil, Luis. *As tapeçarias de D. João de Castro.* Lisbon, 1928.

Kellenbenz, Hermann. *Unternehmerkräfte im Hamburger Portugal- und Spanienhandel, 1590–1625.* Hamburg, 1954.

Keller, Otto. *Die antike Tierwelt.* 2 vols. Leipzig, 1909.

Kernodle, George R. *From Art to Theatre: Form and Convention in the Renaissance.* Chicago, 1944.

Killermann, Sebastian. *Albrecht Dürers Tier- und Pflanzenzeichnungen und ihre Bedeutung für die Naturgeschichte.* Strassburg, 1910.

――――. *Die Miniaturen im Gebetbuche Albrechts V von Bayern (1574).* "Studien zur deutchen Kunstgeschichte." Strassburg, 1911.

Kipling, J. L. *Beast and Man in India.* London, 1904.

Kisch, Wilhelm. *Die alten Strassen und Plätze Wiens.* Vienna, 1883.

Klemm, Gustav. *Zur Geschichte der Sammlungen für Wissenschaft und Kunst in Deutschland.* Zerbst, 1837.

Knappe, Karl-Adolf. *Dürer: The Complete Engravings, Etchings and Woodcuts.* New York, n.d.

Koehler, Wilhelm R. W., (ed.). *Medieval Studies in Honor of A. Kingsley Porter.* Cambridge, Mass., 1939.

Koeman, C. *Collections of Maps and Atlases in the Netherlands.* Leyden, 1961.

――――. *The History of Abraham Ortelius and His "Theatrum orbis terrarum."* Lausanne, 1964.

Kriegk, G. L. *Geschichte von Frankfurt.* Frankfurt, 1871.

Kubler, G., and Soria, M. *Art and Architecture in Spain and Portugal.* "The Pelican History of Art," edited by Nikolaus Pevsner, Vol. XVII. Baltimore, 1958.

Kühnel, Ernst. *Die Arabeske: Sinn und Wandlung eines Ornaments.* Wiesbaden, 1949.

Kühnel, Ernest, and Goetz, Hermann. *Indische Buchmalereien aus dem Jahângîr-Album der Staatsbibliothek zu Berlin.* "Buchkunst des Orients," Vol. II. Berlin, 1924.

Kunz, George Frederick. *The Curious Lore of Precious Stones.* New York, 1938.

――――. *Ivory and the Elephant in Art, in Archaeology, and in Science.* New York, 1916.

Lane, Arthur. *Italian Porcelain.* London, n.d.

Lapeyre, Henri. *Une famille de marchands: les Ruiz. Contribution à l'etude du commerce entre la France et l'Espagne au temps de Phillippe II.* Paris, 1955.

Laufer, B. *The Giraffe in History and Art.* Chicago, 1928.

Lees-Milne, James. *Baroque in Spain and Portugal, and Its Antecedents.* London, 1960.

Legrand, F. C., and Sluys, F. *Arcimboldo et les arcimboldesques.* Brussels, 1955.

Lehmann-Hartleben, K., and Olsen, E. C. *Dionysiac Sarcophagi in Baltimore.* Baltimore, 1942.

Lewin, Louis. *Phantastica: Narcotic and Stimulating Drugs, Their Use and Abuse.* New York, 1964.

Lhotsky, Alphons. *Die Geschichte der Sammlungen.* In *Festschrift zur Feier des fünfzigjährigen Bestandes,* Vol. II, Pts. 1 and 2. Vienna, 1941–45.

Lichtenberg, Reinhold. *Zur Entwicklungsgeschichte der Landschaftsmalerei bei den Niederländern und Deutschen im XVI. Jahrhundert.* Leipzig, 1892.

Lieb, N. *Die Fugger und die Kunst im Zeitalter der hohen Renaissance.* Munich, 1958.

Liverani, Guiseppe. *Catalogo delle porcellane dei Medici.* Faenza, 1936.

———. *Five Centuries of Italian Majolica.* New York, 1960.

Loisel, Gustave. *Histoire des ménageries de l'antiquité à nos jours.* 3 vols. Paris, 1912.

Lopes, Joaquim Mauricio. *Les Portugais à Anvers au XVIᵉ siècle.* Antwerp, 1895.

Lucas-Dubreton, Jean. *Le monde enchanté de la Renaissance: Jerôme Cardan l'halluciné.* Paris, 1954.

Luchner, L. *Denkmal eines Renaissancefürsten: Versuch einer Rekonstrution des Ambraser Museums von 1583.* Vienna, 1958.

McCurdy, Edward. *The Mind of Leonardo da Vinci.* New York, 1939.

McDermott, W. C. *The Ape in Antiquity.* Baltimore, 1938.

Magalhães-Godinho, Vitorino. *Os descobrimentos e a economia mundial.* 2 vols. Lisbon, 1963.

Mahon, Denis. *Studies in Seicento Art and Theory.* London, 1947.

Maiuri, A. *Pompei-Ercolana: I nuovi scavi.* Naples, 1927.

Mâle, E. *L'art religieux après le Concile de Trente.* Paris, 1932.

Marlier, Georges. *La renaissance flamande, Pierre Coeck d'Alost.* Brussels, 1966.

Martin, J. R. *The Farnese Gallery.* Princeton, N. J., 1965.

Masson, Georgina. *Italian Gardens.* New York, 1961.

May, Alfred. *Wien in alten Ansichten.* Salzburg, 1965.

May, Florence Lewis. *Hispanic Lace and Lace Making.* New York, 1939.

———. *Silk Textiles of Spain.* New York, 1957.

Mazzotti, Giuseppe. *Ville Venete.* Rome, 1963.

Meiss, Millard. *French Painting in the Time of Jean de Berry.* 2 vols. New York, 1967.

Menendez-Pidal, Gonzalo. *Imagen del mundo hacia 1570: Segun noticias del consejo de Indias y de los tratadistas espanoles.* Madrid, 1944.

Mercer, Edward. *English Art, 1553–1625.* Oxford, 1962.

Michel, Francisque. *Recherches sur le commerce, la fabrication, et l'usage des étoffes de soie, et d'argent, et autres tissues précieux en occident, principalement en France, pendant le moyen âge.* 2 vols. Paris, 1852–54.

Michiel, Marcantonio. *Notizia d'opere di disegno pubblicata e illustrata da D. Jacopo Morelli.* Bologna, 1884.

Molinier, E. *Venise, ses arts décoratifs.* Paris, 1889.

Murray, David. *Museums: Their History and Their Use.* 3 vols. Glasgow, 1904.

Murray, H. J. R. *A History of Chess.* London, 1913.

Murray, Linda. *The Late Renaissance and Mannerism.* New York, 1967.

Naravane, V. S. *The Elephant and the Lotus.* Bombay, 1965.

Bibliography

Nichols, R. S. *Spanish and Portuguese Gardens*. New York, 1902.

Nissen, Claus. *Die naturwissenschaftliche Illustration*. Bad Münster am Stein, 1950.

———. *Herbals of Five Centuries*. Munich, 1958.

Oakeshott, Walker Fraser. *Some Woodcuts by Hans Burgkmair* (Printed as Appendix to the Fourth Part of "*Le Relationi universali di Giovanni Botero*," *1618*). Oxford, 1960.

Oberhummer, Eugen. *Konstantinopel unter Suleiman dem Grossen: Aufgenommen im Jahre 1559 durch Melchior Lorichs aus Flensburg*. Munich, 1902.

Olmedilla y Puig, Joquin. *Estudio histórico de la vida y escritos del sabio médico, botánico, y escritor del siglo XVI, Cristobal Acosta*. Madrid, 1899.

Olschki, Leo. *Marco Polo's Asia*. Berkeley, 1960.

Orbaan, J. A. F. *Stradanus te Florence, 1553–1605*. Rotterdam, 1903.

Panofsky, Erwin. *The Life and Art of Albrecht Dürer*. 2 vols. Princeton, 1955.

Parr, C. M. *Jan van Linschoten: The Dutch Marco Polo*. New York, 1964.

Pecchiai, Pio. *Il Gesù di Roma*. Rome, 1952.

———. *Roma nel cinquecento*. Bologna, 1948.

Peregallo, Prospero. *Cenni intorna alla colònia italiana in Portogallo nei sècoli XIV, XV, e XVI*. Genoa, 1907.

Pereira, Gabriel. *Estudos eborenses, historia e arqueologia*. 3 vols. Evora, 1947–50.

Petri ab Hartenfels, G. C. *Elephantographia curiosa*. Erfurt, 1715.

Pevsner, N. *Academies of Art, Past and Present*. Cambridge, 1940.

Phillips, J. G. *China-Trade Porcelain*. Cambridge, Mass., 1956.

Phipson, Emma. *Animal Lore of Shakespeare's Time*. London, 1883.

Pinto, A. C. *Cadeiras portuguesas*. Lisbon, 1952.

Piper, Reinhard. *Das Tier in der Kunst*. Munich, 1922.

Plat, Hugh. *The Jewell House of Art and Nature*. London, 1653.

Podreider, F. *Storia dei tessuti d'arta in Italia*. Bergamo, 1928.

Pölnitz, G. F. von. *Jakob Fugger, Kaiser, Kirche, und Kapital in der oberdeutschen Renaissance*. 2 vols. Tübingen, 1949–51.

Pope, John Alexander. *Chinese Porcelains from the Ardebil Shrine*. Washington, D.C., 1956.

———. *Fourteenth-Century Blue-and-White: A Group of Chinese Porcelains in the Topkapu Sarayi Müzasi, Istanbul*. Freer Gallery of Art, "Occasional Papers," Vol. II, No. 1. Washington, D.C., 1952.

Portmann, A. *Die Tiergestalt*. Basel, 1948.

Pouzyna, I. V. *La Chine, l'Italie et les débuts de la Renaissance (XIIIᵉ–XIVᵉ siècles)*. Paris, 1935.

[Powell, Thomas.] *The History of Most Curious Manual Arts and Inventions*. . . . 3d ed. London, 1675.

Praz, Mario. *Belleza e bizzarria*. Milan, 1960.

———. *Studies in Seventeenth-Century Imagery*. 2d ed. Rome, 1964.

Priezac, Salomon de. *L'histoire des éléphants*. Paris, 1650.

Raczynski, Atarazy. *Les arts en Portugal*. Paris, 1846.

Randall, Lilian M. *Images in the Margins of Gothic Manuscripts*. Berkeley and Los Angeles, 1966.

Books

Read, Conyers. *Lord Burghley and Queen Elizabeth*. New York, 1960.

———. *Mr. Secretary Cecil and Queen Elizabeth*. New York, 1955.

Réal, D. *Tissus espagnoles et portugais*. Paris, 1925.

Reidemeister, L. *China und Japan in der Kunstkammer der brandenburgischen Kurfürsten.* Berlin, 1932.

Reinhardt, Hans. *Das Basler Münster*. Basel, 1961.

Reznicek, E. K. J. *Die Zeichnungen von Hendrick Goltzius*. 2 vols. Utrecht, 1961.

Riano, Juan F. *The Industrial Arts in Spain*. London, 1879.

Ricci, Corrado. *L'architecture italienne au XVIe siècle*. Paris, n.d.,

———. *Il tempio malatestiano in Rimini*. Milan and Rome, n.d.

Richards, G. R. B. *Florentine Merchants in the Age of the Medicis*. Cambridge, 1932.

Richter, Christian. *Über die fabelhaften Thiere*. Gotha, 1797.

Ridolfi, Carlo. *Le maraviglie dell'arti*. Venice, 1648.

———. *Vita di Giacopo Robusti detto il Tintoretto. . . .* Venice, 1642.

Riegler, R. *Das Tier im Spiegel der Sprache: Ein Beitrag zur vergleichenden Bedeutungslehre.* Leipzig, 1909.

Robin, P. A. *Animal Lore in English Literature*. London, 1936.

Rodocanachi, E. *La première Renaissance: Rome au temps de Jules II et de Léon X*. Paris, 1912.

Rogers, Millard B. "A Study of the Makara and Kirttimukha with Some Parallels in Romanesque Architectural Ornament of France and Spain." Ph.D. dissertation, Department of Art, University of Chicago, 1965.

Roscoe, W. *The Life and Pontificate of Leo X*. 4 vols. London, 1827.

Rose, W. *The Epic of the Beast*. London, n.d.

Rossi, Vittorio. *Dal Rinascimento al Risorgimento*. "Scritti di critica litteraria," Vol. III. Florence, 1930.

Rowland, Benjamin, Jr. *Art in East and West: An Introduction through Comparison*. Cambridge, Mass., 1954.

Roy, Claude. *Arts fantastiques*. Paris, 1960.

Rozan, C. *Les animaux dans les proverbes*. 2 vols. Paris, 1902.

Rubio, Julián Maria. *Felipe II y Portugal*. Madrid, 1927.

Ruska, J. *Das Steinbuch des Aristoteles.* Heidelberg, 1912.

Russo, Lia. *La fontana di Piazza Pretoria in Palermo*. Palermo, 1961.

Saintenoy, Paul. *Les arts et les artistes à la cour de Bruxelles*. Académie royal de Belgique, Classe des Beaux-Arts, "Mémoires," 2d ser., Vol. II, fasc. 3. Brussels, 1932.

Salis, Arnold von. *Antike und Renaissance*. Zurich, 1947.

Sampayo Ribeiro, Mario de. *O retrato de Damião de Gois por Alberto Dürer, processo e historia de uma atourda*. Coimbra, 1943.

Santos, Reynoldo dos. *O azulejo em Portugal*. Lisbon, 1957.

———. *Faiança portuguesa, séculos XVI e XVII*. Lisbon, 1960.

———. *O estilo manuelino* Lisbon, 1952.

———. *Oito séculos de arte portuguesa: História e espírito*. Lisbon, 1967.

———. *A Torre de Belém, 1514–20*. Coimbra, 1922.

Santos Simões, J. *Os azulejos do paço de Vila Viçosa*. Lisbon, 1945.

Scheil, Gustav. *Die Tierwelt in Luthers Bildersprache in seinen reformatorisch-historischen und polemischen deutschen Schriften*. Bernburg, 1897.

Schéle, Sune. *Cornelis Bos: A Study of the Origins of the Netherland Grotesque*. Stockholm, 1965.

Scherer, Valentin. *Die Ornamentik bei Albrecht Dürer*. Strassburg, 1902.

Schierlitz, E. *Die bildlichen Darstellungen der indischen Gottestrinität in der älteren ethnographischen Literatur*. Munich, 1927.

Schlosser, Julius von. *Die Kunst- und Wunderkammern der Spätrenaissance*. Leipzig, 1908.

Schramm, Percy E. *Sphaira, Globus, Reichsapfel, Wanderung und Wandlung eines Herrschaftszeichens*. Stuttgart, 1958.

Schürer, Oskar. *Prag: Kultur, Kunst, Geschichte*. Vienna and Leipzig, 1930.

Schuette, Maria, and Müller-Christensen, Sigrid. *The Art of Embroidery*. London, 1964.

Schwoebel, Ralph. *The Shadow of the Crescent: The Renaissance Image of the Turk (1453–1517)*. Nieuwkoop, 1967.

Seznec, Jean. *La survivance des dieux antiques: Essai sur le rôle de la tradition mythologique dans l'Humanisme et dans l'art de la Renaissance*. London, 1940.

Shearman, John *Mannerism*. London, 1967.

Shepard, Odell. *The Lore of the Unicorn*. Boston and New York, 1930.

Silva Nascimento, João Filipe da, and Cardoso Pinto, Augusto. *Cadeiras portugueses*. Lisbon, 1952.

Silveira, Luis. *Ensaio de iconografia das cidades portuguesas do ultramar*. 4 vols. Lisbon, 1957.

Skelton, R. A. *Decorative Printed Maps of the 15th to 18th Centuries*. London, 1952.

Slomann, V. *Bizarre Designs in Silks*. Copenhagen, 1953.

Smith, Ronald Bishop. *The First Age of the Portuguese Embassies . . . to the Kingdoms and Islands of Southeast Asia (1509–21)*. Bethesda, Md., 1968.

Smith, William S. *Interconnections in the Ancient Near East: A Study of the Relationships between the Arts of Egypt, the Aegean, and Western Asia*. New Haven, 1965.

Smyth, C. H. *Mannerism and Maniera*. Locust Valley, N.Y., 1963.

Soil, E. *Les tapisseries de Tournai*. Tournai, 1892.

Solier, René de. *L'art fantastique*. Paris, 1961.

Soulier, Gustave. *Les influences orientales dans la peinture toscane*. Paris, 1924.

Sousa Viterbo, Francesco Marques de. *O thesouro do rei de Ceylão. . . .* Lisbon, 1904.

Souza, Luiz de. *Vida de Dom Fr. Bartolomeu dos Martires.*Viana, 1619.

Speth-Holterhoff, S. *Les peintres flamands de cabinets d'amateurs au XVIIᵉ siècle*. Brussels, 1957.

Sponsel, J. L. *Das Grüne Gewölbe zu Dresden*. 4 vols. Leipzig, 1925–32.

Stengel, Walter. *Alte Wohnkultur in Berlin und in der Mark im Spiegel des Quellens des 16.–19. Jahrhunderts*. Berlin, 1958.

Sterling, Charles. *La nature morte de l'antiquité à nos jours*. Paris, 1952.

Sthyr, Jergen. *Dansk Grafik, 1500–1800*. 2 vols. Copenhagen, 1943.

Stockbauer, Jacob. *Die Kunstbestrebungen am bayerischen Hofe unter Herzog Albrecht V und Herzog Wilhelm V*. "Quellenschriften für Kunstgeschichte," Vol. VIII. Vienna, 1874.

Strauss, Gerald. *Nuremburg in the Sixteenth Century*. Bloomington, Ind., 1967.

Strzygowski, J. *Der Bilderkreis des griechischen Physiologus des Kosmas Indicopleustes und Okateuch nach Handschriften der Bibliothek zu Smyrna*. Leipzig, 1899.

——— *et al. Asiatische Miniaturenmalerei*. Klagenfurth, 1933.

Stuart, Dorothy M. *A Book of Birds and Beasts*. London, 1957.

Targioni-Tozzetti, Antonio. *Cenni storici sulla introduzione di varie piante nell' agricoltura e orticoltura*. Florence, 1896.

Taylor, Francis Henry. *The Taste of Angels: A History of Art Collecting from Rameses to Napoleon*. Boston, 1948.

Telfer, W. *The Treasure of São Roque: A Sidelight on the Counter Reformation*. London, 1932.

Tervarent, G. de. *Attributs et symboles dans l'art profane, 1450–1600*. 2 vols. Geneva, 1958.

Thode, Henry. *Tintoretto*. Bielefeld and Leipzig, 1901.

Thoma, Hans. *Kronen und Kleinodien: Meisterwerke des Mittelalters und der Renaissance aus den Schatzkammern der Residenz zu München*. Munich, 1955.

Thompson, James W., (ed.). *The Frankfurt Book Fair: The Francofordiense Emporium of Henri Estienne*. Chicago, 1911.

Thomson, W. G. *A History of Tapestry*. London, 1930.

Tooley, R. V. *Maps and Map-Makers*. London, 1949.

Tormo y Monzó, E. *Os desenhos das antiqualhas que vio Francisco d'Ollanda, pintor português*. Madrid, 1940.

Valenti, D. *Museum Museorum*. Frankfurt am Main, 1703–14.

Vasconcelos, Joaquem Antonio da Foncesca. *Ceramica portuguesa*. Oporto, 1884.

———. *Ourivesaria portuguesa*. 2 vols. Porto, 1914–15.

Vieira da Silva, A. *As muralhas da Ribeira de Lisboa*. 2 vols. Lisbon, 1940–41.

Vilhena Barbosa, Ignacio de. *Apontamentos para a história das collecções e dos estudos de zoologia em Portugal*. Lisbon, 1885.

Vocht, H. de. *History of the Foundation and Rise of the Collegium Trilingue Lovaniense, 1517– 1550*. 4 vols. Louvain, 1951–55.

Volker, T. *Porcelain and the Dutch East India Company*. Leyden, 1954.

Voss, Hermann. *Die Malerei der Spätrenaissance in Rom und Florenz*. 2 vols. Berlin, 1920.

Wagner, Henry R. *Sir Francis Drake's Voyage around the World*. San Francisco, 1926.

Walker, John. *Bellini and Titian at Ferrara: A Study of Styles and Taste*. London, 1956.

Wallis, Henry. *The Oriental Influence on the Ceramic Art of the Italian Renaissance*. London, 1900.

Watson, W. C. *Portuguese Architecture*. London, 1908.

Wauvermans, H. E. *Histoire de l'école cartographique belge et anversoise du XVIe siècle*. 2 vols. Amsterdam, 1964.

Werner, K. *Die Sammlungen Kremsmünster*. Berlin, 1936.

White, T. H. *The Book of Beasts*. London, 1954.

Wichmann, Hans, and Wichmann, Siegfried. *Schach: Ursprung und Wandlung der Spielfigur in zwölf Jahrhunderten*. Munich, 1960.

Wiles, Bertha Harris. *Fountains of Florentine Sculptors and Their Followers*. Cambridge, 1933.

Bibliography

Willett, C. W., and Cunningham, P. *The History of Underclothes.* London, 1951.

Winzinger, F. *Die Zeichnungen Martin Schongauers.* Berlin, 1962.

Würtenberger, F. *Der Manierismus.* Vienna, 1962. English edition, New York, 1964.

Yates, Frances A. *The Valois Tapestries.* London, 1959.

Yerkes, R. M., and Yerkes, A. W. *The Great Apes.* New Haven, 1929.

Yriarte, Charles. *Un condottiere au XVe siècle.* Paris, 1882.

Zimmermann, Max. *Die bildenden Künste am Hofe Herzog Albrechts V. von Bayern.* Strassburg, 1895.

ARTICLES

Åberg, Nils. "The Orient and Occident in the Art of the Seventh Century," *Vitterhets Historie och Antikvitats akademiens Handlingar* (Stockholm), Vol. LVI, Nos. 1–3 (1943–47).

Adhémar, Jean. "The Collection of Paintings of Francis the First," *Gazette des Beaux-Arts,* XXX (1946), 5–16.

———. "French Sixteenth Century Genre Painting," *Journal of the Warburg and Courtauld Institutes,* VIII (1945), 191–95.

Antal, F. "The Social Background of Italian Mannerism," *Art Bulletin,* XXX (1948), 82–103.

Aquarone, J. B. "L'aventure portugaise dans les mers de l'Inde," *Bulletin de l'Association Guillaume Budé,* 3d ser., No. 3 (1953), pp. 62–79.

Aquirre, Emiliano. "Evolutionary History of the Elephant," *Science,* CLXIV (June 20, 1969), 1366–75.

Askew, P. "Perino del Vaga's Decorations for the Palazzo Doria, Genoa," *Burlington Magazine,* XCVIII (1956), 46–56.

Avery, Louise. "Chinese Porcelain in English Mounts," *Metropolitan Museum of Art Bulletin,* N.S., II (1943), 266–72.

Ball, V. "A Commentary on the Colloquies of Garcia da Orta, on the Simples, Drugs, and Medicinal Substances of India," *Proceedings of the Irish Academy,* I (1889), 381–415.

Baltrušaitis, Jurgis. "Monstres et emblèmes; une survivance du moyen âge aux XV et XVI siècles," *Médecine de France,* XXXIX (1953), 17–30.

Bandmann, Günther. "Das Exotische in der europäischen Kunst." In *Der Mensch und die Künste: Festschrift Heinrich Lützeler,* pp. 337–54. Düsseldorf, 1962.

———. "Ikonologie des Ornamentes und der Dekoration," *Jahrbuch für Asthetik und allgemeine Kunstwissenschaft,* IV (1958–59), 232–58.

Bataillon, M. "La cour découvre le nouveau monde." In J. Jacquot (ed.), *Fêtes et cérémonies au temps de Charles Quint,* pp. 13–27. Paris, 1960.

Benesch, O. "The Orient as a Source of Inspiration of the Graphic Arts of the Renaissance." In *Festschrift Friedrich Winkler,* pp. 242–53. Berlin, 1959.

Bentham-Jutting, W. S. S. van. "A Brief History of the Conchological Collections at the Zoölogical Museum of Amsterdam, with Some Reflections on 18th Century Shell Cabinets and Their Proprietors . . .," *Bijdragen tot de Dierkunde,* XXVII (1939), 167–246.

Articles

Bernard, Henri. "Humanisme Jésuite et Humanisme de l'Orient," *Analecta Gregoriana* (Rome), 1954, pp. 187–92.

———. "Le passage de Guillaume Postel chez les premiers Jésuites de Rome (mars 1544–decembre 1545)." In *Mélanges Chamard*, pp. 227–43. Paris, 1951.

Beylen, J. van. "Schepen op kaarten ten tijde van Gerard Mercator," *Duisburger Forschungen*, VI (1962), 122–42.

Bialostocki, Jan. "Les bêtes et les humaines de Roelant Savery," *Musées royaux des Beaux-Arts Bulletin* (Brussels), No. 1 (March, 1958), pp. 69–97.

Blair, Patrick. "Osteographia elephantina; or, A Full and Exact Description of All the Bones of an Elephant, Which Died near Dundee, April the 27th, 1706...," *Philosophical Transactions*, (London), XXVII (1710–12), 53–168.

Born, Wolfgang. "An Indo-Portuguese Painting of the Late Sixteenth Century," *Gazette des Beaux-Arts*, XXX (1946), 165–78.

———. "Some Eastern Objects from the Hapsburg Collections," *Burlington Magazine*, LXIX (1936), 269–76.

———. "Textile Ornaments of the Post-Classical East and of Medieval Europe," *Ciba Review*, No. 37 (1941), pp. 1331–46.

Boxer, C. R. "The Carreira da India (Ships, Men, Cargoes, Voyages)." In *O centro de estudos históricos ultramarinos e as comemorações henriquinas*, pp. 33–82. Lisbon, 1961.

———. "Portuguese Influence in Japanese Screens, from 1590 to 1614," *The Connoisseur*, XCVIII (1936), 79–85.

Braamcamp Freire, Anselmo. "Inventario da guarda-roupa de D. Manuel," *Archivo historico portuguez*, II (1904), 381–415.

———, (ed.). "Cartas de quitaçao del Rei D. Manuel," *Archivo historico portuguez*, I (1903), 94–96, 163–68, 200–208, 240–48, 276–88, 328, 356–68, 398–408, 447–48.

Bretschneider, E. "Early European Researches into the Flora of China," *Journal of the North China Branch of the Royal Asiatic Society*, N.S., XV (1880), 1–186.

Briggs, George W. "The Indian Rhinoceros as a Sacred Animal," *Journal of the American Oriental Society*, LI (1931), 276–82.

Brito, Gomes de. "Os pachidermes do estado d'El Rei D. Manuel," *Revista de educação e ensino*, IX (1894), 80–85.

Burckhardt, Jakob. "Die Sammler." In *Beiträge zur Kunstgeschichte von Italien*, pp. 341–573. 2d ed. Stuttgart, 1911.

Cagnat, R. "La première représentation connue du mode d'embarquement de l'éléphant," *L'ami des monuments et des arts* (Paris), XIV (1900), 67–70.

Calvesi, Maurizio. "Il sacro bosco di Bomarzo." In *Scritti di storia dell'arte in onore di Lionello Venturi*, I, 369–402. Rome, 1956.

Cauwenberghe, E. van. "Quelques recherches sur les anciennes manufactures de tapisseries à Audenarde," *Annales de l'académie d'archéologie de Belgique*, XIII (1856), 271–94, 429–73.

Cesano, S. L. "Le monete di Cesare," *Atti della pontifica Accademia Romana di Archeologia*, 3d ser., *Rendiconti*, XXIII–XXIV (1947–48), 103–51.

Chartrou, J. M. "Les entrées solonnelles à Bordeaux au XVIᵉ siècle," *Revue historique de Bordeaux*, XXIII (1930), 49–59, 97–104.

Bibliography

Châtelet-Lange, Liliane. "The Grotto of the Unicorn and the Garden of the Villa di Castello," *Art Bulletin*, L (1968), 51–58.

Chattopadhyaya, Kamaladevi. "Origin and Development of Embroidery in Our Land." In *Textiles and Embroideries of India*, Pt. 2, pp. 5–10. Bombay, 1965.

Chmelenz, E. "Das Diurnale oder Gebetbuch des Kaiser Maximilians I," *Jahrbuch der kunsthistorischen Sammlungen des allerhöchsten Kaiserhauses*, III (1885), 95–128.

Codrington, K. de B. "Mughal Marquetry," *Burlington Mazagine*, LVIII (1931), 79–85.

Codrington, Ralph, and Edwards, K. de B. "The Indian Period of European Furniture: A Reply to Dr. Slomann," *Burlington Magazine*, LXV (1934), 273–78.

Cole, F. J. "The History of Albrecht Dürer's Rhinoceros in Zoölogical Literature." In *Science, Medicine and History: Essays on the Evolution of Scientific Thought and Medical Practice, Written in Honour of Charles Singer*, I, 337–56. Collected and edited by E. Ashworth Underwood. London, 1953.

Coste, C. "Anciennes figurations du rhinocéros," *Acta tropica*, III (1946), 116–29.

Dainville, François de. "Les amateurs de globes," *Gazette des Beaux-Arts*, 6th ser., LXXI (1968), 51–64.

Delen, A. J. J. "Bücherillustrationen des Peter Coeck van Alost," *Gutenberg Jahrbuch*, 1930, pp. 189–97.

Delisle, Leopold. "L'éléphant de Henri IV," *Bibliothèque de l'Ecole des Chartes*, LIV (1893), 358–62.

De Roover, Florence E. "Lucchese Silks," *Ciba Review*, No. 80 (1950), pp. 2902–30.

Dodgson, Campbell. "The Story of Dürer's Ganda." In A. Fowler (ed.), *The Romance of Fine Prints*, pp. 45–56. Kansas City, 1938.

Doege, Heinrich. "Die Trachtenbücher des 16. Jahrhunderts." In *Beiträge zur Bücherkunde und Philologie: August Wilmanns zum 25 März 1903 gewidmet*, pp. 429–44. Leipzig, 1903.

Dony, Paul. "Der Manuelstil in Portugal (1495–1521)," *Das Münster: Zeitschrift für christliche Kunst und Kunstwissenschaft*, XIX (1966), 229–43.

Druce, G. C. "The Elephant in Medieval Legend and Art," *Archaeological Journal*, LXXVI (1919), 1–73.

Dworschak, F. "Die Renaissancemedaille in Österreich," *Jahrbuch der kunsthistorischen Sammlungen in Wien*, N.S., I (1926), 215–25.

Ehlers, E. "Bemerkungen zu den Tierdarstellungen im Gebetbuche des Kaisers Maximilian I," *Jahrbuch der königlichen preussischen Kunstsammlungen*, XXXVIII (1917), 151–76.

Ehrmann, J. "Drawings by Antoine Caron for the Valois Tapestries," *Art Quarterly*, XXI (1958), 47–65.

Einstein, L. "A Chinese Design in St. Mark's at Venice," *Revue archéologique*, 5th ser., XXIV (1926), 28–31.

Erdmann, K. "Orientalische Tierteppiche auf Bildern des 14. und 15. Jahrhunderts," *Jahrbuch der königlichen preussischen Kunstsammlungen*, L (1929), 261–98.

Erffa, Hans Martin von. "Das Programm der Westportale des Pisaner Domes," *Mitteilungen des kunsthistorischen Institutes in Florenz*, XII (1965), 55–106.

Ettinghausen, Richard. "Near Eastern Book Covers and Their Influence on European Bindings," *Ars orientalis*, III (1959), 113–31.

Articles

Falke, Otto von. "Chinesische Seidenstoffe des 14. Jahrhunderts und ihre Bedeutung für die Seidenkunst Italiens," *Jahrbuch der königlichen preussischen Kunstsammlungen*, XXXIII (1912), 176–92.

Faria de Morais, A. "Les tapisseries de D. João de Castro," *Bulletin des études portugaises et de l'institut français au Portugal*, N.S., XIX (1955–56), 64–138.

Fechner, Jelena. "Die Bilder von Roelant Savery in der Eremitage," *Jahrbuch des kunsthistorischen Institutes der Universität Graz* (Graz, 1966–67), II, 93–101.

Filliozat, Jean. "L'Inde et les échanges scientifiques dans l'Antiquité," *Journal of World History*, I (1953–54), 353–67.

———. "Les premières étapes de l'indianisme," *Bulletin de l'Association Guillaume Budé*, 3d ser., No. 3 (1953), pp. 80–96.

Focillon, Henri. "Quelques survivances de la sculpture romane dans l'art français." In W. R. W. Koehler (ed.), *Medieval Studies in Memory of A. Kingsley Porter*, II, 453–66. Cambridge, Mass., 1939.

Frade, Fernando. "Os animais e seus produtos nos *Colóquios* de Garcia da Orta." *Garcia da Orta*, 400th Anniversary Volume (1963), pp. 695–714.

Francesco, Grete de. "Silk Fabrics in Venetian Paintings," *Ciba Review*, No. 29 (1940), pp. 1036–48.

Friedländer, Max J. "Der Meister mit dem Papagei," *Phoebus* (Basel), II (1949), 49–54.

Gibbs, F. W. "Historical Survey of the Japanning Trade (I–IV)," *Annals of Science* (London), VII (1951), 401–6; IX (1953), 88–95, 197–232.

Giglioli, H. H. "Notes on Some Remarkable Specimens of Old Peruvian 'Ars plumaria' in the Mazzei Collection," *Internationales Archiv für Ethnographie*, VII (1894), 221–26.

Giglioli, O. H. "Jacopo Ligozzi disegnatore e pittore di piante e di animali," *Dedalo*, IV (1923–24), 554–60.

Giuseppi, M. S. "The Work of Theodore de Bry and His Sons, Engravers," *Proceedings of the Huguenot Society of London*, XI (1915–17), 204–26.

Goetz, Hermann. "An Indian Element in 17th Century Dutch Art," *Oud-Holland*, LIV (1937), 222–30.

———. "Oriental Types and Scenes in Renaissance and Baroque Painting," *Burlington Magazine*, LXXIII (1938), 53–60.

Goeze, E. "Liste der seit dem 16. Jahrhundert bis auf die Gegenwart in Gärten und Parks Europas eingeführten Bäume und Sträucher," *Mitteilungen der deutschen dendrologischen Gesellschaft*, XXV (1916), 129–201.

Goitein, S. D. "From the Mediterranean to India: Documents on the Trade to India, South Arabia, and East Africa from the Eleventh and Twelfth Centuries," *Speculum*, XXIX (1954), 181–97.

Gollob, H. "Der Turkismus und die Buchgraphik des 16. Jahrhunderts," *Gutenberg-Jahrbuch*, XXXVII (1962), 425–29.

Gombrich, E. H. "Renaissance Artistic Theory and the Development of Landscape Painting," *Gazette des Beaux-Arts*, 6th ser., XLI (1953), 335–37.

Grabar, André "Le succès des arts orientaux à la cour Byzantine sous les Macédoniens," *Münchener Jahrbuch der bildenden Kunst*, 3d ser., II (1951), 32–60.

Gray, Basil. "The Export of Chinese Porcelain to India," *Transactions of the Oriental Ceramic Society* (London), XXXVI (1964–66), 21–37.

Bibliography

Guerra, Francisco. "Drugs from the Indies and the Political Economy of the Sixteenth Century," *Analecta medico-historica*, I (1966), 29–54.

Haller, R. "The History of Indigo Dyeing," *Ciba Review*, No. 85 (1951), pp. 3077–81.

Hamann, Richard. "Das Tier in der Romanischen Plastik Frankreichs." In W. R. W. Koehler (ed.), *Medieval Studies in Memory of A. Kingsley Porter*, II, 413–52. Cambridge, Mass., 1939.

Hamy, E. T. "Le père de la zoölogie française: Pierre Gilles d'Albi," *Revue des Pyrénées*, XII (1900), 561–88.

Hartt, F. "Raphael and Giulio Romano with Notes on the Raphael School," *Art Bulletin*, XXVI (1944), 67–94.

Hausmann, T. "Der Pommersche Kunstschrank," *Zeitschrift für Kunstgeschichte*, XXII (1959), 337–52.

Heckscher, William S. "Bernini's Elephant and Obelisk," *Art Bulletin*, XXIX (1947), 165–82.

Heichelheim, F. M. "Byzantine Silks," *Ciba Review*, No. 75 (1949), pp. 2742–67.

Heikamp, Detlef. "Zur Geschichte der Uffizien-Tribuna und der Kunstschränke in Florenz und Deutschland," *Zeitschrift für Kunstgeschichte*, XXVI (1963), 193–268.

Hendley, T. H. "Indian Animals, True and False, in Art, Religion, Etc.," *Journal of Indian Art and Industry* (London), XVI (1914), 71–80.

Hochstetter, Ferdinand von. "Ueber mexikanische Reliquien aus der Zeit Montezumas in der K. K. Ambraser Sammlung," Königliche Akademie der Wissenschaften (Vienna), Philosophisch-historische Classe, *Denkschriften*, pp. 83–104. Vienna, 1885.

Hoff, Door Bert van't. "Gerard Mercator (1512–94) en de kartografie van de 16ᵉ eeuw," *Duisburger Forschungen*, VI (1962), 1–27.

Hoogewerff, G. J. "Philips van Winghe," *Mededeelingen van het Nederlandsch Historisch Instituut te Rome*, VII (1927), 59–82.

Huber, Eduard von. "Die Malerfamilie Burgkmair von Augsburg," *Zeitschrift des historischen Vereins für Schwaben und Neuburg*, I (1874), 310–20.

Irwin, John. "The Commercial Embroidery of Gujerat in the Seventeenth Century," *Journal of the Indian Society of Oriental Art*, XVII (1949), 51–56.

———. "Indian Textiles in Historical Perspective." In *Textiles and Embroideries of India*, Pt. I, pp. 4–6. Bombay, 1965.

———. "Indo-Portuguese Embroideries of Bengal," *Arts and Letters: The Journal of the Royal India, Pakistan and Ceylon Society*, XXVI (1952), 65–73.

———. "A Jacobean Vogue for Oriental Lacquer-Ware." *Burlington Magazine*, XCV (1953), 194.

———. "Origins of the 'Oriental Style' in English Decorative Art," *ibid.*, XCVII (1955), 106–14.

———. "Reflections on Indo-Portuguese Art," *ibid.*, XCVII (1955), 386–88.

Ivanov, Nicolas. "Fêtes à la cour des derniers Valois," *Revue du XVIᵉ siècle*, XIX (1932), 96–122.

Ivins, William M. "A Neglected Aspect of Early Print-Making," *Metropolitan Museum of Art Bulletin*, VII (1948), 51–59.

Articles

Jenyns, Soames. "Feather Jacket (*Jimbaori*) of the Momoyama Period (1573–1638) Supposed to Have Belonged to Hideyoshi (1536–1598)," *British Museum Quarterly*, XXXII (1967), 48–52.

————. "The Chinese Porcelains in the Topkapu Saray, Istanbul," *Transactions of the Oriental Ceramic Society* (London), XXXVI (1964–66), 43–72.

Kaufmann, Alexander. "Über Thierliebhaberei im Mittelalter," *Historisches Jahrbuch der Görresgesellschaft*, V (1884), 399–423.

Kenner, Friedrich. "Die Porträtsammlung des Erzherzogs Ferdinand von Tirol," *Jahrbuch der kunsthistorischen Sammlungen des allerhöchsten Kaiserhauses*, XIX (1898), Pt. I, 6–146.

Kiichi, Matsuda. "Armaduras japonesas en la Real Armería de Madrid," *Monumenta Nipponica*, XVI (1960–61), 175–81.

Kish, George. "The Japan on the 'Mural Atlas' of the Palazzo Vecchio, Florence," *Imago mundi*, VIII (1951), 52–54.

Kömmerling-Fitzler, Hedwig. "Der Nürnberger Georg Pock († 1528–29) in Portugiesisch-Indien und im Edelsteinland Vijayanagara," *Mitteilungen des Vereins für Geschichte der Stadt Nürnberg*, LV (1967–68), 137–84.

Kris, Ernst. "Georg Hoefnagel und die wissenschaftliche Naturalismus." In *Festschrift für Julius Schlösser*, pp. 243–53. Zurich, 1927.

————. "Der Stil 'Rustique,'" *Jahrbuch der kunsthistorischen Sammlungen in Wien*, N.S., I (1926), 137–208.

Kurz, O. "A Volume of Mughal Drawings and Miniatures," *Journal of the Warburg and Courtauld Institutes*, XXX (1967), 251–71.

Ladendorf, H. "Zur Frage der künstlerischen Phantasie." In *Mouseion: Studien aus Kunst und Geschichte für Otto H. Förster*, pp. 21–34. Cologne, 1960.

Laprade, Jacques de. "Un inventaire des tentures et des meubles transportés de Pau à Nérac en 1578," *Bibliothèque d'Humanisme et Renaissance*, XXIV (1962), 413–30.

Leix, Alfred. "Early Islamic Textiles," *Ciba Review*, No. 43 (1942), pp. 1573–78.

————. "The Sassanid Textiles and Their Influence on the Western World," *Ciba Review*, No. 43 (1942), pp. 1559–65.

Lemos, Maximiliano. "Damião de Goes," *Revista de história*, IX (1920), 5–19, 208–26; X (1921), 41–66; XI (1922), 34–66.

Lightbown, R. W. "Oriental Art and the Orient in Late Renaissance and Baroque Italy," *Journal of the Warburg and Courtauld Institutes*, XXXII (1969), 228–78.

Liu, James J. Y. "The *Fêng-yüeh Chin-nang*: A Ming Collection of Yüan and Ming Plays and Lyrics Preserved in the Royal Library of San Lorenzo, Escorial, Spain," *Journal of Oriental Studies* (Hongkong), IV (1957–58), 79–107.

Loehr, Max. "The Chinese Elements in the Istanbul Miniatures," *Ars orientalis*, I (1954), 85–89.

Lopes, Carlos da Silva. "As conquistas e descobrimentos na heráldica portuguesa do século XVI," *Armas e Troféus*, 2d ser., I, No. 2 (1960), 107–24.

Lozzi, Carlo. "Cesare Vecellio e i suoi disegni e intagli per libri di costumi e di merletti," *La bibliofilia*, I (1900), 3–11.

Madrazo, Pedro de. "Über Kronungsinsignien und Staatsgewänder Maximilian I. und Karl V. und ihr Schicksal in Spanien," *Jahrbuch der kunsthistorischen Sammlungen des allerhöchsten Kaiserhauses*, IX (1889), 45–51.

Bibliography

Marchesi, V. "Le relazioni tra la repubblica Veneta e il Portogallo dall' anno 1522 al 1797," *Archivio veneto*, XXXIII (1887), 9–42, 283–307; XXXIV (1887), 5–30.

Matos, Luís de. "Forma e natura e costumi del rinoceronte," *Boletim internacional de bibliografia Luso-Brasileira* I (1960), 387–98.

———. "Natura intelletto e costumi dell'elefante," *ibid.*, I (1960), 44–55.

McGrath, R. L. "The 'Old' and 'New' Illustrations for *Cartari's imagini* . . . ," *Gazette des Beaux-Arts*, 6th ser., LIV (1962), 210–20.

Merrill, E. D. "Eastern Asia as a Source of Ornamental Plants," *Journal of the New York Botanical Garden*, XXXIV (1933), 238–43.

———. "Loureiro and His Botanical Work," *Proceedings of the American Philosophical Society*, LXXII (1933), 229–39.

Mez, M. L. "Una decorazione di Daniele da Volterra nel Palazzo Farnese a Roma," *Rivista d'arte*, XVI (1934), 276.

Mitchell, Charles. "Ex libris Kiriaci Anconitani," *Italia medioevale e umanistica*, V (1962), 280–88.

Moeller, M. A. "An Indo-Portuguese Embroidery from Goa," *Gazette des Beaux-Arts*, 6th ser., XXXIV (1948), 117–32.

Münsterberg, Oskar. "Bayern und Asien," *Zeitschrift des Münchener Alterthumsvereins*, N.S., VI (1894), 14–27.

———. "Leonardo da Vinci und die chinesische Landschaftsmalerei," *Orientalisches Archiv*, XII (1910), 92–100.

Müntz, M. "Les collections d'antiquités des Médicis," *Mémoires de l'Académie des Inscriptions*, XXXV, Pt. 2, 140–53.

Nair, V. "A Nair Envoy to Portugal," *Indian Antiquary*, LVII (1928), 157–59.

Naumann, W. "Bark Cloth in the Reports of the First Explorers of the South Seas," *Ciba Review*, No. 33 (1940), pp. 1175–79.

Neumann, Erwin. "Das Inventar der rudolfinischen Kunstkammer von 1607/11." In Swedish National Museum, *Analecta reginensis*. Stockholm, 1966.

Neves Tavares, Carlos das. "A botânica nos *Colóquios* de Garcia da Orta," *Garcia da Orta*, XI, No. 4 (1963), 667–93.

Noack, Ferdinand. "Triumph und Triumphbogen." In *Vorträge der Bibliothek Warburg*, *1925–1926*, pp. 185–90. Leipzig-Berlin, 1928.

Olschki, Leonardo. "Asiatic Exoticism and the Italian Art of the Early Renaissance," *Art Bulletin*, XXVI (1944), 95–108.

Palm, Erwin Walter. "Dürer's Ganda and a XVI Century Apotheosis of Hercules at Tunja," *Gazette des Beaux-Arts*, 6th ser., XLVIII (1956), 65–74.

Panofsky, D. and E. "Iconography of the Galerie François Ier," *Gazette des Beaux-Arts*, 6th ser., LII (1958), 119–30.

Payne, Joseph Frank. "On the 'Herbarius' and 'Hortus sanitatis,'" *Transactions of the Bibliographical Society*, VI (1900–1901), 63–126.

Pessanha, José, "A porcelana em Portugal: Primeiras tentativas," *Archivo historico portuguez*, I (1903), 20–24, 58–64, 89–93, 124–28, 169–76, 236–39.

Picard, G. C. "La mosaique romaine au Afrique du Nord," *Gazette des Beaux-Arts*, 6th ser., LII (1958), 198–203.

Popham, A. E. "Elephantographia," *Index to Life and Letters*, V (1930), 179–91.

———. "On a letter of Joris Hoefnagel," *Oud-Holland*, LIII (1936), 145–51.

Reidemeister, Leopold. "Philipp Hainhofer und die ostasiatische Kunst." In *Festschrift Adolph Goldschmidt*, pp. 109–12. Berlin, 1935.

Reis-Santos, Luis. "Garrofas chinesas de Jorge Alvares," *Belas Artes: Revista e boletim da Academia Nacional de Belas Artes* (Lisbon), 2d ser., No. 18 (1962), pp. 59–69.

Rezende, Marquez de. "Embaixada de El-Rei D. Manuel ao Papa Leão X," *O Panorama: Journal litterario e instructivo*, XI (1854), 219–22, 253–55, 261–63, 271–72, 274–75.

Rinaldi, Stefania Mason. "Appunti per Paolo Fiammingo," *Arte veneta*, XIX (1965), 95–105.

Roethlisberger, Marcel. "La tenture de la licorne dans la Collection Borromée," *Oud-Holland*, LXXXII (1967), 85–115.

Romdahl, Axel L. "Pieter Brueghel der Ältere und sein Kunstschaffen," *Jahrbuch der kunsthistorischen Sammlungen des allerhöchsten Kaiserhauses*, XXV (1905), 85–169.

Rowe, J. H. "The Renaissance Foundations of Anthropology," *American Anthropologist*, LXXVII (1965), 1–20.

Rumpf, Fritz. "Beiträge zur Geschichte der frühen Spielkarten." In *Festschrift Adolph Goldschmidt*, pp. 77–91. Berlin, 1935.

Salerno, Luigi. "Arte, scienza e collezioni nel manierismo." In *Scritti di storia dell'arte in onore di Mario Salmi*, III, 193–214. Rome, 1963.

Santos, Reynaldo dos. "A exposição de arte portuguesa em Londres," *Belas Artes* (Lisbon), 2d ser., No. 9 (1956), pp. 6–9.

———. "A India Portuguesa e as artes decorativas," *ibid.*, No. 7 (1954), pp. 3–16.

Saxl, Fritz. "Die spätmittelalterliche Vermischung orientalischer und europäischer Tradition." In F. Saxl and H. Meier, *Verzeichnis astrologischer und mythologischer Handschriften*, pp. 90–118. London, 1953.

Schlegel, G. "Hennins or Conical Lady's Hats in Asia, China, and Europe," *T'oung pao*, III (1892), 422–29.

Schmidt, Robert. "China bei Dürer," *Zeitschrift des deutschen Vereins für Kunstwissenschaft*, VI (1939), 103–6.

Schuette, Marie. "History of Lace," *Ciba Review*, No. 73 (1949), pp. 2685–98.

Schulze, I. "Zum Problem der Verweltlichung religiöser Bildformen in der deutschen Kunst des 16. Jahrhunderts und der Folgezeit," *Renaissance und Humanismus in Mittel- und Osteuropa*, I (1962), 249–60.

Schurhammer, Georg. "Desenhos orientais do tempo de S. Francisco Xavier," *Garcia da Orta*, Special Number (1956), pp. 247–56.

———. "Die Jesuitenmissionäre des 16. und 17. Jahrhunderts und ihr Einfluss auf die japanische Malerei." In *Jubiläumsband 1933 der deutschen Gesellschaft für Natur- und Völkerkunde Ostasiens*, I, 116–26. Leipzig, 1934.

Seznec, Jean. "Erudits et graveurs au XVIᵉ siècle," *Mélanges d'histoire et d'archéologie*, XLVII (1930), 118–37.

———. "Un essai de mythologie comparée au debut du XVIIᵉ siècle," *ibid.*, XLVIII (1931), 268–81.

Bibliography

Sinor, Denis. "Sur les noms altaïques de la licorne," *Wiener Zeitschrift für die Kunde des Morgenlandes*, LVI (1960), 170–75.

Slomann, V. "Elfenbeinreliefs auf zwei singhalesischen Schreinen des 16. Jahrhunderts," *Pantheon*, XX (1937), 357–60; XXI (1938), 12–19.

———. "The Indian Period of European Furniture," *Burlington Magazine*, LXV (1934), 113–26, 157–71, 201–14.

———. "The Indian Period of European Furniture: A Reply to Criticisms," *ibid.*, LXVI (1935), 21–26.

Soria, Martin S. "Francisco de Campos (?) and Mannerist Ornamental Design in Evora, 1555–1580," *Belas Artes* (Lisbon), 2d ser., No. 10 (1957), pp. 33–39.

Soulier, G. "Les influences persanes dans la peinture florentine du XVᵉ siècle." In *L'Italia e l'arte straniera*, pp. 194–98. Rome, 1922.

Sousa Viterbo, Francisco Marques de. "O orientalismo portugues no século XVI," *Boletim da Sociedade de geografia de Lisboa*, XII (1892–93), Nos. 7–8, pp. 317–30.

———. "O theatro na corte de D. Filippe II," *Archivo historico portuguez*, I (1903), 1–7.

Spinazzola, Vittorio. "Di un rinoceronte marmoreo del Museo Nazionali di Napoli (preteso falso di Pompei)," *Bollettino d'arte*, VII (1913), 143–46.

———. "Pompeii and My New Excavations," *Arts and Decorations*, XVIII (1923), 9–12.

Spriggs, A. I. "Oriental Porcelain in Western Paintings, 1450–1700," *Transactions of the Oriental Ceramic Society* (London), XXXVI (1964–66), 73–87.

Standen, Edith A. "The *Suiets de la Fable* Gobelins Tapestries," *Art Bulletin*, XLVI (1964), 143–57.

Stannard, Jerry. "Dioscorides and Renaissance Materia Medica," *Analecta medico-historica*, I (1966), 1–21.

Steinlein, G. "München im 16. Jahrhundert," *Volkskunst und Volkskunde*, VIII (1910), 49–84.

Sterling, Charles. "Le paysage dans l'art européen de la Renaissance et dans l'art chinois," *L'Amour de l'art*, 1931, pp. 9–21, 101–12.

Stevenson, Allan. "The Quincentennial of Netherlandish Blockbooks," *British Museum Quarterly*, XXXI (1967), 83–87.

Théodorides, J., and Grmek, M. D. "Remarques sur l'utilisation des animaux dans la matière médicale au XVIᵉ siècle," *Analecta medico-historica*, I (1966), 23–27.

Theuerkauff, Christian. "Zum Bild der Kunst- und Wunderkammer des Barock," *Alte und moderne Kunst*, LXXXVIII (1966), 2–18.

Thibout, Marc. "L'éléphant dans la sculpture romane française," *Bulletin monumental* (Paris), CV (1947), 183–95.

Thomas, Henry. "Copperplate Engravings in Portuguese Books of the Late Sixteenth Century," *The Library*, 4th ser., XXII (1942), 145–62.

Tietze-Conrat, E. "Die Erfinding im Relief, ein Beitrag zur Geschichte der Kleinkunst," *Jahrbuch der kunsthistorischen Sammlungen in Wien*, XXXV (1920), 99–176.

Toda, Kenji. "The Effect of the First Great Impact of Western Culture in Japan, Illustrated by the Study of the Introduction of the Western Form of Pictorial Art," *Journal of World History*, II (1954), 429–45.

Torre de Assunção, Carlos Fernando. "A mineralogia nos Colóquios," *Garcia da Orta*, Special Commemorative Volume (1963), pp. 717–21.

Catalogues

Toynbee, Paget. "Tartar Cloths," *Romania*, XXIX (1900), 559–64.

Van Beylen, Jules. "Schepen op kaarten ten tijde van Gerard Mercator," *Duisburger Forschungen*, VI (1962), 131–57.

Varde-Valivlakar, W. "An Account of the Expedition to the Temples of Southern India Undertaken by Martin Alfonso de Souza, the 12th Governor of Portuguese India," *Indian Antiquary*, XLI (1912), 238–48.

Varron, A. "From the History of the Umbrella and the Sunshade," *Ciba Review*, No. 42 (1942), pp. 1519–25.

——. "The Umbrella as an Emblem of Dignity and Power," *ibid.*, No. 42 (1942), pp. 1510–17.

Vetterli, W. A. "The History of Indigo," *Ciba Review*, No. 85 (1951), pp. 3066–71.

Waille, Victor. "Note sur l'éléphant, symbole de l'Afrique à propos d'un bronze récemment découvert à Berrouaghia (Algérie)," *Revue archéologique*, XVII (1891), 380–84.

Ward-Jackson, P. "Some Rare Drawings by Melchior Lorichs," *The Connoisseur*, CXXXV (1955), 88–89.

Wechser, Paul. "The 'Idea' in Giuseppe Arcimboldo's Art," *Magazine of Art*, XLIII (1950), 3–8.

Weitzmann, Kurt. "Icon Painting in the Crusader Kingdom," *Dumbarton Oaks Papers*, No. XX (1966), pp. 51–83.

Weixlgärtner, A. "Die weltliche Schatzkammer in Wien," *Jahrbuch der kunsthistorischen Sammlungen in Wien*, N.S., I (1926), 300–303.

Weller, F. "Buddhistische Einflüsse auf die christliche Kunst des europäischen Mittelalters," *Wiener Zeitschrift für Kunde des Morgenlandes*, L (1954), 65–70.

Wentzel, Hans. "Abseitige Trouvaillen an Goldschmiedearbeiten." In F. Dettweiler *et al.* (eds.), *Studien zur Buchmalerei und Goldschmiedekunst des Mittelalters*, pp. 65–78. Marburg, 1967.

Wildenstein, Georges. "Un fournisseur d'habits de théâtre et de mascarades à Paris sous Henri III," *Bibliothèque d'Humanisme et Renaissance*, XXIII (1961), 99–106.

Winner, Matthias. "Raffael malt einen Elefanten," *Mitteilungen des kunsthistorischen Institutes in Florenz*, XI, Pts. II–III (November, 1964), 71–109.

Winzinger, Franz. "Albrecht Altdorfer und die Miniaturen des Triumphzuges Kaiser Maximilian I," *Jahrbuch der kunsthistorischen Sammlungen in Wien*, N.S. LXII (1966), 157–72.

Wittkower, R. "Miraculous Birds," *Journal of the Warburg Institute*, I (1937–38), 253–57.

——. "Marvels of the East. A Study in the History of Monsters," *ibid.*, V (1942), 157–97.

Yashiro, Yukio. "The 'Oriental' Character in Italian Tre- and Quattrocento Paintings," *East and West* (Rome), III (1952), 81–87.

Zander, Giuseppe, *et al.* "Gli elementi documentari sul Sacro Bosco," *Quaderni dell' Istituto di storia dell'architettura* (University of Rome), April, 1955, pp. 19–32.

CATALOGUES

L'art portugais de l'époque des grandes découvertes au XXe siècle. Published by Exposition portugaise de l'époque des grandes découvertes, . . . Paris, n.d.

Bibliography

Blancken, Gerard. *Catalogue de ce qu'on voit de plus remarquable dans la chambre de l'anatomie publique, de l'université de la ville de Leide. Rangè en ordre selon les nombres suivans par G . . . B . . . .* Leyden, 1704.

Cart, Germaine, *et al. Le paysage en Orient et en Occident.* Paris, 1960.

Castres, France. Musée Goya. Musée Jaurès. *Les plus belles peintures des collections privées du Tarn du XVᵉ au XVIIIᵉ siècle.* Castres, 1956.

Fischer, E. *Melchior Lorck: Drawings from the Evelyn Collection at Stonor Park, England, and from the Department of Prints and Drawings, the Royal Museum of Fine Arts, Copenhagen.* Copenhagen, 1962.

Florence. Esposizione A. Vespucci. *Collection of Maps and Documents.* Florence, 1954–55.

———. Galleria degli Uffizi, Gabinetto disegni e stampe. *Mostra di disegni del Ligozzi (1547–1626).* Florence, 1924.

———. Galleria degli Uffizi, Gabinetto disegni e stampe. *Mostra di disegni di Jacopo Ligozzi (1547–1626): Catalogo.* Edited by M. Bacci and A. Forlani. Florence, 1961.

———. Palazzo Strozzi. *Mostra della caccia nelle arti.* Florence, 1960.

Lisbon. Museu das Janelas Verdes. Esposiçao temporária. *Mobiliario Indo-Portugues.* Lisbon, 1938.

Margaret of Austria. *Margareta van Oostenrijk en haar Hof.* Mechelen, 1958.

Martin-Méry, Gilbert. *L'Europe et la découverte du monde.* Bordeaux, 1960.

Muraro, M. *Catalogue of the Exhibition of Venetian Drawings from the Collection Janos Scholz.* Venice, 1957.

Rogers, Francis M. *Europe Informed: An Exhibition of Early Books Which Acquainted Europe with the East.* Cambridge, Mass., 1966.

Rosas, José, Jr. *Palacio da Ajuda: Catalogo das jóias e pratas da coroa.* Lisbon, 1954.

Sweden. Stockholm Museum. *Dutch and Flemish Drawings.* Stockholm, 1953.

Thoma, H., and Brunner, H. *Schatzkammer der Residenz München: Katalog.* Munich, 1964.

Vienna. Kunsthistorisches Museum. *Sonderausstellung Karl V.* Vienna, 1958.

———. National Museum. *Führer durch die K. K. Ambraser Sammlung.* Vienna, 1879, 1882, and later years.

Illustrations

KATHERINA REGINA FRANCORVM

1. Catharine de' Medici, Queen of France. Engraving by Hans Liefrinck. Now in the National Library, Vienna. From V. von Klarwill, *The Fugger News-Letters, Second Series* (London, 1926), facing p. 68.

2. Engraving of Archduke Ferdinand of Tyrol. Original in Kunsthistorisches Museum, Vienna. From J. von Schlosser, *Die Kunst- und Wunderkammern der Spätrenaissance* (Leipzig, 1908), frontispiece.

3. Engraved portrait of Archduke Ferdinand in a triumph, in Jakob Schrenk von Notzing, *Armamentarium heroicum* (German ed.; Augsburg, 1603). From A. Lhotsky, *Die Geschichte der Sammlungen* (Vienna, 1941–45), Vol. I, Pt. 2, pl. XIX.

4 and 5. Chinese studio paintings from Ambras. Now in Kunsthistorisches Museum, Vienna. Both from Schlosser, *op. cit.* (pl. 2), facing p. 74.

6. East Asian *objets d'art* from Ambras. Now in Kunsthistorisches Museum, Vienna. From Schlosser, *op. cit.* (pl. 2), p. 68.

8. Bezoar stones from Ambras. Now in Kunsthistorisches Museum, Vienna. From Schlosser, *op. cit.* (pl. 2), p. 101.

7. Seashells in settings from Ambras. Now in Kunsthistorisches Museum, Vienna. From Schlosser, *op. cit.*, p. 50.

9. Rock crystal elephant of Indian workmanship in a gold and enameled setting added to it in Renaissance Europe. From W. Born, "Some Eastern Objects from the Hapsburg Collections," *Burlington Magazine*, LXIX (1936), pl. IID.

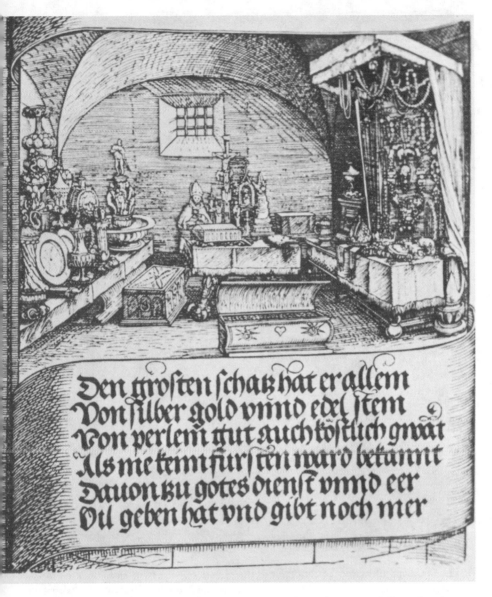

Den grösten schatz hat er allem
Von silber gold vnnd edel stem
Von perlem gut auch köstlich gwat
Als me keim fürsten ward bekannt
Dauon zu gotes dienst vnnd eer
Vil geben hat vnd gibt noch mer

10. Woodcut of treasury of Emperor Maximilian I, from the Triumph by Albrecht Dürer. Now in Kunsthistorisches Museum, Vienna. From Lhotsky, *op. cit.* (pl. 3), pl. IX.

Gottorffifche KunstKammer.

Schleswig in Gottfriedt
Schultzens Buchladen.

11. Engraving of cabinet of curiosities of the princes of Schleswig-Holstein at Gottorp. Originally published in A. Olearius, *Gottorpische Kunstkammer* (Schleswig, 1674). From F. C. Legrand and F. Sluys, *Arcimboldo et les arcimboldesques* (Brussels [1955]), pl. 23. Courtesy of André de Rache, Brussels.

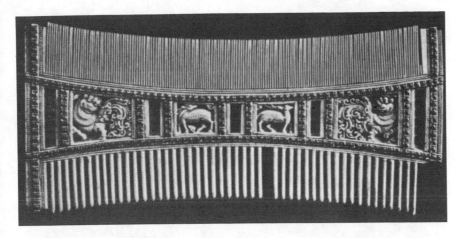

12. Sinhalese comb with reliefs. In Residenzmuseum, Munich. From V. Slomann, "Elfenbeinreliefs auf zwei singhalesischen Schreinen des 16. Jahrhunderts," *Pantheon*, XXI (1938), 19.

13. Front of ivory chest from Ceylon. From Slomann, *loc. cit.*, pl. I.

14. Bezoar cup of Emperor Rudolf II, attributed to Jan Vermeyen. From A. Weixlgärtner, "Die weltliche Schatzkammer in Wien," *Jahrbuch der kunsthistorischen Sammlungen in Wien*, N.S., I (1926), 301.

15. Engraved portrait of Carolus Clusius (Charles de L'écluse) by Jakob de Gheyn. From F. W. H. Hollstein, *Dutch and Flemish Etchings, Engravings, and Woodcuts, ca. 1450–1700* (Amsterdam, n.d.), VII, 152. Courtesy of A. L. van Gendt and Co., Amsterdam.

16. A collection, probably that of Abraham Ortelius. Painting by Hans Francken, now in Kunsthistorisches Museum, Vienna (Inv. No. 1048). From J. Denucé, *De konstkamers van Antwerpen . . .* (The Hague, 1932), pl. 7.

17. Tower of Belém, Lisbon. Attributed to Francisco de Arruda. From R. dos Santos, *O estilo manuelino* (Lisbon, 1952), pl. LXXIII.

18. Monumental archway of the "Capelas imperfeitas," Batalha, Portugal. From Dos Santos, *op. cit.* (pl. 17), pl. XLIX.

19. Manueline window of the Convent of Christ at Tomar, Portugal. Work of Diogo de Arruda. From Dos Santos, *op. cit.*, pl. LIX.

20. Upper portion of the portal of the church of Matriz Golega, Portugal. From Dos Santos, *op. cit.* (pl. 17), pl. XXI.

21. Portal of the Casado Capítulo, convent of the Loios, Evora, Portugal. From Dos Santos, *op. cit.*, pl. CVII.

22. Manueline interior of the Cathedral of Guarda, Portugal. From Dos Santos, *op. cit.* (pl. 17), pl. XIII.

23. Stalls of Santa Cruz, Coimbra. From W. C. Watson, *Portuguese Architecture* (London, 1908), fig. 74.

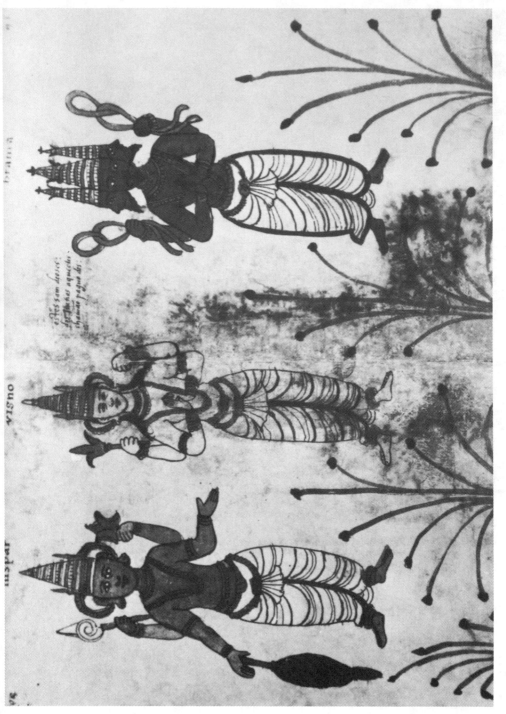

24. Vishnu, Siva, Brahma. Watercolor by an anonymous European artist, *ca.* 1540. Courtesy of the Bibliotheca Casanatense, Rome.

25. Sacrifice and *pagode* in India. Watercolor by an anonymous European artist, *ca.* 1540. Courtesy of the Bibliotheca Casanatense, Rome.

26. Kanarese harvesting rice. Watercolor by an anonymous European artist, *ca.* 1540. Courtesy of the Bibliotheca Casanatense, Rome.

27. Náyar marriage. Watercolor by an anonymous European artist, *ca.* 1540. Courtesy of the Bibliotheca Casanatense, Rome.

28. Kanarese washing clothes. Watercolor by an anonymous European artist, *ca.* 1540. Courtesy of the Bibliotheca Casanatense, Rome.

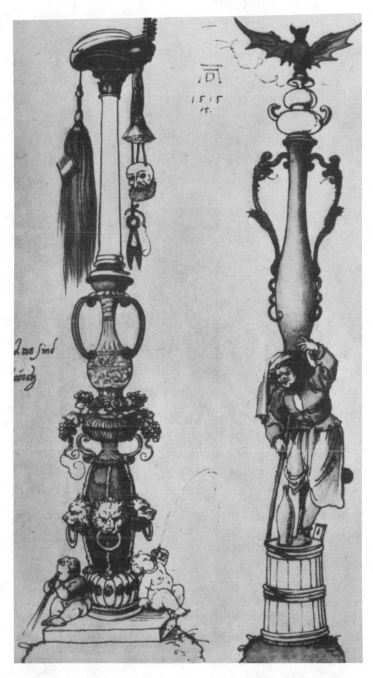

29. Two fantastic columns. Colored pen drawing by Albrecht Dürer. Original in British Museum. From R. Schmidt, "China bei Dürer," *Zeitschrift des deutschen Vereins für Kunstwissenschaft*, VI (1939), 105.

30. Adoration of the Magi by Vasco Fernandes. In Museu Grão Vasco, Viseu, Portugal. From R. dos Santos, *Oito séculos de arte potruguesa* (Lisbon, 1967), fig. 55.

31. Detail from Adoration of the Magi by Gregorio Lopes. From Dos Santos, *op. cit.*
(pl. 30), facing p. 112.

32. Adoration of the Magi, Portuguese school. Cathedral of Evora. From Dos Santos, *op. cit.* (pl. 30), fig. 117.

33. Adoration of the Magi by Francisco Henriques. São Francisco de Evora. From Dos Santos, *op. cit.* (pl. 30), fig. 36.

34. The Triumph of Asia, a fresco painting by Pauwels Franck (Paolo Fiammingo), *ca.* 1584–85. In Schloss Kirchheim of Hans Fugger. From S. F. Rinaldi, "Appunti per Paolo Fiammingo," *Arte veneta,* XIX (1965), 99.

35. The four Japanese envoys to Europe, with Father Diogo de Mesquita. From J. A. Abranches Pinto et al., *La première ambassade du Japon en Europe, 1582–1592* (Tokyo, 1942), following p. xxi.

36. The plant *Datura stramonium*. Painting by Jacopo Ligozzi. From Gabinetto disegni e stampe, Galleria degli Uffizi, *Mostra di disegni di Jacopo Ligozzi (1547–1626)* (Florence, 1961), fig. 6.

37. Mountainous landscape. Painting by Nicolas Manuel Deutsch. From J. Bousquet, *La peinture manieriste* (Neuchâtel, 1964), p. 271.

38. Detail from "The Return of the Herd," by P. Brueghel the Elder. From F. Grossmann, *Brueghel: The Paintings* (rev. ed.; London, 1966), pl. 108.

39. Grotesque head with elephant in center, painting by G. Arcimboldo. Original in Graz Museum. From W. Suida, *Österreichische Kunstschätze* (Vienna, 1911), pl. 51.

40. "The Admiral (?)" Anonymous (sixteenth-century painting), after Arcimboldo. Private collection, Paris. From Legrand and Sluys, *op. cit.* (pl. 11), pl. 17. Courtesy of André de Rache, Brussels.

41. Painting (*Kutūhala*) of composite elephant with rider. Mughul school, *ca.* 1590. In National Museum of India, New Delhi (No. 48. 14/20). Courtesy of Professor Pramod Chandra.

42. Two composite elephants in combat. An Indian miniature. From T. H. Hendley, "Indian Animals, True and False, in Art, Religion, Etc.," *Journal of Indian Art and Industry*, XVI (1914), pl. 3*b*.

43. Composite elephant formed of female musicians and driven by Krishna. From Hendley, *op. cit.*, pl. 7*b*.

44. "People of Calicut." Woodcut by Hans Burgkmair. From G. Hirth, *Kulturgeschicht-liches Bilderbuch aus drei Jahrhunderten* (Munich, 1881–90), Vol. I, pl. 276.

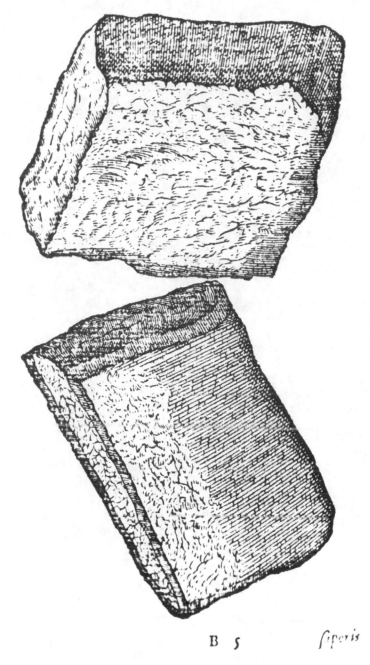

B 5   *ſiperis*

45. Engraving of sago bread. From C. de L'écluse (Clusius),... *Aliquot notae*...
(Antwerp, 1582), p. 25. Courtesy of the Newberry Library.

rebat,

46. Engraving of banyan tree. From L'écluse, *op. cit.* (pl. 45), p. 18. Courtesy of the Newberry Library.

47. "Hunting for Wild Ducks in China." Engraving by Philippe Galle after Stradanus. From R. Caillois, *Au coeur du fantastique* (Paris, 1965), facing p. 145. Courtesy of Editions Gallimard, Paris.

FERDINANDES MAGALANES LVSITANVS *infra sua cuigo superato. Ego? tellari al Austrum paura dele, euisqz navis omnium pritus atqz nessima Solis cursum in terris condata; tervr totus globum circunit. An del. ꝏ·D·XXII·*

48. "Magellan's Discovery of the Straits." Woodcut by Stradanus. From R. Wittkower, "Miraculous Birds," *Journal of the Warburg Institute*, Vol. I (1937–38), facing p. 256, fig. *c.*

49. Etching by Pieter van der Borcht of Portuguese triumphal arch erected for solemn *entrée* at Antwerp of July 18, 1593. From J. Boch, *Descriptio publicae gratulationis . . .* (Antwerp, 1595). Courtesy of the Newberry Library.

50. Tower of Azuchi Castle. After sketch by Philips van Winghe. Engraving from V. Cartari, *Imagini delli dei de gl'antichi*, facsimile of the 1647 edition (Graz, 1693), p. 381.

Il già nominato Filippo Vvinghemio in certo suo foglio disegnò già i Tempij d'alcune Deità Giaponesi, situati sopra alcuni alti rupi. & raccontaua d'hauerli Cauati dalli Pittori. che gl'Ambasciatori Giaponesi portarono à donare à P.pa Gregorio XIII.

51. Gate of Azuchi Castle. Sketch by Philips van Winghe. Engraving from Cartari, *op. cit.*, p. 382.

in Stolber Jauarischer man mit sein Chineischt dolchen auff der seyten desfen hesst oder
nichtheben ist wie ein Teuffel dan diser so hie neben gerissen nach ein rechten dolchen so
n Jaua Komen Conterfait ist Zu der rechten ist ein weib so Reiss gekaust vnd also haia
egt. Die Zur Lincken Jst wol eine von den furnembsten weibern Dess Pfeffers
wechst viel alda an den Cocos oder Nusebeumen etc.

52. People of Java and a god from the hilt of a kris worn by the middle figure. Engraving by Hans Sibmacher. From L. Hulsius, *Erste Schiffart* . . . (Nuremberg, 1598). Courtesy of the Newberry Library.

53. Tapestry of the India series, Tournai. From H. Göbel, *Die Wandteppiche* (Leipzig, 1928), Vol. II, pl. 227. Courtesy of Klinkhardt and Biermann, Brunswick. Tapestries in plates 53 and 57 seem to have a common source.

54. Tapestry of the India series, Oudenaarde. From Göbel, *op. cit.* (pl. 53), Vol. II, pl. 226. Courtesy of Klinkhardt and Biermann, Brunswick.

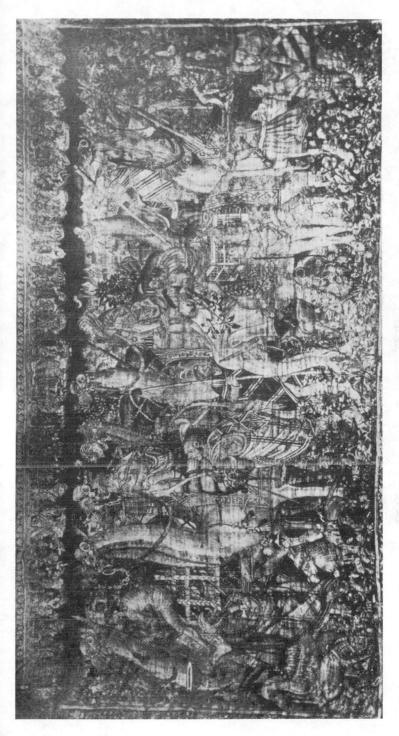

55. "The Camel Caravan." Tapestry of the early sixteenth century in the Museum of Fine Arts of Barcelona. From P. Ackerman, *Three Early Sixteenth-Century Tapestries* (New York. 1932), pl. 20.

56. "The Magi." Tapestry of *ca.* 1550 manufactured in the Low Countries. From Göbel, *op. cit.* (pl. 53), pl. 134. Courtesy of Klinkhardt and Biermann, Brunswick.

57. "Landing at Calicut." Sixteenth-century tapestry. From Ackerman, *op. cit.* (pl. 55), pl. 16. Cf. pl. 53; the tapestries seem to have a common source.

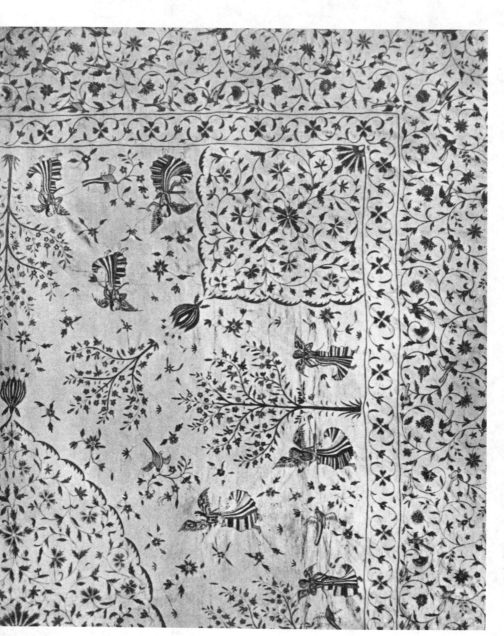

58. Detail from a Gujarati bedspread in chain stitch, late sixteenth century. From J. Irwin, "The Commercial Embroidery of Gujarat in the Seventeenth Century," *Journal of the Indian Society of Oriental Art*, XVII (1949), pl.

OMNIVM PENE

EVROPAE, ASIAE, APHRICAE ATQVE AMERICAE

GENTIVM HABITVS.

Habits de

Diuerses Nations de Levrope, Asie,
Asiqve et Amerioe.

Trachtenbuch:

Der furnembsten Nationen vnd Volcker kley:
dungen beyde Manns vnd Weybs personen
in Europa Asia Affrica vnd
America.

Abraham de Bruyn Excudit A.°
M. D. LXXXI

59. Engraved title page of A. de Bruyn, *Omnium pene* . . . (Antwerp, 1581). Courtesy of the Newberry Library.

Indica mulier cum viro, in America   *Indi et Indiæ Orientales .*

famina in America   *Athabalippa Rex ultimus Americæ*   *Vidua et Virgo Africana*   *Maura Granatensis*

58

60. Engraving of costumes of Africans, Asians, and Americans. From De Bruyn, *op. cit.* (pl. 59). Courtesy of the Newberry Library.

Matrona del-
la China.

61. Chinese matron. Woodcut from C. Vecellio, *Habiti antichi et moderni* . . . (Venice, 1598), facing p. 478.

62. Indian woman of moderate quality. Woodcut from Vecellio, *op. cit.* (pl. 61), facing p. 475.

63. Indian of quality. Woodcut from Vecellio, *op. cit.*, facing p. 472.

64. Chinese nobleman. Woodcut from Vecellio,
op. cit. (pl. 61), facing p. 480.

65. Lady of the Moluccas. Woodcut from
Vecellio, *op. cit.*, facing p. 476.

66. Chinese noblewoman. Woodcut from Vecellio, *op. cit.* (pl. 61), facing p. 479.

67. Chinese of moderate quality. Woodcut from Vecellio, *op. cit.*, facing p. 481.

68. East Indian woman of quality. Woodcut from Vecellio, *op. cit.* (pl. 61), facing p. 474.

69. Woodcut of Japanese youth with staff in figured robe. From Vecellio, *op. cit.*, facing p. 477.

70. Chinese export porcelain, 1557. In Victoria and Albert Museum, London. From J. G. Phillips, *China-Trade Porcelain* (Cambridge, Mass., 1956), fig. 2.

71. Vase of Medici porcelain. Reproduction of a drawing in J. C. Davillier, *Les origines de la porcelaine en Europe* (Paris, 1882), p. 68.

72. Flask of Medici porcelain. From A. Lane, *Italian Porcelain* (London, n.d.), pl. *2c*.

73. Gourd or flagon of Medici porcelain. Reproduction of a drawing in Davillier, *op. cit.* (pl. 71), p. 72.

74. Ewer of Medici porcelain. Reproduction of drawing in Davillier, *op. cit.* (pl. 71), p. 66.

5. Chinese porcelain bowl with silver-gilt mounting added in England, *ca.* 1585. Courtesy Metropolitan Museum of Art, Rogers Fund, 1944. From Phillips, *op. cit.* (pl. 70), fig. 13.

76. Pitcher with grotesque figures, from the ornamental series "Cups and Jugs" (1548) by Cornelius Floris. From S. Schéle, *Cornelis Bos* (Stockholm, 1965), fig. 13.

77. Turtle and shell, from the series "Cups and Jugs" by Cornelis Floris. From Schéle, *op. cit.*, fig. 12.

78. Exotic detail of lid design on chest belonging to Duke Albert V of Bavaria (*ca.* 1560), the work of Annibale Fontana of Milan. From H. Thoma, *Kronen und Kleinodien* (Munich, 1955), pl. 67.

79. Mughul-type chest with ivory inlays (*ca.* 1580). In National Museum, Stockholm. From V. Slomann, "The Indian Period of European Furniture," *Burlington Magazine*, LXV (1934), pl. II*b*, facing p. 114.

80. Studiolo of Francesco de' Medici, Palazzo Vecchio, Florence. From D. Heikamp, "Zur Geschichte der Uffizien-Tribuna und der Kunstschränke in Florenz und Deutschland," *Zeitschrift für Kunstgeschichte*, XXVI (1963), 194.

81. Indian chair with ivory inlays, *ca.* 1580. In University Museum, Uppsala, Sweden. From Slomann, *loc. cit.* (pl. 79), pl. II*b*, facing p. 114.

82. Exotic detail on silver tankard, Antwerp, *ca.* 1525. From Thoma, *op. cit.* (pl. 78), pl. 25.

83. Coconut cup in silver mounting of Emperor Charles V, *ca.* 1530. From Slomann, *loc. cit.* (pl. 12), XX (1937), 323.

84. Cartographic detail on lid ornament of a Rappoltstein goblet (*ca.* 1543) by Master Georg Kobenhaupt of Strassburg. From Thoma, *op. cit.* (pl. 78), pl. 34.

85. Coconut cup in silver setting, Amsterdam, 1590. From M. H. Gans and T. M. Duyvené de Wit-Klinkhamer, *Dutch Silver* (London, 1961), pl. 5.

86. "The Flight from Egypt" in the Book of Hours (1517) of King Manuel of Portugal. From Dos Santos, *op. cit.* (pl. 30), pl. 376.

87. "Elephant and People of Calicut." Woodcut by Hans Burgkmair. From Hirth, *op. cit.* (pl. 44), pl. 277.

NATVRA

Intelletto & costumi de lo Elephante cauato da Aristotele Plinio & Solino:& alcuni exempli de esso Elephante:insieme con vn Capitulo de defettiui de natura in Rima.

O Vel re inleto z excelso Emanuele de Portugallo z de regni acostati distrugitoz del populo infideles glozia z honoz fra tutti e baptizati: banendo el Papa córtese z fidele molti dopi magnifichi manadri: (no me ba dato vn tbema:z fa cb próprio so farui:audito:z:a tutti quanti vn dono

Non expectati de baver pero Perle Rubaz:ouer: Balais:argéto:on aure perche son cose che non pon tenerle chi nón possede richezza z thesauro a Emanuele e facil possederle che acosta la India e il grá paese Mato sto in Italia:z nó bo inito domen Géme ne Perle:z tal volta vn carlin

88. First page of small book of verse, author unknown, dated Rome, 1514. From L. de Matos, "Natura intelletto e costumi dell' elefante," *Boletim internacional de bibliographia Luso-Brasileira,* I (1960), 48.

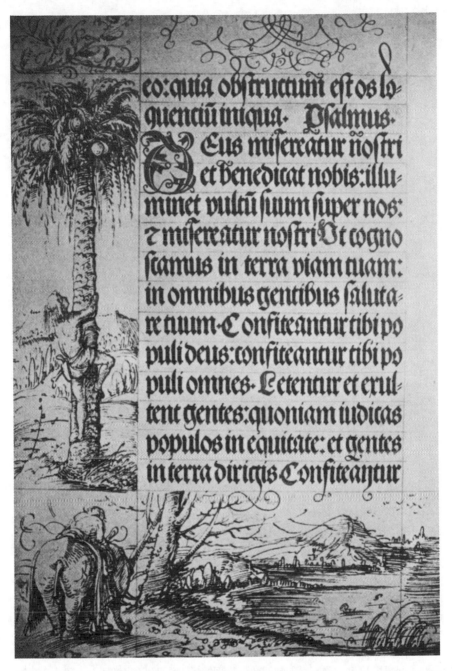

eo: quia obstructum est os lo-
quencium iniqua. Psalmus.
Eus misereatur nostri
et benedicat nobis: illu-
minet vultum suum super nos:
z misereatur nostri Ot cogno
stamus in terra viam tuam:
in omnibus gentibus saluta-
re tuum. Confiteantur tibi po
puli deus: confiteantur tibi po
puli omnes. Letentur et exul
tent gentes: quoniam iudicas
populos in equitate: et gentes
in terra dirigis Confiteantur

89. Drawing of elephant in tropical setting, in Maximilian's Prayer Book. From K. Giehlow (ed.), *Kaiser Maximilians I Gebetbuch* (Vienna, 1907), p. 58v.

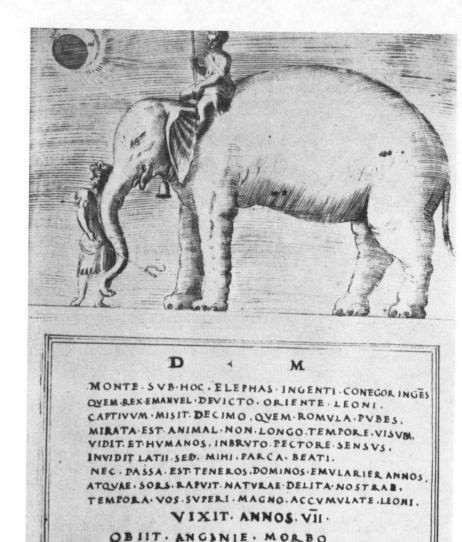

D   M

MONTE · SVB · HOC · ELEPHAS · INGENTI · CONEGOR INGĒS
QVEM · REX · EMANVEL · DEVICTO · ORIENTE · LEONI ·
CAPTIVVM · MISIT · DECIMO , QVEM · ROMVLA · PVBES ,
MIRATA · EST · ANIMAL · NON · LONGO · TEMPORE · VISVM,
VIDIT · ET · HVMANOS , INBRVTO · PECTORE · SENSVS ,
INVIDIT LATII · SED , MIHI · PARCA · BEATI ·
NEC · PASSA · EST · TENEROS , DOMINOS · EMVLARIER ANNOS ,
ATQVAE · SORS · RAPVIT · NATVRAE · DELITA · NOSTRAE ,
TEMPORA · VOS · SVPERI · MAGNO , ACCVMVLATE · LEONI ·

VIXIT · ANNOS · VII ·

OBIIT · ANGINIE · MORBO
ALTITVDO · ERAT · PALM · XII ·
IO · BAPTISTA · BRANCONIVS · AQVILANVS ·
A · CVBICVLO · ET · ELEPHANTIS · CVRAE · PRAEFEC ·
POSVIT ·
M ·   D' ·   X VIII · IVNII ·
LEONIS · X · PONT · ANNO · QVARTO ·
RAPHAEL · VRBINAS · QVOD · NATVRA · ABSTVLERAT
ARTE · RESTITVIT S

90. Pen drawing by Francisco d'Ollanda of Raphael's elephant and its inscription, *ca.* 1539. From E. Tormo y Monzó, *Os desenhos das antigualhas que vio Francisco d'Ollanda* (Madrid, 1940), p. 31v.

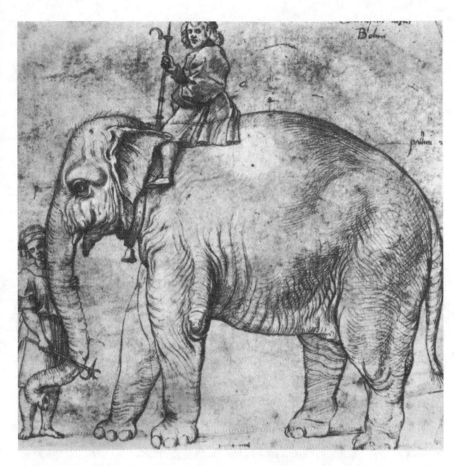

91. Hanno. A pen drawing after a Raphael drawing which is not extant. Courtesy of the
Kupferstichkabinett, Staatliche Museen, Berlin.

92. Hanno in stucco, by Giovanni da Udine. In the loggia of the Vatican. From M. Winner, "Raffael malt einen Elefanten," *Mitteilungen des kunsthistorischen Institutes in Florenz*, XI (1964), 101. cf. pl. 151.

POETA
BARABAL

93. "The Poet Baraballo on Hanno." Intarsia on portal (upper right-hand portion) of
the Stanza della Segnatura in the Vatican. Executed by Giovanni Barili. From E. Rodocanachi, *La première Renaissance* (Paris, 1912), pl. 18.

94. Woodcut of Hanno, published in S. Fanti, *Triompho di Fortuna* (Venice, 1526).

95. Pen drawing of elephant fountain at Villa Madama, Rome, by Marten van Heemskerck. From O. Fischel, *Raphael* (London, 1948), Vol. II, pl. 185A.

96. Elephant in the "Marriage Feast of Cupid and Psyche." Fresco by Giulio Romano in the Sala di Psiche of the Palazzo del Te, Mantua. From F. Hartt, *Giulio Romano* (New Haven, 1958), Vol. II, pl. 254.

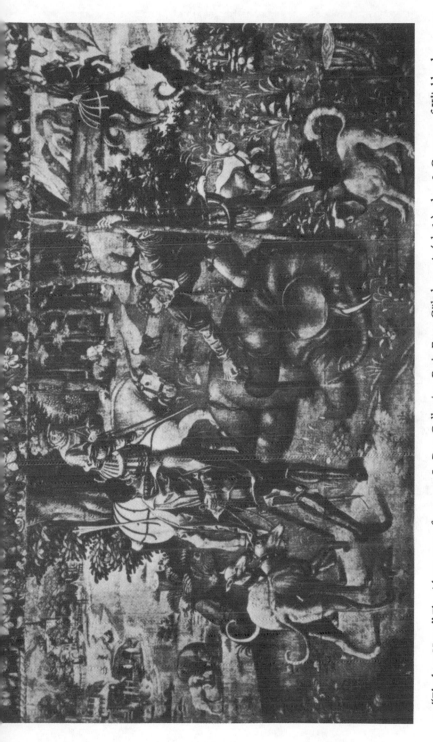

97. "Elephant Hunt." Flemish tapestry of 1535–40, Le Roy Collection, Paris. From Göbel, *op. cit.* (pl. 63), pl. 148. Courtesy of Klinkhardt and Biermann, Brunswick,

98. End relief on Sinhalese ivory chest, *ca.* 1545, showing King Bhuvanaika Bahu VII of Ceylon. From Slomann, *op. cit.* (pl. 12), pl. V.

99. Ivory chest of Ceylon, *ca.* 1545. End view. From H. Thoma and H. Brunner, *Schatzkammer der Residenz München* (Munich, 1964), pl. 46.

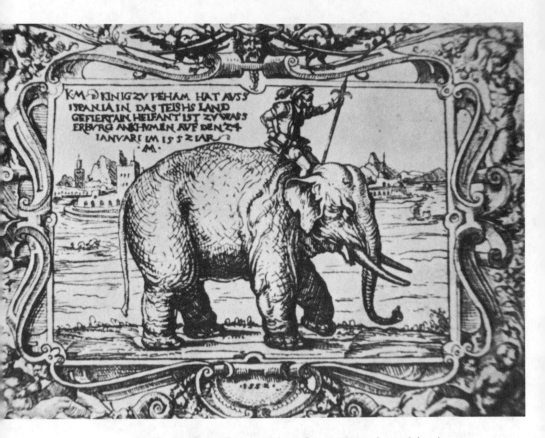

100. *Flugblatt* elephant of 1552. Etching from Winner, *loc cit.* (pl. 92), p. 78.

101. Elephant medal dated 1554, the work of Michael Fuchs. From F. Dworschak, "Die Renaissancemedaille in Österreich," *Jahrbuch der kunsthistorischen Sammlungen in Wien*, N.S., Vol. I (1926), facing p. 220.

102. Elephant and dragon in garden of Bomarzo, Italy. Original photograph by Alma Lach.

103. Elephant in garden of Bomarzo, Italy. Original photograph by Alma Lach.

104. Engraving of an elephant hunt in Stradanus' *Venationes* (Antwerp, 1567). From E. W. Palm, "Dürer's Ganda and a XVI Century Apotheosis of Hercules at Tunja," *Gazette des Beaux-Arts*, 6th ser., XLVIII (1956), 73.

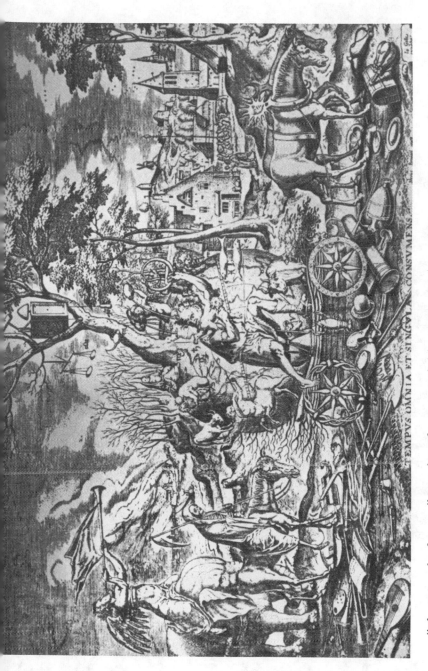

105. "The Triumph of Saturn." Woodcut after P. Brueghel by Philippe Galle, 1574. From Hollstein, *op. cit.* (pl. 15), III, 298. Courtesy of A. L. van Gendt and Co., Amsterdam.

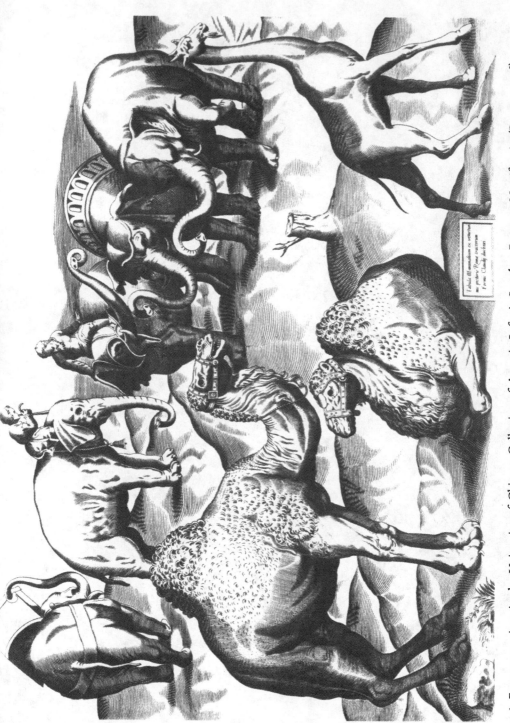

106. From engravings in the University of Chicago Collection of Antonio Lafreri, *Speculum Romanae Magnificentiae* (Rome, 1575?).

107. "Noah's Ark." Painting by Simone de Myle, 1570. From Musée Goya, Musée Jaurès (Castres), *Les plus belles peintures des collections privées du Tarn du XVᵉ au XVIIIᵉ siècle* (Castres, 1956), pl. 24. Courtesy of Georges Alran, Mazamet (Tarn), France.

108. "Night Festival with the Carrousel Elephant." Painting by Antoine Caron, *ca.* 1580. From F. A. Yates, *The Valois Tapestries* (London, 1959), pl. XII. Courtesy of Jean Ehrmann, Paris. See also J. Ehrmann, *Antoine Caron, peintre à la Cour des Valois* (Geneva, 1955), pl. XI.

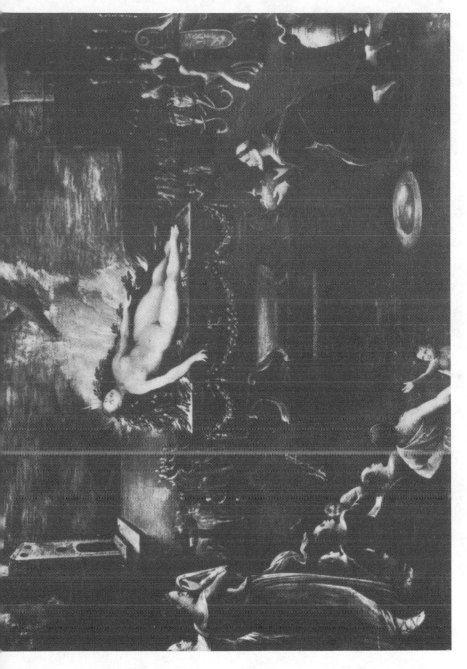

109. "Triumph of Séméle." Painting by Antoine Caron. From Bousquet, *op. cit.* (pl. 37), p. 139.

110. "Elephant with Three Sheep." Etching by Hans Sibmacher. From J. Camerarius, *Symbolorum et emblematum* (1590), Bk. II, p. 4.

11. Ape on the back of an elephant. Black pencil drawing by Roelant Savery. In Crocker
rt Gallery, Sacramento, California. From W. Bernt, *Die niederländischen Zeichnungen*
s 17. Jahrhunderts (Munich, 1958), Vol. II, pl. 532.

112. Elephant hunt. Ceiling painting in the House of the Scribe, Tunja, Colombia. From Palm, *loc. cit.* (pl. 104), p. 72.

113. Detail from Ortelius' map of China (Antwerp, 1584).

114. Woodcut of elephant, by Melchior Lorck, 1580. Department of Prints and Drawings, the Royal Museum of Fine Arts, Copenhagen, Denmark.

115. Woodcut of Antwerp elephant from solemn *entrée* of July 18, 1593. From Boch, *op. cit.* (pl. 49). Courtesy of the Newberry Library.

116. Gilded silver elephant by Christoph Jamnitzer, *ca*. 1600. Courtesy of the Charlottenburg Museum, Berlin. Inventar Nr. K3900.

Von dem Elephanten.

Er Elephant ist vnter allen Thieren/ die auff der Erden gehen/ das grösseste/ wechst biß auff neun Eln-bogen in die höhe/ vnd fünff in die dicke: wirdt in India am grössesten vnd besten gefunden/ vnd lebet auff zwey-hundert Jahr. Die Alten haben jhn zum Kriege in Streitten gebraucht/ vmb die Schnautzen oder Nasen bewaffnet/ vnnd auß sonderbaren Kästen/ so sie jhme auffgeladen/ mit 10. 12. ja etwan 40. wehrhaffter Männern sich ab jhme gewehret vnd gestritten. Darumb hab ich jhne in diesem Buch zuvorderst angesetzt/als das mechtigeste Thier/ einen Baw zu tragen. Der Drack/ ist sein Todt feind/ windet sich vmb seine Füsse/ verstopffet mit seinem Schwantz jhme seine Nasen/ vnd erstecket jhn/ wa er nicht bald einen Baum oder Felsen findet/ daran er den Dracken verdrucke/ vnd sich also seines Feindes erwehre.ꝛc. Solche Dracken werden von 20. biß auff 30. Elnbogen lang in Arabia gefunden. Er hasset die Mauß vber alle Thier/ isset auch kein Futter/ darüber ein Mauß nur geloffen. Ein Künstler wirdt jhne auch wol wissen mit anderm Thierköpffen zubezieren/ als von einem Widder/ oder Schwein: welche des Elephanten Natur auch gantz zuwider seindt.

x

117. Caryatid of elephant and dragon. From J. Boillot, *New Termis Buch* (n.p., 1604). Courtesy of the Newberry Library.

118. "Schauessen" prepared for the wedding of the Duke of Jülich-Kleve-Berg. Engraving from E. Kris, "Der Stil 'Rustique,'" *Jahrbuch der kunsthistorischen Sammlungen in Wien*, N.S., I (1926), 185.

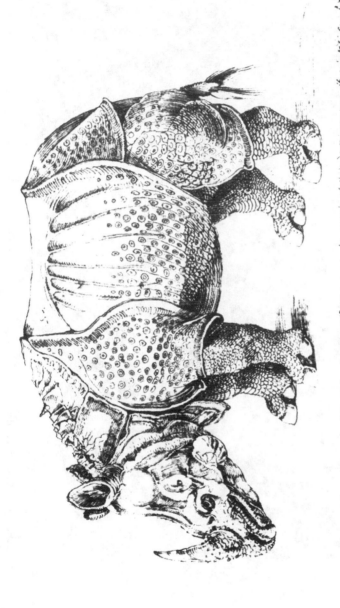

119. Dürer's drawing of the *Rhinoceron*, dated 1515. From C. Dodgson, "The Story of Dürer's Ganda," in A. Fowler (ed.), *The Romance of Fine Prints* (Kansas City, 1938), p. 44.

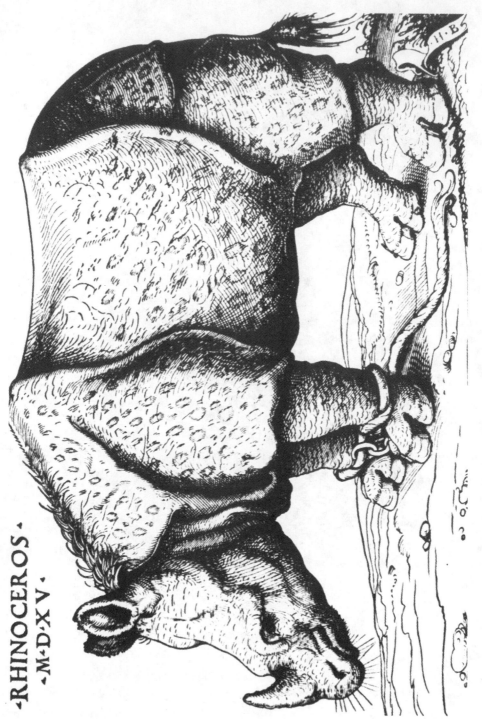

·RHINOCEROS·
·M·D·X·V·

·H·B·

120. Rhinoceros by Hans Burgkmair, dated 1515. Woodcut in the Albertina, Vienna. From Dodgson, *loc. cit.* (pl. 119), p. 54.

121. Rhinoceros in marble relief. Courtesy of the National Museum, Naples.

122. Drawing of rhinoceros in Maximilian's Prayer Book. From E. Chmelanz, "Das Diurnale oder Gebetbuch des Kaiser Maximilians I," *Jahrbuch der kunsthistorischen Sammlungen des allerhöchsten Kaiserhauses*, Vol. III (1885), pl. XXXVIII.

123. Woodcut detail from "Triumphal Arch of Maximilian I," by Dürer. Courtesy of the Albertina, Vienna.

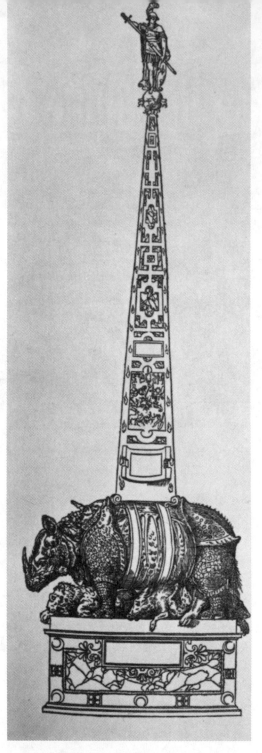

124. Rhinoceros with obelisk. Engraving of monument erected on King Henry II's entry into Paris in 1549. From E. Iversen, *The Myth of Egypt and Its Hieroglyphs* . . . (Copenhagen, 1961), pl. XIII.

125. Grotto in the garden of the Villa Medici in Città di Castello (post 1565). From F. Würtenberger, *Der Manierismus* (Vienna-Munich, 1962), p. 132.

126. Combat between rhinoceros and elephant in *Oeuvres d'Ambroise Paré* (Paris, 1585).
From C. Coste, "Anciennes figurations du rhinocéros," *Acta tropica*, III (1946), 123.

127. Rhinoceros. Ceiling decoration of sixteenth-century House of the Scribe, Tunja, Colombia. From Palm, *loc. cit.* (pl. 104), p. 68.

128. Engraving of caryatid of rhinoceros and elephant. From Boillot, *op. cit.* (pl. 117). Courtesy of the Newberry Library.

129. Emblem of rhinoceros and bear. Etching by Hans Sibmacher. From Camerarius, *op. cit.* (pl. 110), Bk. II, No. V, p. 10.

130. Bacchus and Ariadne with a tiger. Fresco in the Sala di Psiche of the Palazzo del Te, based on a design by Giulio Romano. From Hartt, *op. cit.* (pl. 96), p. 262.

131. Tigers and elephant in Annibale Carracci's ceiling painting "Triumph of Bacchus and Ariadne." From J. R. Martin, *The Farnese Gallery* (Princeton, 1965), pl. 69.

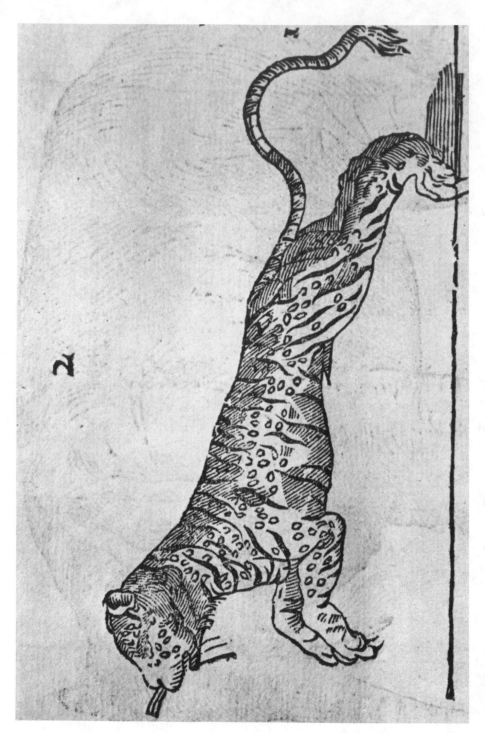

132. Tiger. From J. de Arphe, *Varia commensuracion* . . . (Madrid, 1598), Bk. III.

133. "The Story of the First Human Pair." Brussels tapestry of mid-sixteenth century. From Göbel, *op. cit.* (pl. 53), pl. 396. Courtesy of Klinkhardt and Biermann, Brunswick.

134. "The Ape Laocoön." Woodcut by Titian. From Würtenberger, *op. cit.* (pl. 125), p. 54.

135. "Young Man with a Parrot," portrait by Niccolò dell'Abbate. In Albertina, Vienna. From Würtenberger, *op. cit.*, p. 221.

136. "Madonna and Child with Parrot," painting by "Meister mit dem Papagei." From
M. J. Friedlander, "Der Meister mit dem Papagei," *Phoebus*, II (1949), 54.

137. "German Woman with a Parrot," painting by Bartholomäus Bruyn (?) or Bartel
Beham (?). From E. R. von Engerth, "Über die im kunsthistorischen Museum neu zur
Aufstellung gelangenden Gemälde," *Jahrbuch der kunsthistorischen Sammlungen des
allerhöchsten Kaiserhauses*, III (1885), facing p. 86. Original in Kunsthistorisches Museum,
Vienna. Inventar Nr. 3483.

138. Emblem of musk deer. Etching by Hans Sibmacher. From Camerarius, *op. cit.* (pl. 110), Bk. II, LXIV, p. 128.

139. Emblem of the bird of paradise. Etching by Hans Sibmacher. From Camerarius, *op. cit.*, Bk. III, No. XLIII, p. 86.

140. Emu, the wonderful bird. Engraving by Hans Sibmacher. From Hulsius, *op. cit.* (pl. 52). Courtesy of the Newberry Library.

141. Emblem of crowned bird of Catigan. Etching by Hans Sibmacher. From Camerarius, *op. cit.* (pl. 110), Bk. III, No. XLIV, p. 88.

142. Dodos. Pencil and chalk drawing by Roelant Savery. In Crocker Art Gallery, Sacramento, California. From Bernt, *op. cit.* (pl. 111), pl. 533.

143. "Orpheus with the Animals." Painting by Roelant Savery. Original in the Hermitage, Leningrad. From J. Fechner, "Die Bilder von Roelant Savery in der Eremitage," *Jahrbuch des kunsthistorischen Institutes der Universität Graz*, Vol. II (1966–67), pl. CXXVI.

144. "Garden of Eden." Painting by Roelant Savery. From K. Chytil, *Kunst und Künstler am Hofe Rudolfs II* (Prague, n.d.).

145. "Asia." Woodcut from C. Ripa, *Iconologia* . . . (Padua, 1611), p. 357.

146. Engraved title page of J. T. and J. I. de Bry, *Pars quarta Indiae orientalis...*
(Frankfurt, 1601). The frame is supported by an elephant and Dürer's rhinoceros. The
confronted birds on the top are emus, each facing a parrot. The censers at the sides of the
top level are burning aromatic gums and resins.

DE LANCVAS, FAGARAS,
LACCA ET CVCIFRVCTA.

147. Engraving of products of Asia. Galingale (*Alpinia galanga*), here called "Lancuas" (Malay, *langkvas*), Japanese pepper (*Zanthoxphum piperitum*), lac deposits on twigs of ber (*Zizyphus jujuba*), and gourds. Note the accurate depiction of a banana tree in the background. From De Bry, *op. cit.* (pl. 146), pl. XVIII.

148. Temples and gods of India. Note bathing tank and Hindu idol. From De Bry,
II pars Indiae orientalis (Frankfurt, 1599), pl. XXI.

149. Ornamental panel from the loggia of the Vatican. Planned by Raphael and painted by Giovanni da Udine. From Niccola de Antoni (publisher), *Ornati delle loggie del Vaticano* (Rome, n.d.), fig. II, no. iv.

150. Detail of the elephant from pl. 149.

151. Etching of a decorative panel by the Doetechum brothers(?) (after H. Vredeman de Vries) as published in *Grottesco in diversche Manieren* (Antwerp, 1555). Reproduced from A. J. J. Delen, *Histoire de la gravure dans les anciens Pays-Bas . . .*, 2 parts (Paris, 1935), Pt. II, pl. LXI. cf. pl. 92, above.

Index

Abbate, Niccolò dell', 73; "Young Man with a Parrot," 181
Abelard, Peter, 160
"Abulabaz," Charlemagne's elephant, 130
Acanthus, 71, 194
Acosta, Cristobal de, 154 n., 158; on elephant, 154; *Tractado*, 82, 138 n., 154
Aelian, 127 n., 158; on primates, 175; on rhinoceros, 160; on tiger, 172
Affaitadi, house of, 117
Afonso, Jorge, 68, 69
Africa, 38, 70, 79, 149 n.; apes of, 175, 176, 177; elephants of, 125, 128; and Magi, 75; maps of, 76, 170; monkeys of, 175, 176; parrots of, 179, 180; pictures of natives of, 65; rhinoceros of, 160, 170; symbols of, 79, 128
Agates (cat's eyes), 20, 117
Agricola, Georg: collections, 22
Ahmadābād, 58, 61
Aix-en-Provence, 33
Aix-la-Chapelle, 130, 131 n.
Alberèllo (drug pot), 105
Albert, cardinal, elector of Mainz, 153
Albert V, duke of Bavaria, 24, 110, 153
Al-Biruni: on rhinoceros, 160
Albuquerque, Afonso de, 10, 60, 98, 161; Casa da India of, 12
Alicante, 124, 136
Alciati, Andrea, 85, 149
Aldrovandi, Ulisse, 41, 43, 71, 83, 182; *Ornithologiae*, 92
Alençon, François, d', duke of Anjou, 152
Aleppo, 147, 168 n.
Alessandro, duke of Florence: rhinoceros device, 166, 167
Alexander the Great, 70, 114, 191; at Babylon, 125; defeat of Darius III, 125; in India, 125–26, 172
Alexander Romance, 129, 130
Alexandria, 126, 129, 131; as animal market, 126, 129, 131, 179; and pepper, 4
Alfonso, elephant keeper, 138
Alfonso I, duke of Ferrara, 107
Alfonso II, duke of Ferrara, 107
Alfonso V, king of Portugal, 133
Alicorns (mounted horns and tusks), 39, 159 n.
Allori, Alessandro: "Pearl Fishery," 40
Alost, Pieter Coecke van, 89, 93 n., 165, 196 n.; "Histoire indienne a oliffans et jeraffes," 101; Turkish costumes of, 90
Alps: in landscape painting, 73
Altdorfer, Albrecht, 81, 165, 190; and "People of Calicut," 80; rhinoceros, 164–65
Alvares, Emmanuel, 67
Amann, Jost, 150
Amber, 15, 117
Ambergris, 34, 193
Amboise, 31, 143
Ambras, 30, 75, 167 n.; Chinese paintings at, 27; Ferdinand's collection at, 26; ivories at, 153
America, 76; featherworks of, 18, 195 n.; gold and silver of, 113; Indian products of, 16; nephrites of, 117; in painting, 190 n.; parrots of, 180; relations with Europe, 4–5, 16; symbols of, 155; and tigers, 174 n.
American Numismatic Society, 128 n.
Amethysts, 114, 117
Amsterdam, 17, 18, 22, 79; white elephant at, 158 n.
Ancona, 35, 99
Andrade, Fernão Peres d', 10, 64

Index

Ango, Jean d', 31
Angola, 170
Animals, 93, 132; at Alexandria, 126, 129, 131, 179; of Asia, 123, 156, 191; Assyrian reliefs of, 175; in bestiaries, 129; of Bomarzo, 148; in books, 164; in carpets, 99; Christian attributes of, 129, 179, 184; at Constantinople, 131, 143 n., 168 n., 173; Dürer's studies of, 164, 177; as emblems, 86 n.; as fused and interlocked fauna, 170; as gifts, 136, 183; in Greece, 126; imaginary, 156; and man, 177, 178, 184; as monsters, 158; and Naturalism, 183; in ornament, 154, 184, 196; in paintings, 72–73, 75, 129, 156; in pasquinades, 139 n.; in *Physiologus*, 129; on porcelains, 105; in Portugal, 123; in Romanesque design, 96; in Rome, 133, 138–39; in sculpture, 148–49, 166; secularized, 184; on silverware, 119; symbolism of, 134–35, 173, 177, 178, 179, 184, 191; in tapestries, 99, 100, 101, 134, 165, 184; in woodcuts, 134; at Venice, 131. *See also under names of individual animals, such as* Elephant; Rhinoceros
Anjou, 30
Antioch, 36
Antiochus I, 126 n.
Antiquity, 44; and Asia, 70, 90, 191, 199; D'Ollanda on, 69–70; "phallic ape" of, 177
Antonello, merchant, 37
Antwerp, 13 n., 22, 31, 38, 43, 79, 90, 184, 195; diamonds and pearls at, 117; Dürer in, 17, 195; elephant effigy of, 135 n., 152, 192; elephants in, 124, 151, 152; as emporium, 17, 121; engravers of, 87, 91; engraving of, 16 n.; Florentines at, 39; giant, 152; Gois at, 19; guilds, 100; monkeys in, 177; parrots in, 179; Place de Meu, 19; Portuguese at, 16–17, 19, 93; Portuguese emigration from, 89 n.; silverware, 119; "sinjoren" of, 19; tapestry weaving, 100; triumphal processions, 93–94, 152, 170
"Antwerp Mannerists," 195
Apes, 177–78; in caryatids, 178; in Gothic art, 176; and humans, 177, 178
Apian, Peter, 81
Apollo, 92
Aquila, Giovanni Battista Branconio dell'. *See* Branconio dell' Aquila
Arabia, 65, 116
Arakan, 117
Aranha, Brother, 67
Arbela, battle of, 125
Architecture: *antiga portuguesa*, 62; arches, 59, 62; Asian influences on, 58, 60, 62, 63–64; capitals, 59; caryatids, 150, 170, 174, 178, 196; edifices of Asia, 70, 122; elephants in, 157; façades, 62; Gothic, 58; influence of sculpture on, 59; landscape, 186; Manueline, 57–58; Mexican, 58

Arcimboldo, Giuseppe, 122, 187, 197; and elephant, 156; Indian influence on, 77; at Milan, 77 n.; and Naturalism, 156; *têtes composées*, 77
Ardebil (Iran), 104
Aretino, Pietro: satire on curia, 139
Aristotle, 114, 172, 175; on elephant, 125, 126, 139 n.; *History of the Animals*, 159; on parrots, 179; on rhinoceros, 159
Arles, 30
Armenia, 37 n.
Armor, 10; Asian, 14, 27
Arphe y Villafañe, Juan de: designs, 119; on elephant, 154; on rhinoceros, 169; on tiger, 174
Arras, 148
Arrivabene, Ludovico, 156
Arruda, Diogo de, 59, 60
Arruda, Francisco de, 59, 61
Artists, 45, 121; and Antiquity, 70, 199; Asian, 65, 67; and Asian ornament, 194–95; and Asian products, 56; and collections of curiosities, 188, 190; cooperative works, 68, 91; European amateurs in Asia, 64–66; and foreign beasts, 184–85; and literary sources, 190; and living models, 189; and plant specimens, 83–84; social status, 44, 104, 118; travels, 89–90
Arts: and Asian objects and motifs, 56–57, 114, 186, 188; Byzantine, 36, 120, 131; Cardano on, 45; comparative, 186–87; identifying marks in, 164, 173, 175; imitations, 74, 188; Indo-Portuguese, 10, 99, 107, 110, 119, 187; interrelations among, 123, 131, 142, 164, 171, 184–85, 187, 190, 196–97; and Islam, 96; and Jesuits, 8, 62, 65, 67, 70, 191; and literary sources, 91–93; and living models, 183; and magnifying glass, 83, 118; "migration," 186; monumental, 61, 186; and Neoplatonism, 86; and oriental subjects, 80, 81, 94; pirating, 81, 85; and political propaganda, 23; prototypes, 183; relation to nature, 30, 39, 40–41, 43, 44, 112, 169, 191; relation to science, 147; serpentine line, 187; styles, 57, 58, 59, 68, 118, 187; symbolic representations of Asia in, 192; and tradition, 183, 186, 191; uncertainty in, 45, 121, 191. *See also* Collections; Mannerism; Naturalism; Ornament; Styles in art; Symbolism
Asia, 29, 70, 79, 159; animals, 123, 156, 177, 183, 191; and Antiquity, 70, 90, 191, 199; armor and weapons, 26, 27, 28; artistic traditions, 120; cities, 5, 28 n., 88; costumes, 98; Dutch voyages to, 17, 94; as earthly paradise, 129; European art in, 63, 187 n.; in European art, 65–66, 186; and European artists, 8, 56, 64–66, 88, 188; in European literary sources, 5, 6, 8, 19; on European maps, 8, 19, 40, 76, 80, 87; exotica, 17, 29, 30–33, 187, 191; "export

arts," 98, 107, 110, 121, 187; exports to Europe, 16, 55; featherworks, 18, 69, 195; gold and silver, 113; Jesuit structures in, 63; "land of gold," 113, 191; personifications of, 192, 193–94; plants, 40–41, 109; symbols for, 79, 155, 171, 178, 180, 191, 192, 193, 198; temples, 70, 122. *See also* Arts; Europe; Jesuits

Asia Minor, 96

Asnelli, Carlo, 141

Assyria, 125

Athens, 69, 175; tigers at, 172

Augsburg, 18, 22, 79, 80, 81, 85, 111

Augustus, elector of Saxony, 24, 128 n.

Augustus, emperor of Rome, 156 n., 172

Australia, 113

Avvisi (newsletters), 42

Azores, 34

Azuchi, Nobunaga's residence, 89

Azuchi Castle, 188; representations of, 89

Baboon, 177 n.

Babylon, 125

Bacalhoa, 12

Bacchus. *See* Dionysius

Back scratchers, 188

Bada (rhinoceros): etymology, 168; In Iberia, 169

Baghdad, 116 n.

Baglione, Astorre, 150

Bajus (Indian jackets), 103

Baldung, Hans, 79

Balthazar (Arabia), 75

Baltin, Pieter: "Preaching of St. John the Baptist," 153

Baltrušaitis, Jorge, 73

Bamboo, 40, 109

Banchelli, Paglio, 174

Baraballo of Gaeta, 138, 139

Barbary apes, 175, 176

Barbosa, Duarte, 98; on porcelain, 105; on precious stones, 115

Barcelona, 60

Barhut stupa, 176

Barili, Giovanni: intarsia of Hanno, 139, 148

Bark-cloth, 98

Barnum, P. T., 141 n.

"Barocchus Manuelinus," 58

Baronius, Caesar, 76

Baroque, 58, 64; Asian influence on, 62–63, 187; Costa-Tôrres on, 62; and Manueline architecture, 58

Barros, João de, 10

Bartas, G. de Saluste du, 168, 181 n.

Bastiães (silverworks of animals), 16 n., 162

Batalha, 57, 58; unfinished chapels, 59, 60

Bavaria, 145; and Jesuits, 24–25

Bé, Guillaume le, 90

Beirut, 35

Belém, 57, 118, 148; Jerónomite monastery, 63. *See also* Tower of Belém

Belleforest, François de: *Cosmographie universelle*, 88

Bellini, Gentile, 80, 94, 98 n.

Bellini, Giovanni, 86 n.

Belon, Pierre, 7, 32, 44; on porcelains, 105

Beneventum, battle of, 127

Bengal, 98, 172

Benzoin, 11

Berger, Georg, 119

Bergh, Mayer van den: breviary, 109 n.

Berlin: Charlottenburg, 153; *Kupferstichkabinett*, 141; state library, 83 n.

Bernini, Giovanni Lorenzo: elephant statue, 135

Beroaldo, Filippo, the Younger, 138, 140

Besançon, 24, 164

Bestiaries, 149, 163; on elephant, 129, 130, 131, 147; on monkeys, 176; on parrots, 179; on rhinoceros, 160, 161; on tiger, 173

Bezoar stones, 21, 23, 29, 30, 115; as amulets and antidotes, 12; in mountings, 12, 27, 119

Bhang (hashish), 11, 55

Biblioteca Casanatense, 65, 66, 81

Biblioteca Malatestiana, 132

Bird of paradise, 18, 20, 27, 103, 123, 184; in costume, 102; in emblems, 87, 182; etymology, 181 n.; as gifts, 181; myths, 181; in painting, 156, 181–82; and parrot, 181; plumages, 181; symbolism, 182, 184; in woodcuts, 182

Birds: dodo, 123, 183; of Catigan island, 87; fabulous, 92; "ruch," 92; wild ducks, 92–93

"*Bittacus*" (parrot of Ctesias), 178

Biwa, lake of Japan, 89

Blancken, Gerard, 21

Boboli gardens, 40

Bodin, Jean, 6

Boillot, Joseph, 196; and apes, 178; and *ganda*, 170; *New Termis Buch*, 150, 170, 196; on tiger, 174

Boissard, Jean Jacques, 91, 102

Bologna, 41, 43, 83, 84, 135; Palazzo Fantuzzi, 134

Bomarzo garden, 148–49; as iconographic problem, 149; and Palazzo del Te, 149 n.; "Sacred Wood," 148

Bombay, 67 n.; Elephanta island, 37

Bomberg, Venetian printer, 32

Bonardi, G. M., 180

Bonciani, Francisco, 169 n.

Boniface VIII, pope, 155

Bontius, Jacob: *Historiae naturalis*, 182

Boodt, Anselm Boetius de: *Gemmarum et lapidum historia*, 120

Book of Revelation, 114

Books, 188, 194; animals in, 158, 164, 180; of Barros, 10; bestiaries, 147, 149, 163; costume, 91, 102, 188; of designs, 102, 119, 121; Dürer's rhinoceros in, 166–67; elephants in,

Books—(*continued*)
133, 134–35, 144, 154, 156; hieroglyphic, 78; natural histories, 9, 158, 180; and woodcuts, 78, 81, 180. *See also* Chinese books; Collections; Engraving

Borcht, Pieter van der, 83, 178, 192

Borel, Pieter, 158 n.

Borghini, Raffaello, 39, 191

Boria, Juan de, 182

Borneo, 18

Bosch, Hieronymus, 73, 75, 77, 147 n., 185, 196; "Garden of Delights," 134; and Naturalism, 134; "Siege of the Elephant," 152; transparent globes of, 186

Botany: comparative plant morphology, 83–84; floriculture, 82; herbals, 81–84; *Herbarius, or Ortus sanitatis*, 81, 133; "porcelain flowers," 105; relation to art, 43

Bousquet, Jacques, 73

Bouttats, Gaspar, 152 n.

Boyle, Robert, 113 n.

Boytac, Diogo, 59, 60

Bracciolini, Poggio, 168 n.

Brachmann, Severin, 146

Brahma: portraits of, 65

Branconio dell'Aquila, Giovanni Battista: epitaph on Hanno, 140–41; and Leonardo, 137 n.; and Raphael, 138

Brandão, João: on trade at Lisbon, 11 n.

Brant, Sebastian, 22 n.

Brass, 30

Braun, Georg, 88

Brazil, 111

Breslau, 180

Breton, Richard, 90 n.

Breu, Jorg, 81

Breydenbach, Bernard von, 133 n., 176

Bristol: St. Mary Redcliffe, 60

British Museum: Sloane Collection, 151 n.

Brixen (Bressanone): elephant painting, 145

Brueghel, Pieter, the Elder, 73, 144 n., 181; "Adoration of Kings," 147 n.

Brueghel, Pieter, the Younger, 156

Bruges, 193

Brunfels, Otto: *Herbarum vivae icones*, 82

Brussels, 75, 143; Dürer in, 17; elephants in, 124, 153; gardens, 18; tapestries, 100, 101

Bruyn, Abraham de, 90, 91

Bruyn, Bartholomäus, 180

Buddhism: in elephant legends, 129 n.; Jesuits on, 8; and rhinoceros, 171

Buontalenti, Bernardo, 40

Burgkmair, Hans, 79, 81, 157, 165, 170, 183, 190, 195 n.; and elephant, 134 n.; "King of Cochin" series, 80, 134, 164; "People of Calicut," 18, 80, 100, 164; and Prayer Book of Maximilian I, 80; rhinoceros of, compared to Dürer's, 164; sources, 164

Burgundy, 30

Burma (Pegu), 112 n., 117

Bushidō, 187

Byōbus (Japanese folding screens), 14, 18, 42, 89, 187–88; as sources of motifs, 74

Byzantium, 35, 36, 96, 97, 109; artistic traditions, 120; collections, 9; glass jewels, 114. *See also* Arts

Cabral, Pedro Alvares, 61

Caccini, Matteo, 40

Cadamosto, Luis de, 147; on elephants, 133

Caesar, Julius, 127, 128 n.

Cairo, 104 n., 105, 168

Calceolari (Calzolari), Francesco, 18, 43

Calicos, 34

Calicut, 32, 88, 180, 192; exotica from, 10, 17; Zamorin, 10

Cambay (Gujarat), 10, 65, 98; colchas (quilts) of, 98; elephants in, 135; *ganda* of, 158; Portuguese mission of 1513 to, 60, 161; precious stones, 115, 117

Cambodia, 18; rhinoceros in, 168 n.

Cambridge (Mass.): Fogg Museum, 141

Camels, 75, 119, 144, 164, 166; on tapestries, 101

Camerarius, Joachim, 28, 170, 180, 182; on birds, 182; *Hortus medicus et philosophicus*, 84; relations with Ortelius, 20; on rhinoceros, 169; *Symbolorum ac emblematum*, 86–87; on tiger, 174

Camillo, Francisco, 148 n.

Camoëns, Luis de: on bird of paradise, 181 n.

Canigiani, Lorenzo, 61

Cannanore, 88

Cano, Juan Sebastian del, 12

Capaccio, Giulio Cesare: on parrots, 180

Capito, Giovanni, 139 n.

Caracalla, emperor of Rome, 160

Caravaggio, Polidore da, 143

Cardano, Girolamo, 43, 105, 121, 145, 191; on arts, 45; on bird of paradise, 181 n.; on elephant, 145; on precious stones, 120; on rhinoceros, 168

Cardinal-King (Henry of Portugal), 148

Carnelians, 20, 21, 117

Caron, Antoine: "Night Festival with the Carrousel Elephant," 152; "Triumph of Séméle," 152

Carpaccio, Vittore, 98 n.

Carpets, 15, 32, 34, 56, 188; French, 99; in Venetian paintings, 36

Carracci, Annibale, 76, 177, 178 n.; and tiger, 174; "Triumph of Bacchus and Ariadne," 155

Cartari, Vicenzo: *Imagini*, 89 n., 150

Carthaginians, 127

Cartography, 44; of Asia, 8, 80, 87; in cosmographies, 88

Caryatids. *See* Architecture

Casanatense. *See* Biblioteca Casanatense

Caspar (India-Ethiopia), 75

Cassowary. *See* Emu

Castanheda, Fernão Lopes de. *See* Lopes de Castanheda
Castello, 148; gardens and grotto, 166; sculptured animals of, 166
Castiglione, Saba, 39
Castilho, João de, 59
Castreata, Isabella, 102 n.
Castro, Gilles de, 100
Castro, Dom João de, 66; Pinha Verde, 12; tapestries of, 101–2
Catalonia, 70
Catania: elephant, 135 n.
Catharine, queen of Portugal, 13, 102 n.
Cathay, 76
Catigan island (Philippines), 87 n.
Cavallerius, Thomas, 144
Cavendish, Thomas, 34
Cecil, William (Lord Burghley), 33, 35, 120
Cellini, Benvenuto: on Turkish ornament, 194–95
Ceramics: history, 104; imitations of Asian wares, 104–5; Indo-Portuguese, 107; influence of textile designs on, 105; majolica, 104; motifs, 74; pottery painting, 104; terracotta, 104; true porcelain, 107–8
Cesena, 132
Ceylon, 116; and elephant, 125; ivories in Europe, 14, 25; and Portugal, 10; precious stones, 117
Chalcedony, 115
Chalderia, Francesco, 136 n.
Charlemagne, 96; apes of, 176; chess set of, 130, 149 n.; elephant of, 129–30, 155
Charles of Spain, 25
Charles I, king of Spain. *See* Charles V, Holy Roman Emperor
Charles II, archduke of Graz, 25
Charles V, Holy Roman Emperor, 4, 12, 15, 19, 118, 174 n.; as collector, 13–14, 17, 22; triumphs, 93 n.
Charles V, king of France, 30
Charola, Mestre de, de Tomar, 178 n.
Chattra. See Parasols
Chaucer: on parrots, 179
Chaul, 98
Chess sets and pieces, 30, 32, 110, 130, 131 n., 149 n.
Chimpanzee, 175
China, 90, 156; bedsteads, 110 n.; block printing, 78; chairs, 110 n.; conical hats, 103; and cormorants, 182; customs, 37–38; "export furniture," 110; "export porcelains," 13 n., 106; featherworks, 18; jade, 117; land route to, 64; landscape painting, 73–74, 187; and Leonardo, 37; map of, 34; Ming blue-and-white porcelains, 108; paper, 21; pictures of natives of, 65; relations with Europe, 4–5; and rhinoceros, 127; silks, 98; silver, 113; and tiger, 173 n.; and wild ducks, 92–93; writing, 21

Chinese books: in European collections, 13, 41, 74 n., 188; as sources of motifs, 74
Chinese coins: in collections, 28; engravings in Hulsius, 95
Chinese paintings, 46; in European collections, 10, 15, 27, 28, 29, 64, 75, 187; influence in Europe, 64, 75, 91, 187
Chinoiseries, 6, 107 n., 187, 194, 196
Christian, prince of Anhalt, 24
Christian I, elector of Saxony, 24
Christian I, king of Denmark, 132
Christian IV, king of Denmark, 24, 158 n.
Cinnamon, 88
Civitavecchia, 124, 137
Claesz, Cornelis, 94
Claudius, emperor of Rome, 172
Clement VII, pope, 118
Clock, Pieter, 103
Cloisonné, 27
Clusius, *See* L'écluse, Charles de
Cochin, 12, 66, 161, 168 n.
Cock, Hieronymus: "Siege of the Elephant," 152
Cock, Jean de, 73
Coconut palm, 110
Coconuts, 17, 25, 30, 31, 32, 34; in mountings, 27, 119, 120
Coimbra, 67; church of Santa Cruz, 61
Coins and medals, 22, 25, 28, 35; of Alexander the Great, 126; and elephant, 126 n., 128, 132, 146; of Julius Caesar, 128; of Metelli, 127; of Nero, 126 n.; of rhinoceros, 160, 163, 164, 164 n.; of Socrates, 126 n.
Colchas (quilts), 98, 99
Collections: at Ambras, 26–27; and artists, 56, 188; at Besançon, 24; and bird of paradise, 181; *byōbus* in, 14, 42; 89, 187–88; of Camerarius, 84; Chinese books in, 13, 188; Chinese paintings in, 10, 15, 27, 28, 29, 64, 75, 187; at Copenhagen, 21, 24, 27 n.; of costumes, 90, 102, 103; at Dresden, 24; of dried plants, 83; in Florence, 37, 39–40, 108; of Francis I, 31; and gardens, 82; of Gesner, 84; at Graz, 25–26; of Habsburgs, 23, 101; at Halle, 28; history, 9; of "Indian" furniture, 110–11; of Indian miniature paintings, 77, 188; of lacquerware, 15, 24, 110, 112, 188; at Lisbon, 10–11; of maps, 32, 34, 37, 40, 88, 94, 188, 192 n.; meaning of, 44; in medieval treasuries, 9; of mounted curiosities, 119–20, 153, 188; at Munich, 25; of Ortelius, 19–20; in paintings, 73; of Paludanus, 20; of porcelains, 11, 13 n., 16, 19, 26–27, 30, 31, 33, 36, 38, 39, 41, 104, 108; at Prague, 26; private, 20, 28, 39; and the public, 187, 188; of Rudolf II, 28–30; as sources of illustration, 35, 44–45, 122; of tapestries, 101; types of collectors, 8–9, 42–44; Vatican, 42–43; Venice, 36, 38; *Wunderkammer*, 9, 30, 198

Cologne, 28, 87, 88; elephants at, 133, 153; emu at, 183; Portuguese at, 89 n.
Colombia, 169
Colombo, Fernando, 163 n.
Colonna, Francesco, 135; and elephant, 134; *Hypnerotomachia Poliphili*, 134, 165
Columbus, Christopher, 93 n., 192 n.
Comanini, Don Gregorio, 156
Conflans, Antoine de, 143 n.
Constantine the Great, 173
Constantinople, 31, 33, 35, 36, 89; animal market, 143 n., 168 n., 173; Busbecq's mission to, 90; elephants at, 131, 147 n., 156; as emporium, 36, 64; European artists at, 64; glass jewels of, 114; Latin conquest of, 96; Lorck in, 89–90; mosaics, 131 n.; porcelains in, 104; triumphal arch of Arcadius, 131 n.
Conti, Nicolò dé, 87, 168 n.; on rhinoceros, 161 n.
Cope, Walter, 34, 35
Copenhagen, 21, 24, 27 n.
Corcquires, Gerardus Suberinus, 162 n.
Cormorants, 182
Corneto, 137
"Coromandel": lacquerware, 112
Corrêa, Gaspar: as artist, 66; *Lendas da India*, 89 n.
Corsali, Andrea, 37 n.
Cort, Cornelis: "The Battle of Scipio against Hannibal," 144, 152, 154
Cortes, Hernan, 17, 192 n.
Corvinus, Matthias, king of Hungary, 181 n.
Cosimo I, duke of Florence, 39–40
Cosmographies, 8, 45; illustrations in, 88
Costa-Tôrres, Raul da, 58, 59 n., 61; on origins of Baroque, 62–63
Costume, 30, 32, 35; Asian influences on, 102–3, 122; of Asians, 65, 72, 81, 90–91, 98, 102; bark-cloth, 98; in Bavaria, 25; books, 90, 91, 102, 188; from Chinese paintings, 91; cotton clothes in Europe, 103–4; differences in, 91; in engraving, 93; of feathers, 28, 69; of Japanese emissaries, 72, 91 n., 102; in Linschoten, 66; Lorck's woodcuts of, 90; of Magi, 75; national, 90; Orientalized, 102, 122; in paintings, 68, 103; pearl decorations on, 117; pleating and starching of, 103–4; as source of design ideas, 102; in Spain, 15; on tapestries, 100, 101; transparent smocks (*bajus*), 103; turbans, 98; in triumphs, 93; Vecellio on, 91; in Venice, 102
Council of Trent, 42
Cousin, Jean, 88
Cranach, Lucas, 79, 177
Cremona, 130
Crescentio, P. de, 147 n.
Crivelli, Carlo, 98 n.
Crusades, 96; and apes, 176; elephants from, 130; and Europe, 4
Cruz, Gaspar da, 110 n.; on Chinese lacquer, 113 n.; on porcelain, 106 n.; on rhinoceros, 168 n.

Crystals, 39, 117
Ctesias of Cnidus, 125, 175, 176; on Asia, 114; *Indica*, 159, 178; on parrots, 178; on rhinoceros, 159; on tiger, 172
Cunha, Tristão da, 136; engraving of, 137 n.
Cyprus, 97, 116
Cyriac of Ancona, 36, 132

Dabhul, 101
Dacca, 98
Damascus, 35
Danti, Ignatio, 40
Darius III, king of Persia, 125
Dartmouth, 34
Datura (thorn apple or strammony), 12
De Bry brothers, 156, 157, 190, 193
De Bry, Theodor, 81; *India orientalis*, 94
Decorative arts. See Ornament
Delasso, Francisco, 146
Delsenbach, J. A., 145 n.
Demetrius, Emanuel, 20
Denmark: Order of the Elephant, 132–33; royal canopy of, 133 n.
Dentatus, Curius, 127, 128 n.
Desprez, Francois: *Recueil*, 90
Deutsch, Hans Rudolph Manuel, 88
Diamonds: engraving of, 118; of four castes, 120; of India, 116; in Lisbon, 116; sources, 116
Dieppe, 31, 124, 155
Diez, Ernst, 58
Dio, 172
Dionysius, 76, 150; triumphs of, 126, 155 n.
Dioscorides, 82, 147
Diu, 88, 101, 161
Dodo birds, 123, 183
Dodoens, Rambert, 83 n.
Doesborch, Jan van, 81
Doetechum, Baptista à, 94, 95
Doetechum, Joannes à, 94, 95
D'Ollanda, Francisco, 191; on art of Antiquity, 69–70; and Hanno's portrait, 140, 141, 148; and Mannerism, 70; and Michelangelo, 69–70; in Rome, 140; sketch of elephant fountain, 142; writings, 69–70
Domitian, emperor of Rome, 172
Double coconut, 23; in silver mount, 120 n.
Dragons, 158; and elephant, 129, 132 n., 149, 161; in Musée Cernuschi, 74 n.; in ornament, 150; in paintings, 74; and rhinoceros, 161; symbolism, 161
Drake, Sir Francis, 33
Dresden, 102; collections, 24, 153
Drugs, 12
Duarte, Diego, 19
Du Bartas, G. de Saluste. See Bartas, G. de Saluste du
Du Halde, Jean-Baptiste, 92
Duisburg, 19

Dürer, Albrecht, 22, 44, 81, 82, 86 n., 121, 158, 161, 166, 167, 168, 169, 182, 185, 188, 190; "Affentanz," 177; at Antwerp, 17, 195; and Chinese porcelains, 80, 195; collection of, 17; diary, 17; drawings of Asian animals, 80, 163, 180; influence of rhinoceros woodcut of, 171; and lacquer varnish, 112; Prayer Book of Maximilian I, 80; print of whale, 193; rhinoceros woodcut of, 163–64; "St. Jerome in Meditation," 16; "subtle *ingenia* of people in distant lands," 18; and triumphs of Maximilian I, 79–80, 165

Dyeing, 38; resist technique, 103 n.

East Indies: birds of, 181, 182

Ebersdorf: menagerie, 23, 146

Ebony, 29, 32, 34, 39, 40, 109, 111; symbolism of, 109, 111

Eden, Richard: on precious stones, 116 n.

Egypt, 36, 37, 96, 105, 124, 126, 132; animal markets, 160; hieroglyphs, 84; porcelain in, 104

Elephanta island, 37

Elephants, 14, 30, 41, 75, 76, 79, 81, 123, 155, 164, 183; "Abulabaz," 130; in agriculture, 147 n.; and apes, 176, 178; in Apocrypha, 129 n., 131 n.; armchair, 146; in Asia, 126 n., 135; in Babylon, 125; Bernini's statue, 135; in bestiaries, 129, 130, 131, 147; of Bomarzo, 148; in books, 133, 134–35, 144, 154, 156; in Burgkmair, 134; in Byzantine art, 131; and Cardano, 145; carried by bird, 92; as caryatids, 150, 196; at Castello, 166; and castle, 130, 131 n., 133, 137, 148, 153; characteristics of African, 125; characteristics of Asian, 125; of Charlemagne, 129–30; 155; chess pieces, 130, 131 n., 149 n.; Christian attributes of, 129; chronogram, 133, in circuses and games, 127, 129; as clocks, 153; on coins and medals, 126, 127, 128, 132, 146; "deer elephants" of India, 147 n.; dissection of, 147, 158 n.; and dragons, 129, 132 n., 149, 150; in drawings, 144, 151; in Egypt, 126; as emblems, 85, 87, 131 n., 132, 134, 149, 192; in engravings, 93, 137 n., 144, 145, 149, 157; etymology, 126; in Europe, 23, 124, 127, 128, 129–30, 133, 135, 137–39, 144–45, 151, 153, 157, 158 n.; evolution, 125; fantasized, 142, 143, 144, 150, 157; *Flugblatt* portrait of 1552, 145, 146; as fountains, 142, 148; in frescoes, 143, 145–46, 151 n., 155; genera, 125; as gifts, 144, 154, 155; of Giulio Romano, 142–44; in Greek art and literature, 125, 126; "Hanno," 138; Hindu beliefs about, 127; hooks (*ankus*) for, 142, 145 n., 155; houses and inns named for, 138, 145–46; howdah, 130 n.; hunts, 93, 129, 133; influence in European art, 142–44; intarsia of, 139, 141, 148; intelligence, 128, 135, 136, 139, 151; in ivories, 25, 126 n., 130, 153; jointless,

127, 129, 148; in literary descriptions, 135, 147; mahouts, 124, 127, 128, 155 n.; as Malatesta insignia, 36, 132; of Mantegna, 81, 133, 149, 152 n.; and Manuel of Portugal, 135–36, 140; in manuscript paintings, 130, 131 n., 132, 136; on maps, 131, 167 n.; maritime transport of, 124, 136 n., 137, 150–51; in medieval depictions, 129–31; in miniatures, 142; in monastery of Jerónimos, 148; moral virtues, 124, 128, 129, 150; in mosaics, 131 n., 137 n.; myths, 127, 128, 129, 132, 136, 145, 158; in natural histories, 124, 133, 147, 154, 158; and Naturalism, 147–48, 150–52, 154, 155, 157, 189; and Neoplatonism, 134; and obelisk, 134–35; in ornament, 130, 135, 143, 154, 194; in paintings, 133, 134, 144, 147, 148, 149, 152, 153, 155, 156, 157; in *Panchatantra*, 128 n.; in pasquinades, 139 n.; in Persian designs, 131; physical attributes, 124, 127, 128, 129, 135, 141, 146, 147, 148, 151, 152, 153, 154, 168; in *Physiologus*, 129; poems and comedies on, 138, 139 n., 146; as poppy heads, 130 n., 149; in processions, 127, 134, 136, 138, 145; in quadrigas, 126, 134, 144 n., 149; range, 125; of Raphael, 141–43; in relief, 143, 146; in religion, 129, 156; and rhinoceros, 128, 159, 161, 162, 163, 165, 167, 168, 170; in rock crystal, 27; on Romanesque monuments, 131; in Rome 127, 137–39; on sarcophagi, 126, 144 n.; in satire, 139, 151 n.; in sculpture, 130–31, 132, 133, 148; secularized, 138, 157; in silverworks, 155; in Sinhalese carvings, 147 n.; with soldier in trunk, 126, 148, 149 n.; stuffed, 153; in sugarwork, 153; as symbols, 92, 93, 125, 128, 129, 132, 133, 134, 149–50, 154 n., 157, 161, 184, 192; in tapestries, 101, 134, 144, 148, 152, 157; on tavern signs, 131 n.; and tiger, 173; on tower of Belém, 136; trinkets 153; in triumphs, 132–33, 134, 149, 152; in Vienna, 124, 145–46, 147, 152; in Vienna inscription, 146; in war, 125, 126, 131, 135; as watermarks, 131; white variety, 128 n., 151 n., 156, 158 n.; of woodcut type, 92; in woodcuts, 133, 134, 147, 149, 150, 151, 154, 156, 157, 168

Elizabeth I, queen of England, 33; collections, 103, 120; costume, 102; and elephants, 155; jewels, 102, 118; plumage of bird of paradise, 102, 181 n.; porcelains of, 120

Emblems, 86 n., 154 n., 186; and bird of paradise, 182; of Asia, 191–92; of Camerarius, 86–87; composers and compilers of, 85–88; and divine revelation, 86; of elephants, 85, 87, 131 n., 132, 134, 149–50, 192; hieroglyphs in, 84–86; and Jovius, 167; of maps, 87; of Medici, 165, 167; of parrots, 180; and philosophical speculation, 84; and rhinoceros, 85, 86, 167, 171, 192; sources, 85; tigers in, 174; Torquato Tasso on, 86 n.; vulgarization, 86

Embroideries, 16, 26, 121; designs, 98–99; pictures, 29; quilts, 99
"Eme." *See* Emu
Emeralds, 117
Emu, 123, 193; eggs, 30, 183; etymology, 95 n., 183; in Europe, 182–83; in Hulsius, 95; in paintings, 183
Encyclopedism: in natural history, 84
Engelhardus, Daniel, 117 n.
Enghien, 100
England, 113, 118, 120; Asian exotica in, 33–35; capture of "Madre de Dios," 34; costume, 103; elephants in, 130, 155; relations with Turkey, 33
Engraving, 79, 94, 95: "The Battle of Scipio against Hannibal," 144; of betel leaf, 88; in book illustration, 78–79, 123; of clove tree, 88; of coconut, 120; of costumes, 90; by De Bry, 94–95; of Dürer's rhinoceros, 166–67; of elephants, 93, 127, 144, 145 n., 149, 150, 152, 157; of gems, 114; history, 78; in Hulsius, 95; influence on design ideas, 106; in Linschoten, 94; from literary sources, 91–93; of Magellan, 91–93; and magnifying glass, 118; of maps, 78, 79; of musk deer, 88; oriental subjects in, 91 n., 93, 95; of parrots, 88; of pepper plant, 88; of sago bread, 34; symbolism in, 92, 193–94. *See also* Woodcuts
Enkhuizen, 20, 21
Epirus, 127
Erasmus, 23
Erlach, J. E. Fischer von, 145 n.
Erlangen: university library, 182
Ernest, archduke of Austria, 20, 26, 96, 192
Escalante, Bernardino de, 110 n.; on Chinese paintings, 64 n.
Escorial, 69, 110, 140; Chinese books in, 13; Portuguese carrack at, 15
Este family, 37
Este, Alfonso d': and Raphael, 142
Este, Ercole d', 167
Este, Isabella d': and Raphael, 141
Estoile, Pierre de l', 33
Estrées, Gabrielle d', 32
Etchings: in Camerarius, 87; of bird of paradise, 182; in book illustrations, 79; of elephant, 151; of monkeys, 178
Ethiopia, 93, 113, 116, 168 n.
Etruscans, 114, 137 n.
Euphrates, 125 n.
Europe: apes in, 176; "art of Japanning" discovered, 113; artistic traditions, 9, 120–21; Asian animals in, 12, 123, 183; Asian arts in, 187; Asian books in, 13, 41, 74 n., 188; Asian influence in, 5–6; Asian plants in, 12, 82–83; Asian products in, 7, 9, 16, 55, 64, 98, 99–100, 103, 110, 113, 114, 118, 119, 121, 187; Asian traditions in, 120, 176; Asians in, 34 n., 37, 188, 192; bathing and personal hygiene, 103–

4; and bird of paradise, 181; block books in, 78; Chinese paintings in, 10, 15, 27, 28, 29, 64, 75, 187; cities, 5; conical hats of, 103; cormorant in, 182; costume, 16, 102; Crusades, 4; cultural bias, 3–4, 122; elephants in, 23, 124, 128, 129–30, 133, 144–45, 153, 157; emu in, 182–83; fairs, 16, 133; gem engraving, 114; history of collecting, 9; Indian words in, 138 n.; Indians in, 127, 136, 161; invention of typography, 78; lory in, 180–81; maps of, 76; orangutan in, 177; Oriental paintings in, 64; Oriental slaves in, 64; parrots in, 179–80; peacocks in, 182; reactions to America, 4–5; reactions to Asia, 3–5, 7, 81, 94; rhinoceroses in, 158, 168–69; silkworm introduced, 93, 109; sweet oranges in, 12, 40; tigers in, 173–74; uses of lac, 112; weaving of silk textiles in, 96–97. *See also* Asia; Renaissance; *and under the names of individual European countries and cities*
Eurasia: overland route, 4
Evelyn, John, 113 n.
Evora, 12, 67
Exoticism. *See* Ornament; Symbolism; *and under names of individual products and animals*

Fabri, Alexandre di: *Diversarium nationum ornatus,* 103
Faenza, 105
Fans, 35, 103; in engravings, 94
Fanti, Sigismondo, 142
Fantuzzi, Antonio: elephant fresco, 143
Faria, João de, 136 n.
Faria, Nicolau de, 136
Farnese, Cardinal Alessandro, 63
Favolius, Hugo, 87
Featherworks, 13, 17, 29, 35, 121, 187, 188; of America, 18, 195 n.; of Asia, 18; at Brussels, 18, 195 n.; in ornament, 18 n., 195; in paintings, 69, 72, 75, 155; as pictures, 182
Fedrici, Cesare, 156
Ferdinand, archduke: at Ambras, 26–27; at Prague, 26
Ferdinand I, Holy Roman Emperor, 19, 23, 144
Ferdinand I, grand duke of Tuscany, 24
Fernandes, Andreas, 168 n.
Fernandes, Diogo, 60
Fernandes, Garcia, 68, 69
Fernandes, Mateus, 59, 60
Fernandes, Tomas, 60
Fernandes, Valentim: on *ganda,* 162 n., 163
Ferrara, 141; "porcelains" of, 107; tigers at, 173
Feyerabend, Sigismund, 150
Ficino, Marsilio, 84
Fickler, J. B., 25
Figueiredo, Cristóvão de, 68
Filiberto, Emanuel, 150
Fitch, Ralph, 67

Index

Flanders: "Spanish Fury" of 1576, 19; verdures of, 99. *See also* Netherlands

Florence, 43, 71, 155, 163; Boboli gardens, 40; luxury trades of, 111; Palazzo Vecchio, 39; relations with Portugal, 38–39; as rival of Venice, 39; Santa Croce, 61; studiolo of the Medici, 40, 111; triumph of Camillus, 138; Uffizi palace, 182. *See also* Medici

Floris, Cornelis: ornamental experiments of, 195–96

Floris, Franz, 151 n.

Flower painting, 72, 73, 122

Fonseca, Pedro da, 168

Fonseca, Vicente de, archbishop, 14

Fontainebleau, 157, 159; *Cabinet des singularitez*, 32; collections, 31–32; elephant fresco, 143

Fontenay-le-Comte (Vendée), 32

France, 70, 71, 113, 155; Asian exotica in, 30–33; Dürer's rhinoceros in, 170; elephants in, 130, 155; *entrées* of kings, 149, 165; "great names," 32; Portuguese commercial agents in, 16; relations to Turkey, 31; symbols for, 165; textile industry, 99, 102; voyages to East, 31, 33

France, Jean de, duke of Berry, 31

Francesco I, grand duke of Tuscany, 24, 40, 66, 77, 108; gifts to Saxony, 24; studiolo, 40, 111

Francis I, king of France, 118, 184; agents, 31; allegorical portrait of, 143; correspondence with Portugal, 31, 143 n.; menagerie of, 143 n.; and rhinoceros, 162; tapestries for, 143, 144

Franck, Pauwels, 76, 192

Francken, Frans, the Elder, 181

Franco, Giovanni Battista, 144 n.

Frankfurt, 22, 94; elephants in, 133, 158 n., fair of 1480, 133

Frederick I, duke of Württemberg, 20

Frederick II, emperor, 133 n.; elephant of, 130

Frederick III, duke of Schleswig-Holstein-Gottorp, 21

Frescoes: Asians in, 155; elephants in, 143, 143 n., 145–46, 151 n., 155, 158 n., 159 n.; at Marissa in Palestine, 159 n.; monkeys in, 177; in Palazzo Vecchio, 155; rhinoceros in, 159 n.

Fröschl, Daniel, 29 n.

Fuchs, Leonhard, 82

Fuchs, Michael, 146

Fugger, house of, 22, 34, 88, 117; newsletters, 28; and tapestries, 101

Fugger, Anton, 16

Fugger, Hans, 76

Fugger, Mark, 25

Fugger, Octavius, 153

Furniture, 24, 34, 121, 187; bedsteads, 10, 110; cabinets, 110; chests, 110; in collections, 110–11; Indo-Portuguese, 107; lacquered, 112;

Linschoten on, 110; at Munich, 25; ornamentation, 110, 111; at Prague, 30; in Spain, 13

Fustat (Egypt), 104 n.

Gaddi, cardinal, 43

Gaddi, Niccolò, 40

Galen, 175

Galingale, 34

Galle, Philippe, 87, 90, 144 n.

Gama, Francisco da, 15

Gama, Vasco da, 10, 12, 37, 61, 101, 118; portrait, 68

Ganda (rhinoceros of Cambay), 172; and Hanno, 162; death, 162; Dürer's drawing of, 163; Dürer's woodcut of, 163–64; etymology, 158 n.; harness for, 162; in India, 161; influence in art, 163–64, 168, 171; Jovius on, 162 n., 167; literary description of, 163; Lisbon sketches of, 163, 165; in Portugal, 161

Gardens, 28, 83; Boboli, 40; at Bomarzo, 191; of Camerarius, 84; at Castello, 166, 191; as collections of curiosities, 82; Gothic, 73; and landscape architecture, 166, 186, 191; at Leyden, 83; at Lisbon, 191; at Malines, 180; at Padua, 82; at Rome, 138, 142, 148; of Tuileries, 189 n.

Garnets, 117

Garthe, Richard, 35

Garuda (Indian solar bird), 92 n.

Gastaldi, Giacomo, 87

Gaudi, Antonio, 60

Gaultier, Leonard, 88

Gems. *See* Precious stones

Genoa, 162; elephants in, 124, 144; Palazzo Doria, 143 n.

Geography: connection with astronomy, 44

Germany: collectors of, 22, 28, 30; Dürer's rhinoceros in, 170; lacemaking in, 121; relations with Netherlands, 22; silverware, 119. *See also under names of individual states and cities*

Gerritsz, Dirck (alias "China"), 20

Gesner, Konrad, 28, 84, 158, 174 n., 182; *Historiae animalium*, 166; woodcuts, 166

Gesù, church at Rome, 43, 62; influence in Asia, 63; relics from East in, 63

Gheeraerts, Marc, 86 n.

Ghent, 95

Ghini, Luca, 83

Gilles, Pierre, 32, 147, 158

Giovio, Paolo. *See* Jovius, Paulus

Giraffe, 158, 166, 177

Glanvil, Bartholomew, 161

Goa, 14, 65, 88, 89 n., 90, 101, 161; Archaeological Museum, 66; churches of, 67; embroideries of, 99; goldworkers at, 118 n.; Jesuit structures at, 63, 65; lacquerware of, 107 n.; paintings of Portuguese fortresses, armadas, and viceroys at, 66; as "Queen of the

Goa—(*continued*)
East," 13; ship-building at, 15; tiles (*azulejos*) of, 107; trade in ceramics from China, 107 n.; transparent smocks (*bajus*) of, 103; Western paintings at, 69
Gois, Damião de, 18, 20; on porcelains, 105
Gold and goldworks, 11, 13, 16, 30, 38, 43; in Asia, 113; crown of, 10; custodial of Belém, 118; at Goa, 118 n.; Manueline creations in, 118; price of, 113
Golden House of Nero, 70, 194
Gonçalves, Nuno, 67
Gonzáles de Mendoza, Juan. *See* Mendoza, Juan Gonzáles de
Gorilla, 175
Gorlé, Abraham, 153
Gothic art, 59, 61, 62, 96; apes in, 176; Asian influences on, 187; church ornament in, 197; garden in, 73; and Naturalism, 97
Goujon, Jean, 165
Grand Khan of Tartary, 37 n., 90
Granvelle, Antoine Perrenot de, cardinal: collection of, 23–24, 29
Granvelle, Nicholas Perrenot de: collection of, 23–24, 29
Graphic arts, 56; depictions of Chinese in, 122
Graz: collections at, 25–26
Greece, 69, 96, 175; collections, 9; and elephant, 125, 126
Gregory XIII, pope, 42, 72, 89, 91 n., 192
Grenier, Jehan, 100, 134
Grotesques, 77, 119, 195; from Golden House of Nero, 70
Guicciardini, Ludovico: on elephant, 151
Guise, house of, 32
Guissoni, Andrea, 108
Guitter, Parisian collector, 33
Gums and resins, 20, 193
Gustavus I Vasa, king of Sweden, 110
Guyon, Loys: on porcelain, 106

Habsburgs: and Asian trade, 22; collections, 22, 23, 25–30; portraits, 150
Hainhofer, Philip, 18, 24
Hakluyt, Richard, 35, 44, 64, 98 n., 106, 157 n.; catalogue of prizes from "Madre de Dios," 34
Halle, 28
Hamel, Alart du, 152 n.
Hangchow, 42
Hanno, 148, 152 n., 157, 158, 172, 198; and Baraballo, 138; bell of, 141; death, 139; in engravings, 144 n.; epitaph, 140–41; etymology, 138 n.; fantasized, 142; influence in European art, 141, 143–44, 147, 150; intarsia of, 139, 141; and Leo X, 139; at Mantua, 143; proportions, 141; public appearances, 138; Raphael's portrait of, 140; in stucco relief, 143; in woodcuts, 141–42

Harun al-Rashid, 96, 130 n.; gift of elephant to Charlemagne, 129
Haupt, Albrecht, 58
Heemskerck, Martin van: sketch of elephant fountain, 142
Heere, Lucas de, 152
Heliogabalus, emperor, 173
Henriques, Francisco, 68, 69
Henry II, king of France, 32, 103, 135 n., 147, 165, 168, 192, 196
Henry III, king of England, 130
Henry III, king of France, 152, 153, 168
Henry IV, king of France, 32; as collector, 33; elephant of, 155
Henry VIII, king of England: porcelain of, 33; tapestries of, 100
Hereford map, 131
Herodotus: on Asia, 114
Herwart, house of, 22, 116 n.
Hidalcão (sultan of Bijapur), 101
Hides, 38, 39
Hieroglyphs: and emblem books, 78, 84–86; and painting, 86 n.; and philosophical speculation, 84
Hinduism: elephant legends of, 129 n.; Jesuits on, 8; and rhinoceros, 171; and transmigration of souls, 77
Hirschvogel, house of, 116
Hoefnagel, Georg, 72, 76, 183; animal drawings of, 156 n.; and Chinese paintings, 75
Hoffmann, Lorentz, 28
Hogenberg, Franz, 87, 192; engravings of Asian cities, 88–89
Holbein, Hans, the Younger, 88
Holland. *See* Netherlands
Hollar, Wenzel, 158 n.
Holtzwart, Matthias, 180
Holy Land, 35, 64, 76, 130
Horapollo, 85, 86, 134; *Hieroglyphica*, 84
Hornick, Erasmus, 119
Hradchin (Prague), 29
Huetstocker, Sebastian, 146
Hulsius, Levinus: German travel books of, 95
Humanism, 3, 22, 23; and Antiquity, 69–70; and Asia, 40, 70, 191, 199; and Asian art, 70; and barbarians, 199, 199 n.; and elephant, 124, 151, 157; and painting, 190, 191; and porcelain, 106 n.; and rhinoceros, 172. *See also* Renaissance
Hutten, Ulrich von: on Hanno, 139

Iconography, 36; of Asian animals, 123; and emblems, 86; of Goa, 89 n.; and maps, 87; of Romanesque ornament, 96; unity with poetry, 85
Il Riposo (villa near Florence), 39
Imhof, house of, 28
Imperato, Ferrante, 43
India, 149 n.; Alexander's invasion of, 125–26,

172; animals typical of, 30, 123; apes and monkeys of, 175, 177; castes of diamonds and rubies, 120; composite paintings of, 187; diamonds, 116, 117; drawings of life in, 61, 65, 134 n.; elephant hooks, 142; elephants of, 125, 128, 135, 147 n., 156; European artists in, 61–62, 63, 87 n.; Europeans in, 7; export wares, 14, 110; goods and temples of, 30, 88, 148, 199; as "the land of the elephant," 127; and Magi, 75; maps of, 24, 87; "noble sages" of, 142; occupations, 65; orangutan of, 175 n.; parrots of, 178; pearl divers of, 38; precious stones, 114, 117; quilts of, 99; religious processions, 88; rhinoceros of, 159, 161; and rhinoceros in art, 171; ritual bathing in, 104; stone elephants of, 148; symbols of, 170, 171, 192; textiles produced in, 98, 99; traditions about precious stones, 115–16, 120; uses of lac, 112; "wild men" of, 176. *See also* Asia; *and under names of individual principalities and cities*
Indian "dog": as emblem, 87
Indian hemp (hashish), 11
Indian miniatures: and Arcimboldo, 77 n.; and Rembrandt, 77
"Indian objects," 7, 29, 46, 188
"Indians," 41 n.
Indicopleustes, Cosmas: on rhinoceros, 161
Indigo, 103, 188
Indochina: pictures of natives of, 65
Indonesia: pictures of natives of, 65
Indo-Portuguese arts. *See* Arts
Ingolstadt, 24
Innsbruck, 153
Iran: porcelain in, 104
Irises, 193
Isidore of Seville, 129
Islam, 4, 96; artistic traditions of, 120; influences in Indian and European art, 61; and migration arts, 194
Isotta, of Rimini, 132
Istanbul: Museum of Antiquities, 175 n.
Italy, 113; ceramics of, 104; costume of, 103; Dürer's rhinoceros in, 170; elephants in, 127, 128, 137, 144–45; faience of, 107; furniture of, 111; garden of Bomarzo, 148; Japanese emissaries in, 72; jewels in, 115 n.; majolica, 107; natural history collections of, 43; relations with Levant, 35–36; relations with Netherlands, 22; silk trade of, 36; textile industry of, 96, 99. *See also under names of individual cities*
Itō, Mancio, 72
Iviza island, 137
Ivories, 14, 17, 25, 29, 30, 32, 34, 37, 39, 128, 133, 188; "Apotheosis of Romulus," 126 n.; bedsteads, 110 n.; cages, 179; Charlemagne's chess set, 130; designs, 131; elephants in, 25, 126 n., 130, 153; Sinhalese, 25
Jade: etymology, 117; Marco Polo on, 114;

Odoric of Pordenone on, 114; of Turkestan, 114; virtues, 114, 117
Jaffa, 35
Jahangir: and European engravings, 187 n.
Jamnitzer, Christian, 154
Jamnitzer, Wenzel, 120
Japan: Azuchi Castle, 89; birds of, 182; *byōbus* (folding screens) of, 14, 42, 89, 187, 188; embassy to Europe of 1615, 89 n.; feather-works of, 18; gods of, in Cartari, 89 n.; Kano school, 89 n.; Nishiji lacquerware of, 198; silver, 113; Urushi ware, 110. *See also* Asia; Japanese legates
Japanese legates of 1584–86 in Europe: in art, 72, 91 n., 189; costumes of, 91 n., 102, 189; and elephant, 169; engravings of, 91 n.; in Florence, 41, 111; gifts to Francesco de' Medici, 111; gifts to papacy, 42; gifts to Philip II, 14, 110; and rhinoceros, 169; at Rome, 42; in Spain, 14; and Vecellio, 72 n.; at Venice, 72; at Verona, 18
Japanning, 113
Java, 95; emu from, 95, 182, 183
Javanese kris: engraving of, 95
Jerónimos (Order of St. Jerome): church of the, 60; congregation in Italy, 63; custodial of, 118; monastery of, 57;
Jerusalem: European artists in, 35, 64
Jesuits: and art, 65, 67, 70; art style called "Jesuit," 62; on Asia, 5, 191; on Asian arts, 8, 63, 106, 191; and Gesù, 42, 43, 62, 63; gifts to patrons in Europe, 67 n.; at Goa, 65; lacquered furniture of, 112–13; letterbooks of, 19, 25; letters, 63, 67, 168 n.; at Mughul court, 187 n.; paintings in Europe, 71–72; and Pinto, 65–66; and plants, 82; on porcelains, 106; relations with Bavaria, 24–25; on the rhinoceros, 168 n.; in Rome, 43, 62, 63; sarcophagi of, 187; on statues and temples of Asia, 8, 63
Jewelry, 15, 36, 112; Asian pieces in Europe, 118; patronage of jewelers, 118. *See also* Precious stones
Jewels. *See* Precious stones
John George I, elector of Saxony, 24
John III, king of Portugal, 68, 69, 140, 144; symbolic investiture of the Sinhalese prince by, 10
Jordan of Severac: on rhinoceros, 161
Jovius, Paulus (Giovio, Paolo), 162; and Hanno's portrait, 140; *History of My Own Times*, 140; and emblems, 167; museum, 167; on rhinoceros, 162 n., 167
"Jumbo," 141 n.
Justinian: engraving of, 93

Kano school, 89 n.
Katchadourian, Sarkis, 67 n.
Khevenhüller, Hans Christopher, 26, 29

Index

Kingfisher (*Halcyon chloris*), 18
Kirchheim, 76, 192
Kleberger, Hans, 165
Knieper, Hans, 133 n.
Knights of Christ, 59
Kobenhaupt, Georg, 119
Kotte (Ceylon), 10
Krafft, Hans Ulrich, 24 n., 29 n.; on jewelry, 116; travels in the Levant, 116
Kremsmünster: Stiftsbibliothek, 146
Krishna Dēva Rāyya, ruler of Vijayanagar: collection of jewels, 116

Lac, 112
Lace, 96, 99, 121
Lacquer and lacquerware, 27, 30, 32, 56, 107; in Asia, 112; commerce in, 112 n.; "Coromandel," 112; decorations on, 196; at Dresden, 24; etymology, 112; European imitations of, 121; furniture, 112; imports into Europe, 112; in paintings, 69; in Philip II's collections, 15, 110; recipe for, 112; screens, 14, 42, 89, 112, 187–88; as sources of motifs, 74; Urushi ware, 110
Lafreri, Antonio, 152 n., 154 n.; *Speculum Romanae magnificentiae*, 144
Lancaster, James, 168 n.
Langrens, Arnoldus F. à, 94, 170
Lapis lazuli, 114
Laocoön, 70
Laureati, Tommaso, 192
Laz, Wolfgang, 145
L'écluse, Charles de (Clusius), 8, 34, 82, 83, 154, 158; collections of foreign plants, 28; on elephant, 151, 153; on emu, 95, 183
Lees-Milne, James, 58
Leipzig, 24
Leo X, pope, 31, 41, 101, 137; Chinese book of, 41; and *ganda*, 161–62; and Hanno, 138, 139, 140 n.; and Hanno's portrait, 140; and Manuel of Portugal, 16, 162; Manuel's letter to, 10; Portugal's mission of obedience to, 136–37; and Raphael, 140
Leonardo, Camillo di: *Speculum lapidum . . .*, 115 n.
Leonardo da Vinci, 71, 77, 86 n., 191; on ape, 177 n.; on Asian customs, 37–38; books of, 37; and elephant 129 n.; and lacquer varnish, 112; letters, 37; *Notebooks*, 37; pearl recipe, 117; *Prophecies*, 38; in Rome, 137; travels, 37; as vegetarian, 37
Levant, 96, 116, 124, 126; animal markets of, 123, 160; Breydenbach in, 133 n.; elephants in, 147; porcelain, 104
Leyden, 21, 83
Leyden, Lucas van, 74, 79, 83
Leyte, 87 n.
Lião, Duarte Nunes de, 199
Liberale, Giorgio, 82

Ligozzi, Jacopo, 41, 71, 155; and bird of paradise, 182
Lille, 132
Linschoten, Jan Huygen van, 20, 66; on Cambay, 117; engravings, 66; on furniture of India, 110; influence, 94–95; *Itinerario*, 21, 94; on lacquer, 112 n., 113 n.; on lory, 181; on paintings at Goa, 66; and Paludanus, 20–21; on porcelain, 106; sketches of Asia, 21, 66
Lipsius, Justus: on elephant, 151
Lisbon, 9, 22, 31, 39, 43, 67, 162, 169, 192, 196; Academy of Sciences, 66; as artistic center, 57; Casa da India, 161; combat of rhinoceros and elephant at, 159, 161–62; diamond cutters of, 117; diamond trade at, 116–17; earthquake of 1755, 16, 57; elephant stable, 135; elephants in, 124, 135–36, 150–51, 154; as emporium, 10, 11, 116, 117, 121; entry of Philip II in 1581, 13; Florentines in, 100 n.; "Indian" furniture at, 110 n.; jewelers of, 118; Jews in, 38; monkeys in, 177; Nicot in, 32; Paço d'Estãos, 135; Paço da Ribeira, 13, 161; pharmacists of, 11; prices at, 38; renovation, 11; Rossio of, 11; Rua Dourivesaria, 118; Rua Nova das Mercadores, 11, 118; slaves in, 38; silversmiths of, 118; Torre do Tombo, 110 n.; triumphal arches and pedestals, 13
Livro das Armadas, 66
Livro de Lizuarte de Abreu, 66, 89 n.
L'Obel, Mathias de (Lobelius), 35, 83 n.
London, 94; porcelain exhibition of 1956, 106 n. *See also* England
Lopes, Gregório, 68, 69
Lopes de Castanheda, Fernão, 87
Lorck, Melchior, 89, 191; sketches of, 90; Turkish costumes of, 90
Lory, 180–81
Louis IX, king of France: elephants of, 130, 155
Louis XIV, king of France: elephants of, 158
Louvre: Cabinet des Dessins, 151; exhibition of landscape painting in 1960, 74
Lucca, 36; silk weaving at, 97
Lufftvogel (bird of paradise), 181
Luther, Martin: and Leo X, 139
Lyons, 102, 165
Lyskirchen, Konstantin von, 28, 88

Mabuse, Jan Gossaert, 75
Macao: Jesuit structures, 63
Macedonia, 116
Macer, Jean, 76, 190
Machiavelli: on Baraballo, 139
Mactan (Philippines), 88
Madagascar, 92
Madras: painted calicoes, 98
"Madre de Dios," 34
Madrid, 13; Armería, 14; elephants in, 124, 154; and Japanese emissaries, 14, 110; menagerie, 14; rhinoceros at, 169

Magellan, Ferdinand, 87 n., 88, 192 n.; and Apollo, 92; portraits, 26 n., 92
"Magellanica," 193
Mahabharata, 92 n.
Mahouts, 124, 127, 128, 155 n.
Mainz, 133
Majolica, 105, 106, 107
Majorca, 137
Malacca, 98, 112 n.; elephants captured at, 135; pictures of natives of, 65
Malatesta, family of Rimini, 36, 134; elephant symbol of, 132; "temple," 132
Malatestiana. *See* Biblioteca Malatestiana
Malayālam word for "elephant," 138 n.
Malines, 71, 180
Malpighi, Marcello, 158 n.
"Mamuco Diata" (*Manuk dewato* in Malay), 181 n.
Manaar, straits of, 117
Mandeville, Sir John, 37, 113; on precious stones, 115
Manila, 110
Mannerism, 57, 69; and animals, 177–78, 184; at Antwerp, 195; Asian influences on, 122, 187; and D'Ollanda, 70; and elephant, 155, 157; and landscapes, 73; and Naturalism, 189; and neo-Pythagorean beliefs, 199; and ornament, 71, 195, 198; in Portugal, 69; and symbolism, 198. *See also* Ornament; Symbolism
Mantegna, Andrea, 81, 86 n., 149, 152 n.; "Triumph of Caesar," 133
Mantua: and elephants, 142; ducal palace, 143, 174; Palazzo del Te, 143, 174
Manuel I, king of Portugal, 10, 31, 41, 57, 64, 106, 161; armillary sphere, 59; *Book of Hours*, 11 n., 136, 162, 165; decrees on gold- and silversmiths, 118; "elephants of state," 135; and *ganda*, 162; gifts to papacy, 16, 140 n.; goldworks of, 118; and Hanno, 140; letter to Leo X, 10 n.; as Oriental potentate, 135–36; and tapestries, 110 n.
Manzor, sultan of Tidore, 88 n.
Maps: animal landmarks on, 131, 167; of Asia, 32, 80, 87; at Caprarola palace in Viterbo, 192 n.; of China, 34; conventional signs, 87; in cosmographies, 88; Dürer's rhinoceros on, 170; of Elephanta island, 37; as emblems, 87; engravings of, 79; in Florence, 40; of Gastaldi, 87; iconographical elements, 87, 196; in Linschoten, 94; at London, 34, 94; on medals, 88 n.; as ornaments, 34, 88 n., 192 n., 198; of Ortelius, 88; in Paris, 32; portraits on, 192 n.; and print makers, 190; on silverware, 119; sources, 87; on tapestries, 101
Marbodius: *De Lapidibus*, 114
Marche, Oliver de la, 132 n.
Margaret of Austria, archduchess, 19, 180
Maria, empress, 146

Maria, of Graz, 26
Marseilles: *ganda* at, 31, 162
Martaban, 112 n.
Martaban jars: at Djakarta, 13 n.; in engravings, 94; at Leeuwarden, 13 n.
Martial, 170; on rhinoceros, 167
"Martichoras" (tiger), 172
Martires, Bartolomeu dos, 41
Mascarenhas, Leonor, 67 n.
Mascarenhas, Francisco de, viceroy, 14
"Master B.," 151
Matarazzo, Federico, 37
Mattioli, Pier Andrea, 40, 43, 83, 154, 193; commentaries on Dioscorides, 82, 147
Maura, Miguel de, 15
Mauritius island, 183
Maxentius, 126 n.
Maximilian I, Holy Roman Emperor, 19, 100, 149, 184; collections, 23; Prayer Book, 80, 134 n., 164, 177; "triumphs," 79–80
Maximilian II, Holy Roman Emperor, 82, 145, 146, 150, 153; elephant of, 144–45; in Spain, 144
Maximilian of Transylvania, 87, 181 n., 182
Medici, house of, 37, 121, 184; Castello, 148, 166; collections, 39, 174; emblems, 149, 165, 167, 167 n.; festival of Saints Cosmas and Damian, 138; and Hanno, 142, 143
Medici, Catharine de', queen of France, 32, 165; costume, 103
Medici, Giovanni de', 167
Medici, Giuliano de', 37 n.
Medici, Ippolito de', cardinal, 37
Medici, Lorenzo de' (the Magnificent), 37, 138
Medici, Marie de', queen of France, 33
"Medici porcelains," 108, 121
Medina del Campo, 12
Meetkerke, Adolf van, 193
Megasthenes, 175; *Indica*, 127
Melchior (Persia), 75
Menageries, 36, 44, 124; at Amboise, 31, 143; in Brussels, 18; at Ebersdorf, 146, 153; human, 37; in Italy, 37; at Palermo, 130 n.; at Prague, 183
Mendoza, Don Hurtado de, 12
Mendoza, Juan Gonzáles de, 87; on *bada*, 169; on Chinese paintings, 64 n.; on porcelain, 106 n.
Mercati, Michele, 43
Mercator, Gerhard, 8, 19 n., 28, 44, 79
Merchant-Adventurers, 34
Metellus, Lucius Caecilius, 127
Meteren, Emanuel van, 34 n.
Mexico, 110; birds of, 182
Meyerpeck, Wolfgang, 82
Michelangelo, 70, 71, 191; and D'Ollanda, 69
Milan, 37 n., 110, 143; elephants in, 124, 145, 149
Mithra, 75
Mnemon, Artaxerxes, 125

Index

Mocquet, Jean, 32
Modafar II, sultan of Cambay, 161
Mohenjo-daro civilization, 171
Moluccas, 18, 32, 39, 87, 102, 180, 181; pictures of natives of, 65
Monardes, Nicholas, 11 n., 87
Mongols, 4, 191
Monkeys, 22, 72 n., 80, 123, 166, 183; Assyrian reliefs of, 175; in frescos, 177; and humans, 176; in *Physiologus* tradition, 176; symbolism of, 176, 177, 184; tailed and tailless, 175; in tapestries, 177
Monstier, Etienne, 33
Montaigne, 6
Montalboddo, Francanzano da, 133 n.
Montalto, cardinal (elected Pope Sixtus V in 1585), 99, 137
Montano, Benito Arias, 8, 13 n.; collection, 20; relations with Ortelius, 20
Monte Cassino, 102 n.
Montezuma, 17
Montmorency, house of, 32
Morandini, Francesco (Poppi), 40
"Moresques," 71, 198
Morgan, Dr. Hugh, 34
Moryson, Fynes, 156
Mosaics, 197; parrots in, 179; tigers in, 173; of Ravenna, 35; of rhinoceros, 160
Mostart, Jan: "The Discovery of America," 190
Moyen, Van der, weaver of Brussels, 89
Mudéjar (folk art of wall ornament), 62
Münster, Sebastian, 87; *Cosmographia universalis*, 88, 116 n., 166; on diamonds, 116 n.; on parrots, 180; on rhinoceros, 166; woodcuts of, 166
Münsterberg, Oskar, 73
Mughul arts: furniture, 111; and Jesuits, 187 n.; miniatures, 77
Mulberries, 40
Munich, 24; cabinetmakers of, 111; collections at, 25
Murer, C.: *Animaux au paradis*, 156 n.
Musk, 17, 34
Musk deer: as emblem, 87
Myle, Simone de: "Noah's Ark," 144
Myrobalans, 11, 17

Naga (snake), 92 n.
Nagasaki, 72
Naldini, Battista, 40
Naples, 43, 127; National Museum, 166, 178 n., 179 n.; rhinoceros of, 166
"Narsinga" (Vijayanagar), 88
Narwhal, 164
Nascherino, Michelangelo, 148 n.
Naturalism: and apes, 176, 177; of Arcimboldo, 156; and artistic prototypes, 183, 189; and Asian animals, 183, 184; and Asian objects and motifs, 186, 189; at Castello, 166; and ele-

phant, 124, 133, 141, 144, 147–48, 150, 151–52, 154, 155, 156, 157; and fantasizing, 183; and live models, 189; in minor arts, 189 n.; in ornament, 72, 194, 196, 197; in painting, 155; in prints, 190; and rhinoceros, 166, 169–70; trends, 186
Nature: chronological and geographical unity, 77; conceptions of, 74; in landscape painting, 73; relation to man, 77
Nautilus shell, 119, 120
Navagero, Andrea, 38
Nāyar warriors: portraits of, 65
Nazzaro, Matteo del, 118
Nearchus, Jacobus, 19 n., 179
Neckam, Alexander, 161, 176
Needlework: chain stitch, 99, 121; embroideries, 98–99; quilting, 99
Negro: and ape, 176
Neoplatonism, 84; and art, 86; of Colonna, 134
Nepal: rhinoceros emblem, 171
Nephrites, 117
Nero, emperor of Rome, 126 n.
Netherlandish ornament, 72, 196
Netherlandish paintings: of Magi, 75–76
Netherlands, 33, 113, 183; blockbooks, 78; costume, 103; Dürer's rhinoceros in, 170; elephants in, 124, 151, 152, 153, 158 n.; grotesques of, 195; silverware, 119; tapestries, 100–101
Nève, Henri de, 101 n.
New Guinea, 181
Nicholas V, pope, 36
Nicolay, N. de, 90
Nicolo, Giovanni, 67
Nicot, Jean, 32
Nineveh, 114
Nonsuch Castle, 102
Noort, Lambert van, 151
Notre Dame de Paris, 130
Nova Reperta, 93 n.
Nuremberg, 22, 79, 84, 95, 116, 154, 161; collections of curiosities at, 120; elephants at, 158 n.; silverware, 119
"Nuri" (Malay for lory), 181

"Oçem" (Indian elephant keeper), 161
Oda Nobunaga, 14, 89
Odoni, Andrea, 38
Odoric of Pordenone, 114 n.
Olearius, Adam, 21
Onyx, 120
Opium, 11, 12 n.
Oporto, 69
Oranges: in Europe, 12, 40
Orangutan, 177
Order of Christ (Portugal), 57
Order of the Elephant (Denmark), 132–33
Orissa, 116
Ormuz, 88; carpets of, 98; pearl fishing at, 88

Index

Ornament, 56, 57, 186; acanthus motifs, 71, 194; *alla porcellana*, 105; animals in, 105, 154, 184; arabesques, 71, 105, 194; in architecture and sculpture, 60, 121, 196; Asian influences on, 71, 97, 105, 121, 197–98; birds in, 105, 195; in books, 72, 150, 194; books of designs, 102, 119, 121; in borders, 72, 105; of caryatids, 196; Cellini on, 194–95; in ceramics, 105; and chinoiseries, 6, 97, 105, 170 n., 187, 194, 196; cloud motif, 74; dragon motif, 194; and Dürer, 17, 195; elephants in, 130, 135, 143, 150, 154, 194; on European daggers and sheaths, 95 n.; and exoticism, 71, 97, 105, 194; exotic vocabulary of, 196; "façon d'Inde," 32; of fantastic birds and animals, 71; floral design, 97; foliages, 194; on furniture, 110, 111; on goldworks, 118; grotesques, 70, 77, 119, 195, 198; hieroglyphs, 86; by Hoefnagel, 76; and Indo-Portuguese arts, 187; in Italy, 194; on lacquerware, 112–13; and Mannerism, 71, 195, 198; Manueline, 57–59, 118, 121, 196; on maps, 87, 88 n., 192 n., 196; maritime motifs, 60, 118, 194, 196, 198; of Medici porcelains, 108; medieval motifs, 194, 197; in minor arts, 198; "moresques," 71, 198; *mudéjar*, 62; and Mughul art, 187 n.; and Naturalism, 72, 194, 196, 197; Netherlandish, 72, 196; in painting, 71; palmettes, 71, 105; on playing cards, 87 n.; porcelains in, 195–96; in quilt design, 73, 197; rhinoceros in, 169; Romanesque, 96–97; seashells in, 196; and serpentine line, 187; on silverworks, 119; tigers in, 174; traditional motifs, 194, 197, 198
Orpheus, 76, 185
Ors, Eugenio d', 58
Orsini, Vincino, 148
Orta, Garcia da, 87; on aromatic woods, 109–10; *Coloquios*, 82, 154, 158; on the elephant, 154; on pearls, 116; on precious stones, 116
Ortelius, Abraham, 8, 21, 34 n., 40 n., 43, 44, 66, 72, 79, 90, 117 n., 162 n.; as collector, 19–20; correspondents, 19; *Theatrum orbis terrarum*, 88, 192
Osório, Jerónimo, 10
Ostendorfer, Michael, 81
Oudenaarde: tapestries of, 100
Oxford: Ashmolean collection, 144 n.

Padua, 43; university, 82; Villa Cornaro, 143 n.
Paintings: "Adoration of the Magi," 68–69, 75–76, 190; of animals, 72, 76, 77, 156, 176, 178, 184; apes in, 176; of Asia in Biblioteca Casanatense, 65–66; Asian arts and products in, 68–69, 122; Asian designs and motifs in, 71; Asian influences in, 73–74; Asians in, 68–69, 75, 189; and bird of paradise, 181; of birds, 181, 182, 183; borrowing of motifs, 74; carpets in, 99, 189; on ceramics, 106–7; of Christian converts in Asia, 67; cooperative

works, 66, 68; costume in, 103; elephants in, 133, 134, 144, 147 n., 148, 152, 153, 155, 157; of emu, 183; and engravings, 94; fans in, 103; featherworks in, 69, 72, 75, 155; of "the flight from Egypt," 190; of flowers, 72, 73; of "four parts of the world," 76, 190; of Garden of Eden, 190; and Humanism, 190, 191; of insects, 72; Islamic and Persian miniatures, 99; of Japanese legates, 72; of Jesuits, 67, 71–72; landscape, 73, 74, 122, 181, 187; of lory, 181; and Mannerism, 69; miniatures, 29, 36, 64, 72, 99, 142, 190; of Noah's ark, 190; Oriental subjects, 64, 67; and ornament, 71; parasol in, 103; parrots in, 180; and perspective, 74, 197; of plants, 66, 72, 73; of porcelains, 67, 72 n., 73, 107, 109, 189; on porcelains, 31 n., 106, 108, 196; in Portugal, 67–70; of religious subjects, 67; rhinoceros in, 171; of seashells, 73; still life, 72 n., 73, 122; *têtes composées* of Arcimboldo, 77; of textiles, 68, 73, 97–98, 189; tigers in, 174; traditional themes, 190, 198; of triumph of Bacchus in India, 76, 190; of *Wunderkammer*, 9; of Xavier in Asia, 71
Palanquins, 24 n.; in engravings, 94
Palermo, 35, 127, 130 n.; fountain elephant, 148
Palestrina, 160
Palissy, Bernard, 32, 189 n.
Palmyra, 96
Paludanus (Bernard ten Broecke), 84, 151; collections, 20–21, 94; epigram about, 21; on porcelain, 106 n.
Panchatantra: on elephant, 128
Panciroli, Guido: on porcelains, 105, 109
Papacy: and Council of Trent, 42; legations to, 41, 42, 136–38. *See also* Rome; Vatican
Paradiseidae (bird of paradise), 181
Parasol (*chattra*), 81, 103; in engravings, 94
Paré, Ambroise, 147, 168, 181 n.
Parentino, Bernardo, 134 n.
Paris, 90, 168, 189 n.; Cabinet des Medailles, 130 n.; collections at, 32; costumers of, 102; Louvre exhibitions of 1960, 74; Musée Cernuschi, 74 n.; Portuguese at, 32
Paris, Matthew, 130
Parrots, 17, 22, 41, 72 n., 80, 123, 145, 183, 193; in bestiaries, 179, 180; and bird of paradise, 181; in Egypt, 179; as emblems, 87, 180; etymology, 181 n.; in Europe, 17, 22, 179–80; as gifts, 17, 22, 179–80; of India, 178; in mosaics, 179; in natural histories, 87, 180; in paintings, 180; in Rome, 179; speech and tricks of, 178–79; symbolism, 179, 180, 184; in woodcuts, 180
Pasquinades: animals in, 139 n.
Pathan warriors: portraits of, 65
Patinir, 73
Paul VI, pope: and Hanno's portrait, 140
Pausanias: on ebony, 109

Index

Peacock, 182

Pearls, 10, 16, 22, 30, 34, 38, 40, 115, 121, 187; comparison of European and Oriental, 117; on costumes, 117; infusions of, 117; inlays, 117; mother-of-pearl, 117; in mountings, 27; in pendants, 119

Pegu (Burma), 88, 117, 156

Peiresc, Claude de, 33

Penni, Gianfrancesco: drawings for tapestries, 144

Penni, Giovanni Giacomo, 162, 163

Pericoli, Niccolo, 166

Persia, 96, 172; cormorant in, 182; costume, 102; and Magi, 75; pictures of natives of, 65

Persian Gulf, 32, 117

Perugia, 160

Peutinger, Konrad, 182; collections, 22

Philip II, duke of Pomerania-Stettin, 111

Philip II, king of Spain, 105, 118, 152, 187; arboretum at Aranjuez, 14; Chinese chair of, 110; as collector, 13–15, 27; elephants of, 14, 124, 154, 155; emblems, 15, 154 n.; as king of Portugal, 154, 192; and Japanese emmissaries, 14, 110; letters to daughters, 14; at Lisbon, 14, 192; medal, 15; porcelain collection, 27, 105; rhinoceros of, 169; triumphs, 13, 193

Philip III (Philip II in Portugal), 107

Philip of Burgundy, 132

Philippine Islands, 13, 14, 87 n., 90; birds of, 182

Philoenus, Manius, 138 n.

Phoenicians, 114

Phoenix, 181 n.; in Musée Cernuschi, 74 n.; in paintings, 74

Physiologus, or The Naturalist, 129, 157, 166

Pigafetta, Antonio, 92

Pignoria, Lorenzo, 89 n.

Pina, João de, 162

Pina, Ruy de, 10

Pineapples, 193

Pinheiro, Manuel, 61

Pinto, Fernão Mendes, 65

Pinturicchio, 86 n.

Pirckheimer, Willibald, 180 n.; collections, 22

Pisa: cathedral, 130, 170

Pius IV, pope, 16, 41; and elephants, 150 n.

Plantin, Christopher, 19, 79, 83, 90, 152 n.

Plants: in botanical books, 81–84, 123; drawings of, 83; dried specimens of, 82, 83; in engravings, 94; geographical distribution of, 82; in *Herbarius* (also called *Ortus sanitatis*), 81, 133; illustrations of, 82; imported into Europe, 82, 83; and Jesuits, 82; living specimens of, 83; in ornament, 71, 97, 105, 194–95; in painting, 66, 72, 73; in woodcuts, 81, 188

Plateresque style, 62

Platter, Thomas, 34, 35, 102

Playing cards, 87

Pléiade, 199

Pliny the Elder, 37, 96, 114, 138 n., 147, 154, 157, 159, 167, 176; *Natural History*, 128; on elephant, 128, 132 n., 139 n.; on parrots, 179; on rhinoceros, 160; on tiger, 172, 173

Plutarch, 144 n., 173

Pluto, 40

Pock, Georg, 116

Poetry: birds of paradise in, 181; and elephant, 124, 138–39, 146; of Favolius, 87; parrots in, 181; and rhinoceros, 162–63; unity with iconography, 85

Poggi, G., 40 n.

Poissonnier, Arnold, 100

Poitiers, Diane of, 103 n.

Poland, 153

Polo, Marco, 36, 92, 114, 160 n., 192 n.; on rhinoceros, 161

Pompeii, 126 n., 166, 179

Pompey the Great, 159

Porcacchi, Thommaso, 87

Porcari, Metello Varro, 166

Porcelain, 10, 13, 17, 28, 31, 33, 35, 39, 43, 56, 121, 187; admiration of, 199; at Ambras, 26–27; arabesques on, 105; at Bologna, 16 n.; celadons, 37, 104; Charles V's set of plates (now at Dresden), 13 n.: chemical composition of, 104–5, 108; clay, 21; cost, 105, 187; debates over, 105; decorations, 31 n., 105 n., 106, 108, 196; in England, 33; etymology, 105; European imitations of, 104–6, 107, 108, 121; export wares of China, 106; in Florence, 39, 41; in France, 31; in Italy, 37, 38; "louças da India," 106; of Margaret of Austria, 19; in medieval Europe, 104; as models for Dürer, 75, 80; in mountings, 33, 119, 120; in ornament, 195–96; in paintings, 69, 72 n., 73, 107, 109, 189; and papacy, 16, 42; of Philip II of Spain, 27, 105; in Portugal, 11; at Prague, 30; and seashells, 105, 107; as sources for design ideas, 91, 195; in Spain, 13; in Venice, 36. *See also* Ceramics

Porta, Giacomo della, 62

Portugal, 69, 70, 113; Asian animals in, 123; carpet and rug imports, 100; Chinese paintings in, 10; costume, 102; elephants in, 14, 124, 150–51; and export porcelain, 106; furniture, 110; guilds of gold- and silversmiths, 118; Italian artistic influence in, 119; and Mannerism, 69; missions to papacy, 16, 41, 136–37, 162; national style of painting, 68; painting, 67–70; "policy of secrecy," 4–5, 8, 68; potters, 107; relations with Flanders, 67; relations with Florence, 38–39; relations with Venice, 38; relations with Vijayanagar, 116; silverware, 119; spice monopoly, 11; suzerainty over Ceylon, 10; textile industry, 99. *See also* Lisbon; Manuel I

Porus, an Indian prince, 125, 126

Postel, Guillaume, 8, 32

Index

Prague, 22, 120 n., 196; artists and scientists at, 29; cabinetmakers of, 111; collections, 46–54, 77; Ferdinand at, 26; menagerie, 174; paintings at, 29, 76–77; *Wunderkammer* of Europe, 28. *See also* Rudolf II

Praun, house of, 22

Praun, Paul von, 28

Praun, Stefen von, 28 n.

Precious stones, 8, 9, 10, 11, 22, 29, 30, 34, 36, 38, 40, 43, 120, 121, 187; Asian traditions about, 115; of Ceylon, 116; engraved gems, 114, 153; in engravings, 94; and Herwarts, 116 n.; history, 114; in India, 116; in lapidarial writings, 114, 115; medicinal and magical properties of, 114, 115; symbolism, 115, 120; on tapestries, 117; in theological minerology, 114, 120; in trade, 115–16

Printing: in China, 78; Chinese influences on, 78, costume books, 90–91, in Europe, 78; of herbals, 83; image prints, 78; of news-letters, 81; of playing cards, 78, 87 n.; of textiles, 78

Provins, 155

"Psittace" (parrot): of Aristotle, 179

Ptolemy, Claudius, 37, 44, 81

Ptolemy II, of Egypt, 126, 179

Pyrrhus II, king of Epirus, 127

Quadrigas: on coins, 132 n.; on decorative stuccos, 143 n.; of elephants, 126, 134, 144 n., 149; of tigers, 173; wall painting of, 126 n.

Quellin, Erasmus, 71

Quickeberg, Samuel, 25

Quinsay (Hangchow), 42

Rabanus: *De universo*, 129

Rabelais, 6, 32, 165

Rama: in Christian sculpture, 67

Ramayana, 92 n.

Ramusio, Giovanni Battista, 87, 105 n.; medal honoring, 88 n.; on rhinoceros, 168 n.; as source for artists, 92

Raphael, 70, 71, 76, 124, 158, 183, 188, 189, 190, 197; "Acts of the Apostles," 101; and Alfonso d'Este, 142; and Berlin elephant, 141; and elephant fountain, 142; and Hanno's portrait, 140, 141; and Isabella d'Este, 141; and Naturalism, 157; "Triumph of Bacchus in India," 142

Raphia, battle of, 126, 128 n.

Rathgeb, Jakob, 20

Rauwolf, Leonhard, 84 n., 168 n.; on Indian gems, 116 n.

Ravenna, 35

Rem, Lucas, 163 n., 177; jewels of, 117 n.; in Lisbon, 22

Rembrandt, 77 n., 158 n.

Renaissance: and Antiquity, 6, 69–70, 149; and ape, 177; artistic experiments, 64, 121, 193–94; artistic preconceptions, 57, 187 n.; artistic trends, 186; and Asian animals, 185; and Asian arts, 4, 6, 74, 122; and bestiary tradition, 129 n.; and elephant, 125; and emblems, 84–88; and gem engraving, 115; individualism, 44; jewelry, 115; lapidarial writings, 115; ornament, 197; in Portugal, 119; relations between art and nature, 44; and rhinoceros, 161; silverworks, 119; social status of artists, 104; triumphs, 132–33; virtuosity, 39, 44, 45. *See also* Antiquity; Humanism

René the Good, duke of Anjou, 133

Rewick, Erhard, 133 n.

Reynolds, Sir Joshua, 142

Rhaponticum (rhubarb), 83

Rhinoceros, 30, 79, 80, 123, 183, 185, 193; African variety, 160; Altdorfer's drawing, 164–65; in bestiaries, 160, 161; biblical references to, 159; in books, 166–67; Burgkmair's woodcut, 164; in caryatids, 170, 196; at Castello, 166; in China, 127 n.; on coins and medals, 160, 163, 164, 167; combat with elephant in Lisbon, 161–62; death, 162; dorsal horn, 164, 168; Dürer's woodcut of, 163–65, 172, 190; and elephant, 128, 159, 161, 162, 163, 165, 167, 168, 170; as emblems, 85, 86, 167, 171, 192; in Europe, 158, 160, 161, 168–69; fantasized, 170; in frescoes, 159 n.; in games, 159; as gifts, 158, 161–62, 169; hunt, 160; Indian variety, 160; jointless legs, 127 n.; literary descriptions of, 159, 167; in Manuel's Book of Hours, 162; on maps, 167; marble relief of Naples, 166; maritime transport of, 161, 162; at Marseilles, 31, 162; Martial on, 167; medicinal virtues, 159; in mosaics, 160; myths, 159, 159 n., 164; and Naturalism, 166, 169–70; with obelisk, 135 n., 165; in ornament, 169, 170, 196; in paintings, 156, 169, 171; physical attributes, 127 n., 159, 163, 164, 167, 168; *plicae*, or folds, of skin, 159, 164, 168; in poetry, 162–63; at Rome, 159–60; in sculpture, 166; stuffed, 162; as symbol, 79, 160–61, 165, 166, 167, 171, 172, 184, 196; as symbol of Asia, 79, 93; as symbol of India, 170; in tapestries, 165; in triumphs, 192; at Tunja, 169; and unicorn, 159, 160, 161; and virgins, 160; in woodcuts, 159, 163, 168, 169. See also *Bada*; *Ganda*

Rhinoceros bird, 182

Rhinoceros hide, 30

Rhinoceros horns, 30, 115, 159 n.; as amulets and antidotes, 12; in gold or silver mountings, 12

Rhubarb, 11, 81; Chinese origin, 83

Ricci, Simone de, 100 n.

Rice, 40

Richard, earl of Cornwall, 130

Rimini, 36; Biblioteca Gambalunga, 132 n.; Malatesta of, 132; *Regalis Ystoria*, 132 n.

Ripa, Cesare: *Iconologia*, 156, 193; on symbols of Asia, 193
Ripon (England): cathedral, 130 n., 149 n.
Robertet, Florimond de, 31
Rococo: Asian influences on, 187
Roger II, of Sicily, 97
Roiz, Diogo, 118
Romano, Giulio, 152, 154 n., 157, 183, 188; "Bacchus and Ariadne," 174; and elephant, 154; elephant fountain, 142; fantasized elephants, 143; "Marriage Feast of Cupid and Psyche," 143; tapestry drawings, 144; and tiger, 174
Rome, 69, 70, 71, 99, 175, 195; "African beasts," 127; African empire of, 128; animal shows and combats at, 127; antiquities of, 22, 69; Asian imports in, 41, 96, 114; Augustan era, 114, 156 n.; Biblioteca Casanatense at, 65, 81; Campo dei Fiori, 138; capitol, 138; Castel San Angelo, 137, 177; Chinese silks in, 96; church of Maria Sopra Minerva, 133; cloister of St. John Lateran, 59; coins, 126, 127, 132, 158; collection of Metello Varro Porcari, 166; collections, 9, 114; elephants in, 124, 127, 128, 133, 136–37, 158; exotic woods, 109; Farnese gallery, 76; festival of Saints Cosmas and Damian, 138; gem engraving, 114; Gesù, 43, 62, 63; Golden House of Nero, 70, 194; hospital for "Indians," 41; importation of precious stones, 114; Indian embassy to, 172; ivory carving at, 126 n.; Japanese legates in, 42; Jesuit archives at, 67 n.; myrrhine vases of, 106; parrots in, 179; Piazza Minerva, 135; Porta del Popolo, 137; Portugal's mission of obedience to Pope Leo X, 41, 136–38; revival, 42–43; rhinoceros at, 159–60, 170; sack of 1527, 41; Saint-André-en-Quirinal, 72; sarcophagi, 126, 132; stuffed rhinoceros in, 162, 165 n.; Tiber, 137; tigers at, 172; torchlight parades, 127, 128 n.; white elephant in, 128 n., 156 n.
Root of China, 11, 23
Rosso Fiorentino, 157; Fountainbleau fresco, 143
Rott, Konrad, 24 n.
Rouen, 192; *entrée* of Henry II, 94, 149
Rovellasca, house of, 20 n.
Roz, Felipe, 155
Rubies, 21, 117; of four castes, 120
"Ruch" (rook): as symbol, 92
Rudolf II, Holy Roman Emperor, 76, 188; collections, 28–30, 156; inventories of collections of, 46–56
Ruiz, Simon, 12
Ruspagiari, Alfonso, 167

Sago bread, 33–34
Sago palm, 34
Saint-Malo, 33

St. Mark (church of Venice), 35, 36; mosaic, 160 n.
St. Paul, 160
St. Petersburg: collection, 21
St. Thomas (Madras), 98
Salmanassar II, king of Assyria, 125
Sambucus, Joannes, 87, 153
Sandalwood, 17, 109
Sansovino, Francesco 43
Santos, Reynaldo dos, 61
Sanuto, Marino: on elephant, 139
Sapphires, 117
Sarrazim, Dom Jean: on *bada*, 169
Sassetti, Filippo, 24 n., 40 n., 61, 66, 100 n., 108; on elephants, 156; in Lisbon, 11 n.; on parrots, 180; on porcelains, 106
Savery, Roelant, 76, 183, 185; animal paintings of, 156; and apes, 178; "Garden of Eden," 182; and tiger, 174
Saxony: collections, 24; silk weaving in, 102
Scaliger, J. C., 105, 106 n.; and plumage of bird of paradise, 181 n.
Schäufelein, Hans, 79, 85
Schaller, Georg, 156
Schelling, Friedrich W. J. von, 58
Schewl, Paulus, 111
Schmitt, Konrad, 88
Schoenberger, Anton, 120 n.
Schongauer, Martin, 76, 94, 134, 147, 149, 176; woodcut of African elephant, 133
Schuren, Johann von, 16, 117
Schwenkfeld, Caspar, 174
Sculptures: of animals, 184; apes in, 176; in Asia, 67; Dürer's rhinoceros in, 166, 170; elephants in, 128, 130, 131, 132, 133, 135, 136, 142, 148, 157; influence on Manueline architecture, 59; of rhinoceros, 165; in Rimini, 132; of tiger, 174; of "wild men," 176
Scythia, 116
Seashells, 22, 25, 30, 32, 39; in mountings, 27; in paintings, 73; and porcelain, 105, 107; symbolism, 109, 120
Sebastian, king of Portugal, 32, 148, 150 n.
Secularization: of animals, 184; of apes, 177; of elephant, 157; of symbolic meanings, 191–92
Seleucids, 126
Seleucus, Nikator, 172
Sequeira, Diogo Lopes de, 10
Seram island, 95 n.
Setubal, 12
Seville, 11 n., 12, 169; Biblioteca Colombina, 163 n.
Seychelles Islands, 23
Shiva: portraits of, 65
Siam, gifts to Portugal, 10
Sibmacher, Hans, 170, 182, 183, 190; engravings, 95; etchings, 87; and rhinoceros, 169
Sicily, 35, 36; silk weaving, 97

Siculus, Diodorus, 125; on rhinoceros, 160
Sidayu (Java), 95, 183
Siena, 43, 137
Sigismund I, of Rimini, 132
Silks, 10, 34; for bedsteads, 110; of China, 36, 98; Chinese motifs in, 96–97, 131; in European costumes, 102; of Florence, 36; history of, 95–97; of Levant, 36; of Lucca, 36; of Persia, 36; of Sicily, 36; tussore, 98; of Venice, 36
Silver and silverworks, 11, 30; in Asia, 113; *bastiães*, 16 n., 162; designs, 119; Dürer's rhinoceros in, 170; elephants in, 155; exotic detail, 119, 197; monkeys in, 175; in Spain, 119
Sind, 98
Sintra, 12
Sirigatto, Ridolfo, 39
Sirkej: tombs of, 61
Sita: portraits of, 67
Sixtus V, pope, 42
Skelton, John, 181 n.
Snyders, Frans, 72
Society of Jesus. *See* Jesuits
Solinus, Julius: on elephant, 139 n.; on rhinoceros, 160
Solis, Virgil, 87, 150
Sousa, Diogo de, 118
Southeast Asia: gold in, 113; and elephant, 125
Spain, 69, 70; ceramics, 104, 107; Chinese books in, 13; church ornament of, 197; costume of, 15; elephants in, 14, 144; furniture, 110; menagerie, 12; Plateresque style, 62; rhinoceros in, 190; silk industry of, 96–97; silverware, 119; sumptuary laws, 15–16, 99; textile industry of, 99; textiles in, 12; tigers in, 174; Western books on Asia in, 13
Spices, 11, 34, 38
Spinels, 117
Spränger, Bartolomäus, 29 n.
Springer, Balthasar, 80, 164
Steinbeck, Catherina, 110
Sterling, Charles, 73, 74
Stockholm: National Museum, 100
Storey, Ralph John, 67
Strabo, 37; on the rhinoceros, 159
Strada, Ottavio da, 29 n.
Stradanus (Jan van der Straet), 40, 92; collaborative engraving with Galle, 93; in Florence, 92 n.; and maps, 91 n.; and Persian miniatures, 92 n.
Strassburg, 79, 119
Studiolo of Florence, 40, 111
Styles in art: Baroque, 58, 62–63, 164, 187; flamboyant Gothic, 57; Gothic, 58, 59, 61, 62, 96, 97, 187; Manueline, 57–59, 118; national, 62, 68; Plateresque of Spain, 62; Rococo, 187; Romanesque, 58, 96–97; "rustique," 189. *See also* Mannerism; Naturalism; Ornament

Sugarwork: elephant, 153
Sumatra, 67 n.; birds of, 180; names used for elephant and rhinoceros in, 167
Switzerland: Dürer's rhinoceros in, 170
Symbolism, 57, 186; of Africa, 79, 128; of animals, 134–35, 173, 177, 178, 179, 184, 191; of apes and monkeys, 177, 178; of Asia, 79, 93, 155, 171, 178, 180, 191, 192, 193, 198; of bird of paradise, 182; of dragon, 129, 149, 161; of ebony, 109, 111; of elephant, 92, 93, 125, 128, 129, 132, 133, 134–35, 149–50, 152, 154 n., 157, 161, 184, 192; of emblems, 84–88; of hieroglyphs, 84–86; of "Hunting for Wild Ducks in China," 92; of Magellan engraving, 92; of Magi, 75–76; and Mannerism, 198; of parasol (*chattra*), 81, 103; of parrots, 179, 180, 184; of porcelain, 108–9; of precious stones, 115; of rhinoceros, 79, 93, 160, 161, 165, 166, 167, 170, 171, 172, 184, 196; of seashells, 109, 120; of tiger, 173, 174, 175; in triumphs, 79–80, 192; of unicorn, 161; of *Wunderkammer*, 77, 198
Syria, 147

Talavera, 107
Tamarinds, 11
Tamerlane, 26
Tapestries, 43, 89, 198; "à la manière de Portugal et de l'Indye," 100; animals in, 99, 100, 101, 134, 165, 184; of Arras, 99, 148; Asian influence on, 100–101; and discoveries, 122; Dürer's rhinoceros in, 165, 170; elephants in, 101, 134, 144, 148, 152, 157; "Elephant Hunt," 144 n.; of Flanders, 99, 100; at Graz, 26; Indian series, 100; and literary sources, 190; monkeys in, 177; and precious stones, 117; themes of, 100–101; "The Triumph of Fame," 134; triumph of Scipio Africanus, 143; triumphs of João de Castro, 101–2; verdure and hunting scenes, 99, 101; and woodcuts, 100
Taprobane: and "Mandelaph," 88; maps of, 87
"Tartar cloths," 97
Tartars, 191
Tartary: maps of, 87
Tasso, Torquato, 86 n., 150, 167 n.
Teak, 15, 109
Tenasserim, 88
Tetzel, Anton, 180 n.
Textiles, 8, 11, 15, 19, 24, 25, 27, 30, 34, 36, 38, 43, 56, 187; block prints, 78; in "breakfast pieces," 73; brocades, 10, 96, 98; canopies, 98; Chinese motifs in, 96, 97, 194; for clothes, 102; *colchas* (quilts), 34, 98, 99; collective weaving, 97; counterpanes, 98; damasks, 98; designs in, 74, 96, 102, 131, 196; drawn work, 96; dyeing, 103, 121; elephants in, 130; embroideries, 98, 99; of Europe, 36; European imitations of Asian, 121; "export embroideries," 98;

Index

Textiles—(*continued*)
history of, 95–97; Indian centers of production, 98; Indo-Portuguese, 98, 107; influence on ceramics, 105; muslins, 98; in paintings, 68, 73, 97–98, 189; quilting of, 99, 121; Romanesque ornament in, 96–97; satins, 98; *sinabafos* of Bengal, 98; in Spain, 12; taffetas, 32; "Tartar cloths," 97

"Therse," 76

Thevet, André, 44; collection, 168; *Cosmographie universelle*, 167; on ebony, 111 n.; engravings, 88; at Fontainebleau, 32; on rhinoceros, 167; voyage to Levant, 88; woodcuts, 88

Thuringian company, 24 n.

Thurzo, Johann, 180

Tigers, 76, 123, 188; in bestiaries, 173; Capaccio on, 175; in caryatids, 174, 196; in China, 173 n.; description, 172; and elephant, 173; as emblems, 87, 174; in games, 172; as gifts, 172; of Giulio Romano, 174; in Greece, 172; hunt, 173; myths, 173; as ornament, 174; in paintings, 156, 174; as predators, 173; in quadrigas, 173; range, 172; in Rome, 172; symbolism, 173, 174, 184; in woodcuts, 174

Tiles (azulejos), 106, 107

Tintoretto, 72

Tiraqueau, André, 32

Titian, 142; "the Ape Laocoön," 177

Toggini, Gianpaolo, 15 n.

Tomar, 57, 58, 60, 118; Capitular window, 60; paintings at, 68

Topaz: symbolism of, 115

Torre, Giulio della, 88 n.

Tournai, 100, 101, 134

Tower of Belém, 57, 60; elephant on, 136; Indian influence on, 61–62; rhinoceros on, 165

Trazzo, Jacopo da, 118

Trenchard, Sir Thomas, 33

Tribolo (Niccolo Pericoli), 166

Tri-mūrti (Sanskrit for "three forms"): portraits of the gods, 65

Trismegistus, Hermes, 84

Triumphs (*trionfi*): of Alexander the Great, 126; at Antwerp, 93–94, 152, 170; of Asia, 76, 101; automatons in, 132; of campaigns in India, 101; of Dionysius, 126, 155 n.; Dürer's rhinoceros in, 170; in Egypt, 126; and elephant, 79, 132, 134, 144 n., 149, 152; in engravings, 193; at Florence, 138; at Lisbon, 13; of Maximilian I, 79–80, 149, 165, 192; of Philip of Burgundy, 132; in Renaissance art, 126; and rhinoceros, 79, 165, 170; in Rome, 126; symbolism, 192; on tapestries, 101, 134, 143; of Venetian painters, 76

Tuileries, 189 n.

Tulip, 86, 193

Tunja (Colombia), 171; rhinoceros mural at, 169

Turbans, 101

Turin: tigers at, 173

Turkestan, 76

Turkey, 46, 86, 89; costume of, 102; and porcelains, 104, 108; relations with England, 33; relations with France, 31

Turks, 4, 37 n., 38; in caryatids, 196 n.

Turrecremata, cardinal: *Meditations*, 133

Tuscany, 105; collections, 39; menagerie, 174

Tyrol: elephants in, 145

Udine, Giovanni da, 71, 77, 143 n., 194; and elephant, 142, 143

Uffizi: Valois tapestry of, 152 n.

Unicorn, 158, 166, 184; biblical references to, 159; and rhinoceros, 159, 160, 161; and virgins, 160 n.

Urbino, Camillo da, 107

Urreta, Fray Luis de, 172

Urzidil, Johannes, 158 n.

Vaduz, 29 n.

Vaga, Perino del: "Triumph of Bacchus in India," 143 n.

Valencia, 104

Valeriano, Giovanni Pietro, 86; on elephant, 136 n., 149; *Hieroglyphica*, 85, 167; on parrots, 180; on tiger, 174

Valignano, Alessandro, 14, 70, 89 n., 158

Valois, Margaret of, 32

Valori, Baccio, 11 n.

Varchi, Benedetto, 71

Varthema, Ludovico, 81, 87, 98; *Itinerario*, 135; on rhinoceros, 168 n.

Vasari, Giorgio, 86 n.

Vatican, 69, 188; Belvedere gardens, 138; Castel San Angelo, 137, 177; collections, 42, 43; elephant diplomat at, 137; elephant intarsia in, 139, 148; Galleria delle Carte geografiche, 42; Japanese screens at, 42, 89, 188; library, 42; loggia, 143, 194; Loggia della Cosmographia, 42; natural history collection, 43; renovation, 140; Stanza della Segnatura, 139. *See also* Papacy; Rome

Vaz, Gaspar, 68

Vecchietti, Bernardo, 39

Vecellio, Cesare, 72 n., 102; class distinctions in costume, 91; *Habiti antichi et moderni di tutte il mondo*, 91; Japanese youth of, 91; realistic Chinese of, 91

Veii, 137 n.

Venice, 22, 35, 43, 71, 82, 90, 105, 131; Burgkmair at, 80; cathedral of St. Mark, 160 n., 194; collections, 9, 36, 38; as commercial rival of Portugal, 38; costume, 102; costume books, 90–91; as emporium, 36, 38, 117; glass jewels of, 114; importation of Oriental textiles to, 97, 100; Japanese emissaries at, 72; lacemaking at, 121; lacquerware of, 112; Leonardo at,

37 n.; Museo Correr of, 139 n.; porcelains, 107; silk weaving at, 97

Verona, 18, 43

Veronese, Paolo, 98 n.

Vesalius, Andreas, 177

Vespasian, Titus Flavius, emperor of Rome, 160

Vespucci, Amerigo, 81, 192 n.

Vicente, Gil, 118

Vicentino, Valario Brilli il, 118

Vicenza: church of San Corona, 135 n.; white clay from, 108

Vienna, 22, 75, 90; Albertina, 164; Chinese paintings at, 27; collections at, 23; elephants in, 124, 145–46, 147, 152; Graben, 145; hunting lodge of Ebersdorf, 23, 146; Kärntner Gate, 145; Kärntnerstrasse, 146; Kunsthistorisches Museum, 101; Michaelsplatz, 145; "Elephant House," 145

Vignola, Giacomo da, 63

Vijayanagar: diamond mining at, 116; elephants in, 135

Villa Madama (Rome), 148; elephant fountain, 142, 143, 144

Villafañe, Juan de Arphe y. *See* Arphe y Villafañe, Juan de

Villa-Viçosa, 102 n.

Villefranche, 162

Vincent of Beauvais: on the bird of paradise, 181

Viseu, 67, 68

Vishnu: portraits of, 65

Viterbo: Caprarola Palace of, 192

Voorn, Jakob, 21

Voragine, Jacobus de, 75

Vries, Hans Vredeman de: *Grottesco in diversche Manieren*, 196

Warham, Archbishop, 33

Wasserberg: elephants in, 145

Watson, W. C., 58

Wax, 14, 38

Wedel, Leopold von, 33

Weiditz, Hans, 81

Weisberg, Hermann, 153 n.

Welser, house of, 22, 28, 80, 177

Welser, Philippine, 26

Weyden, Roger van der, 75

White elephant, 128 n., 151 n., 156, 158 n.

Whitehall, 34

Wild ducks: hunting of, in China, 92–93

William V, duke of Bavaria, 24, 25

Winghe, Philips van, 188; in Rome, 89; sketches in Cartari, 89 n.

Winner, Matthias: on Raphael's elephant, 141

Wittelsbach, house of, 25

Wittenberg, 79

Woad, 103, 188

Wolfe, John, 94

Woodcuts: of animals, 94, 184; of apes, 176, 177; of Asian cities, 88; of Asian plants, 82; of bird of paradise, 182; in books, 78, 81, 88; Burgkmair's India series, 164; Chinese in, 189; in cosmographies, 88; of costume, 90; of customs of Turks, 89; and discoveries, 122; of Dürer, 79; of Dürer's rhinoceros, 163–64, 167; of elephants, 133, 134, 139 n., 141–42, 147, 149–50, 151–54, 156, 157; of emblems, 85; and engravings, 79; in Germany, 79; of Gesner, 84; of Hanno, 141–42; in hieroglyphic books, 78; history, 78; influence of, 171; "King of Cochin" series, 80; and literary sources, 190; of maps, 87, 94, 190; of parrots, 180; "People of Calicut," 80, 81; of plants and flowers, 81, 88, 188; of rhinoceros, 159, 163, 164, 167, 168, 169; of rhinoceros fighting elephant, 168; in southern Europe, 79; and tapestries, 100; of tigers, 174; of triumphs of Maximilian I, 79–80

Woods, 11, 20, 22, 31, 38, 63; aloe, 109; aromatic, 109; cabinetmakers, 111; camphor, 11, 109; commerce in, 109–10; ebony, 29, 32, 34, 39, 40, 109, 111; joinery, 111; as medicaments and dyes, 109, 110; ornamentations on, 111; sandal, 17, 109; teak, 15, 109

Wunderkammer, 28, 198; definition, 9; meaning, 30; of Paludanus, 20

Wyftel, Robert, 100

Xatim, Raulu, 118

Xavier, Francis, 70; in painting, 71

Yuccas, 193

Zaltieri, Bolognino, 150

Zane, Matteo, 38 n.

Zeeland, 151

Zimarra (black Venetian robe), 102